A Concise History of the Parish and Vicarage of Halifax, in the County of York

John Crabtree

NAPLES.

A

CONCISE HISTORY

OF THE PARISH AND VICARAGE

OF

HALIFAX,

IN THE COUNTY OF YORK.

BY JOHN CRABTREE, GENT.

HALIFAX:

PUBLISHED BY HARTLEY AND WALKER.

SIMPKIN, MARSHALL, AND CO., LONDON.

MDCCCXXXVI.

ENTERED AT STATIONERS' HALL.

HARTLEY AND WALKER, PRINTERS, HALIFAX.

TO

THE REVEREND CHARLES MUSGRAVE, B. D.

VICAR OF THE PARISH OF HALIFAX,

AND

PREBENDARY OF THE PREBENDAL STALL OF GIVENDALE,

IN THE

CATHEDRAL CHURCH OF SAINT PETER'S, YORK,

THIS VOLUME IS (BY HIS PERMISSION)

DEDICATED,

AS A HUMBLE TRIBUTE OF SINCERE RESPECT

TO HIS PASTORAL OFFICE,

THE ARDUOUS AND IMPORTANT DUTIES OF WHICH

HE HAS

(UNDER DIVINE PROVIDENCE)

FOR NINE YEARS SO ABLY FULFILLED;

AND ALSO AS A SMALL TOKEN OF ESTEEM AND REGARD,

BY HIS FAITHFUL PARISHIONER

AND DEVOTED SERVANT,

JOHN CRABTREE.

Halifax,
March 1, 1836.

PREFACE.

WHEN it is considered that many important changes and improvements have taken place in this extensive parish since Mr. WATSON's valuable "History and Antiquities" issued from the press; that its circulation is at the present very circumscribed: that new discoveries have been brought to light; and, above all, that much local information of an interesting nature may be found in the elegant and elaborate works of Dr. Whitaker, Hunter, and other eminent topographical writers, (works too costly to find a place in the library of the general reader,) the Compiler of the following pages is induced to hope that a Concise history of the Parish and Vicarage of Halifax, founded on the labors of her able and zealous antiquary, and embodying additional information gleaned from the rich and fertile fields of literature before referred to, will not be unacceptable to those for whose peculiar use the present volume was intended, namely, the parishioners of Halifax.

It has been his endeavour to make such selections as appeared to him best calculated to illustrate the general history of the parish, not omitting matters of minor detail; and to arrange the whole in a manner adapted to edify, to instruct, and to amuse. It is highly probable that defective information, or too great a regard for brevity, have caused him to pass over many things which would have materially illustrated the various subjects of the history, and particularly matters of legal detail. An adherence to facts has been his primary object.

There is no royal road to the knowledge of the law. No man can render an obscure and intricate disquisition of title either perspicuous or entertaining. While it has been the Compiler's endeavour to afford general satisfaction, there are two classes of readers whom he fears he shall have some difficulty in pleasing. To the first class, (whom without intending any offence) he must term the superficial reader, he fears his selections will frequently appear injudicious or ill-chosen; this class in general have a rooted aversion for any thing that savours of antiquity; to them the very word is bodied out in the form of a spectral old man, poring over some rust eaten weapon, or handling with affection some crazy vessel, which they could scarcely bring themselves to touch; or if they can fancy him unrolling ancient records, and attempting to decipher old characters, they regard him as a vision of the past, a being who has buried himself alive, and over whose living remains it is seemly and decent to draw the veil of forgetfulness. The other class run into an opposite extreme, and whose displeasure he fears he shall incur by the omission of pedigrees, armorial bearings, and family genealogies; he is free to confess that his own inclinations and pursuits would have led him to conciliate this class by entering fully upon enquiries of this sort, had his limits permitted him so to do: but he looks for some extenuation of his error (if such it be) in the confidence that the omission will be both ably and fully supplied in a forthcoming work on a larger scale.*

It is stated by Dr. Whitaker, that "the antiquary who looks through this extensive district for those appearances which most delight him, will be disappointed. In a tract of more than 124 square miles there exists not the remnant of a castle; there never was a monastic foundation. He must therefore content himself with a few earth-works which in-

---

* Proposed "History and Antiquities of the Parish of Halifax, by E. N. Alexander, F. S. A. &c. &c."

dicate that some inconsiderable fortresses once existed within it; and with respect to ecclesiastical antiquity, he must take up with the appropriation of its rectory to a remote house, and with a few scattered donations of acres and ox-gangs to such neighboring convents whose popularity extended beyond their own immediate bounds." Be it so. Does it thence follow that all is barren? The labors of Watson attest the contrary. Do they not present us a field for enquiry—a storehouse of relics from whence we may glean some memorial of generations who breathed two thousand years ago; that if the dust of the valley could spring to life, the sounds which our mountains and moorlands reverberated, in years of which scarcely a tradition remains, would again awaken the slumbering echo, and the wild solitude would be once more peopled with human beings.

If it be asked—Are there no memorials in existence to indicate that aught but the forest tree or the heath has tenanted the soil, since the retiring waters crept into the ocean? The learned Doctor has proved the contrary, as may be seen by his opinions, embodied in the following pages, to which the Compiler craves, with all humility to refer; opinions which encouraged him in this attempt, from a conviction that they contained interesting local information, too valuable to slumber on the shelves of the antiquary and topographer. The past state of a country cannot be known, until its antiquities have been thoroughly and accurately investigated. Disclaiming the arrogant assumption of one single qualification necessary to constitute a true antiquary, save a guileless enthusiasm, the Compiler has ventured occasionally to offer an hypothesis or conjecture when connected with the early history of the parish, in the hope that it might conduce to stimulate the reflection, and to guide the researches of others; and should he have succeeded in the attempt he shall hereafter reflect with honest pride that his labors have not proved fruitless. His own personal conviction has been strengthened by the opinions of individuals, for whose judgment he has the highest respect, (among the number he may be permitted to mention the late Mr. Watkinson, who was well acquainted with the localities of this extensive parish,) that notwithstanding much has been done of a valuable character, and the ground comparatively cleared of many of its obstructions, and the journey of future historians rendered comparatively easy, an unexplored field of enquiry is yet open in which both pleasurable occupation and honor may be gained.

Already have the inmost recesses of her woods been penetrated for the advancement of science, and trodden by the foot of the naturalist. That there are few districts which afford opportunities so valuable for the cultivation of natural philosophy, the labors of a Bolton bear ample testimony.

If we descend into the bosom of her moorlands and her mountains. Are we not presented with an instructive field for geological examination in its varied and interesting characters? Ask the Geologist, he will not only tell us of the treasures that are hidden under the surface, and of their value in a scientific and commercial point of view; but he will pause and ponder over the mysterious things which have already been brought to light as tending to illustrate some of the most imposing theories of that sublime science.

But why mention these facts to stimulate the exertions of others when it is borne in mind that a great desideratum has been attained for Halifax in the union of literary feeling and sentiment. Already is the ivy clinging to the oak, and the admirer of nature, in the cultivation of his favorite pursuit will in the end have the satisfaction of finding that she " never betrayed the heart that loved her."

It was the intention of the Compiler to have added a Chronological Table of the principal events connected with the parish; but finding so many opportunities in the course of his progress for introducing matter originally set apart for this table, he was induced to embody it in the work rather than add it in the form originally intended, which would have considerably increased the bulk of the volume. He begs most explicitly to state that no information which he contemplated inserting in that table, has been omitted here.

To some of his professional friends the Compiler is under great obligations for much valuable information; particularly to Mr. James Edward Norris and Mr. Edward Nelson Alexander his best thanks are due; to the former gentleman for several important historical facts relating to the early history of the Advowson, and other ecclesiastical matters of much and valued interest: the latter for some additional information relating to matters of title, and for correcting some errors connected with that intricate subject. To Mr. F.A. Leyland, jun. he also tenders his acknowledgements for some information relating to the antiquities of the Parish.

He can neither forget nor be ungrateful for the very kind and flattering manner in which his proposals for publication were honored by his subscribers; he shall ever reflect with pride on the confidence reposed in him, assuring them that it has been not only the highest object of his ambition, but that of his Publishers, to merit their approbation.

It is with extreme reluctance that the compiler adverts to a personal affliction which precludes him from enjoying the pleasures of colloquial society; nor would he have intruded the subject in these his prefatory remarks had not that affliction prevented him from obtaining much information that might have proved both interesting and instructive, and driven him to seek for that in the society of books, which others more favored obtain by the "hearing of the ear."

He is not impervious to criticism. To those who are inclined to censure he cries, "your mercy gentlemen." "Do not pursue with a weighty scourge the man who deserves only a slight whip."

TABLE OF CONTENTS.

LIST OF ILLUSTRATIONS.

A CONCISE HISTORY

PARISH AND VICARAGE OF HALIFAX.

GENERAL DESCRIPTION.

THE Parish of Halifax, within the Wapentake of Morley, in the West Riding of the County of York, comprises a mountainous and bleak region of country forming a portion of what are sometimes termed the English Apennines. It extends seventeen miles from East to West, and on an average eleven miles from North to South, and contains an area of 75,740 English Statute Acres: it is considered the largest Parish in England, and the population thereof at the last census was computed at 109,899 souls. Its boundaries on the North-West, West, and South-West, are the Parishes of Rochdale, and Whalley, in the County of Lancaster; on the South the Parish of Huddersfield; on the South-East the chapelry of Hartishead; on the East the Parish of Birstall; and on the North that of Bradford, in the County of York. It is divided into twenty-three Divisions or Townships; viz. Halifax, Barkisland, Elland with Greetland, Fixby, Erringden, Heptonstall, Hipperholme with Brighouse, Langfield, Midgley, Norland, North Owram, Ovenden, Rastrick, Rishworth, Skircoat, South Owram, Sowerby, Soyland, Stainland, Stansfield, Shelf, Wadsworth, and Warley.

The town of Halifax, from whence the Parish takes its name, may be considered the centre of the populous manufacturing district of the North of England, it lies fourteen miles from Leeds, seven

B

from Bradford, sixteen from Wakefield, and twelve from the borders
of Lancashire; and on the direct line of communication between
the ports of Liverpool and Hull.

Various have been the conjectures as to the true origin of the
name. CAMDEN says "all ancient records that ever were, do give it
the name of Halifax, the reason of which seems to have been this:
that at first it was a hermitage of very great antiquity; the Church
that now is built from, or rather added to, a Chapel long since built,
was consecrated and dedicated to Saint John Baptist, who is styled
by some ancients the first father of hermits, and in which place, as
they pretend, was kept the real face of Saint John Baptist; hence
was it named Halifax or Holy-Face." "The place is situate at the
foot of a mighty and almost inaccessible rock, [for so doubtless at
the first it was,] all overgrown with trees and thick underwoods,
intermixed with great and bulky stones, standing very high above
ground, in a dark and solemn grove, on the bank of a small murmuring rivulet; for such places were always chosen by ancient and
solitary hermits, where, being removed far from all human converse,
they found every circumstance thereunto appertaining very much to
contribute to, and heighten contemplation, insomuch that whoever
was the first that set this place apart, [as the face of things then stood]
could not in all these parts have found out a place of greater privacy
and retirement." So much for the learned author of the *Britannia*.

This opinion, notwithstanding it has been received and adopted
by all authors who have hitherto attempted a history of the Parish,
with the exception of the late Dr. WHITAKER, has been so successfully combated by that learned antiquarian, and with such sound
reasoning as to carry conviction at once to the mind of the reader,
and dispel all doubt relative to the true origin of the name.

"The name of Halifax" he observes, "is a singularly compounded
name, half Saxon, and half Norman; which, not having been
understood, has occasioned the invention of an idle fable to explain
it.* It appears, however, to have been no fable that in the deep
valley, then embosomed in woods, where the Parish Church now

---

* The fable here alluded to, is the story told by CAMDEN, for the change of the name
from Horton, which it is alledged the place was formerly called, to that of Halifax.

I should have given the story verbatim, but finding its leading features so fully embodied in honest FULLER's reason for omitting all mention of the Maid alluded to in the
story, in his Catalogue of Yorkshire Saints, and so quaintly commented on by him, I

stands, was an Hermitage dedicated to St. John the Baptist; the imagined sanctity of which attracted a great concourse of pilgrims in every direction. Four ways, by which the modern town of Halifax is entered, still distinctly point at the Parish Church as their common centre, though at one extremity of the place. These were the roads by which the pilgrims approached the object of their devotion, and hence the name 𝕳𝖆𝖑𝖎𝖋𝖆𝖝 or 𝕳𝖔𝖑𝖞-𝖜𝖆𝖞𝖘; for fax, in Norman French, is an old plural noun, denoting high-ways. Thus Car-fax in Oxford (a case exactly in point) is the four roads; and Fair-fax, whatever may be pretended to the contrary, is neither more nor less than the fair roads."

"This hermitage, however, (continues my author) the approaches to which must have received their name very soon after the conquest, became, at a short period afterwards the parent of a Parish Church, to which was attached a wild, and almost unpeopled district of vast extent. The inconveniences of superstition have, in this instance, been felt during seven centuries; for the Church, which, after a vast increase of population, continued for half its duration to the present time without the aid of more than two Chapels, is situated almost in a corner of the Parish; and the genius of commerce itself, which usually despises ancient prejudice and attends to its own convenience alone, has, in this instance, been made to bend to the ancient religion of the place. The respective situations of a great

here insert his Remarks, trusting that my readers will pardon the digression, many of them probably thinking that I might with impunity have omitted all mention of the story for the reason assigned by that "Worthy of worthies," namely, "because the judicious behold the whole contrivance devoid of Historical truth."

"Expect not here," (says FULLER) "that I should add to this Catalogue that Maiden, who to secure her virginity from his unchaste embraces that assaulted it, was by him barbarously murdered, whereby she got the reputation of a Saint, and the place the scene of his cruelty, (formerly called Horton) the name of Hali-fax or Holy-hair. For the credulous people conceited that the veins, which in form of little threds spred themselves between the bark and body of that Yew-Tree (whereon the head of this maid was hung up,) were the very hairs indeed of this Virgin head, to whom they flock in pilgrimage." "Oh! how sharp sighted, and yet how blind, is superstition! Yet these country folks fancies had the advantage of Daphne's being turned into a laurel tree."

In frondem crines, in ramos brachia crescunt.

Ovid's Metamorph. lib. 1. *fol.* 9.

"Into a bough her hair did spread,
And from her arms two branches bred."

"But here she is wholly omitted, not so much because her name and time are un-known, but because the judicious behold the whole contrivance devoid of Historical truth."

B 2

trading town, and of a sequestered hermitage, might appear to be little adapted to each other, and an early separation might have been expected between them ; yet so it is, that within two miles of a fine open valley, the great line of communication between the Eastern and Western seas, and on a navigable stream, the principal town of this extensive and populous district, after every improvement which wealth and skill could apply in the diversion of roads, can only be approached by ascending or descending a precipice."*

"Nature and common sense would have pointed out Elland as the proper site for the capital of the Parish."

"The whole district now comprising this great Parish, may be considered as one valley, with its numerous collateral forks, bounded at very unequal and constantly varying distances, by two high and barren ridges of moor stone. The general appearance of the bottoms is pleasing and picturesque ; scarcely a foot of level ground appears, except the alluvial lands which are unusually fertile. The sides of the hills immediately above are hung with woods of native oak, which delights in the clefts and crevices of sand stone, though it rarely attains in such situations, the bulk and majesty of form which it acquires in deeper soils."

"So various is the course of the principal valley, that the eye is never fatigued by resting on one uniform and protracted expanse, but delights in sudden and unexpected turns, producing new and varied beauties. Above these are long and widely extended slopes, where art and expense, which manufactures alone could have afforded, have triumphed over what otherwise would have been deemed unconquerable barrenness, and produced a verdure not unequal to that of native fertility. Above all appear the purple ridges of the mountains, defying all the power of man, and destined for ever to contrast the original face of savage nature, with the effects of toil and industry. On the brows of these hills frowns many a sturdy block of free stone, sometimes perhaps worn away by storms to a narrow and immovable point, which the fondness of antiquarian fancy has decreed to be druidical. From the boundary of Lancashire to the valley which separates the townships of Halifax and Ovenden from

* Twenty years have elapsed since these remarks were written ; considerable improvements have taken place, and the Town can now be approached on all sides without inconvenience : the entrance from Bradford by the Godley Lane Road is a fair specimen of what art can accomplish when difficulties of the description alluded to are in the way.

North Owram the whole basis of the Parish is grit-stone. Immediately to the East of this valley, argillaceous strata, with their general concomitants, stone and iron, once more appear; and to this cause, together with the copiousness and rapid descent of its numerous brooks the Parish of Halifax is indebted for its wealth and population. Unequal surfaces, rapid streams, and plentiful fuel, are the soul of manufactures."

"The antiquary who looks through this extensive district for those appearances which most delight him will be disappointed. In a tract of more than 124 square miles, there exists not the remnant of a Castle; there never was a monastic foundation. He must therefore content himself with a few earth works which indicate that some inconsiderable fortresses once existed within it; and, with respect to ecclesiastical antiquity, he must take up with the appropriation of its rectory to a remote house, and with a few scattered donations of acres and ox-gangs to such'neighbouring convents whose popularity extended beyond their own immediate bounds."

"The unfavorable situation of Halifax may serve to prove how completely the wealth, and industry of man can trample over the most stubborn indispositions of nature. In a farming district the whole Township must have lain waste for ever. A basis of quartz not half covered by a few stunted bushes of ling, would have held out no temptation to the husbandman, and would have been im-moveable by all his efforts, because animal manures, the *egesta* of a large town must have been wanting. Yet how astonishing is the effect actually produced! Look on one side of a fence and you have nature yet remaining in the state not exaggerated by this account. Look on the other, and you have a creation of vegetable mould, covered with a rich and abundant coat of artificial grasses. In short, it is here the tiller who has made the soil, and not the soil which has enriched the tiller."

" It appeared to CAMDEN a singular fact, that in this Parish then peopled according to his own account by about twelve thousand souls, there were more human beings than beasts of any kind.

" This is unquestionably true at present, when the human species has increased nearly six fold, and sheep have greatly diminished in number, by means of enclosures. But at the close of the sixteenth century, I strongly suspect the number of quadrupeds to have preponderated. Suppose the Parish of Halifax, (and it will approach the truth,) to consist of 120 superficial square miles, [124 is the real size] or 76,800 acres, one half, at least, must have lain in common; yet barren as these commons for the most part were two acres would have depastured a sheep in summer, and we are not to suppose so thrifty a race would have left their own commons unstocked, so that there must have been an excess of sheep above mankind, of at least one third."[*]

The Parish of Halifax may be considered as the valley of East Calder with its several auxiliary streams for nearly the first eighteen miles of its course. The obscurity, and almost inaccessible nature of the country through which this river passes, until within the last fifty years, has occasioned great uncertainty among topographers with respect to its name and source. Various as are the conjectures as to the origin of the word Calder; the account given by WATSON is much more probable than that of any other historians, that at the coming of our Saxon ancestors this river having only the common appellation Dūr, they added the epithet Ceald or Cold. Perhaps after all, observes Dr. WHITAKER, the word is simply the Danish adjective Kaldur, *frigidus*.

"The source of both the East and West Calders is a marsh in Claviger Dean, in the adjoining Parish of Whalley, where anciently stood a Cross called Cross i'th' Dean, or in the Dean, and from which the several springs, according to their situation to the East or West of the ridge, run to the East or West seas." The hills which constitute this ridge form part of the grand ridge, or as it is popularly termed, the back bone of England, the West Calder taking its course Westward, joins the Ribble and enters the Irish Sea; the East Calder pursuing an Easterly course enters the Parish at Todmorden, running through a valley rich indeed in the grand and the romantic, where in some places so narrow are its confines, that the river, the turnpike road, and the Rochdale canal are within a few yards of each other, passing the populous hamlets of Mytholm, Hebden-Bridge, Mytholm Royd, and Sowerby-Bridge, to within two miles of the town of Halifax, thence by Elland and Kirklees Park, in the vicinity of which it receives the Colne, proceeding onward by Brighouse, Mirfield,

* Whitaker's Loidis et Elmete, p. 266, et seq.

Dewsbury, and Horbury to Wakefield and from thence to Castleford it unites with the broad Aire. It is impossible to traverse the vale of Calder without pleasure; at its commencement there are two scenes, one West of Hebden-Bridge and the other of Todmorden, truly magnificent and which may be compared to the finest highland glens.

So obscure was the greater part of this valley in the earlier part of Queen Elizabeth's reign, that HARRISON, in his description of Brittaine, A. D. 1577, speaks of it with amusing hesitation and uncertainty, which to an ear familiar with its local names is heightened by the mistakes in orthography.

"There is a noble water that falleth into Are, whose head as I take it, is about Stanforde, (it is in fact within a mile of the Western extremity of Stansfield,) from whence it goeth to Croston Chapel, to Lingfield, (Langfield) and thereabout receyving one ryll near Elfabright Bridge, and alsoe the Hebden, it goeth to Breareley Hall, and so taketh in the third by North, it proceedeth on Eastward by Sorsby Bridge Chappel, and there a ryll from South-West, and so to Coppeley Hall. Beneath this place I finde alsoe that it receyveth one ryll from Hallyfaxe which ryseth of two heades, and two other from South-West, of which one cometh by Barealande and Stainlande in one channel, as I reade, so that after this confluence, the aforesayde water goeth on toward Cowforde Bridge, and as it taketh in two rylls above the same, on the North side, so beneath the Bridge there falleth into it a pretty arme encreased by sundry waters comyng from by South, as from Marshden Chapel, from Holmesworth (Holmfirth) Chapel, and Kirkheaton, like one growing of sundry heads, whereof I would say more if I had more intelligence of their several gates and passages." He then traces it "finally into the Aire west of Castleworth as I learn" and concludes, "what the name of this river should be, as yet I heare not, and therefore no mervaile if I do not sett it down, yet it is possible such as dwell thereabout are not ignorant thereof, but what is that to me, if I be not partaker of their knowledge."

This dry detail of HARRISON's is versified by DRAYTON in his *Polybion*, in the following strain:

"And leading thence to Leeds that delicatest flood
Takes Calder coming in by Wakefield, by whose force
As from a lusty flood, much strengthened in her course

But Calder as she comes, and greater still doth wax,
And travelling along by-heading Halifax,
Which Horton once was called, but of a Virgin's hair
(A Martyr that was made, for chastity that there
Was by her lover slain) being fastened to a tree,
The people that would needs it should a relic be,
It Halifax since named, which in the northern tongue
Is holy hair."

The principal rivulets and streams within the Parish tributary to the Calder are in number, nine.

The first takes its rise on the moorlands of Stansfield, and in its course divides that Township from Heptonstall, and falls into the Calder at Mytholm.

Second.   The Hebden or Hepton; this river rises in the mountainous district of Heptonstall, and dividing that Township from Wadsworth, falls into the Calder at a place called Black Pit, near Hebden-Bridge.   There is a Charter mentioned in DODSWORTH'S MSS., wherein this river is thus referred to "Sup. Stagnum de Heptonstall ultra aquam qua vocatur "Hepton" (not Hebden,) qua currit inter Heptonstall et Wadsworth."

Third.   A Brook, which rising near Blackstone Edge meanders through the romantic and beautiful vale of Turvin, partly dividing the townships of Sowerby and Erringden, falls into the Calder at Mytholm Royd Bridge.

Fourth.   A Brook, from Luddenden, which dividing the townships of Midgley and Warley, and passing under the Rochdale canal at Luddenden Foot, enters the Calder there.

Fifth.   The Riburn.   This is a considerable stream, and is composed of several heads, the valley through which it passes is remarkable for the fineness of its scenery; it unites with the Calder at Sowerby Bridge.

Sixth.   The river Hebble, Halig, or Halifax Brook.   This is formed by the union of the waters of Skirden and Ogden or Oakden in Ovenden, where passing through the vale of Wheatley it unites with another stream (which rises in Illingworth,) about half a mile from the town of Halifax, at a place called Lee Bridge, where forming one stream it passes round the North and East sides of the Town, dividing it from the townships of North and South Owram, and empties itself into the Calder at Brooksmouth.

Seventh. The Blackburne or Black-Brook, above Elland, which rises in the Parish of Huddersfield and separates the townships of Stainland and Barkisland.

The Eighth is a stream called the Red Beck, which rises in North Owram, and dividing that Township from South Owram, falls into the Calder at Brookfoot.

The Ninth and last stream within the Parish which discharges itself into the Calder, is Clifton Beck, it rises in the township of Shelf and divides that Parish from the chapelry of Hartishead.

Nearly the whole of these streams are made subservient to the purposes of manufactures.

There are also several minor streams; the country indeed abounds with springs of water, and the valleys through which they take their course present some beautiful and matchless changes of landscape, which if but divested of the inelegance of manufactories, and their unsightly but necessary appendages, to say nothing of those threatened nuisances—railways and tram roads, would afford situations for residence rarely to be met with in more favored districts.

With the exception of the Hebble, the water of which is too much impregnated with the refuse of the mills, and dyer's works on its banks; the majority of these streams, particularly the Hepton, produce most excellent trout, and other fish, and would afford delightful sport to the angler, were it not that the breed is gradually decreasing in consequence of the impunity, with which poaching, and poisoning the water by an infusion of lime, is carried on in the vicinage of the manufactories.

The Parish also possesses the advantage of some mineral springs, which are not unworthy of notice. In the township of Soyland is a strong chalybeate, called Swift Cross Spaw, the water from this spring was found, by experiment, to be eighteen grains in a pint, lighter than at Swift Place, a few hundred yards below. At a place called the Cragg, in Erringden, there is another with an impregnation slightly sulphureous as well as chalybeate. At Horley Green, about a mile and a quarter North-West of Halifax, a mineral water has lately been discovered, on which a pamphlet has been written by Dr. GARNETT, of Harrogate; it appears from his experiments to contain a large proportion of vitriolated iron, besides alum, salenite, and ochre, and it is stated by him to be the strongest water known.   In the township of Shelf, there is said to be a petrifying water.   These mineral springs are much resorted to by the laboring classes, who experience great benefit from the use of them.

The great advantages to be derived from internal commercial navigation have ever induced the legislature to promote, and facilitate, the views of those who may have been willing to advance their capital in this description of undertaking.

The Aire and Calder Navigation was the first of the kind in England; and with the exception of the canal at Languedoc in France; the first in Europe.

The great benefit which the trade and commerce of the country derived from the former, led those who were more immediately connected with the district, to apply to Parliament for its sanction to extend that navigation, from its termination to within a short distance of the town of Halifax.   By an Act 31 Geo. II. this was speedily effected.   The line was surveyed by John Smeaton, Esq., in 1757, and the works were carried into execution under his superintendence, until the year 1765, when he was suceeded by Mr. James Brindley; but before the line was completed, such of the works as were then made, were, by the violence of repeated floods, destroyed or very greatly damaged, more particularly by a great flood, which occurred in the night between the 7th and 8th October, 1767.   At this juncture the late Sir George Savile rendered many important services to the undertaking, and was one of its most ardent promoters.   Application was made to Parliament in the following year, the 9th Geo. III. by the proprietors; and an Act was obtained "for extending the navigation of the river Calder to Salterhebble Bridge, and Sowerby Bridge, in the county of York, and for repealing an Act for that purpose."   By this Act the Proprietors of the canal were incorporated by the name of "The Company of Proprietors of the Calder and Hebble Navigation;" under its provisions, several alterations and improvements were suggested by Mr. Smeaton, in the years 1770, and 1779; of whose eminent talents the company again availed itself.   At the first general meeting of the proprietors for carrying the new Act into execution, held in Halifax on the 18th May, 1769, the following expressive acknowledgment was made of the services of Sir George Savile; it was resolved—

" That the unanimous thanks of the Company of Proprietors of the Calder and Hebble Navigation be paid to Sir George Savile, Baronet, for his generous patronage and important services to their navigation, and that the chairman, Colonel Townley, be desired humbly to present the most respectful acknowledgments of the said company to Sir George, for the same; and earnestly entreat his favorable acceptance of this small pledge of their gratitude for his great attention to the general good, at the same time that they cannot but admire his singular moderation and complacency with regard to such things as concern himself alone."

This navigation from its junction with that of the Aire and Calder at Fall Ing Locks, near Wakefield, to the basin at Sowerby Wharf, where it communicates with the Rochdale canal, is 22 miles in length, with a fall of 192 feet 5 inches, by thirty-eight locks.

A considerable portion of the line occupies the original bed of the river, and the remainder consists of cuts, to avoid its circuitous course, and for the purpose of passing the mill weirs.

It was first projected with the sole object of giving facility of intercourse with the populous and manufacturing districts, westward of the town of Wakefield; but it has subsequently by its connection with the Rochdale and Huddersfield canals become a very important part of the line of inland navigation between the ports of Liverpool, Goole, and Hull, thus connecting the German Ocean and the Irish Sea. This spirited and important undertaking may be looked upon as one of the greatest improvements that could possibly be effected in this part of the country; and at the period of its formation, its benefits must have been incalculable; nor is it less so at the present day. We have only to imagine what were the state of the roads between the large manufacturing towns of which Halifax was the centre, when we are informed that the " carriage of raw wool and manufactured goods was performed on the backs of single horses, at a disadvantage of nearly 200 to 1, compared to carriage by water."

The country through which the line passes has also partaken of the great advantages arising from a well regulated navigation: agricultural lime, has by its means, been carried to fertilize a sterile and mountainous district; stone and flag quarries have been opened at Cromwell Bottom and Elland Edge, which furnish inexhaustible supplies for the London markets. Ironstone, and coal works have been, and continue to be worked on its banks; and from the collieries at Flockton and Kirklees, railways are laid to this navigation. Many other collieries and stone quarries have been opened in its vicinity, in consequence of the facility it gives for exportation.

In 1825, the proprietors applied for and obtained " an Act to make a navigable cut or canal from Salterhebble Bridge to Bailey Hall, near to the town of Halifax, in the West Riding of the county of York; and to amend the Act relating to the said navigation." By this Act the company were empowered to raise among themselves or by the admission of new proprietors, the sum of £40,000, for carrying into execution (the works proposed being only one mile and three-eighths of canal) with further power to raise by way of loan or by creating new shares, an additional sum of £10,000; but which sums of £40,000 and £10,000, might be raised upon promissory notes, or on mortgage of the tolls and duties authorized to be collected.

The cut authorised to be made by the last Act, is nearly one mile and three eighths in length, with a rise of one hundred feet and a half. It commences in the Salterhebble basin and proceeds up the valley to the East side of the town of Halifax, where there are capacious warehouses, convenient wharfs, and basins, for the accommodation of the trade. The water for supplying it is procured by means of a drift eleven hundred and seventy yards in length from the basin of the canal at Salterhebble, to a reservoir beyond the uppermost lock from which it is raised by a powerful steam engine, into the head level. This novel and expensive mode of procuring the lockage water was resorted to by the late Mr. Bradley, the company's engineer, for the purpose of avoiding disputes with the numerous mill owners on the line of the Hebble Brook, below Halifax. The work was begun on the third day of May, 1826, and the canal was opened on the twenty-eighth day of March, 1828, when rejoicings and festivities characterized the day. A short account of these festivities, &c. will be given in the chronological table.

Again the company have found it necessary to apply to Parliament and during the present Session, (1834) an Act has been obtained, entitled an Act " to enable the Company of Proprietors of the Calder and Hebble Navigation to improve their navigation and to amend the Acts relating thereto." The improvements contemplated are those which may be effected by making new canals and substituting them for the present river in such parts of the line as are at present subject to interruption from floods and other inconveniences attendant upon river navigation.

In that part of the Parish lying Eastward of the Hebble, including the townships of North Owram, South Owram, and Shelf, are to be found considerable beds of good Coal. The produce of these collieries, together with those of the adjoining Parishes; (for the transmission of which every facility is afforded by the line of navigation) always ensures a constant supply of that invaluable mineral, not only for domestic purposes, but also for the use of the manufactories.

The heights in the immediate vicinage of the town afford an inexhaustible supply of valuable stone capable of being adapted for every purpose. The produce of these quarries is brought down to the navigation, (on the banks of which the proprietors have wharfs,) and is from thence shipped in considerable quantities to all parts. St. James's church in the town is an excellent specimen of the stone from the quarries in Shibden dale. The produce of the Ovenden quarries is brought down to the Rochdale canal at Luddenden Foot, and from thence transmitted to its places of destination, and finds a ready market in the adjoining county of Lancaster.

The high ridge above Mytholm, in the township of Heptonstall, also affords good stone for building, a specimen whereof may be seen in the new church at Mytholm.

Suffice it to say, that if proof be wanting of the excellent quality of the stone with which the Parish abounds, " look around it."

On the confines of the Parish, but actually within the adjoining Parish of Bradford, are the extensive and well known iron works of the Low Moor Company.

Agriculture, as a scientific pursuit, is little followed in the Parish, the soil being altogether unfavorable to it. Since the passing of the Enclosure Acts, much of the land has undergone considerable improvement, and the facility afforded by the local navigation for the conveyance of tillage from distant parts, (neither lime, marl, nor other products of the earth adapted to the purpose being to be obtained within the district,) has been the means of introducing cultivation by the plough to a much greater extent than formerly;

but notwithstanding these improvements, the arable land bears but a very small proportion to the whole, and the grain produced is principally oats and wheat, the latter preponderating. The cultivation of potatoes has also much increased of late; nor amidst the general improvement, has the spirit of planting been neglected in those parts were waste land has recently been enclosed. The greater part of the land is exclusively kept in grass.

The farms throughout the Parish are generally small, and principally occupied by the inhabitants, as a matter of convenience, for the use of their families. The manufacturer has his enclosure, .wherein he keeps his milch cow for the use of the family, his horses for carrying goods to market and bringing back the raw material.

The tenure by which most of the farms are held is from year to year; and leases are unusual.

The moorlands which are very extensive abound with grouse, and in general are well preserved; portions of the moors are devoted to the feeding of sheep and cattle, which are afterwards brought down to the pastures to fatten.

Much as the present system of turnpike road management is in general to be deprecated, the principal roads throughout the Parish with one or two exceptions may be considered in sound repair compared with their state a few years ago; still it cannot be concealed that much remains to be done, and until a system more in unison with the improved mode pursued in other parts of the country be adopted, much may be expected. But the line between Manchester and Leeds certainly affords a striking contrast to the description given of it by our amusing friend, TAYLOR, the Water Poet, who travelled in these parts in 1639. In his book called "Part of this summer's travel, or news from Hell, Hull, and Halifax" he says, "when I left Halifax I rode over such ways, as were past comparison or amendment, for when I went down the lofty mountain called Blackstone Edge, I thought myself in the land of breaknecke, it was so steep and tedious;" and again, in 1649, we find Mr. Ainsworth, then curate of Lightcliffe, in a sermon preached by him at Halifax, (and printed) exciting the tender feelings of his congregation in the following sympathetic strain " the highways did lament and mourn as he came that day, because they were deprived of Mr. Waterhouse's legacies, and whereas their seasonable repair would magnifie the dead, their deepnesse and unpassableness did shame the living." The exceptions to the general rule do indeed at certain seasons afford instances of "deepnesse and unpassableness" which unquestionably call for censure, more in the shape of indictments than sermons.

The air of the Parish is decidedly salubrious, and epidemical diseases may be considered as rare. Of the contagious disorders which have at various periods raged in England, the inhabitants appear to have suffered most from the *sudor anglicanus*, or English Sweat, which appeared in the fifteenth century, it is said of this disorder that it "mended or ended" its victims in twenty-four hours. Of that dreadful epidemic *the plague* it appears from the Register at Halifax, that there died in the township of Ovenden of the pestilence, and were buried near their own dwellings, in 1631, sixty persons; and in the same year, one hundred and seven persons are said to have died of that disorder at Heptonstall, several of whom were buried at home, but all entered in the Register there. In the year 1675 there prevailed an epidemic distemper profanely called the *jolly rant*, it was a severe cold and violent cough, which visited York, Hull, Halifax and other places, and affected all manner of persons so unusually that it was almost impossible to hear distinctly an entire sentence of a sermon. In the year 1681 the *small pox* is said to have been very fatal at Halifax, also at a subsequent period. I should not omit to mention that in the year 1832, when the whole country was visited by that awful scourge *the malignant cholera*, the Parish was happily preserved by a gracious Providence from the afflictive visitation.

The West and South-West Winds usually prevail in this district, and are generally attended with rain and tempest, sometimes to a degree most severe in their effects. The incessant rains which at times fall upon the mountains, may be attributed to the effect produced by the conflict of the East and West Winds, which generally takes place in the Western moorlands, arising from their elevated situation. Blackstone Edge and the mountains of Craven, are said to be the most foggy, rainy and stormy districts in England. These Winds have certainly a tendency to purify the atmosphere and perhaps the best evidence of the salubrity of the climate is the general healthful appearance of the inhabitants.

There are some instances of extraordinary longevity recorded by WATSON.

In the Halifax Register is this entry, "sepult. 1568, 11th Oct. Roger Brook, of Halifax, aged six score and thirteen years,"

1700. —— Littleton, of Rishworth, aged 100.

1704. Dec. 25th, Nathan Wood, of Soyland, aged 108.

1708. Dec. 3rd, Peter Ambler, of Shelf, aged 108.

1721. Nov. 10th, John Roberts, Hipperholme, aged 114.

And in 1757, John Firth, of Sowerby, supposed age 107, who left seven sons and daughters living, the eldest of whom was 87 years old, and the youngest 69.

1805. Elias Hoyle, Sowerby, 113.

1830. John Shepherd, Soyland, 100.

1830. John Logan, Halifax, 105.

Unfortunately, accounts of extraordinary longevity in general rest upon such unsatisfactory evidence, that there is much ground for scepticism when we hear of these instances of the marvellous.

To come down to the present time, it appears from the Parish Register that out of the number of 17,315 persons, buried in the Parish during eighteen years, viz. from 1813 to 1830 there

Died between the ages of 70 and 80 - - 1613.

,,   ,,   80 and 90 - -   837.

,,   ,,   90 and 100 -   89.

,,   ,,   100 and upwards - 1.

Ecclesiastically, the Parish is a Vicarage, (in the gift of the crown) within the province and diocese of York, and the arch-deaconry of the West-Riding.   It is divided into three ecclesiastical districts; viz. the Parish of Halifax, in the township of which name stands the mother Church of the whole Parish, comprising ten townships: the parochial chapelry of Elland, comprising six townships: and the parochial chapelry of Heptonstall, comprising five townships.   When this arrangement took place we have nothing to shew, the sub-divisions of the great Saxon Parishes form one of the most obscure subjects of English antiquity.   This may in a great measure arise from the equivocal signification of the word *parochia*, which anciently meant a bishopric or diocese, as well as a large Parish.   However interesting an enquiry into the time of dividing Parishes might be to the antiquarian, I shall not weary my reader with the dry detail of conjectures on the subject, he must in this instance rest satisfied with the simple fact, that these ecclesiastical divisions have existed long beyond the time whereof the memory of man runneth not to the contrary.

Shortly after the erection of the Parish Church, there arose, in the twelfth century, two ecclesiastical edifices called Parochial Chapels, viz. Elland and Heptonstall, these in common with the mother Church, possess the rights of baptism, the nuptial benediction, and of sepulture, but do not participate in the tithe of the land around them. Ten ecclesiastical Chapels were erected in the out-townships, between the twelfth century and the reformation. Trinity Church in the town, in the year 1798, a Chapel in Erringden in 1815; St. James's, in the town, and the Chapels of Brighouse and Mytholm, during the incumbency of the present Vicar, making a total of eighteen ecclesiastical places of worship throughout the Parish, to these may be added a Chapel at King Cross, in Skircoat, licensed by the Arch-bishop for the celebration of divine service. With the exception of the modern erections, none are contemporary with the period to which I have assigned them, but built on the sites of old foundations, or near them, and the majority have been rebuilt within the present century. Until the late and present incumbencies, too little attention appears to have been evinced in providing anything like an adequate church accommodation for the rapid increase of the population. That new Churches are much wanted in many of the out-townships is a truth that must be apparent to the most superficial observer. Many of the present Chapels are built on the verge of the Townships where located, or remote from the more populous parts; the consequence of which is, that a large portion of the inhabitants are prevented from attending, with any regularity, the stated services, by reason of the distance. This is an evil much to be deplored; and probably has been one cause of the growth of dissent in this extensive Parish, affording a plea not only for separation from the Church, but also for the erection of Meeting-Houses, the force of which it seems impossible to repel.

"It is a very remarkable circumstance," observes Dr. WHITAKER, "with respect to several of the ancient Townships, within the Parish, that though swarming with population they have no villages.

There is no single assemblage of houses called Stansfield, Langfield, Wadsworth or Warley; but the name denotes the whole district. The consequence of this is bad, the police must be comparatively inefficient, where, though the dwellings of the poor are numerous, they are yet so many solitudes. Objects of depredation are always near at hand, where observation is difficult and escape easy."

This is true to a certain extent but it is an evil beyond the reach of police regulations; we can only look to the improved habits and morals of the people to counteract the evil consequent on a state of society such as is here represented. The best system of Police must prove abortive. Since the introduction of what are termed "Beer Shops" into districts of this description, (putting out of the question the more centrical parts of the Parish, where they swarm) there has been a lamentable increase of crime. It is almost impossible to devise a system more pregnant with mischief. The resort of the idle and the dissolute in the day, and the haunt of the poacher and the thief at night, the one is sure to find his fellow. In the day is planned the succeeding night's spoliation; the house is too often made the receptacle of their plunder, and the tap is kept in a constant state of replenishment arising from the profit of their illicit depredations. Here, the incendiary and the unionist fraternise together; from hence, under the influence and excitement of their too often adulterated beverage, they turn out at midnight to consummate the mischief they have been plotting in the day, the one to fire the corn stack and the barn, the other to imbrue his hands in the blood of a fellow workman, or peradventure, the man to whom he was formerly indebted for his daily bread. That this is not an exaggerated statement, the proceedings of our Courts of Justice bear me witness. While the charges of the judges, the reports of grand jurors, and the calendars of crime, proclaim aloud the demoralizing influence of the national nuisance; the opinions of the resident magistracy, and the annals of the local police confirm the awful truth in every district of the country.

It has been a subject of frequent remark, and indeed it cannot have escaped the notice of the most superficial observer that in some of the remote parts of the Parish, particularly on the verge of Lancashire, (into which county the evil also extends,) that the standard of manners and morals among a great portion of the laboring population is disgustingly low. The advantages which usually result from an extended intercourse with commercial towns, and more populous places, have not been produced. However rapid may be the "march of intellect" elsewhere, it certainly "ascends but slowly up these mountain valleys." I am free to admit, that under any circumstances we are not to look for a high state of cultivation in districts of the description here alluded to, far from it, that can only be expected in large cities and towns; and even then it is but partial; this holds good in every civilized state; but in the present day, in whatever part of the country we may chance to locate, or roam, we have a right to expect that our ears shall not be polluted by language the obscenity of which, is only surpassed by its blasphemy; nor our eyes be doomed to witness scenes and exhibitions of so revolting a nature, that the pen shrinks from describing them.

It has been urged in extenuation of this evil, that the working classes have not the means of educating their children; this may be true to a certain extent, and it is to be regretted such is the case; the evil is not so much to be attributed to the want of schools as to the system itself. Here, (and it is the same in nearly all the manufacturing districts where the population is dispersed,) the Sunday school is the only place for instruction afforded to the children of the laboring poor; hither the child is sent, no sooner however has it arrived at an age capable of being employed in a lucrative way and before it has sufficient discrimination to choose the good, and refuse the evil, than it is transplanted into the manufactory. It requires no labored argument to prove, that neither virtue nor morality are indigenous to these places; the temperature is ungenial to the growth of either. The favorable impressions which have been made upon the child at school are speedily obliterated; the good implanted on the first day of the week, is stultified, by the influence of evil example, during the remaining six days. The result is obvious—yet such is the system.

This may, in some measure, account for the state of society before alluded to: how far the adoption of the new system, under the provisions of the late Factory Act, may prove beneficial to the rising generation, time will shew; we must not expect immediate effects, the looked-for improvement must be gradual, to be efficient.

c 2

"The biography of the Parish will prove, that it has given birth or residence to more talent, in various departments, than has fallen to the lot of some entire Counties. It is no small matter of boast that one country town has afforded an habitation to two such writers as Daniel de Foe and Sir Thomas Brown; and the birth-place of Tillotson will ever be regarded with veneration, by all who know how to estimate religion without bigotry, and reason without scepticism." I have made such selections from Watson's temple of fame, and such additions to it, as will fully justify the truth of the foregoing remark; and to that selection the reader is referred.

With respect to her eleemosynary foundations, scholastic institutions, and public charities, there are few (if any) provincial parishes that can compete with her; these she may consider her proudest boast. On a subject so interesting in a local point of view I have endeavoured to collate all the information in my power, and must refer to the chapter in a subsequent part of the work devoted to their consideration, and embodying the last report of His Majesty's Commissioners for enquiring into public charities.

There is a peculiarity in the dialect of the Parish, which has not escaped the notice of our earlier historians; and it will be found that Thoresby's observation is applicable to a certain extent at the present day.

"The ancient British way of using the father's and grand-father's christian names, instead of the *nomina Gentilitia* is not yet wholly laid aside in these parts of England. In the Vicarage of Halifax 'tis yet pretty common among the ordinary sort, A friend of mine asking the name of a pretty boy that begged relief, was answered, it was William o' Bill's o' Toms o' Luke's. In which spacious Vicarage, they have the remains of many ancient customs and names, evidently deduced from the British and Saxon times, as might have induced some of the learned men (for whom it has been deservedly famous) to give a particular description thereof: I shall only instance in what relates to the present argument, persons who dwell in the country villages are almost universally denominated from the place of their habitation. The ingenious gentleman before mentioned inquiring for Henry Cockroft, could hear of no such person, though he was within two bow-shots of the house, till at long run he found him under the notion of the *chaumer mon*, as he did William Thomas, though not without like difficulty, under that of the *hoo-hoil mon*, which manner of pronunciation of *mon* for man is the result of the Danish dialect, when Lords paramount or Lord-Danes in these parts; of which conversion of *a* into *o* there are many instances, in the learned Dr. HICKE's most elaborate *Thesaurus*. By the bye, *chaumer mon* is not to be taken for *camerarius*, but the inhabiter of the chambered house, which probably was a rare matter, of old, amongst the *sylvicolæ* of the forest of Hardwick."

"A tincture of early puritanism" says DR. WHITAKER "continues to appear in the manners, and in the christian names of the people; and perhaps there is not a Parish in the kingdom where old Testament names have so nearly superseded those of the new."

The peculiar dialect of that part of the Parish bordering on the confines of Lancashire has maintained its ground, from the earliest period of our language. "Besides a curious and singular nomenclature which has been collected with great industry and exactness by WATSON, (and which has a place in the appendix,) this dialect is most strongly marked by a peculiar corruption of the vowels and diphthongs, better learned, if it were worth while, by the ear than the eye. Long patronymical names (not indeed peculiar to this Parish, for they prevail in the adjoining ones of Whalley and Rochdale) are so generally in use, that a man is almost completely unknown among his neighbours by his legal surname."

As education and civilization advance, these modes of recognition fall into disuse: in the more central parts of the Parish, constant communication with persons of education has completely done away with it: but the practice referred to by THORESBY of using the fathers' and grandfathers' christian names, instead of the surname, is still maintained on the whole line of the County bordering upon Lancashire; and the observations of DR. WHITAKER apply with equal force at the present day, except that the custom of using old Testament names is not so generally followed.

The two following letters appeared in the "Halifax Union Journal" at the period they bear date, and have been instanced in the present day as a fair specimen of gooid Halifeighs. They are here inserted for the amusement of my readers, to whom (however uncourteous it may appear) I leave their translation, claiming an exemption from the task on the plea that I am not a native.

Halifaighs, Maartch 14th, 1758.

Maister Dorbee,

     Yawl vorre mitch abieege me, an eal print this letter e yawr neuspaper neist Wik, thoa sen yawr a gooid mon e dooin sitch a thing for a poor bodde, an i sware I'm reight poor ; i'm but a poor jurneeman croppar man, an its a trade noght gooid too, yawn work twelve aares for ten pinse; thmorohens al ha wage enogh, but its tCuntre Meisters mon at runs awei wit. But what i want yaw to doe for me is, om in a deeol o truble abaet a Pointer, yaw nawn what e mean, som fok calls em Spaniards, at aaer Meister broght me to keep for on oth Morchens at e works for, an yusturday whoei i wor at mi wurk, mo woef, a gaumless fooil, laate im run awei. Meister wold not loize him for twenty ginniz ; for mon thei setten more store o ther dogs than o ther men, an one on em ligs e more keepin then one o mo childer, or where the dule maught one get it aaeto laaeze ten pinse oth dey ? besaed aaer Meister sez at Meister————laekt this dog better than onne e haz, an o dor sei heez ommost thurte o one mak on other, haaends, an beigles, an pointers ; but heez lent this dog at o had monne a taem toth Porson, an e laeks im reight weel, thei sen heez a vorre gooid Shoiter, but i think sur e mught foend summet else to do, but sum on om ez nobbed loek like other fok at i see ; bui this dog sur, heez a braaen on whoet on, he corries a gooid teil, an heez a brass collar abaaet iz neck, wi Meister————z name on, for tha takken a praed man a keepin a deal o dogs ; heez not a vorre grut dog, nor a vorre little on, but ov a middle soez : An if yaw com hear ov onne bodde at haz im, yaw needen not be feared but yawl get paid, an weel too, prei a na sur put it in, for om ommost field aaet me wit abaaet it ; tho o think we sall hear on im agean too, for if Meister———— get to hear heez lost, heel get awther Porson orth Clark to cro im ith Chappil or else daub up a paper at Chappil doore abaaet it. So sur i think o neod to sei no more, yawl doit for me, o dor sei, an ost be vorre mitch ableeged tooya.

        "FRANK FORFEX, tho croppar."

     For Maister Dorbee at prinstt Halifaghs Jurnal with aul Haste.

Maister Dorbee, Surr.

     What om bewn to rite iz abewt dog at yaur news teld on. For mon a Tuaday at neet we wor gone a drinking too ith Ale hews, an we heard Joss o maister sam's reed tnews abewt a dog at wor lost, an at talm at faint moot ha sommot for tackint up. So we sed tone toth tother at weeld watch tLoin oth Wednesday Caus we wor gravin at toms oth dobhill ith faur de wark an it Liggs meet att Loin aide, So we gate up meeterly soyn oth Wednesday at morn on went to or wark an I Daraay weed not dun aboon five or seighs foors afore joss Chonst to be starin abewt im, ast most part o poolers don an saghim eom trotting up at Cruckt turn ith lower Loyn. So ee ran and fot him, but we eud not tell att furst whether it wor a rang on for it ad more marks nor yawr news teld on an it did not hold up it teil abit an beside ad gret ribs in it side ant Bally wor meet at it for Leggs ant Coller wor far to wide fort ant Letters wor Speld wit rang aide up for we eud not make om ewt, hewiver I tookt home an put it ith coyt imangth fiaghths an teld Matty to git som draff but t plagy bitch gat aul toth ould hen and so thpoor dog wor ther while fride at Neet afore any body thought ont or saghit but hur when owent to fot fiaghths to lay oth fire an oo took no notice ont athewt twur to git a nock wi or Clogg so o fride at Neet oo sed tew gret slane wat walt to doo we this rotten nasty thing so joss an me went an cauld out but it coom none Ewt cause we new not wat to caulit but wee cauld Pointer an Spaniard an Dol an Jet an Nance an Tobe an aulth dog names at we cud think on but th sluberon son ov a ***** ald not stir an ten Joss went tot an pausd it an palld it but ee wor no better for itld moove noan nor hasnt dun Eat. So any mon at naws wat to Caulit av a mind to come an give os a groat ee may hat for its nobbut ith gate hear.

New Maister Dorbee an yawl print tis yawl ma poor Frank fain or an yaw Cud tellim bewt printin it may happen doo os weel But yawm be sure to dooth tone.

SAWRBY TUPP.

The trade and manufactures of the Parish, or in other words her commercial history, is a subject not less interesting than important, and entitled to a prominent place in her local history. The chapter devoted to this inquiry will at once shew the extent and value of her manufactures, and the importance of her commercial relations.

In whatever point of view we glance at the modern history of this extensive Parish there is matter for congratulation, as the subsequent pages will shew. I am afraid that this Chapter exceeds the limits usually assigned to the subject on which it professes more immediately to treat, but embodying as it does a considerable portion of Dr. WHITAKER's valuable remarks, these, I hope, will be accepted as an atonement for its length.

THE BRITISH ÆRA.

THE Parish possesses some interesting remains of antiquity which may be safely assigned to the Brigantian Æra. Of these the Druidical remains form the prominent feature. On this subject DR. WHITAKER has forborne to enlarge "because he thought them all equivocal, excepting those which were clearly natural" but in adverting again to the subject he says that "to such purposes it is certainly possible they may have been adapted: those wonderful architects did not waste their unknown and astonishing powers where nature had prepared the way, and where a little excavation or the removal of a slight preponderance would suffice to produce a moveable fulcrum, and a perceptible balance. The powers which erected Stonehenge would in such instances be suspended, and the effect would be the same. Still, where the hand of man is not distinctly visible; where it is possible that nature, or time, or accident may have produced the same appearances, positive evidence is required to prove that they have been employed by the first ministers of superstition, to astonish and overawe the first rude inhabitants of the country."

With all deference to the opinion of the learned Doctor I cannot subscribe to the position, that positive evidence is required to prove cases of this description; and, notwithstanding he has rejected the reasoning of WATSON as vague and unsatisfactory, I certainly think that gentleman's sentiments on this subject are entitled to respect, although unsupported by that description of evidence which the learned Doctor considers essentially necessary to establish the fact; WATSON's many opportunities of examining these supposed remains, and his abilities in searching into antiquity, render his authority very respectable, to say the least of it; and as his conjectures on the present inquiry are plausible, so it is not likely we shall ever see any hypothesis better grounded than that with which he has favored us. GROSE, in his *Antiquities* classes some of these remains among the curiosities of Yorkshire. I have availed myself of WATSON's description where it applies, but abridged some of his remarks.

In the township of Barkisland is a ring of stones, supposed to be druidical, called the Wolf-fold, which from the name, says WATSON, I at first imagined to be the ruins of either a decoy for taking wild beasts, or a place to keep them in; but on a more particular view, was rather of opinion that it had belonged to the Druids. The stones of this circle are not erect, but lie in a confused heap like the ruins of a building, and the largest may have been taken away. It is but a few yards in diameter, and gives the name of Ringstone-edge to the adjacent moor.

Not far from Ringstone-edge is a parcel of rocks, on a common, called Whole Stone-moor, a supposed corruption of Holy Stone, or Hole Stone; devoted in all probability to druidical purposes. These stones which were in general about five or six feet in height above ground, and about six feet in circumference, were perforated at about three feet from the ground by a round hole, sufficient to admit a common-sized hand. In some parts of Ireland stones of this des-cription are common, particularly in the burial grounds attached to very ancient churches. We are informed that perforated stones are not uncommon in India: and devout people pass through them when the opening will admit, in order to be regenerated. If the hole be too small they put the hand or foot through it, and with a sufficient degree of faith, it answers nearly the same purpose!

At the edge of Norland-moor, among a large ridge of rocks, is a very ponderous stone, which projects over the side of the hill, and has a very uncommon appearance. It is called the Lad-stone, but for what reason no inhabitant of the place can tell. WATSON con-jectures the name is British, and it may come from *Lladd*, to kill, or slay, denoting persons were put to death here by a regular court of justice. If it be Anglo-Saxon, it may come from laðe, a purgation by trial, and therefore points out this place, as one where justice was administered. The Druids had undoubtedly this power, and they exercised it amongst rocks. The name also of the district lying below these rocks, is Butterworth, which might be so called from the bods, or bodes, the common appellatives of the abodes of people in the druidical times. A Ladstone in Sowerby is mentioned in a copy of a court-roll at Field-house in Sowerby, dated 6 Henry VIII. near the borders of Erringden, it is now destroyed.

In Rishworth is a group of stones laid seemingly one above another to the height of several yards, called the Rocking Stone.[*] Tradition says, that it once would rock, but that quality is lost. The form of it is not very unlike the Wring-cheese in Cornwall, described by Borlase, p. 165, and perhaps might serve for the same purposes.

The neighbourhood of this rocking stone, notwithstanding it is now a wild, uncultivated waste, WATSON conjectures to have been inhabited in the times preceding Christianity. The first reason for this opinion, is taken from its name. ROWLAND's, in his *Mona Antiqua*, p. 28, edit. 1766, has shewn us, that fixed dwellings were in this island originally called bods, a word yet used where the primitive language of the country is kept entire from that of the Anglo-Saxons. Where those people settled, bod would be wrote, and pronounced-bode or bothe, in modern spelling, booth, the very name by which this place is now distinguished. Another reason is, because there are yet to be seen the foundations of a large building, not far from the above rocking stone, by a place called Castle-dean, near which are many rocks of various shapes and sizes, where it is supposed a Druid might have exercised every part of his religion. There are also many other curious rocks and stones on the adjoining common, which are worth the inspection of the antiquarian. It may be thought a mistake to suppose that the Druids were settled here, because groves were essential to their worship, and there is not a tree, or even a bush, in all the neighbourhood; but there is sufficient proof that it once was woody, the name of Catmoss adjoining to it, helps to establish this fact. Coed is the British for a large number of trees growing together; hence THORESBY, p. 213, makes Cat-Beeston to be Woody-Beeston; and WRIGHT, in his Rutlandshire, p. 94, after Camden, explains Catmoss, by a field full of woods. But to put the matter quite out of dispute, the mosses hereabout that are cut into for fuel, are full of the fragments of trees.

[*] Loggon, or Rocking Stones, were huge stones so exactly poised on a point, as to be easily caused to rock or vibrate, if touched at a certain place; some of these are artificial, and others natural rocks cleared of the circumjacent earth.

The immense rocks and stones within the township of Stansfield, and its very retired situation, affords an ample field for antiquarian conjecture, that the Druids had a settlement here; and the Hawk-stones, Humberds, Bride-stones, &c. have been assigned by WATSON, as their temples or places of worship. The Bride consists of an upright stone or pillar, whose perpendicular height is about five yards, its diameter in the thickest part about three yards, and the pedestal about half a yard; near this stood another large stone, called the Groom, now thrown down; which in all probability might have been used by those ancient people for some religious purpose; at short distances are several others, of different magnitudes, and a vast variety of rocks and stones scattered about the common, presenting an appearance not unlike those remains to be found in Wiltshire, and other parts of the country, which our most eminent antiquarians have decreed to be strictly druidical.

At the end of the second edition of ROWLAND's *Mona Antiqua*, is a description of a druidical remain in Staffordshire, called also the Bride-stones, which affords a presumptive argument that this in Stansfield was made use of by the same people. They have been known by the name of Bride stones from time immemorial and are so described in a deed, temp. Henry VII.

Sowerby has in it a rude stone pillar, called the Standing Stone, near six feet high. It is conjectured that stones of this description are of more ancient date than Druidism itself; and were placed as memorials recording different events; it might have been an idol of the heathen inhabitants of this land.

On a swampy common called Saltonstall-moor, in Warley, is a fine large altar, called by the country people the Rocking Stone, the height of which on the West side, is about three yards and an half. It is a huge piece of rock, with rock basins cut upon it, one end of which rests on several stones, between two of which is a pebble of a different grit, seemingly put there for a support, and so placed that it could not possibly be taken out without breaking, or removing the rocks; these in all probability have been laid together by art. The stone in question, from the form and position of it, could never be a rocking stone, though it has always been distinguished by that name: the true rocking stone lies at a short distance from it, thrown from its centre. The other part of this stone is laid upon a kind of pedestal, broad at the bottom, but narrow in the middle; and round this pedestal is a passage, which from every appearance, seems to have been formed by art, but for what purpose is uncertain. BORLASE, p. 166, has given an account of something of this sort, called in Cornwall, and Scilly, Tolmen, or hallowed, which signifies the hole of stone, formed by a large orbicular stone, supported by two smaller, between which there is a passage or aperture, conjecturing, that whoever passed through these, acquired a kind of holiness, and became more acceptable to God; also that the cavity might be a sanctuary for the offender to fly to; but chiefly that such were intended and used for introducing proselytes, people under vows, or going to sacrifice, into their more sublime mysteries.

At the distance of about half a mile from this huge rock are the remains of a Carne, formed of loose stones, which for centuries has been called by the country people, Sleepy Low. Several broken fragments of rock are strewed over the moor, these are rendered more remarkable from the fact that the common is one vast morass.

On the right side of the road leading to the village of Luddenden there was formerly the remains of an altar, called Robin Hood's Penny Stone, who is said to have used this stone to pitch with at a mark for amusement, and to have thrown the Standing Stone, in Sowerby off an adjoining hill with his spade as he was digging! Report says that it was surrounded with a circle, but a few years ago this relic of antiquity was broken up for building purposes.

There are other presumptive proofs that the Druids inhabited this parish, such as a considerable part of the township of Wadsworth being formerly called Crimlishworth, now Crimsworth, from Cromlech, a sepulchral monument of that people, now destroyed. The term Cromlech is said to be derived from the armoric word crum, crooked or bowing, and leh, stone, alluding to the reverence which persons paid to them by bowing. That this was a woody part of the country, is not improbable, as appears from the name of Wadsworth or Woodsworth. It is said to have been an essential amongst the Druids to worship in groves of oaks, and such this country was once famous for, though at present few remain. Large tracts, which now are waste, are proved by tradition, and by their names, to have been covered over with trees, so that there was no want of the sacred misletoe. But the finest druidical remain in these parts, and what incontestably proves that these people were actually settled hereabout, is what is called the Rocking Stone, which is so situated as to be a boundary mark, dividing the two townships of Golcar, and Slaithwaite, in the Parish of Huddersfield, adjoining to the Parish of Halifax, on Whole-stone moor; which last circumstance seems to confirm the conjecture before made, that the Druids once worshipped in Barkisland. This stone is ten feet and an half long, containing nearly six cubits, druidical measure; nine feet, four or five inches broad, containing nearly five cubits; and five feet three inches thick, answering to three cubits or thereabout. Its weight, supposing seventy pounds to a square foot, is eighteen tons, and one hundred and ninety pounds. It rests on so small a centre, that at one particular point a man may cause it to rock, though some years ago it was damaged a little, in this respect, by some masons, who endeavored, but in vain, to throw it from its centre, in order to discover the principle on which so large a weight was made to move.

The tale that is told of Stonehenge, is also related by the people hereabout, namely that no one has ever been able to count the stones of which the circles here are composed so as to make the numbers of two successive reckonings agree. Although a baker once essayed to do it by placing a loaf on every stone, and afterwards counting the loaves, yet on a second trial he always found the same number of loaves either too many or too few.

In connection with the first period of society that existed in these mountains Dr. WHITAKER refers to "one discovery which must" he says, "without hesitation or controversy, be assigned to the aboriginal Britons. About the year 1779, a countryman in digging peat on Mixenden-moor, struck his spade through a black polished stone, resembling a hone or whetstone; adjoining to this was discovered the most beautiful and perfect brass celt I ever saw, it had apparently never been used, the edge being very sharp and uncorroded, from its whiteness the copper appeared to have been alloyed with tin. These remains were accompanied by four arrow heads of black flint, or basalt; by another light battle axe, of a beautiful green pebble, speckled with white; and lastly by a hollow gouge or scoop of hard grey stone, evidently intended for the excavation of canoes, or other wooden vessels.   This last is an unique, no implement for this purpose having ever been discovered before. Altogether they seem to have formed the imperishable part of the arms and implements of some British soldier, who by some other means than in battle perished among these wastes, where all remains of the body, together with the handles of the weapons, had long since perished, while the more ponderous and durable parts sunk beneath the spongy surface, to be disclosed by a fortunate accident at the distance perhaps of two thousand years."

Such are the memorials which still exist of the ancient British inhabitants of this district, that there are others yet undiscovered is by no means improbable. It is with diffidence, but without distrust, that I assert, it is my firm belief, (and herein I am not singular,) that a large portion of this district was inhabited by the primeval inhabitants of our isle.

Indeed if we look at the present aspect of the Parish, its general appearance, the sequestered valleys with which it abounds, and the brooks and springs by which they are fertilized, and compare it with the description given by early historians, particularly by Cæsar, of the sites usually selected by the aboriginal Britons for their habitations, there is much room for probable conjecture that such was the case, supported as that conjecture is by the evidence of the memorials before adverted to. But further than this. I know that in a part of our moorlands, there is an ancient highway still in existence, the original formation of which there is little reason to doubt may be safely assigned to this Æra, notwithstanding it may have been subsequently converted by the Romans into a vicarial way, for we are informed, that many of the roads supposed to be Roman are really formed in the line of British Trackways. I have inserted a description of the highway, to which I particularly allude, in the next chapter, for a cause purely deferential. Time will shew whether my hypothesis be correct.

THE ROMAN ÆRA.

NOTWITHSTANDING the County of York from its central position in Great Britain, was the favorite seat of the Romans, while under their yoke, there is not the visible remains of a Roman Station, within the bounds of this extensive Parish. Two military ways are supposed to have gone through it, one leading from Manchester to York, and the other from Manchester to Aldborough. The first of these has been described by MR. WHITAKER, in his *History of Manchester*, p. 81-86, who traced its course until it came to the township of Stainland, very near which, at a place called Slack, are the manifest traces of an ancient settlement, "which I had the honor" says WATSON "of being the first discoverer of, and of shewing to the Rev. Mr. Whitaker aforesaid." The wild and barren nature of this district unquestionably suggested to the Romans a motive for prolonging the usual distance between their stations. Hence in an interval of fifty miles, they had only one station noticed in the Itinerary of Antoninus between Mancunium (Manchester) and Calcaria (Tadcaster.) This was Cambodunum.

That WATSON, our own historian and antiquarian had the merit of having discovered the real site of Cambodunum, is confirmed by the testimony of that able antiquary, DR. WHITAKER, and the result of WATSON's enquiry was transmitted to the Society of Antiquaries by whom the communication was printed in the first volume of their Archaeologia.

"Excited probably by Camden's vague account of the celebrated altar, DVI CIV BRIG having been found in Greetland, as well as the report of roman bricks discovered at Grimscar, and upon a very accurate research finding nothing ancient or curious in that township, he extended his enquiries into Stainland, on the confines of which, but actually within Longwood, in the Parish of

Huddersfield, he found, I think beyond a doubt, the long lost Cambodunum of Antonine. On this subject, however differing on others, Mr. Whitaker and himself agreed; nor indeed could it be otherwise, for the distance from Manchester is exact, the line, near that of the great military way, and the remains decisive of Roman antiquity."

This testimony of Dr. WHITAKER's is at once so decisive, that I shall not trouble my reader with the proofs brought forward by WATSON in support of his argument.

That Cambodunum was not at Almondbury, is clear from more reasons than those assigned by WATSON. "Burgh and Borough are of the same origin, and denote in general the same idea, viz; that of a fortified hill; but in the North of England there is a distinction between the two which has not been sufficiently attended to, namely that Borough describes for the most part a Roman, and Burgh, a Saxon fortification." I concur with WATSON in opinion that Almondbury is merely a Saxon fortification, but the following memorial will prove that a prison at least upon the site of the old castle there was kept up until the beginning of the fourteenth century. "Almondbury, Huddersfield, Elmsley, &c. pres. quod quidam extraneus occisus est in prisona quondam Castri de Almondbury habens corpus quasi devoratum vermibus, avibus et canibus, et dicunt quod alibi occisus est et ibidem postea positus et projectus." "An horrid picture" observes the Doctor.

"High on the verge of the bleak moors which divide the Parishes of Huddersfield, Halifax, and Rochdale, but screened by a higher ridge to the West and South, is a sloping piece of ground, containing about twelve statute acres, and divided into several enclosures, some of which bear the name of the eald (or old) fields. The South side of this is formed by the deep and precipitous channel of Longwood Brook, the West by another nameless streamlet, the East by one still more inconsiderable but evidently deepened by art, and the fourth by a trench still visible, though partly covered by buildings, and partly effaced by the operations of husbandry." The inhabitants there have a tradition, that on these fields there formerly was a great town. This tradition, WATSON observes, is amply confirmed by many appearances, and from carefully considering where the plough is said to meet with obstructions, and where not, he thought that the range of a street or two might be made out, there are not any appearances of a Camp." Amongst these buildings WATSON was directed to the fine altar of Fortune (a vignette of which is presented to the reader) which he afterwards gave to his friend and brother antiquary, MR. WHITAKER; the place where it was found, is near the centre of the station, beside a perennial spring, and where from many symptoms, there must have been a bath with an hypocaust, near this are still remaining many mossy fragments of Roman mortar mixed with pounded bricks, apparently parts of the floor of the bath.

Of this spot MR. WHITAKER observes very judiciously "the station must have been placed in the neighbouring fields, immediately beyond the channel of the Western streamlet. This is a proper site for a Camp, a *lingula* formed by the union of two brooks, and defended by their deep channels on two sides." "With submission to Mr. Whitaker's judgment," says WATSON "I can see nothing to incline me to think that there ever was a camp here, or that if there had, the two insignificant currents of water above-mentioned could not have been any defence to it." "But had he" observes DR. WHITAKER, "directed a critical or even an attentive eye to the banks of these currents, he could not have failed to perceive the remains of a deep *agger*, and on the line of Longwood brook of two, where the North-East angle is very conspicuous, and turned entirely in the Roman

D

manner.   Both our antiquaries omitted to observe a small circus
of earth on the common to the North-West, which is now nearly
destroyed by a Turnpike Road, and there is a similar one in the hill
above.   Both these were by the people of the place denominated the
Camps : but they are evidently *gymnasia*, or places of exercise for
the Roman Soldiers.   On the side of a lane below, leading towards
Barkisland Hall, I saw, observes Dr. WHITAKER, an entire barrow
heretofore unobserved.   Such are the few visible remains of Cambodunum, of which I regret, after diligent and thrice-repeated
searches, I can add no more to the discoveries of my predecessors.
The present obscurity of Cambodunum may be imputed to a cause,
the very reverse of that which has occasioned the destruction and
disappearance of so many stations, viz. that their sites were so well
chosen in fertile districts, and on the banks of considerable rivers,
that after their abandonment by that sagacious people, later settlers
could find no other ground so eligible for the foundation of their
Parish Churches, their towns and fortresses, in preparing for which
they first destroyed all that remained of Roman architecture, and
then worked up the materials in their own constructions.   On the
contrary nothing can be more bleak and ungenial than the site of
Cambodunum, on a barren soil, and an high unsheltered eminence,
then wholly unenlivened by those cheerful hues of cultivation which
now clothe the country below, the natives of Italy and Gaul, condemned to garrison duty within its walls, must have thought themselves exiled to the extremity of the habitable globe.   The truth
seems to be, that at the first distribution of stations in the North of
England, this site was chosen, and fortified merely as a place of rest
from Calcaria (Tadcaster) to Mancunium (Manchester), but as the
country became better cultivated, and more inhabited, this cold and
inconvenient settlement was abandoned, the stages on the line were
multiplied; and Castleshaw, in Saddleworth, the small Roman camp
near Kirklees, the Roman town mentioned by Dr. Richardson, near
Kirkheaton ; and lastly, Wall flat, near Leeds, were planted on the
same line, for the better accommodation of the Roman troops on
their marches.   Let not this be thought a chimerical hypothesis ;
the obscurity of the remains at Cambodunum, where they can never
have been destroyed by future colonists, and the strong fact that
the coin found here with the altar, was of Hadrian, while the altar

bore strong internal evidence (as Mr. Watson has well shewn) that it belonged to the same period, all point to the same conclusion. And if we add to this, that no coins of a *later* date have ever been found here, and that all the coins found at or near the other Roman settlements above mentioned, are uniformly of the lower empire, my hypothesis must be allowed to be highly probable, that Cambodunum was abandoned at an early period of the Roman Empire in Britain."

"With respect to the dimensions of this encampment, it should not have been confounded by WATSON with those minor stations, which from the centurial inscriptions usually discovered within them, he very rightly judged to be adapted to a century only, as they seldom exceed 100 or 120 yards square; whereas there is a space of 240 paces within the ramparts of Cambodunum on one direction, and of 200 to the other. Such an outline could not have been defended by less than a cohort. But there was another objection to Cambodunum, as a post in time of war; which was that it could scarcely be defended from missile weapons at all, as it is commanded on two sides by higher grounds immediately beyond the brooks. On the whole, it was an untenable post, as well as an uncomfortable lodging, and therefore early abandoned. In short, though decidedly Roman, this site of an encampment is an anomaly in Roman castrametation."

Should any antiquary have the curiosity to trace the Roman way by Slack, it is necessary to caution him against a mistake " that it becomes the boundary to the parishes of Halifax and Huddersfield, and passes within two hundred yards from the station and the town." The boundary between these two parishes, is in the public road, called the Outlane, but the military way runs nearer to the station, through the fields called the Bents, having there frequently been turned up with the plough, and being composed of gravel.

Dependent upon the station of Cambodunum, appears to have been the Roman work on Lee Hill, near Slack, which Mr. Watson considers as Saxon. The work referred to, is a circular remain of an ancient encampment, about eighty yards each way, measuring to the outside of the *agger*, it commands a fair view of Castle Hill, near Almondbury, as well as of the adjoining country. There is a tradition of a battle having been fought here, which is borne out by the appearance of *tumuli* scattered here and there upon the common.   Upon these remains Dr. Whitaker remarks " the *castra æstiva* of the Romans, which were generally on elevated points, commanding like this very extensive views of the country around, were frequently oval or circular, adapting themselves to the shape of the hill on which they were placed.   The long connecting trench running over Linley Moor to Watch hill, which has evidently been an artificial specular mount, has more the appearance of a Roman than a Saxon Work."

We are informed by Camden, that at Grimscar have been dug up bricks with the inscription, COH. IIII. BRE, which Horsley judges to be " Cohors quarta Brittonum."   Bricks with the same inscription on them have also been found in the neighbourhood of Slack since Camden's time.   Mr. Watson is of opinion, that a detachment of the fourth cohort must have been quartered at Slack, and that the probability is, they went to Grimscar to make bricks, on account of the clay.

The most valuable remains of the Roman times which this district has presented is the votive altar, (of which the following is a vignette,) dug up in Greetland, and referred to by Camden.

The following is the inscription thereon, DVI. CI BRIG. ET NVM. GG. T. AVR. AVRELIANVS DD. PRO SE ET SVIS S. M. A. G. S.   On the reverse. ANTONIO III ET GETA COSS

The altar appears to have been dedicated by Titus Aurelius Aure-
lionis, to the God of the state of the Brigantes and to the Deities
of the Emperors, on behalf of himself and his followers, in grateful
remembrance of the success of their undertaking. The reverse shews
the time when the altar was set up, that is, when Antonius was
consul the third time with Geta. And the altar of Fortune before
referred to, (p. 33) discovered by our antiquary, Mr. Watson ; the
reading on this altar is said to be " Fortunæ sacrum. Caius
Antonius Modestus Centurio legionis sextæ victricis posuit et votum
solvit lubens merito." From which it appears to have been erected
by Caius Antonius Modestus, centurion of the sixth legion, in discharge of a vow. It was discovered in 1736, among the ruins of a
building manifestly composed of Roman bricks, many of which are
yet to be seen in the common fence walls there.

Roman coins either in single pieces or hoards, have at various
times been discovered in different parts of the Parish. In August,
1769, a quantity of coins of the small size were found in Elland
Wood, in a cavity of a rock under a stone. A considerable number
were also discovered at one time, at a place called Beestones, in
Stainland, about two miles from Slack ; also some in Sowerby and
Warley, also two or three at High Greenwood, in Heptonstall.
These, it must be observed, cannot be received as evidence of the
permanent residence of the Romans, on any particular site. Single
pieces may be dropped any where, and as the intention with which
hoards of money were sometimes buried, was, that protection might
be gained by concealment, they might be deposited at a distance
from the owner's residence.

The fragment of a Roman lattice, made of iron, was found at a
place called Hall Body, in the Eald Field, at Cambodunum, among
a large quantity of Roman tiles and bricks, which apparently were
the remains of a building.

I have embodied within this chapter the most interesting
portion of what has been written by former historians respecting
the remains of the Roman Æra within the Parish, or rather bordering upon it.

In the preceding chapter I referred to an ancient trackway,
which had not been previously noticed by them. It is a singular
fact that it should have escaped the attention of WATSON, because

in his time much of what is now destroyed, by the operations of husbandry and other causes, might then be distinctly traced.

Accompanied by a few friends on a fine morning at the commencement of the last spring, and bending our course to Ovenden Common, where by previous appointment we found our guide, (an old man upwards of eighty years of age, who had, he said "known the way from his childhood, as also his father before him.") We proceeded to a place called Cockle, or Cock Hill, in Ogden, an elevated spot on Ovenden Common, where are distinctly visible the remains of an ancient trackway; on examination, the material, of which it appeared to have been constructed were stones varying in size from a diameter of five inches to sixteen inches, the interstices between which had been filled up with a kind of mortar so tenacious even at the present day, that it was with difficulty the stones could be severed; many of them, which from time to time had been turned up, were used in building the adjoining walls. The way here is elevated and about the average breadth of fourteen feet; from this spot it takes a direction due West, to a place a little below, called the Peat Holes, a marshy spot where the way may be distinguished by its firmness; proceeding in the same direction over the common, it crosses an highway leading to a farm-house, and passes through two fields, at the bottom of one of which the waters of Skirden and Ogden meet; from this spot may be discerned at the distance of about two hundred yards to the right, two mounds, which two of our party were induced to inspect; the one resembled a cone, the other was still larger, and there was a smaller one on each side, the whole presented an artificial appearance, but time would not permit a fuller examination of them. From Skirden Clough, the way proceeded through some cultivated land, where the operations of husbandry had nearly effaced it, indeed the plough was then in full operation, the men at work informed us that they had sometimes met with obstructions from stones and stuff, which had been thrown in a heap. Passing through these lands we came to a place called Mixenden Ings, where our guide informed us, Farmer Tattersall had dug the road up, and formed with the stones a causeway to Brookhouse. Crossing a small brook, and ascending a moor called the Carrs, we reached the evident remains of a Camp, which if any reliance is to be placed on the authority of those versed in antiquarian lore, was in all probability formed by the Romans; the remains in question form a considerable circle, covered with heath and ling, and are surrounded by a ditch or *agger*, this is nearly filled up, but still distinctly marked: there is also a rampart or *vallum* composed of the earth dug out of the *agger*, the remain is divided into two parts by a way, which the Romans called the *Principia*, one of these divisions is considerably larger than the other, From this spot the way passes through Hunter Hill Lands, thence into Barrett's Lands, where, entering the township of Warley, at a place called Noah's Ark, in Coldedge, it is intersected by the high road from Halifax to Haworth, and along which road we proceeded homewards, anticipating the pleasure of a closer examination of these remains at a future period, which I regret to say has not yet occurred.

Generally speaking, in some places the way cannot be traced without difficulty, the vestiges being extremely faint and obscure; in others it continues firm and distinct, though covered with earth and grass, its height does not present that fine bold rampart which generally characterises the Roman Itinera in this country, though its breadth is in some places considerable; with respect to these remains it may be observed that the Romans never passed a night even in the longest marches without pitching a camp, and fortifying it with a rampart and a ditch; if they staid but one night in the same camp, or even two or three nights, it was called *castra*; if for a considerable time it was called *castra stativa*, a standing camp; *æstiva*, a summer camp, and *hiberna* a winter camp. This in all probability was only a *castra*.

I cannot pretend to give an opinion as to what *iter* or vicinal way, (if such it be) the road in question, may form a part. I must leave that to others better versed in antiquarian research. If I might venture on a conjecture, I should say, that it might be a portion of the way mentioned by Mr. WHITAKER, as issuing from the Roman road, which may be traced in a broken causeway over the wild moors of Heptonstall pointing towards Ilkley; or it may be a part of the Roman line of road leading from Ilkley to Cambodunum, "so conspicuous on the high grounds between Keighley and Halifax." Or, if these conjectures fail, I may perhaps be permitted to indulge in the harmless speculation, that it may be the remains of an ancient British Trackway, passing on from the place where we left it, over Saltonstall Moor, along the high grounds of Warley and Wadsworth, by Old Town to Crimsworth, and thence into Stansfield. I say passing in this direction, because these places have been assigned as stations occupied by the aboriginal Britons, (Ogden, or rather Oakden, the valley of Oaks, where the halig, or holy brook is formed by the junction of the waters before alluded to, being doubtless inhabited by the ancient Britons or their Druids.) My readers will bear in mind the important fact that the celts and arrow heads, referred to in the preceding chapter, were found in the district through which the way passes, and this circumstance, it is submitted, has a tendency to confirm the plausibility of my speculation. I fear, however, after all that can be said, the matter must be left involved in that glorious antiquarian uncertainty in which it was found. Happy shall I be if the account here given be an incentive to others to follow up an enquiry, (which if providence permit I intend to pursue,) and from which I can confidently assure them they will derive much gratification.

THE SAXON ÆRA.

THE commencement of the fifth century introduces us to a new Æra. At a time when the ferocious hordes of Picts and Scots were harrassing the island wherever they could penetrate, the Anglo Saxon invasion of England occurred. This invasion, says Mr. TURNER, in his *History of the Anglo Saxons*, "must not be contemplated as a barbarisation of the country. They brought with them a superior, domestic, and moral character, and the rudiments of new political, juridical, and intellectual blessings. An interval of slaughter and desolation unavoidably occurred, before they established themselves and their new systems in the island. But when they had completed their conquest, they laid the foundation of that national constitution, of that internal polity, of those peculiar customs, of that female modesty, and of that vigour and direction of mind, to which Great Britain owes the social progress which it has so eminently acquired. Some parts of the civilization, which they found in the island, assisted to produce this great result. Their desolations removed much of the moral degeneracy which at that time prevailed." For an historical, impartial, and interesting account of the Anglo Saxons, the reader is referred to Mr. Turner's work before alluded to. At the period of their establishment in this country, Britain was unhappily divided into numerous petty sovereignties. "Fallen into a number of petty states, in actual warfare with each other, or separated by jealousy, Britain met the successive invaders with a local not with a national force; rarely with any combination. The selfish policy of its chiefs, often viewing with satisfaction the misfortunes of each other, facilitated the successes of the Saxon aggressors."

Into their general history I have not the inclination (were it indeed within my province) to enter: and with regard to their contests, my readers must, in this instance, rest satisfied on the authority of MILTON, that they " are no more entitled to remembrance or recital, than the battles of crows and hawks in a summer's day."

Neglected and abandoned as were the Roman remains in this district, by the Saxons, they certainly colonized the more fertile parts of the Parish of Halifax, for the villare is generally Saxon ; there are also several earth-works, which can scarcely be ascribed to any other people.   Evident traces of these entrenchments and fortifications are still visible, none of them however are of any great extent; "a poor and barren district, at the very extremity of cultivation in the island, never afforded a residence to any of the great chiefs of the heptarchy, or a scene for any great action likely to be marked by permanent remains," but these remains on the contrary can only have been relics of domestic precaution or of petty discord, where the savage chief of one hamlet dreaded or attacked that of the next.   Conygarth will scarcely be considered an exception to this remark.

A few of the most noted places which are supposed to be remains of the Saxon Æra are here pointed out.

On Greenhalgh, a hill above Hoohoile, in Erringden, is a circular remain, which WARSON, from its name and appearance, judged to have been Saxon, the diameter of which is about sixteen yards; it has been walled round, and seems to have been a fort; the place is called Tower Hill.   There are the appearances of two breastworks, the first of which is about twenty-five yards from the remains, towards the South, East, and North sides thereof, of a circular form, the centre of which faces the east. . The other is at a greater distance, running along the South verge of the hill, which is very steep. It is remarkable that no breastworks appear to the West, where the ground is level, but no danger might be apprehended from that quarter. It is conjectured to have been raised for the purpose of opposing some irruption from the side of Sowerby, wherein, on an opposite hill was another fort, at a place near Hollinhey, called Conygarth, the site of which is still to be seen, but so situated, as plainly to be intended for a short use.

Near Ripponden, in the township of Barkisland, is a remarkable high hill, called the Conygarth, from the Anglo-Saxon, Cyniȝ, a king, and the British Garth, a mountain; as if some crowned head had encamped here with his forces, in the Saxon times. We have indeed no tradition or annals to shew this, but many facts of this sort are buried in oblivion, and others only to be discovered from a number of concurring circumstances. This hill is well situated for a thing of this sort, both on account of its being sufficiently spacious, having a good command of the country, and being on several parts of it very difficult of access.

In the depth of Rawtonstall Wood, within the township of Stansfield, is a deep moat, which appears to have surrounded an old manor house; and on the pointed and rocky summit of the hill above, tradition forty years ago, preserved the memory of a castle. On the side of this hill, towards the South, there has been a very large shoot of earth, which destroys the regularity of it; part of this earth was, in 1768, cut through to make a turnpike road. This breach shews that the whole hill was natural, as a large rock appears very near the summit of it. At the foot of the hill is a house called the castle, which in all probability takes its name from the hill. Whether the place was formed by our Saxon ancestors is altogether matter of conjecture, nothing antique having ever been found near it. It may have been used for the purposes of war by the inhabitants of Yorkshire, to stop the incursions of the Lancastrians; nothing could be better situated for that purpose, as it is within a mile of the borders, and stands in a pass between two very high ranges of hills; but no tradition of this kind remains. The valley below it has the name of the Castle-nase-bottom.

At Rastrick, in this Parish, was lately a mound called Castle-hill, which Dr. Johnson, who surveyed this neighbourhood in 1669, said was trenched about, and hollow in the middle, as if many stones had been got out of it. The circumference of it he measured to a hundred and eighty-eight yards within the trench, and on the top a hundred and seventeen, which shews the form of it. It has lately been destroyed, for the sake of the stone it contained, and it appeared upon examination that the top of it, for a few yards perpendicular, was cast-up earth, the rest a natural hill, the whole being left hollow at the top, seemingly with design. If this was a work of the Saxons, its name may come from Rerꞇ, a bed, or sleeping, and piᶾe, the ridge of a hill, meaning the hill where travellers or others used to lodge; and such a situation as this was very necessary in troublesome times, either for the neighbourhood to retire to upon alarms, or for way-faring men to make their nightly habitation; for being hollow at the top, it formed a kind of breast-work to protect the men in case of an assault; there was also a considerable ascent to it on every side, and there was no rising ground about it, from whence it could be annoyed. It must be owned that the words come very near to Rastrick. Several of the northern nations use rast for rest, in particular the Swedes and Germans. Raste also has the same meaning in the Belgic, or Low Dutch.

Works of this kind, I know, are generally attributed to the Danes, who, being few in number, in comparison of the Saxons, used this kind of fortification, to the end that, when alarms were given, they might repair thither, and remain in safety, until they could assemble themselves in greater strength. Now, if this was a Danish settlement, probably its name may be Danish too. It is certain, that all circular forts raised by this people, were called by the Irish, Raths, as they were also by the ancient Cornish men, and perhaps other inhabitants of this island, from the word Radt, which in the Celtic, signified a wheel, and by adding to this the Danish word Ryg, the ridge of an hill, such as this mount stood upon, we have Rath's-Ryg, which would easily be softened into Rastrick.

WATSON conjectures that the Danes spread themselves all over this neighbourhood, and is supported in his hypothesis by the fact of an urn having been found, with two others, at the gates at the bottom of the walk near Shaw Hill, leading to a house in Skircoat, called Heath. They lay in a line, one yard deep, and one yard asunder, with their mouths downwards. This urn contained calcined bones, and dust; the two others were broken in pieces. It was eight inches deep, stood upon a bottom of four inches diameter, and where there was no moulding, measured from twenty-one inches, or thereabouts, to twenty-three inches in circumference.

It appeared to that Gentleman, from a passage in the Saxon Chronicle, that the Danes under Cnute, (or Canute,) their king, made a grand march by the borders of this Parish. It is stated that this Cnute went against Uhtred, the Earl of Northumberland, through Buckinghamshire, Bedfordshire, Huntingtonshire, Lincolnshire, Nottinghamshire, and towards York; and the said Uhtred being slain, "deinde regressus est austrum versus, alia via per plagam occidentalem, adeo ut venirit totus exercitus ante pascha ad naves;" he returned to the south by the western coast, a different way from what he had gone before. But what way so likely as this which the Romans had made between Manchester and York? It might be then in good repair, and if the king chose to march by the western coast, was the next and best way. This was in the year 1017. There is a circumstance which confirms the opinion that this Danish king did actually march along this road, for several places on the line of it do still retain his name, such as Knot-lane in Saddleworth, and by the side of this, Knot-hill, which is a remarkable round-topped hill, from the top of which this king is said to have harangued his army. Also Knot-Mill near the Castlefield, by Manchester, where possibly the Danes might halt for some time ; and lastly, Knots-ford, called by Camden Canuti vadum. The road which branches off from this great military way, at Slack above-mentioned, and which has the name of the Danes-road, might have been used by part of this army, and have thence acquired its name; for having no enemy to fear in these parts, it might be more convenient for the army to take two different routes from thence to Manchester ; if they did, that division which fell in with the road between Ilkley and Manchester, might possibly march to the place of rendezvous, along the street called the Danes-gate, if indeed that name did not come from the Deans of Manchester, as the head clergy there were formerly called.

That the parish was in some places desolated by the Saxons, and made the arena of their contests, the memorials here exhibited sufficiently shew, but to what extent we have no account. In what further relates to their connexion with this Parish I have nothing to add. No coin or other interesting memorial of their presence, has ever been turned up within its precincts.

In this part of our subject we are walking over the country of the departed, whose memory has not been perpetuated by the commemorating heralds of their day. A barbarous age is unfriendly to human fame. When the clods of his hillock are scattered, or his funereal stones are thrown down, the glory of a savage perishes for ever. In after ages, fancy labors to supply the loss; but her incongruities are visible, and gain no lasting belief. But I cannot take my leave of this obscure and barbarous æra, without looking back

upon it, and comparing in imagination, the then prospects of the
Country with its present flourishing condition, though it is not
easy for a mind familiarized to its present state to conceive of the
other even in fancy.   But would my reader carry himself nine or ten
centuries back, and ranging the high ground of Skircoat, or taking
his position at King-Cross, survey the vale of Calder; instead of the
populous village, the well-built residence, the modern villa, the
comfortable cottage, the elegant mansion, the artificial plantation,
the enclosed park and pleasure-ground, instead of uninterrupted
enclosures, which have driven sterility almost to the summit of the
distant hills, how great must have been the contrast, when at a
distance, or immediately beneath, his eye must have caught vast
tracts of forest ground, stagnating with bog or darkened by native
woods, where the wild ox, the roe, the stag, and the wolf had
scarcely learned the supremacy of man; when, directing his view
to the intermediate spaces, to the windings of the valley, or the
expanse of plain below, he could only have distinguished a few in-
sulated patches of culture, each encircling a village of wretched
cabins, among which would still be remarked one rude mansion of
wood, (scarcely equal in comfort to a modern cottage) rising proudly
eminent above the rest, where the Saxon Lord, surrounded by his
faithful *coterii*, enjoyed a rude and solitary independence, owning
no superior but his sovereign.   This was undoubtedly a state of
simplicity, such as the admirers of uncultivated nature may affect
to applaud; yet no good man can lament the subversion of Saxon
polity, for that which followed.

THE NORMAN ÆRA.

The earliest period of written and authentic information relative to this Parish commences with Domesday*, the most ancient record that exists in the Archives of the United Kingdom. We there find the following members of the Parish thus described as Berewicks of the Manor of Wakefield, to which they still belong.

Terra Regis in Eurewickscire. In Wachefeld cu' ix Ber'. Sandala, Sorebi, Werla, Fealei, Miclei, Wadesuurde, Crumbetonsetan, Lanfeld, Stanesfelt. Sunt ad g'ld LX Car t're 7 iii bovat 7 tercia pars uni' bovat. Hanc t'ram poss. arare xxx Caruce. Hoc manes' fuit regis Edw. in Dnio. modo in manu regis. Sunt ibi iiii vill. 7 iii Pb'ri 7 ii Eocli" æ 7 vii Sochi'i 7 xvi bord. Simul ht vii Car. Silva pascua 7 c. From this it will be seen that the number of Carucates in each Berewick is not particularized.

In the Terra Ilberti de Lacy, Elland and Overe (North and South Owram) were thus surveyed;

M"'. In Elant hb' Gamel. iii Car. tre 7 dim ad g'ld ubi ii Caruce poss. e e. Ilberr'. ht. nc' 7 wast e. T. R. E. val xx sol. Silva past. dim leug. lg 7 iiii q' 2 lat 7 iiii acr. pti.

In Overe h"b Gamel iii Car. car tre ad g"ld ubi iii Car. poss. e'e'. Ilberr" ht 7 wast e. T. R. E. val xx sol. Silva past. iii q' 2 lg" 7 iii lat.

"In the foundation of the Parish of Halifax (observes Dr. WHITAKER) it appears that the two great houses of Warren and

---

Lacy concurred. The former permitted eight of the berewicks specified above to be detached from the parish of Dewsbury, and the latter, from the vicinity of their situation to the new church, permitted North and South Owram, in which are to be included Shelf, Hipperholme, &c. and Elland to be separated from Morley, the only Saxon church in the hundred beside Dewsbury. It is remarkable that these portions of the Lacy fee are described as waste, whereas all the townships in the *terra regis* were in a state of cultivation. Was it that the conqueror in his dreadful devastation of Yorkshire, spared his own demesnes? Scarcely so; for almost all the townships within the soke of Wakefield, as distinct from its berewicks, are stated to have been depopulated. The probability therefore is, that these remote townships lying at the very extremity of population, had escaped those ravages with which first the Danes and afterwards the Conqueror had visited the more open and fruitful parts of Yorkshire."

Of the places described by Domesday in this district, corrupted as many of them are, there can be little doubt with the exception of Feslei, which is meant for Fesebie, Fekisbe, or the modern Fixby, and Crumbetonsetun, which has been supposed to be Cross Stone; but this is not only no hamlet within Stansfield, but never was included within it, I deem it therefore much more probable, that it is meant for the valley, bounding on one side the township of Heptonstall, now called Crimsworthden or Crimsworth (especially as Heptonstall itself is not mentioned in Domesday) for WATSON was mistaken in supposing that place to be meant for Hepton, which is in the Wapontake of Agbrigg.

We have, however only ten townships in the Parish of Halifax, which by subdivisions have gradually increased to twenty-three. Of these Erringden, having been first a chace and afterwards a park, formed no part. The sub-divisions of Overe have already been

stated; according to some, 1083, 17 WILL. I. According to the Saxon Chronicle, 1085, but the Red Book of the Exchequer states its commencement to be the 14th WILLIAM 1st, 1080, and its completion in 1086. The pound mentioned in Domesday Book (says Sir Robert Atkins) for reserved rent was the weight of a pound in silver, consisting of 12oz. which is equal in weight to £3 2s. of our present money; the same weight in gold is now worth £48. The shilling mentioned in the same book, consisted of twelve pence, and is equal in weight to 3s. of our money: A caracute, hide, or plow of land, was a certain quantity of land, about 120 acres. An ox was then valued at 7s. 6d.; about 1770 it was worth £7 10s., its present value in England is nearly £30.

mentioned; Soyland may be assigned to Sowerby; Norland, Stainland, Greetland, and Barkisland together with Rastrick and Rishworth, to Elland; and Skircoat and Ovenden, with Halifax the capital, must have been taken out of Warley. No such name as Horton, which an idle tradition has delivered down as pre-existing on the site of Halifax, is mentioned in Domesday. CAMDEN therefore, who too credulously took up with a vague report, and has given a credit and currency to it which it did not deserve, was wholly misinformed.

"When the Domesday survey was taken, all the cultivated lands of the parish within the Warren fee, which is more than two-thirds of the whole were contained in seven berewicks or vills, and consisted of less than thirty carucates, or 3000 acres. These were mere spots and patches of culture, selected for their native fertility, by the first settlers, either from the alluvial lands on the banks of the Calder, or from the higher slopes, such as Langfield, where the soil is deep, and comparatively productive.

"From some cause or other, for trade had not yet been introduced, a great increase in population (and consequently in culture) had happened, otherwise the erection of the two parochial chapels would not have taken place. But now the old and fertile enclosures (the oxgang land of their forefathers) became inadequate to the wants of the inhabitants, the process of ridding or essarting the native woods on the steep brows, which is the origin of the rood land, began; the circles of cultivation in the neighbouring townships began, at their lower extremities, to touch each other, and the commons were gradually confined to the stony summits of the hills, where nature will for ever continue to vindicate her rights against all the encroachments, and all the opulence of man."

THE MANOR.

The history of Halifax is so inseparably connected, in an historical point of view, with that of the Manor of Wakefield as forming an extensive part of it, that an enquiry into the history of the one naturally includes the history of the other.

Of the precise date when the Manor of Wakefield with its dependencies, passed from the Crown into the hands of the Earls Warren, we have no legal evidence. The first William de Warrenne married Gundred, daughter of the Conqueror, with whom, according to some accounts, he had the Manor of Wakefield, to which Halifax was an appendage; but this is improbable, because in Domesday Book, which was only finished in 1086, about two years before the Earl's death, (and after the decease of Gundred,) this manor with the nine berewicks thereto belonging, are said to be in the king's hands. The second earl enjoyed the honor and possessions of the family nearly fifty years, dying in 1138. "Between the years 1091 and 1097, when he was yet young in age and new in his possessions, the second earl gave the church of Coningsborough and all its dependencies, and the church of Wakefield, to his father's monastery of Lewes, in Sussex. The date of this donation, about which there has been some misconception, is to be collected from the names of the witnesses, among whom are three bishops, named Ralph, Gundulph, and Wakeline. These bishops were contemporary in their respective sees, only during that interval. The grant is very extensive, both in new donations and confirmations of the gifts of his father :—" In Eborasira vero, dedi eis ecclesiam de Conynge-burg cum aliis ecclesiis decimis et terris et omnibus suis appendiciis; et ecclesiam de Wakfeld cum pert. suis." In these few words and simple terms an interest is conveyed, which in these times would be estimated too low at ten thousand pounds a year."

The gift of the church of Wakefield plainly shews that Wakefield

had been granted to the Warrens before the time of Henry I,
A. D. 1100; and brings the date of that grant within a narrow
compass. The donor does not specify the *alias ecclesias* which
went with the churches of Coningsborough and Wakefield but there
is a grant, which MR. HUNTER attributes to the *third* earl, (not the
second) in which they are specifically mentioned. This grant I
shall have occasion more fully to refer to, in treating of the advowson,
and under that head I beg to refer the reader, inasmuch as it is
more intimately connected with the ecclesiastical affairs of the Parish.

It is to be observed that all these charters are without date, and
throw little light on the precise period at which the Warren family
became possessed of these advowsons, or the manors to which they
were regardant. WATSON quotes a MS. by a Mr. Nalson, dated
1665, entitled "Miscellanea, sive Observationes, Collectaneæ"
where the writer affirms, that the Manor of Wakefield was parcel
of the possessions of the Crown of England, until the grant of
Henry I to Earl Warren, A. D. 1116. "Whence (adds WATSON)
this writer got his intelligence I cannot say, but I have met with
nothing to invalidate it." "Neither indeed have I" continues DR.
WHITAKER, In the Warren family these manors remained, until
the death of John, the eighth and last earl, in 1347.

A circumstance occurred during the reign of Edward I, whereby
the spirit of John the seventh earl was put to the test. "King
Edward standing in need of money devised a newe shift to serve
his tourne" as HOLINSHED has expressed it, he issued a proclamation
"that all suche as helde any landes or tenementes of hym shuld come
and shewe by what right and title they helde the same, that by suche
meanes their possessions might returne unto him by escheate, as chiefe
lord of the same, and so to be solde or redeemed agayne at his handes."
This was a cause of much complaint on the part of the people. "Many
were thus called to answere, till at lengthe the lorde John Warren
earle of Surrey, a man greatly beloved of the people, perceyving the
king to have caste his net for a praye, and that there was not one
whyche spake against him determined to stand against those so bitter
and cruell proceedings, and therefore being called afore the justices
aboute this matter, he appeared, and being asked by what right he
helde his lands, he sodenly drawing forth an olde rusty sworde; by
this instrument [sayd he] doe I hold my landes, and by the same I

E 2

intende to defend them." The earl's answer is put down in the
following expressive manner ;—" Produxit in medium, gladium anti-
quum, evaginatum et ait, Ecce Domini mei, ecce meum warrantum !
Antecessores mei vero cum Willielmo bastardo venientes, conquesti
sunt terras suas gladio, et easdem gladio defendam a quocunque eas
occupare volente ; non enim rex terram per se devicit, et subjecit,
sed progenitores nostri fuerunt cum eo participes et coadjutores."
It has been well observed, that in this unimaginative age when we
are in danger of being deprived of every thing which tends to mark
and individualize the members of the old baronage of England,
attempts have been made to represent this as a mere technicality
of law, and not an effusion of a bold and indignant spirit. But it
was something more than a cool plea, *per gladium.*

Shortly after this event it appears, from the pleas of assizes and
jurats, at the borough of Scarborough, that this earl was summoned
to answer by what warrant he appropriated to himself as a forest *inter
alia,* all the divisions of Halifax, Skircote, Ovenden, Haldesworth,
Saltonstall, Miggeley, Wadesworth, Heptonstall, Rowtonstall,
Stansfield, and Langfield ; and by what warrant he refused to permit
the king's bailiffs to enter his lands to perform their offices, except his
own bailiffs were present ? To which the earl answered, that he
claimed gallows at Coningsborough and Wakefield, and the power of
doing what belonged to a gallows in all his lands and fees, and that he
and all his ancestors had used the same from time immemorial ; with
regard to his appropriation of a forest, he claimed no forest in the
aforesaid lands, but that he and his ancestors, had free chace in the
same, from time immemorial, as well in fees as demesne lands, viz.
inter alia, Wakefield, Halifax, Langfield, Miggeley, Skircote,
Saltonstall, Northland, Rishworth, Rastrick, Heptonstall, Hipperholme, Ovenden, Haldesworth, Wadsworth, Rowtonstall, Stansfield,
Northowram, and Shibden. He also claimed to have free warren
as well in his fees as in demesne lands, which he had of ancient
tenure, viz. the same lands, and that King Henry III. granted to him
free warren in all his demesne lands, which he then had or which
he should acquire. Besides all these manors, it appears from Kirby's
inquest, in this king's reign, that the earl was possessed (as chief
lord) *inter alia,* of Fixby, Sowerby, and Warley.

King Edward I. gave his grand-daughter Joan de Barr, in marriage to the eighth earl. The marriage was issueless, and not a happy one, both parties sued for a divorce, but the law of the church was uncompromising; she was alive in the year of the earl's death, when, under the title of Countess of Surrey, she presented a clerk to one of the Warren's churches; so that it is probable there is no pretence for naming any second wife; Isabel de Houland standing, we may presume, in the same relation to him with Maud de Neirford, who produced him a numerous offspring. In all that relates to the marriages real or supposed, and issue of this Earl, observes MR. HUNTER, Mr. Watson's book, which was written to support an hypothesis must be read with great caution. One intrigue of this earl produced consequences which threatened for a time a premature separation of Wakefield from the possessions of the house of Warren.

"The northern border of the lands in Yorkshire, forming the Warren fee, touched in a great extent of its course on the fee of the Laci's, Lords of Pontefract. Disputes seem to have from time to time arisen between these great chiefs; and in the year 1268, it appears that, in a dispute about a pasture, the Warrens and Lacis had armed each their retainers, and prepared for one of those lawless encounters, of which there are several instances in our baronial history, but were prevented by the king. Alice de Laci, the heiress of Pontefract, was of about the same age with the eighth Earl of Warren. She was given in marriage to Thomas, Earl of Lancaster, grandson to Henry III., who lived for the most part at her castle of Pontefract. This lady, on the Monday before Ascension day, A. D. 1317, was carried off by violence, to a castle of the Earl of Warren, at Riegate, in Surrey. There was much mystery in this affair at the time, and much scandal. Certain it is, she was divorced by her husband, and the Earl of Lancaster proceeded to avenge himself by laying siege to the castles in Yorkshire, belonging to the Earl of Warren. But the king commanded he should cease from doing so; and further it is certain, that when in 1318, the Earl of Lancaster engaged to pardon every one all trespasses and felonies done against him, he made an exception of the trespasses and felonies of the Earl of Warren. In the same year, 1318, the Earl of Lancaster, who was then in the plenitude of his power, took from the Earl of Warren a grant of his Manor of Wakefield, for the life of the Earl of Warren, if a make peace it must be

allowed a noble one.   The Earl of Lancaster also obtained Coningsborough, thus banishing his rival entirely from the North.   In 1322,
the discontents of the Earl of Lancaster drove him into open rebellion.
Amongst others to whom the king's warrant issued, to pursue and
take the earl, was the Earl of Warren, who was among the peers
present in the castle of Pontefract, when sentence of death was
passed on the Earl of Lancaster, and he was led forth to execution.
On his death these lands escheated to the Crown, nor did the Earl
of Warren recover possession till some years afterwards.   In the 1st
Edward III. 1327, a warrant was issued to the king's escheator,
north of the Trent, not to meddle with the castles of Sandal or
Coningsborough, and the Manors of Wakefield, Sowerby, &c. to
which the Earl of Warren laid claim, they being by consent of
the said Earl, and of Henry Earl of Lancaster, who was brother of
Earl Thomas, and his next heir, to remain in the king's hands, to
be delivered to the said Henry.   The grant of his Yorkshire Lands
to the Earl of Lancaster had been made by the Earl of Warren only
for his own life; indeed he only possessed a life interest at the time
of the grant, for a little before he had settled the remainder after
his own decease on certain parties who must now be mentioned.

   " Estranged from his wife, the Earl took to his bed Maud de
Neirford, a lady of a family of rank in the County of Norfolk.   By
her he had two sons, John and Thomas de Warren, and on these
sons it was the desire and design of the Earl, that Wakefield, and
his other property North of the Trent, should descend.   For this
purpose he conveyed to the king, by charter dated on the Thursday
next after the first of St. Peter and St. Paul, in 9th Edward II. 1316,
inter alia "castra et villas meas de Coningsburgh et Sandal; et
maneria mea de Wakefield, Hatfield, Thorne, Sowerby, Braithwell,
Fishlake, Dewsbury, et Halifax;" and on the fourth of August
following, the king by charter, tested at Lincoln, made a regrant
of the same lands to the Earl for life, remainder to Maud de Neirford
for life, remainder to John de Warren and the heirs male of his
body, remainder to Thomas de Warren and the heirs male of his
body, (both sons by the said Maud,) remainder to the heirs of the
body of the said Earl, lawfully to be begotten, and in default of such
issue, to revert to the king; this disposition however did not take
effect.   Maud, and her two sons, died without issue in the life time

of the Earl, on which account, says WATSON, "he married Isabel de Houland, and previous to this marriage the king seems to have been prevailed upon to secure to the said Isabel, what before had been settled upon Maud." This Earl died A. D. 1347.

As a difference of opinion seems to exist, whether this Isabel de Houland was ever Countess of Warren, I have introduced an interesting extract from the Earl's will; "jeo devys a Isabel de Houland ma compaigne mon avel d'or oue le bonne ruby." The precise form of the word *compaigne*, observes Mr. HUNTER, as applied to Isabel de Houland, is not apparent. Joan de Barr, was beyond question then alive, and bearing the title of Countess of Surrey, but it is thought by many that the marriage was dissolved, and that Isabel was in truth his wife, a relation which was expressed by the word *compaigne*, of which we have a proof in the will of Richard Fitz Allen, Earl of Arundel and Surrey, nephew to the Earl of Warren, who desired to be buried in the priory of Lewes, "pres de la tombe de ma treschere compaigne Alianore de Lancestre." WATSON also says she is found in the court rolls of Wakefield, after the Earl's decease, as Isabel, Countess of Warren. At her death which happened A. D. 1359, (33 Edward III,) the Manor with its dependencies again reverted to the Crown in the person of Edward III. I am at a loss how to reconcile this statement of WATSON "that the king seems to have been prevailed upon to secure to Isabel what had before been settled upon Maud" with the fact, that on the 6th of August 1347, only thirty seven days after the death of the Earl, a royal patent was signed at Reading, "per manus Lionelli filii nostri carissimi custodis Angliæ" (the king being then in France) by which, "omnia castra, maneria villas, terras, et tenementa cum pert. quæ fuerunt Johannis de Warrenna nuper comitis Surr. in partibus ultra Trentam, et quæ occasione mortis ejusdem comitis in manu nostra existunt" were settled on Edmund of Langley, a younger son of the king, and heirs male of his body, with remainder to John of Gaunt, and Lionel of Antwerp, and their heirs male respectively, remainder to the crown. This grant was confirmed by Parliament, but Edmund not being more than six years of age, his mother queen Phillipa, was allowed to receive the profits for the education of this and her other younger children. Edmund had been created by his father, Earl of Cambridge, but in the 9th Richard II, he was advanced to the title of

Duke of York. He died 1st August, 3rd Henry IV., 1402, seised *inter alia* of the Manor of Sowerby, and the Lordship or Manor of Wakefield, of which Halifax was a parcel, leaving Edward, Earl of Rutland, his eldest son and heir, aged twenty-six years, who, on his father's death, became Duke of York.

This Edward, Duke of York, accompanied Henry V. in his great expedition to France, and lost his life at the battle of Agincourt, leaving a widow, Phillipa Mohun, daughter of the Lord Mohun, of Dunster, sans issue; from whose will, dated 1430, it appears she held the Manor of Sowerby, *inter alia*, in dower. The duke dying without issue, his honors and estates descended to his nephew Richard, of Coningsborough, as he was usually called, after the fashion of the Plantagenets naming themselves from the places of their birth, the younger of the two sons of his brother Edmund, of Langley, who is usually called Earl of Cambridge. He married Anne Mortimer, the daughter of Roger, Earl of March, and Phillipa, the daughter and heiress of Lionel, Duke of Clarence. This marriage brought the claim to the crown to the House of York; for her brother Edmund Mortimer, the last of the Mortimers, Earls of March, died without leaving issue, but not till after the death of Anne, so that she is not, in strict propriety, called the heiress of Lionel, Duke of Clarence. In her issue, however, the rights of Lionel inhered entire. Richard appears not to have been insensible to the wrong which was done to the house of Mortimer, by the accession of Henry IV. to the throne. A little before King Henry the V. left England, to prosecute his war in France, this Richard was engaged in a real or supposed conspiracy, and was attainted. The treason alledged in the act of attainder was, conspiring to lead his brother in law Edmund, Earl of March, to the borders of Wales, and there proclaim him king; and countenancing the imposture of Thomas de Trumpington, *de Scotiá ideotam*, who personated King Richard II. The Earl was beheaded 3rd Henry V. 1415, leaving issue a son Richard, Duke of York, by Anne Mortimer, who died some time before her husband. There being no issue of Edmund, Earl of March, at his death, his nephew Richard was his undoubted heir, and the equally undoubted heir to the rights of Lionel's posterity. A long period elapsed before he ventured to assert them. Richard of Coningsborough after the death of Anne Mortimer, married a second wife, who survived him; and died A. D. 1446, and on her death Richard Duke of York entered into possession of the Manor. He married Cecily Nevil a daughter of the Earl of Westmoreland by whom he had issue. The Duke did not forget the right which had descended to him from his mother, and he gave indications of his aspiring disposition before his conduct ceased to be equivocal. The issue of the struggle is well known; he lost his life in the encounter between the houses of York and Lancaster, at Wakefield. The spirit and object of the father descended to his son, the Earl of March. In the year after his father's death, was fought the great battle of Towton, in which the fortunes of the house of York prevailed, and the Earl became seated on the throne as king Edward IV.

The Lords of the Manor of Wakefield thus became kings of England. On the marriage of Henry VII, with Elizabeth of York, the ancient rivalry of the white and red rose became extinguished, and there being no probability of the right of succession of the issue being questioned, the whole of what had been settled upon Edmund of Langley was declared to be resumed and for ever annexed to the crown.* This was done in Parliament, 2nd Henry VII, and the Manor continued parcel of the royal possessions until the year 1554 the time of the marriage of king Philip and queen Mary, when as it is said, it was united to the Duchy of Lancaster.

In the reign of Charles I. the Manor was granted to Henry, Earl of Holland, who was beheaded 1649 by a sentence of the high court of justice, for attempting the restoration of Charles II. It subsequently passed into the family of Rich, Earl of Warwick. Robert, the first Earl gave it as part of the marriage portion of Penelope his daughter, to Sir Gervase Clifton, Bart., who sold the Manor to Sir C. Clapham, about the year 1663. The heirs of Sir C. Clapham sold it to Peregrine, the third Duke of Leeds from whom it has descended to George William Frederick, Duke of Leeds, its present most noble possessor.

The most accurate Villare of this district which has ever been exhibited is an inquisition of survey for the honor or lordship of Wakefield which was taken in the 19th Elizabeth, A. D. 1577. It derives an additional value from having preserved the names of several hamlets of which the names have since become obsolete;

* Hunter's South Yorkshire, vol. 1. p. 113.

and being compared with the Domesday Survey of the same district, will shew in how large a proportion the villare of that tract had been extended between the eleventh century and sixteenth. The following extract relates to the district within this Parish. In this Survey it is remarkable, that the rectories of Wakefield, Dewsbury, Kirkburton, and Lewes, (Halifax) were considered as Manors; and as they were vested in the crown on the dissolution of the religious houses to which they had been appropriated, they are very distinctly stated as holden of the crown *in capite*, not as of the Duchy of Lancaster, and parcel of the possessions of Earls Warren, though originally granted by them.

Langfield, like the other members of this great fee, was originally parcel of the possessions of the Earls Warren, but having been granted out and forfeited by the mesne lord, Sir Stephen Hamerton, it was not considered as a portion of those estates, though all of them were vested in the crown and members of the duchy of Lancaster—but as immediately in the Queen's hands.

The places marked v. are townships and those marked with the letter H. or not marked, are hamlets, the word pars, with a connecting mark, denotes two places constituting an hamlet together. Under whatever tenure they were held, whether of the crown *in capite*, or as of the Duchy of Lancaster, all owed suit and service at the great leet of Wakefield.

Inter alia.
v Halifax
v Skercoate
v
v Hopperholme
v Northowram
Shipden ⎫
Horley Green ⎬ pars
v Brighouse
v Ovenden
Misenden
v Warley
Saltonstall

Infr. Dnum & Man. de Wakefield & Dna Reg. est cap. Dn͞a jure Dnii de Wakefield quondam parcel. possession. Comitum Warren. Except maner. de Halifax cu' Heptonstall modo in tenura Rob͞t Waterhouse & tent. de Dn͞a Regina in Cap. & nuper erant parcel. terr. & poss. nuper Priorat. de Lewis in Com. Sussex.

v Midgeley
v Heptonstall
 Wadsworth cum
ʜ Shackleton et
 Weddophead
v Erringden alias
 Aringden
v Sourby
ʜ Soyland
v Stansfield
v Blackshaw
v Rowtenstall
v Rishworth and
v Norland
v Langfield
v Rastricke cum
ʜ Toothill
v Fixby
v Barkisland

Ut supra. Quondam parcel terr. & possess. Comitum Warren. Except maner. de Halifax & Heptonstall—necnon terr. & ten. vocat, Erenden tent. de dict. Regina in Cap. & certas terras. & ten. vocat. vill. de Langfield in Man. Dne Regine per attincturam. Steph[i] Hamerton mil. Quæ quidem terr. & tenementa quovis alio modo de Regina teneantur adhuc sunt infra visum Dnii prædict.

Inter alia.
v Golkar cum
 Old Lindley

Ut supra. Parcel poss[m]. Comit. Warren.

In this inquisition is no mention of the Graveships, but in the 7th James, there is specified the Graveship, (*inter alia*) of Soyland quarter.

The last authentic Villare of this district comprises above one hundred and fifty places within this Parish, all owing suit and service at the great leet.

This manor may be divided into three branches, distinguished by the names of Wakefield Branch, Holmfirth Branch, and Halifax Branch.

The Halifax Branch is disjoined from the other branches by the Honor of Pontefract. The most eastern part is about two miles from Wakefield Branch, and commences at Hartishead, extending thence Westward to the County of Lancaster, about twenty-three miles. It is bounded by High-town, Robert-town, and Mirfield, to the East;

Kirkheaton, Bradley, Huddersfield, Lockwood, South Crossland, and Slaithwaite, to the South; Marsden and the County of Lancaster, to the West; Haworth, Thornton, Clayton, North Bierley, Wike and Scholes, to the North.

The Lord of the Manor has the return of all writs within his liberty, the direction being "*To the Lord of the Manor of Wakefield, and his deputies.*" There is a gaol for the imprisonment of debtors, appertaining to the Manor, kept at Halifax.

The Court Baron which is held at the Moot-hall in Wakefield, holds plea for recovery of debts under £5, and in matters of *replevin.* The jurisdiction of the Court was extended by an act of the 17th George III, c. 15. The rolls relating to the copyhold estates holden of the manor and manorial records, are kept at the rolls office, in Wakefield, in the custody of the deputy steward.

Within the Manor are holden four courts leet, or sheriff-turns, viz. at Wakefield, Halifax, Brighouse, and Holmfirth.

Under the leet at Halifax are the following Constableries :—

HALIFAX	STANSFIELD
SOWERBY	RISHWORTH CUM
SKIRCOAT	NORLAND
OVENDEN	LANGFIELD
WARLEY	HEPTONSTALL
WADSWORTH	ERRINGDEN
	MIDGLEY.

Under the leet at Brighouse ;

NORTHOWRAM	DALTON
SHELF	FIXBY
HIPPERHOLME CUM	STAINLAND
BRIGHOUSE	BARKISLAND
RASTRICK	HARTISHEAD CUM
QUARMBY	CLIFTON

Indeed the whole of this extensive Parish with the exception of the townships of Elland-cum-Greetland and Southowram is included within the Manor.

THE GIBBET LAW.

The exact period of time when the jurisdiction anciently exercised by the Lords of the Manor of Wakefield, namely, the *jus furcæ* was first called into operation within this Manor is involved in great obscurity. It does not appear that any other mode of punishment than that of decapitation was ever resorted to at this place. The word *gibbet* is of doubtful derivation; it is said to be a French word as well as an English one, and a French author declares himself uncertain whether the French borrowed it from the English, or the English from the French. A MS. note in my possession informs me that this mode of punishment was not unknown to the ancients, and was considered by them as a mark of the grossest infamy. That the term was known in this country as early as the year 1223 is certain; thus the king orders *Gibbetum grandem preparari!* where the Gibbet meant what is now called a gallows, or the machine made use of for suspending a criminal in chains. As modern legislation has happily discarded from our Statute book the use of this Instrument, and as the interest and pleasure to be derived from an extended enquiry as to its antiquity, is, after all, rather of a doubtful nature, putting out of the question the value of the information to be ultimately derived from an enlarged discussion, I shall proceed at once to the custom of the place.

As the *jus furcæ* at Wakefield was actually claimed by the Earls Warren, in their returns to *quo warrantos*, and never claimed for Halifax. "I think," says DR. WHITAKER, "the consequence is that the custom did not commence here till a later period, perhaps not till the general introduction of the Woollen Manufactory rendered a special protection necessary for that species of property." The History of Halifax, published by Bentley, 1712, in "a true account of their antient and customary Gibbet Law; and their particular form of trying and executing criminals, the like not used in any other place in Great Britain," sets forth that the inhabitants within the forest of Hardwick, claimed a custom from time immemorial, "that if a felon be taken within their liberty, with goods stolen out or within the liberty or precincts of the said forest, either hand habend, backberand, or confessand, cloth or any other commodity of the value of thirteen pence halfpenny, that he should, after three markets or meeting days within the town of Halifax, next after such his apprehension, and being condemned, be taken to the Gibbet, and there have his head cut off from his body." These liberties had their beginning on the West, from the boundaries of Yorkshire and Lancashire.   On the East, Salterhebble Brook as the same runneth from Illingworth to the river Calder.   On the North, they bordered on the vicarage of Bradford.   And on the South, on the rivers of Riburn and Calder, and contained within their circuit the townships and hamlets of Halifax, Ovenden, Illingworth, Mixenden, Bradshaw, Skircoat, Warley, Sowerby, Rishworth, Luddenden, Midgley, Erringden, Heptonstall, Rawtonstall, Stansfield, Cross Stone, Langfield, and Wadsworth.   The Lord Bailiff of Halifax, was called the Sheriff of Sowerbyshire, and in the execution of criminals acted as Sheriff.

When an accused person was apprehended he was forthwith brought to the bailiff, who, by virtue of his authority, kept a common jail in the town, had the custody of the axe, and was the executioner. On receipt of the prisoner, the bailiff issued out his summons to the constables of four several towns within the aforesaid precincts, to require four Frith-burghers within each town to appear before him on a certain day, to examine into the truth of the charge laid against the prisoner; at the time of appearance, the accuser and the accused were brought before the jurors, face to face, and the thing stolen produced to view; and they acquitted or condemned, according to the evidence, without any oath being administered.

Bishop Hall, in his Satires, insinuates, that among the jurors of this court integrity was something like an exception to a general rule.

> "Or some more straight-laced juror of the rest,
> Impanelled on a Holy-fax Inquest."

If the party accused was acquitted, he was directly set at liberty on payment of his fees; if condemned, he was executed forthwith, provided it was the principal market day, if not, he was kept till then, in order to strike the greater terror into the neighbourhood, and in the mean time set in the stocks, on the lesser meeting days, with the stolen goods on his back if portable, if not, before his face. The party from whom the goods were stolen was not allowed to compound the felony, but was bound to bring the prisoner with what he had taken, to the chief bailiff at Halifax, and prosecute the thief according to ancient custom; otherwise the goods became forfeited to the lord of the manor.

After every execution, it appears to have been the custom for one of the coroners for the county to repair to the town of Halifax, and there summon a jury of twelve men before him, (sometimes the same persons who condemned the felon,) and administer an oath to them, to give in a true verdict relating to the felony for which the said felon was executed, to the intent that a record might be made thereof in the crown-office, "which gracious and sage proceedings of the coroner in that matter, ought," (as the author of the book alluded to, most sagaciously observes) "one would think, to abate in all considering minds, that edge of acrimony which hath provoked malicious and prejudiced persons to debase this laudable and necessary custom." A mode of proceeding very highly satisfactory to the poor criminal.

The proceedings at the trials of the last malefactors who suffered at this Gibbet, are fortunately preserved in Bentley's Book, and are intitled :—

A true and impartial narrative of the trials of Abraham Wilkinson, John Wilkinson, and Anthony Mitchell, for felony, by them committed within the forest of Hardwick and liberty of Halifax.

"About the latter end of April, 1650, Abraham Wilkinson John Wilkinson, and Anthony Mitchel, were apprehended within the manor of Wakefield, and liberties of Halifax, for divers felonious practices, and brought into the custody of the chief bailiff there, to have their trials for the same, according to the custom of the forest of Hardwick, at the complaint, and prosecution of Samuel Colbeck, of Warley, and John Fielden, of Stansfield, both within the liberty of Halifax, and John Cusforth, of Durker, in the parish of

Sandal, within the manor of Wakefield; on which, the bailiff did forthwith issue out his summons to the several constables of Halifax, Sowerby, Warley, and Skircoat, requiring that without fail they should make their appearance, with each of them four men of the most antient, intelligent, and the best ability, within their several constableries, at his house in Halifax, on the 27th day of April, 1650, to hear, examine, and determine the several cases between the said prosecutors and felons. Accordingly those who attended were

For Halifax.	*For Sowerby.*
JAMES HOLLAND.	FRANCIS PRIESTLEY.
RICHARD NICOLLS.	HENRY RILEY.
ISAAC HOOKER.	JAMES DOBSON.
JOHN EXLEY.	JOSEPH PRIESTLEY.

For Warley.	*For Skircoat.*
JOHN BIALLS.	JAMES WHITAKER.
MICHAEL WOOD.	JAMES ELLISON.
JOHN HOLDSWORTH.	ANTHONY WATERHOUSE.
HENRY MIRRIEL.	THOMAS GILL.

These being impanelled by the bailiff in a convenient room in his house according unto custom, and the prosecutors and felons being brought face to face before them, and the stolen goods there, to be viewed and apprized, the said bailiff thus opened to them the occasion of their summons :

"Neighbors and friends,

"You are summoned hither and impanelled according to the antient custom of the forest of Hardwick, and by virtue thereof, you are required to make diligent search and inquiry into such complaints as are brought against the felons, concerning the goods that are set before you, and to make such just, equitable, and faithful determination betwixt party and party, as you will answer it between God and your own consciences.

"After this, the several informations were brought in, and alledged against them, as follows :

"The information of Samuel Colbeck, of Warley.

"This informant saith, and affirmeth, that upon Tuesday the 17th of April, 1650, he had feloniously taken off from his tenters, by Abraham Wilkinson, John Wilkinson, and Anthony Mitchell, sixteen yards of russet-coloured kersey, part of which cloth you have here before you, and of which you are to inquire of its worth and value, and take their confession here before you.

"The information of John Cusforth, of Durker, in Sandal parish.

"This informant saith, and affirmeth, that Abraham Wilkinson and Anthony Mitchell, did feloniously take off from Durker Green, the 17th day of April, 1650, at night, one black colt, which colt, as well as the prisoners, are here presented before you; and also at the same time, one other grey colt belonging to Paul Johnson, of Durker, was feloniously taken by these men from off Durker Green, and is here produced to your view.

"The information of John Fielden, of Stansfield.

"This informant saith, and doth affirm, that he had one whole kersey piece feloniously taken from the tenters at Brerely Hall, by Abraham Wilkinson, about Christmas last, which he the said John Fielden hath found in the hands of Thomas Brown, bailiff, in Wakefield, six yards of which kersey being dyed cinnamon color, and eight yards thereof white, and frized for blankets; which dyed piece he affirms that Isaac Gibson's wife, of Wakefield, did affirm to the said Fielden, that Abraham Wilkinson did deliver unto her : also William Ellison's wife doth affirm the same ; and John Roberts doth affirm that he knoweth the man, and his name to be Abraham Wilkinson.

"These three informations being thus given in, Abraham Wilkinson, accused by Fielden, alleged in his own defence that he did not confess the aforesaid piece unto Gibson's wife, but was present when John Spencer, a soldier, in Chesterfield, did deliver the said piece unto Gibson's wife. On this point some debates arising among the jurymen, they, as customary in such cases, adjourned to the 30th day of April, when being again assembled in like manner, at the same place, after a full examination, and hearing of the whole matter, with united consent, gave in their verdict in writing in these words :

F

"An inquisition, taken at Halifax, the 27th and 30th days of April, 1650, upon certain informations hereunto annexed.

"To the complaint of Samuel Colbeck, &c. we whose names are hereunto subscribed, being summoned and impanelled according to antient custom, do find by the confession of Abraham Wilkinson, of Sowerby, within the liberty of Halifax, being apprehended and taken, that he the said Abraham Wilkinson took the cloth in the information mentioned, with the assistance of his brother John Wilkinson, from the tenter of Samuel Colbeck, in Warley, being sixteen yards of russet colored kersey, nine yards, at the least, thereof, being brought before us, with the prisoner, the said Samuel Colbeck doth affirm to be his own cloth, and part of the sixteen yards aforesaid, and is so confessed to be by the prisoner, which nine yards we do value and apprize to be worth nine shillings at the least.

"To the complaint and information of John Cusworth, &c. we the aforesaid impanelled jury do find, by the free confession of Anthony Mitchell, that John Wilkinson did take the black colt of John Cusworth's, from Durker-Green, and that himself and Abraham Wilkinson were there present at the same time; and also that Anthony Mitchell himself did sell the aforesaid colt to Simeon Helliwell, near Hepton-Brigg, for forty-eight shillings, whereof he received in part twenty-seven shillings; and we do apprize and value the same colt to be worth forty-eight shillings. Likewise we do find by the confession of the aforesaid Anthony Mitchell, that Abraham Wilkinson did take the grey colt of Paul Johnson's, from off Durker-Green aforesaid; and that John Wilkinson was with his brother Abraham Wilkinson when he took him, and that the said Anthony Mitchell was by, and present, when Abraham did stay, and bridle the grey colt: Also he confesseth, that himself and John Wilkinson did leave the said colt with George Harrison, of Norland, which colt we have seen; and do value and apprize him at three pounds.

"The determinate sentence.

"The prisoners, that is to say, Abraham Wilkinson and Anthony Mitchell, being apprehended within the liberty of Halifax, and brought before us, with nine yards of cloth as aforesaid, and the two colts above mentioned; which cloth we apprized to nine shillings, and the black colt to forty-eight shillings, and the grey colt to three pounds: All which aforesaid being feloniously taken from the above-said persons, and found with the said prisoners; by the antient custom, and liberty of Halifax, whereof the memory of man is not to the contrary, the said Abraham Wilkinson, and Anthony Mitchell, are to suffer death, by having their heads severed, and cut off from their bodies, at Halifax Gibbet; unto which verdict we subscribe our names the thirtieth of April, one thousand six hundred and fifty. James Holland, &c."

"After this, the said Abraham Wilkinson and Anthony Mitchell were, the same day, *(because it was Saturday, or the great market,)* conducted to the said gibbet, and there executed in the usual form. These felons were the last who suffered by this mode of punishment.

I am at a loss how to reconcile this fact with what Bentley says. "As touching the manner of the felon's death, you'll find great kindness and christian compassion to be discovered. In that he hath six days allowed him after his condemnation to prepare himself by the best means he can devise, or shall make choice of, to fit and prepare himself for his latter end religiously and devoutly, as being well assured that his death is unavoidable." But I have taken the account as I find it.

This peculiar and humane mode of punishment, was probably introduced by the great Norman Barons out of their own country, where it had lately been made the instrument of the most compendious and expeditious massacres that ever disgraced the forms of justice. It may be traced as appurtenant to the right of outfangtheof and infangtheof in the domains of the Lacies, both in Cheshire and Lancashire. In the laws of Edward the Confessor, which William the Bastard afterwards confirmed, the 21st chapter is entitled, " De Baronibus qui suas habent curias, et consuetudines," and therein is express mention made of infangtheof, which in chapter 26th is thus explained, " Justitia cognoscentis latronis sua est, de homine suo, si captus fuerit super terram suam." Here is nothing said "de homine extraneo," or such as did not belong to the manor, whom the lord had power to execute, by the privilege of outfangtheof, if taken as a thief within his manor, let the robbery have been committed where it would. This power, however, was certainly exercised at Halifax, as appears, amongst other instances, from the

F 2

following entries in the register there: "Quidam extraneus capitalem subiit sententiam, 1° die Jan. 1542"—"Richard Sharpe, and John Learoyd, beheaded the 5th day of March, 1568, for a robbery done in Lancashire."

"Our early text writers are not agreed as to the power of infangtheof, and outfangtheof; the truth is what Spelman has asserted, "certissima interpretatio a locorum usu petitur." The proof of certain facts appears to have been essentially necessary, before a felon was condemned to suffer.

" 1st. He was to be taken within the liberty; and it appears that if he escaped out of the liberty, even after condemnation, he could not be brought back to be executed; but if ever he returned into it again, and was taken, he was sure to suffer; as was the case with one Lacy, who, after his escape, lived seven years out of the liberty, but returning, was beheaded on his former verdict, A.D. 1623. This man was not so wise as one Dinnis, who having been condemned to die, escaped out of the liberty on the day destined for his execution, (which might be done by running about five hundred yards) and never returned again; meeting several people, they asked him if Dinnis was not to be beheaded that day; his answer was, " I trow not;" which having some humour in it, became a proverbial saying amongst the inhabitants, who to this day use the expression, " I trow not, quoth Dinnis."

" 2dly. The fact was to be proved in the clearest manner; the offender was to be taken either handhabend, or backberand, having the stolen goods either in his hand, or bearing them on his back, or lastly confessand, confessing that he took them. This is what writers have called by the name of furtum manifestum, answering to the Open Dyꝼb in the 61st chapter of the laws of the Danish King Cnute, which is there said to be a crime not to be atoned for; and perhaps the bad opinion which our ancestors had of this offence, might give rise to the Baron's power of punishing it; for nothing surely could more effectually deter from the practice, than to take off the offenders without much trouble, or expence to the prosecutors, in this public, summary way, without a possibility of either pardon, or reprieve, if they were found guilty. It is worth remarking, that neither of the last executed criminals were taken either handhabend, or backberand, but that both were convicted on their own confession; and it seems that John Wilkinson escaped, merely by not confessing; for Anthony Mitchell charged him directly with stealing the black colt; and Abraham Wilkinson, with assisting him to rob the tenter of Samuel Colbeck. Does it not therefore follow, that the two others might likewise have saved their lives, had they used the same precaution? But if so, there was a great defect in this mode of proceeding, for unless a man was taken with stolen goods in his actual, and immediate possession, (which would very seldom be the case) his silence was sure to bring him off, and the person injured had no farther redress; for it is to be presumed that the criminal could not be again arraigned for the same offence in the king's court. There is a mistake in the register book at Halifax, which has John Wilkinson beheaded, instead of Abraham; for if this be right, then Abraham Wilkinson was acquitted, though he confessed that he stole the cloth, and John was executed merely on the information of the two others, which is directly subversive of the very foundation on which this custom is said to stand."

The expression in the determinate sentence, "that the two colts, and cloth were found with the prisoners," appears foreign to the purpose, if the nature of this privilege is rightly handed down to us; for they were not found with them either handhabend, or backberand; neither could they have been found guilty from the manner of the discovery, for if they could, John Wilkinson must also have suffered with them.

"3dly. The value of the goods stolen must amount to thirteen pence halfpenny, or more; (and if at the judgment of the jury, it be but at the utmost value worth thirteen pence halfpenny, and no more, or of less value, by this custom they are to acquit the felon, and he shall not die for it.) The opinions about this, however, have differed, some fixing the value at thirteen pence; others that it was to exceed thirteen pence halfpenny. DR. GREY, in his notes on Hudibras, vol. ii. p. 288, seems to think that thirteen pence halfpenny may have been called hangman's wages, in allusion to the Halifax law; if so, might not the Scotch mark, which was made current in England, in the reign of King James I. for thirteen pence halfpenny, have been made the standard value for convicting capitally at this place, and this piece, or the value of it, be the usual gratuity to the executioner? Nothing renders this improbable, but that the custom must then have undergone an alteration, without its being known by what authority; but it will be shewn by and by, that it has undergone a greater change than this.

" 4thly. The accused person was, after three markets, or meeting days, within the town of Halifax, next after such his apprehension, and being condemned, to be taken to the gibbet. This is not very clearly expressed, but the meaning is, doubtless, that after he was delivered to the bailiff, no time was to be lost in proceeding to his trial, for the said bailiff was immediately to send his summons for the speedy bringing in of those who were to try him, which might be effected in two or three days; his execution, if he was found guilty, depended on the day when the sentence was passed,' for he was not to be beheaded but on a Saturday, which was the great meeting; thus if he was convicted on a Monday, he would be kept three market days; if on a Saturday, he would, as some have asserted, be led directly to the block. This was the case of the two last malefactors, who were condemned, and executed the same day.

" 5thly. When brought to the gibbet, he was to have his head cut off from his body. This gibbet stood a little way out of the town, towards the West end, on an ascent still distinguished by the name of the Gibbet Hill, and which at that time formed the principal Western entrance to the town; where, to this day, is to be seen a square platform of earth, considerably raised above the level of the road, walled about, and ascended by a flight of stone steps; on the summit of this hill were placed two upright pieces of timber, five yards in height, joined at the top by a transverse beam; within these was a square block of wood, which HARRISON, in his *Description of England*, vol. i. p. 185. Lond. 1587, says, was of the length of four feet and a half, which rose up and down, between the said uprights, by means of grooves cut for that purpose; to the lower end of this sliding block an iron axe was fastened, which is yet to be seen at the jail in Halifax; its weight is seven pounds twelve ounces; its length ten inches and a half; it is seven inches broad at the top, and very near nine at the bottom; its centre is about seven inches and a half; at the top are two holes made to fasten it to the block above mentioned. The axe thus fixed was drawn up to the top by means of a cord and pulley, and at the end of the cord was a pin, which being fixed either to the side of the scaffold, or some part below, kept it suspended, till either by pulling out the pin, or cutting the cord, it was suffered to fall, and the criminal's head was instantly separated from his body. This proceeding has been differently related. Harrison tells us, that every man present took hold of the rope, or put forth his arm as near to it as he could, in token that he was willing to see true justice executed, and that the pin was pulled out in this manner; but if the offender was apprehended for stealing an ox, sheep, horse, &c. the end of the rope was fastened to the beast, which being driven, pulled out the pin."*

TAYLOR, in his book before alluded to, asserts, that the line was cut, and that no man might cut it but the owner of the stolen goods, which if he did, he had all again; but if he would not cut it, he lost all; the goods were employed to some charitable uses, and the thief escaped. CAMDEN says, if the execution was not done by a beast, the bailiff, or his servant, cut the rope; this last in all probability, was the fact, and is so represented in Bentley's account. The time of the execution was known by the jurors (if they could properly be so called who were not sworn) holding up one of their hands; for it seems they were under the necessity of being present at the execution of those whom they had found guilty, doubtless to give it the greater appearance of justice, and accordingly, "the bailiff, jurors, and the minister chosen by the prisoner, were always on the scaffold with him." WRIGHT adds, "that the fourth psalm was played round the scaffold, on the bagpipes; after which, the minister prayed with him a while, till he underwent the fatal stroke."

* Wright, in an extract from a work entitled "a Tour through the whole Island of Great Britain," has a story "of a countrywoman who was riding by the Gibbet, on her hampers to the market, just at the execution of a criminal, when the axe chopt his neck through with such force, that the head jumpt into one of her hampers, or (as others say) seised her apron with the teeth, and there stuck for some time." It is useless employing words about this affair, but the circumstance may serve to shew with what apathy the country people regarded this mode of punishment; their minds were evidently hardened by such exhibitions, and the fact developes the inadequacy of such awful administrations of justice to produce that proper moral, and salutary effect which might have been anticipated;—such scenes, oft repeated, appear to harden, rather than soften—to stupify, rather than awaken the sensibilities of man's nature.

"Having now completed the circumstantial account of this curious custom, it is time, says WATSON, to enquire how long it may have been exercised.

"In Domesday-book, the manor of Halifax (with several others in that neighbourhood) is put down, though not expressly by that name, as having been part of the demesne lands of king Edward, but at the making of that survey, in the hands of the crown; probably therefore nothing of this sort was exercised then, nor till the manor of Wakefield (of which this was part) was bestowed on Earl Warren; for in the reign of king Edward I. at the pleas of assizes and jurats at the borough of Scarborough, John, the 7th Earl, in answer to a writ of *Quo warranto*, said that he claimed gallows at Coningsborough, and Wakefield, and the power of doing what belonged to a gallows in all his lands and fees, and that he, and all his ancestors, had used the same from time immemorial; to which it was answered, on the part of the king, that the aforesaid liberties belonged merely to the crown, and that no long *seisia*, or prescription of time, ought to prejudice the king; and that the earl had no special warrant for the said liberties, therefore judgment was desired, if the *seisia* could be to the said earl a sufficient warrant."

From hence it is plain, that the charter containing these privileges could not be produced, even about the year 1280; the prescriptive right was, however, deemed good, for upon the inquisition taken afterwards, it does not appear that any thing was found for the king.

It seems to have been universally agreed, that theft was the only thing cognisable in this court; and yet in a manuscript in the Harleian collection in the British Museum, No. 797, under the title Halifax, is the following entry: "The court of the Countess, held 30th January, 33 Edw. III. It is found by inquisition, that if any tenant of this lordship of Halifax be beheaded for theft, *or other cause*, that the heirs of the same tenant ought not to lose their inheritance, notwithstanding any lease made in the mean time by the steward."

It has been stated that the custom was appurtenant to the forest of Hardwick; and Bentley refers to Manwood's discourse of forest laws, for an elucidation on this subject; but it is clear that the custom had nothing to do with a forest at all. Halifax seems not to have stood in a forest; for at the above mentioned pleas of assizes and jurats at Scarborough, earl Warren being summoned to answer by what warrant he appropriated to himself the divisions of Halifax, &c. his reply was, that he claimed no forest in the said lands, only free chase, and free warren. 2dly. Because these privileges were so commonly exercised in other places, where there was not the least pretension to a forest. In fact, they are in themselves older than any known forest laws, except those of Knute are genuine, which Sir Edward Coke says are to be suspected. Now if these proceedings at Halifax were not in consequence of a forest being there, how can it be thought that they were allowed, as mentioned in Wright, for the preservation either of the King's, or Baron's deer? If of the King's, then would the King's officers have exercised that power; if of the Barons, why did they execute for every kind of theft, provided the proofs were manifest? and why were two men beheaded for a robbery committed in Lancashire? The truth is, that this power was annexed to a manor, and not a forest; but being within the purlieu of a forest, the preservation of the venison might amongst others, be one object of it.

It has generally been supposed, that the punishment by decollation was practised in no part of England but at Halifax, upon common offenders; but in the Harleian MSS. No. 980. fol. 355, is the following remark: "Aunciently the several customes of places made in those dayes capitall punishments severall. Apud Dover infalistatus, apud Southampton submersus, apud Winton demembratus, vel decapitatus, ut apud Northampton, &c." WATSON refers to a MS. relating to the earls of Chester, containing extracts from some records, wherein it is said, that "the serjeants or bailiffs of the earls had power to behead any malefactor, or thief, who was apprehended in the action, or against whom it was made apparent by sufficient witness, or confession, before four inhabitants of the place, or rather before four inhabitants of the four neighboring towns." Then follows an account of the presenting of several heads of felons at the castle of Chester, according to custom, by the Earl's Serjeants (Servientes pacis.) And it must have been the usual way to behead malefactors in this county, because in a Roll 3 Edw. II. it is called the Custom of Cheshire. These are direct, and evident proofs, that the beheading of criminals was

not peculiar to Halifax, but was exercised likewise in other parts
of the kingdom; and accordingly it seems to have been known to
be so, even in later times; for in the second volume of Hollinshed's
Chronicle, printed in 1577, at p. 654, is a wood cut, representing
the execution of a man who attempted to murder king Henry III.
The criminal is laid within such a gibbet as that at Halifax, only
the axe is suspended from the top by a cord, which the executioner
is cutting with a knife, similar to an engraved representation of the
Halifax gibbet in Moll's set of fifty maps of England and Wales,
Lond. 1724, where the bailiff, or some other person is cutting the
rope. Also in Fox's book of Martyrs, vol. i. p. 37. Lond. 1684,
is a plate of this sort.

From whence the custom of beheading criminals with an engine
originally came, is not easy to say. It seems that Earl Morton,
the Regent of Scotland, carried a model of the Gibbet from Halifax to
his own country, where it remained so long unused, that it acquired
the name of the maiden. The Scots have a tradition, that the first
inventor of this machine, was the first who suffered by it. So far
is certain, that Earl Morton, who was executed June 2, 1581, had
his head taken off by such an instrument as this; for in the Continuation of Hollinshed's Chronicle of Scotland, we read, "that having
laid his necke under the axe, he cried, Lord Jesus receive my spirit,
which words he spake, even while the axe fell on his necke."

It is evident that such a contrivance was known in Germany
before the execution of Earl Morton; for there is a small print, by
Aldegraver, one of the German masters in 1553, representing Titus
Manlius standing by to see the execution of his son, for fighting contrary to his orders. The axe hangs over his neck, suspended by a
cord; there are hollows cut in the two uprights, to direct it in its
descent, but being a side view, the method made use of to cause it
to fall, is not represented. An officer who stands by the side of
Manlius, has his left hand on the criminal's head.

There are engravings of it in books printed so early as 1510.
In Evelyn's memoirs (1645) is the following; "At Naples they use
a frame, like ours at Halifax. The next day I saw a wretch executed,
who had murther'd his master, for which he had his head chop'd off
by an axe slid down a frame of timber, the executioner striking at
the axe with a beatle, and so the head fell off the block."

And from a Polish journal it appears that not long since two ancient benches, to which two small tables with carvings in wood were
attached, stood beneath the choir of St. Nicholas' church in Kalisch.
One table represented the martyrdom of St. Lawrence, and the other
the death of some unknown martyr by an engine similar in every
respect to the Gibbet in use here. The table is deposited in the
museum of Polish antiquities at Pulawy.

It was first introduced into France during the revolution, by Dr.
Guillotine a physician, and hence its name there.

It is a circumstance worth remarking, that this power of the
Barons, to inflict capital punishment, was kept up at Halifax, a
considerable time after it had ceased in every other part of the
kingdom. This, however, as I take it, (says WATSON) was merely
accidental; the privilege (as it is called) was not taken away from
any place, by act of parliament, but dropt by degrees, as the motives
for its continuance became less necessary. And surely it was but
right, as the tenures *in capite* ceased, that the liberties therewith
granted should cease also. As Halifax however was a place of so
much trade, this custom which struck such a terror into thieves in
general, was found to be so highly beneficial to the honest manu-

THE GIBBET.

facturers there, that they kept it up as long as they dare: And
it is very probable that it had not ceased when it did, if the bailiff
had not been threatened, after the last executions, that if ever he
attempted the like again, he should be called to a public account
for it.

.The foregoing account appears to have been drawn up by WATSON
with so much accuracy that I have in few places presumed to alter
it.   The records of executions before the time of Elizabeth are lost;
but during her reign twenty-five persons suffered under it, and from
1623 to 1650 there were twelve executions.   This is certainly a
formidable catalogue, for the time it takes in, and has doubtless given
rise to the expression, "From Hell, Hull, and Halifax, good Lord
deliver us," which says FULLER "is part of the Beggars' and Vagrants'
Litany: of these three frightful things unto them, it is feared that
they least fear the first, conceiting it the furthest from them.   Hull
is terrible unto them as a town of good government where they meet
with punitive charity, and 'tis to be feared are oftener corrected than
amended.   Halifax is formidable unto them for the law thereof,
whereby thieves, taken in the very act of stealing cloth are instantly
beheaded with an engine, without any further legal proceedings."

THE ADVOWSON.

The following grant may be considered as the oldest evidence on record relating to the Parochial Church of Halifax. It is printed in the *Monasticon*, vol. i. p. 617, and the following is extracted from Archbishop Corbridge's Register at York, fo. 9. It purports to be a grant and confirmation, from an Earl of Warren to the Priory of Lewes in Sussex, of certain churches within the Manor of Wakefield, and other places. I have before had occasion to refer to it in connection with the manorial history.

In LELAND's *Collectanae*, vol. i. p. 238, is the following "William the first (Earl of Warren) cam into England with William Conquerour, and foundid the priorie of Lewis the xii yere after the conquest in the yere of our Lord 1078."

"Sciant presentes & futuri, quod ego Willielmus, Comes de Warrena, dono, concedo, & hac presenti carta mea confirmo, Deo & S. Pancratio,* de Lewes, & monachis ibidem Deo servientibus, pro salute animæ meæ, & Willielmi patris mei, et omnium successorum nostrorum; Ecclesiam de Conningburgh, cum ecclesiis, capellis, terris, et decimis, & omnibus ad eas pertinentibus; scilicet Ecclesiam de Braythewell cum pertinentiis. Ecclesiam de Donigthon cum pert. Ecclesiam de Herthill cum pert. Ecclesiam de Fislak cum pert. Ecclesiam de Hetfeld, cum capella de Thorne, et omnibus pert. Ecclesiam de Parva Sandale, cum capella de Hernoldesthorp, cum omnibus pert. Ecclesiam etiam de Wakefeld, cum capella de Horbyry, & omnibus pert. suis, Ecclesiam de Halyfax cum omnibus pert. suis,

---

* Sir Henry Spelman in his treatise of ancient deeds and charters observes that it was ordinary, in ancient times, to make grants to persons intellectual and invisible, as God himself, the blessed Trinity, the Church, the Apostles, the Saints, &c. who had been long dead : but after the time of Henry iii (he observes with little delicacy of expression) God's omnipotency was in point of law disabled to purchase, or to take by grant, &c. ; and so also was the spouse, the church; for the law thinks it no reason the wife should be in better condition than her husband. The whole army of saints were likewise disabled.

Ecclesiam de Dewesbyry, cum capella de Herteaheved, & omnibus pert. suis Ecclesiam de Birton cum pert. suis, Ecclesiam de Majori Sandale cum omnibus pert. suis.   Et si forte terræ in quibus sitæ sunt predictæ ecclesiæ in alterius alicujus dominium quam in meum, sive per homaſium et servicium, sive per maritagium, sive alio quocunque modo devenerint, volo nihilominus et percipio, ut prædictæ ecclesiæ, et omnes aliæ quas habent de feodo meo, prædictis Monachis ad sustentionem eorum libere et quiete semper remaneant, ita ut nullus omnino hominum in eisdem ecclesiis aliquod jus advocationis sive presentationis sibi posset vendicare preter ipsos Monachos meos, quibus totum jus quod unquam habui, vel habere potui, in eisdem ecclesiis, dedi et concessi, nullo mihi vel heredibus meis in eisdem ecclessiis jure retento.   Hiis testibus Radulpho de Warren, Hugone de Petroponte, Radulpho de Playz, Rob. de Frivele, ·Reginaldo de Warren, Adam de Poning, Gwyd de Mencecourt, Will. de Drosaio, et multis aliis."

It will be observed that this grant, like most of our charters at that early period, is without date; and hence has arisen the doubt, to which of the Earls Warren it is to be attributed.   At this distance of time it certainly imports but little who was the donor; I have given the opinions both of our ancient and modern historians as they bear upon the question; ·they may be read with interest, but yet leave the point involved in a little obscurity.

DUGDALE has attributed the grant to the *first* Earl of Warren, who died in 1088, shortly after Domesday was finished, although no notice is taken of a Church at Halifax in that return; on the contrary it is said "In Wachefeld, &c. sunt duo Ecclesiæ;" the churches of Wakefield and Sandal being at that time in existence.

"I would rather" says WATSON "attribute the grant to the *second* Earl of Warren, who died in 1138, and who, I have reason to believe, was the first of that family who ever possessed any estates in Yorkshire, except Coningsborough and its dependencies."   In Watson's Memoirs of the Earls Warren, this grant is certainly placed among the charters of the second Earl, and is there stated as having been so entered in the Chartulary of the Priory of Lewes, and confirmed as the grant of that Earl, in a charter of Thomas, Duke of Norfolk, at the request of John Ok, prior of Lewes and the convent there, in the Castle of Lewes.

Mr. HUNTER is of opinion* that the grant was that of the *third* Earl, and not the second, and assigns as a reason for transferring this important charter to the third Earl, from the second, to whom it had theretofore been usually assigned, that "in the *Monasticon,* vol. i. p. 15 of the second edition, is a charter of a William, Earl Warren, who must be the third, because one of the witnesses is Theobald, Archbishop of Canterbury. Among the lay witnesses to this charter we find the names which are appended to the charter before referred to (when treating of the Manor, p. 50) namely, the three bishops, Ralph, Gundulph, and Wakeline, and some others, and placed nearly in the same order. Secondly, in a Chartulary of the priory of Lewes, then in possession of the Earl of Dorset, DODSWORTH read an account of the donation of the above churches, accompanied by the ceremony of cutting a lock of hair from the heads of the Earl and Reginald his brother,† in the presence of Archbishop Theobald and other distinguished ecclesiastics. Theobald was not seated in the archiepiscopal throne, till some time after the death of the second Earl."

This point being settled, it remains to prove to which of the Saxon parishes this wild and waste district, now constituting the Parish of Halifax, had antecedently belonged. It could only have belonged to Morley, or to Dewsbury, which were the parents of all the filial churches in the hundred, (wapontake?) but its dependance upon the latter is not proved by any ancient pension, like those due from Bradford, Thornhill, Mirfield, Huddersfield, and others. We must therefore have recourse to other evidence.

Now in the endowment of the vicarage of Dewsbury, A. D. 1349, is a recital of the great tithes, out of which certain payments are reserved to the incumbent of the church of Dewsbury, and among these are included "decimæ et portiones garbarum de Halifax debit, et ab antiquo solvi consuet." How or when the payment ceased is immaterial—it once existed. In confirmation of this WATSON says "I have seen a deed at Plaintrees, in Shelf, wherein mention was made of tithes in the township of Hipperholme, which was parcel

---

* Hunter's *South Yorkshire.* Vol. i.

† Mr. Ellis speaks of this as the most curious mode of investiture he had seen. De Vaines notices a charter which was attested thus: "presenti scripto sigilli mei robur apposui cum tribus pilis barbæ meæ."

of the rectory of Dewsbury." The Parish of Halifax therefore was taken out of Dewsbury, which there is every reason to believe was the mother church of this part of the country, Paulinus, Archbishop of York, having preached there in the year 627.

The Church seems to have been endowed with an ample glebe, and the rector had certainly a Manor, which by degrees came to be described as the Manor of Halifax. This is proved as follows. In the general survey of the Duchy of Lancaster, A. D. 1577, is this return; "Halifax cu' Heptenstall.—Maneriu' ib'm parcel. possession nuper Prior' de Lewes com. Sussex est infra cur. visus franc pleg. cum turno Dom. de Wakefield, ad manum nup. Regis Hen. VIII. devent. ratione dissolutionis nuper Prior. de Lewes, modo in manu Rob. Waterhouse.

It was the manor of the rectory therefore which the Waterhouses held, by grant from the crown, after the dissolution of the priory of Lewes. But why Halifax cum Heptenstall? At the time of the endowment of the Vicarage of Halifax, A. D. 1273, there must have been a glebe belonging to the parochial chapel there, which was considered as part of the glebe of the rectory, and consequently of the rectory manor. From the foundation of the Church to this time, a period perhaps of 160 years, the benefice, though the advowson had been granted to the monks, was rectorial and presentative. Accordingly we find it, not very long after the Conquest, yet after Domesday, going under the name of a rectory, and Adam de Copley, a younger son of Hugh de Copley, of Copley, in Skircoat, near Halifax, named as one of the Rectors, if not the first, for he was grandson of Adam de Copley, who was slain at the siege of York, in 1070.* Whether any thing particular was given to the rectors of this church, besides the tithes and other dues, to which they were entitled by law, no evidence remains to shew, except in the instance of an undated deed, a copy of which WATSON stated to have been in his possession, and ran thus: "Ego Rob'tus filius Ric. de Talvas, dedi, &c. Tho. fil. Ric. de Coppley totam illam terram quam Ricardus pater meus quondam tenuit de Deo et Soc'. Johanne Baptista et ecclesia de Halifax in villa de Hipperhome;" And in

* "Now certainly, it is a fact capable of proof that there might be an Adam, rector of Halifax, about the year 1130, reckoning according to the order of nature, from his grandfather's death; and he might be 'born at Copley, but the age of local surnames was not yet.'—Dr. Whitaker's *Loidis et Elmete*, p. 331.

another deed, without date, there is mention made of land lying " inter assartum sacerdotis, et magnam viam in Hipperhome ;" but whether the same as the above is not clear. This latter deed seems to be older than the founding of any chantry in Halifax church, and the former, doubtless, belonged to the Rectors or Impropriators, otherwise it had still belonged to the Vicars, which it does not. There is reason to believe the income was something considerable, both from the very large extent of the parish, and because we find persons of no mean account possessed of the living, such as Adam de Copley, whose family was the most flourishing at that time in these parts. Its wealth rendered it an object to foreigners, and other improper persons, who were obtruded on the monks, as they complained, by great men, meaning no doubt their own patrons, the Earls Warren. This is intimated in the endowment itself.

Of these wealthy and too useless ecclesiastics little is known. The last rector, however, we know to have been William de Chameur, a Frenchman, who ceded the rectory of Halifax on being promoted to the bishopric of Lofon in his own country. On his resignation the appropriation took place, and the prior and convent of Lewes presented to the newly endowed vicarage one Ingolard de Turbard, who, after the celebration of high mass by Gilbert de So'to Leofardo, Vicar General to Archbishop Walter Gray, was solemnly inducted into the same in the presence of Gilbert de Angell, rector of Thornhill, Tho. de Boleau, rector of Birstall, Thomas, rector of Heaton, then rural dean, and others. From this period the succession of incumbents (with one or two exceptions) is clear and certain. The endowment of the vicarage, as will hereafter appear, was ample; from the extent of the parish, and the value of the patronage, the benefice has always been an object of ambition to considerable men, their memories have been well preserved; and there is perhaps no parish church in the kingdom in which the arms of the incumbents have been continued through a period of more than 500 years. I by no means assert that they are contemporary with the period to which they are respectively assigned

In the year A. D. 1273 the rectory of Halifax became impropriate, and the vicarage fixed in one clergyman, who was called the perpetual vicar thereof—being obliged to perpetual residence. By the deed of endowment (a copy of which will be found in the

G

Appendix (A,) as also a Bull of Pope Alexander's issued about the same time, together with the mandate empowering the Abbot of St. Alban's to give possession of the church to the prior and convent of Lewes,) the vicar was to receive certain portions of the revenue, amounting to fifty marks per annum, according to the accustomed and common taxation. There was granted to him a piece of land, extending itself in length, from the road along the river side towards the East, to another road towards the West, and in breadth from a way on the South side of the church yard or cemetery, to the land then held by one Richard de Gumar : on this piece of ground a vicarage house was to be built, in which the vicar for the time being should reside. He was also to have "omnes obventiones et proventus spectantes ad alteragium, excepta decima lane et agnorum, et hedorum; cetera omnia ad alteragium spectantia, in usum Vicarii cedere decernimus absolute," but at his own expence to provide for the service of the mother church and its chapels, the repair of the chancel, the procurations and synodals, and all the ordinary burthens.* And the vicar was further bound by the same instrument to pay the salaries to the officiating ministers at the chapels within the vicarage, (viz. Elland and Heptonstall) which is done at this day, each of them receiving the annual stipend of £4. A dispute having afterwards arisen between the prior, the convent, and the vicar, a composition real was made between them in 1275, by Walter Gifford, archbishop of York, and it was decided with the consent of both parties that the vicar and his successors for ever should enjoy the tithes of mills and calves, and also mortuaries, paying yearly to the prior and convent the sum of £4 13s. which the impropriator still receives from the vicar annually. And this appears to have been the ancient endowment of the vicarage.

The following is extracted from the taxation book of Pope Nicholas, (taken for the province of York A. D. 1292,) and

---

* The repair of the chancel, as well as some of these ancient provisions have been by long usage otherwise provided for; the parish has repaired the chancel, as may be seen by the accounts kept at the Town's Committee Room, for more than a century, although at a vestry held in 1831, the parishioners passed a resolution that they were not liable to the repairs of the chancel. When this onus was taken from the vicars does not appear by any records which I have been able to find, neither is it material now to enquire, since the usage and provisions of the vicarial tithe commutation act are in unison.

is curious as shewing the value of the living at that time, p. 322, b.

	£.	s.	d.
"Ecclesia de Halifax	93	6	8
"Vicarius ejusdem	16	0	0

The prior and convent of Lewes continued to present every vicar, from the period of the endowment until the suppression of the monastery at the reformation, when the rectory became vested in the crown. On the happening of that event we find the value of the living thus set forth in the Valor Ecclesiasticus, Henry VIII. " Comit Ebor Halifax Vicaria Robertus Holdesworth Incumbent, et rectoria ib'm appropr' Priori St. Panoraria de Lewes, in Com : Sussex ! Vicar ib'm valet in exit Vicar ib'm mane cum gardino et divers stop eidem adjacent per ann : 8s. oblac ib'm com̄'bus annis XLlb. Xs. Od. minut ac privat decimi com̄'bus annis LIXlb. decimi annis mollend ib'm per ann : IIs.

In Toto C Lib. &c. &c. &c.

The next authentic document states the value of the living at the time of the Commonwealth ; the document is curious, shewing, as it does, that the coarse and rude hand of lawless violence had already wrested from our Church her patrimony.

In the Parliamentary Survey, Vol. 18, p. 270, *et sequitur*, is the following : "Halifax.—We finde that belonging to this great parish there is a vicarage presentative with cure of souls, the small tythes and other profits thereunto belonging worth about £240 per ann., when the dues were paid, which are now withdrawn by most of the chapelryes in the parish. The rectory is impropriate, formerly in the Crown, and now in the State, the customary tythe thereof worth £28 and a noble per annum.

In the 27 Henry VIII, (1535) a money composition was agreed upon between the Prior and Convent of Lewes on the one hand, and the parishioners on the other, confirmed by the ordinary, for the Tithes following, "tritici, selignis, hvrdei, avenarum, fabarum, piscarum et fæni" within the Parish.

In the 15 Elizabeth (1572) by orders indented, taken by the Earls of Sussex and Leicester, commissioners of the Court of Star Chamber, to hear and determine the causes of controversy between certain persons, inhabitants of the parish of Halifax, plaintiffs, and

G 2

the Waterhouses, (the lessees of the prior and convent) defendants. It was ordered 1st, That all actions should cease, &c.   2nd, That, it appearing that the above recited composition had been in some parts corrupted, &c. it was ordered, for avoiding all doubts in future touching the said composition, that the same composition should remain in force in future, and 3rd, It was ordered, that all manner of persons, their heirs and assigns, that had any Lands, &c. within the said vicarage of Halifax, should have, hold, and enjoy their tithes of corn and hay, and other tithes whatsoever, without interruption, of the said Waterhouses or their assigns, and pay yearly during the interest of the said Waterhouses therein, such sum of money as is particularly expressed in the said composition.

In the 18 Elizabeth (1576) an act of Parliament was passed for establishing this composition, and so the rectorial or great tithes of the Parish were commuted ; since which time no alteration has been made.

The present owners of this commutation payment are the lessees of the Crown, who are now in treaty for the purchase thereof, with a view to a subsequent sale either to the respective townships or to individuals.

Happily both for the church and people in this parish there are now "neither great nor small tithes in the vicarage of Halifax ;"* the former having been commuted in the reign of Elizabeth, and the latter in that of his late Majesty, by an act more particularly noticed hereafter.   I say happily, because I believe that there is neither a clergyman nor layman who will not hail it as the dawning of a brighter and happier day for the Church of England, when her ministers shall cease to derive remuneration from a source equally obnoxious to both parties.

The parish register contains a table of customary payments which for a considerable time are stated to have been made to the vicar. This table is also set forth in Watson's history, together with an elaborate explanation ; from which it appears that the parish was anciently divided into two divisions, comprising various townships, called *in* and *out* of Hardwic, or *in* Hardwic Forest and *out* of Hardwic Forest.   I have omitted its insertion in this work, because those

* An expression used in the Terrier of Mr. Burton, when vicar of Halifax, more prophetic than true, in 1790.

payments are now extinguished, and any reference to them may only have a tendency to mislead, if they were ever correct, which is a question much doubted.

A copy of the last Terrier will be found inserted in the Appendix (A.)

On the incumbency of the present vicar, in the year 1827, that gentleman endeavoured to inform himself as correctly as possible, as to the rights and interests of the living as they at that time existed; and a communication was made by him to the parishioners thereon, which gave rise to considerable discussion at the period. As to the nature of the claim made on the one hand, and the resistance contemplated on the other, it is not my intention to offer any observation. The question was happily arranged with the assistance of the legislature, and the future rights of the Church clearly defined and rendered more satisfactory to all parties interested.

By an Act of Parliament, which received the Royal Assent on the 13th April, 1829, intituled "An Act for extinguishing tithes, and payments in lieu of tithes, mortuaries, and Easter offerings, and other vicarial dues and payments, within the parish of Halifax, in the diocese of York; and for making compensation to the vicar in lieu thereof, and enabling him to grant certain leases of lands belonging to the vicarage," the tithes and vicarial dues formerly payable to the vicar were extinguished; and thereby (after reciting the divisions of the parish into the twenty-three townships thereinafter named, and the expediency of providing an annual stipend thenceforth to be paid to the vicar of the said parish for the time being, in lieu of all vicarial tithes, mortuaries, Easter offerings, and dues or payments in lieu of vicarial tithes, or dues arising or payable within eighteen townships, and in lieu of all mortuaries, Easter offerings and dues arising or payable to the said vicar within three of the townships.) It was enacted that the respective churchwardens for the time being of the several townships should yearly thereafter pay or cause to be paid in the proportions thereinafter mentioned, to the vicar for the time being, one clear annual stipend or sum of £1409 15s. 6d. free from all taxes, except the ancient annual payment of £4 13s. payable by the vicar to the King's most Excellent Majesty as rector of the parish.

The act directs the proportions to be raised in each township, as set forth in the following table.

A Table showing the proportions to be raised in each township, and paid to the vicar of Halifax for the time being, in lieu of tithes, &c.

		£.	s.	d.
1	Erringden	35	1	6
2	Fixby	8	15	3
3	Halifax	243	13	6
4	Heptonstall	80	0	10
5	Hipperholme-cum-Brighouse	78	0	0
6	Langfield	38	18	8
7	Midgley	39	3	0
8	Norland	25	3	9
9	Northowram	151	1	6
10	Rastrick	45	10	6
11	Rishworth	27	5	6
12	Shelf	38	3	2
13	Skircoat	65	8	2
14	Southowram	83	13	2
15	Sowerby	111	14	5
16	Soyland	61	3	0
17	Wadsworth	93	0	0
18	Warley	89	17	10
19	Barkisland	15	17	3
20	Ovenden	57	12	0
21	Stainland	20	12	6

£1409 15 6

These payments are to be made by the respective churchwarden or churchwardens of each township, on Easter Monday in every year, in the vestry room of the church, or in such other place as may be agreed on.

The proportions are to be raised and paid for the first eighteen townships by an assessment on all inhabited houses, corn mills, arable, meadow and pasture lands, orchards and gardens, and the proportions to be paid by the last mentioned three townships are to be raised by a charge on all inhabited houses, rateably in proportion to their value: the mode in which the property is to be rated is set forth in the 10th sec. of the act. This annual stipend is in lieu of and for all manner of tithes, mortuaries, Easter dues, oblations, obventions, and other dues and offerings of every denomination whatsoever, (save and except surplice fees usually accustomed to be paid in respect of marriages, christenings, churchings, and burials within the parish,) and all compositions prescriptive and customary, or other payments whatsoever, payable to the vicar, in respect of the messuages and lands, &c. in the first eighteen townships, and in lieu, &c. of all manner of mortuaries, Easter dues, oblations, and other dues and offerings of every denomination whatsoever (save and except surplice, &c.) within the three last mentioned townships. The respective townships may redeem their respective proportions on payment of a sum in gross, not being less than twenty-eight years' purchase. The townships of Elland-cum-Greetland and Stansfield were at liberty to become parties to the act within twelve months after its passing, of which privilege they did not avail themselves: they are not precluded, however, from redeeming their Easter dues on the same terms as the other townships, and there is a proviso in the act that nothing therein contained shall extend to interfere with the vicar's rights in Elland and Stansfield, unless they shall bring themselves within the operation of the act.

By this act, the vicar, and his successors for the time being, with the consent of the Crown, and the Diocesan, is empowered to grant building leases for ninety-nine years, to take effect in possession (without fine) of the land belonging to the vicarage described in the following schedule. The vicar is also empowered, with the same consent, to grant improving leases for terms of sixty years, of the lands marked with an asterisk in the same schedule, being the commons and waste lands allotted to the vicar, under the several inclosure acts.

In the Township of Halifax:

A close of land in Lister Lane, containing 2 acres 1 rood and 7 perches.

In Southowram:

A close of land called Hawkins Royd, adjoining the Gas Works, containing 2 acres 3 roods and 30 perches.

In Barkisland :

* A piece of land situate at Ringstone-Edge, containing 150 acres and 35 perches.

In Ovenden :

* A piece of land situate on and being parcel of Harewood-Well Moor, containing 216 acres.

In Stainland :

* A piece of land situate on Crow-Edge otherwise Cross-Edge, containing 52 acres.

* A piece of land called the Vicar's Pen, situate at or near Great Penam-End at the bottom of Lindley Moor, containing 7 acres.

In Elland-cum-Greetland :

* A piece of land called the Vicar's Park, situate on Greetland Moor, containing 75 acres.

In Stansfield :

* A piece of land situate on and being part of the Blackmoors, containing 408 acres and 20 perches.

* A piece of land situate at Birdstones, containing 77 acres and 18 perches.

* A piece of land situate at Clunters, containing 25 acres and 3 roods.

* A piece of land situate at Chisley Stones, containing 90 acres and 3 roods.

There is a proviso in the act that nothing therein contained shall extend to prevent, after the termination of the present ncumbency, a division of the parish into district parishes.

Independently of the land specified in the foregoing schedules of the act, and allotted to the vicar under the several enclosure acts that have been passed in connection with the parish, the vicarage is endowed with a close of land, containing about two acres, two roods, and sixteen perches, called Shack Field or Vicar's Field, between Southgate and the manufacturer's hall. By an act of Geo. III. passed in 1781, part of this field was vested in trustees for making a road from Southgate to the manufacturer's hall ; and the vicar and his successors were enabled to grant building leases of the other parts of the said close for any term not exceeding 99 years from the making thereof, so as such leases should take effect in possession and not in reversion, and so as there should be reserved the best and most improved yearly ground rents that could reasonably be obtained for the benefit of the vicar. This land has been let on building leases accordingly.

The vicar is also entitled by custom to a small proportion of surplice fees from the several chapelries in the parish.

There are a few benefactions to the vicar arising from different sources; for preaching sermons on certain occasions, and the performance of other duties, which are clearly defined, the whole emoluments whereof are very inconsiderable.

These are the principal resources whence the vicar of this extensive parish derives his income. The patronage immediately connected with the vicarage is the right of presentation to all the episcopal chapels within the parish. The right of presentation to Trinity Church is at present in the representatives of the late Rev. Dr. Coulthurst, who have three nominations after the present incumbent, when the right vests in the vicar. Christ Church, in Skircoat, is private property.

The vicar for the time being is also a trustee of Waterhouse's and Smyth's Charities, and a governor of the Free Grammar Schools at Skircoat, and at Hipperholme; but from these he derives no income, and the duties attached to some of them, are at times arduous.

The present fabric of the vicarage house was erected A. D. 1712, during the incumbency of the Rev. Thomas Burton, but not at his expence, as has been erroneously stated, and as the following extracts from the parish books will shew.

"*Memorandum.*—That the ould vickeridge house was pulled down July the twelfth day, 1712, and was rebuilded by ye liberall contributions of neighbouring gentlemen, and ye inhabitants of the town of Halliffax, and ye inhabitants of ye neibouring towns within the parish of Halliffax, the charge of which was disbursed by Samuel Stead, and the house was thacked the 11th December, 1712."

"*Memorandum.*—That upon 21st of December, 1713, Mr. Thomas Burton, then vicker of Halliffax, did with his family goe to dwell in ye new vickeridge house, it being finished; and ye whole charge of rebuilding it, besides ye ould materials about it, and work given, amounted to about £350, payd by me Samuel Stead."

Perhaps a more suitable spot in the whole township could not have been chosen for the residence of the vicars, if we recur to the period of its first erection: seated, as we may imagine it to have been, " in a dark and solemn grove, on the bank of a small murmuring rivulet, with every circumstance thereunto appertaining very much to contribute to, and heighten contemplation." It is perhaps one of the best and pleasantest vicarage houses within the diocese, possessing sufficient accommodation to enable the vicar for the time being to " maintain hospitality" as his station demands. It is conveniently situated with regard to the church, and lies retired from observation, with a frontage towards the pleasure grounds. The removal of a cluster of low and ill built houses, which at present appear to encroach upon its retirement, is a consummation much to be desired: the site they occupy would not only render the approach to the church both handsome and commodious, and also afford ample room for carriages, without inconveniencing pedestrians; but would lay open to the distance a view of that venerable building. The subject is well entitled to the consideration of the proper authorities.

THE MANOR OF HALIFAX.

It now becomes necessary that we advert to the history of the Manor of Halifax, or in other words the Manor of the Rectory to which we have had occasion to refer in the preceding chapter. I shall endeavour to be as concise and clear as possible. Mr. WATSON observes that at Halifax there has of long standing been a Manor within a Manor. In Kirkby's inquest, being an inquisition taken by John de Kirkby, treasurer to king Edward I. and his fellows, commissioners assigned to enquire of the fees holden in chief in the county of York, of the said king, and the rents of assize then due to him, being the 24th year of his reign, the prior of Lewes was found to hold Halifax ; this must have been then by grant from some of the Earls of Warren. To this priory it continued to belong until the reformation, when, by one sweeping grant the House and its possessions were given in 29th Henry VIII. to Thomas Lord Cromwell, who, being attainted two years afterwards, his lands reverted to the Crown, the manor was made part of the dower of the Lady Ann Cleve, 32 Henry VIII., and she held it until her death, in 1555. Mr. *Watson* mentions that several exceptions were made in the granting of the Rectory Manor to Lady Ann, a lease thereof having been granted by the Priory to Robert Waterhouse, of Halifax, 27 Henry VIII., the said Robert paying the same rent to the Crown which he paid to the convent. Mr. WATSON also refers to a written account which says, that the premises being of the value of sixteen pounds fourteen shillings, were granted to Lady Ann Cleve, for the term of her life, by the king's majesties letters patents without any thing paying for the same; also that there was an annual rent of twenty-one pounds six shillings going out of the King's Manor of Wakefield,

to this Manor of Halifax, and parcel of the lease of Robert
Waterhouse, not charged in this value, neither any parcel of the
possessions assigned to the said Lady Ann Cleve, but remained
in the king's hands extinct.   The king had also in spiritualities
in Halifax, and other the members of the same, to the yearly value
of ninety-five pounds six shillings and eight pence which were
letten in farm to John Waterhouse and others, by indenture,
under the convent seal of the monastery of Lewes, and not charged
in the said value.   The benefices of Coningsborough, Braithwell,
Sandal, Harthill, and Dinnington, are in this account said to be
members of the Manor of, Halifax and not to be granted to the
said Lady Ann, but to have been made over to Robert Waterhouse
as often as they should happen to be void during his term.   By
letters patent dated 14th June, in the 37th Henry VIII., the
reversion of the premises expectant upon the decease of the Lady
Ann, was granted to John Waterhouse, of Halifax and Shipden
Hall, gent. son and heir of Robert Waterhouse, (by Sybil, daughter
and coheiress of Robert Saville, second son of John Saville, of
Hullenedge,) and Robert Waterhouse, son of the said John, Barrister
at Law and Justice of the Peace, for the sum of one hundred and
fifty pounds, five shillings, and ten-pence, to hold to the said John
and Robert, their heirs and assigns, for ever, *in capite,* by the
service of the hundredth part of a knight's fee.   Robert survived
his father, and held the same of Henry VIII., Edward VI., Philip
and Mary, and lastly, of Queen Elizabeth, in whose reign he died
seized, and the Manor descended to Edward Waterhouse, (afterwards Sir Edward,) his son and heir, who held the said Manor in
his demesne, as of fee of the said Queen Elizabeth, and subsequently
of King James, by the said service, the Advowson still remaining
in the Crown, The family of Waterhouse appear to have had
several transactions with the Priory of Lewes.   By leases of lands
and churches under the Priory they obtained great wealth, and
became persons of considerable weight and interest in this parish.
They had their principal seat at the Moot Hall, in the town;
Shipden was also theirs.   Sir Edward Waterhouse is said to
have been a consumer of the property.   Having obtained the
king's license, he sold the Manor to Sir Arthur Ingram, who granted
deeds of infranchisement to several copyholders, reserving yearly

quit rents, fines on deaths of principal tenants, and alienations in fee simple, or fee tail. The lessees also covenanted to appear and do suit and service at the Lords Courts in Halifax, there to be impanelled and sworn of juries, as often as should be needful, to enquire and present misdemeanors, and other things inquirable and presentable within the said Manor; and to perform and keep all reasonable orders, by-laws, and directions, at such courts to be made, for good order and government, within the said Manor; or else to satisfy and pay such reasonable essoigns, and amerciaments, wherein they should at any court be essoigned, amerced, or pained, for their default of suit, or other defaults or offences. Also that they would grind all their corn and grain which they should buy, or bring into the said Manor, to be spent in their houses, upon any part of the premises, or within the said Manor, at the corn mills of the said lords, their heirs and assigns, situate within the parish of Halifax aforesaid, and that they, their heirs and assigns, would not, at any time hereafter, erect any corn mill or mills within the said Manor, or do anything to the prejudice of the lord's mill, or mills, in Halifax aforesaid. The tenants to be well and orderly used in the grinding of their corn and grist, and to have their grinding dispatched in reasonable and convenient time, and no greater mulcture to be taken for the grinding thereof than the twentieth part of every stroke, or half bushel, and after that rate for any greater or lesser measure, of and for all the corn of the growth within the said Manor of Halifax; and the four and twentieth part of every stroke, or half bushel, of hard corn; and the thirtieth part of every stroke, or half bushel, of all other corn; and after that rate, for any greater or lesser measure, of and for all the said kinds of corn to be brought, or bought to be spent, within the said Manor of Halifax: A mulcture dish to be made for taking of that mulcture, and no more, and to be yearly viewed and reformed in the court of the said Manor, as need should require, or complaint be made. Oats to be dried at the lord's kilnhouses there, at the rate of fourpence for each horse-load.

From Sir Arthur Ingram the Manor descended to Charles the Ninth, and last Viscount Irwin, who died at Temple Newsome A. D. 1778. By his will he bequeathed the Manor of Halifax, with other estates, to his daughter Isabella Lady Beauchamp, for life, with remainder to her second and every other son except the eldest, with shifting uses, remainder to his daughter Frances, and her issue male, remainder to other daughters in succession, and their respective issue male remainder to his right heirs.   Whoever succeeded was to take the name of Ingram.   In pursuance of this will they became the property of the late Isabella Dowager Marchioness of Hertford, the Lady Beauchamp named in the will; at whose decease in 1834 they became vested in her sister, the present Lady Gordon.

THE PARISH CHURCH.

Drawn by J. HORNER, Engraved by G. BONNER.

THE PARISH CHURCH.

The present fabric of the Parish Church is a handsome and venerable structure, dedicated to St. John the Baptist, standing at the East end of the town, on a gentle declivity from West to East; rivalled by many, but surpassed by none of the same description within the county of York; it presents to the beholder an air of majestic dignity, or, as THORESBY has observed of its Leeds contemporary, "a very spacious and strong fabric, an emblem of the Church militant, black but comely."

"Its fabric (observes DR. WHITAKER) is entitled to a particular examination." My reader will therefore permit me to enter with him its consecrated precincts, and if I trespass too long on his attention, I hope that it may be attributed to a feeling of respect for the subject under investigation, than from a supposition that I wish to make an invidious distinction between the Parish Church and the more humble temple of the Dissenter. I have too high an opinion of the parishioners of Halifax, to believe that there are any among them who can look with indifference on that sacred pile, and contemplate it as an object unworthy of his regard, whatever may be his creed. To a member of the Church of England, let his station in life be what it may, from the peer to the peasant, high or low, rich or poor, his "PARISH CHURCH" is connected by some more than ordinary tie, some solemn recollection, or some pleasing association. He takes a pride in its prosperity; and regards it as an object of his peculiar care.

The former visits the consecrated spot, he contemplates the sculptured marble of ages past, the monumental effigies of the

H

illustrious dead, now alas! surrounded by the pomp of heraldry, without its glitter; time has not yet erased from the polished surface the recorded virtues of a noble race of ancestors, entombed within the sacred mausoleum; he gazes upon the scene, the days of chivalry pass in review before him, their recollection excites him to honorable actions, he is reminded that virtue alone is true nobility, and forms the pious resolve to devote his life to deeds of benevolence and charity. His untitled neighbour visits the monument which affection has reared to record the memory of one he loved; it speaks in solemn silence the christian hope in which the departed spirit took its flight, in one simple but expressive word, *"resurgam,"* the tear of affection steals down the cheek, it drops upon the grave; and is rendered holy by the sanctity of its depositary. Who can linger among such scenes, and not feel what Addison has so beautifully expressed. "When," he says, "I look upon the tombs of the great, every emotion of envy dies in me; when I read the epitaphs of the beautiful, every inordinate desire goes out; when I meet with the grief of parents upon a tombstone, my heart melts with compassion; when I see the tombs of the parents themselves, I consider the vanity of grieving for those whom we must quickly follow; when I see Kings lying by those who deposed them; when I consider rival wits placed side by side, or the holy men that divided the world with their contests and disputes, I reflect with sorrow and astonishment on the little competitions, factions, and debates of mankind: when I read the several dates on the tombs, of some that died yesterday, and some six hundred years ago, I consider that great day when we shall all of us be contemporaries, and make our appearance together." These may be solemn recollections, but are there no pleasing associations which draw the tie still closer? Yes! the churchman gazes upon his "PARISH CHURCH," and is reminded that at its baptismal font he was signed with the sign of the Cross, and admitted a member of a Christian community; that, in the spring time of youth he there received the Episcopal Benediction, and renewed the solemn vow that was pledged for him in his infantine days; that, at its sacred altar he became united with the dearest object of his earthly affections, in one unbroken, one indissoluble bond of union; that there, on every returning Sabbath has he joined in the sublime and holy liturgy, and heard the grand truths of revealed religion proclaimed from its pulpit; and finally, when he has finished his earthly pilgrimage, does he hope to be gathered to his fathers within its sacred walls.

> " A silent, solemn, sacred spot,
>   The mouldering realms of peace;
> Where human passions are forgot,
>   Where human follies cease."

" The precise date of the original foundation of the Church cannot now be ascertained; neither to which of the Earls Warren the good work is to be attributed. The silence of Domesday forbids us to believe that it existed at that period. Neither is it probable that it was erected while the Lordship of Wakefield remained in the Crown. All the neighbouring Churches, not of Saxon origin, were built by the great Norman lords, soon after their accession to the estates severally granted to them. The reign of Henry I. (viz. from 1100 to 1135) in particular was a general æra of church building in the North, and the probability is that the first Church was erected during that period." Among the principal features of the national character at that early period, a proper attendance upon the duties of public worship might be justly reckoned among the most prevailing; whatever might be the apparent ignorance of the people, " all had devotion at least, and would resort to their Parish Church with an eagerness and regularity not always imitated by those who are more enlightened."

Of the first or Norman building not a vestige remains. This seems to have been destroyed as being too small, or having become dilapidated, about the time of Edward I; for the windows of the North wall of the Nave, surrounded by demi cylindrical mouldings, and with only a single ramification, may be safely assigned to that age. This is the only remnant of the second Church. It is evident that when the plan of the third, that is, the present edifice, was adopted, the parish which had then the Chapels of Elland and Heptonstall, must have become opulent as well as populous. Zeal in those days was never wanting. With respect to the precise time at which the work was begun, all evidence, internal as well as external, concurs in fixing it to the time of Henry VI., and the

H 2

whole work to the incumbency of one vicar, Thomas Wilkinson."*

On entering the South porch we are introduced into a lofty and spacious edifice, consisting of a lobby, nave, side aisles, and chancel. "Though the general proportions which are singularly light and airy, the mouldings of the columns remarkable for their cavettoes, and the precise turn of the arches is so completely maintained throughout, as to prove a general adherence to the original plan; yet two afterthoughts appear to have occurred in the progress of the work. The workmen seem to have begun at the West end, and with the intention of mounting a tower on the wall of the West front, and on the two next columns Eastward. An evidence of this is the beginning of the staircase in the wall, which now leads to nothing. It seems, however, that, as in consequence of the low situation of the Church a very lofty bell tower was required, the constructors of the work very prudently distrusted the strength of these two columns, and began the entire steeple from the ground westward of the Church. Hence they proceeded eastward, intending, as it should seem, to carry the Church no farther than the entrance of the present choir; for on the springers of the second columns West from thence are cross springers North and South, evidently intended for arches to divide the nave and choir: nay, more, in the more northerly of these two columns is actually remaining the groove for the great beam to support the rood loft, which shews that this arrangement had actually taken place; yet before the work was quite completed, or very soon after, the work was extended three arches further, and on exactly the same plan with the parts already finished." These are described by Mr. WATSON as broken arches, as an evidence of the alterations which the Church has undergone.

"This produced the bold and lightsome choir, of which the East window, according to the inscription upon his arms, was erected at

* The following extract from an original MS. referred to by Wright and Watson written by John Waterhouse of Shipden, and sometime Lord of the Manor of Halifax, may be considered as the best information that can be obtained as to the precise era of the present erection. "In the time of John Waterhouse of Halifax, deceased, who died about Candlemas 96 years since, (i. e. 1540,) at his death being near 100 years of age, I trowe three years under, and when he was a child, about 6 or 7 years of age, was the Church of Halifax begun to be builded, and he and many more children stood upon the first stone of the steeple. It was 20 years in building. By this it appeareth that John Waterhouse was born in 1443, and in 1637, it is 207 years since the foundation of Halifax Church was laid."

the expense of Vicar Wilkinson A. D. 1480: according to my hypothesis, therefore, the West end must have commenced, and the first columns erected some time before, and probably as early as the first years of Wilkinson's incumbency, whom, from an original attestation to a charter I know to have been vicar A. D. 1440."

There are two side chapels connected with this Church, that on the North is known to have been erected in conformity with the will of Archbishop Rokeby, who died A. D. 1521; it is eleven yards and a quarter in length, and five yards and a quarter in breadth, and was ordered by the Bishop to be erected and used as a chantry. The insertion of the masonry into the former wall is sufficiently conspicuous, and the arches within, which have a kind of torus moulding instead of cavettoes, prove that it is of a different æra from the body of the Church, to which it is attached. Nearly opposite, but of much greater extent, is the chapel of Dr. Holdsworth, the twelfth vicar, who was unhappily murdered in the vicarage house A. D. 1556. This chapel is sixteen yards and a half in length, and five and a quarter broad, within is a tomb in which the vicar lies interred.* The arches of this chapel are precisely the same with those of Rokeby's chapel. Without, it is distinguished by perpendicular detached buttresses, on a rhomboid base, surmounted by spouting monsters, which discharge the water from the roof, and exceedingly resemble the fantastic architecture of King James V. buildings at Falkland, Linlithgow, &c. On the whole, the chapel may be assigned to the earlier years of Dr. Holdsworth's incumbency.

At the entrance of the chancel stands the skreen, dividing it from the " aula," or body of the church; this, as in many of our ancient parochial churches, is of excellent workmanship, and too well known to need any description, it is surmounted in the centre by the royal arms of Queen Anne, which are executed in a superior manner, and present a handsome appearance, viewed on either side. At the South end of the skreen, is the entrance of a small staircase, which leads up to a door at a moderate height from the pavement, (by which door we now enter the High Sunderland gallery.) If I might be permitted to indulge in the hypothesis, I should say

---

* Mr. Watson says, p. 365, he was buried under the great tomb-stone in the South chapel, without any inscription.

that at this door was formerly the place for the pulpit, probably the
rood loft, as appears from the following rubrics: "Incepta vero
ultima oratione ante epistolam subdiaconus per medium chori ad
legendum epistolum in pulpitum accedat.   Quando Epistola legitur
duo pueri in superpelliciis, facta inclinatione at altare ante gradum
chori in pulpitum per medium chori ad gradale incipendium se pre-
parent et suum versum cantandum."   The pulpit to which these
stairs led, might indeed be the rood loft, for it is highly probable
that the rood loft which formerly existed in this Church was placed
over the skreen, occupying the entrance to the choir, that that was
the case sometimes, is manifest from the will of Henry VI., where
there is mention made of a "reredosse (skreen) bearing the rood
loft departing the choir and the body of the Church; and the upper
stair usually ascends nearly even with the top of the skreen."   On
pursuing my inquiries on this truly interesting subject, I am led to
believe that from this place the sermon was made, the curate being
obliged to preach four times in the year, by an ecclesiastical constitution of Archbishop Peckham, in which is this injunction,
"Exponat populo vulgariter absque cujuslibet subtilitatis textura
fantastica."   From which reading and preaching to the people
assembled in the nave "ubi insident ipsi parochiani laici," a
learned antiquary observes, the body of the Church received the
name of "auditorium."   That this staircase did not lead to any
place devoted to the use of the people is, I think, highly probable,
for not only does the chancel seem to have been considered in all
ages, the most sacred part of the Church, but by the Laodicean
Canon none were admitted but those of the priesthood during the
oblation; and women were totally excluded by another Canon of
the same Church.

Upon entering the chancel from the nave, we observe on either
side the remaining stalls, appropriated formerly to the use of the
priest and his clerks, where, and at the altar, the church service
was performed, prior to the reformation; the stalls are now
divided off into pews for the use of the vicar, and the clergy
officiating at the Church.

. Proceeding onward we ascend three steps; here formerly stood
the high altar, now occupied by the communion table.   The table
itself has nothing worthy of note, and is of modern date, the former

having in all probability been destroyed during the civil wars. There is nothing connected with the present appearance of the altar to claim more than ordinary attention.

Within the chancel are deposited the remains of many of the late vicars, who now rest from their labors, and of the major part of whom it may be truly said, their works do follow them; for there is no parish in the United Kingdom which has more reason to boast of the sound orthodoxy of her clergy than the parish of Halifax.

On the North side of the Church is a gallery, the seats or pews in which belong to the adjoining out townships, and are let by them at considerable rents. The township to which each pew belongs, has its name painted on the front. At the rear of this gallery is another, which runs back into Rokeby's chapel, and is commonly called the Calf Gallery.

At the West end of the Church over the entrance to the nave is the Organ Gallery. In the year 1764 a subscription was set on foot for purchasing the present valuable organ, for providing a salary for the organist, and keeping the organ in repair; the amount raised was upwards of £1,200, out of which sum the organ loft was purchased. Considerable opposition appears to have been manifested by the township of Sowerby, to the erection of this organ, on the plea, that it would entail additional expense upon the township, and their churchwardens appeared by Proctor to oppose the faculty; a suit was instituted, but such was the strong feeling of the parishioners generally in favor of the organ, that a subscription was entered into amounting to upwards of £720, to defray the expenses of the suit. The call on the subscribers amounted only to twenty-five per cent. The sum received was £194 5s., when the law suit was happily terminated, and on the 11th July, 1766, the Faculty for playing the organ was granted by the Archbishop of York.*

* Among the organists who have presided at the Parish Church, it may be well to record that the celebrated and renowned astronomer, Dr. Herschel, was foremost. Having come to England along with a German regiment as a performer on the hautboy in the military band, his extraordinary musical genius and abilities attracted the attention of Dr. Miller, the historian of Doncaster, on whose solicitation he left the corps, and became an inmate in the family of his new acquaintance. Soon after this event, the present magnificent and powerful organ, equalled by few and excelled by none for the full and exquisite richness of its tone, came new from the hands of *Snetzler*. Many were the competitors

On the North side of the Church under the middle window, (observes Mr. WATSON) "is a cavity in the wall, and a projecting stone, where probably some chauntry priest officiated." At the present day it is not visible, having been probably covered over by the wood work there, rendered necessary by the damp state of the wall. Mr. WATSON also observes "that on the right hand of what is called the sun door was a cavity, now filled up, where tradition says the holy water was kept."

On the South side of the Church is a handsome circular painted window, erected in the year 1830 at the expense of Christopher Rawson, Esq. of this town: its shape is oval, and the first series of panels are in imitation of the beautiful window in the South entrance of York Cathedral, known by the name of "The Marygold Window," from the circumstance of its containing representations of that flower, which was a great favorite with the ancients. In the central compartment is emblazoned the Rawson's Arms and Crest, and the intermediate panels are filled up with a wreath of foliage, after the Herba Benedicta, a plant much copied by the members of the early English style of Ecclesiastical Architecture. The window was executed by BARNETT, of York.

On an escutcheon over the entrance to the South porch are the arms of the Lacis. This may be considered as the principal entrance to the Church, (although that on the North side is apparently of greater antiquity;) on each side is found a bench extending its

---

for the organist's situation, and on the arrival of the day of trial, Herschel and six others entered the lists. Mr. (afterwards Dr.) Wainwright preceded Herschel, and so rapid was his execution, that old Snetzler ran about the Church angrily exclaiming: "Te Tevel, te Tevel, he run over te kee'sh like one cat, he will not gif my piphes room for to shpeak." During Wainwright's performance Dr. Miller enquired of his friend Herschel what chance he had of following this performer. " I don't know," replied Herschel, "but I am sure fingers alone won't do." When it came to his turn, Herschel ascended the organ-loft, and produced so uncommon a richness, such a volume of slow harmony as astonished all present: and finishing this extemporaneous effusion with a steady, harmonious, and dignified performance of the Old Hundredth Psalm, he drew from the delighted builder the exclamation, " Aye, aye, tish is very goot, very goot indeed, I will luf tish man, he gifs my piphes room for to shpeak." Herschel, on being asked how he contrived to produce so astonishing an effect, observed, " I told you fingers alone would not do ;" and producing from his waistcoat pocket two pieces of lead, remarked, " One of these I placed on the lowest key, and the other upon the octave above, (pedals not being then invented,) and thus by accommodating the harmony, I produced the effect of four hands instead of two." This superiority of skill obtained Herschel the situation; but he soon after removed to Bath, where he burst forth from obscurity, and rose to the highest pitch of celebrity in the dignified science of astronomy.

whole length; it appears to have undergone some modern reparations, which may perhaps account for the absence of those appearances that are sometimes found in the porches of our ancient churches. However it may in general have been passed over as a matter of ornament, it is without doubt a very ancient appendage to the Church, and upon inquiry we shall find that it had its especial uses; an enquiry, I can assure my readers, far from being devoid of interest. Here (on the right of the entrance to the Church) was placed a stone bason, the receptacle for holy water, used by every one about to enter the sacred edifice. It was also used for the christening of children, and weddings, as may be seen from the will of Henry VI. before mentioned, where referring to the foundation of his college at Eton, is this article: "Item, in the South side of the body of the Church, a fair large door with a porch, and the same for christening of children, and weddings." Somner relates, that in 1299, Edward I was married at Canterbury to Margaret, sister to the King of France, by Archbishop Winchelsea, "in ostio ecclesiæ versus claustrum." That it was also used for the churching of women appears from a rubric in existence printed at Paris, 1515; but its most particular use was in administering baptism; here the necessary questions being asked, and prayers being said, the parties were led into the church to receive the blessing. Nothing can be more apparent that had it not been for the porch, the performance of these rites would have been many times impracticable.

Within the lobby, and opposite the entrance to the nave stands the Font, which is of stone, the bason is in the ancient octagonal form, and of the usual capacious dimensions; the faces of the octagon are at present blank, although it is evident something has been cut upon them. The cover of lattice, is of excellent workmanship, and worthy the attention of the curious; its height is sixteen feet, the form spiral, and richly carved with crockets. The register informs us that it was re-erected in the year 1660.

Within the lobby is also a figure of wood representing an old man, holding the poor box. The man here represented was designated by the familiar appellation of "Old Tristram." He was for a considerable time dependant upon the parish for parochial relief; and if any reliance is to be placed on tradition, the workhouse was the place of his birth, parentage, and education. From the same source, it appears that it was his practice to carry a box appended to some part of his person, with the memorable inscription thereon, "Pray remember the Poor," much after the present fashion, but I know not why he was thus immortalized. His son followed the same occupation, and their names occur in the parish books during the sixteenth century. The great grandson was interred in December, 1833. Peace to their manes.

The steeple at the West end is a fine substantial turret, thirty-nine yards from the ground to the summit of the pinnacle. It is of the same date as the rest of the fabric, and MR. WRIGHT informs us that the principal contributors to it were the Lacis, and the Savilles. The South East pinnacle of it was destroyed by lightning in the year 1558. MR. WATSON conjectures that the old steeple was at the South West corner of the Church; and observes that the arches on which it was built are still standing, and very strong, although they have little or nothing to support. This, it will be observed, differs from DR. WHITAKER's hypothesis, who attributes the present appearance of the building to two after thoughts, which appear to have occurred in the progress of the work, as before mentioned. Below the windows in the present steeple are two angels holding escutcheons made of stone, but at this date there are no arms upon them. The window appears by an inscription there to have been made at the charge of Dorothy, widow of Mr. Nathaniel Waterhouse, of Halifax, A. D. 1657. The steeple contains ten fine musical bells, which are allowed by connoisseurs and competent judges to be inferior to none in the North of England, both with regard to tune and tone. Eight of them were erected in the year 1787, by voluntary subscription; the cost, &c. amounting to upwards of £350. A list of the subscribers is painted on a board in the belfry. The remaining two, which are the first and second of the peal, were erected in the year 1814, and have no mottos.

MOTTOS ON THE BELLS.

On the third.

"Mortals with us your voices raise,
And shout abroad Jehovah's praise."

On the fourth.

"With sweetest voices we will sing,
And loudly cry God save the King."

On the fifth.

"Let PARKER'S liberal deeds be known,
To future ages yet unborn."

On the sixth.

"Ye Ringers who wou'd happy be,
In concord live and unity."

On the seventh.

"When Britons are with laurels crown'd,
We'll make the hills and vales resound."

On the eighth,

William and Thomas Mears, late Lister, Pack, and Chapman, Bell
Founders, White Chappel, London; as such, there is no motto on it.

On the ninth.

"Attend ye sons for worship bent,
Your prayers put up, your sins lament."

On the tenth.

"All ye who hear my mournful sound,
Repent before you lie in ground."

Thomas Holden, }
William Birkby, } Church-Wardens.—1787.

On a board, within the Church, near the steeple, is inscribed,
"In the years 1804 and 1805, new Chimes were erected, which cost
£154.   In the years 1807 and 1808, the Church was perfectly repaired, the Church aisles, choir, South and North Chapels.   The
several pews and galleries were raised and made even, the church-
yard and burial grounds were put into complete repair, the old
causeways were widened, and new ones laid; the gateways repaired,
and new gates put thereon.   Total cost of the works, £137 19 11."

And on another board, "In the years 1817 and 1818, the uppermost part of the church steeple, including the whole of the pin-
nacles, parapet, walls, and stone figures, were entirely renewed.
The roof of the steeple was also then covered with lead.   The
whole of which work cost £490."

On the outside, this Church, with the exceptions already
noticed, bears every mark of one progressive but consistent plan.
There are no appearances of separation externally between the
tower and West end, or between the intended termination of the
original choir and its present one. The battlements are crocketted
in a peculiar, but not unornamental manner, which for the sake of
uniformity has been copied in Archbishop Rokeby's chapel, though
not in that of Dr. Holdsworth. Another singularity in this Church
is, that having been built on a site declining rapidly to the East,
without any unusual ascent to the communion table, a crypt of
three rooms, formerly used as a vestry and library, now as a library
and Sunday school room bnly, has been constructed at the East
end, and in these, two vicars, Dr. Clay and Dr. Legh lie interred.

CHURCH CHANTRIES.

In all that relates to the Chantries formerly founded in this
Church I shall be as brief as possible, there is but little interest
attached to the subject, otherwise than as it developes the state of
gross ignorance and mental darkness which obscured the understanding in those dark ages of popish superstition.

To such of my readers who may not be familiar with the purposes to which these Chantries were appropriated, it may perhaps
be necessary to state "that Chantries consisted of salaries to one or
more priests to say mass daily, for the souls of their founders
deceased : which, not subsisting of themselves, were generally
incorporated and united with some parochial, &c. church," as there
were forty-seven Chantries in the Old Church of St. Paul, at
London, and but fourteen altars, it was possible for several to be
founded at the same altar. They were generally endowed with
houses and lands. When a person was not sufficiently rich to
endow a perpetual Chantry, it was common for an anniversary
chaplain to sing masses for the repose of his soul during a certain

space, for which a stipend was left, as appears by the will of Robert Wolsey, the father of the Cardinal.—See Fiddes' *Life of Wolsey.*

Mr. Watson's hypothesis that the cavity in the wall, and the projecting stone before referred to, was a Chantry altar, is not improbable; the projecting stone being used as an altar, and the cavity or niche was doubtless what was called *piscina.* The use of this receptacle is thus specified in the Archæologia, Vol. XI.: "That should a fly or spider, &c. fall into the chalice, before consecration, it was directed to be thrown, together with the wine, into this receptacle; but should this happen afterwards, it was directed to be burnt *super piscinam.*"

By the certificate of Robert, Archbishop of York, and others concerning Chantries, &c. 2 Edward VI. it appears that in Halifax Church were, 1. The Chantry of the Trinity, founded by John Willoughby, yearly value, four pounds. 2. Hunter's Chantry, yearly value, four pounds thirteen shillings. 3. The perpetual stipend or service at the rood altar there, yearly value, three pounds eighteen shillings. 4. Brigg's Chantry, yearly value, four pounds thirteen shillings and four-pence. 5. Firth's Chantry, yearly value three pounds six shillings and eight-pence. To which Stevens, in his Supplement, vol. 1. page 68, adds, the service of the morrow mass in the said Church, yearly value, fifty one shillings and ten-pence; differing in nothing else from the above, except making the yearly value of Brigg's Chantry four-pence less, and that of Firth's eight-pence. "As to the first of these," says Watson, "I find that Thomas Willeby founded a Chantry on the south side of Halifax Church, and to endow it, feoffed Sir John Nevil, Knt., Thomas Nevil, Esq. his son and heir, Thomas Willeby, his kinsman, and others, in lands in Priestley, in Hipperholme, to the yearly value of six marks, in June, 9 Henry VII. In Halifax Register is the following entry, "Dom. Thomas Gleydheyll Cantarist. in Cantar. voc. Wylbe Chantre, ac quondam Vicarius de Cunnesburghe, sepult. Maii, 1541." The lands belonging to this Chantry were granted by Edward VI in the third year of his reign, to Thomas Gargrave, Knt. and William Adam, jun. In Willis's History of Mitred Abbies, vol. ii. p. 292. in a list of pensions paid in 1553, to incumbents of Chantries, under Wylby's, one Richard Northend was then in possession thereof, but his annuity, on some account or other, is only put down at three pounds twelve shillings, which gives room to suspect that the rest are undervalued."

The original institution of this Chantry is fully set forth in WATSON's History. Those who take an interest on such subjects will doubtless feel greatly edified by the perusal of a Latin transcript, from an old MS. occupying no less than four quarto pages. Its length of course precludes its insertion here.

In a list of the compositions for tithes paid in Halifax parish is the following entry : " John Paslew, Chaunter of the Chauntry called Hunter's, for five closes in Halifax and Skircoat, near Shasike, (Shaw Syke,) to the said Chauntry belonging, 18d."

The perpetual stipend, or service, at the rood altar, is thus described in the certificate of the Archbishop of York and others, dated 14 Feb. in the secounde yeare of his Grace's reygne, (Edw. VI.) Hallifaxe Parish. " The Rode Obite, or perpetual stypend of a Preyst in the parish church there.—John Waterhouse, incombent, 47 yeares of age, hath nothing else to live upon but the profitts of the said Chauntry. Goods, ornaments, and plate belonging to the said service, as appyth by the inventorye. Goods, 2l. Plate, 2l. The yerely value of the freehold land belonging to the said service, as particularlie appyth by the rentall, 5s. Coppiehold by yeare, 77s. whereof resolutes, viz. of the freehold by yeare, 4s. resolutes of the coppiehold by yeare, 4s. So remains clere of the coppiehold yearly, 73s. and to the King's Majestie clere of freehold yerely, 12d." This, in all probability was founded to celebrate the death of Christ.

In the Harleian Manuscripts in the British Museum, N°. 797, under Halifax, it is said, that in 1532, (24 Hen. VIII.) William Brigg founded a Chantry in the north part of Halifax Church, adjoining to Rokeby's chapel. Mr. WATSON says "I have seen mention made of the Chaplain who celebrated or said divine service at the altar of St. George, in the parish church of St. John Baptist, of Halifax, but which of the above Chantries it belonged to I cannot say."

The officers of Earl Warren having charged the Monks of Halifax, (the Prior and Convent of Lewes,) with Argent, Bladez, Furnage, Cervise, and divers repasts, they were quitted thereof, 6 Edward III.

MONUMENTS, EPITAPHS, &c.

THE several Monuments, Brasses, and Inscriptions, within the Church, next claim our attention. I have selected from WATSON's copious List a few of those which are most worthy of notice; and of these none can boast of any great antiquity: whether any ever existed in the Church prior to these is very uncertain, though not improbable; the testamentary burials would lead us to infer that such was the fact, but if so, no traces of them are visible at the present day.

Exclusive of these burials the earliest Monument is that of

ROKEBY.

On a monument formerly in the Chapel on the north side of the Church, but now removed; "Orate pro anima WILLIELMI ROKEBY, Jur. Can. Profess. ac etiam Episcopi Medensis et deinde Archiepisc. Dublin. Capellæ fundatoris istius, qui obiit 29 Novembris, An. Dom. 1521."

SAVILE.

In the Chancel, round the border of a stone, in ancient characters: "(Pray) for the (Sa)wl of THOMAS SAVILE, of Coplay, Esquyer, the . . . . of July, (and) in the yeire of ower Lord God, MCCCCCIXXX."

This was in all probability the first burial in the Chancel, for it is only since the Reformation, except in cases of superior sanctity, that they had recourse to burial in the Chancel.

WATERHOUSE.

In the middle aisle of the Church, on brass plates, fixed to a seat near the pulpit, which are all torn off except the heads, a man kneeling, with a book in his hand, and opposite to him a woman kneeling, and a string of beads hanging down from her waist. On a label over the man, in old characters; "Miserere mei Deus, et salva me." On another label near the woman, in like characters: "Miserere mei Deus, secundum magnam misericordiam." On a brass plate over their heads: "I am the resurrection and the life, saith the Lord. He that believeth in me, though he were dead yet shall he live, and he that liveth and believeth in me shall never die." Underneath, in the above characters; "JOHN WATERHOWS, of Halyfax, and AGNES, hys wyff, which John dep͡ted from thys worlde the XXVII day of January, anno Dn͡i MCCCCCXXX." Something wanting both at the beginning and end. On a close inspection of this plate, it occurs to me that it has been taken off some monument, in all probability at the time of the civil wars, that it escaped the fate of its contemporaries, of which doubtless it had many in this church prior to that event, and that it was fixed in its present place the better to preserve it.

On the North side of the Church, where the deceased particularly desired to be buried, is a tomb, on which is written; "Here lieth the body of Mr. JOHN WATERHOUSE, of Lower Ranns, (or Rands,) in Northowram, who died April 4th, 1759, aged 60." On the West end of the tomb :—

Oh Christian Reader! often think

Christ will appear,

How shall I then in judgment stand!

LACY.

DR. JOHNSON, in his MS. Collections for Yorkshire, says, that in Halifax Church was the following, in ancient characters: "Here lieth enclosed the body of JOHN LACYE, of Brerely, Esq. who was buried the 19th day of August, in the year of our Lord God . . . . " (This date should be 1585.) "Part of this stone I saw in 1764; it had cut upon it the figure of a man in armour laid on his back, a cushion under his head, and a lion at his feet; on one side hung a large sword, and a small one on the other; his hands were joined on his breast in a praying posture; on his left arm a shield, with the following coats of arms: 1. Argent, six ogresses, three, two, one, for Lacy. 2. Gules, three crescents argent, on a chief of the second three garbs or. 3. Gules, an eagle displayed argent, for Soothill, of Soothill. 4. Argent, three bendlets sable; all these quarterly impaled with Argent, a chevron between three crosses formée, fitchée gules, for Woodrove, of Woolley. Under the arms of Lacy were in old characters, "Orate pro anima Magistri Joannis

Lacye." It is not improper to mention here, that on a grave-stone in the chancel is a large cross, on one side of which is a sword of lead laid in the stone, and on the other, in a shield, the ogresses as above.

WATERHOUSE.

In the North Chapel, on a stone with a man in armour upon it, in old characters; "Here lyeth the body of ROBERT WATERHOUSE, of Halyfax, Esquyer, which departed this life the . . . of June . . . (hav)ying lyved as one that should dye."

Near the above, but now destroyed (as supposed) was another figure of a man in armour, with this inscription round, in old characters: "Here lyeth the body of BRYAN WATERHOUSE, of Halyfax, Gentleman, which departed this life the iv day of October, in the year of our Lord God, 1589. Humanius est deridere vitam quam deplorare."

In Dr. Johnson's MS. Collections is the drawing of a tomb said to have been removed out of the North Chapel when the stairs were made which lead to the North gallery there, at the head of which was a shield of arms, viz. Waterhouse, Or, a pile ingrailed sable, quartered with Savile, parted per pale quarterly, 1. Bosseville, of Gunthwaite. 2. Bendy of thirteen pieces, or and argent. 3. . . . A lion rampant. . . . over all a bend gules; fourth as first. Under these a scroll and motto, "Virtus vincit omnia." On the top of the tomb lay the figure of a man in armour, holding on his breast a shield with the same arms as above. On one side of his head were, on a shield, the arms of Waterhouse, on the other the coats of Waterhouse and Savile, quartered; on one side of his feet, Waterhouse, impaled with Bosseville, and on the other, Waterhouse, impaled with the same quarterings as are impaled in the shield on his breast. The above stairs were made in 1700.

SUNDERLAND.

Dr. Johnson says, that the following was in the South aisle of the Chancel: " Here lieth the bodies of ROBERT, son of RICHARD

I

Sunderland, of Coley, Esq.; and Judith, his daughter, who died January 19th, 1623. February 8th, 1623." This was round a stone, on which were cut, in bad proportion, the figures of a man and woman kneeling down together; over their heads, on a shield, three lions passant; and for crest, on a helmet a goat's head.

TILLOTSON.

In the Chancel, in letters of gold, on a tablet, with the arms of the Archiepiscopal See of Canterbury impaled with his own:

· Johanes Tillotson, Archiepus Cantuar. natus Sowerbiæ, renatus Halyfaxie, 3^{tio} 8^{bris}, 1630. Denatus Lambethæ, 22o Novebris, A. D. 1694. Ætatis suæ 65."

BENTLEY.

On a gravestone in the South Chapel: " Eli Bentley, son of Richard Bentley, of Sowerby Dene, M. A. some time Fellow of Trinity College, in Cambridge, and late Minister of the Gospel at Halifax, departed this life July 30th, 1675, in the 45th year of his age."

RAMSDEN.

On a pillar in the Chancel: " Hic jacet Hugo Ramsden, filius Galfridi Ramsden, de Greetland, infra Vicariam de Halifax, Bacc. in S. S. Theol. olim Socius Collegii de Merton in Ac. Ox. postea Rector de Methley, in Comit. Ebor. demum Vicarius de Halifax. Vir dubium sanctior, an doctior, ingenii acris, judicii subacti, eruditionis multiplicis, qui omne tempus deperire existimabat quod non aut templo aut musæo inpertiabatur; qui dum vixit toti circumjacenti Regioni doctrina sua prælucebat, et magis exemplo; atq; moriens triste sui apud omnes bonos, pacisq; Ecclesiæ cultores reliquit Desiderium. Inductus est Vicarius de Halifax Non. Octob. An. Salutis 1628, et decimo septimo Calend. Augusti sequentis vitam cum immortalitate commutavit. Hoc mœrens monumentum posuit Frater ejus natu minor, ejusq; in Vicaria de Halifax impar successor, Henricus Ramsden."

To the word "commutavit," there is the same on a tablet in Methley church, put there in 1680 by one Robert Nalson.

On a pillar opposite to the above, is a long inscription to the memory of Henry Ramsden, a brother of the above, also vicar of this parish.

DUN.

On a marble monument upon the wall of the South side of the Chancel :

M. S.

Hic juxta conditur

Quod reliquum est Joshuæ Dun,

Filii Joshuæ et Mariæ Dun, de Halifax,

Collegii Christi dum apud Cantabrigienses floruit Alumni

Quin et Collegii et Academiæ decoris et ornamenti,

Nunc proh dolor ! tristis iisdem desiderii ;

Juvenis erat, si ætatem : si spectas dotes, vir eximius ;

Si quem eximium reddere valeant

Probitas, summum ingenii acumen, acre judicium,

Artium scientia, morum suavitas, urbanitas.

Sese quantumvis ad omne literarum genus aptum natum,

In Medicina presertim excolenda, seu potius ornanda,.

Exercuit ;

In qua tam mirificos fecit progressus,

Ut brevi istius Facultatis peritus admodum prodierit :

Summatim,

Nisi quod tantum mortalibus fata invidissent virum,

Ad morbos propulsandos,

Et ad redintegrandas labefactatas hominum vires

Plane natus videbatur :

Ast heu ! quam aliis potuit sibi-metipsi non concessum est

Opem afferre ;

Variolis enim correptus, post duodecem dies,

Cum spes jam eum revaliturum effulserat,

Inter seros nepotes vix æquiparandus,

Haud certe unquam superandus, occubuit,

Die 13 Sept. MDCCIX, annos natus xxv.

Nec procul ab illo recumbit

Pater ejus Joshua Dun,

Qui obiit 7° Aug. A. D. 1715.   Ætatis suæ 80.

Et mater ejus Maria Dun,

Quæ obiit Apr. 5°, A. D, 1729,

Ætatis 87.

Mr. Wright says, this epitaph was drawn up by the celebrated Nicholas Sanderson, Professor of Mathematics in the University of Cambridge.

FAVOUR.

On a gravestone in the Chancel: "Hic dormit JOHANNES FAVOUR, Doctor sanctissimus hujus Ecclesiæ....

Occubuit seris, heu! quod non serius, annis;
Nec longæva magis quam bona vita fuit.
Quam sacre velavit speciosum pectore corpus,
Dignum equidem tumulo nobiliore tegi.
Qui quidem extremam fidus permansit ad horam,
Non illi tumulus, sed diadema decus.
Theologus Medicusq; obiit, Jurisq; peritus:
I, sequere in cœlos, qui modo salvus eris."

On a pillar on the South side of the quire is a monument, erected to the memory of the above Dr. Favour, who is placed as in a pulpit, drest in his robes, surplice and hood, and in an attitude of preaching, with one hand on his breast, and the other on a skull, which rests on the cushion before him.

Jo. FAVOUR, LL. Doct. Medici peritiss.   et hujus
Ecclesiæ Pastoris vigilantissimi.

"Corpora et ægrotant animæ; fremit undiq: rixa,
Scilicet oba suo turba FAVORE jacet.
En Pastor, Medicusq; obiit, Jurisq; peritus:
I, sequere in cœlos, qui modo salvus eris."

HOOKE.

On a marble monument in the Chancel: "P. M. RICHARDI HOOKE, S. T. P. Regimini tam ecclesiastico quam sæculari Anglicano fidelissimi, qui per viginti sex annos huic Ecclesiæ præfuit Vicarius, tribus Archiepiscopis Eborᵇᵘˢ a sacris, Hospitiorum sancti Johannis beatæq. Mariæ Magdelenensis sub agro RIPPONENSI Magister, Ecclesiæ EBORᵗⁱˢ SOUTHWELLᵗⁱˢ RIPPONENSISQ. Canonicus. Obiit 1ᵐᵒ Jan. Ætatis suæ 66.   Anno Domini 1688-9.

HOUGH.

The following inscription was put over Vicar Hough, who was buried in the Chancel: "Sacrum memoriæ EDMUNDI HOUGH, A.M.

e Coll. Jesu Cant. quondam Socii, Parochiæ de THORNTON postea Rectoris, tandemq; hujus Ecclesiæ Præsidis; qui concionandi perspicuus, disserendo facundus, pietate catholicus, post exiguum autem Olicanæ temporis impensum morienti hanc desideratam requiem sibi dedit Dedus. Obiit 1mo die Aprilis, 1691. Anno ætatis 59."

There is an English one to the memory of the same, on a stone in the Chancel, taken from part of the above.

It was a great mistake in the writer of the above epitaph to call Halifax by the name of Olicana, for that was undoubtedly the Roman station at Ilkley.

ROBERTS.

On a stone in the Church-yard, opposite the great door : "Here lieth the body of JOHN ROBERTS, of Hipperholme, who departed this life the 10th of November, in the year of our Lord 1721, and in the hundred and fourteenth year of his age."

SHARP.

On a tablet in the Chancel, an angel in clouds, blowing a trumpet, and on a cloth hanging from it, these words : "JOHANNES, Dominus Archiepiscopus EBORUM, 1704." Arms of Sharp painted near the inscription, impaled with those of the See of York.

This was put up in honour to his memory, as he was born in the parish of Bradford.

STEAD.

" Near this place is interred the body of Mr. VALENTINE STEAD, Merchant, who died May the 16th, 1758, aged 70. Also NAOMI, his wife, who died October the 9th, 1740, aged 47. And seven of their children. Also two children of Valentine Stead the younger, who erected this monument."

Near the font, on a grave-stone : "Here lieth the body of MARY, the wife of SAMUEL STEAD, of Halifax, who was buried the 29th of May, 1734, aged 82 years and six months. She was wife of the abovesaid Samuel Stead, Salter, 58 years and 6 months.

Also SAMUEL STEAD, husband to the abovesaid Mary, who departed this life the 4th day of December, 1736, aged 80 years, 10 months, and seven days.

Mr. Wright, p. 195, remarks, that this gentleman lived to see of his children, grand children, and great grand children sixty-one in number.

WATKINSON.

On a pillar on the South side of the Chancel: "H. M. Memoriæ sacrum MARIÆ, filiæ unicæ Rev^di Dn^i EDWARDI WATKINSON, Capellæ de Luddenden in hac Vicaria Curat. Quæ nata vesperi præcedente Pascha, Anno 1723, febre perquam maligna correpta occidit (heu nimium fugax et multum flebilis) Augusti 24to, 1726.

WILKINSON.

On a grave-stone in the Chancel: "JOSEPH WILKINSON, A.M. quondam Vicarius de Chapel-Izod, juxta Dublin, in Hibernia, et Prebendarius de Castroknock, Ecclesiæ Cathedralis Sancti Patricii Dublin, postea Rector de Wigginton comitatu Ebor. et tandem huic Ecclesiæ per viginti annos præfuit Vicarius. Obiit 28 die Decembris, Anno Dom. 1711. Ætatis suæ 60."

LEGH.

In the Chancel of the Parish Church is an ill executed monument bearing the following inscription: " Near this place in the same vault, are deposited the remains of the Rev. GEORGE LEGH, LL.D. and his two beloved wives Frances and Elizabeth, to whose joint memory this monument is erected; he was Vicar of this Parish of Halifax above forty-four years: during which time he interested himself with laudable zeal in the cause of liberty and sincerity, being the last survivor of those worthy men who distinguish^d themselves by their opposition to Ecclesiastical Tyranny, he defended the Rights of Mankind, in that memorable Hoadlian Controversy. The Bible he consider^d as the only standard of Faith and practice, to the poor and distress^d and Public Charity^s, he was a generous Benefactor, by his Will order^d Bibles to be given for the benefit of the poor. He did honor to his Profession as a Clergyman and Christian. Esteem^d when liveing, in death lamented. He died compos^d on the 6th of Decem^br, 1775, in the 82d year of his age; his wife Frances died Decem^br 9th, 1749; Elizabeth Feb. 8th, 1765."

I much regret that my limits will not permit me to give a more elaborate description of some of the modern monuments and tablets within the Church. To transfer in every instance from the marble to the paper, the simple fact "that he died," would be neither instructive nor entertaining. I must be content with mentioning a few; there are others however I cannot pass over. Memorials of those who in one sense may be said to live with us.

COULTHURST.

On the left side of the altar is a beautiful monument, executed by Westmacott, and erected at the expense of the parishioners. The workmanship is finely executed, a bust of the Dr. surmounts the following epitaph, from the pen of the late DR. WHITAKER:—

A X Ω

HENRICO WILHELMO COULTHURST, S. T. P.

Ab ingenuâ inter Cravenses stirpe oriundo
Ex scholari coll. divi Johannis Cantabrigiae Sidn, Sussexiensis socio:
Ibidemque juventute academicâ, qua domi instituenda qua
scholis in Jublices regendâ
Nomen inter equales haud vulgare consequito
Deinde per annos 27 hujus Ecclesiae vicario pervigili
Conscionibus, non hoc pro suggesta tantum verum etiam per
amplissimae parochiae saella
Assidue habitis, simplici ac flexanimo;
In jure dicundo, citra omne supercilium,
Omnem præjudicatæ mentis propensionem acqui bonique arbitro:
In convictu jucundo, faceto, peraleganti,
Tamen up Oɩ KOΔOMH'N semper intueretur,
Christi servus, linguâ vita que atque intineo corde Domino
mancipatus,
Qui cibo licet interetum parco, vino percissimo
Apoplexiâ perculsus excitium vitae habuit, repentinum quidem
At sanctae, et tranquillae, coelum qui spiranti animæ haud
intempesturim
11 die Dec. A. D. 1817 annum aetatis agens 65 in

Quene vivum coluerunt, extinctum lugentes
Imaginem hanc, acre conlato,
P P
Halifaxiensis sui.

The following is a translation of the above :—
   (Christ.—" Alpha and Omega.")

HENRY WILLIAM COULTHURST, D. D., descended from an
ancient and respectable Family in Craven, formerly Scholar of St.
John's College, afterwards Fellow of Sidney Sussex College, Cambridge. As Tutor in his College, as Moderator in the Public
Schools, he acquired among his contemporaries no common celebrity.
For 27 years he was a most vigilant Vicar of this Church. His
discourses (assiduously delivered not from this pulpit only, but in
the several Chapels of this extensive Parish,) were simple and
persuasive. As a Magistrate, he was the dispenser of equity and
justice, without superciliousness or prepossession. In social intercourse, pleasant, facetious, elegant, yet ever with a view to edifica-
tion. As a servant to Christ, in words, in actions, in heart, devoted
to his Lord. Though temperate in diet, abstinent in wine, he was
removed by a stroke of apoplexy, sudden indeed, but to a soul holy,
tranquil and heaven-aspiring, not untimely, on the 11th day of
December, A. D. 1817, in the 65th year of his age. To him, revered
in life, in death lamented, his Halifax Parishioners raised by public
subscription this memorial.

KNIGHT.

Upon a neat marble monument in the chancel is the following
inscription.

To the Memory of
The Reverend SAMUEL KNIGHT, M A.
formerly Fellow of
Magdalene College Cambridge ;
The first Incumbent of Trinity Church
in this Town,
And afterwards Vicar of this Parish.
He was a Man
Endowed with a vigorous and penetrating Mind ;
and was intimately conversant with

the various branches of science and literature,
but what things were gain to him
those he counted loss for Christ.
The Gospel was that in which alone he gloried ;
its precious truths he preached
With fidelity and affection
Its holy precepts he exemplified
in his Life and conduct ;
and
Its everlasting consolations he realized
in the solemn prospect of Eternity.
He departed this life January 7th, 1827,
in the 68th year of his Age,
and lies interred in this Chancel.

This monument is erected with feelings of
affectionate regard by his surviving Widow.

RAWSON.

In the South aisle is an elegant marble monument by Westmacott, with emblematical sculpture, erected to the memory of J. M. Rawson, and bearing the following inscription.

To the memory of
JOHN MARKLAND RAWSON,

Eldest son of John Rawson, of Ash Grove,
Who perished with 8 seamen, in Simon's Bay, Cape of Good Hope
by the swamping of the pinnance of H. M. S Owen Glendower,
on the 10th March, 1826,
In the 19th year of his age.
His afflicted parent dedicated this monument.

Near the above is also a beautiful Tablet with a basso-relievo of the good Samaritan, by the same sculptor.   The following is the inscription.

Sacred to the memory of
WILLIAM RAWSON,

Who was born in this Parish, and died 25th Aug. 1828, aged 79,

Earnestly endeavouring to follow the example of
his blessed Saviour,
" Who went about doing good,"
He passed a long life in unwearied exertions
To promote the best interests of his fellow creatures ; and
in the conscientious discharge of every christian duty,
sought humbly the approbation of
his God.
Reader, " Go thou and do likewise."

SAYER.

On one of the pillars in the North aisle a monument affixed,
on which the following is inscribed :

Near this place are deposited the remains of MARY, the wife of
Thomas Sayer, of Halifax, gentleman, and co-heiress of William
Cockroft, of Mayroyd, Esq.   She died the 12th of May, 1779,
aged 36 years. This monument is erected to her memory by an
affectionate and afflicted husband, as a respectful token of his esteem for those virtues which adorned her heart and endeared her to
him, and to all who had the happiness of an acquaintance with her.
Ask not, pensive reader, a recital of those virtues which her humility wished to conceal; this silent marble refers thee for information
to the cries and tears of the sick and needy, who lost in her a sympathetic attendant on their distress, and a generous reliever of their
wants ; and to the regret of that concourse of every age and rank,
who paid an honourable and voluntary tribute to her merit, by accompanying her remains to their interment.   If her amiable example
excite thy imitation, forget not to adopt her noblest praise : by
fulfilling every duty of Nature and Society, from a principle of
affection and gratitude to GOD, the Friend, the Parent, the Redeemer
of mankind.

THOMAS SAYER, Gent.   Ob. 12 May, 1781.   Aetat. 44.

CAYGILL.

On the right of the Altar is a handsome white marble monument,
on which is executed, in basso-relievo, a representation of an angel
with wings expanded, raising a dying Christian from his couch, and
pointing to heaven.

Sacred to the Memory of
JANE
Relict of John Caygill, Esq. of Shay, Halifax,
And last remaining issue of William Selwyn, Esq. formerly of
Down Hall, Essex,
who was lost to her afflicted family the 25th Day of July, 1806,
Aged 84 years.
Her heart was the favorite residence of all the gentle and peaceful
virtues:
warm affection, sincere piety, benevolence and humanity dwelt there,
In mental as well as bodily sufferings she was patient and resigned;
To her numerous virtues, held in constant exercise
her relations and friends bear the most ample and sincere testimony,
and availing ourselves of her good example, may we endeavour
to tread
with religious cheerfulness her peaceful footsteps,
for they lead to everlasting happiness.
As a tribute of filial veneration and affection
her only immediate descendant, Lady Jane Ibbetson
caused this monument to be erected, A. D. 1807.

HULME.

On a plain tablet in the North East corner of Rokeby's chapel, is
inscribed :—

Near this place, in the grave of the late Richard Taylor, Esq.
are deposited the remains of JOSEPH HULME, M. D. who departed
this life on the 2nd day of February, 1806, aged 92 years. He
practised Physic in this town, with great success, about 63 years.
To his patients he was very attentive and humane; to the poor,
benevolent and charitable. He was ready in lending pecuniary
assistance, to most who applied to him, but slow in calling in debts.
He was a man of few words, yet affable and pleasant with his friends.
From his medical abilities, his general knowledge, and gentle manners, he was much respected by all who knew him. He was a rare
instance of temperance and sobriety, water being his common drink
from his youth, and for many years he never tasted animal food.
This strict regimen did not prevent his taking much exercise, and

undergoing great fatigue: for he was almost daily on horse-back, over the neighbouring hills, in every season and in all weather. Though so far advanced in life, yet his hand continued steady, and his judgment clear, so that he died not of old age, but of an acute disease: and in the blessed hope that he should not dwell for ever with corruption.

Also,

In the same grave, are deposited the remains of his beloved wife, BATHSHEBA, a daughter of the above named Richard Taylor, Esq. who departed this life on the 25th day of Feb. 1786, aged nearly 51 years.

CLAYTON.

In the Chancel, a plain but neat marble tablet, surmounted by the family arms.

In memory of RALPH CLAYTON, Sergeant at Law, who was on his way towards Malvern, for the recovery of his health, was prevented by increase of illness from continuing his journey, and after enduring the severest pain with Christian patience and resignation, died in this town, on the 11th of October, 1813, in the 55th year of his age. He was an active and useful member of society, able and learned in his profession, and justly esteemed and respected by all who knew him.

ALEXANDER.

A plain unornamental marble tablet is erected in the family pew, in the South Chapel, on which is inscribed the following memorial.

Beneath this pew are deposited the mortal remains of Elizabeth, wife of Lewis Alexander, of Hopwood Hall, Halifax, Esquire, who died 18th January, 1832, aged 61 years. In pious commemoration of a conjugal love and maternal tenderness, which time served but to strengthen and death only could impair,—and with the Christian hope of being again united, where all tears will be wiped away, and where no second separation can be known, this Tablet is inscribed by her afflicted husband and children.

WATERHOUSE.

There is affixed on the wall to the right of the communion, a monument to NATHANIEL WATERHOUSE, Esq. on which are inscribed the various gifts and charities, &c. of the deceased, but as they will be found in a subsequent part of the work their repetition here may be deemed unnecessary.

The Church is surrounded with a spacious burial ground, enclosed by a stone wall and iron railing, it has latterly been considerably improved; its appearance is clean, and reflects a credit on those to whose care it is more immediately entrusted. From the hill that overlooks the town, it presents the appearance of a paved yard. Few of the tomb stones are prior to the reformation, and some of those of early date are in very good preservation.

TESTAMENTARY BURIALS AT HALIFAX.

FROM MR. TORR'S MS.

July 12, 1402, John del Burgh, of Halifax, made his will, and left his soul to God Almighty, St. Mary, and All Saints, and ordered his body to be buried in the Parish Church of Halifax.

Nov. 21, 1437, Henry Savyle, of Halifax, Esq. Soul and body as above.

March 3, 1439 Richard Pek, of Southowram. Soul as above, body in the quire of the Parish Church of Halifax.

April 20, 1459, John Sayvell, of Copley, Esq. Soul as above, body in the church, or church-yard of Halifax.

June 1, 1481, Tho. Wilkinson, Vicar of Halifax, already mentioned.

April 4. 1482, William Marshall, Rector of Kirk-Sandal.—Soul as above, body in Halifax Church.

Feb. 3, 1484, Richard Waterhouse, of Warley. Soul as above, body in the Church or Church-yard of St. John Baptist, Halifax.

April 29, 1510, Henry Savile, of Copley. Soul as above, body in the New Warke of Halifax.

Feb. 15, 1530, Tho. Savile, of Bladeroyd, in Southowram —
Jan. 5, 1533, Thomas Savile, of Copley, Esq.—1533, John Waterhouse, of Skircoat.—1535, Edward Waterhouse, buried in the
Church-yard at Halifax.—1538, Richard Waterhouse, of Shipden,
body to be buried in the Church of the holy prophet St. John Baptist, of Halifax.—1541, John Illingworth, of Illingworth.—1543,
Edward Waterhouse, of Skircoat —1543, William Illingworth,—
1545, Humphry Waterhouse, of Shelf Soul to God Almighty,
hoping through Jesus Christ to be saved. " Here Protestantism
began to shew itself, and mankind began to act more from principles
of reason, and common sense, than to bequeath their souls to the
Virgin Mary, and all the Saints, who are only in the same condition
that all living Saints will shortly be placed in, and who cannot help
if they are applied to."

1545, John Waterhouse, of Skircoat.—1554, Henry Savile, of
Copley.—1556, John Waterhouse, of Thollinges, in Warley.—
1556, Richard Midgley, of Midgley.—1569, Thomas Savile, of
Copley —1570, Hugh Lacey, of Brearley, in Midgley, Esq.—
1570, Thomas Savile, of Southouram, Gent.—1578, Anthony
Waterhouse, of Warley, Gent.—1586, Abraham Sunderland, of
High Sunderland, Gent.—1620, John Holdsworth, of Astey, Gent.

A LIST OF THE VICARS.

1. INGOLARD DE TURBARD was instituted the first vicar by the
prior and convent of Lewes, who continued to present every vicar
until the time of Dr. William Rokeby inclusive. This vicar's
presentation bears date 25th Jan. 1273; he was inducted May 3,
1274, and died May 28th, 1315.

2. JOHN AARON DE GRYDINGTON, instituted 21st June, 1315;
death uncertain.

3. THOMAS DE GAYTINGTON, instituted 5th June, 1321; died
Sept. 10, 1349.

4. JOHN DE STAMFORD, instituted Feb. 7, 1349; died October
29, 1362.

THE PARISH CHURCH. 127

One Richard de Ovenden is stated by Mr. Watson to have been vicar about this time, but no mention is made of him in any authentic list, nor are his arms emblazoned on the roof of the Church.

5. RICHARD DE HEATON, instituted Nov. 3, 1362; died March 9, 1389. Mr. Watson states that he was of the family of Heatons of Over Shibden, in Northowram.

6. JOHN KYNGE, inducted March 13, 1389; died March 14th, 1438. Mr. Watson states that in his MS. List occurs Dominus Thomas Eland, as vicar of Halifax, said to be instituted May 20, 1438, but he is not noticed either in Wright, or on the roof of the Church. In the Townley MSS. 914, says Dr. Whitaker, I find a Joh. Piper, Vic. Eccl. de Halyfax, 11th Hen. 4ᵗ.

7. THOMAS WILKYNSON, born, as tradition informs us, at Brackenbed, in Ovenden, and instituted May 16, 1438; died Jan. 25, 1480. "Thomas Wylkinson Vicarius Eclie de Halifax," is witness to a deed in my possession, dated May 7, 19 Hen. VI, or A. D. 1440.

8. RICHARD DE SIMMS, instituted Feb. 11, 1480; died Nov. 11, 1496.

9. THOMAS DE BRONT, L.D. instituted Nov. 27, 1496. He resigned the vicarage, and it was the first instance of its having become vacant any other way than by death.

10. WILLIAM ROKEBY, Bishop of Meath, and afterwards Arch-bishop of Dublin, in Ireland, instituted 14th June, 1502; died Nov. 29, 1521.

11. JOHN TAYLOR, LL.D. Master of the Rolls and Chancellor, instituted some time in the year 1521. Mr. Wright thinks he resigned the vicarage before his death, which happened in 1534, but of this there is no proof.

12. ROBERT HOLDESWORTH, LL.D. the time of whose institution is uncertain. He was of the family of the Holdsworth's, of Astey (or Ashdale,) in Southowram, and was possessed of an estate in that township. He was slaine of thieves in the night time, in the vicarage house, which stood on different ground from the present one, in the third year of the reign of Philip and Mary. An old MS. says, this event happened at the great chamber of the North, at the vicarage, at the lower part of the house, in the part thereo

turning towards the East. He built the South Chapel of the Churches at his own charges, and was buried under the great tomb-stone there May 10, 1556, as appears by the register.

13. JOHN HARRISON, instituted July 13, 1556; buried at Halifax 15th Feb. 1559.

14. CHRISTOPHER ASHBURN, or ASHBORNE, instituted in the beginning of Lent, 1559, and resigned it 1573. He was the first Protestant Vicar here. He defaced and sold much of the housing belonging to the vicarage; was buried at Halifax Dec. 7, 1584.

15. FRANCIS ASHBURN, his son, of Trinity College, Cambridge, instituted June 3rd, 1573, on the presentation of Queen Elizabeth; died July 18th, 1583.

16. HENRY LEDSAM, or LEDSHAM, D.D. Fellow of Merton College, Oxford, presented by Queen Elizabeth, was instituted Sept. 15, 1583; resigned Nov. 29, 1593. He was slaine in London in 1598, by one that was afterwards hanged at Tyburn, as the party confessed at his death.

17. JOHN FAVOUR, LL.D. of New College, in Oxford, who, according to Watson, was instituted Dec. 3, 1593, on the presentation of Queen Elizabeth; inducted Jan. 1594; died March 10, 1623. He was a justice of the peace for the West Riding.

18. ROBERT CLAY, D.D. of Merton College, Oxford, of the family of Clay, of Clayhouse, in Greetland, where he was born. He was instituted to the vicarage March 20, 1623, having been presented thereto by Sir Henry Savile, Knt. and Bart. He died April 9, 1628, and was buried in the library (which he is said to have built) in Halifax church, April 14, 1628, with the following inscription on his grave-stone: " Robertus Clay, S. T. P. Vicarius de Halifax, obiit Aprilis nono die, Anno Domini 1628."

The Register contains the following entry: " Robertus Clay, D.D. Oxoniensis Merton, post quadrinum apud Halifax multa cum diligentia et pastorali cura in zodiaco animarum cursum attigiaset, dulciter et quiete placida [this should be placidam] vitam transmisit in celestia. Obiit Aprilis nono, et sepultus decimo quarto ejusdem mensis, Anno Dom. 1628." Mr. Watson has extracted certain articles said to have been exhibited against this gentleman, which might with impunity have been omitted, considering that they were never proved.

19. HUGH RAMSDEN, B.D. also of Merton College, of which he was Fellow; inducted Oct. 7, 1628, on the presentation of King Charles I; died at York, July 16, and was buried in Halifax chancel, July 19, 1629.

20. HENRY RAMSDEN, his brother, was instituted on the presentation of King Charles I. Aug.–19, 1629, and inducted the 23rd. Died March 25, 1638. He was a justice of peace for the West Riding.

21. RICHARD MARSH, D.D. instituted on the presentation of King Charles I. April 12, 1638; inducted April 17, following. He was obliged to fly from his living in 1642, to which he did not return until after the King's restoration. He was a Justice of Peace and Dean of York. A memoir of him will be found in the Parish Biography.

After the Doctor's departure, says Watson, one Wayte was appointed vicar by the Lord Fairfax, but how long he officiated is uncertain. Mr. Wright says that Mr. Root was minister here in 1643 and 1644. John Lake, in 1647 and 1649, (which is proved by a mem. of his at the end of vol. III. of the Register). Then Robert Booth, in 1650, who was buried at Halifax, July 28, 1657. Lastly, Eli Bentley, born at Sowerby, who was assistant to Booth, and after his death continued in the place until he was ejected for refusing to comply with the Act of Uniformity, as we are told by Mr. Wright, who has taken his statement from Calamy's account of ejected ministers, vol. II. p. 804, 2nd edition. This writer says, that Bentley was bred at Cambridge, and was Fellow of Trinity College; that he became assistant to Booth in August, 1652—that he fled before the Five-mile Act, but in 1672 returned to Halifax, and preached in his own house; and that he died July 31, 1675, aged 49. The character he gives of him is, that he was a man of good parts, a solid, serious preacher, of a very humble behaviour, and very useful in his place; he lived desired, and died lamented.

It is stated that after the removal of Mr. Root, Halifax was served, till the return of Dr. Marsh, by stipendiary priests, which in all probability was the case.

22. RICHARD HOOK, D.D. instituted June 10, 1662, on the presentation of King Charles II. and inducted the 29th. He was also rector of Thornton, in Craven. He died Jan. 1, 1688-9.

K

23. EDMUND HOUGH, M.A. also rector of Thornton, inducted June 26, 1689, on the presentation of King James II.   It is probable that he was at no time a very rigid conformist, for Calamy says that he died of a broken heart, in consequence of the persecutions of the Ecclesiastical Court.   In Halifax Register is this entry: "Edmundus Hough, A.M. inductus erat in Vicar. de Halifax per Jacobum Roberts, Vicar. de Bingley, 26º die Junii 1689.   Sepultus 3º Aprilis, 1691.—Vir de tota ecclesia tam pietatis quam doctrinæ ergo optime meritus, industrius Pastor, et efficax Evangelii Concionator, quondam dignus Coll. Jesu Cant. Socius, et Ecclesiæ Thorntonensis doctus et diligens Rector, tandem vixit Ecclesiæ sedulus per biennium Vicarius."

24. JOSEPH WILKINSON, A.M. instituted Sept. 7th, or 17th, and inducted Oct. 26, 1691, having been presented by King William III.   He was first vicar of Chapel-Izod, near Dublin, and Prebendary of Casternock, in the Cathedral of St. Patrick's, Dublin, afterwards rector of Widdington, Yorkshire.   Notwithstanding these preferments, he is said to have been necessitous, and to have lived, for a considerable time, in the library of the church, in order to secure himself from arrests.   He died Dec. 28, 1711, and was buried in the Chancel at Halifax.

25. THOMAS BURTON, M.A. rector of Lofthouse, and curate of Yarum, in Yorkshire, was instituted on the presentation of Queen Ann, March 28, and inducted April 3d or 4th, 1712.   March 1, 1715, he was made Prebendary of the Prebend of Givendale, in the Cathedral of York.   He died July 22, 1731, and was buried in the Chancel at Halifax, without any memorial of him.

26. GEORGE LEGH, LL.D. inducted, as Mr. Wright says, on the presentation of King George II. October 2nd, 1731.   He was subsequently made Prebendary of York, in the Bottevant-Stall. Died 6th Dec, 1775, and was interred in the library of the Parish Church.   An ill executed monument has been erected to his memory, in the Chancel.   "He was (says Dr. Whitaker) a low churchman, and popular among the dissenters, a disciple of Bishop Hoadley and his coadjutor, in what was called the Bangorian Controversy; about which he seems to have been more in earnest than his duty as a preacher, which he is said to have performed in a very careless and languid manner.   He was a man of great singularity

of character, subject to fits of absence and forgetfulness, which not unfrequently exposed him to ridicule."

27. HENRY WOOD, D.D. of Jesus College, Cambridge, also rector of Hemsworth. He was inducted on the 14th Feb. 1776; died October 1790, and was buried at Hemsworth.

28. HENRY WILLIAM COULTHURST, D.D. Scholar of Saint John's College, and afterwards Fellow of Sidney Sussex College, Cambridge, was inducted December 4th, 1790, and died Dec. 11th, 1817. Of Dr. Coulthurst, it was truly said by his excellent successor, " that he possessed an admirable combination of qualities to render his society both delightful and profitable ; he was cheerful without frivolity, grave without moroseness, and instructive without pedantry. His deportment was ever affable and courteous ; in his social intercourse he was the decided friend and advocate both of morality and religion; his conversation was such as became the gospel of Christ,—an affectionate husband,—an indulgent master,— a kind neighbour,—a generous friend,—a dutiful subject,—and a true lover of his country. Integrity, clemency, and the fear of God ever influenced him in the discharge of his magisterial duties; in short, his name will long be remembered in the parish of Halifax, and as long as it is remembered, will be revered." The parish is indebted to this excellent divine for the Holy Trinity Church, in this town, which he erected at his own expense, thus evincing in the most decided manner his laudable anxiety for the best interests of his parishioners.

29. SAMUEL KNIGHT, M.A. of Magdalen College, Cambridge ; the first incumbent of Trinity Church above mentioned, was instituted on the 29th Dec. 1817; died on the 7th January, 1827, and lies interred in the Chancel. Being a native of the parish, the reader is respectfully referred to the Biographical Notices for a short memoir of this most exemplary divine.

30. CHARLES MUSGRAVE, B. D. of Trinity College, Cambridge, Vicar of Whitkirk, in this County, the present respected Vicar, was instituted on the 30th of March, 1827, and inducted on the following day. This Gentleman has since been presented to the Prebendal Stall of Givendale, in the Cathedral of York.

THE MIDDLE AGES.

THERE is little on record respecting the history of the Parish, during the middle ages, to call forth any historical remarks. Situated in a rugged and mountainous district; and in a remote part of the country, out of the direct line of communication between the Metropolis and the capital of the North; the parish of Halifax, does not appear to have been involved in any of those calamitous wars which at various periods of our national history, but more particularly during the middle ages, desolated the populous and fertile districts of Yorkshire: not forgetting "that fatal quarrel, which was not finished in less than thirty years—which was signalized by twelve pitched battles—which opened a scene of extraordinary fierceness and cruelty—and which was computed to have cost the lives of eighty princes of the blood; and to have almost annihilated the ancient nobility of England."

A commission was issued the 12th Henry VI, the main design of which was to obtain a return of the number of Gentry within the County who were favorable to the house of York. The return is altogether disproportionate to the extent of numbers, there are only two gentlemen returned as residents within this Parish, viz.

Robt. Pylkington de Ayringden, arm:

Thos. Radcliffe de Bradley, arm:

During the civil war between Charles the First and the Parliament Halifax identified itself with the cause of the latter, (this was generally the case with the manufacturing towns:) but it does not appear to have suffered to the same extent with some of its contemporaries, and this may have arisen, in a great degree, from the cause I have before stated, namely, its untoward situation. From its locality it was ill fitted by nature to act on the defensive in a state of warfare; we are nevertheless informed, that it was made use of as a garrison against the king, and CLARENDON, in speaking of the strength which the Parliament had in the North in the year 1642, says "Leeds, Halifax and Bradford, (three very populous and rich towns, which, depending wholly upon clothiers, too much maligned the gentry) were wholly at their disposal;" and he represents the Lord Fairfax as quitting Selby, Cawood, and Tadcaster, and retiring to Pontefract and Halifax, and DRAKE in his *Eboracum*, observes, that in that retreat,(which was after the battle at Tadcaster,) "Sheffield, Wakefield, Leeds, Halifax and Bradford, and several other towns and garrisons against the king, were in six weeks' space, by the valour and conduct of the Lord General (Newcastle) reduced to his Majesty's subjection; but by the various chance of war, lost and won again, sometimes by one party, and sometimes by another," and Yorkshire spite of all precautions, was for some time a scene of bloodshed and misery. An obstinate action is stated to have taken place on the top of Halifax Bank, adjoining the old road leading to Wakefield, and the ground retains the name of the bloody-field, to this day. DUGDALE in his Baronage, vol, iii. page 421, says, that William earl of Newcastle, obtained victories among other places, at Tadcaster, Sheffield, Rotherham, Yarum, Beverley, Cawood, Selby, Halifax, Leeds, and Bradford, all in Yorkshire; indeed the forces in these parts must have been considerable, to have given them the name of the Halifax army. The town appears to have been strongly infected with republican principles; for VICARS in his *Parliamentary Chronicle*, p. 240, says, that in December, 1642, when Bradford was attacked by part of the earl of Newcastle's army, succour came in speedily from Halifax, and other parts, and that they had borrowed a commander of Halifax; and in the next page, that "there came to their aid from Halifax, some firemen and clubmen." Also when Leeds was taken by Sir Thomas Fairfax, many of his men are said to have been inexperienced fresh-water soldiers, taken up about Bradford and Halifax, on the Saturday before the action. Again, when the attack on Wakefield was resolved on by Lord Fairfax, an order was given for a party of a thousand foot, three companies of dragoons, and eight troops of horse, to march from the garrisons of Leeds, Bradford, Halifax, and Howley. Lastly, it appeared from a letter in the possession of colonel Goring, who was taken prisoner at Wakefield, that his father, lord Goring, had advised him to get, with his forces, between Bradford and Halifax, to separate the friends of the parliament, in all their designs.   Heptonstall, it appears, was a garrison for the king.   There is an entry in the register at Halifax in these words, "Jan. 4, 1643, two soldiers were hanged on a gallows made near the gibbet, who were taken by Sir Francis Makworth's company, from Heptonstall forces.   They had deserted from the Halifax army to Heptonstall, for which they were hanged the same night they were taken prisoners."   Tradition informs us that an action was fought in that neighbourhood, between the roundheads and cavaliers, and a great part of the town of Heptonstall was burnt; but as there are no written memorials to be found concerning this encounter, we may suppose that it was not of much consequence.

The intrenchments, remains of which are still to be seen at Camp-end, above Warley, were doubtless thrown up at that time; as also were two small redoubts on each side of the old road over Blackstone-edge, just at the summit of the hill, which are said to have been formed with great military skill.   That they were thrown up in these troublesome times, appears from the following extract, taken from the 16th page of a pamphlet entitled, "An historical relation of eight year's services for king and parliament, done in and about Manchester and those parts, by Lieut. Col. John Rosworm, London, printed in the year 1649."   "About July 4th, (1642) the earl of Newcastle, with no small force, made an angry approach towards Lancashire, our men (at Manchester) were sent out to oppose his passage; the issue was, our men were soundly beaten at Wisket-hill, in Yorkshire, and pursued into Lancashire by the enemy, who quickly also possessed himself of Halifax.   When I had received this sad intelligence, I informed myself of the nature of the passes, by which the enemy most easily could come in upon us; and finding them capable of a sudden fortification, by the consent of the deputy lieutenants, I quickly helped nature with art, strengthening Blackstone-edge, and Blackegate, and manning them with soldiers, to prevent the earl's dangerous approach, by which means being diverted, like an angry storm with a gust, he went to the siege of Hull."

In the parliamentary history of England, Col. Birch is thus represented as writing to the Parliament from Newcastle, Sepr. 9,

1657. "I think the Scots King (Charles II) came this day with Lieutenant General Lesley, and Lieutenant General Middleton, who were taken on Blackstone-edge, in the moors between Rochdale and Halifax, and we believe that he escaped towards Yorkshire in some disguise." This was immediately after the battle of Worcester.

It appears from WILLIS' *Notitia Parliamentaria*, that Halifax returned a representative to Parliament at the time of the Commonwealth, in the person of Jeremy Bentley, gent., in a parliament which began at Westminster, Sepr. 3, 1654. He was also returned a second time by the title of Jeremy Bentley, Esq., in 1656, but it does not appear that he took part in any of the strange debates which characterized the times. The reason for these unprecedented returns may be seen in Rapin, Clarendon, and other historians.

In treating of this unhappy period of our national history, I have exclusively confined myself to such matters of narrative, as related more immediately to the history of the place.

Notwithstanding the part which the population of the manufacturing districts took in the great Rebellion, there is every reason to believe, from the narratives of the best informed historians, that it was with feelings of satisfaction and joy the great majority of our countrymen in these parts, hailed the return of Charles II. to the throne of his ancestors; and well they might. They had seen the destruction of order and the evil of confusion to their fullest extent; they had seen the possession of power thrown into the hands, not of the best, but of the strongest; they had seen the laws over-ruled, and their rights abolished; they had seen the soldier seize upon their property, and the fanatic rush into the church; they had seen the power of faction, commenced by clamour, promoted by rebellion, and established by murder, the atrocity of which was only equalled by its cruelty, by murder not necessary even to the safety of those by whom it was committed, but chosen in preference to any other expedient for security;* such were the evils they had seen, well might they consider the "happy restoration" of their exiled monarch an "unspeakable mercy."

To this period of our history may be traced the introduction of Nonconformity into the district. In shortly treating of its rise and progress, I shall as far as practicable confine myself to a simple narration of facts.

* Dr. Johnson.

It may be necessary to premise that on the restoration of king Charles II, the terms of communion were purposely narrowed in order to exclude many of the old ministers, who by remaining in possession of their pulpits would have had too much influence over the minds of the people. This exclusion arose from a non-compliance, or in other words a non-conformity, with the requisitions of the Uniformity act. This act enjoined that all those ministers who would not comply with its terms should resign their situations in the establishment, on the 24th August, 1662, and that their places should be filled by others, in the same manner as if they were deceased. In public commotions, as well as private contentions, it is too frequently found that there have been grounds for censure on one part, as well as the other. With respect to the occurrences now referred to, a great diversity will be found in the sentiments of writers of eminence and respectability. Bishop Burnet says, "many of the ejected ministers were distinguished by their abilities and zeal;" and Mr. Locke remarks "Bartholomew day was fatal to our church and religion, as throwing out a very great number of worthy, learned, pious, and orthodox divines, who could not come up to some things in the act of uniformity." On the other hand, Dr. Whitaker observes that "in this rigorous and exclusive requirement, the government were justified by the necessity of the case: many of these men were not only avowedly hostile to the new Government, but joined in a perpetual confederacy against it, and therefore deservedly excluded." The real hardship of the case was that of the Presbyterians, who wished well to a limited monarchy, but could not bring themselves to submit to an episcopal hierarchy. Two thousand ministers at that time vacated their livings, many of them very valuable, without any prospect of support, so, that in the judgment of charity, there is reason to believe they were influenced by principle, and not by sinister motives.

A great majority of the ejected ministers were attached to the Presbyterian discipline, and the churches they formed were of that denomination. Among the number of those who, in this district, were ejected from their pulpits, in consequence of their non-conformity, the name of Oliver Heywood occupies a prominent place. The public are indebted to the biographers of that gentleman, for much information relating to the local history of these times, selected from his diary.

The Reverend OLIVER HEYWOOD was descended from a highly respectable family, the youngest branch of the house of Heywood, an ancient esquire's seat between Rochdale and Bury; at the age of 18 he was entered of Trinity College, Cambridge; where he remained until he had taken his bachelor's degree, and then returned to his father's house.   In the year 1650 he was invited to accept the incumbency of Coley in this Parish, to which he acceded. The Presbyterian form of church-government being at the time predominant in England, he was ordained after the form of that church, by the second class of Lancashire ministers at Bury.   At the time he undertook the charge of Coley he attempted to establish, as far as existing circumstances permitted, the presbyterian discipline, in which he partly succeeded: and when licences were granted, in 1672, he formed a church at Northowram, and conducted it on the principles of moderate presbyterianism.

The arbitrary measures of Cromwell and his adherents had induced the more respectable portion of the presbyterians to feel anxious for the return of their lawful sovereign ; among the number of these was Mr. Heywood, who really wished well to the reigning monarch, but could not conscientiously comply with the requisitions of the Uniformity Act, in consequence whereof he was ejected from his incumbency, and his excommunication published in Halifax Church.

In the year 1672, a Royal declaration was issued, suspending the laws that had been passed against the non-conformists ; this declaration acknowledged "that there was very little fruit of all those forcible methods which had been used for reducing erring and dissenting persons."

In the Northowram Register, p. 16, there is a considerable blank, and at the bottom of the page, Mr. Heywood has written, "This long interval of almost ten years I was parted from the exercise of my ministerial functions by the act of Uniformity in August, 1662: restored again to my work, by the king's declaration, March 12th, 1672, to ministerial employment in my own house."   In the following May he received the Royal licence, and accordingly made use of it; and on the 12th June, a covenant was entered into between Mr. Heywood, and his congregation at North-owram, and a church formed on presbyterian principles.

Prior to the formation of this church a congregational society had been established at Sowerby Bridge, under the care of a Mr. Root, of Magdalen College, Cambridge, who was for some time a preacher at Halifax Church, and who collected a congregational society at Sowerby Chapel in 1645. These two churches of Sowerby and Northowram joined in communion, and gained a considerable accession of members, the society meeting at the house of Mr. Heywood in Northowram.

This may be considered as the foundation of the first dissenting society in the parish. Dr. Hook, at that time vicar, has been repre-sented as manifesting a violent spirit of hostility against Mr. Heywood and his followers; but after all that can be said, his hostility (if the performance of a duty can be deemed an hostile act) never exceeded a very proper request that he might have a sight of Mr. Heywood's licences. In Mr. Heywood's diary is the following entry; "Mr. Horton having erected a meeting place at Sowerby, and having procured a licence, desired me to begin a weekly lecture, on Tuesday, May 6th, 1673, which accordingly I did." This Mr. Horton is represented in the Northowram Register, as a pious man, a justice of the peace who had £1000 a-year. The father of Archbishop Tillotson is stated to have been a member of this society. Scarcely a year had elapsed since the issuing of the King's Royal declaration, but we find, from the Rev. Gentleman's diary, that places of worship were erected by the non-conformists, not only at Leeds, Bradford, Halifax, (this in all probability was Northgate Chapel) and Wakefield; but dissent-ing Chapels were also built in the adjacent villages, at Warley, Sow-erby, Eastwood, Mixenden, Kipping, Bingley, Idle, Pudsey, Cleckheaton, Heckmondwike, &c, besides the chapel at Northowram. The episcopal chapel at Morley, venerable for its antiquity, at that time fell into the hands of the dissenters.

The liberty enjoyed by the non-conformists was not of long duration. The king had unadvisedly outstretched his royal preroga-tive; the house of Commons voted the royal declaration illegal, and were quieted only by the assurance that it should not be brought into a precedent. At the close of the year 1674 the licences that had been granted were recalled, the restrictive laws again put in force, and the privations and persecutions of the non-conformists were carried on in some places with increased severity. Among other instances the following is recorded:—"Yesterday, August 19th, (1675) the pursuivants took up several persons at or about Halifax, and are taking up others to day to carry them to York, before the duke, on what account is not known."

In the year 1685 sentence of excommunication was pronounced against Mr. Heywood in Halifax church; and he was convicted at Wakefield on the charge of having a riotous assembly in his house, fined £50 and ordered to enter into recognisances for his good behaviour, and in default he was committed to York Castle, from whence he was afterwards released on the payment of £30.

During his imprisonment, Charles II. died and was succeeded by his brother JamesII. Little as the non-conformists had to hope from Charles, they had no reason to anticipate more favorable treatment from his royal successor, who was an acknowledged papist; but their fears do not appear to have been well founded. About two years after his accession a declaration was issued, entitled "his majesty's gracious declaration" "for liberty of conscience," in which he gave liberty "to all his loving subjects to meet and serve God after their own way and manner in private houses and places hired and built for that purpose." No sooner was this declaration issued than Mr. Heywood rented a large room near Halifax Bank Top, where he commenced preaching, July 3rd, 1687, and officiated every Sunday; here it appears "he had great attendance of people." Emboldened by the liberty enjoyed through the king's declaration, and encouraged by their increasing numbers, the dissenters turned their thoughts towards the erection of a permanent convenient place for public worship. Hitherto Mr. Heywood's hearers had assembled in his own house which was not sufficient to accommodate them; various attempts appear to have been made to erect a chapel, which was at last effected through Mr. Heywood's personal exertions, and he had the satisfaction of opening for divine service on the 8th July, 1688, the chapel in Northowram, which continues in existence to this day.

We have now brought down the period of our history to the glorious revolution. "The alarm and danger (says Dr. TOULMIN) which the church of England felt during the reign of James II, arising in a great measure from his precipitate and violent attempts to introduce popery, contributed much to prepare the way for the act of toleration; by disposing the members and the clergy of the establishment to make a common cause with the dissenters as against a common enemy." "The prince of Orange" (says Burnet,) "always thought that conscience was God's province; and that it ought not to be imposed upon; and his experience in Holland made him look on toleration as one of the wisest measures of government." Previously to the revolution, the bishops and clergy with great unanimity had acknowledged the necessity of widening the ecclesiastical foundation, and of forming a closer connection with foreign protestants. In the language of lord Mansfield, "The toleration act rendered that which was illegal before, now legal; the dissenting way of worship is permitted and allowed by that act; it is not only exempted from punishment, but rendered innocent and lawful; it is *established*; it is put under the protection, and is not merely at the *connivance* of the law." The act unquestionably reflected a glory on the æra to which it gave a date, and laid the basis of that religious liberty which has been the felicity and honour of succeeding times; "I will maintain toleration inviolable!" was the ever memorable declaration of the "father of his people;" a declaration which it has been the pride of his royal successors to confirm, and which we have no reason to fear will be abrogated under the paternal sway of the royal descendants of his illustrious house.

It is now my duty to return to the order of dates. About the year 1693 a school was erected in Northowram, of which Mr. David Hartley was the tutor; Lord Wharton, a noted puritan of the time, maintained six scholars at this school.

Public worship among the Dissenters being at this time protected by the law, the number of meeting houses increased. In Mr. Heywood's diary for 1697 he says, that at Halifax the people have built a large meeting place, and that several of his hearers at Northowram were gone from them to Halifax. The following fact may not prove uninteresting to some of my readers, shewing, as it certainly does, not only what a minister was expected to tolerate at that period; but also the income of one who was exceedingly popular among the non-conformists. At the close of the year 1697, Mr. Heywood thus writes "I think I am put to more charges than any minister, my

house standing near my synagogue, there is scarcely a Lord's day
but I have six, eight, or ten persons at dinner at my table, besides
many others who have bread and broth. On sacrament days,
which are every eight weeks, we have usually about twenty that
eat with us :" speaking of his income he adds, "I have some yearly
rents coming in from Lancashire, about £14 a year ; £7 a year from
Sowerby ; and of late £7 15s. from Holdsworth. Lady Hewley
hath usually given me £5 a year, and Lord Wharton £3." Mr.
Heywood was a preacher fifty two years, and only about half that
number were years of liberty. From a regular statement it appears
that from 1665, at which time the conventicle act passed, till 1701
inclusive, a term of thirty seven years, seventeen of which only were
years of public liberty, and most of them after he had reached sixty
years of age, he preached on week-days, besides his regular work
on the sabbath-day, 3027 sermons, kept 1256 fasts, observed 314
thanksgiving days, and travelled on preaching excursions 31,345
miles. Mr. Heywood died May 4th, 1702, aged 73, and it is generally supposed he was interred in Houldsworth's chapel, on the
south side of the Parish Church. For a detailed account of this
excellent man, the reader is referred to his Memoirs, they may be
perused with considerable interest as giving an account of a most exemplary Christian, who amidst a series of privations and sufferings
maintained a consistency of conduct, in every respect worthy of his
high profession.

The name at first given to the dissentients from the church of
England, after the re-establishment of the reformation from Popery
in the reign of Queen Elizabeth, was that of Puritans. When the
Prince of Orange came to the throne, he found these dissentients
divided into several bodies, each respectable for number and influence,
and which, during the civil wars, and in the reign of the second
Charles, had risen to importance : these were Presbyterians, Independents and Baptists : to them was added a sect of recent origin,
the society of Friends commonly called Quakers.

About the year 1735 there arose a sect called the Wesleyan
Methodists; their origin may be considered as the commencement
of a new era in the religious world : comprising, as they now do, a
considerable portion of the population of this Parish, it may be
expected that I should shortly advert to their introduction here.

The first society was formed in the year 1742, by the venerable founder of Methodism, at the village of Skircoat Green; and in 1748 he again visited Halifax, and commenced preaching at the Market Cross, but was compelled to desist, in consequence of the tumult occasioned by persons throwing money among his audience. Notwithstanding the opposition thus manifested, Methodism grew apace—a meeting house was erected in Church Lane, in the year 1752, at the cost of £300; and we find that in the year 1758, another meeting house existed in Sowerby. To trace the growth and progress of Methodism, from its first commencement down to the present period, is foreign to my purpose. The summary in the Appendix will suffice to afford a tolerable estimate of its present state in the Halifax circuit.

It would be unjust to withhold from this respectable body the meed of praise to which they are so eminently entitled; their zealous but persevering efforts to afford religious instruction in all places, but more particularly in these populous manufacturing districts, have not only been productive of great good, but present in many respects, an example truly worthy of imitation: a real and lasting benefit has been imparted, a moral influence has been spread among the poor and uneducated, and a great reformation has consequently been effected. The same remark will apply to the strenuous and successful efforts of the dissenters both at home and abroad.

Having thus shewn the introduction of non-conformity into the Parish, it may be necessary to state, that notwithstanding it exists to a considerable extent, the prevailing sentiments do not assume variety of modification and graduation in the thermometer of that enthusiasm which is to be found in many of the manufacturing towns. The want of sufficient church accommodation has unquestionably been one great cause of the rapid increase of dissenting meeting-houses within this district, whatever may be said of the growth of dissent in general. I have condensed into the form of a statistical table to be found in the Appendix D, the number of places of worship belonging to each sect, as they existed in 1758, and as they now exist. With the points of doctrine, the modes of discipline, and the principles of Christian philosophy, on which the various seceders from the establishment differ, these pages have no connection. The non-conformist is no longer precluded, by the laws of the realm, from a full participation of the same civil honors that a member of the church of England exclusively enjoyed previous to the repeal of the Corporation and Test acts.

Within these few years the general body of the dissenters have urged upon the attention of the Legislature their claims, not only for domestic relief in relation to an authorized register of births, the celebration of marriages in their own meeting houses, and a full participation of university honors and privileges, without being required to conform to the established usages of those seats of learning, but a separation between church and state has been solicited by a considerable portion of them, substituting in the place of an establishment, the "*voluntary principle*." How far it may be expedient to concede certain privileges which belong exclusively to the establishment, without endangering that establishment, is a question for legislative discussion, and not within the compass of my enquiries. Nor should I have adverted to the subject had not the voluntary principle been recognised in a petition to Parliament, from a portion of the dissenters of Halifax. That every grievance of which the dissenter can complain, with the least appearance of justice, should be considered and disposed of, and that he should be placed on a perfect equality with the rest of the king's subjects, no reasonable mind can entertain a doubt; but that the paramount claims of *public principle* should be abandoned to gratify the air-built theories and empty declamations of religious sciolism, reason informs us is neither consonant with the laws of abstract right nor conducive to the welfare and happiness of mankind. "By *principle* is not meant the airy speculations of vague and delusive theory; but that code of moral law, which is the joint result of reason and experience." Upon principle then, thus created and established, we found our attachment to all that is high and honorable in the contracted paths of private life, to all that is venerable and noble in the more expanded prospect of public duty. If the exclusive principle (for upon the vantage ground of *public principle* do I take my stand) be once allowed to be relaxed, who shall prescribe any bounds to its relaxation? Who shall presume to draw the line of indulgence, and to say to importunity,—thus far and no farther! It may indeed be considered as a general maxim, (and happy would it be for mankind if the maxim were never lost sight of) that in no instance can relaxation of principle be unaccompanied with danger. For the human mind is sure to lose its respect for principle when it ceases to regard it as inviolable, and it is soon led to view with indifference, what it before looked upon as sacred.

Upon *principle*, the fabric of our constitution both in church and state is reared and supported, and by *principle* alone can it be strengthened and maintained. This is the high ground upon which every pure and patriotic mind must take its stand, and upon this we must rest our defence of all that is dear to us as Englishmen and as Christians. The political and the ecclesiastical establishments of a state mutually support and maintain each other, it is the state which protects, honors, and cherishes the church; it is the church which defends, adorns, and consecrates that political body with which she is so intimately connected. So long as Christianity is "part and parcel of the law of England," so long as it forms a constituent part of the body politic, so long is it essential to its general and easy reception, that an establishment should exist, not for the sake of rendering the church political, but the government religious; and experience teaches us with how powerful a bond of united interest the ecclesiastical and civil institutions of our native land are cemented and confirmed: it should be borne in mind, that it has ever been the constant policy of those who have aimed at the destruction of all civil government, to direct the first blow at the church establishment; for as long as the church remains unpolluted, the bonds of civil union are uninjured. The history of our own country in former years, and the records of other nations, will bear a powerful and overwhelming testimony to the practical truth of these opinions; may that truth never be confirmed by our own practical experience.

THE MODERN ÆRA.

1662.—In this year several of the inhabitants of the Parish, but more particularly tradesmen and victuallers, coined copper pieces, penny and half-penny tokens. For this there was an urgent necessity, since at that time but few brass half-pennies were coined by authority, and no great quantity of farthings. This money was coined by the tradesmen and victuallers, at pleasure; it was struck for necessary change; the figure of the coin was sometimes octagon, but generally round, the devices various, and the materials lead, tin, copper, or brass. All tradesmen who issued this useful kind of specie, were obliged to take it again, when brought to them, and they usually kept a sorting box, into the partitions whereof (which, we may suppose were as numerous as there were people in the place that coined) they put the money of the respective coiners, and at proper times when there was a competent quantity of one person's money, sent it to him to be changed into silver. Specimens of these sorting boxes are said to be very scarce. A few of these *Nummorum Famuli* are still in existence, one in the museum of the Halifax Literary and Philosophical Society, the most proper place for their reception and preservation. One of these coins bearing the inscription, "John Farrar, in Halifax, his halfpenny, 1667," was exhumed lately in digging the foundation of the new Chapel in King-Cross Lane, in Halifax.

The best account of these Tokens is to be found in Leake's Historical Account of English Money, London, 1745, 8vo.; Mr. Thoresby's Museum, p. 379, and Mr. Drake's Eboracum, in the Appendix. The halfpence are represented by Thoresby " as shameful light, a common halfpenny of the King's outweighing twelve of them." They were cried down by proclamation in the year 1762.

1745.—At the time of the rebellion Halifax manifested most

unequivocal proofs of loyalty to the house of Hanover. A voluntary association of the gentry and tradesmen of the Town was formed, for the patriotic defence of the Altar and the Throne, against the attacks of popery and arbitrary power. The accounts of the victories from time to time obtained over the rebels by the king's forces were welcomed by the inhabitants with every demonstration of public joy: the money expended by the Churchwardens in distributing ale to the troops as they passed through the town to the battle of Culloden; and the sums paid to the ringers for their services, form no inconsiderable item in the Parish accounts at that period.

A loyal and patriotic club, designated, the Union Club, was at the same time established under the auspices of Sir George Saville, Bart, a name ever to be remembered in the Parish of Halifax; and in the year 1759, the first local Newspaper, called the Union Journal, or Halifax Advertiser, was published, under the patronage of the worthy Baronet, in support of the principles of the club.

We may infer from this fact that the Schoolmaster was then abroad in Halifax: to shew the progress he has since made, a short description of the Union Journal, and a comparison of the intelligence conveyed in its first number, with the publications of the present day, may not prove uninteresting.

The paper was embellished with two plates; one representing Britannia seated on a Woolsack, her left arm resting on a cage supported on her knee, from which cage three birds appear to have just escaped; on the dexter side of the Woolsack stands a little chubby fellow, emblematical of Liberty; and on the sinister side a bee-hive surrounded with bees, emblematical of Industry. Motto—Britannia loves Freedom. The other plate represents a warrior trampling on two French flags, supporting in his right arm a spear, his left arm bearing a shield charged with the arms of England, resting on his thigh. The paper was published weekly, and advertisements taken in at 3s. 6d. During its continuance, it contained little local information, being principally filled with extracts from the London Journals, Gazette, &c. The first number is very barren of local news, it merely consists of the following intelligence :—that a "wager had been determined for a considerable sum, that a mare did not draw three packs of goods from the Hanging Gate, below Blackstone-Edge, to Halifax, in eight hours; which she performed in 6h. and 2m. with great ease, and what is remarkable, she did not sweat an hair in coming in. "May 4th, Sunday, was observed with the usual diversions, the annual wake or tide in the pasture ground near the river Calder in Skircoate, where under the pretext of viewing the grazing animals, was assembled an amazing multitude of people, who spent the greatest part of the day in running, wrestling, and leaping, &c., somewhat resembling the Olympic Games of old; and to refresh fainting nature, hucksters, tiplers, .&c. were present with their wares." The amusements of our gentry have decidedly progressed with the march of intellect. "July. The inhabitants of the town were for three days amused with a grand cock match between Robert Stansfield and Robert Hawkesworth, Esqrs., and William Southern and —Harvey, Esqrs., when twenty two battles were won by the former, and thirteen by the latter."— The following "curious wager was this year made, for £50, between Mr. Hoyland, of this town, and Mr. Oldfield, of Chester. Mr. Hoyland betted that his black Galloway would walk round Skircoat Common on its hind legs, in ten minutes, without its fore legs ever touching the ground. Mr. Oldfield offered £5 to be off the wager on seeing the galloway perform its exercise."

1760.—To the honor of the Parish be it recorded, that Halifax could at this time boast of having three independent companies of Militia, clothed at their own charge. I have no wish to disturb the gravity of my readers, at the expense of their forefathers, but I much doubt whether their appearance on parade, clothed in their new regimentals, would not at the present day relax the risible muscles of many a loyal and dutiful son. That they may not plead the want of precedent in the selection of a Regimental Uniform, should their country require their services in the field, the soldier like appearance of their honored sires may serve as an instruction. The following will suffice :—

"The independent companies of Militia of this town, under the command of Colonel Spencer, Captain William Ingram, and Captain John Tarlton, were reviewed by the Earl of Scarborough in Price's Square, (now the Manufacturer's Hall,) and went through their manual exercise, platoon, and street firing; the companies were clothed in their new uniform, provided at their own expense. The Colonel's company in blue, lapelled and faced with buff. Cap-

tain Ingram's company in scarlet coats, and scarlet breeches, (!) lapelled and faced with green, green waistcoats, gold laced hats, and
cue wigs.   And Captain Tarlton's company in blue, with gold vellum button holes.   Captain Johnson's company of the train of Ar-
tillery wore the uniform of the heavy blue and buff, with gold laced
hats."

1769.—The attention of the country was this year drawn to a
circumstance which occured within the Parish, and excited much
notice, namely, the capture of a most notorious and desperate
gang of Coiners, who were apprehended in the vale of Turvin, a
romantic and beautiful spot in the township of Erringden ; the scene
of their operations.   It was their practice, (which it seems they
had carried on with impunity for six years, at the time of their apprehension,) to diminish guineas by clipping and filing them,
while the clippings and filings were melted down and re-struck in
rude dies resembling Portugal coin of 36s. and 27s. pieces.   They
had no screw presses for the purpose, but fixed their dies in heavy
blocks.   The impression was produced by the stroke of sledge ham-
mers, which were nightly heard on every side, no one daring for
some time to interrupt so powerful and desperate a gang ; indeed
the practice had become so common, that large undiminished
Guineas were openly bought by the gang, at twenty-two shillings
a-piece.   Their illicit proceedings did not escape the notice of government : through the instrumentality of Mr. Deighton, a Supervisor
of Excise, acting under the advice of Mr. Parker, an eminent solicitor in the town, some of the gang were brought to justice.   At
the York Spring and Summer Assizes, 1770, several were arraigned
on the charge of high treason, tried, and convicted, but only two
were executed, viz. James Oldfield, of Warley, and David Hartley
of Erringden, the latter was called—King David, by his fraternity.
They had another chief named David Greenwood, of Hill Top, in
Erringden, distinguished by the appellation of Duke of Edinburgh,
this man used to provide the cash, sometimes as much as one hundred guineas at a time.   At a subsequent Assizes he was also tried
convicted, and ordered for execution, but he died in York Castle,
before the sentence could be carried into effect.   There was another
indictment against him at the same Assizes for a fraud in obtaining
£20 from the widow of David Hartley, under a pretext that he had

paid that sum to Mr. Parker, the Crown Solicitor, at the preceding Assizes, as a bribe to get Hartley acquitted. Upwards of forty men were connected with the gang, who appear to have been a most daring set of villains: nineteen of them were liberated on entering into recognizances with sureties to appear when called upon. The leniency of the Crown upon this occasion seems to have been misplaced, for it is a fact, that the major part of those who were liberated were subsequently convicted of a second offence; and notwithstanding two of that number were then acquitted on account of a flaw in their indictments; before the expiration of four years from their acquittal, they were a third time tried, and convicted for fresh offences of a similar nature, although their operations were principally confined to shillings and half-pence. One of these, named Thomas Greenwood, was a Woollen Manufacturer, residing in Wadsworth. He was usually called Great Tom, or Conjuror Tom, from his expertness in coining, which he had carried on for twenty years. I shall give some account of him in a subsequent part of the work. The gang used to have an annual supper at Mytholmroyd Bridge at Michaelmas, called the coiner's feast.

The apprehension of the principals in this affair, was followed, not only by the murder of Mr. Deighton, who was shot in Bull Close Lane: but of another person at Heptonstall, who was instrumental in their apprehension.

1783.—In this year a riotous mob assembled in the town to demand a reduction in the price of grain, and to compel the dealers to sell at such prices as the mob thought fit to dictate: they seized upon large quantities of corn, sold it at their own price, and the owners received the money when they could get it. Two of the ring leaders named Spencer and Saltonstall suffered the full penalty of the law for their temerity, and were executed on Beacon Hill. Both of these men were connected with the gang of coiners, before-mentioned; Spencer, it is believed, hired Thomas and Norminton to murder Mr. Deighton.

1795.—The Parish does not appear to have been altogether free from the taint of republicanism, which spread through the country at the period of the French Revolution. The turbulent spirit, and the levelling principle, manifested itself in a considerable degree; and the same incendiary methods to inflame the minds of the lower class of people, and to efface every remaining impression of either allegiance to the sovereign, or submission to the laws, were too successfully practised by emissaries from the corresponding society. A considerable quantity of muskets, bayonets, and other weapons of warfare were sent from Birmingham to Elland, and the disaffected in those parts were trained in the night, to the use of arms. By the vigilance of the local Magistracy, the designs of the disaffected were happily frustrated, and a company of Volunteers was formed in the town, to repress any local disturbance.

1799.—In this year, the crops throughout the country generally failed, and in the following year, much distress prevailed in the Parish in common with other places. The poor at that time lived principally on oatmeal, very little flour being then used: yet such was their extreme state of destitution that many were compelled to live upon Barley or Bean Meal, neither could they obtain a sufficiency of those articles. Oatmeal was sold in the town as high as £5 5s. per load, and Flour £6 per pack ; and to add to the general distress, work was very scarce. A royal proclamation was issued, recommending economy in the use of grain, in private families: parliamentary enactments followed: general subscriptions were entered into for the relief of the distressed : but all proved inadequate to arrest the progress of the famine, until a gracious Providence was pleased to restore a period of plenty. It is called Barley-time in some parts of the Parish, to this day.

1811-12.—Were rendered remarkable in the manufacturing districts, by a daring spirit of insubordination and riot that manifested itself among the workmen connected with machinery. This lawless system, which assumed the name of Luddism, first broke out at Nottingham, and spread into Yorkshire and Lancashire. The destruction of Machinery was the principal object of these deluded men ; and to effect this, every species of crime was resorted to, fire arms were seized, illegal oaths were administered, and nocturnal meetings held. At Huddersfield they began their operations, which ultimately spread in all directions.

Among the particular instances of resistance they met with ; and which are worthy of record, the bravery of Mr. Cartwright, of Rawfolds, near Cleckheaton, should not be passed over unnoticed. On the night of Saturday, April 12th, 1812, nearly two hundred men surrounded the mill of this gentleman. Mr. Cartwright had prepared for the attack, and with four workmen and two soldiers determined to resist the lawless band. The assailants marched to the attack in companies, armed with pistols, hatchets and bludgeons, and attempted to break into the mill; they were completely defeated by the gallant little garrison, and were compelled, after a contest of twenty minutes, to retire in confusion, leaving two of their number mortally wounded upon the field. The firmness and resolution of Mr. Cartwright did not pass unrewarded; the manufacturers of the district duly appreciated his conduct, and as an instance of their approbation, presented him with the sum of three thousand pounds, which they had raised by subscription.

Defeated in this attempt to effect the destruction of property, they had recourse to assassination; Mr. Horsfall, of Marsden, an extensive manufacturer, was shot in open day, on his return from Huddersfield market; several other attempts at murder were also made. For a more particular description of these unlawful proceedings the reader is referred to the works of Mr. BAINES, who has entered fully into the subject, and treated it with great ability.

Happily, in this country, miscreants of the description here alluded to, seldom escape the retributive arm of justice. The assistance of the legislature was called into operation; sixty-six persons were in the course of the latter year apprehended and committed to York Castle. The public were much indebted to Joseph Radcliffe, Esq. an active and intrepid Magistrate, who was afterwards created a baronet for his services: a special commission was issued for the trial of these prisoners in January 1813. Eighteen were condemned to death: three of them, the murderers of Mr. Horsfall, were executed on Friday, January 8th, and fourteen on the Saturday week afterwards, some were sentenced to transportation; and a few liberated on bail. The example thus made soon put a stop to these diabolical proceedings, and shewed that the adoption of vigorous measures by the constituted authorities, is the best preventative against popular excess.

1815-20.—With the exception of the seditious meetings holden in various parts of the district, at which the lowest and basest of the people were encouraged, by men a little higher than themselves, to lift their hands against the constituted authorities of the land;

no circumstance of importance occurred in connection with the history of this place worth recording. How far those proceedings might admit of extenuation, in consequence of the distress which at that time generally prevailed, is not my province to enquire; the country had just emerged from a long, arduous, and expensive struggle with the despot of France, for the support of which it had been found necessary to tax our resources to the fullest extent; the reduction of that taxation, and the lightening of the public burthens, could not be effected in a moment; it required not only time to renovate our national prosperity, but that the best energies of our legislators should be directed to that important end. That the illustrious statesmen who at that time held the reins of government, were not unmindful of the duty they owed their country, her present renown and glory sufficiently testify.

1825.—This year was prolific in various schemes for the investment of capital, of which there was a considerable surplus in the country. It might have been expected that the history of the South Sea scheme would have been a good lesson on the subject of adventures for several generations; and that the various projects of extracting silver from lead, making butter from beech trees, deal boards from saw-dust, and air-pumps for the brain, which at that time gulled the public, would have rendered the most credulous dupe cautious of engaging in air-built speculations. To such an extent did the epidemic rage in the month of January in this year, that it presented schemes for twenty rail-road companies, twenty-two banking, loan, investment and assurance companies, eleven gas companies, eight British and Irish and seventeen foreign mine companies, nine shipping and dock and twenty-seven miscellaneous companies. The rise in the public funds and on the original stock in various public companies was beyond all precedent; the original shares of £100 in the Navigation Company connected with this Parish rose to £650, and several purchases were made at that price. It is not disputed that some of the foregoing schemes proved advantageous, but the majority of them were decided failures, and involved not only the projectors but the dupes of their confidence in one common ruin, producing in conjunction with secondary causes what has been not unaptly termed, a "general panic." From the best information I have been able to obtain on the subject, this district was not involved

in the speculations of the day to the extent that prevailed in many
parts of the kingdom; and the commercial distress that did prevail
here, during this, and the subsequent year, was rather a consequence, than a first cause, aggravated in no ordinary degree, by
the failure of some considerable Banking Establishments in the
county, who had long possessed the public confidence. The establishments connected with the town of Halifax remained unshaken,
either as regarded their credit, or the confidence which has been
invariably and deservedly placed in them.

1830.—Among the local events of this year, the "Halifax Musical
Festival forms too important a feature to be passed over in silence.
I am indebted to "An historical Record" of that interesting and
joyous occasion, for the following facts.

The funds of the Halifax Dispensary (to which I shall hereafter
have occasion to advert) having been found inadequate to meet its
increased expenditure, (the consequence of its extended usefulness,)
a meeting of the inhabitants was held on the 12th June, to discuss
the expediency of organizing a Musical Festival, for the benefit of
that excellent institution; this meeting was attended by upwards of
fifty gentlemen of the highest respectability and opulence in the
parish; our worthy and patriotic townsman, Christopher Rawson,
Esq. taking the lead: resolutions were unanimously adopted, that
in the ensuing autumn, a musical festival should take place—a
guarantee fund formed—the co-operation and assistance of the gentry resident in the parish requested—and the Archbishop of the
Province, the Lord Lieutenant of the Riding, and other Noblemen
and Gentlemen connected with the Riding, solicited to become the
Patrons; a committee of management was nominated to carry the
intentions of the Meeting into effect; and upwards of £500 was subscribed instanter, towards the guarantee fund. The spirit and zeal
which characterized this meeting, was responded to in the out-
townships; sub-committees were formed, and a spirit of emulation
excited, well befitting the benevolent object it had in view. Wednesday, Thursday, and Friday, the 29th and 30th September, and
the 1st of October, were the days fixed upon for holding the festival,
which it was resolved, should be celebrated by three morning performances in the parish church, two Evening Concerts in the Assembly Rooms, and a Grand Fancy Ball at the same place, on the

evening of the third day. The principal vocal performers whom the good taste of the committee had catered for the gratification and amusement of an audience fully capable of appreciating their merits, were Madame Stockhausen, Mrs. Wm. Knyvett, and our talented young towns-lady, Miss Farrar, Mr. Braham, Mr. Wm. Knyvett, Mr. Bennett, and Mr. Phillips. Mr. White was engaged to lead the instrumental performers, Dr. Camidge to preside at the organ, M. Stockhausen at the harp, the veteran Lindley at his violoncello, and Mr. Nicholson on the flute. The instruments consisted of 15 violins, 6 violas, 7 violoncellos, 3 contra basses, 4 flutes, 4 oboes, 2 clarinetts, 4 bassoons, 4 horns, 3 trumpets, 4 trombones, 2 bass horns, a serpent and drums. The vocal performers comprised 19 soprano, 12 alto, 16 tenore, and 20 basso. The judicious arrangements made by the committee, to accommodate all parties, and to give effect to the performances, were of the first order; the fine old organ in the church was altered so as to make it chord with the instruments when at concert pitch; an extensive and commodious orchestra was constructed at the west end of the church, and temporary seats at the east end, extending across the chancel from the screen to the railing of the altar; outside the church, a large awning, of ample width and accommodation, was erected, extending across the church yard, from the vicar's gate, to the chancel door. The proprietors of the New Assembly Rooms, with a laudable spirit, caused an elegant new orchestra to be erected expressly for the occasion, enlarged the orchestra appropriated to the musicians for the dance; and made other arrangements for giving eclàt to the fancy ball. The publicity given to the proceedings of the committee of management served but to increase the spirit of enthusiasm which animated all who were interested in the event. It is true that after the preliminaries of the festival had been completed, the time fixed for its commencement, and the performers engaged, a pamphlet, entitled " Strictures on Musical Festivals" was fulminated from the press, the object of which was to characterize these festivals as " combining an unhallowed mixture of things sacred and profane," and induce a belief that they were calculated to become "inadvertently, contributors to that baneful dissipation inseparably connected with these fascinating entertainments." It is difficult to imagine what could be the motives of the author in this gratuitous publication of his opinions, happily, the pamphlet not only served to stimulate the zeal of the committee, but its tendency upon the festival was to increase its funds, thus producing a contrary effect to the author's benevolent intention.

A rehearsal having taken place in the Church, on the Tuesday preceding, to the satisfaction of a numerous audience; the anticipated day at length arrived: eleven o'clock was the time appointed for the commencement of the performances in the church; while "the seats in the chancel, and the pews in the centre aisle, were crowded by a brilliant array of fashion and rank," the orchestra was filled by nearly all the musical talent of the West Riding, in addition to the eminent performers before mentioned. The morning's performance consisted of selections of sacred music from Handel, Haydn, and Beethoven. The concert in the evening, in the New Assembly Rooms, consisted of a most judicious miscellaneous selection, in which all the performers acquitted themselves beautifully, chastely, and effectively.

The audience, on the second morning, were gratified by the performance of Handel's sublime oratorio "The Messiah," the popularity of which, combined with a reduction of the prices of admission to the body, and the North gallery, filled the church to overflowing. The evening's concert again consisted of a judicious selection; the audience was more brilliant than on the preceding evening; upwards of ninety carriages set down company at the door.

The third morning's performances in the church, consisted of the first part of Haydn's "Creation," with a selection from the works of Handel, Mozart, and other celebrated composers. The extraordinary fact is worthy of record, (as illustrative of the extent to which musical science is studied in Halifax,) that, with the exception of two, the choristers were natives of the parish, or its immediate neighbourhood. In concluding this notice it may be permitted to remark, that the oldest musical professors present on the occasion, stated that they did not remember a performance of the various selections having drawn forth a greater number of beauties, or gone off with a less proportion of blemishes: indeed the celebrated vocalist, Braham, confessed on the occasion, that he had never heard finer choral singing.

The fancy Ball that concluded the Festival passed off with considerable eclàt: it diversified the amusements of the week, and left nothing that could be wished for, presenting an attraction to all who enjoy this truly innocent and fascinating amusement; giving animation to age, and warming with pleasure, even the stoic and the misanthropist. Above 500 persons attended the assembly and embraced all, or nearly all, the *elite* of the district.

It is not the least interesting feature in this imperfect sketch, that the nett proceeds for the sale of tickets and books amounted to £1512 18s. 4d.; the expenses to £1188 16s. 3d. leaving a balance of £324 2s. 1d., to which was added donations received, amounting to £354 5s. The cash paid to the Treasurer of the Dispensary amounted to £654 5s., leaving a surplus of £24 2s. 1d, to satisfy certain contingencies.

The efficient and important services rendered to the Festival Committee by their honorary Secretary, (Mr. W. Craven) were appreciated by the presentation of a piece of plate, of the value of thirty guineas.

The public events of subsequent years, down to the Reform Æra, have relation principally to political topics, which it is not the province of the local historian to discuss, excepting so far as the annals of the place are involved in the enquiry; and I am not aware that any circumstances transpired, beyond the excitement which is usually produced by a county election, worth adverting to, so far as regards the parish of Halifax.

The Reform Æra having a more immediate connection with a prescribed district, than the whole of the Parish, particularly as regards the enfranchisement of the new borough; I shall therefore proceed to the consideration of those matters which relate generally to the Parish, before entering upon a more detailed account of particular districts.

THE PUBLIC CHARITIES.

I HAVE before had occasion to remark, that the Public Charities connected with this Parish were her proudest boast: they are unquestionably the honor point in her escutcheon, and will reflect a lustre upon her historic page, when her wealth, manufactures, and commerce shall have passed away.

The Commissioners for enquiring into Charities having visited Halifax in the year 1826, I have inserted so much of their Report as relates to this Parish, inasmuch as it conveys all the information necessary for the general reader, in a less prolix, but more interesting form, than the bare recital of old wills and deeds; these will be found set forth in Watson's History. There are other Charities referred to by that gentleman, which I shall have occasion to notice. The benefactions to the preachers at various chapels are here omitted, but hereafter mentioned in connection with their history.

I have now before me an interesting document entitled "The Enquirie and Presentment of the Jurye charged upon the Comission directed for finding out of things given to pious uses." Happy shall I be if it put any of my readers upon the "finding out of things given to pious uses" which have been diverted to other purposes. The paper is without date, but I conclude it is the document referred to by Mr. Watson, as formerly in the possession of Mr. John Brearcliffe, who was an apothecary of this town, if so, the date of the enquiry is about the year 1651.

WATERHOUSE'S CHARITY.

"By letters patent under the great seal, dated the 14th September, 11th Charles I, reciting that *Nathaniel Waterhouse*, gent. had given a large house, within the town of Halifax, to be employed

as a workhouse, to set the poor within the town and parish to work,
it was granted and ordained that the said house should be employed
for the said purpose, and that thirteen of the ablest and most discreet persons in the town and parish should be a body corporate,
by the name of "Master and Governors of the Workhouse for the
poor, within the Town and Parish of Halifax," and have power to
make rules for the governing and ordering the workhouse, and the
poor therein to be maintained and employed, and to examine all
persons idly wandering within the town and parish of Halifax, and
compel them to labour in the workhouse for their living, and to
appoint officers in the workhouse to oversee and provide that the
poor might be well ordered and provided for.

"The said Nathaniel Waterhouse, by his will, dated the 1st of
July, 1642, devised to Richard Marsh, D. D. then vicar of Halifax
and fifteen other persons, as trustees, and their heirs, all his houses
buildings, lands, and hereditaments in Halifax, Skircoat, and Southowram, and in Siddall and Exley, and elsewhere, in the county of
York, (except such as are thereinafter devised to the master and
governors of the workhouse,) to the intent that the trustees should
employ the same to the purposes therein after mentioned, viz. first
that part of the houses and buildings situate at or near the Over-
church Steele and Causey Head, in Halifax, which the testator had
made into twelve several dwellings, should be used for the habitation of twelve aged or impotent poor persons, whereof three should
be of the town of Halifax, and one out of each of the other nine
towns within the Parish, viz. Sowerby, Midgley, Warley, Ovenden,
Skircoat, Northowram, Southowram, Hipperholme, and Shelfe,
there to continue without paying rent during their respective lives,
or so long as by the trustees should be thought fit, and that after
the decease or removal of any of them, the trustees should choose
out of the ten towns other aged or impotent poor people, to be
placed in their room; and the testator directed, that the trustees
should pay to the twelve poor persons, yearly, £18, viz. to each of
them 30s. per annum towards their maintenance, and £6 to array
them in black; and he further directed, that a house, with the appurtenances, in Halifax, in the will described, should be employed
for bed rooms and working rooms, for ten boys and ten girls, and
the habitation of a person, to be elected by the trustees, for train-

ing up, and teaching the twenty children in such employment and work as they should be most apt for ; and that the trustees should bestow £1 a year in keeping in repair the said house and the twelve dwellings for poor persons : and that they should choose the overseer of the workhouse to be overseer and master of the twenty children ; and that the twenty children should be such as were fatherless and motherless, and should be taken into the house at the age of six years, and there kept at work and maintained, with all necessaries, till they should accomplish the ages of thirteen or fourteen years, that they might be fit for putting out apprentices at the discretion of the trustees, and the vicar and churchwardens of the parish of Halifax, and justices of the peace for the time being, or others whom it might concern, to have anything to do about the disposing of the children after they should attain that age ; and that such of the children as should, for want of strength, be unmeet to be bound apprentice at the age of thirteen or fourteen years, should be maintained in the house till they should be fifteen years of age, and should then be left to the provision of their friends, and the parish of Halifax ; And he willed, that the ten boys and ten girls should be taken as follows ; of the town of Halifax five, of Southowram two, of Northowram two, of Hipperholme two, of Skircoat one, of Shelfe, one, of Ovenden two, of Warley two, of Midgley one, and of Sowerby two : and that as any of the twenty children should die, or be removed, the trustees should take in another such child, whose parents were dead, of the same sex and township as the child so dead or removed ; and that the trustees should allow to the overseer and superintendant or master of the children, for their meat, drink, clothing, and all other necessaries, and his pains in training them up in work, the yearly sum of £45 and also £5 a year to buy them blue coats withal, and should permit him besides to take the gains which he could make of the reasonable service of the children : And touching a house and buildings, at the Causey Head in Halifax, therein mentioned, with the garden, west part of the croft adjoining, and a new house, then lately built on the north part of the croft, and the rents and profits thereof, the testator directed the same to be employed by the trustees for the benefit of the person who from time to time should be the stipendiary preacher or hired lecturer, in the parish church of Halifax, which lecturer he directed should resort to the poor persons in the twelve dwellings, and the poor employed in the workhouse, and the twenty children, and admonish them to repair to church, to prayers and sermons, at convenient prayer times, and should catechize them, or the younger sort of them, weekly in the summer time, at the trustees discretion; and the testator directed, that the trustees should, towards their charges, at their meetings about the execution of his will, keep to themselves, out of the rents and profits of the premises, the annual sum of 40s.; and that during the time there should be no lecturer at the parish church of Halifax, the said house, buildings, garden, west part of the croft and new house, and the rents and profits thereof should be employed towards the maintenance of the poor people within the town of Halifax and Sowerby, Midgley, Warley, Skircoat, Ovenden, Southowram, Northowram, Shelfe, and Hipperholme, at the discretion of the trustees; and that the trustees should pay, out of the rents and profits of the said premises, lands, and hereditaments, devised to them, the following stipends and annual sums, that is to say, to the preachers, hired at the several chapels or churches within the parish of Halifax, called Sowerby Bridge Chapel, Illingworth Chapel, Cooley Chapel, Lightcliffe Chapel, Chapel in the Greaves or Bryers, Rastrick Chapel, Elland Chapel or Church, Ripponden Chapel, Sowerby Chapel, Luddenden Chapel or Church, Heptonstall Chapel or Church, and Cross Stone Chapel, upon the feast days of Pentecost and St. Martin, by even portions the stipends following; viz. to the preacher of Sowerby Bridge Chapel 5l., the preacher of Illingworth Chapel 4l., at Cooley Chapel 4l. at Lightcliffe Chapel 4l., the preacher of the chapel in the Greaves 3l., at Rastrick Chapel 40s., Sowerby Chapel 4l,, at Elland Chapel, 4l., at Ripponden Chapel 3l., the preacher of Luddenden Chapel 3l., at Heptonstall Chapel 40s., and at Cross Stone Chapel 40s , towards the augmentation of the respective stipends of the preachers; and he desired that for their stipends the preachers should preach a sermon in rotation in the parish church of Halifax, every first Wednesday in each month in the year, and in default thereof, that the trustees should employ so much of the yearly stipends as should for that time be payable to any of the preachers, to the overseer or master of the twenty children for their better education and maintenance : and that the trustees should pay the yearly sum of 20s. to the churchwardens and overseers of the poor of the parish of Huddersfield, and 20s. a year to the churchwardens and overseers of Mirfield, for the time being, to be by them respectively distributed amongst the poor of the said respective parishes at Pentecost and Christmas, and that in default of such distribution, the respective annual sums should be distributed by the trustees to the poor of the parish of Halifax; and that the trustees should employ the yearly sum of 40s. in repairing the highways on the banks called Northowram Banks and Southowram Banks, (one leading from Halifax towards Bradford, another from Halifax towards Wakefield, and another from Halifax to Southowram), and 20s. a year in repairing the highway between Spright Smithey and Southowram Bank; and that the trustees should also pay the annual sum of 40s. to the governors of the possessions, revenues and goods of the free grammar school of Queen Elizabeth, within the parish of Halifax, for the use of the school; and the testator thereby gave to the master and governors of the workhouse, for the poor within the town and parish of Halifax, all the residue of the rents and profits of his said messuages, lands, tenements and premises, and also the messuage called the Workhouse, and a close called Hatter's Close, with the appurtenances, in Halifax; to hold the same to the said master and governors, to the use of the workhouse, and for setting and employing the poor therein on work, according to the intent of the said letters patent; and he declared his will to be, that the trustees, and the several preachers of the twelve chapels or churches should, twice a year view the repairs of the said houses, and other the premises, whence the said annuities, stipends, and allowances were to be raised, and should take special care that they should not decay for want of timely looking into and repairing, and should demise them to the tenants thereof, at such easy rents that the occupants might sufficiently repair and uphold them; and he directed, that after the death of six of the trustees, the others surviving should make an election of so many other honest and sufficient persons of the parish of Halifax (whereof the vicar for the time being to be one, if the former were then dead) as might supply the number of fifteen trustees, and then make a conveyance of all the things devised in trust as aforesaid, to the use of themselves and those other elected persons and their heirs, in trust to perform his said will and

M

charitable intentions; and he declared his mind to be, that the trustees should take especial care that none of the wood or trees growing upon any part of his said lands should be cut, sold or destroyed, but that the same might by all means be preserved till it should be strong timber, and then be carefully made use of for repairing and amending all his said houses, lands and tenements, devised to his said trustees, and by them to be built for the pious uses aforesaid: And he gave to the master and governors of the workhouse £200 to be bestowed on lands and tenements for the benefit of the workhouse and poor therein set on work, to be paid by his executors, when the master and governors should have procured lands and tenements to be purchased therewith; and if his personal estate should extend to discharge the several legacies in his will mentioned, and any thing remain, he gave the clear residue to the said trustees, to be bestowed on lands merely for the benefit of the poor of the ten townships in the parish of Halifax; and he entreated the justices of assize for the county of York for the time being, to compose and determine by their order, whatsoever differences doubts and questions might arise at any time, touching that his will and meaning, or any thing therein contained.

"By a decree of commissioners of charitable uses, made in the fifth year of King George the First, reciting an inquisition, whereby it was found that such letters patent had been granted, and such will made as aforesaid, and that the sum of £200 bequeathed by the testator to the master and governors of the workhouse, had been laid out in the purchase of lands and tenements in Northowram, called South Howcans, Holling Hay, and Tenter Croft, and a small parcel of land used for a lane, all then of the yearly value of £10, or thereabouts, and that the workhouse had been misemployed, and the rents and profits of the said tenements and premises misconverted and divers other abuses committed in the trust, the commissioners decreed that the surviving governors of the workhouse, and the legal representatives of the deceased governors, should pay divers sums of money, amounting in the whole to £641. 5s. 10d. to the Rev. Thomas Burton, clerk, and others therein named, and did adjudge the places and offices of the then surviving governors of the workhouse to be void, and that the said Burton and others should be trustees of the workhouse, and receive the rents and profits of the said Hatter's close and tenements in Northowram, and apply the same to the use of the workhouse, and the employment of the poor of the town and parish placed therein, and that they should apply for new letters patent of incorporation, to be granted to them, with such powers as to the crown should seem meet, and apply so much of the money thereby to them decreed, towards defraying the expense of obtaining such letters patent, or soliciting for the same, as should be requisite, and that the workhouse should be conveyed to the said Burton and others.

"On the hearing of exceptions taken to the decree in the Court of Chancery, an order was made by the court, bearing date the 18th February 1722, that the sum of £641. 5s. 1d. should be reduced to £604 8s. 5d. and with some other variations the decree was confirmed.

"By another decree of commissioners of pious uses, dated the 4th October 1749, after reciting the previous decree and order of the Court of Chancery, and stating conveyances of the workhouse and trust estate to the trustees appointed in pursuance of the order, and that the trustees had received the said sum of £604. 8s. 5d. and entered upon the trust premises, and had received the rents and profits thereof, and had applied the same, and also the sum of £604. 8s. 5d. except £149. 7s. 8d. which then remained in the hands of the surviving trustees, to the repairs of the workhouse, and maintenance of the poor of the town of Halifax kept and employed therein, and that the said trust premises were then of the yearly value of 17l. 5s. or thereabouts, exclusive of the workhouse, and that the trustees had not been able to procure any letters patent or charter of incorporation, and that for want thereof the trustees could not compel any of the poor of the parish not resident in the town of Halifax to come into the workhouse, so that the poor of that township only had been maintained therein, the commissioners named ordered and decreed, that from thenceforth the workhouse should be employed as a workhouse for the poor of the towns of Ovenden, Northowram, Southowram, Hipperholme, Shelfe, Skircoat, Warley, Midgley and Sowerby, as well as of the town of Halifax, and that the rents and profits of the Hatter's Close, and of the tenements in Northowram, should be employed for the maintenance of the poor of the said several townships kept in the workhouse according to

M 2

the intent of the letters patent, and of the will of Nathaniel Waterhouse.

By an Act of Parliament for better regulating the charities of Nathaniel Waterhouse, passed in the year 1777, after reciting the matters aforesaid, and other matters, and setting forth, that the trust estates had in general been sufficient to answer the trusts reposed in the trustees, but had not yielded any surplus profits for the benefit of the trusts reposed in the governors of the workhouse, and that the feoffees or trustees had no surplus in hand; but on the contrary, their trust estates were then indebted the sum of £100 and upwards, for monies borrowed, and disbursed in the repair and improvement thereof; and that at the time of obtaining the letters patent, establishing the workhouse, the poor of the parish in general, were maintained at the common charge of the whole parish; but some years afterwards the several townships, which constituted the parish of Halifax, were separated by an Act of Parliament, passed in the 13th and 14th years of king Charles 2d, with respect to their poor, and afterwards each township distinctly supported its own poor, by monthly payments, or in workhouses established by each township respectively, by means of which separation and alteration, the exercise of the powers in the letters patent was rendered difficult, and could not be conveniently carried into execution; yet, in case the several trusts, vested in the governors and feoffees, or trustees respectively, were united and vested in the same persons, with proper powers, it was conceived that the purpose of both the trusts would be more completely answered, the execution of those trusts facilitated, and the several objects of the bounty of the donor be greatly benefitted thereby. It was enacted, that all the messuages, lands, and premises, comprized in the letters patent, and given and devised by the will of Nathaniel Waterhouse, and also the lands and tenements in Northowram, should be vested in William Walker and four others in the Act named, upon trust, to convey the same to the use of the vicar of Halifax, and his successor, vicars of Halifax for the time being, and of the said William Walker and eight others, therein named, their heirs and assigns, upon trust that the said governors and trustees of the said premises, together with the six governors and trustees to be elected as thereinafter mentioned, should, out of the rents and profits of the trust estates, and the monies in the hands of the governors, and such other trust monies as should come to their hands in pursuance of that Act, pay the expenses attending that Act, the debt of £100 and upwards, and all other debts due from the charity estates; and that the governors and trustees should from time to time pay and apply the residue of the rents and profits of such of the trust premises as were devised by the will of Nathaniel Waterhouse to the feoffees or trustees therein named, and also the residue (if any) of the monies in the hands of the governors, according to the directions expressed in the will regarding the same, except in such instances where a different application was by that Act directed; and it was enacted, that when the clear rents and profits of the trust premises should be sufficient to answer the several annual payments directed by the will, and to yield a sufficient surplus, there shall be paid annually out of the surplus, the several further sums thereinafter mentioned, in augmentation of such annual payments respectively; that is to say, the further sum of £6 yearly, to the said twelve aged or impotent poor persons: the further sum of 20s. yearly, for the maintenance of the house and twelve dwellings in the will mentioned: the further sum of £20 yearly, to the overseer and master of the twenty children in the will mentioned: the further sum of 40s. yearly, to the governors of the school; and the further sum of £20 yearly, to the several preachers in the will mentioned, in augmentation of their several stipends, thereby provided, and to be divided amongst them, in proportion thereto respectively: And after reciting, that since the separation of the ten townships, with respect to their poor, each of such townships had established, or was desirous to establish within itself, a workhouse, for the better ordering, setting to work and providing for its own poor separately, it was further enacted, that the residue and surplus of the rents and profits of all the other trust premises, vested and to be vested in the governors and trustees, in pursuance of that Act, should be by the said governors and trustees respectively paid on the first Wednesday in March, annually, to the overseers of the poor of the said ten several townships, who should pay and apply the same for the better ordering, setting to work, and providing for the poor in the said workhouse of such ten townships respectively, in the following proportions; (that is to say), out of every £48 there should be paid to the overseers of the poor of Hali-

fax, 12l. 1s. 6d. : to the overseers of the poor of Sowerby, 6l. 0s. 9d.
to the overseers of the poor of Midgley, 2l. 18s. ; to the overseers
of the poor of Warley, 5l. 13s. : to the overseers of the poor of
Ovenden, 4l. 17s. 9d. ; to the overseers of the poor of Skircoat,
2l. 2s. 10d. ; to the overseers of the poor of Northowram, 5l. 17s. 9d. ;
to the overseers of the poor of Southowram, 3l. 13s. 6d. ; to the
overseers of the poor of Hipperholme, 3l. 13s. 6d.; and to the
overseers of the poor of Shelfe, 1l. 1s. 5d. ; and so in proportion
for any greater or lesser sum than 48l., which might from time to
time be in the hands of the governors and trustees ; and it was further
enacted, that the vicar of Halifax for the time being, should be one
of the governors and trustees of the said united charity ; and that he
and the said William Walker, and eight others, in whom the said trust
estates were thereby directed to be vested, should, within one month
next after the conveyance to their use, elect six other persons to be
governors and trustees, along with them, of the said united charity :
and that one of the new governors and trustees should be elected
from or out of the inhabitants of the township of Midgley, another
from the inhabitants of the township of Warley, another from the
inhabitants of the township of Ovenden, another from the inhabitants
of the township of Skircoat, another from the inhabitants of the
township of Northowram, and another from the inhabitants of the
township of Southowram ; and that there should be at all times
thereafter (besides the vicar of Halifax for the time being) five of
the governors and trustees resident in Halifax, two in Sowerby, and
one resident in each of the other eight townships of Midgley,
Warley, Ovenden, Skircoat, Northowram, Southowram, Hipperholme and Shelfe respectively ; and that on the death, resignation,
or removal out of such townships respectively, of any of the governors
and trustees, the remaining governors and trustees should elect
another inhabitant of the township where such death, resignation
or removal, should happen; and if the remaining governors and
trustees should for three calendar months after any such vacancy,
neglect or omit to elect a proper person to be governor and trustee,
it should be lawful for such of the inhabitants of the township from
whence the vacancy or vacancies was or were to be filled, as should
be assessed to the church and poor, for £10 a year or upwards, to
elect such governor and trustee, governors and trustees, to fill up

the vacancy or vacancies so neglected to be supplied, such previous
notice being given of the time and place of such election as therein
mentioned, and the then right of election should be in the majority
of such inhabitants assessed as aforesaid, who should attend such
meeting; and it was further enacted, that it should be lawful for
the governors and trustees, by indentures executed by all the
governors and trustees, or twelve of them at the least, in the presence of, and attested by two or more credible witnesses, to make
any grants, demises or leases, of any parts of the trust premises,
(except the workhouse in Halifax, during the time the inhabitants
in Halifax should choose to use or enjoy the same in manner thereinafter mentioned), to such person and persons as should at any
public auction, within the town of Halifax, of which one month's
notice at the least, should be previously given, as therein mentioned,
be the highest bidder, or offer to give the greatest yearly rent for
the same, so as every such grant, demise or lease be executed by
all the governors and trustees, or twelve of them at the least, and
be not made to continue for a longer time than twenty one years,
to take effect in possession and not in reversion, or by way of future
interest, and be made without taking any fine, premium or foregift;
and after reciting, that several parts of the trust estates were very
conveniently situated for building upon, for the use of the inhabitants
of the parish of Halifax, and on some parts of such trust estates,
very old houses and other buildings were standing, which were subject to frequent repairs, It was enacted, that it should be lawful for
the governors and trustees, by indenture under their hands and seals,
duly executed by all the governors and trustees for the time being,
or twelve of them at the least, in the presence of and attested by
two or more credible witnesses, to demise any such parts of the trust
estates not built upon, as might appear to the governors and trustees,
or twelve of them at the least, to be fit and proper to grant and
lease out for the purpose of new building, and also such parts of
the houses and other buildings then or thereafter to be erected on
the trust estates, as might appear to the governors and trustees, or
twelve of them at the least, to be fit and proper to lease out, for
the purpose of effectually repairing, re-building, or new-building
the same, (the said workhouse in Halifax excepted during the time
before in that behalf mentioned,) yet nevertheless so as the lands or

buildings to be leased should be let by public auction, after one month's notice thereof as aforesaid, and the highest bidder or bidders should be the lessee or lessees thereof, and so as every such lease be executed by all the trustees or twelve of them at the least, and be made for such number of years, not exceeding ninety-nine, for the purpose of re-building, or erecting new buildings, and not exceeding forty-one years, for the purpose of effectually repairing any part of the trust estates, as to the governors and trustees should be thought reasonable, with full power for them, from time to time in like manner to renew the same, or any subsisting lease or leases, so as all such leases be made to take effect in possession or immediately after the determination of the then subsisting leases, and so as every such lease be made without taking any fine, premium or foregift in respect thereof, and so as in every such lease there be contained such conditions as therein mentioned; and that it should be lawful for the governors and trustees to sell and convey such part of the trust premises within the township of Halifax, as they should think proper, for the scite of a new church, and for a convenient churchyard to be enjoyed therewith, in the township or parish of Halifax, for such prices as the trustees should think fit, and to sell and convey such parts of the trust estates, for the making any public roads within the township or parish, as the governors and trustees for the time being, should think proper; and also to sell and convey any such small parts of the trust estates unto and in order to accommodate any private person or persons, who were or might be owners of estates adjoining to the trust estates and premises, or any part thereof, and for such prices as the governors and trustees should think fit; provided, that no one such sale to any one owner of adjoining or contiguous estates, contain more than one hundred square yards of ground, to be annexed to any such adjoining or contiguous estate; and that all the governors and trustees, or twelve of them at the least, should agree to such sales and execute such conveyances, and that all sums of money received by the governors and trustees, as the price of such parts of the trust estates, should be by them either applied and disposed of in such manner as is thereby directed, concerning the rents and profits of the trust estates and premises, or otherwise, at the election of the trustees, be laid out in the purchase of other lands or hereditaments, within the parish of Halifax, and be conveyed and settled to the same uses as the trust estates; and it was enacted, that the workhouse given by Nathaniel Waterhouse, should, so long as the overseers of the poor of the township of Halifax should think fit, be a workhouse for the poor of the township of Halifax only; and that the overseers of the township of Halifax should pay to the governors and trustees, out of the poor rates, the yearly rent of £10 for the same, which rent should not be varied; but in case the overseers should be desirous to quit the workhouse, and discontinue to use the same as a workhouse, then it should be lawful for the governors and trustees to demise the same as the other parts of the charity estates; and it was further enacted, that one of the governors and trustees should be president, governor and treasurer for one year; and that the governors and trustees should each in his turn be president, governor and treasurer; and that every new-elected governor and trustee should be invested with power to act in the trusts without having the trust estates conveyed to him, until the number of governors and trustees in whom the trust estates should be vested should be reduced to five, and then so soon as conveniently might be after such reduction, the trust estates should be conveyed to the use of themselves, and such new-elected governors and trustees; and that it should be lawful for the governors and trustees, or the major part of them, at any public meeting, whereof fourteen days' notice should be previously given, to make such regulations and orders for better executing the powers vested in the governors and trustees, and regulating the charity and management of the trust estates, as to the governors and trustees, or such majority, should seem meet; and that two books should be kept by the governors and trustees, in one of which should be entered all regulations and orders made respecting the charity; and in the other should be fairly entered, all receipts, payments, and disbursements respecting the trust estate, and the affairs thereof; and that the accounts of the charity should be settled and passed by the governors and trustees, on the first Wednesday in March annually, at which time, or within twenty-one days after, all and every the clergymen, receiving or taking any benefit or interest under the will of Nathaniel Waterhouse, and also the churchwardens and overseers of every of the townships, and also any two or three of the inhabitants of every township, should have liberty to examine and inspect the said books and accounts, from ten in the forenoon till four in the afternoon; and that the balance on settling the accounts should be paid in the manner before directed, except £40, which it should be lawful for the governors and trustees to retain and keep in hand, to answer such future payments as might from time to time become due before the next rents of the trust premises should become payable.

"Since the passing of the Act of Parliament, the trust has been managed by governors and trustees elected in the manner thereby directed, and the estates have been conveyed in the manner prescribed from time to time, and regular meetings of the governors and trustees are held twice a-year, at which the accounts are examined and passed.

"The governors and trustees are in possession of the several estates and property mentioned or referred to in the act of Parliament, with the exception of some parts that have been sold or disposed of under the authority of the clauses or provisions contained in the Act with reference to that subject.   A rental of the property in the occupation of tenants, with the names of the tenants, has been supplied by the clerk of the governors and trustees, and from this it appears that the rents for the year 1826 amounted to £1,181. 3s. 4d. As to the course of letting and management, it may be stated, that the directions of the Act are followed, and it is represented, that the property is all let for its full annual value, or at least, that the several parts of it have been let on the best terms that the governors and trustees at the time of letting could obtain.

"Some small parts of the property have at different times been sold, and buildings have been given-up for streets for the improvement of the town; and the wood, of which there is a considerable quantity growing on that part of the estates which is situate in Skircoat, is sold from time to time when fit to be cut.   It has been the course to carry the produce arising during each current year from the sale of property which has been sold, and of the wood, to the general yearly account of the trust, and to apply the annual funds both to the purpose of answering and defraying the general exigencies of the trust, and carrying into effect the charitable purposes mentioned in the will, and also to the purpose of making such buildings and improvements upon the trust estate as the governors have considered necessary or proper, and the annual surplus, which as directed by the Act of Parliament, is payable to the overseers of the poor of the ten several townships, is divided and paid to them in the proportions mentioned in the Act, and applied to the maintenance and relief of the poor of the several townships, with their poor rates.

"As to the several charities mentioned in the will of Nathaniel Waterhouse, we find that the specific annual sums directed by the will to be paid to the preachers at the different chapels, and for the free grammar school, together with the augmentations thereof respectively, directed by the act, and the annual sums payable to the churchwardens and overseers of the poor of Huddersfield and Mirfield, and for repairing of highways, are annually paid, without alteration in amount; but as to the maintenance or repairs of the almshouse, and the house or school for orphan children, and the support of those institutions, the governors and trustees finding the allowance made by the act insufficient, have not confined themselves to that allowance, but have laid out annually such sums of money as appeared to them necessary or fit to be expended upon those objects.

"The almshouse was rebuilt in 1812 or 1813 with money arising from the sale of timber, and it is occupied by twelve poor widows, who are usually appointed on the recommendation of the overseers of the poor of the several townships from which they are directed by the will to be taken, and they receive each of them an allowance of £2 a year, and are supplied with gowns. The house for children usually called the Blue Coat Hospital, is kept up as a workhouse and school for the habitation, maintenance, employment and training up of orphan children, viz. ten boys and ten girls, chosen from the places mentioned in the will, and the allowance for their maintenance is regulated by the governors and trustees, with reference to the price of the necessaries of life, and is at present about £80 a year; and the expense of clothing the almswomen and the children amounts, on an average, to about £50 per annum. The profits arising from the children's work constitute the emoluments of the master, who has them under his care; and the lecturer attends to the catechizing of the children and admonition of the almswomen.

"The accounts of the charity are annually made out by the clerk of the governors and trustees, and settled and passed by them, and liberty is given to examine and inspect them, as directed by the act of parliament.

"It appears to us, on the examination of this charity, that so far as concerns the several specific charitable payments and objects mentioned in the will of Nathaniel Waterhouse, the trust is duly performed; and indeed with reference to the almshouse and the hospital for orphan children, the governors and trustees have contributed more largely out of the income arising from the trust estates than was, perhaps, without further legislative authority, in strictness justifiable. As the surplus income of the trust estate, after providing for the charitable payments and objects mentioned in the will, and the augmentation directed by the act, is payable to the overseers of the poor of the several townships, for setting to work and providing for the poor of those townships in the same way in which funds raised by a poor rate are applicable, we apprehend, that the administration of this trust beyond what relates to the specific charities mentioned in the will, is scarcely within the scope of the enquiry which we are authorized and required to make, and that a more enlarged statement has perhaps already been made than was necessary, for explanation of what concerns the individual charities mentioned in the will. It may be proper, however, to add, that as some topics of complaint and animadversion, respecting the administration of the trust and management of the property, were presented to our notice, we deemed it expedient at the time, and were induced, by consideration of the combined nature of the trust, to investigate its management in a general way, and to examine and bring to the consideration of the governors and trustees, the several objects of animadversion which had been suggested to us, imparting to them such observations on various points, as the occasion appeared to us to require; and it may be proper to state, that although some recent improvements of the trust property, on which there has been a large expenditure, appear to have been injudicious and the expenditure thereon has been unproductive of an adequate return, and a different mode of letting part of the property, and greater attention to economy in some branches of expenditure, may perhaps be properly recommended, and in an equitable point of view some method should be adopted of applying the periodical produce from the sale of wood, so as to equalize, during successive years, the surplus annually divided among the overseers of the poor of the several townships, we have not discovered any real grounds of inculpation, on the score of misconduct, wilful neglect, or inattention on the part of the governors and trustees."

SMYTH'S CHARITY SCHOOL.

"*John Smyth*, formerly of Heath, esquire, by his will, dated in 1726, reciting that he had built a school at Halifax, devised the same to the governors of Mr. Waterhouse's charity there, and their successors, for them from time to time to elect such a schoolmaster as should be approved of by his son, John Smyth, and his heirs, or such persons as should thereafter be owner or owners of his estate at Halifax, to be upon every vacancy nominated and put into the school by him or them, to teach six poor boys or girls whose parents pay no assessments therein, to read; and he gave to the governors, and to their successors, a house in Halifax, then let at the yearly rent of £4 in trust, to let and dispose thereof as would be most advantageous, to any person, other than the schoolmaster for the time being and to pay the rents and profits thereof to such master, for teaching six poor boys or girls as aforesaid, there to be placed by the governors, or the major part of them, with the advice and assistance of the churchwardens and overseers of the poor there, if desired : And he abrogated that his devise to the governors, in case they should ever suffer the schoolmaster to live in the said school, or schoolhouse, for so long a time as they should permit him to inhabit either of the said houses : And he devised to his son, John Smyth, a farm in Reavey, held by lease, for a term of which there were eighty years to come, (the lease expired in 1806) upon trust during the lease, to pay 40s. per annum, to the vicar of Halifax; for preaching two charity sermons, and catechizing the boys or girls taught in the school; (and he desired the churchwardens of Halifax to go about the church, when such sermons should be preached, to collect charity for the benefit of the poor children in the school;) and also, upon trust, to pay other 40s. a year for buying bibles and religious books for the children.

"The school built by the testator having fallen into decay, was rebuilt in 1821, at the expense of £100 raised partly by savings of income, and partly by subscription.

"The premises devised by the testator consist of a house in Northgate, let to Timothy Netherwood, as yearly tenant, at £8, 15s. a year, and a small tenement or warehouse adjoining, let to Robert Mitchell, as yearly tenant, at £1. 10s. a year, and the whole is let at the fair value.

"The following funds also belong to the charity; viz.—£100, secured on the tolls of the Halifax and Wakefield turnpike road, at interest of five per cent. and £50 secured on the Halifax water-works, at interest of five per cent., which funds are supposed to have arisen from money collected at charity sermons for the school, and £21 on the security of the waterworks, at the same interest, being a legacy bequeathed by Dr. Legh, formerly vicar of Halifax.

"The total income is £18. 16s. a year; and of this the sum of £8. 6s. a year, made up of £7. 5s. which was formerly the rent of the houses, and £1. 1s. the interest of Legh's legacy, is paid by the governors to a schoolmaster appointed by them, for teaching as free scholars, six children to read and write; and the surplus of £10. is appropriated to supplying an allowance of 16s. a year to the schoolmaster, for every child beyond the six, whom he instructs in the same way; and the whole of it, except a small sum occasionally deducted for repairs of the school, is applied in making such allowance. The school is properly conducted and attended to.

THE FREE GRAMMAR SCHOOL AT SKIRCOAT.

"By letters patent of Queen Elizabeth, bearing date 15th February 1585, her majesty, at the suit of the inhabitants of the parish and vicarage of Halifax, for the bringing up and teaching of children and youth of the said parish and vicarage, and other villages and hamlets near adjoining, ordained, that there should be a grammar school, to be called the Free Grammar School of Queen Elizabeth, for the bringing up of children and youth in grammar, and other good learning, to consist of a master and usher, and to be under the direction of 12 governors, to be chosen from the discreetest and honestest men dwelling within the parish and vicarage of Halifax;

and the governors were thereby incorporated; and it was directed, that when any of them should die or dwell out of the parish or vicarage, the survivors should elect others, from other meet persons dwelling within the same, being of the age of 24 years and upwards, and failing such election within one month from the time of any vacancy, then the Archbishop of York, with the consent of two of the governors, should have the power to fill up the vacancy; and the governors were thereby empowered to choose and appoint a master, who should have been a student in one of the Universities of England for the space of five years at the least, to be presented to and approved of by the Archbishop of York; and it was ordained, that failing such election of a master, within six months from the vacancy, it should be lawful for the Archbishop to nominate and appoint a fit person qualified as aforesaid, to the office of master; and the governors were also thereby empowered to appoint and admit an usher, taking to them the master, to judge of the sufficiency in learning and aptness of the usher, so that the election were made within one month after the place of usher should become void; and power was also given to the governors, to make ordinances in writing, for the government of the master and scholars, and possessions of the school, the same being allowed under the seal of the Archbishop of York.

"In consequence of neglect to appoint new governors to fill up vacancies, their number was reduced in 1726 to one, and a question arose, whether the corporation was not dissolved; but on application to the crown, a new charter, dated 7th July 1730, was granted, incorporating as governors, certain persons nominated by the Archbishop of York, and confirming in all respects the former charter, and the number of governors has since been regularly kept up.

"The property belonging to the school has been derived partly from gifts of the Earl of Shrewsbury, and other benefactors, and partly from purchases made with funds raised by subscription of the inhabitants of Halifax, for the school, and it consists of the following particulars;—

Situation and Description of Premises.	Number of Acres.	Present Occupants.	Annual Rent.	Observations.
At Skircoat :—	A. R. P.		£. s. d.	
A school, dwelling-house, garden and offices	.. .. ..	The Rev. John Wilkinson master of the school	0 0 0	Rent free.
Four closes of land adjoining the school, containing 16½ days' work, equal to about..	11 0 0	Ditto	27 0 0	
At Ovenden :— A house and farm called Hutt Farm	8 2 32	James Sutcliffe....	12 12 0	Let from year to year.
In Northowram :— A house and 14½ days work of land, called North Field Gate Farm about	10 0 0	Jos. Midgley.......	42 0 0	Ditto.
In Stansfield :— The Hartley Royd estate, containing 158½ days, or about 102A. 2R. 23P., and an allotment on Stansfield waste of 14A. 1R. 27P., thus divided, viz.				The wood is stated to be all in a thriving state, and likely to become very valuable, care having been taken by the governors to keep up a succession of timber. There has been no fall for the last 30 years.
Woodland, about	40 2 0	In possession of the Governors..		
Three farms, with houses and outbuildings, about	62 0 23	John Barker, Widow Barker, Jas. Greenwood in severalty	89 9 6	
Part of the allotment.	0 1 16			
Part of the allotment .	14 1 11	Unoccpd. at present		Let from year to year

Also two water-course rents of four guineas and five guineas per annum, paid by the owners of land adjoining the above estate, for the use of parts of the stream of the river Calder, and another stream called Harkley Clough .... £9 9s.

These rents are payable under leases granted by the trustees in 1802, and 1806, to Anthony Crossley and Richard Naylor, for securing the enjoyment of the respective water-courses, for terms of 999 years, subject to be determined on the water to be restored to its ancient course.

RENT CHARGES, &c.

		£. s. d.
Payable under the gift of Robert Saltonstall, in 1593, out of a tenement, called Brooke, in Hipperholme	.. ..	1 0 0
By the will of Benjamin Thornhill, in 1598, out of Almonroyd Close, in Lightcliffe	Sir Joseph Radcliffe, Bart............	1 0 0
Quit-rent under gift of Robert Wade, for land in Sowerby.	Richard Stansfield, Esq...............	2 10 0
Under gift of Nathaniel Waterhouse, out of his charity estates	Trustees of Waterhouse's Charities....	4 0 0

Total income £157 0s. 6d. per annum.

The farms are all let at their full annual value, and the rents are received by a steward or receiver appointed by the governors.

The governors pay to the master of the school a salary of £80 a year, and the residue of the rents, after providing for ordinary annual repairs of the school buildings, and those on the trust estates, and other necessary outgoings, is deposited, by the governors, in the bank of Messrs. Rawson & Co. in Halifax. Interest is allowed on cash balances in the bank, and added to the principal, and at the time of this inquiry the fund accumulated amounted to £643 and upwards.

"The school is conducted as a free grammar school for the instruction of the sons of the inhabitants of the parish of Halifax, in grammar and classical learning, the only qualification required on admission being, that the boys should be able to read a little in the English testament; and the scholars are instructed in other branches of education on moderate terms. The present master was appointed in 1788, and the average number of free scholars at a time, since his appointment, has been about 35. The master has also several boarders in his house, with whom the free scholars are instructed. The school appears to be creditably and satisfactorily conducted.

"The governors used to appoint an usher, but that practice was discontinued in the time of the late master, in compliance with his desire to receive himself the usher's salary, and provide an assistant of his own appointment, and the same course has been since followed.

"The object of the governors in accumulating the surplus rents, is represented to be the making of improvements on the school property, the principal improvement in contemplation being that of making a road through the woods on the Hartley Royd estate, to unite the three farms with the Burnley turnpike road; which it is represented would very considerably increase the annual value of that property. The governors have half-yearly meetings to manage the business of the trust, and settle the accounts; but they appear to us to have been somewhat remiss in not having had a survey and estimate made of the contemplated improvements, to effect which the fund accumulated is already probably more than sufficient. The good circumstances of the present master have probably been the cause why the governors have not taken into their consideration the propriety of advancing his stipend, to which no addition appears to have been made for upwards of thirty years; but it appears to us, regard being had to the amount of the revenues, and to the services of the present master, that he has a fair claim to a very considerable

N

increase of salary, and that however commendable it may be to provide for the future prosperity, in point of revenue, of the charity, that object has in this instance obtained too exclusive a degree of attention, at the expense of him who is to be considered principally interested in the trust property, as tenant for life."

By the Statutes which are said to have been drawn up by the Rev. Dr. Hayter, successively Bishop of Norwich and of London, it is ordained,—

That none shall be chosen schoolmaster of this school, who is not well affected to the present settlement in church and state, has not been a student in one of the Universities of Oxford or Cambridge for five years at least, and during his stay there conducted himself with discretion and sobriety, diligently pursued his studies, and is well skilled especially in Grammar, and the Latin and Greek tongues.

The master on his election, is to be presented to the Archbishop of York, to be licensed to teach school by his Grace.

And shall take an oath before the president governor and governors, that he will instruct the youth of this school, in religion, learning, and good manners, and will be faithful and careful for the good of the school in all things belonging to his office and charge, according to the trust reposed in him.

And for the improvement of his scholars in learning, he shall in the most familiar manner teach them grammar, and the Latin and Greek tongues, by reading to them all or some of the Classic Writers, which follow,—as in Latin, Phœdrus' Fables, Cornelius Nepos, Cæsar's Commentaries, Terence, Livy, Tully, Ovid, Virgil, and Horace,—and in Greek, the Greek Testament, Xenophon, Isocrates, Demosthenes, Hesiod, Homer, and Sophocles. And he is strictly charged, to make his scholars, according to their age and capacity, perfect grammarians, and not to carry them on too hastily from prose to verse, or from latin to greek, and especially to be constant and strict in the examination of their exercises.

These duties by the master thus performed, yet lies there upon him at least the duty of informing his youth in *good nature and good manners, which are of themselves an ornament to good learning*. We adjudge it, therefore, a part of the master and usher's duty, respectively to instruct their scholars to reverence their betters in all places; to be courteous in speech to all men; in their apparel always cleanly; and in their whole carriage joining decency with modesty, and good manners with good learning.

No one shall be admitted as a scholar, upon any pretext whatever, unless he be able to read English tolerably well, and be promoted to the Accidence. And for the admission and teaching of every scholar of the town and parish of Halifax, of what condition soever, NOTHING SHALL BE DEMANDED.

Both the Eton and Westminster grammars are used.

Mr. Staincliffe, who received his education at this seminary, left £100 to repair the school.

Brian Crowther, of Halifax, by his will dated the 9th September 1606, bequeathed to the governors, to the use of the Free Grammar School, an annuity of £20, issuing out of lands and tenements, within the manor of Armyn, to be paid half yearly, for ever, by even portions.

Thomas Milner, Clerk, Vicar of Bexhill, in Sussex, formerly fellow of St. Mary Magdalen College, in Cambridge, by will and codicil, bearing date in 1722, gave to the said College, a reversionary grant of £1000, for the maintenance of three bachelor scholars, till masters of arts or fellows, to be chosen from the schools of Heversham, Halifax, and Leeds.

And in the year 1736, Mrs. Mary Milner, his sister, added £200 to his benefaction, to be applied by the College to the same uses.

A scholarship is now about £40 a year.

Among the eminent men, who have been educated at this school, may be enumerated:—John Milner, B. D., the learned divine. Dr. Cyril Jackson, the late venerable Dean of Christ Church. William Jackson, D. D., his brother, late lord bishop of Oxford. The Revd. Edward Ellis, M. A., the present second master of Westminster School. The Revd. Mr. Sharpe, the present Vicar of Wakefield.

SOMERSCALE'S CHARITY.

"*Richard Somerscale*, by will, dated 17th March 1622, devised his estates in Halifax and Ovenden, in the occupation of the persons in the will named, to six trustees, in trust, after deducting the

N 2

necessary charges for repairing the buildings on the estates, and other disbursements in defence of the trust, to distribute the yearly rents and profits among the poor and needy of the towns of Ovenden and Halifax, at the discretion of the trustees and their heirs, and of the churchwardens of the said two towns for the time being.

"By an agreement of the trustees, acting on behalf of the townships of Halifax and Ovenden, dated in 1644, it was arranged that such part of the charity estates as lay within the township of Halifax, should be held and appropriated to the use of the poor of Halifax; and that such parts as lay within the township of Ovenden, should be appropriated to the poor of that township, and this agreement and division have ever since been acted upon.

"The property in the township of Halifax consists of a messuage, barn, and 7a. 2r. of land, and also two small tenements in the town of Halifax, and is let to William Fletcher, as yearly tenant, at the rent of £36 per annum, being the full annual value.

"For many years previous to 1813, the estate was under the management of the churchwardens and overseers, and the rents were applied in aid of the poors' rates; but in pursuance of an order of the court of Chancery, made on a petition presented for the purpose in that year, by some of the inhabitants, five new trustees, four of whom are now living, were appointed, and a conveyance of the estate was made to them by the heir at law of the last surviving former trustee. The rents have been regularly received by the trustees, but owing to the expenses incurred in the proceedings in Chancery, and consequent thereon, and the outlay required to put the buildings and fences on the farm, which have been much neglected, into proper condition, there has been hitherto little or no surplus left for distribution; there was a balance, however, in the hands of the trustees, in October 1826, of £14 9s, which it was intended to distribute among the poor at Christmas following, together with the rent which would then become due.

It appears, from the account of the receipts and disbursements of the trustees, from the time of their appointment, that the receipts, including the rent which would be due at Christmas 1826, amounted to £403 14s. 10d. and the disbursements altogether to £353 5s. 10d. leaving a surplus of £50 9s. to be distributed as above mentioned.

"The property in Ovenden appropriated to the poor of that township, consists of a farm-house, barn, outbuildings, and 16 days' work, or between 11 and 12 acres of land, and is under the management of four trustees chosen as vacancies occur, by the survivors, from inhabitants of Ovenden. The premises are let to Joseph Wilson, as yearly tenant, at a fair annual rent of £20, and the rent is distributed, yearly, on Christmas day, at the chapel in Ovenden, among poor persons of the township, not receiving parochial relief, at the discretion of the trustees.

HOPKINSON'S AND CROWTHER'S ALMSHOUSES AND SCHOOL.

"These almshouses and school, which are situate near the old church, in Halifax, were originally founded, as appears by an inscription in front of the building, by Mrs. *Ellen Hopkinson*, and Mrs. *Jane Crowther*, for the residence of 18 poor widows of Halifax, and a master to teach poor children, and consisted at first of twenty rooms only, but they have been rebuilt at the township's expense, and contain at present 24 apartments, 21 of which are appropriated to the use of as many almswomen, and three to the use of the school-master and school.

"No provision appears to have been made for the support of the almswomen: but by custom, an allowance has been made to them out of the church-rates, and they now receive out of that fund 2s. 6d. each, once a month, and a gown once in two years. They are appointed by the churchwardens, being usually poor widows of the township.

"The sum of £100 appears to have been given by Mrs. Jane Crowther for the school; and in satisfaction thereof, a rent-charge of £5 a year was granted by Thomas Lister, by deeds dated the 16th May, 1657, out of a farm in Southowram, called Haines, now the property of Mrs. Prescott. This rent-charge the master receives, and also the interest on £160 secured on the rates for lighting and paving the town of Halifax, with interest at £5 per cent; but we are not informed from whence the latter fund arose. The master instructs the poor children who reside in the almshouse, (each of the widows being permitted to take a child to reside with her,) and the poor children sent to school from the workhouse by the church-wardens.

ALICE CROWTHER'S CHARITY.

"*Alice Crowther*, by will, dated 12th October 1722, devised a cottage, outhouse and four other cottages, situate in the Dean Clough, in Halifax, unto Joshua Mercer and Timothy Scholefield, and their heirs, in trust, to distribute the rents and profits among poor housekeepers and other poor people within the town and town-ship of Halifax, having no relief from the township.

"Of the premises devised three cottages only now remain, which are occupied as almshouses for poor persons put in by the church-wardens and overseers.

"A fourth cottage, which was standing in 1792, appears, from a memorandum in the overseer's book, to have been sold and taken down about that time, in order to make a road to a mill belonging to Messrs. Waterhouse, of Halifax; but to what purpose the purchase money was applied is not stated, and cannot now be ascertained.

"The charity has long been under the management of the church-wardens and overseers, the repairs of the cottages being provided for out of the township rates.

BRIAN CROWTHER'S CHARITY.

"*Brian Crowther*, by will, dated 9th September 1606, devised to John Favour, then vicar of Halifax, and other trustees, a yearly rent of £10, out of messuages and lands in Armyn, to be yearly distributed amongst the poor of the town of Halifax, at the discretion of the vicar and churchwardens, and three other honest and sufficient persons of the town.

"By indenture, dated 16th August, 9th Charles 1st, the rent-charge was, with the consent of divers of the inhabitants in Halifax, released to Sir Arthur Ingram the elder, and Sir Arthur Ingram the younger, and in lieu thereof, a yearly rent-charge of the same amount was granted by them to Henry Ramsden, then vicar of

Halifax, and others, their heirs and assigns, out of two messuages and two water corn-mills, in Siddall, Southowram, and Skircoat, or some of them, payable at Michaelmas and Lady-day; and the rent-charge is paid in respect of the Flour Mills estate, belonging to the Marchioness of Hertford, and distributed by the churchwardens yearly, among poor persons of the township of Halifax.

"The yearly sum of £6 15s. is also paid out of land in Halifax, called Goldsmith Grave Closes, being a rent-charge secured by an indenture, dated 4th January 1654, and granted in obedience to a decree of commissioners of charitable uses, in satisfaction of certain arrears of the former rent-charge.

"This annuity is paid by the owner of the premises charged to the overseers of the poor, and has hitherto been applied in aid of the poors' rates, but the amount will in future be distributed with the annuity of £10.

BATES'S GIFT.

"The yearly sum of 20s. is mentioned in the benefaction table for Halifax, to have been given by *Brian Bates*, out of an estate in Blackledge Steel (called Yeathouse) formerly the property of Sir Watts Horton, of Chadderton, bart., by whom the payment was made for many years. There are entries of the receipt of the payment in the overseer's account book, down to the year 1813, since which time it has not been received. The estate is now the property of Captain Rhys, who married the only daughter of Sir Watts Horton, but is stated to be in the possession of J. B. S. Morritt, esquire, as mortgagee, and an application has been made to the agent of that gentleman on the subject of the charity.

HAWORTH'S AND TURNER'S GIFTS.

"The sum of 20s. a year, given by *Alice Haworth*, to the aged and impotent poor of Halifax, is paid as a rent-charge out of houses in Halifax, called Parkinson's houses, the property of Holroyd

Spencer, esquire, and is distributed accordingly; and the sum of 40s. a year given by *John Turner*, for bread, to poor prisoners in Halifax gaol, is paid out of premises in Back-lane, formerly called Cheapside, in Halifax, belonging to Nathaniel Waterhouse, esquire, and is applied according to the intent of the donor.

BOWCOCK'S CHARITY.

"*Isaac Bowcock*, by will dated the 11th February 1669, gave to the townships of Halifax and Ovenden, his lands in Osset, that the rents might be yearly bestowed by his feoffees in the will named, being seven in number, 'for preferring and putting forth five poor men's sons to trade, yearly, as are not to be put forth town prentices, or for the relief of such as are in necessity, not through wasteful expense, or such as have relief from the parish or for setting up in trade, or stocking hopeful young persons to make good use of it, at the discretion of the said trustees, and that £6. thereof should yearly be given to Ovenden.

"New trustees of this charity have been appointed from time to time, the last appointment being in 1825.

"The charity estate consists of a farm called Osset Street Side, comprising a house, a barn lately erected, and a garden, croft and some closes of land, containing, in the whole, 23A. 3R. 26P.

"The farm is let to Timothy Wheatley and Charles Wheatley, on lease, for 29 years from the 2nd February, 1826, at the annual rent of £60; and, by a lease dated 13th January, 1826, the trustees also demised to the said Timothy and Charles Wheatley, the upper or top bed of coal underneath the farm, (except the buildings, garden and croft,) for the term of 29 years, at the yearly rent during the first $10\frac{1}{2}$ years, of £35 per annum, for half a statute acre of coal, whether wrought or not; and in case of the lessees getting more than half an acre, then at the rate of £70 an acre for all the coal taken; and also at the rent, during the last eighteen years of the term, or until the whole of the coal should be gotten, of £70 for every statute acre of coal whether taken or not; and in case the lessees should get more than one acre of coal during the last eighteen years, then, during those years, at the rate of £70. an acre for every acre of coal dug or taken.

"The lease of the farm was granted for the above-mentioned length of time, in order to enable the lessees to work the coal, and the land has been let, and the coal sold on proper and advantageous terms, for the benefit of the charity.

"Previous to 1826 the farm was let for £60. a-year, which was the full annual value.

"Out of the rents of the charity estate are paid the following yearly sums : viz. £6. distributed among poor persons of Ovenden ; £3. for the expense of a dinner for the trustees and their assistants ; and £1. 5s. 6d., or thereabouts, as an allowance to the deputy constable and overseer of the poor, for assisting the trustees in the selection of proper objects for the charity, and for other necessary expenses ; and the remainder of the rents is distributed among poor people of the township of Halifax, not receiving parochial relief, in sums varying from 1s. to £1.

"The accounts are settled by the trustees at a yearly meeting. It has never been usual to apprentice children, or set up young persons in trade by means of the charity.

"It is proposed to invest the money arising from the sale of the coal in the purchase of stock, and to distribute the annual dividends with the rent of the farm ; and, when a purchase of land can be made with advantage to the charity, to apply so much of the stock as may be necessary in effecting such a purchase ; and it appears to us, that such a scheme is proper to be carried into effect.

TOWNSHIP OF HIPPERHOLME-CUM-BRIGHOUSE.

THE FREE GRAMMAR SCHOOL.—SUNDERLAND'S CHARITY.

" *Matthew Broadley*, of London, gentleman, by will, dated 15th October, 1647, devised to his brother, Isaac Broadley, and his heirs, his tenements, with the appurtenances, in Hipperholme, provided he pay out of the same, yearly, £5. per annum towards the maintenance of a free school, to be erected near Hipperholme, where his executor should appoint ; and he gave, towards the erecting of the said free school, the sum of £40 ; and he gave to his nephew,

Matthew Broadley, £1,000, provided that he should bestow £500. thereof, partly upon settling a convenient yearly means for the said free school, and partly in providing 52s. in bread, yearly, to be given by 12d. each Sunday, at Coley Chapel, to the poor of Hipperholme town, and the Lane Ends; and he constituted the said Matthew Broadley sole executor, and made Mr. John Drake, of Brazenose College, in Oxford, overseer of that his will.

"By indenture, dated the 22d May, 1661, reciting the will of Matthew Broadley, and that the said Matthew Broadley, the nephew, having received the said sum of £1,000, and being willing to perform the will and good intention of Matthew Broadley, deceased, had with the advice and consent of William Farrar, Esq.; John Lake, clerk; Abraham Mitchell, Stephen Ellis, Richard Langley, Nathan Whitley, Joshua Whitley, Joseph Hargreaves, Henry Brighouse, John Scholefield, and Joseph Lister, being principal inhabitants in Hipperholme and Halifax, contracted with Samuel Sunderland, for the purchase of the messuages, lands and hereditaments therein mentioned, for £500. bequeathed by the said Matthew Broadley, for settling a convenient means for the said free school, and for providing 52s., to be given in bread, yearly, according to the tenor of the said will; it is witnessed, that the said Samuel Sunderland, in consideration of the said £500. granted and enfeoffed unto the said Matthew Broadley, and William Farrar, and others above named, their heirs, &c. two messuages, with the appurtenances, in Hipperholme, two barns, two stables, two gardens, two folds, and all the lands and hereditaments to the said two messuages belonging, and one close in Lightcliffe, called Brookroyd, then made into three closes; another close called Highroyd Ing; another close, called Heyroyd Ing; and a yearly rent-charge of £11, issuing out of a messuage at Brookfoot, in Southowram, with the lands thereto belonging; and a water corn mill, at Brookfoot, which had been granted by deed, dated the 15th February, 1650, as therein mentioned; and another yearly rent-charge of £1 10s. issuing out of the messuages, lands and hereditaments, in Shelfe, in the county of York, therein mentioned, which rent-charge had been bought by the said Samuel Sunderland, as therein mentioned; all which said messuages, lands and annuities, were then together of the clear yearly value of £25, to hold the same to the said Matthew Broad-

ley, William Farrar, and others, their heirs and assigns, upon trust
to dispose of the said messuages, lands, rents, and premises, at the
best yearly value, so as no lease of the premises should exceed
twenty one years in possession, or at least not above two years
before the expiration of the old leases thereof, and that at the ancient and accustomed rents; and upon trust, to apply the rents and
income of the premises and annuities, as well for the yearly payment of 52s. at the chapel of Coley, by 12d. to be laid out in bread
every Sabbath day, for the most poor, aged, and impotent people
of Hipperholme and the Lane Ends, or so many of them as the said
Matthew Broadley, &c. should think meet to be relieved therewith
so as at no day there should be under the number of four poor persons to have the weekly allowance, and also for the maintenance
and keeping in repair of the school-house for the said free school,
to be erected and established in or near the town of Hipperholme;
and to employ the residue of the yearly rents, profits and income,
together with the annual sum of £5, issuing out of the tenements
of Isaac Broadley, in the will mentioned, for the maintenance and
wages of a learned and sufficient person, being a graduate of the
degree of bachelor of arts at the least, of one of the universities, to
be schoolmaster of the said free-school, to educate and instruct in
grammar and other literature and learning, the scholars and children
of the township and constablery of Hipperholme-cum-Brighouse,
only, gratis, and without any other reward: and it was thereby
concluded and agreed, that every increase of the rents and profits
of the said premises, should be employed for the maintenance of
the schoolmaster, except that the expense of any suits or other
trouble concerning the premises, should be deducted out of the
yearly profits; and that whenever the place of schoolmaster should
be void, the trustees for the time being, should, within one month
after such avoidance, by writing under their hands and seals, appoint
another learned and fit person, qualified as aforesaid, in the room
of such schoolmaster; and in case of their not appointing a schoolmaster within two months after such avoidance, it should be lawful
for the vicar of Halifax for the time being, by writing under his
hand and seal, to appoint a fit person, qualified as aforesaid, to be
schoolmaster; and it was thereby agreed, that the schoolmaster
should be allowed, ordered, directed, placed or displaced by the

said Matthew Broadley, &c. according to such rules and orders as should be appointed and made by the trustees, or the survivors of them for the time being, or the greater number of them, for the rule and government of the said free school, schoolmaster, and poor people, under their hands and seals, in writing; and that such rules should be binding upon all persons concerned; and that the trustees, or the greater number of them, should have power to visit the schoolmaster, and reform all abuses in the school, or in the schoolmaster or poor people; and that whensoever there should be but three of the trustees living or resident within the township of Hipperholme or vicarage of Halifax, the three survivors, together with the non-residentiaries of the said trustees, should convey the rents and premises to nine other sufficient persons inhabiting in Hipperholme, or the vicarage of Halifax, to the use of such nine persons, and of the survivors and residentiaries of them the trustees, so as there should be at least six of the trustees inhabitants of Hipperholme, upon the trusts above declared.

"By an inquisition, dated the 29th August, 1662, under a commission of charitable uses, it was found, that the testator, Matthew Broadley, had made his will to the effect aforesaid, and that the sum of £40 in the will mentioned, had been laid out in erecting a free school; and that the sum of £500 had been laid out upon lands for the maintenance of the same: and that the sum of 52s. part thereof, was bestowed weekly in bread at Coley Chapel; and that the lands and tenements, in the will mentioned, came to the possession of Isaac Broadley, but he had not paid the said sum of £5, to the use for which it was intended, in respect that the free school was not erected until Michaelmas then last past; and by the decree of the commissioners in the commission named, it was ordered, that the several sums of £40. and £500. disposed of according to the will of the said donors, should stand firm for the maintenance of a schoolmaster, to teach the said free school within and for the township of Hipperholme, whereof 52s., be laid out in bread, to be given by 12d. on each Sunday at Coley Chapel, to the poor people of Hipperholme and the Lane Ends; and that the said charitable gift of £5. per annum, should be kept up for ever; and that the said Isaac Broadley, his heirs and assigns, should pay unto Wm. Farrar, John Lake, Abraham Mitchell, Stephen Ellis, Richard Langley,

Nathan Whitley, Joshua Whitley, John Scholefield, Henry Brighouse, Joseph Hargreaves and Joseph Lister, feoffees, for the use
of the free school, nominated and appointed by the commissioners,
the yearly sum of £5. for ever, towards the maintenance of the free
school, to be paid out of the rents and profits of the lands and
tenements in Hipperholme aforesaid.

"By indenture, dated 30th. June, 1671, Samuel Sunderland,
of Harden, in the parish of Bingley, Esquire, enfeoffed and granted
unto Richard Hooke, vicar of Halifax, Stephen Ellis, Richard
Langley, Nathan Whitley, Joshua Whitley, William Brook, and
Joseph Lister, their heirs, &c. a messuage, part whereof was converted into a school house, and the buildings, gardens, lands and
hereditaments usually occupied therewith in Hipperholme, in the
occupation of John Coates : and also another messuage, with the
buildings, lands and hereditaments, commonly occupied therewith
at Norwood Green, within the township of Hipperholme-cum-Brighouse, in the occupation of Samuel Waddington, to the use of the
said Samuel Sunderland, for life ; and after his decease, as to the
said messuage, lands and hereditaments in Hipperholme, in the
occupation of John Coates, to the use of the schoolmaster for the
time being, teaching a free grammar school within the said school-
house for the township of Hipperholme-cum-Brighouse, the same
schoolmaster being thereunto lawfully licensed, and being of the
degree of bachelor of arts, at least, provided that the said schoolmaster should pay forth of the profits of the said lands and tenements,
the yearly sum of £6. to an usher master, to be nominated by the
feoffees therein named, and their successors, and to be lawfully
licensed and admitted thereunto ; and as to the messuage, lands
and premises at Norwood Green, in the occupation of Samuel Waddington, to the use of the most indigent poor people of and within
the township of Hipperholme-cum-Brighouse, the yearly rent thereof
to be distributed unto the said poor people, on the feast days of St.
Thomas and St. John the Baptist, at the school-house, by the
minister, churchwardens and overseers for the poor within the chapelries of Coley and Lightcliffe ; and to the intent, that as the seven
feoffees should by death be decreased to two, the survivors should,
within three months afterwards, appoint the vicar of Halifax for
the time being, if not one of the surviving feoffees, and six of the

most discreet inhabitants of the township of Hipperholme-cum-Brighouse, or seven, if the vicar be one of the two surviving feoffees; and that the two surviving feoffees should, at the request and costs of the said minister and churchwardens of the said chapelries, convey the said messuages and premises unto the said seven persons so nominated, and the survivors of them, for the uses above mentioned; and that the same order for electing of feoffees, &c. should be observed as occasion should require; and that the feoffees should take care, that the buildings and fences upon the lands should be kept in sufficient repair.

PARTICULARS AND RENTAL OF THE PROPERTY :—

Property.	Tenant and Term.	Rent.	Remarks.
		£. s. d.	
Under Broadley's gift, in Hipperholme township, & hamlet of Lightcliffe :—			
House and land, 3 acres .	James Batty, year to year..	20 0 0	
Cottage	John Naylor, year to year.	5 5 0	
Cottage .... {	Richard Mitchell, year to year.............. }	5 6 2	
Cottage	Nat. Hirst, year to year .	2 12 6	
Cottage .... {	Thomas Illingworth year to year }	2 12 6	Part of the property, leased by Sir Joseph Radcliffe, being one acre less by about 900 yards, has been taken for the Huddersfield and Bradford turnpike road; the compensation to be paid is not yet settled, but is expected to be about 100l.
Cottage ....:	Wm. Gray, year to year ..	2 12 6	
Building used for a Sunday School .... {	Wm. Priestley, as trustee, year to year .... }	3 10 0	
In Lightcliffe :—			
Four closes, being the property formerly called Brookroyd, Hieroyd Ing, and Allenroyd Ing Ida. .... {	Sir Joseph Radcliffe, bart under lease for 900 years from 2nd February, 1657, granted by Samuel Sunderland, the donor .... }	6 0 0	
Rent charge of £5 mentioned in the will of Mr. Broadley .... {	Paid out of estate at Lane Ends, Hipperholme, the property of Miss A. Walker }	5 0 0	Recognized in a deed respecting the property, dated the 16th of April, 24 Charles II.
Rent charge of £11 a year {	Paid by William Barnshaw, owner of the property charged.... }	11 0 0	
Rent charge of £1 10s. a year .... {	Paid by Mr. Greenwood, of Leeds, owner of the property charged .... }	1 10 0	
Under Sunderland's endowment :—			
1st for master, &c.			This last lot, in the occupation of Joseph Brook, was let in 1806 for £14 a year. In January, 1827, it was let for 20l. a year, the sum of 190l. having been laid out in buildings, &c. arising from surplus rents, and money from sale of wood. It was afterwards let at 30l. a year but the tenant left the property in very bad condition; it was necessary to turn him out by ejectment, and the suit cost about 100l.
The school-house, with a cottage, barn, garden & 7 closes, containing altogether, 17A. 3R. 11P. {	Rev. Richard Hudson, master of the school	Rent free worth about £90 a year	
A house, barn, & garden, and 2 closes, containing altogether, 2A. 1R. 23P. now called Helliwell Syke .... {	Richard Woodhead, year to year....................	full value 13 2 0	
2nd. for the poor.			
A dwellinghouse, barn & 7 closes, containing, in the whole, 15A. and 17P. called Birks close Farm and situate at Norwood Green .... {	Joseph Brook, under lease for 11 or 14 years, at £28 a year. This lease was granted about two years ago }	28 0 0	

"The school estates were last conveyed to new trustees in 1824.

"The property which is in the occupation of tenants, is let for the full annual value.

"The rents and income of the school estates and property are received by the agent of the trustees, and are paid by him to the master of the school.

"In 1804, some coal, under part of the school property, was sold for £705, part of which was laid out in converting an old malt-kiln and barn into cottages, and the remainder, amounting to £437 0s. 3d. was placed and remains in the bank of Messrs. Rawson and Co., of Halifax, at interest, and the interest is paid to the master. It was the intention of the trustees to lay out the fund in a purchase of land, and the money was placed in the bank, to be ready for that purpose.

"The school has been kept up as a grammar school by the masters for the time being, with the assistance of an usher, appointed by the master, and properly qualified to instruct boys in the elements of a classical education; boys of the township of Hipperholme cum Brighouse being admitted as free scholars, to be instructed in Greek and Latin. The school has also been attended by boarders or foreigners the number of whom has at different times been very considerable; but, since Midsummer 1826, the master, who is of advanced age, has discontinued to receive boarders. The boys are also instructed in writing and accounts, by masters for that purpose; the charge for such instruction to the free scholars being 1s. a week, for writing and arithmetic, and 9d. a week, for writing only.

"It is represented, that the number of free scholars has been frequently from 20 to 40; and that at the time of this enquiry there were about 20 attending the school: but that number, we apprehend, exceeds what may be fairly considered the fair average attendance of scholars at the present time.

"Some complaint has been urged as to the management of the school in this particular, that the boys entitled to the freedom of the school are not instructed gratuitously in writing and arithmetic, and instances are referred to, as having occurred, of boys of the poorer class not having been required to pay for such instruction; allowing, however, that such instances have occurred, we find no reason to conclude, that the school has ever been conducted in the main otherwise than as a regular grammar school ; and regard being had to the conduct of it, and more particularly to the footing on which it was placed as a grammar school, by the deed of 1661, and the recognition of such its establishment by the decree of the commissioners of charitable uses, it appears to us that the school cannot otherwise be properly conducted than as an institution for teaching the superior branches of education in the usual way, and that the master cannot be required to supply gratuitous instruction in such elements of knowledge as are not properly subservient to that general purpose.

"As to that part of the property at Norwood Green, now called Berks close Furze, which was given by Samuel Sunderland, by the deed of 1671, to the use of the most indigent poor people of and within the township of Hipperholme-cum-Brighouse, we find that it had been let for a term of 200 years, which expired in 1806, at £8 a year ; that in 1806, the rent was advanced to £14 ; that in January 1807, the sum of £120, arising partly from the sale of wood, was laid out in buildings, &c., and the rent was advanced to £20 a year ; and that some time afterwards the farm was let for £30 a year, but that the tenant having mismanaged the property, and refusing to give up possession, a considerable expenditure was incurred in law charges to recover possession, and a further expenditure was made in buildings and repairs ; and that there was due at the time of this inquiry, to the executors of the late James Lister, esquire, who was one of the trustees, and to another person, for money advanced for the above purposes, the sum of £86. 8s. 1½d. Notwithstanding the advance of the rent, the trustees have never distributed more than the old reserved rent of £8 a year among the poor since the expiration of the term of 200 years, the management of the trust having been involved in considerable difficulty, and attended with considerable loss. It appears to us, from the accounts exhibited, and the explanation given on the part of the trustees, that the loss has not been occasioned by neglect or misconduct of the trustees for the time being, although they have not held regular meetings at stated times, as they ought to have done."

BROOKSBANK'S GIFT.

"*James Brooksbank*, by will, dated 25th January 1706, gave the yearly rent-charge of 6s. 8d. out of a messuage, with the lands and appurtenances thereto belonging, at or near Norwood Green, in the township of Hipperholme, payable at Midsummer and Christmas, by equal portions, unto Samuel Riddlesden and Eliezer Tettley, their heirs and assigns, upon trust, to distribute the same to the poorest inhabitants in and about Norwood Green, most in need.

"This annuity is paid out of a farm, the property of John Holland, in the occupation of William Rhodes, and is regularly distributed.

WHITLEY'S GIFT.

"By indenture, dated 3d February, 32d Charles 2d, reciting that *Thomas Whitley*, by will dated 17th November, 7th Charles 1st, gave to the poor of the township of Hipperholme £40, to be distributed amongst them, by Francis Oates, Michael Whitley and John Whitley, all then deceased; and that the interest thereof having been neglected to be distributed, the inhabitants of the township had applied to Sir John Armitage, bart. and others, the commissioners under a commission of charitable uses, who, by decree, dated 29th August 1662, had decreed that Joseph Fournish, and Phœbe his wife, and Judith Whitley, Richard Law, and Esther his wife, and Grace Whitley and Joshua Whitley, and Thomas Lister, should pay to the poor of Hipperholme £40 and three years' interest, to be kept as a stock, the interest thereof to be distributed, yearly, amongst the poor people there, with the assistance of the churchwardens and overseers of the said town; and further reciting, that neglect having been made in payment of the said interest, and thereupon complaint having been made to the said court, a writ of subpœna, in the nature of a *scire facias*, had been granted against the persons therein named, to show cause why they should not perform the said decree; and further reciting, that the said Samuel Lister, Joshua Whitley, James Oates and Benjamin Law, being served with copies of the said writ, and having inquired after and informed themselves concerning the truth of the premises, and being rather inclinable to promote so charitable a gift, and having met together, had agreed to perpetuate the said charitable gift out of their own estates equally, not knowing they had any assets belonging to the said legacy in their hands; it is witnessed that the said Samuel Lister, for his part of the said sum of £40, and in pursuance of the said decree, granted unto Richard Langley, Stephen Ellis, Jonathan Priestley, and six others, therein-named, their heirs and assigns, a yearly rent-charge of 10s. out of a messuage called Kirktrees, in Lightcliffe, with the ground thereto belonging, payable at Martinmas, with power of distress, to the intent that the said yearly sum of 10s. should be yearly distributed by the said Samuel Lister and others, on St. Thomas's day, at the Free School at Hipperholme, to the poor people of the said township, with the assistance of the churchwardens and overseers of the town; and if none of the trustees should be present before the hour of ten o'clock on the said day, then by the churchwardens and overseers; and also to the intent, that when the feoffees should by death be decreased to the number of two, the survivors should, with the assistance of four of the principal inha- bitants of the township, appoint seven of the most able and discreet inhabitants within the township, and assign the rent-charge of 10s. unto the said seven inhabitants, and the surviving feoffees, in trust for the use above-mentioned.

"It does not appear that the residue of the yearly interest of the gift of £40 was charged or secured in a similar manner, with the sum of 10s. a year, secured by the above deed, but the payment of the whole interest of the £40 has been usually made as a rent-charge issuing out of lands, in the proportions and out of the estates following; viz.—ten shillings a year out of an estate called the Harby Head, in Hipperholme, now the property of John Walker esquire; 10s. a year out of the Yew Tree Farm, in Hipperholme, now the property of Captain Lister, both which payments are regularly made; and £1 a year which used to be paid out of a farm called Dearden's farm, in Hipperholme, now the property of Mrs. Susan Holroyd, widow of the late Mr. Joseph Holroyd, and which was purchased by her husband from Mr. John Dearden, in 1814, but since the time of the purchase, the sum of £1 a year has not been paid.

"The money paid has been duly distributed by the churchwardens, and overseers of the poor, amongst poor persons of Hipperholme-cum-Brighouse.   We have applied to Mrs. Holroyd, respecting the sum of £1 a year, formerly paid out of her property, and have intimated to her, that the payment ought to be resumed and continued.

GIBSON'S GIFT.

"*Michael Gibson*, esquire, left by will, dated 17th April, 1731, the sum of 1s. a week, to be distributed in bread every Sunday, among twelve poor persons resident in Hove Edge and Upper-lane, by the minister and chapelwardens at Lightcliffe chapel.

"The yearly sum of £2 12s. is charged on an estate called Pear Trees, in Lightcliffe, and the money is duly distributed in bread by the churchwardens.

SUTCLIFFE'S GIFT.

"The Rev. *Richard Sutcliffe*, by will, dated in 1782, gave 20s. a year to William Walker, esquire, of Crow-nest, and the minister and chapelwardens of Lightcliffe, and their successors, to be by them distributed to 20 poor persons, not receiving parochial relief, at Lightcliffe chapel on Christmas day.

"This yearly sum is paid in respect of an estate at Sheard Green, in Hipperholme-cum-Brighouse, belonging to the incumbent of Lightcliffe Chapel, having been purchased with Queen Anne's bounty, in 1749, and the money is duly distributed.

GLEDHILL'S GIFT, AND WILLIAM WALKER'S GIFT.

"*James Gledhill*, by will, dated in 1789, gave to William Walker, esquire, of Crownest, and his successors, the sum of £50, to the intent that one half thereof should be distributed in linen cloth to eight poor women, and the other half be applied to the use of the Sunday schools, but if the Sunday schools should be discontinued, it should be distributed to the poor at Lightcliffe chapel, on Christmas day.

"*William Walker*, of Crownest, esquire, by his will, dated the 19th August 1809, gave to his executors and trustees, and their heirs, an annuity, clear yearly rent or sum of £10, upon trust, that they or the survivors or survivor of them, and his heirs, should distribute the same at the chapel at Lightcliffe, on Christmas day, in every year, amongst such poor persons of the township of Hipperholme, as they should think fit: the sum of £2, part thereof, being the interest of £50 paid to him under the will of the late James Gledhill, and the residue thereof he declared to be a donation from himself; and he also charged his estates thereafter given to his brother John Walker, with the payment of the same; and as to all the remainder of his real estates, subject to the payment of his debts, annuities and funeral expenses, he devised the same to his said brother John, his heirs and assigns; and he appointed his brother John Walker, and his nephews William Priestley and John Priestley, joint executors of his will.

"The residuary real estates devised to the testator's brother, John Walker, are now the property of John Walker, esquire, son of the devisee, who is entitled also to the testator's personal estate, subject to the payment of debts, &c.

"The sum of £10 a year is regularly paid, and £8 thereof is distributed by the executors of the testator at Christmas day, among poor people of Hipperholme, in money or clothing, and the sum of 40s. a year, under Gledhill's gift, is applied, one half in linen, to eight poor women, and the other half to the use of a Sunday school.

LOST CHARITIES.

"We find that a *Mrs. Mary Bedford*, in or about the year 1735, gave £200 to a school at Brighouse, and that several proceedings were had, under a commission of charitable uses, concerning the charity; but on examination of the documents which exist relating to this subject, we find that the fund has been long irrecoverable.

"We also find it mentioned in Watson's History of Halifax, that *William Birkhead*, in 1638, gave £5 for charitable purposes in Lightcliffe and Hipperholme, and that in 1651, the money was in the hands of Samuel Hoyle, but of this charity we can obtain no further account.

TOWNSHIP OF OVENDEN.

BOWCOCK'S CHARITY.

"The yearly sum of £6 received for the poor of Ovenden, under this charity, of which an account is given among those for the poor of the township of Halifax, is distributed by trustees chosen for the township at Christmas, yearly, among such poor persons thereof, as have received no parochial relief within the year.

SOMERSCALE'S CHARITY.

"An account of this donation is given among the charities in the township of Halifax.

FOURNESS'S CHARITY.

"By indenture, dated the 3d June 1701, *Phœbe Fourness* enfeoffed unto William Illingworth and four other trustees and their heirs, a cottage in the township of Ovenden, and a parcel of common land, containing by estimation one acre, adjoining upon Somerscale's charity lands, upon trust, to pay the yearly sum of 10s. to some ecclesiastical person, as should every Sunday read divine service, and preach in Illingworth chapel, and to dispose of the residue of the yearly rents and profits of the premises amongst such poor persons, inhabitants of the township of Ovenden, as should frequent the said service and sermons on the feasts of Saint John the Baptist and Christmas day, yearly by equal portions; and it was directed, that when the trustees should be reduced to two, the premises should be conveyed to three, four, or more substantial persons, inhabitants of the township of Ovenden, upon the like trust.

"It does not appear, that new trustees were ever appointed, and it is unknown in whom the legal estate is vested.

"The cottage mentioned in the indenture is supposed to be the same with a cottage now divided into two tenements, in the occupation of Thomas Mitchell, and Thomas Robertshaw, in respect of which, the yearly sum of 10s. is paid to the minister of the chapel in Ovenden, but the same annual sum having been invariably paid by Mitchell and his ancestors, in possession of the cottage, he claims the property as his own, subject only to a fixed payment; and though little doubt exists as to the insufficiency of his title, from the small value of the property, and the expense of proceedings to recover it, an attempt to regain the cottage by process of law, would scarcely be warranted.

"The acre of land is let with Somerscale's charity land adjoining and is in effect treated as part of that estate.

POOR'S COTTAGE.

"A cottage at Swillhill, in Ovenden, understood to be given by *Isaac Walton*, for the poor of Ovenden, is at present occupied by poor people, put in by the overseers.

TOWNSHIP OF NORTHOWRAM.

THE FREE SCHOOL.

"This school, which is under the management of trustees chosen from the inhabitants, was established under the will of *Joseph Crowther*, in or about the year 1711, for the teaching of 12 poor children of Northowram, whose parents are least able to pay for their education, and its emolument consists of a school, dwelling-house and croft, in the occupation of the master, rent free; and a farm, comprising a house, barn, cottage, and 10½ acres of land, in the township of Northowram, let by the trustees to Abram Toodolf, as yearly tenant, at the rent of £21 per annum, which is the full annual value. The trustees out of the rent of the farm, pay a stipend of £16 a year to the master of the school, and he teaches 12 poor children, nominated by the trustees, as free scholars, to read, and instructs them in writing and arithmetic, on payment of a moderate quarterage, together with others, who attend as pay scholars.

"The stipend of the master was increased from £7 to £16 in

the year 1811, at which time the rent of the school estate was raised from £8 to £21, and the surplus rents have been since retained, for the purpose of making repairs and improvements on the farm and buildings thereon: these have been partly applied, and it is apprehended that the balance remaining in hand, which, at the time of this inquiry, was £20 14s. 11d., will not be more than sufficient for their completion.

"The account of the rents and expenditure is kept by one of the trustees, and examined by the others, at meetings held for the purpose.

HALL'S CHARITY.

"*Jeremiah Hall*, M. D, by his will, dated in 1687, directed two sums of £50 each, to be laid out by his executors and trustees, in purchasing ground in Booth Town, and erecting dwellings thereon, for two old men and two old women, natives of Booth Town, and a schoolhouse; and he gave the further sum of £100, and the sum of £230, then secured upon mortgage, to provide for the maintenance of the poor people, and for payment of a stipend of £5 to a person who should teach ten poor children, natives of Booth Town, in the school, gratis.

"This charity is under the management of twelve trustees. The almshouse and school, erected in pursuance of the testator's direction, were rebuilt about twenty-five years ago, and comprise four tenements for the almspeople, a school and house for the master; and the estates purchased with the funds given for the support of the almspeople and teacher, consist of the following particulars, and are let by the trustees, as follows:—

"1.—A farm called Moor Falls, in the township of Northowram, containing 14 acres of land, or thereabout, let to James Wood, as tenant from year to year, at £36 per annum.

"2.—Two farms in Ovenden, called Brockholes, one containing a house and 17A. 2R. 16P. of land, and the other a house and 12A. 2R. 12P. of land, let respectively to John Bancroft, and James Priestley, as yearly tenants, at rents amounting together to £78 per annum.

"3.—Two allotments on Ovenden Moor, containing together about five acres and a half, awarded about seven years ago.

"These allotments are held by the tenants of the farms in Ovenden, rent free, on consideration of their inclosing and bringing them into cultivation, which has been partly done.

"The farms are let for their full annual value. The trustees pay to each of the four almspeople, who dwell in the almshouse, and are chosen by the trustees, £10 a-year, and to a schoolmaster £28 a year, as a salary for teaching five poor children to read and write, and twenty-five others to read. The remainder of the rents has been retained for and laid out by the trustees in making some recent considerable repairs and improvements upon the charity estates, and as these are nearly completed, it may be expected, that the stipends of the almspeople will shortly be increased.

"The accounts are kept by one of the trustees, as treasurer, and are examined by the trustees at their meetings, held half-yearly.

TOWNSHIP OF SOWERBY.

THE ALMSHOUSES.

"*Elkana Horton*, of Thornton, in the parish of Bradford, by will, dated September 19th, 1728, after setting forth that he had erected six apartments at Sowerby for the habitation of three men and three women, born in the chapelry of Sowerby, and inclosed some ground before the same, to be divided into six gardens for their several uses, and a middle room, or oratory for their daily assembling in for prayers, he gave the same to the six men and women in the apartments and their successors, to be chosen by his trustees, and such other as their counsel should advise; and he willed, that the three men and three women should be of the age of sixty and unmarried, and remain so during the continuing in their apartments; and he gave unto each of the six two shillings and sixpence a month, to be paid to them at the end of each calendar month; and he willed that one of the three men should, twice every day, assemble the other five persons, by ringing a bell, and read a chapter out of the New Testament, and a proper prayer, to which reader he gave five shillings quarterly for doing it; and he willed, that so much of his real estate, or as much other estate be purchased, as would raise yearly sufficiently for paying the said allowances clear, and also keep the buildings in good repair for ever; and if more be set out than will do it, the overplus to be divided equally amongst the said six, and be settled in trust as counsel should advise.

"The almshouse mentioned in the will, consists of six small houses, and a building in the centre, called an oratory, and is inhabited by six poor persons, three men and three women, all unmarried, the almspeople being placed therein from time to time, by the occupier of the mansion and estate of Sowerby Hall, for the time being, which property belonged to the family of Horton, and now belongs to Captain Charles Rhys, of Bath, in right of his wife, who was the daughter and heiress of the late Sir Watts Horton, bart. The stipends of the poor people are paid by Mr. David Jennings, the present occupier, and are allowed to him by way of deduction from his rent, the sum of 2s. 6d. a month being given to five of the almspeople, and 4s. 2d. a month, to one of the men who read prayers to the rest.

"It is represented, that the almshouses and the oratory in particular, are very much out of repair, and require to be new roofed; that the windows want new leading, and that those in the oratory which are broken, are made or filled up with stones, and that the latter room is in such bad condition, that the reader cannot officiate in it.

"We find, that previous to the year 1819, when Captain Rhys came into possession of the property, the almshouses had been always kept in repair by the occupier of Sowerby Hall, and that the expense was allowed as a deduction from his rent, but that since 1819, when Mr. Kershaw became steward, nothing has been allowed for repairs, and that payment has been refused of a sum of £1 3s. which was laid out by Mr. David Jennings, in 1825, in rebuilding the chimney, and repairing a part of the roof, broken by the fall of the chimney.

"We have met with no evidence of any particular part of the founder's estate having been settled after his death for the support of the almspeople or the almshouses; but the liability to maintain the charity, appears to have been thrown as a charge upon the

Sowerby Hall property, and it appears to us, that in default of the due performance of that duty, recourse should be had to a court of equity for its directions, as to the maintenance of the charity, according to the intention of the founder.*

FOURNESS'S CHARITY.

"*John Fourness*, on the 19th October, 13th James 1st, surrendered to trustees, two cottages in Sowerby, to the use of three poor men of the said town.

"The two cottages are let to two poor families, at £2 and £2. 2s. a year respectively, being moderate rents. The rents have been usually paid to the overseers of the poor, and applied with the poor's rate; the expense of repairing the cottages, defrayed by the by the overseers. It seems to us, that the rents, after deducting the expense of repairs, should be separately distributed among poor persons.

BENTLEY'S GIFT.

"*John Bentley*, some time before the year 1651, gave £20, to be lent to four honest tradesmen of Sowerby-cum-Soyland, £5 to each, for four years together, providing sureties to repay the same, with interest.

"George Priestley, of Whitewindows, Esq. and the Rev. Robert Webster, of Ripponden, act as trustees of this charity. Loans are made of £5 each, and security taken for the same, by way of promissory note, with two sureties, and agreeably to the custom which has prevailed, three of the portions are advanced to inhabitants of Sowerby, and one to an inhabitant of Soyland.

* Since this Report was prepared, we have had a communication with Captain Charles Rhys, on the subject of the Charity, and he states, that as being the owner of the Sowerby Hall Estate, he will take care that arrangements shall be made with his tenant at Sowerby, for putting the hospital in proper repair, and for providing for the repairs in future.

GREENWOOD'S CHARITY.

"*Daniel Greenwood*, by will, dated 11th March 1672, charged his lands in Crowell Shaws, in the township of Sowerby, with the yearly sum of 40s. to the minister of Sowerby Chapel, and 40s. to the poor of the chapelry.

"These annuities are paid by Mrs. Clayton, the occupier of the property charged, and the sum of 40s. for the poor, is received by G. Priestley, esquire, and laid out by him in buying linen, which he distributes among about fourteen poor persons.

PAUL BAIRSTOW'S CHARITY.

"*Paul Bairstow*, by will, dated the 31st March 1711, devised a farm and lands, in the parish of Meopham, in Kent, after the decease of the persons therein named, unto John Tillotson and others, upon trust, to sell the same, and lay out the produce in the purchase of an estate of inheritance in or near the parish of Halifax; and he directed, that the trustees should stand seised thereof, upon trusts, out of the rents and profits, to pay to the master of the school at Sowerby the yearly sum of £16, for and in consideration of his teaching twelve poor children living within the chapelry of Sowerby, whose parents should not be worth, in real and personal estate, above £50, to be chosen by the minister and churchwardens, or chapelwardens, of the parish or chapelry; and also, that the trustees, out of the residue of the rents and profits, should repair the tomb of his father, Michael Bairstow, and Ann, his wife, in Sowerby church or chapel yard; and pay 20s. a year to the minister of Sowerby, for preaching a sermon on the feast-day of St. Michael the archangel; and distribute the remainder of the rents and profits, if any there should be, to and amongst such poor persons of the parish or chapelry of Sowerby, not receiving alms, in the parish or chapelry, as the minister and churchwardens, or chapelwardens, should direct; and be ordered, that the trustees should transmit the estate to be purchased down to posterity, subject to the trusts aforesaid.

"By indentures of lease and release, of the 28th and 29th April, 1735, reciting the will of Paul Bairstow, and that Henry Barrell,

the then surviving trustee, had sold the farm and lands in Meopham
for £630, which with £15 15s. more had been laid out in the
purchase of £600 South Sea annuities, and that the said Henry
Barrell had received out of the rents of the Meopham estate, and
from the dividends of the stock, and by sale of the stock, in all £831
and that he had agreed with John Stansfield, and Israel Wilde, for
the purchase of the messuages, lands, and hereditaments therein
mentioned for £660, and that by an account then stated and allowed
by the trustees, parties thereto, of all monies received and disbursed
it appeared that there was due to the said Henry Barrell, £171,
which with the said £660 amounted to £831; it is witnessed, that
for the considerations therein mentioned, the said Stansfield and
Wilson conveyed to the said Henry Barrell and George Stansfield,
and thirteen others, and their heirs, the premises therein mentioned
upon the trusts declared by the will, and upon trust, that when
nine of the trustees should die, the two last remaining trustees
should convey the premises to nine or more other trustees, to the
use of themselves and such nine trustees, and their heirs, upon the
same trusts, and so from time to time.

"By indentures of lease and release, dated 7th and 8th December
1804, reciting the will and previous indentures, and stating, that
a succession of fresh trustees had been appointed, and the real estate
so purchased had been conveyed; and that George Stansfield and
James Riley had become seised of the estates so purchased, and had
appointed the persons therein named to be co-trustees with them of
the said estate, the said George Stansfield and James Riley conveyed
unto the Rev. Joseph Ogden, and twenty-six others, and their heirs,
a messuage called Nether Headley in Thornton, in the parish of
Bradford, in the county of York, with the appurtenances and several
closes in Thornton, near the messuage, containing together, by
estimation, forty days work, and a piece of woody ground, called
the Clough in Thornton, near the closes, and a piece of ground
called Morton End, lately inclosed from the commons in Thornton,
containing 13 acres, and a piece of ground called the Upper Common,
lately inclosed from the commons in Thornton, containing eight
acres, with the minerals and appurtenances, to the use of the said
George Stansfield, James Riley, and Joseph Ogden and others,
their heirs, &c. upon the trusts of the will, with a proviso for con-

tinuing the trusts by election of twenty new trustees, when twenty of the said trustees should die or resign.

"Several of the trustees named in the deed of 1804 are now living.

"The property consists of the particulars, and is let in the manner following :—

"A farm house, two barns, some cottages, and certain lands called Headley, in the township of Thornton, the lands containing altogether 38A. and 37P., are let to Jonas Greenwood, as yearly tenant, at the annual rent of £90.

"An allotment of about twenty days' work, or 13 acres, in the township of Thornton, is let to Valentine Smither's, as yearly tenant at £12 per annum.

"An allotment of Moor land near Denholm Gate, in the township of Thornton, containing about eight day's work, or about 5 acres, is let to Valentine Smithers, at £1 a year.

"The whole of the property is let at its full annual value; but the two allotments would be greatly improved in value, if a small house and barn were erected upon each.

"There are beds of coal and stone under the estate at Headley, the value of which is not ascertained; but it is represented by the trustees that it would not be expedient at present to sell the coal for working.

"As to the application of the rents, we find that the sum of £16 a year is paid to the master of the school at Sowerby, who is appointed by the trustees, for teaching to read twelve poor children, chosen by the minister and chapelwardens, and that, after defraying the the occasional charges, of keeping the tomb in repair, and paying 20s. a year to the minister for a sermon, the residue of the rents is distributed in sums of 5s. a piece, by the minister twice a year, on the first Sunday in February, and the first Sunday in August, among poor people nominated by him and the chapelwardens and overseers, being such as have not received parochial relief in the preceding year; but of late years a portion of the rents has been retained for the purpose of repairs, buildings, and improvements, and there is a balance in hand of £147 19s.

"The school is now kept in a building which was erected in 1817, by subscription, for a Sunday school; but an old township school still remains, which is occasionally used by the master for the purpose of keeping up the right of possession : and there is a pew in Sowerby chapel, supposed to belong to the school, which the master uses for the boys whom he takes to chapel.

WAINHOUSE'S CHARITY.

"*Edward Wainhouse*, by will, dated September 18th, 1686, gave to the old people and poor persons of the town of Sowerby, such as did not receive allowance from the town, the yearly rents and profits of a house in Sowerby Dean, and he ordered, that the rents should be paid at Christmas to the overseers of the poor of Sowerby, and that they should take one or two of the heads of Sowerby, to see the distribution of the rents ; and he empowered the overseers, and one or two of the heads of the town, to let the house for the use of the said poor persons, as often as there should be occasion.

"The premises devised by the will, now consist of two cottages, at Style, in Sowerby, which are let at £1 16s. and £2 2s. a year respectively, being as much as they are worth.   The cottages are in a ruinous condition, but the site of them might be converted to a profitable purpose, if means were found of erecting new buildings on the ground.

"The rents (which however are occasionally in arrear) are distributed with the funds arising under Bairstow's charity.

LOST CHARITIES.

"*Thomas Foxcroft*, in 1617, gave £10 to be lent without interest on security.

"*Thomas Mitchell*, in 1621, gave £10 for a similar purpose.

"*Robert Brooke*, left a house at Hunslet, near Leeds, for the poor of Sowerby, the rents to be paid yearly, which house was sold for £10 and the money placed out at interest.

Of these charities no further account can be given, and the funds are lost.

TOWNSHIPS OF SOWERBY, MIDGLEY, & RISHWORTH.

WADSWORTH'S CHARITY.

"*Mary Wadsworth*, on the 14th May, 1793, surrendered a copyhold dwelling-house called Jack Hey, in Sowerby, with a cottage, and the buildings and appurtenances, and certain closes usually occupied with the messuage, containing together, by estimation, fifteen days' work, to the use of nine trustees, three of whom were of each of the townships of Sowerby, Midgley, and Rishworth, upon the trusts mentioned in an indenture of the same date, by which it was declared; that the trustees should distribute the rents and profits of the premises, after deducting necessary expences, as follows: one third part thereof, in equal moieties, on the first Sunday in May, and the first Sunday in November, yearly, amongst such poor persons resident and legally settled in the township of Sowerby, not receiving alms, or town's pay, and in such proportions as the trustees for that township should appoint; one other third part at the same time, amongst similar poor persons of the township of Midgley, as the trustees for that township should appoint; and the remaining third part on the same day, among similar poor persons of the township or hamlet of Rishworth, as the trustees for that township should appoint; and it was directed, that when the trustees in any of the townships should be reduced to one, the remaining trustees should elect other proper persons, inhabitants of such township, to be co-trustees with them, and convey the premises to the use of the remaining and new-elected trustees.

"On the 24th October, 1807, a new election of trustees having taken place, the estate was surrendered, and an indenture declaring the trusts thereof, was executed.

"The charity estate, which is properly described in the surrender, is let to John and Philip Pickles, as yearly tenants, at £21. per annum, which is the full annual value, and the rent is duly divided and distributed in the manner directed by the donor.

TOWNSHIP OF SOYLAND.

HOYLE'S GIFT.

"*Elkanah Hoyle*, by a codicil to his will, dated 28th March, 1718, charged a messuage and barn in Soyland, called Hollins, now the property of Henry Lees Edwards, esquire, with the payment of 40s. a year, to be distributed by John Hoyle, and his heirs, and the owner of Upper Swift Place, on Easter-day, yearly, among poor people of Soyland not receiving parochial relief : and he charged a farm at Lightazels, called Lower Hoyleheads, now the property of Henry Richards. esquire, with £3 a year, to be paid to the curate of Ripponden, for a Sermon on Ascension-day ; in default whereof the testator gave the said yearly sum to the poor of Ripponden during such neglect.

"The latter annuity is paid to the minister, but since the purchase of the Hollins by Mr. Edwards, which occurred about ten years ago, the rent-charge of 40s. has not been paid or distributed, Mr. Edwards having purchased, without notice of the incumberance ; the liability of the estate however being now shown, Mr. Edwards has consented to renew the payment of the rent-charge, that the charity may be continued."

BENTLEY'S GIFT.

"Of this gift an account is given among the charities of Sowerby chapelry ; and it may here be added, that the sum of £5, part of the charity fund, is advanced upon loan to a poor inhabitant of Soyland, and duly secured by a promissory note."

CHAPELRY OF HEPTONSTALL.

THE GRAMMAR SCHOOL.—GREENWOOD'S CHARITY.

"The Rev. *Charles Greenwood*, by a deed dated 14th July 1642, and by his will of the same date, made in execution of a power reserved by the deed, conveyed and appointed to John Greenwood, and four other trustees, and their heirs, a house built by him for a school-house, and two messuages and farms, in Colden, in Heptonstall, to the intent that after his decease, the house should be used for the purpose of a free grammar school, for the children of the inhabitants of the town and township of Heptonstall, and that the trustees, and the survivors of them and his heirs, should be seised of the two messuages and premises in Colden, to the use and maintenance of a schoolmaster, who had well profited in learning, to teach the children of the inhabitants of Heptonstall within the school-house.

"New trustees have been appointed from time to time, and the estates have been conveyed to them; the last conveyance however is dated in 1786, and there is occasion for the appointment of new trustees.

"The rental and annual value of the school property is about £77 a year, two tenements adjoining the school-room, in Heptonstall, being let at £8. 2s. a year, and the two farms in Colden, which, besides buildings, contain together 56¼ days work, or about thirty-four acres of land, being let to yearly tenants, at rents amounting together to £69 per annum.

"The rents of the property, after payment of expenses of repairs of the school premises and farm buildings, are paid to the master of the school. The school has always been and continues to be mainly conducted on the footing of a grammar school, and the sons of the inhabitants of the town and township of Heptonstall are instructed in the learned languages, as free scholars, and according to the master's account, the school has been long of great utility, in providing the means of suitable education for persons to whom some knowledge of the dead languages was requisite. Other branches of instruction are also taught on moderate terms, by an usher, employed for the purpose, and the school is attended generally by the children of the inhabitants of the chapelry, principally for instruction in English, reading, writing and arithmetic. The average number of scholars is from fifty to sixty, and at the time of this inquiry, seventeen boys were receiving instruction from the master in Latin, as free scholars.

PAUL GREENWOOD'S GIFT.

"*Paul Greenwood*, by will, dated the 4th April 1609, gave 20s.

P

a year to the poor of Wadsworth, and 20s. a year towards the maintenance of a preacher, being a master of arts at Heptonstall, out of a farm called Rawholme, in Wadsworth, now the property of Mr. John Crossley Sutcliffe.

"The sum of 20s. a year for the poor is distributed among poor persons of Wadsworth, by or under the direction of Mr. Sutcliffe, but there has been no preacher at Heptonstall of the degree of M. A. for several years, and the annuity for the preacher has not been called for, or paid for a considerable time.

NAYLOR'S GIFT.

"*Richard Naylor*, by will, dated the 6th May 1609, gave £3. 5s. a year, payable out of a messuage and lands in Mixenden, now the property of William Mitchell, esquire, one moiety for a preacher in Heptonstall, being a master of arts, who should preach a sermon on St. John Baptist's day, and the other moiety, or in case of there being no such preacher, then the whole for the maintenance of poor children of and within the parish of Heptonstall.

The sum of £3. 5s. a year is distributed under Mr. Mitchell's direction, among poor persons of the Chapelry of Heptonstall, a certain proportion being assigned to the poor of each township.

WALL'S GIFT.

"*Abraham Wall*, by will, dated 13th September 1638, gave £8 a year, part of an annuity of £20 payable out of houses and premises in Ironmonger-Lane, London, now belonging to the representatives of the late Mr. Alderman Boydell, to be appropriated yearly, as follows ; 20s. by the churchwardens of Heptonstall, for purchasing Bibles for poor men's children ; £4 for teaching poor children of Heptonstall ; and £3 for apprenticing one poor child, so taught, to a trade in London, the child to be chosen by the chapelwardens and vestry.

"The sum received under this donation, land-tax being deducted, is £6 8s. a year, of which the sum of 16s. 8d. is laid out in Bibles, which are distributed among poor children once in three years, and the remainder, as the object of putting out an apprentice in London, cannot, from the smallness of the sum, be carried into effect, is applied in obtaining instruction for poor children in reading and writing, by the usher, at the grammar school.

JOHN GREENWOOD'S GIFT.

"*John Greenwood*, of Learings, by will, dated in February 1687, gave out of a messuage in Stansfield, called Drew's Court, now the property of Mr. Jeremiah Horsfall, 40s. a year one half of it to the curate for a sermon on the first Wednesday in June, and the other half for putting out poor children of Heptonstall apprentices at the discretion of the chapelwardens and overseers, and the owner of Learings, for the time being.

"The annuity is applied to the purposes directed, the moiety for apprenticing being accumulated till a sufficient fund is raised for putting out an apprentice.

JOHN GREENWOOD'S GIFT.

"*John Greenwood*, of Hoppings, by will dated 13th December, 1705, gave out of a messuage and farm in Wadsworth, called Grimsworth, now belonging to Mr. Henry Pickles, 20s. a year, to the minister of Heptonstall, for a sermon on the first Wednesday in August, and 20s. a year to the poor of Stansfield, to be distributed in canvass cloth to those not having relief from the parish.

"These payments are made to the minister of Heptonstall and the overseers of the poor of Stansfield respectively, and 20s. a year is laid out by the latter in cloth, which is given to poor persons.

JOHN GREENWOOD'S CHARITY.

"By indentures, dated the 11th and 12th March, 1814, enrolled in Chancery, *John Greenwood* conveyed to the Rev. Joseph Char-

nock, and thirteen others, and their heirs, certain dwellinghouses,
called Mount-Pleasant, with the lands thereto belonging, and two
fields, called the Learing Commons, adjoining the former premises,
the whole containing, by admeasurement, 13A. 2R. 23P., in Heptonstall, upon trust, out of the rents and profits, after payment of
taxes, except window tax, charged on the premises to pay 1s. 4d.
per Sunday to a master, to be appointed by the trustees, to attend
in Heptonstall church, or any place near there, morning and afternoon, on each Sunday in the year, to teach four boys and two girls
to read, write and sing, till divine service commences, and the master and scholars to attend such service, both morning and afternoon
and to the scholars attending and learning the catechism, 2d a piece
each Sunday; and on being examined in the said church once every
year, by the minister thereof in the catechism, 6d. a piece; also,
to pay 8s. a year for coals, to be used in the room where the sunday scholars meet to learn; and 5s. shillings a year for lighting the
fire; and 5s. a year to the minister of the church to preach a sermon
yearly, on Whit-sunday in the afternoon, for a collection to be
made by the churchwardens, to buy testaments and singing books
for the use of the sunday scholars, and the singers of the church,
as the trustees should direct; and to pay to two instrument players
of music, to be appointed by the trustees, 2s. each, for attending
the Sunday scholars, and teaching them to sing, and attending
divine service with them; and for any default in the morning or
afternoon, to deduct 6d. for each default, such deductions to be
applied along with the collections to be made annually on Whitsunday; and £5 4s. a year to be laid out and distributed in bread each
Sunday in the church, by the minister and churchwardens equally,
to such twenty-three poor persons, and the sexton thereof as may
attend divine service; and to pay the sexton for annually cleaning
and keeping the monument legible on the wall, along the south
gallery in the said church, 2s. yearly; and one guinea annually as
a subscription to the singers of Heptonstall church; and to pay all
costs and charges of repairing or rebuilding the buildings on the
said premises, with power to the trustees to augment the allowances
or payments for the purposes aforesaid, as often as should be found
necessary in order to continue the same, and pay such augmentations
out of the rents of the trust estates; and upon further trust, to pay

the remainder of the rents and profits to the persons in the said indenture mentioned, provided that when there should be only five acting trustees, the vacancy should be supplied by the appointment of so many additional persons, being protestants of the church of England, as would make up the number of fifteen trustees, such appointment to be made by the major part of the protestants of the township of Heptonstall, with the consent and approbation of a majority of the surviving trustees, present at a vestry meeting, convened for that purpose.

"The several sums or payments to charitable uses, mentioned in the deed, amounting in the whole to £18. 13s. 6d. a-year, have been regularly paid since the death of the donor in 1823, by the trustees, out of the rents of the estate, and applied according to the directions contained in the indenture.

"The master of the Sunday school performs the duty enjoined, and a sermon is preached yearly, on Whitsunday, in aid of the charity.

"The sum of £5. 4s. directed to be laid out in bread, is applied by the churchwardens in a weekly distribution of loaves at the church every Sunday morning, among 23 poor persons, if so many attend divine service, each poor person receiving a cake or loaf. The surplus, if any, is given amongst the children attending the Sunday school.

TOWNSHIP OF STANSFIELD.—POLLARD'S DONATION.

"*Henry Pollard*, by will, dated in 1608, gave the yearly sum of £2 7s. out of a farm in Stansfield, called Jump's Farm, the property of Mr. Richard Naylor, 9s. thereof to the minister of Cross Stones Chapel in Stansfield, and £1 18s. to the use of the poor of Stansfield.

"These payments are duly made and applied.

CHAPELRY OF LUDDENDEN.

WATKINSON'S CHARITY.

"The Rev. *Edward Watkinson*, D. D. by deed dated June 2,

1732, conveyed to John Dearden, and Stephen Atkinson, and their heirs, a messuage with the appurtenances in Vicar Lane, Leeds, of the yearly rent of £4, and two cottages, with the appurtenances belonging to the said messuage, and standing in the fold adjoining, of the yearly rent of £1. 6s., and two cottages with the appurtenances, at Hunslet, in the parish of Leeds, of the yearly rent of £1. 10s. in trust, that they should, with the rents and profits, purchase twelve two-penny loaves, weekly, for the benefit of 12 poor widows; viz. six within the township of Midgley, and six within the township of Warley; and in default of such number of widows there, then for the benefit of the most necessitous persons in the said townships to be distributed by the chapelwardens of Luddenden, every Sunday in the year, soon after morning service; six of the widows or necessitous persons to be chosen out of the township of Midgley, by the chapelwarden of that township, and six of them out of the township of Warley, by the chapelwarden of that township, the poor to be personally present at the distribution of the bread, unless prevented by sickness or some bodily infirmity; and that each poor person should have, upon Trinity Sunday, 6d., and upon Sunday next before Christmas, 12d., and upon Easter Sunday, 6d., over and besides the bread; and the remaining clear yearly rent should be detained by the person who should take the trouble to collect the rents, and look after the said premises.

"There has been no conveyance of the property to fresh trustees since the execution of the deed above mentioned, and the charity is under the management of the minister and chapelwardens of Luddenden.

"The premises in Vicar-lane, in Leeds, now consist of a house and some cottages behind, and those at Hunslet, of six small houses. The whole property was held by a person named Whitehead, under a long lease, which expired about ten years ago, the rent being about ten pounds a year; and after the expiration of the lease, it continued to be held for some time by the representative of the lessee, at the old rent; and then the premises in Vicar-lane were let to James Kaye, by lease, for 21 years, at the rent of £21 a year, subject to a condition to rebuild, but that condition not being performed, and Kaye having become insolvent, the chapelwardens, in 1824, entered into an agreement with Joseph Pickering, to let the premises in Vicar-lane to him, on a building lease for 21 years, to commence the 1st May 1826, at the yearly rent of £21, on condition that he should previously rebuild that part of the premises which adjoined Vicar-lane, and the remainder of the premises within four years after the commencement of the lease; these terms being the best that could be obtained. The house fronting into Vicar-lane was built before the lease was executed, and the lease was executed in April 1826. The six cottages at Hunslet are let to different persons, at rents amounting to £13 16s. a year; but the tenants being poor persons the rents cannot be regularly or fully obtained, and the cottages being in bad condition, it would be expedient to let them on a building lease, which is intended to be done, when a proper opportunity arises.

"'There was no rent received for the Vicar-lane premises for one year previous to November 1825, and Messrs. Robert Midgley, and Thomas Kitchen the chapelwardens, advanced £10. 10s. each, for the continuance of the charity during the year 1825, and the sum of £6. 12s. 8d. received lately for rent of the Hunslet cottages, has been applied towards re-payment of the money advanced by them.

"Part of the rents of the property have been applied in buying bread for poor widows, distributed weekly in the church at Luddenden, and since the rent has been advanced, the number of widows has been increased to twenty, and such part of the reht as has not been applied in buying bread, has been distributed among the poor widows in money, on the days mentioned in the will, no charge having been made hitherto for collecting the rents.

CHAPELRY OR TOWNSHIP OF RASTRICK.

LAW'S CHARITY.

"*Mary Law*, by will dated February 4th, 1701, devised her real estates at Lower Woodhouse, and in Rastrick, to Thomas Hanson, his heirs, and assigns, and to the minister of Rastrick, and his successors, in trust, as to a messuage and tenement at Lower Woodhouse, to the maintenance of four poor widows, to be

chosen within the town and township of Rastrick, at the discretion
of the said Thomas Hanson and his heirs, and the minister of Rastrick, and his successors; and as to all the testatrix's messuages,
lands, and tenements in Rastrick, to the use of a school at Rastrick,
for teaching 20 poor children to read and write, to be chosen within
the town of Rastrick and Brighouse, at the discretion of the trustees
above mentioned.

"The present trustees are Messrs. John Pitchforth and Samuel
Freeman, as the husbands of the two co-heirs of Thomas Hanson,
and the minister of Rastrick.

"The property at Lower Woodhouse, which comprises a house,
barn, fold, garden, cottage, and about 5A. and 10P. of land, is let
by the trustees to James Iredale, as tenant from year to year, at
£18 a year, the full annual value, and the rent is divided equally,
and paid in pensions among four poor widows, properly selected by
the trustees. The property in Rastrick consists of a house, outbuildings. and 11A. and 39P. of land, let to John Preston at £28
a year, the fair value; two cottages, let at £9. 2s. a year, the fair
value; and two other cottages, lately erected by the trustees, and
not yet occupied, but worth, to let, about £14. a year.

"The trustees pay a stipend of £22..10s. a year to the master
of Rastrick school, for instructing 20 poor children of Rastrick and
Brighouse, nominated by the trustees, two thirds being usually
from Rastrick, and one-third from Brighouse, in reading and writing.
The number of free scholars is properly kept up; they are taught
arithmetic when required, on payment of a charge for such instruction, and are taught with other children, brought up at the expense
of their friends.

"The trustees have of late years expended the whole of the
surplus rents, and also a sum of money arising from the sale of stone
out of a quarry in a close, called the School Croft, in rebuilding
the school and farm-house, and one of the cottages, erecting the two
new cottages, and effecting other repairs and improvements by which
the value of the property has been greatly augmented. The
repairs are not quite completed, but it is expected that means will
shortly exist of increasing the stipend of the schoolmaster. Part
of the money produced by the sale of stone, amounting to £83 9s.9d.
was placed in the bank of Messrs. Brooks and Co. of Huddersfield,

who lately became bankrupts. Some dividend has been paid, and at the time of this induiry there was a balance of £5 or £6 only in the hands of the trustees.

CHAPELRY OF RIPPONDEN.—TOWNSHIP OF BARKISLAND.

THE FREE SCHOOL.

"*Sarah Gledhill*, by will, dated 13th October, 1657, bequeathed £200 to be laid out by her Executors in the purchase of lands to be vested in feoffees, in trust, to pay the yearly rents to a school-master in the town or township of Barkisland, to teach such number of poor children of the town and township to read English, and write or cast accounts, or further learning, as the feoffees and their heirs should think meet, and the funds would extend to.

The legacy was laid out in 1658, in the purchase of an estate at Gomersall, comprising a house, barn, and about 14 acres of land, which is vested by deeds, dated in 1822, in the Rev. Joshua Horton and William Horton, Thomas Norton, Francis Hackitt, and Nathaniel Wainhouse, esquires, the present trustees.

"The estate is let to——Wooller, by lease granted in 1807, for twenty-one years, at the yearly rent of £31 10s., and on the expiration of the lease may probably be let at £40 a year.

"The rent is paid with the sanction of the trustees, to the master of a school, kept in an ancient school-room at Barkisland, to which a dwelling-house for the master, a garden and play-ground are annexed. The dwelling-house, it is stated, was built about 40 years ago, at the expence of the late Mrs. Bold and Joshua Horton, esquire, the then proprietors of Barkisland Hall.

"Twelve poor children, the number determined by the trustees, are instructed as free scholars in reading, writing, arithmetic, and other branches of learning, and have the opportunity of being taught Latin when required, and the school is attended by upwards of 40 other children, educated at the expense of their friends.

DOLES AND RENT CHARGES.

Gifts.	Yearly Amount.			Property charged.	Application and Remarks.
	£.	s.	d.		
By will of Elizabeth Horton, 13th July, 1670, for the poor	5	0	0	The Pearce Hay farm at Barkisland, the property of P. Patten Bold, Esq.	Distributed according to the will ....
Ditto for minister of Ripponden, for a Sermon on Good Friday	5	0	0	....Do...............	Paid to the minister ..
By will of William Horton, 8th October, 1713, for poor of Barkisland.	1	10	0	Jackson's Ing, in Sowerby, the property of Mr. Clay	Applied according to the will ....
And for minister of Ripponden for a Sermon on the 24th of June.....	1	10	0		
By will of James Riley 8th May, 1723, for the poor of Barkisland....	1	0	0	Farm at High Moor, belonging to Sir George Armitage, baronet	Duly applied and distributed by the respective overseers of the poor ......
And for seven widows, or widowers, or poor persons of Sowerby..	1	0	0		

"Mention is made, in the returns of 1786, of a further donation of 30s. a year to the poor of Barkisland, under the name of Mary Turner's charity; and from Watson's History of Halifax, p. 556, the annuity appears to have been secured by a deed, dated 16th February 1743, enrolled in Chancery, out of a messuage on Stainland green, called the New Laith, and three closes of land, thereto belonging; but we do not find that the charity was ever paid, nor have we been able to ascertain the identity of the premises described in the deed, as charged with the payment.*

THOMAS GLEDHILL'S CHARITY.

"The sum of £170, given for the minister of Ripponden chapel, and £50, given for the poor of Barkisland, by the will of *Thomas Gledhill*, in 1656, were laid out in the purchase of a farm, consisting of a house, barn, and 11A. 3P. of land, and the rents thereof are appropriated, in due proportion, to the use of the minister and of the poor.

"The farm is let, by the minister of Ripponden, and the overseers of the poor of Barkisland, to John Wilson, as tenant from year to year, at the yearly rent of £34, being the fair value: and the sum of £10 a year, being the portion of rent for the poor, is distributed

---

* Watson says "the money is yearly distributed by the present owner of Howroyd. The original deed is at the seat of Sir Watts Horton, at Chaderton."

at Christmas, by the overseers and some of the principal inhabitants, among poor persons of Barkisland, not receiving constant parochial relief.

THE ALMSHOUSE.

"An almshouse in Barkisland, containing two tenements, occupied by two poor widows, has an endowment attached of £3 a year, issuing, as supposed, out of a farm called Cat Edge, the property of the family of Bold, and the annuity is divided between the widows; but no writings are known to exist respecting the origin of the charity, or the endowment.

CHAPELRY OF SOWERBY BRIDGE.

EDWARD WAINHOUSE'S CHARITY.

"*Edward Wainhouse*, by will, dated September 18th, 1686, gave to the old people and poor persons of the town of Norland, a messuage or tenement, called Butterise, in Norland; and he directed that the rents should be paid to the overseers of the poor of the town, and that they should take one or two of the heads of the town to the distribution of the rents, and that but a little thereof should go to those persons which should have allowances, or nothing at all of it; and he authorized the overseers of the poor, with one or two of the heads of the town, to let the messuage or tenement as often as need should require.

"The devised premises now consist of three cottage houses, and between two and three acres of land, with a barn, in Norland.

"The land, two of the cottages, and barn are let to Thomas Howard, as yearly tenant, at the annual rent of £17; and the other cottage to the overseers of the poor for the use of the township, at the yearly rent of £1 1s.; and the property is let at its fair annual value. The rent is distributed by the overseers of the poor, with the assistance of some of the inhabitants, among poor persons of the township of Norland, a preference being shown and larger sums given to such as do not receive parochial relief; from the sum distributed each time, however, a deduction of from 5s. to 10s. has been usually made, for the expense of refreshment allowed to the persons who attend at the distribution, with the overseers. Some allowance for refreshment is probably expedient, as an inducement to attend at the distribution; but an allowance to more than three persons, at the most, seems scarcely requisite for effecting the testator's object."

All the charities included in the foregoing Report, with one or two exceptions, are referred to by WATSON; but there are several Benefactions mentioned by that gentleman, which are omitted in the Report: these it will be proper to notice. Mr. WATSON's account is considerably abbreviated, but without altering the material facts.

CHAPELRY OF ELLAND.

FRANCES GRANTHAM'S BEQUEST.

Frances Grantham gave and bequeathed, by will, to the poor of Elland and Fixby, to be paid on Christmas day, yearly for ever, one shilling a piece to twenty poor men, and twenty poor women, and one shilling a piece to twelve poor boys: and to secure the payment of the money directed that fifty-two pounds should be placed in such hands as her sister Thornhill should think meet, that the interest thereof might yearly pay the same.

It is also said, that Mrs. Grantham gave ten shillings yearly to the poor of Elland, and the same sum to the poor of Rastrick and Fixby.

Joseph Brooksbank, citizen and haberdasher of London, by indenture, dated Oct. 4th, 1712, conveyed to trustees, a messuage or tenement, with a barn, an orchard, a yard, and a croft, containing one acre, in or near a street in Elland called the Westgate: and also four selions of land in a field at Elland, called Longmanslands, or Lowmost-town-field; and also four lands in the middle or Stainland-steel-field: and also four lands lying in the High-town-field: and two other lands, lying from Oyl Mabb-top; also six messuages or tenements at the west end of the town of Elland, in a street called the Town-end; also a messuage or tenement called the Little Upper Harper Royd, in the township of Norland, containing, by estimation, ten days work: in trust that the said trustees,

and the survivors and survivor of them, and the heirs and assigns
of such survivor, should permit a certain messuage or tenement in
Elland, (mentioned in the above indenture as having been in the
occupation of one Lawrence Manknowles, school-master, and intended by the said Joseph Brooksbank to be settled as for a free
school, for the educating and teaching forty poor children, boys
and girls, belonging to the town of Elland,) to be from time to
time, for ever hereafter, used and enjoyed as and for the school-
house of the said free school.   And should yearly out of the rents
and profits of the said messuages, lands, and premises, (after the
necessary charges in repairing and supporting the same should be
from time to time deducted) pay by equal quarterly payments, unto
a schoolmaster, for teaching the said forty poor children to read
the English tongue, till such time as they could readily read the
bible, and repeat without book the catechism, (commonly called the
assembly's catechism) the clear sum of ten pounds, without deduction.   And upon farther trust yearly to expend the sum of thirty
shillings in buying ten bibles and twenty catechisms, (commonly
called the assembly's catechisms,) to be yearly distributed amongst
the said forty poor children, in such manner as the major part of
the trustees, for the time being should think fit.   And if, after the
above-mentioned trusts should be fully satisfied and discharged,
there should out of the clear yearly rents, issues, and profits of the
said premises, remain in the hands of the said trustees more monies
than were sufficient to discharge the said trusts, and such necessary
charges of repairs as aforesaid, and after incident charges in execution of the said trusts, then upon farther trust to pay yearly the
overplus, if any, unto such schoolmaster, for the time being, as an
addition to his allowance, or salary, for teaching the forty poor
children above-mentioned, and for no other use, intent, or purpose
whatsoever.   And to the end the trusts mentioned in the said indenture might be the better performed, it was therein declared, that
the school-master of the said free school should be, from time to
time, chosen by the said trustees, or the major part of them ; and
that upon every vacancy of the schoolmaster's place, or office, by
death or otherwise, another school-master should by them be elected
within three calendar months next after such vacancy.   Also, that
the said trustees, or the major part of them, for the time being,

should have the sole power, of nominating and electing the said forty poor children, to be taught to read as aforesaid, and of removing or displacing the same, from time to time, and of putting others in the room of those who die, or are dismissed, or go away from the said school.   And also that in case the said schoolmaster should be negligent or careless in the discharge of his duty, or otherwise misbehave himself in his said office, it should be lawful for the said trustees, or the major part of them, for the time being from time to time to remove such schoolmaster, and to elect another in his room.   The said schoolmaster also, for the time being, was not at any time to receive or take any fee or reward from the parents, relations, or friends, of the said poor children, for or in respect of their being taught to read as aforesaid, (the wages, or salary thereby allowed him only excepted,) under the pain of forfeiting and losing his place or office of schoolmaster.   When the trustees were reduced to two or under, the survivor or survivors were to convey to others; and if at any time the trustees for the time being, should not be suffered to perform the trusts reposed in them, or the said school-master should in any wise be obstructed in the performance of his office, then, and in either of the said cases, the said trustees for the time being might, and they were directed and enjoined, to re-convey and assure the above messuages, lands, and premises to the use of the said Joseph Brooksbank, his heirs and assigns for ever.

FRANCES THORNHILL'S BEQUEST.

Frances Thornhill by will, dated July 31st, 1718, gave and bequeathed nine hundred pounds to be laid out to pious and charitable uses in the manner following; the sum of one hundred and fifty pounds, and the interest thereof, into the hands of the heir and chief of her family of Fixby, her nephew, Thomas Thornhill, Esq; to be the first trustee.   And her will was, that his heirs, being the principals of her name and family of Fixby aforesaid, should successively for ever be trustees to see the said one hundred and fifty pounds laid out in a purchase, for building or making a proper habitation for teaching and improving ten poor girls in spinning wool, knitting,

sewing, reading, and writing, and to be taught the catechism of
the church of England, and private prayers for them every morning
and night. And for the continuance of that her good intention for
ever, she devised four hundred pounds, being further part of the
said nine hundred pounds, to rest in the heir of Fixby's hands for
the time being, whom she desired to consult with the minister of
Elland for the time being, to chuse a proper master and dame to
teach and instruct the said ten poor girls; the interest of which
said sum of four hundred pounds to be annually laid out, and paid
for the salaries of the said master and dame, and maintenance of
the said poor girls, in such manner and proportion as the said heir
of Fixby, or trustee for that her charity for the time being, should
see proper and convenient. And the said testatrix's desire was
that the said poor girls might, from time to time, be chosen out of
the greatest objects of charity which should then be living in Fixby,
and the town and parish of Elland, so as the said school may be
preserved and kept up for ever for the purposes aforesaid; and that
the heir and owner of Fixby for the time being, should take great
care in his choice of a master and dame as aforesaid, for the good
teaching and looking after these ten poor girls, so that they may
have all necessaries provided for them, and that the said master
might read unto them the prayers of the church of England every
night after the girls gave over work. And the said testatrix also
devised two hundred pounds more, part of the said nine hundred
pounds, to rest in the heir or owner of Fixby land for the time
being, for ever, to the end that the minister of Elland, for the time
being, might receive the interest thereof, as an augmentation for
his better subsistence: and that in consideration of the said interest
to be paid to the said minister, he should read every morning, in
the church of Elland, the common prayers of the church of England
at six o'clock in the morning in summer, and at eleven o'clock in
the morning in winter, and the charity girls, with their master and
dame, might attend and be present at the said times and hours of
devotion: and in case the minister of Elland refused to attend and
read prayers, according to this request and intent, then the said
interest of the said two hundred pounds, designed for the minister
aforesaid, should go to the said poor girls, for their better maintenance and subsistence. Also, her will and mind was, that that

part of her will only that related to the charity school of Elland, and the minister of the same, should be read every Christmas-day in the morning, between prayers and sermon, in the parish church of Elland.

CHAMBERLAIN'S GIFT.

Thomas Chamberlain, of Skipton in Craven, who died October 29, 1721, gave by will twenty shillings per annum, for ever, to be distributed amongst four poor widows in Elland, by the minister and churchwardens, on the 6th day of June yearly; the payment whereof is charged on a house at the south end of Elland, belonging, in 1727, to William Chamberlain, salter, in Halifax.

RAMSDEN'S CHARITY.

Mrs. *Grace Ramsden*, of Hawksworth in Yorkshire, by will dated December 13, 1734, after bequeathing to the trustees named in her will, one clear annuity or yearly rent of three pounds ten shillings, and after the decease of certain persons mentioned in the said will, and failure of issue, one other annuity or yearly rent of thirteen pounds, issuing out of several tenements in the parish of Bingley, and reciting that her sister (Mrs. Susannah Ramsden) had it in intention to found a school at Elland, for the instruction of poor boys in the English tongue, but died without founding the same, she the said testatrix did thereby give and devise to Sir John Lister Kay, bart. and others (her trustees) and their heirs, all those her several farms, lands, tenements, and hereditaments, in the parish of Bingley, then in the occupations of William Jennings, and Thomas Laycock, or their assigns, with the appurtenances, of the yearly value of thirty-two pounds, upon special trust and confidence, that her devisees, and their heirs and assigns, at all times after her decease, should receive the rents and profits of the said premises, and order and dispose thereof in manner following:

First, that in case she should not, in her life-time, purchase a convenient house or building in Elland, and settle the same in trust,

to be made use of as a school for the instruction of such poor children
as were thereinafter described, then that her said devisees should,
with all convenient speed, out of the clear rents and profits of the
same premises, raise money, not exceeding forty pounds in the
whole, and should apply the same, or so much thereof as to her
trustees should seem requisite, to the purchase of a house in Elland
aforesaid, and near to the church there, such tenements so to be
purchased to be of the nature of freehold, and the estate therein to
be purchased to be an absolute fee-simple in possession,   And if an
house or building, which she would rather have to be purchased if
it conveniently might be, could not be purchased in convenient
time, then that her said trustees, having purchased such plot of
ground as aforesaid, should apply the residue of the said money,
remaining after payments of the consideration of such purchase, to
the erecting an house or building thereon, convenient for the purpose
thereinafter mentioned: and that such building, so purchased or
erected as aforesaid, (all which she desired might be done within the
space of one year next after her decease,) should at all times thenceforth be made use of as a school-house for the teaching of poor
boys of the township of Elland with Greetland, the children of such
parents lawfully settled there, who in the judgment of her said
trustees should not be of ability to pay for the teaching of their
children: and to that intent she willed, that her said trustees,
should, immediately after the purchase or erecting of the said school-
house, elect a grave man, of good life and conversation, a true
member of the church of England as by law established, a good
grammar scholar, and an expert writer & arithmetician, well qualified
to teach English, writing and arithmetic, and should appoint the
person so elected to be master of the said school; and at all times
thenceforth, so long as he should continue master of the said school,
should pay to him, out of the rents and profits of the said devised
tenements, yearly, the sum of twenty pounds of lawful British
money, without any deduction thereout on any account whatsoever,
at two usual feasts in the year, that is to say, the feasts of the
annunciation of the blessed Virgin, and St. Michael the archangel,
by equal portions, the first payment to be at such of the said feasts as
should first happen next after his being instituted master as aforesaid.
And that upon the death or removal of the said master, or his ceasing

Q

to be master of the said school, the trustees of the said school-house
for the time being should assemble at the said school-house, or the
greater number of them who should there assemble, on public notice
of the vacancy of such school, or place of master, to be given in the
church or church yard, on a Sunday, immediately after the morning
service ended, and within fourteen days after such vacancy, of the
time of meeting at such school house, for a choice of a new master
which time of meeting should not be within less than fourteen days
after such notice, should elect and appoint another such fit person, so
qualified as aforesaid, to be master of the said school, and so from time
to time, and as often as the place of the master should be vacant,
a new master so qualified as aforesaid, should and might be elected
and appointed, in the manner, and by the trustees of the said tenements, for the time being, as was therein before directed touching
the election and appointment of a master, upon the first vacancy of
the school or place of master.   And that her said trustees and devisees, and their heirs and assigns, should, out of the rents and profits
of the said tenements, as aforesaid, pay to the master of the school,
for the time being, such annuity or salary of twenty pounds, as was
therein before directed to be paid to the first master of the said school,
and at the same days therein before provided for payment thereof.
And if any master of the said school should die, remove, or be displaced by her said trustees as was therein after provided, then that her
said trustees, their heirs and assigns, should and might apportion
the salary to become payable at such of the said feasts as should
first happen next after such vacancy of the said place of master,
between the said master so removing or being displaced, or the
executors or administrators of such deceased master, and the person
or persons by whom the place of master of the said school should be
supplied till the appointment of a new master, and such succeeding
master, as her said trustees for the time being, or the major number
of them, in their discretion should think meet: and forasmuch as
the said testatrix would have the school duly attended, she recommended that immediately upon the vacancy of the place of master,
the minister of the church of Elland for the time being should provide
a fit person to teach and instruct the poor children therein, until
the appointment of a master as aforesaid : the person so provided by
the said minister to have a share of the said twenty pounds yearly

salary, proportioned to the time he should so serve the said school. And her will also was, that her said devisees, their heirs and assigns, or the major part of them, at all times after the erecting of the said school-house, and electing and appointing a master thereof, might at their will and pleasure, to be expressed in writing, signed by them or the major number of them, and to be notified to the master of the said school for the time being, remove or displace not only such first appointed master, but any other person or persons who thereafter should be appointed master or master, or serve as master or masters, either by her trustees for the time being, or by the minister of the said church of Elland, and in manner therein before directed for the appointment of a new master upon a vacancy, elect and appoint another fit person to supply the place of master of the said school, in the place and stead of the master so by her trustees removed or displaced. And her will and mind was, that the master of the said school, for the time being, should on every day in the week throughout the whole year, (not being the Lord's day, or other days appointed by the church or state to be observed as a holy day, except the last ten days of the month of December, and except three days before and three days after either of the great festivals of Easter Sunday and Pentecost, and except also the afternoons of every Saturday in the year,) both the forenoons and afternoons of such days, (except as before excepted,) diligently apply himself at the said school to the teaching of poor boys, the children of such poor persons lawfully settled in Elland with Greetland, as aforesaid, which boys the said testatrix would have to be twenty-four in number, to read the English language, and write a plain, legible hand or character, and to understand common arithmetic, so as the said children might be thereby better qualified to gain a livelihood than the children of such poor parents usually are : and that the poor boys to be first admitted after erecting the said school-house, and so taught there, should be nominated by her said trustees, and that all other the said boys to be thereafter admitted to be taught there, should be nominated thereunto by the trustees for the time being, or the greater number of them, or in case of default of such nomination by the space of one month next after the said boys there taught shall not be in number twenty-four, then by any two or more of such trustees : and that the master of the said school, for the

time being, should also faithfully instruct the said poor children in
the principles, doctrines, and precepts of the christian religion, and
should particularly oblige them to learn the catechism of the church
of England, and to repeat the same to him without book, at least
once in every week, after they have so learned that they should be
able to repeat the same to him, and that on such occasions he should
explain the same, or some parts thereof, to the said children, in a
manner suited to their capacities; and that at all times whilst the
said children were under his care, he should watch their behaviour,
and in a proper manner, by gentle means if it might be, and if not
by moderate punishment, restrain them from all immoralities and
indecencies.   And her will and mind also was, that the master of
the said school, for the time being, on every day of the week in
which the morning service, according to the liturgy of the church
of England, should be read in the said church of Elland, should
devoutly attend the same service there, and oblige his said scholars
to attend there with him, and take care that they behave themselves
there decently, and with due reverence, as their respective ages
would admit.

And the testatrix willed that her said trustees should apply the
residue of the rents and profits of the said tenements, after satisfying
thereout the master's said salary, to the buying of books as should
be requisite for the learning of the said boys, till they could read well
the English bible, and for the buying of paper, quills, and ink, for
such of them as should be taught writing and arithmetic, which
writing and arithmetic she would have taught to every of the said
boys, after he could read well in the Bible, for the space of six months
next after: and she willed also, that there be given to every one of
the said boys that should be taught and instructed at the said school
till he could read well in the bible, besides his bible, a new common
prayer book, and a "whole duty of man," at his quitting the said
school, which books her trustees for the time being, should provide
out of such residue of the rents and profits of the said farms to them
devised, after payment of the said salary to the master as aforesaid.

And as for and concerning the said annuity of three pounds ten
shillings therein before devised to her said trustees, the same was to
them devised upon trust, that so much of the sum of fifty shillings,
part thereof, as should be requisite, should be yearly and every year,

expended in providing and laying in coals for a fire to be kept in the
said school-house, during the winter season, for the benefit of the
master and scholars there; and that the residue of the said fifty
shillings, or so much of such residue as should be needful, be laid
out, as occasion should require, in the supporting and keeping in
repair the said school-house. And as to the sum of twenty shillings
residue of the said annuity of three pounds ten shillings, the same
should be expended by her said trustees, for the time being, at any
meeting or meetings to be had by them, or the greater number of
them, in Elland aforesaid, touching the said school, or the trust
thereof, which she desired might be at the least once in every year,
and as often as her said trustees in their discretion should see meet.
And she recommended to them and every of them, that at such
their meetings, or on any other occasion, they, or any one more of
them, do visit the said school, and enquire into the conduct of the
master of the said school, and the proficiency of the poor boys there,
in their learning and knowledge: and for the encouragement of the
said poor boys, she willed that so much of the said annuity of three
pounds ten shillings as should not be expended in any year, should
be distributed to and amongst such of the said boys, as in the
judgment of her said trustees, or the major number of them, should
appear to have best behaved themselves.

And as for and concerning the said annuity of thirteen pounds,
therein before devised to her said trustees, in case the same should
become payable, she willed that the same be expended and disbursed
for the benefit of the poor children thereafter to be taught and
instructed at the said school, in such manner as to her trustees for
the time being should seem meet, only she willed that from and after
such annuity of thirteen pounds should take place, the number of
poor boys to be taught in the said school-house should be increased,
and that such additional boys be children of like poor parents, and
and be in like manner nominated, taught, instructed, governed, and
provided, as was therein before limited, of and concerning the poor
boys to be admitted to the said school, before the falling of the said
last mentioned annuity.   And for the better continuance of the said
trust, her will was, that her said trustees of the said school-house,
within three months next after the decease of any two of them,
should elect two other honest men, of good real or personal estate,

and, if to her said trustees should seem meet, residing in or near
Elland aforesaid, to be with such survivors co-trustees of the said
school-house, farms, and annuities, and should convey the same to
the use of themselves, and such like new elected trustees, and their
heirs and assigns on the trusts therein thereof before limited; and
that in the like manner, from time to time, and at all times, so
often as any two of the trustees of the said school-house, farms,
and annuities, for the time being should die, the survivors of them
should, within three months next after, elect two such other honest
men of good estate, (and if to such survivors it should seem meet,)
residing in or near Elland aforesaid, and to be with them co-trustees
of the said premises, and convey the same to the use of such survivors and new elected trustees, and their heirs and assigns.   And
the testatrix also willed that the trustees for the time being, of the
said school-house and premises, or any two or more of them, should
have power and authority, at their will and pleasure, to turn out,
and remove from the said school, any poor boy there admitted to be
taught and instructed, on complaint to them of the misbehaviour of
such poor boy; and her will was, that the master and scholars of
the said school should at all times conform themselves to such rules
and orders as the trustees should institute and appoint, so as the
same rules and orders were not repugnant to what she had directed.
And it was by the said will provided that it should be lawful for
the trustees to retain their expenses, &c. and that they should not
be answerable for the acts or defaults of each other.

RISHWORTH.

WHEELWRIGHT'S CHARITY.

John Wheelwright, formerly of North Shields, in the county of
Northumberland, gentleman, by his will dated Oct. 14th, 1724,
gave, devised, and bequeathed all and singular his messuages, houses, lands, tenements, and hereditaments whatsoever, situate in the
county of York and elsewhere, unto John Wheelwright, of Norland
in the county of York, Miller; Ely Dyson, of Clay House, in the
county of York, merchant; and Abraham Thomas, of Dewsbury, in

the said county of York, clothier; upon trust, for the building a
school at Dewsbury. And upon farther trust also, that the said
John Wheelwright, Ely Dyson, and Abraham Thomas, should with
all convenient speed after his decease, out of his personal estate
therein after devised to them, pay and apply the sum of one hundred
and fifty pounds for the building of a school at Rishworth, in the
said county of York, and that his said trustees for the time being,
should also out of his real estate pay the yearly sum of ten pounds
to a school-master for ever, at four equal quarterly payments, to
wit, at Candlemas, May-day, Lammas, and Martinmas, in every
year, for the teaching and instructing of twenty boys and girls, to
be chosen by his said trustees, from time to time, out of the poorest
tenants' children, living on any of his estates; and so many of the
boys and girls as should not be elected out of his said tenants'
children, should be chosen by his trustees, for the time being, out
of the poor of the parish where the said school stood, the said master
to teach them to read and write, and to prepare as many boys for
the Latin tongue as his said trustees should judge to have capacity
to learn the same, and he thereby ordered that the said twenty
children should always consist of more boys than girls: and his will
further was, that his said trustees should, out of his said estate, pay,
at four equal quarterly payments, to wit, Candlemas, May-day,
Lammas, and Martinmas, in every year, the clear yearly sum of
forty pounds to a school-master for ever, sufficiently instructed and
skilled in the Latin and Greek languages, and of sound principles,
according to the doctrine of the church of England by law established,
who should teach and instruct as many of the aforesaid poor boys as
should from time to time become fit to learn the Latin and Greek
tongues, and that the said number of twenty boys and girls to be
taught by the said two masters as aforesaid, be from time to time
kept up, and consist of a majority of boys; and he gave full power
to his said trustees for the time being, or any two of them, to choose
such schoolmaster and schoolmasters, and from time to time to place,
and for any misdemeanor, neglect, or other just cause, to displace
them, or any of them, according to their discretion.

And his will further was, and he did thereby order, direct, and
appoint, that his dwellinghouse, commonly called by the name of
Goat-house in Rishworth aforesaid, be fitted up and made convenient,

and so continued by his said trustees, for the lodging of the said
two masters, and also for the lodging, boarding, and entertaining
of the twenty boys and girls before-mentioned, for ever; and the
testator ordered, willed, and directed, that his said trustees, and such
other person and persons as should be duly elected in their or any
of their steads and places, after their, any, or every of their deaths
and deceases, should yearly, for ever, pay and apply out of his said
estate, the sum of five pounds for the maintenance of each of the
said twenty boys and girls at the said Goat-house, the same to be
paid at equal payments, to such person and persons as should from
time to time have the care and management of the said boys and
girls, at the end of every week: and also that his said trustees did
and should yearly for ever, pay to a sober, discreet, and careful
woman, to be employed in the dressing of victuals, washing, bed-
making, and other the necessary looking after the twenty boys and
girls aforesaid, the sum of ten pounds at four equal quarterly payments
to wit, at Candlemas, May-day, Lammas, and Martinmas, in every
year, such woman to be chosen and displaced, from time to time,
by his said trustees, as they should see cause; and his will also was
that the said Goat-house should be sufficiently furnished, and kept
furnished, by his said trustees, with beds, bedding, and all other
necessary furniture, for the entertainment and intent aforesaid, out
of his said estate. And he did also thereby will, order, and direct,
that each and every of the said boys should, at the age of sixteen
years, or thereabouts, have the sum of five pounds paid or applied
by his said trustees, out of his said estate, for and towards the fitting
him for, or putting him an apprentice to some trade, occupation or
business, such trade or occupation to be in the choice of the boy and
his parents, or relations, except only one of the said boys, that
should be best capable of University education, which he did thereby
order should, at the age of eighteen years, or so soon as he should
have school learning sufficient, be sent to Cambridge or Oxford,
and should be there maintained by his said trustees, out of his said
estate, at the rate of forty pounds per annum for four years, and no
longer; after the expiration of which four years another boy should
be sent on the same footing as the former, and so to be continued one
after another for ever; all and every such boy and boys to be from
time to time chosen and elected by the said trustees, or the majority

of them, with advice of the head schoolmaster for the time being.
The testator gave all his household goods whatsoever, with all his
books that belonged to him, either at North Shields, or any where in
Yorkshire, towards furnishing the aforesaid Goat-house, the said
books to be catalogued, and carefully placed in some fit room,
towards the foundation of a library, for the use of the twenty boys
and girls aforesaid, and the said two schoolmasters. And his will
was, and he did thereby direct, that in case the said John Wheelwright should die without heir male, that then it should be in the
power of his other two trustees, or their successors, to elect and
appoint another person of the surname of Wheelwright, who should
be invested with, and entitled unto, the same powers, profits, and
privileges, as the said John Wheelwright was by the testator's
said will, in all respects whatsoever. And he did also order,
that upon the deaths of the other two trustees, Ely Dyson and
Abraham Thomas, the survivor of them, and the said John Wheelwright, or his heir male, or such other person of the name of
Wheelwright as should be appointed as aforesaid, did and should
elect and appoint other trustees, whom he desired might be honest,
able, and faithful persons, living in the tenements wherein the said
Ely Dyson and Abraham Thomas then dwelt, in case there be any
such, and for default of such, the two surviving trustees to choose
such other person and persons as they should think fit to be trustees from time to time, as often as occasion should require; and the
said testator did thereby order, will, and declare, that in case of
any neglect or defaults happening by his said trustees or their successors, elected as aforesaid, in not making such elections of trustees
as aforesaid, or in the not duly performing the several trusts in them
reposed, or the non-payment of any of the bequests and charges
thereby made by him upon his said estates, or any misapplication
thereof, contrary to the true intent and meaning of his said will,
that then, and upon any such complaint made, and not otherwise,
he authorized and empowered the archbishop of York, for the time
being, to enquire into, and rectify all and every such abuse or default,
and to put the same again upon the footing thereby intended, but
without further power to intermeddle therein; and he did thereby
will, order, and appoint, that the clear yearly sum of one hundred
pounds per annum should be from time to time paid out of his said

estate, to such person and persons who should more immediately be concerned in the managing and looking after the several trusts aforesaid, the said sum to be paid at four equal quarterly payments in every year; and he appointed the said John Wheelwright, during his natural life, to manage and look after the same; and after the death of the said John Wheelwright, it was his mind that the said other trustees should choose the son of the said John Wheelwright to manage the several trusts aforesaid, and after his decease, should choose of the issue male of the body of the said John Wheelwright, and for default of such issue, should choose and elect another person of the surname of Wheelwright, to manage and look after the trust aforesaid. And his will was, that all his estates both real and personal, should be chargeable with and subject to the several uses, trusts, legacies, devises, and charges therein-before mentioned; and whatsoever surplus might arise out of and from his said real and personal estate, over and above the discharge of the several trusts, legacies, orders, directions, and devises aforesaid, the same should be applied by his said trustees to the purchasing of lands, and it was his will, that the profits thereof should always be applied to and for the better maintenance and support of the said twenty children, or to the enlarging of the number of scholars there, or for the sending of more of them to the university, as the said augmentation might allow of, in such manner as his said trustees should think fit. And he did also thereby will and desire, that constant prayers might be read in the said schools every morning and evening, by the masters thereof, and that the said children be religiously and virtuously brought up and educated, according to the doctrine of the church of England as by law established; and the testator further willed, and thereby ordered, that his said executor and trustees, or any of them, should not demise or grant any part of his several estates, for any term or terms exceeding twenty-one years, nor should they, or any of them, receive any greater or other rents upon any such lease or demise, than the same were then actually rented at, or let for; and the testator appointed the said John Wheelwright, sole executor of his will.

In the year 1822 an information was filed in the high court of Chancery, by his majesty's Attorney general, at the relation of Robert Wheelwright and others, against John Dyson and others,

the then trustees of the charity, the complainant Robert Wheelwright
claiming as of right to be entitled to the vacant trusteeship occasioned
by the death of Mr. Wheelwright, the surviving trustee : after this
suit had been contested for some time, an arrangement was come
to ; and by consent of parties a decree was made in the cause on the
28th May, 1824, and it was referred to Wm. Courtenay, esquire,
one of the masters of the honourable court to appoint three proper
persons to be trustees, and to settle a proper scheme for the future
regulation of the charity.   In pursuance of this decree, the master
reported, in reference to the appointment of new trustees, that after
a due consideration of the facts and proposals laid before him, by
the informants and the defendants, he conceived the balance of testimony was in favor of the Rev. Samuel Knight (the late vicar) and
George Priestley, esquire, of White windows, and he appointed
them to be trustees of the charity in the room of the deceased trustees;
and he recommended the court to appoint Mr. John Wheelwright,
(formerly called Hoyle, who had assumed the name of Wheelwright
by royal licence) as the third trustee, he having undertaken to act
as such without any salary ; and the master authorized the trustees
to employ Mr. James Wheelwright in the business of the charity,
and to pay him the sum of £100 annually, being the sum intended
by the testator to be appropriated for a managing trustee of the
surname of Wheelwright ; and the master further reported that he
had proceeded upon that part of the decree last stated ; and found
that the annual rents and profits of the said charity estates had been
greatly increased, since the decease of the said testator, and that the
rental of the charity estates amounted to the annual sum of £1939
or thereabouts, and that there was then, standing in the name of
the accountant-general of the court, in trust in the said cause, in
bank three per cent annuities £7476   7s. 9d., and in cash the sum
of £1521 10s. 1d. after payment of the costs of all parties of the
said suit, pursuant to the said decree ; and he found that the building
used as the school at Rishworth aforesaid, and containing one room
only, was then in a very delapidated state, and the farm house called
Goat house, which the said testator by his said will appropriated for
the residence of the schoolmasters and children, was a very old farm
house situated upon the summit of a hill, and was then in a very
delapidated state, and was much too small, and not at all calculated

for the accommodation of so many children, and that it was desirable that a new school and convenient buildings should be erected upon the scite of the present school, or on some other more convenient and eligible part of the charity estates within the said township of Rishworth at the discretion of the trustees; and upon due consideration of the several schemes and proposals brought in before him, and the evidence in support thereof, and such information as had been laid before him by the several parties, he had thought fit to adopt and approve of the following as a proper scheme for the application of the said surplus funds, accumulations, and increased rents in the augmentation and extension of the said charities according to the said directions contained in the said testator's will, that is to say, that there should be maintained at Rishworth, out of the trust funds, two schools to be conducted respectively upon the following plan (that is to say) first, a preparatory school to consist of 15 girls, and 25 boys; the boys and the girls to be admitted at $5\frac{1}{2}$ and the boys to remain until $8\frac{1}{2}$ or 9, and the girls to remain till 13; all to be taught reading, writing, and arithmetic, and the girls to be taught plain work and be accustomed to domestic work, and that there be allowed the sum of £10 to be given with one girl in each year, either as an apprentice fee or to be applied for her use upon her going into service, at the discretion of the trustees: that a suitable building should be provided for this first or preparatory school, and a master and matron appointed for the conduct thereof, by the trustees for the time being, and with such salaries respectively as the said trustees should from time to time consider proper to be given to such persons respectively, but in no case exceeding the sum of £800 in the whole, and to be kept as much below that sum as circumstances would admit.

Second.　A grammar school, to consist of at first 30 boys to be elected in the first instance by the trustees according to the directions of the will, and upon future vacancies to be selected from the boys at the preparatory school; the boys in this school to be divided into three principal divisions or classes, with such further subdivisions as the master with the concurrence of the trustees might think right. That the first class should consist of the boys from their first entrance into the school to the age of 12 years or such other age at which the master might think them fit to begin Greek; this class to be well grounded in Latin and English and to be taught writing and arithmetic; that at the age of 12 the parents or guardians of the boy should be called upon to declare whether they wished the boy to be placed in the second or third division. That in the second division the boys should remain until 16, when they must quit the school; in this division they should not learn Greek, but be made as perfect as possible in arithmetic and be well taught in Latin, they should be well grounded in mathematics, and carried as far as their age would permit in the practical part; provision should be made for teaching some of them mensuration and surveying, and for teaching others the rudiments of chemistry.

The master upon communication with the parents or guardians and observations of the boys themselves, would class them for their branches of education respectively. That in the third division should be placed those boys whose parents have expressed a wish that they should receive what is properly called a classical education; they would be here carried on in Latin and taught Greek, and accustomed to composition in Latin and English, they would also be carried forward in arithmetic, and in the last year or two would be grounded in mathematics. That the boys in this division should also leave the school at sixteen except those selected as candidates for the university the number of which candidates to be determined from time to time by the trustees with the advice of the master, one to be selected every second year from the number of the candidates, and sent to one of the colleges at Oxford or Cambridge, with an exhibition of £150 a year for four years; that upon the examination of the candidates for the university the trustees should be at liberty to apply £100 for the benefit of the boy who shall appear next in merit to the successful candidate. That for this school there should be appointed at first two masters, viz. a head master and a second master which second master should teach writing and arithmetic and take such other part in the school as the head master should direct, with the approbation of the trustees; that if upon experience the trustees found a third master necessary for the conducting of this school, then they might at their discretion appoint a third master to teach writing and arithmetic, and who should also be competent to teach mensuration and the rudiments of mathematics. That the salary of the head master should not exceed £200.; that of the second master should not exceed £100.; and that of the third master (if appointed) should not exceed £70; but the trustees should fix the respective salaries within the above-stated limits, at such sum as they might think proper, with reference to the number of boys educated and the qualifications of the masters respectively. That the trustees should be at liberty to procure and pay for instruction in modern languages or other branches of education, for such of the boys as the master might find well qualified to receive it, to be allowed by way of reward for diligence and industry, provided that they should not expend upon this object in any one year more than £60.

That the trustees should be at liberty to lay out a sum not exceeding the sum of £4000, under the direction of the master, to whom the said cause was referred, in the erection of a new school-house, at Rishworth aforesaid, with proper accommodation, and with a good play ground, and suitable outbuildings attached thereto and with suitable dwellings for the master or masters, mistress, matron, and other persons engaged in the conduct of the said school. That there should be appointed by the Archbishop of York, for the time being, an able and sufficient person to examine, in public, before the trustees and the master, all the boys in their respective classes, once a year, on the feast day of Saint John the Baptist, who should state in writing to the Archbishop, and to the trustees, his unbiassed opinion of the progress of the boys, for which and his expenses he should receive £20.; such examiner to be a graduate M. A. or higher, of Oxford or Cambridge.

That each and every boy and girl should appear at their respective schools, clean and decently clothed, and that no child should be continued in either of the schools having any infectious disease, or of natural filthiness, nor any child who should be evil or wickedly disposed or of lewd conversation, and who after reasonable correction should not be reformed and that it should be in the power of the said trustees for the time being, or the majority of them, to expel from the said school any child for the causes aforesaid or any of them or for any other just and reasonable cause.

That at the annual meetings to be held on the feast of Saint John the Baptist as aforesaid, the said trustees or the majority of them might make such rules and orders for the better regulation of the said schools and the masters thereof, and the boys and girls to be admitted therein as they should think proper, which rules and orders should be submitted to the Archbishop of York for the time being, for his sanction and approbation, and that such of the said rules and orders only as should meet with his Grace's sanction and approbation, should be binding and have effect.

That the said trustees should twice in every year, viz. on the first day of February and first day of August, make out or cause to be made out, an account in writing of all sums received and paid for and on account of the said charity, up to the first day of February and first day of August, which accounts should at the annual meeting before mentioned, in every year be submitted, if required, to the Archbishop of York for the time being, who might require the vouchers to verify the truth and accuracy of the same, to be laid before his Grace whenever he might think proper.

That the surplus rents and profits should be invested to accumulate, and that such accumulations with the balance of the funds in court in trust in this cause, after payment of the costs of this suit, and the expenses of the school and buildings, therein proposed to be erected, together with any increase in the rents by a change of the times, or from letting part of the charity estates on building leases, or from letting the coal mines or stone quarries in and under the charity estates or some part thereof, and from the sale of the timber, should go and be applied by the said trustees to the enlarging the number of boys in the said school, or for the sending of more of them to the university, as the said augmentation might allow of, in such manner as the said trustees for the time being or the majority of them might think fit.

That inasmuch as the testator appeared to have intended to maintain a school-house and schoolmaster, at Dewsbury, the said trustees should be at liberty to expend a sum not exceeding £100 a year, in maintaining the school-house now there, belonging to the said charity, and in paying the salaries of a master and mistress to be employed in the education of as large a number of boys and girls, children of poor parents at Dewsbury, as the said sum would enable them to educate, such children to be nominated by the trustees, and to be taught reading, writing and arithmetic, according to the national plan of education, and the girls to be taught plain work.

This Report was confirmed by the court, and the trust estates were accordingly vested in the new trustees, who proceeded forthwith in the discharge of their important duties. A handsome and commodious building has since been erected on the charity estates, at Rishworth, under the superintendance of the late Mr. John Oates, the architect; and opened for the admission of scholars.

The present trustees are the Rev. Charles Musgrave; George Priestley, and John Wheelwright, Esquires. The head master is the Rev. R. Younger, and there is a second master in the upper school. Mr. Earnshaw is the master of the lower school; and Mrs. Maslam is the matron of the establishment.

RISHWORTH SCHOOL.

TOWNSHIP OF RASTRICK AND BRIGHOUSE.

BIRKHEAD'S CHARITY.

William Birkhead, of Brookfoot, in Southowram, as appears, (says WATSON) from an inquisition taken at Halifax, Feb. 16, 1651, and which belonged to the late Mr. Stead, of Nottingham, gave by will, dated December 29, 1638, out of the last third part of his personal estate, commonly called the Death's part, unto Edward Hanson, of Netherwoodhouse, in Rastrick, and Richard Law, of Shelf, the sum of five pounds, in trust, that they should bestow the same on some parcel of land, or yearly rent of inheritance, to be yearly paid to the poor people of Rastrick and Brighouse, from time to time, to succeeding generations for ever.

This money was not come to the hands of the trustees at the time of taking the above Inquisition.

TOWNSHIP OF SOYLAND.

JOHN RILEY'S CHARITY.

John Riley, of Brigroyd, in Soyland, (as appears from the copy of a court roll, dated at Wakefield, at the court baron of Wm. Craven, knt. and Edwin Wiatt, esq. lords of the manor of Wakefield, in trust, for the use of Elizabeth Clapham, widow, held there Feb. 24, 34 Car. ii.) surrendered, on the 25th of January, 34 Car. ii. into the hands of the lords of the manor, the reversion (after the death of the said John) of a messuage or tenement called Field-end in Soyland, with appurtenances, and also of a mansion-house at Farrowheight, with two inclosures lately taken from Soyland moor, containing, by estimation, six acres and a half, to the use of John Gawkroger, of Flathead in Soyland, and Jeremy Riley, of Warley, and their heirs in trust for the use of Martha Riley of Brigroyd, and her lawful heirs; and for want of such, in trust, to pay the rents and profits thereof to the overseer of the poor of Soyland, for the use of the poor of the said town, for ever, to be paid and distributed to the said poor, at the discretion of the said John Gawkroger and Jeremy Riley and their heirs, and the overseer of the said poor, for the time being for ever.

R

"This charity (says WATSON) is withheld, and has been so for some time. I cannot even find that it was ever paid. A complaint was lodged at the last commission for pious uses in the West Riding, but was offered too late to have proper notice taken of it."

JAMES RILEY'S CHARITY.

James Riley, of Kirklees, clerk, by his will, dated May 6, 1723, after giving to his brother, Joseph Riley, an estate in trust, to pay out of the same five pounds yearly to several persons and purposes, willed as follows :—"Item, I will that one pound, further part of the said five pounds, be paid by the said Joseph Riley, and his heirs, yearly and every year for ever, upon the second day of February, to the overseer or overseers of the poor of the township of Soyland for the time being, and to their successors, overseers of the poor of the same township, for the use of and to be distributed to seven poor widowers or widows, and for want of such to the most necessitous persons of the said town of Soyland, at the discretion of the master or owner of Kirkcliffe, and of the overseers, and one or more of the chief inhabitants of Soyland aforesaid."

Mr. WATSON says, this charity is regularly distributed. The testator charged some trust property in the township of Barkisland with the payment of certain sums to the poor of that township.

TOWNSHIP OF HALIFAX.

"The inquirie and presentment of the jurye charged upon the commission directed for finding out of things given to pious uses," before referred to, is entitled to some attention. With regard to its date, it is necessary to correct an error into which I have inadvertently fallen, in assigning it to the year 1651 ; on re-consideration I am induced to fix it about the years 1618-19, and for this reason, it refers to a bequest of as late a date as 1618, but it does not include one of 1619, (viz. that of John Boye's hereinafter mentioned) nor indeed any of a later date than 1618 : that it is not "the inquisition taken at Halifax, February 16, 1651" mentioned by WATSON, is to be inferred from the fact, that in more than one instance the date of the "*yeare of the king's majestie's reigne that now is*" is mentioned, which expression would not have been adopted had the "inquirie" been executed under the authority of a commission issued by those who had then usurped the ruling power.

Notwithstanding Mr. WATSON has given the substance, I prefer stating the fact, or in other words, adopting the language of the "inquirie", more particularly as it includes "things given to pious uses" not mentioned by that gentleman ; and defer any observations until the end of the chapter.

BRIAN OATES'S CHARITY.

"Imprimis; wee fynde that *Brian Otes* late of Hallifax, by surrender and copy of court-roll, bearing date, which was in the seconde yeare of King Henry viii (1511) surrendered one close, containing two acres of land by estimation, with the appurtenances, in Hallifax, to the use of certain feoffees and their heirs ; and by his will, bearing date April the 28th, 1529, reciting that, whereas he had made a surrender of a cottage and two closes containing, by estimation, three acres of land with the appurtenances in Hallifax, to the feoffees in trust, his will was that they should stand seised thereof, to the use of the said Brian for his life, and after, to the churchwardens of Hallifax and their successors for ever, they paying six shillings and eightpence yearly, to the amending of an highway between Hallifax and Shipden Brook, six shillings and eightpence for a dirge or mass, in the parish church of Hallifax, to be sung or said, and the rest of the profits to the morne priest there."

Mr. WATSON says that from a manuscript, written by Mr. John Brearcliffe an apothecary in Halifax, called "Halifax Inquiries, for the finding out of several gifts given to pious uses, by divers persons deceased, Dec. 22, 1651," it appears, that the above land lay below Goldsmith's grave, in the way from thence towards the Bull Close; that the cottage was taken away, and that the charity was detained by one John Exley, who at that time had the land.   Mr. WRIGHT, page 105, says, none of the charity was paid in 1738, except that for repairing the highway.

BATES'S GIFT.

With reference to "Bates's gift" before-mentioned, (page 183) Mr. WATSON observes "the messuage lands are said in Brearcliffe's MS. to go by the name of Yeathouse, and to lie at Blackledge Steel; they are also called by the same name in the register-book at Halifax. This charity both Mr. Brearcliffe and Mr. Wright have attributed to one widow Pymond, who was no other than Elizabeth Bates above-named. Nov. 7, 1547, she married her second husband, Brian Bates, and was buried Jan. 20, 1552. In the above MS. of Mr. Brearcliffe, are the informations of two evidences, to prove that the sum payable out of Yeathouse, to the poor of Halifax, was forty shillings yearly; and one of them, the wife of one Robert Dean, of Priestley, said she had gone with her sister-in-law, Mrs. Blythman, who was buried at Elland, March 7, 1633, to help her to distribute the same."

In the "inquirie" it is thus set forth :—"Item, wee fynde by the report of Robert Deane of Exley that there was given, by one widdow Pymount, twenty shillings yearly for ever, to be paid in or upon the Friday before Easter day called Good Friday, out of certain land called Yeathouse in Hallifax, which hath been paid every year hitherto."

CLARKE'S CHARITY.

"Item, wee fynde by a coppy of court roll in the tyme of Robert Waterhouse, esquier, dated the 15th day of April, anno Elizabeth 39mo that *Richard Clarke* of Hallifax did surrender to John Black-wood and George Atkinson and their heirs as feoffees in trust, out of his house where the said Clarke dwelt, near Loveledge lane (now called George street) in Hallifax, sixe shillings eight pence for ever to the poore of Hallifax towne. And the said sixe shillings eight pence is likewise confirmed by a Hariott coppie to Thomas Blackwood, son and heir to the said John Blackwood, being the surviving feoffee."

"In Mr. Brearcliffe's MS. (says WATSON) it is said, that Richard Clarke gave this house to one Robert Cunliffe, who either sold or mortgaged it to Humphry Drake, and that in 1651 it was in the hands of John Drake, minister, son of Humphry, who paid the six shillings and eight-pence yearly, since which I have seen no account of it."

SALTONSTALL'S CHARITY.

"Item, wee fynde given by the will of *Sir Richard Saltonstall*, knight, alderman of London, (who was sheriff there in 1588, and lord mayor in 1597,) as appeared by a note shewn unto us, being part of the will, the sum of one hundred pounds to buy rents withal; which rents should be yearly distributed, in the parish church of Hallifax, to the poore of the said towne and parish, in money or bread, at the discretion of the churchwardens then being, and we further fynde the same confirmed by an award, bearing date July 8, 43 Elizabeth, by John Morris, Thomas Middelton, and William Bruce, esquires, by the consent of dame Susan Saltonstall, Samuel Saltonstall, and others her children; that the said Dame Saltonstall, and Samuel, being executors to the said Sir Richard, bestow the said hundred pounds to the most profit, before the 25th day of March next after the said award."

LISTER'S GIFT.

"Item, wee fynde that John Lister of Hull, alderman, did give fortye pounds to be employed upon the poore of Hallifaxe parish or otherwise to be distributed at the discretion of Mr. Doctor Favour, Mr. Sunderland, and Daniel Foxcroft."

HUGH ATWELL'S GIFT.

"Item, wee fynde that one *Hugh Atwell*, parson of St. Tewe in Cornwall, did give (March 10, 1605) thirty three shillings and four-pence, to the use of the poore of Hallifaxe towne, to be lent to some poore man for a year, to be disposed of by the magistrates and officers of the said towne, which money was for a time lent accordingly: and we finde that in 1608 it was lent by Symon Binns and Thomas Taylier, then constables, unto one Allan Pennington; and Jane Crowther, widow, gave her word for it." In Halifax register under the year 1605, it is said to have been given to keep the poor in work, the stock to remain for ever, the gain to be the poor's; to be at the disposition of the magistrates and officers of the town of Halifax, or else such as they shall think fit, for the true disposition thereof. Mr. WATSON says he has seen no farther account of this.

HENRY SAVILLE'S GIFT.

"Item, wee finde that *Henry Saville*, late of Shaw hill and since of London, gent., by his will dated 20 April, 1617, gives to the poore of Hallifax, and towns adjoining, twenty pounds; and to certain poore men by name, 17s. and 10s. to be paid within four yeares after his death."

ISABEL MAUD'S CHARITY.

"Item, wee finde that *Isabel Maud* late of Halifax, widow, deceased, by her will, dated June 12, in the eleventh yeare of the king's majestie's reigne that now is (i. e. James i. 1613,) did give to the late erected schoole in the almshouses in Halifax, ten pounds, for the buying of some annuitye towards the maintenance thereof, to be disposed of by the overseers of her last will (who were Dr. Favour, Samuel Lister, Samuel Mitchell, and John Clough.) And to the poore of the town of Hallifax eight pounds, to be lent, from year to year, to fower tradesmen for ever; and that her overseers, or the most part of them, should take such order that the continuance thereof might remain: her executor was Thomas Butterfield."

Mr. WATSON says "the above is entered in Halifax register, and in Halifax inquiries, written by Mr. Brearcliffe. She also gave twenty pounds to Coley chapel, but for what purpose I have not seen. Query, if she was not widow of John Maud of Halifax, who gave, in 1608, one hundred and twenty-one pounds four shillings to pious uses, but in what particular manner is now unknown?"

NORMAN'S, WATERHOUSE'S, WHITTAKER'S AND CROWTHER'S GIFTS.

"Item, wee finde by the relation of Robert Law that *Anne Norman* late of Hallifax deceased, did by her will give fortye pounds, and which was confessed to him the said Robert by Dr. Favour; but we neither see will nor writing to manifest to what uses and in what manner the same was given.

" Item, we heare by the report of Mr. John Bowyer and others, that *Michaell Waterhouse,* clerke, did by his will give twenty pounds to good uses, and as we learne Clerk Waterhouse of Woodhouse was his executor.

. "Item, wee fynde by the relation of Roger Bolton, that about five years ago *William Whittaker* gave £3 to be lent to three poor tradesmen of Hallifax from year to year by the churchwardens there. It rested in Nathaniel Waterhouse and Michael Maude's hands, when they were churchwardens, and now these churchwardens have but received thirtye shillings.

" Item, wee fynde that *Jane Crowther* did by her will (dated 18 Jany, 1613) give the sum of ten pounds to be lent from tyme to tyme for ever, to the godliest poor people of the town of Hallifax upon security, at the discretion of her executors and overseers, to remayne for ever."

NICOLL'S AND BOYES' GIFTS.

"Item, wee finde that *Richard Nicoll,* late of Halifax, deceased, by his will (dated March 20, in the seventeenth yeare of the king's majestie's reigne that now is) did give and devise unto Robert Lawe and Thomas Holden and their heirs, as feoffees in trust, a yearlye rent of thirteen shillings and four pence for ever, out of an house and certaine lands in Halifax, to bee, by and with the consent or the churchwardens for the time being, paid to the most needful poore of Halifax towne."

Mr. WRIGHT, p. 114, says that this house and lands lie at Mount Pellon, quoting Mr. Brearcliffe for his assertion, "but (adds WATSON) I can find nothing of this in his manuscript, which only says farther that the money was detained by Richard Nicoll, the son, who was executor to his father."

John Boyes, clerk, minister of Halifax church, gave by will, dated July 14, 1619, the sum of eighteen pounds, to be lent to the poor of Halifax, at the discretion of his overseers, or the greater part of them, viz. Dr. Favour, William Boyes, his brother, John Boyes of Halifax, Humphry Drake, Samuel Lister, John Whiteley, and William Whitaker.   See Halifax register, Anno. 1620.

ALICE HAWARTH'S CHARITY.

Alice Hawarth, widow, (as appears from an inquisition taken at Halifax, Feb. 16, 1651,) gave by her last will, dated Feb. 6, 1622, twenty pounds, to be paid by her executors to Anthony Foxcroft, and others, to purchase lands or rents, and with the assistance of the churchwardens of Halifax, to distribute the profits thereof among the poor, impotent, and aged people of the said town; and by the said inquisition it was found, that Abraham Parkinson and Ellen his wife were executors of the said will, which Abraham acknowledged the said twenty pounds to be in his hands, also that neither principal nor consideration had been paid, though the said Alice had been dead twenty-eight years; alleging for himself that he was never required by the said Anthony Foxcroft or others in the will named, to pay in the same; in respect however that the same had continued so long in his hands, he was willing to pay, in lieu thereof, the sum of twenty-five pounds, or else by good and sufficient assurance, to convey to the said Anthony Foxcroft, and such other persons as the commissioners should think meet, and their heirs, one annuity or rent-charge of twenty-five shillings, to be issuing out of his lands and tenements in Halifax for ever.   The commissioners therefore decreed, that the said Abraham Parkinson should pay to the said Anthony Foxcroft, Richard Blacket, John Brearcliffe, and Robert Allenson of Halifax, or some of them, the sum of twenty-five pounds, before the twenty-fourth day of June next following, and that they, as trustees, should purchase with the same, to them and heirs, for the use of the poor of Halifax, and according to the intent of the last will and testament of the said Alice Hawarth, one annuity or rent-charge of twenty-five shillings, or else some lands or tenements of the same annual value; or else the said Abraham Parkinson was to make to them the like conveyance and assurance.   In obedience to which decree, Abraham Parkinson did, by his indenture executed August 25, 1652, give and confirm to the said Anthony Foxcroft, Richard Blacket, John Brearcliffe, and Robert Allenson, their heirs and assigns, for ever, as trustees of Alice Hawarth's charity, one annuity or yearly rent of twenty-five shillings, issuing forth of all that one messuage or tenement, and of all houses, barns, buildings, and gardens thereto belonging, lying on the south side of a lane leading from Goldsmith's grave to Brainthwaites on the moor; and also forth of four closes of land, all adjoining to the south side of the said lane, some of them adjoining on the said house, payable yearly at the feasts of St. Martin and Pentecost. WATSON says "the minutes of the above inquisition, written by Mr. Brearcliffe, were in the hands of the late Mr. Valentine Stead of Nottingham.

BEQUESTS FOR SERMONS, PRAYERS.

Godfrey Walker gave forty shillings a year, for ever, to the vicar of Halifax, for a sermon to be preached in commemoration of him, in the parish church of Halifax in the month of April for ever. He was buried April 4, 1633. This account is taken from Mr. Wright, p. 114. WATSON says "a paper which he met with in the box belonging to the trustees of Crowther and Hopkinson's charity, says, that Henry Riley of London, esq. by will (confirmed by Gill's bargain and sale)gave forty shillings per annum, for ever, to the vicar of Halifax, for a sermon to be preached in commemoration of Godfrey Walker and Catharine his wife, in the parish church of Halifax, in the month of April for ever, to be paid on the third Wednesday in April, yearly, out of a tenement called Netherhouse in Hipperholme cum Brighouse."

Ann Snydall, of Halifax, gave by will, dated June 23rd, 1638, twenty shillings yearly, for ever, to have a sermon preached in Halifax church, every St. Peter's day, by the vicar, or his substitute.

William Chamberlain, by will dated September 22, 1728, gave, devised and bequeathed the sum of twenty shillings per annum, of lawful money of Great Britain, yearly from and after his decease, to be paid to the person that reads prayers twice every day in Halifax, and for want of such usage or reading prayers twice every day, then the said testator did thereby give, devise and bequeath the said sum of twenty shillings yearly unto the lecturer or afternoon preacher in Halifax church for ever: and he did thereby charge the same should be paid forth out of the housing then in Mr. James Ingham's occupation. Mr. WATSON says, he was credibly informed "that Mr. Chamberlain left also six shillings yearly, for which the twelve widows in the almshouses are to have each a dinner and a pint of ale every Christmas-day; likewise twenty shillings yearly for ever, payable out of the whole estate given to his daughter Mary, for teaching the blue-coat children in Mr. Waterhouse's charity to write, at the discretion of the said Mr. Waterhouse's feoffees." This benefactor died May 15, 1729.

Elizabeth Bingley, by will dated May 12, 1729, gave and devised all those her two cottages in or near the lane leading to Mount Pellon, at the upper end of Halifax town, with their and every of their appurtenances, then in the several tenures or occupations of her the said Elizabeth Bingley and John Morris, the rents, issues and profits thereof to go and be to and for the reader of prayers twice every day in Halifax church for ever; and if prayers should cease to be read twice every day, then to the lecturer or afternoon man in Halifax for the time being for ever. Her executor was John Holt of Halifax. This benefactress was born in 1684, died May 14, 1729, and was buried on the 16th following. These premises being copyhold, were conveyed by Lord Irwin, by deed, to trustees, for the uses mentioned in the will.

Mary Drake of Halifax, widow, (who was buried, as Mr. WRIGHT says, in June, 1729) left twenty shillings yearly for ever, to the lecturer at Halifax, and his successors, for preaching a sermon every second Wednesday in June for ever.

John Tenant of Halifax, grocer, left the interest of ten pounds yearly for ever, for reading prayers twice every day in the parish church of Halifax. He died about the year 1729. A messuage or dwellinghouse in Bury-lane is the security for this.

In addition to these charities, various bequests appear to have been made, but particularly about the time of Doctor Favour, to the "*poore of Halifax*" and other townships; and also "*to good and godly uses*" viz.

Clerk Waterhouse gave £10; (the purpose is omitted in the inquirie.) *Robert Wade*, gave unto the poor of Halifax and Sowerby £30, to witt, £xx at Halifax and £x at Sowerby, and that by the advice of Mr. Henry Farrar and Mr. Edward Maud and his executors, or the most part of them, either for setting them to work or otherwise. *John Hogg*, £6 13s. 4d. to good and godly uses. *Edward Broadley*, £10 to good uses, either the free school or poor. *John Smith*, £15 to the poor. *John Maud*, £40 to the poor and £40 to ten of the most honest, decayed, poor tradesmen. *Michael Waterhouse*, £20 to good uses. *Sir A. Ingram*, £10 to the poore. *Wm. Harrison*, £20 to the poor, and £10 "towards bringing of the water into Hallifax towne in lead;" this in 1618.

<hr />

THE FREE SCHOOL

Also appears to have been an object of considerable bounty, in former years. Several legacies and bequests have at various times been given to it, and WATSON says "in 1634, £196 6s. 8d. was collected in order to purchase lands for the use of this school; the following perpetual benefactions have at different times also been made to it, viz. *Brian Thornhill* of Fixby, esq. gave by will twenty shillings yearly. *Robert Wade* of Fieldhouse gave five pounds yearly out of Fieldhouse in Sowerby, but the title being disputable it was agreed, by the parties concerned, that three pounds ten shillings should be paid yearly. *Gilbert Saltonstall*, of Rookes in Hipperholme, gave twenty shillings yearly out of Rookes, in fee, to be confirmed by his son Samuel, of Hunstwick. *Edward Maud*, vicar of Wakefield, gave ten shillings yearly out of a tenement." This account WATSON has extracted from the Register.

The "Inquirie" contains the following, which are also mentioned in an old church book. "Item, wee finde, by the information of Thomas Wilkinson, that one house, and one lathe or barn, at a place in Halifax called Back-lane-end, is given to the free school of Halifax; and wee finde that the same is assured to the governors to the use of the said free-school for ever. Item, wee heare by William Whitacre, that Robert Cunliffe reporteth, that the governors of the free-school demanded eight shillings a year, which was given out of his lands in Blackledge, to the use of the free-school, and also he saith he bought the rent out for eight pounds of the governors. Item, wee finde that there is given out of the house of Robert Hargreaves, in Bury-lane in Halifax, four shillings a yeare for ever, towards the use of the free-school of Halifax. Item, wee fynde Mr. Thornhill, late of Fixbye, did give twenty shillings yearly for ever to the free-school of Hallifax, which hath been paid in former tymes, and hath now rested unpaid this five years or thereabouts. Item, wee fynde xxs. given out of a tenemente called the Rookes in Hipperholme to the free-schole yearly, and hath continued and beene paid by a tenant there, called Roger Bancrofte."

TOWNSHIP OF NORTHOWRAM.

HEMINGWAY'S CHARITY.

Robert Hemingway, of Overbrea in Northowram, by his will, dated March 3, 1613, gave the sum of ten pounds, to be lent from time to time, to certain of the most religious and honest poor, or decayed tradesmen, of the township of Northowram, at the discretion of his executors and overseer, and after their decease at the discretion of the vicar of the parish church of Halifax, and the churchwarden of the town of Northowram for the time being, with the assistance of one honest and sufficient man of the said town, whom he requested to take, from time to time, sufficient security for the continuance thereof.

He also gave £10 to the Free Grammar School, at Halifax, and £40 towards the maintenance of a preacher at Coley chapel.

TOWNSHIP OF SOWERBY,

Independently of the £10, left by *Robert Wade* to the poor of Sowerby, for setting them to work as before-mentioned, he also surrendered "fower pounds yearly out of his lands for eighty years to be given to the poor of Sowerby, and fower other honest men of the same towne."

"Item, we fynde that George Foxcroft, by his will, dated the 20th day of May, in the 17th year of the king's majestie's reign, that now is, did give £10 towards the building of a chapel, at Sowerby, to be paid by his executor within two months next after the said building shall begin : also he gave £10 to the poore of the Chappellrye of Sowerby, to be lent from year to year by the minister, churchwardens, and swornmen of the said chappell, for the time being, to the poore people of Sowerby quarter, Westfield quarter, and Blackwood quarter, taking security for the same, and nothing to be paid for it."

CHAPELRY OR TOWNSHIP OF HEPTONSTALL.

JOHN GREENWOOD'S CHARITY.

"Item we fynde as it appeareth by the copy of a Deed, dated Feb. 20th, in the 40th year of Queen Elizabeth, (1598,) shewn unto us, that *John Greenwood*, of Cottingley, did give three score pounds, to wit, forty pounds to be lent from year to year, for ever, to the poor of Heptonstall parish, and twenty pounds to the poor of Bradford-dale, by the discretion of the churchwardens for the time being of the said parishes."

"The above" says WATSON, "is mentioned both in Mr. Brearcliffe's manuscript, and in Halifax Register, vol. ii."

CALEB COCKROFT'S CHARITY.

Caleb Cockroft, of London, by his will, dated Nov. 2nd, 1643, gave £20 to the parish of Heptonstall, whereof £10 of it for Wadsworth, and £10 for Heptonstall and Erringden, which money should be lent to twenty poor men, to buy them bread corn, from two years to two years, and with one sufficient surety, and to be lent by the advice of the minister, churchwardens, and overseers of the poor, and to be lent where they saw most need to lend, and to be lent to such men who have no relief from the parish at all, and this in the least not to be any hindrance to the charity of those townships, but a help to poor men to buy corn at best hand, and cheapest. The original of this will is in the prerogative court of Canterbury ; the above was copied from Heptonstall register. By an inquisition at Halifax, Feb. 16, 1651, it appeared that in 1647 the minister and churchwardens distributed the money according to the donor's will, but it was not found that they made any account thereof, to their successors or others.

The "Inquirie" refers to a charity connected with Bingley: a devise of land towards the building of a chapel in a place called Dean's head in the parish of Huddersfield: and a rent-charge of £10 a year out of certain messuages for the maintenance of a minister there. Of the following I cannot find any mention in the calendars of either university.

"Item, wee fynde that *William Aykroid*, parson of Long Marsden, by his will, dated the 13th day of September, 1715, gave certain lands in Grimston, Brearley, and Batley, for the maintenance of a scholar of his name at the universitie of Oxford or Cambridge, as by the said will may more clearly appear."

In the foregoing account I have endeavoured to be as accurate as possible, and have adhered to a simple statement of facts. It includes, I believe, all the eleemosynary foundations, scholastic institutions, and public charities, connected with the Parish, with the exception of such as may be more properly denominated ecclesiastical endowments, these are included in the "inquirie," and will find a place in connection with their respective chapels. There are two or three benefactions to Protestant Dissenters, which it will also be proper to notice.

The Report of the Commissioners is silent as to all the charities connected with Elland; and also to some other benefactions referred to by WATSON; for this I am unable to assign a satisfactory reason.

It is highly gratifying to observe that none of the endowed schools connected with this parish have been suffered to decay, (but two fellowships and two scholarships in University College, Oxford, given by the founder of Heptonstall school, were unfortunately lost by the mismanagement of his executors) nor does it appear that the funds applicable to the support of these schools have been diverted from their legitimate course; although the same observation will not apply to some lands given to charitable uses.

The Parish can boast at present of not less than five endowed free grammar schools, being more than are to be found in some entire counties. The first, QUEEN ELIZABETH's free grammar school at Heath, "for the continual bringing up, teaching, and learning of children and youth of the parish and vicarage of Halifax, and also of other villages and hamlets near adjoining unto the same, and of other our faithful and liege people whosoever they be," &c. Second, the free grammar school at HIPPERHOLME, "to educate and instruct in grammar and other literature and learning, the scholars and children of the township and constablery of Hipperholme-cum-Brighouse only, gratis and without any other reward." Third, HEPTONSTALL free grammar school "for the children of the inhabitants of the town and township of Heptonstall." Fourth, BARKISLAND free school, "to teach such a competent number of poor children of the town and township of Barkisland to read English, and to write or cast accounts or farther learning, as the feoffees should think meet and convenient and as the funds would extend." And fifth, RISHWORTH SCHOOL: the peculiar beneficial effects likely to result from this establishment, places it among the first class of scholastic institutions, and cannot but afford much satisfaction to all who take an interest in the success of our public seminaries; the attention of the masters connected with this school is exclusively confined to those who are entitled to the benefit of the charity, nor are they permitted to take other boarders. Much of the useful learning which has so remarkably enlightened the middle ranks of the English nation, and rendered us a moral and an understanding people, has proceeded from our numerous public schools. It is in these truly respectable nurseries of literature, that education has effected its most generous and valuable purposes; the mind, which might otherwise have been confined by sordid habits, has been expanded: genius, which might have been hidden from the world, has been called forth to the honor of human nature; and the general manners, from rudeness and vulgarity, have been rendered easy, courteous, and polite.*

It may appear presumptuous to enlarge on the merits of our local public seminaries, to many who have experienced their beneficial effects; their peculiar regulations having pointed out a particu-

---

* Wilson's History of Merch. Taylor's School.

lar mode to be observed in the instruction of youth, of which their education *is the principles of the EstablishedChurch* forms a prominent feature, it will be conceded that the election of persons properly qualified for their management is a matter of the first importance, to preserve those institutions from the intrusion of ignorant or fanatic trustees.

Sensible of the advantages to be derived from the extension of education, and the diffusion of religious knowledge in this manufacturing parish, may the noble example which has been set by our forefathers animate us to follow in their steps! If, as Dr. Johnson has asserted, the chief glory of every people arises from its authors, it is no less true "that public establishments, which are formed for the advancement of literature, are the highest ornaments of a nation in every state of refinement." Nor can there any surer pledge be given for a durable loyalty to be transmitted to posterity, than a conscience rightly informed by a good education. "I tell you, Sirs" said Henry the Eighth to his hungry courtiers, fleshed with abbey lands, and wishing to spoil colleges also ;—"I tell you, Sirs, that I judge no land in England better bestowed than that which is given to our universities."

BIOGRAPHY.

The Biography of the parish next claims our attention ; and the selections from Mr. Watson's "Temple of Fame," together with a few additions, will fully justify Dr. Whitaker's remark, "that the parish has given birth or residence to more talent, in various departments, than has fallen to the lot of some entire counties." This will apply particularly to her divines, some of whom have not only filled the highest offices in the church, and imparted an unsullied sanctity on the lawn, but by the purity of their precepts and example have shed an hallowed lustre on those important truths they were called upon to preach ; not forgetting her martyr, Farrar, who sealed them with his blood.

AINSWORTH, WILLIAM, curate of Lightcliffe in this parish, published "Triplex memoriale, or the substance of three commemoration sermons. Preached at Halifax in remembrance of Mr. Nathaneel Waterhouse, deceased. By William Ainsworth, late lecturer at St. Peter's, Chester. York, printed by Thomas Broad, 1650." In one of these sermons, he says "the ministry in this church of England s, for the most part, the poorest trade that any man drives, the iinferiour sort of ministers having neither a competency while they live, nor provision made for their families after their death, contrary to the practice of other reformed churches. Every man thinks he is at liberty to pay to the minister or forbeare, though he be content to be bound in every thing else. Men would have ministers to burne like lamps, but will afford them no oyle to keep in the light ; . like Pharoah's hard task-masters, they think we should make brick without straw. The poorest ballad-singer and piper in the country live better of their trades then ministers do."

BREARCLIFFE, JOHN, an apothecary born in Halifax, where he died Dec. 4, 1682, aged 63. He wrote collections relating to the antiquities of Halifax, a manuscript which the late Mr. Wilson of Leeds (author of the manuscript collections of the lives and writings of English, Scotch and Irish historians, their several editions, and where their manuscripts are deposited, now lodged at the free-school in Leeds) said, Mr. Thoresby the antiquary saw in the library at Halifax church, but which, in Mr. Watson's time, had not been there for more than twenty years. The title of one of these papers was, "A particular survey of all the houseinge and lands within the townshippe of Halifax, accordinge to the best information that could be had, taken the the 22d day of Novr. 1648."

This Mr. Brearcliffe seems to have been fond of collecting together every thing which fell in his way, relating to the affairs of his native town and parish. Among the rest were twenty pages in folio in his own hand writing, intitled "Halifax inquieryes for the findeinge out of severall giftes given to pious uses by divers persons deceased. Written Dec. 22, 1651."

THORESBY, in his Vicaria Leodiensis, p. 68, mentions Mr. Briercliffe's MS. catalogue of the Vicars of Halifax, and inscriptions under their arms painted on tables in the library of that church, by the care of that industrious and (which is infinitely better) religious antiquary.

BENTLEY, WILLIAM, born in Halifax, and the reputed author of a book, called "Halifax and its gibbet law placed in a true light. Together with a description of the town, the nature of the soil, the temper and disposition of the people; the antiquity of its customary law, and the reasonableness thereof; with an account of the gentry and other eminent persons, born and inhabiting within the said town, and the liberties thereof.—To which are added, the unparalleled tragedies committed by Sir John Eland, of Eland, and his grand antagonists. London, printed by J. How, for William Bentley, at Halifax, 1708." It contains 174 pages in 8vo. The son of the above William Bentley caused another edition to be printed at Halifax, by P. Darby in 1761. The first edition (which is esteemed scarce,) is that which Wright in his history of Halifax, quotes by the name of the old gibbet-law book.

This William Bentley was clerk of the parish church of Halifax.

BROWN, SIR THOMAS, is said, in Bentley's history, p. 89, to have fixed himself in this parish, in his juvenile years, as a physician, and to have written here his Religio Medici. Wright, p. 152, asserts the same, adding that he composed this piece at Shipden-hall, near Halifax, where he lived about the year 1630.

JOHN OF HALIFAX, commonly called DE SACRO BOSCO, was born, says FULLER, "in the town of Halifax so famous for cloathing, bred first in Oxford, then in Paris; being the prime mathematician of his age. All students of astronomy enter into that art through the door of his book "De Sphæræ." He lived much beloved, died more lamented, and was buried with a solemn funeral at the public cost of the university of Paris. THORESBY affirms that he lay on his back on the hill at Halifax, to observe the motion of the stars, when he wrote his celebrated book, "De Sphæræ." He died A. D. 1256.

BRIGGS, HENRY, an eminent mathematician, was born at a house called Daisy bank, adjoining to Warley Wood, in the township of Warley, (not, as A. Wood has expressed it, in an obscure hamlet called Warley Wood,) about the year 1556. In Halifax register is the following entry, "Henricus, filius Thome Bridge, de Warley, bapt. 23, Feb. 1560." The different spelling of the name is easily accounted for, when it is considered what little care was used to be taken in this respect, and also that Bridge is generally, in this part, pronounced Brigg or Briggs.

"He received his first education at a grammar school, and was thence sent to St. John's College, Oxford, of which he was ultimately elected a fellow. He was particularly attached to the study of mathematics, and when Gresham college was established in London, was appointed the first geometry professor. About this time he constructed a table for finding the latitude, from an observation of the variation of the compass. In 1615 he was engaged on the subject of eclipses and the noble invention of logarithms, then recently discovered, the theory of which he explained to his auditors at Gresham college. He soon after paid a visit to Lord Napier in Scotland, to whom he proposed an alteration in the scale of logarithms, from the hyperbolic form of the discoverer, to that in which one should be the ratio of ten to one. This proposition was adopted, and on his return from a second visit in 1616, he published the first chilia or thousand of his logarithms in octavo. In 1619 he was appointed Savilian professor of geometry at Oxford, and settled at Merton college, where he resided for the remainder of his life, employed in the most laborious compilations of logarithms and other useful works. In 1622 he published a small pamphlet on a north-west passage, which production was followed by his great work, the "Arithmetica Logarithmica," London, 1624, containing the logarithms of 30,000 natural numbers to fourteen places of figures, besides the index. He also completed a table of logarithms, sines, and tangents, for the whole quadrant; for every hundredth part of degree, to fourteen places of figures, besides the index, with a table of natural sines for the same to fifteen places, &c. These celebrated tables were printed at Gouda, and published at London in 1631, under the title of "Trigonometria Britannica." This great man and eminent benefactor to science died at Merton college in 1630, leaving behind him a high character for probity, as well as for genius and scientific invention. In the works already mentioned, we meet for the first time, with several important discoveries, which have been deemed of later date; such as the binomial theory, the differential method, &c. as ably pointed out by Dr. Hutton, in the preface to his mathematical tables. Mr. Briggs wrote many other works besides the foregoing, the principal of which are " Tables for the Improvement of Navigation;" "Euclidis Elementorum vi libri priores," 1620; " Mathematica ab Antiquis minus cognita; "Commentaries on the Geometry of Peter Ramus;" "Duæ Epistolæ ad Celeberrimum Virum;" "Animadversiones Geometricæ;" "An English Treatise of Common Arithmetic," &c. Some of these are still unpublished.

BATES, JOAH, a musician of considerable eminence was born in Halifax, in the year 1740. His father, Henry Bates, was for many years clerk in the parish church. Joah's musical talent having gained him some celebrity in his native town, he determined upon visiting the metropolis. Here he rose in his profession, and had the good fortune to obtain the special notice of his majesty, king George the third. Such was his reputation that, at the commemoration of Handel in Westminster Abbey in the year 1784, he was unanimously selected to superintend the performance; in fact the plan is said to have originated with himself, in conversation with his patron the late Earl Fitzwilliam, and another distinguished individual.

It may be of interest to the musical reader to state the fact, that there was but one general rehearsal for each day's performance, and though this was the first instance of a band of such magnitude being assembled together, the performances were no less remarkable for the multiplicity of voices and instruments (535) employed, than for accuracy and precision. It is no less astonishing that this band moved in exact measure, without the assistance of a *Coryphæus* to beat time, either with a roll of paper or a noisy baton. Dr. Burney remarks, concerning the precision of the performers, "the pulsations in every limb, and ramifications of veins and arteries in an animal, could not be more reciprocal and isochronous, or more under the regulation of the heart, than the members of this body of musicians under that of the conductor and leader. The totality of sound seemed to proceed from one voice and one instrument; and its powers produced not only new and exquisite sensations in judges and lovers of the art, but were felt by those who never received pleasure from music before." "But (as another able writer has observed) to the encomiums so justly bestowed on the able manner in which the band was conducted, Joah Bates, Esq. solely entitled himself; his labors were unremitting, and his reward, complete success."

Till the year 1793 he conducted, with much skill and energy, the choral performances of ancient music, at which period he retired and was succeeded by Mr. Greatorex. His wife was a prima donna singer, celebrated for the excellence of her voice (a fine contralto,) and the clearness of her tones and articulation. Her execution of Purcell's celebrated song of "Mad Bess" is said to have been inimitably fine. The husband died in 1799.

Bois, William, born in Halifax, and (as we are told in Peck's *Desiderata Curiosa*, lib. viii. p. 38.) according to the custom of the time and place, instructed in music and singing, wherein he afterwards attained to great proficiency. He was educated at Cambridge but having a dislike to popery, was obliged to retire to some place of safety in the reign of Queen Mary, and he seems to have pitched upon Nettlestead, near Hadley in Suffolk, where, though he was in orders, he took a farm, and lived as a layman, marrying there

Mirable Poolye, a gentlewoman of good family, who survived him about ten years. In the reign of Queen Elizabeth, he resumed his sacred calling and served the cure of Elmesett near Hadley; and after the death of the incumbent was presented by the lord keeper to the rectory; and not long after to the rectory of West Stow, at the presentation of Mr. Poolye. He died in the 68th year of his age, leaving several children by his wife, one of whom proved an ornament to his country, viz. Dr. John Bois, born Jan. 3, 1560, and had a considerable hand in the present translation of the Bible, and the sketch of whose life may be seen in Peck, as above. In this sketch we are farther told, p. 40, that the Doctor's father was a great scholar, being excellently well learned in Hebrew and Greek, which considering the time he lived in, was almost a miracle.

BURTON, THOMAS, A. M. sometime Vicar of Halifax. He published a sermon preached in the parish church, from Psalm xlvi. 10. on Tuesday, July 7th, 1713, being the day appointed by her majesty for a public thanksgiving for the peace. London, 1713, containing 16 pages in 8vo. The principles advanced in this discourse, which Mr. WATSON calls "something extraordinary" are nothing more than the common tory principles of the time.

CRABTREE, HENRY, sometimes written Krabtree, was born in the village of Sowerby, where he was initiated in school learning with Archbishop Tillotson. He has left behind him the character of being a good mathematician and astronomer. DERHAM, in his *Astro-Theology*, lib. iv. cap. 3. sais, in a note, "In their letters (now in my hands) there is an ingenious controversy between those two great men, Mr. Gascoigne, the inventor of the micrometer, and Mr. Crabtrie, concerning the solar spots that appeared about the year 1640, which Mr. Gascoigne imagined to be great numbers of small planets revolving round the sun, at a small distance from him. Mr. Crabtrie's answer and opinion may be seen in his letter, which is published with my own observations about the solar spots, from 1703 to 1711, in the Philos. Trans. No. 330."

He published "Merlinus Rusticus or a Country Almanack, yet treating of courtly matters, and the most sublime affairs now in agitation throughout the whole world. 1. Shewing the beginning, encrease, and continuance of the Turkish or Ottoman Empire. 2. Predicting the fate and state of the Roman and Turkish Empires. 3. Foretelling what success the Grand Seignior shall have in this his war, in which he is now engaged against the German Emperor. All these are endeavored to be proved from the most probable and indubitable arguments of history, theology, astrology, together with the ordinary furniture of other Almanacks, by Henry Krabtree, Curate of Todmurden in Lancashire. London, printed for the Company of Stationers, 1685."

He married —— Pilling, widow, of Stansfield Hall.

DEANE, RICHARD, D. D. bishop of Ossory. In WOOD's *Athenæ Oxonienses*, p. 722, it is said that this Richard was son of Gilbert Deane of Saltonstall in this parish, by Elizabeth his wife; that he was born at Saltonstall, and having been educated in grammaticals in his own country, became at seventeen years of age, a student in Merton college, in 1587, where continuing about five years as a portionist, he retired to Alban-hall, where he took the degree of bachelor of arts in October 1592, and that of master three years after, which was the highest degree he took in this university. He was made Dean of Kilkenny in Ireland, and in the year 1609 succeeded Dr. Horsfall in the bishopric of Ossory. He died on the 20th of February, 1612, and lies buried in the cathedral at Kilkenny under a marble monument near the bishop's throne.

DEANE, EDMUND, brother to the above Richard, entered a student of Merton College, in lent term, 1591, aged nineteen, where (as we are told by Wood, p. 602) he took one degree in arts, and then retired to Alban-hall, where he became bachelor and doctor of physic. He settled in the city of York, and practised there till about the beginning of the civil wars.

FAVOUR, JOHN, L. L. D., sometime vicar of Halifax, was born at Southampton, where he was educated in grammatical learning, but finished for the university at Archbishop Wykeham's school at Winchester. He was elected fellow of New College in 1578. June 5, 1592, he proceeded doctor of the civil law, and was made vicar of Halifax, Decr. 3, 1593. The beginning of March, 1618, he was made warden or master of St. Mary Magdalen's hospital at Ripon. March 23, 1616, he was collated to the Prebendship of Driffield, and to the Chantership of the church of York. He was also chaplain to the Archbishop, and residentiary.

It is reported of this divine, that he preached every Sunday, lectured every day in the week, exercised justice in the commonwealth, and practised physic and chirurgery. That he was a good divine, a good physician, and a good lawyer. He died March 10, 1623, and was buried in the parish church. See his epitaph, p. 116.

FARRAR, ROBERT, Bishop of St. David's, the Martyr, was born in the parish of Halifax is certain, but unfortunately the family pedigree originates about a generation too low to comprehend him. "Happy should I have been to prove, (says DR. WHITAKER,) that Ewood Hall, a large substantial gentleman's house, rebuilt about a century ago, (the residence of the late Dr. Fawcett,) is one on the scite of that which gave birth to Robert Farrar, Bishop of St. David's, the Martyr."

"Though his nature appears to have partaken of the ruggedness of the soil and climate from which he sprung, and though he may in every respect be regarded as inferior to Cranmer, Ridley, and Latimer, yet we are bound to venerate the understanding and conscience of a man upon whom the light of the gospel dawned, in the twilight of a cloister, and who resolutely followed that light when it guided him from a throne to a stake."

He was condemned and burned at Caermathen, on the south side of the market-cross there, March 30, 1555. It was remarkable that one Jones coming to the bishop a little before his execution, lamented the painfulness of the death he had to suffer; but was answered, that if he once saw him stir in the pains of his burning, he should then give no credit to his doctrine. And what he said he fully performed, for he stood patiently and never moved, till he was beat down with a staff.

Fox in his *Book of Martyrs*, says that the first persecution against him was malicious, and that the second was commenced because he was a protestant. It is certain that some of the articles which he was put to answer in the reign of Edward the vi. were to the last degree frivolous, and shewed themselves to be the offspring of a revengeful mind, such as riding a Scottish pad, with a bridle with white studs and snaffle, white Scottish stirrups, and white spurs—wearing a hat instead of a cap—whistling to his child—laying the blame of the scarcity of herrings to the covetousness of fishers, who in time of plenty, took so many that they destroyed the breeders; and lastly, wishing that at the alteration of the coin, whatever metal it was made of, the penny should be in weight worth a penny of the same metal.

FAWCETT, JOHN, D. D. The late Dr. Fawcett though not a native of this parish, may justly be considered as identified with it, the whole of his long life, after he had attained to maturity, with the exception of occasional visits to other parts, having been spent in its precincts. He was brought up within the pale of the established church, and though he afterwards, from conscientious motives, connected himself with another denomination of christians, he retained a high respect for many distinguished individuals in that church, and preserved, through life, a friendly intercourse with them. In him orthodoxy and charity were happily united. From his earliest year he shewed an ardent thirst for knowledge, denying himself many of the comforts of life that he might spend the money in books, and often retrenching upon the hours of repose, that he might devote them to literary pursuits.

He commenced his labours as a minister, at Wainsgate, in the township of Wadsworth, situated in a mountainous district, and on the verge of an extensive moor, where a small place of worship of the humblest structure, had been erected by the neighbouring inhabitants. In this secluded spot, amidst many discouragements, and often exercised with heavy afflictions, he continued to officiate, though he had frequent invitations to places in a pecuniary point of view greatly superior, and where there was a prospect of more extended usefulness, till the gradual increase of the congregation, from the surrounding hamlets, rendered the erection of a new meeting house at Hebden Bridge, a central situation in the valley below very desirable, which was accordingly effected in the year 1777. In addition to the discharge of his pastoral duties, he opened an academy at Brearley Hall, in which he met with great encouragement, both during his residence there, and afterwards when the establishment was removed to Ewood Hall. Not to mention many others who availed themselves of pursuing their studies under these academic shades the names of FOSTER a native of this parish, writer of the celebrated Essays, and other valuable publications; and of WARD, the missionary, and co-adjutor of Dr. Carey, in translating and printing the holy scriptures into a variety of eastern languages, in which the attempt had never before been made, will be handed down to posterity. Numerous and pressing as Dr. Fawcett's engagements were, both before and after his removal from Wainsgate, he published a variety of books, many of which have passed through several editions; among which may be enumerated : "The Sick Man's Employ" written on recovering from a severe and tedious indisposition. " The Advice to Youth" " Hymns adapted for public worship and the closet :" "Essay on Anger ;"* "The Life of Oliver Heywood ;" "Christ precious to those who believe ;" "The history of John Wise," intended for young children, which has been widely circulated, and in which he shewed that versatility of talent by which Dr. Watts was so eminently distinguished : also a periodical work entitled "Miscellanea Sacra," printed at his own private press, with many other books, which the limits of this notice will not admit to be specified. When near seventy years of age, having retired from the superintendence. of the Academy, at the earnest request of several friends, he employed his leisure, in writing a Comment on the Bible, which was afterwards published, with the appropriate title of a "Devotional Family Bible." To this work, which, at his time of life, may well be considered as an Herculean labour, he steadily devoted his attention, without the aid of an amanuensis, and lived to complete it, though it was evident towards the close, that the unremitted application preyed upon his constitution; but in accordance with his favourite motto, "*Dum vivimus, vivamus*," he was anxious to be usefully employed, so long as his mental and corporeal powers would admit, and that he might not disappoint those who had patronized the publication, by leaving it in an unfinished state. He was born near Bradford, Jany. 6, 1740-1, and

---

* A copy of this Work, accompanied by a humble and dutiful address, expressive of his attachment to his Sovereign, was presented to his late Majesty George III., which the Author had the satisfaction of knowing was graciously received, and perused with approbation.

died July 25th, 1817, in the 77th year of his age.—Some time after his decease an octavo volume appeared, containing a detailed account of his life, ministry, and writings, comprehending many particulars relative to the progress of religion in Yorkshire and Lancashire.

Foe, Daniel de, a writer of great natural ingenuity and fertility, was born in London in 1663, being the son of a protestant dissenter who followed the business of a butcher. His father simply called himself Foe, and why Daniel prefixed the De to his name is not known. Being forced to abscond on account of his political writings, he resided some time at Halifax, in the Back-lane, at the sign of the Rose and Crown, being known to Dr. Nettleton the physician, and the Rev. Mr. Priestley, minister of the dissenting congregation there. It appears that he employed himself in writing his largest poem, "Jure Divino," being a satire on the doctrine of divine right; he is also here said to have written the most popular of all his performances, "The life and surprising adventures of Robinson Crusoe," which was published in 1719; the imputation of his founding it upon the papers of Alexander Selkirk, the Scottish mariner, left on the uninhabited island of Juan de Fernandez, appears to be altogether untrue.

Among the number of his political works he published "The shortest way with the Dissenters," an ironical recommendation of persecution, so gravely covered that many persons were deceived by it. The house of Commons voted it a seditious libel, and sentenced him to fine, imprisonment and pillory; so far from being ashamed of the latter he wrote "A hymn to the pillory," allusive to this circumstance. Pope thus characterizes him in his *Dunciad*:

"Careless on high, stood unabash'd Defoe."

This indefatigable and industrious writer died in April, 1731, at his house in Cripplegate, London, insolvent, leaving a widow and six children.

Gibson, William, M.D. was born at Slead hall in this parish, and educated in Jesus College, Cambridge, where having taken both the degrees in his faculty, he was elected Professor of Anatomy: here he might have continued with profit to others, and honor to himself, but having the misfortune to succeed to a moderate paternal estate, he quitted the liberal society, and with it the liberal habits of an university.   It might be said of him, as it was of another Cambridge professor, "erat ei magnum ingeneum non sine mixtura dementiæ :" —he was a man of genius, with a strong tincture of what, in the tenderness of modern language, is called derangement.   This was aggravated by brandy, to which he abandoned himself with as clear and calm a foresight of its consequences, as if he had been studying the case of a patient : he predicted the long life of his friend (Dr. Joseph Hulme, also a native of this parish) who was a water drinker, and with much more certainty the speedy termination of his own. Meantime he continued to practise in his own Faculty, sometimes with that felicity which is inseparable from genius, and often with a caprice and extravagance that rendered it dangerous to consult him.   At length he betook himself to a paltry inn at Brighouse, whence on one occasion he issued forth, in his scarlet robes and ermine hood, to meet and mortify a bachelor of his own faculty. At this house he became a prey to the destructive habit already mentioned, at the age of 39, and was interred in the parish church.

Greenwood, Daniel, D.D., was born in the township of Sowerby ; was first fellow, and afterwards made principal of Brazen Nose College, in Oxford, by the parliamentary visitors in 1648, and was vice-chancellor of that University in 1650 and 1651 ; in this latter year he was at the head of an association for the parliament, raising, at the charge of the heads of houses, &c. one hundred and twenty horse, and allowing the governor of Oxford to acquaint the counsel, that they had engaged to raise a regiment of foot out of the university and city.   This place he held no longer than the restoration, when he was ejected from it. After his wife's death, he lived in the house of his nephew, Mr. Daniel Greenwood, rector of Steeple-Aston, in Oxfordshire, where he died Jan. 29th, 1673, aged 71, and was buried in the chancel of the church there.

Greenwood, Daniel, son of John, and nephew of the above, was born in Sowerby, became scholar of Christ's college, Cambridge and in 1648 was made fellow of brazen noze college, Oxford, by the endeavours of his uncle, the principal of the said college, several fellows being that year ejected on account of their attachment to the king. In 1653 he was presented by the college to the rectory of Steeple Aston, in Oxfordshire, which he held until his death in 1629, and was buried near the grave of his uncle above-named.

GUEST, ———. It is said that General Guest, who bravely defended Edinburgh Castle against the rebels in 1745, was once a servant at the Angel Inn, at Halifax, which greatly redounds to his honor, as probably he was promoted for his merit. His parents lived at Lidgate, in Lightcliffe.

HARTLEY, DAVID, M.A. was born at Illingworth, in this parish; his father was curate there, and married May 25, 1707, a daughter of the Rev. Edward Wilkinson, his predecessor. His son David received his academical education at Jesus College, Cambridge, of which he was fellow. He first began to practise physic at Newark, in Nottinghamshire, from whence he removed to St. Edmund's Bury, in Suffolk. After this, he settled for some time in London, and lastly went to live at Bath, where he died Sept. 30, 1757, aged 53. He left two sons and a daughter. His elder son got a travelling fellowship, and his younger was entered at Oxford in Michaelmas term, 1757. He published " A View of the present Evidence for and against Mrs. Stephen's Medicines as a Solvent for the Stone, containing 155 cases, with some experiments and observations." London, 1739. This book, which contains 204 pages in 8vo. is dedicated to the president and fellows of the Royal College of Physicians, London. He was the chief instrument in procuring for Mrs. Stephens the £5000 granted by Parliament.

Dr. Hartley was allowed to be a man of learning, and reputed a good physician; but too fond of nostrums: his most considerable literary production is a work entitled "Observations on man, his frame, his duty, and his expectations, in two parts." London, 1749. 2 vols. 8vo.

HOYLE, JOSHUA, D.D. was born at Sowerby, received his first academical education in Magdalene-hall, in Oxford, and being afterwards invited to Ireland, was made fellow of Trinity Coll. Dublin: there he took the degree of D.D. and was elected Divinity Professor in that University. In this office he expounded the whole bible through in daily lectures, and in the chiefest books ordinarily a verse each day, which work held him almost fifteen years. Some time before he ended that work, he began the second exposition of the whole bible in the Church of Trinity College, and within ten years ended all the New Testament (excepting one book and a piece) all the Prophets, all Solomon, and Job. He preached also and expounded thrice every Sabbath for the greater part of the year, once every holyday, and sometimes twice. To these may be added, his weekly lectures (as Professor) in the controversies, and his answers to all Bellarmine's writings. On the breaking out of the Irish Rebellion, in 1641, he came into England, and was made vicar of Stepney, near London, but being too scholastical, he did not please the parishioners. He was constituted about this time one of the assembly of divines, and furnished evidence against Archbishop Laud on his trial, as to matter relating to the University of Dublin, whilst he was Chancellor thereof. At length by the favour of the committee of parliament for the reformation of the University of Oxford, he became Master of University College, and the King's Professor of Divinity. He was respected by Dr. Usher, the learned Primate of Ireland, in whose vindication he wrote "A Rejoinder to Will. Malone, Jesuit, his reply concerning the real presence." Dublin, 1641, in a thick 4to. He died Dec. 6, 1654, and was buried in the little old chapel of University College, which was pulled down in 1668.

Hulme Joseph, was born in the township of Little Horton, the second son of Samuel Hulme, a dissenting minister, of whom it is enough to say he was a friend and correspondent of Dr. Doddridge; under this excellent man Joseph Hulme was educated for the ministry; but, changing his purpose, was placed as a pupil with the amiable Dr. Nettleton, to learn the first rudiments of medical science. Hence he removed to Leyden, where he had the advantage of studying the different departments of his future profession, under Albinus and Muschenbrock. Here he took the degree of M.D. and published on that occasion an inaugural thesis, "De distillatione catarrhosa," which bears date 1743. He next proceeded to Paris, to complete his studies, and then returned to Halifax to succeed his old preceptor: here he continued to his death, which happened

Feb. 2, 1806, in the 92nd year of his age. He was interred in the North Chapel of Halifax Church, where a tablet has been erected to his memory.

HULME, NATHANIEL, M.D. lived for some time in Halifax with his uncle Joseph Hulme, M.D., and wrote "Libellus de natura, causa, curationeque Scorbuti. To this is annexed a Proposal for preventing the Scurvy in the British Navy, 8vo." London, 1768.

KNIGHT, TITUS, was born in this parish, December 17, 1719; he began to preach in the year 1749, being then among the Methodists. In 1762 he withdrew from that connection, and joined the Independents. In the year 1764 he was appointed one of the preachers at the Tabernacle, in London. He afterwards settled in Halifax, at a Chapel in the Fold; the place which was formed of two cottages thrown into one, becoming too small for his congregation, the handsome erection, called "The Square Chapel," was built by voluntary subscriptions, and opened in 1773, wherein he ministered until his decease, which happened in the year 1793. As a minister among the Independents he attained considerable eminence and popularity; and his name and character are still held in veneration by that numerous and respectable body of Christians.

KNIGHT, SAMUEL, A. M. was born at Halifax, on the 9th of March, 1759: he was the eldest child, (by the second marriage) of the above Titus Knight. There is a "circumstance (says the Rev. William Knight in the brief memoir of his father, accompanying his sermons and miscellaneous works,) rendered remarkable by events in after life, and which I cannot, on that account, omit mentioning, that my father was a child of delicate constitution; for, on being presented by his parents at the baptismal font, Dr. Legh, who then held the living of Halifax, and who officiated on the occasion, refused, in the first instance, to administer the ordinance, under the impression that the infant had actually expired before it was given into his arms! How profoundly ignorant are we of futurity: little did the vicar of Halifax imagine that the child he was about to exclude from the initiatory rite of the christian church, was destined, one day, to occupy the very situation, in that church, which he himself then filled."

He received the rudiments of his education at the Free Grammar School at Hipperholme, and on completing his twentieth year, he was entered a fellow of Magdalen College, Cambridge. With respect to his proficiency in literature, and his attainments of academical honors, it may simply be remarked, that his classical knowledge was not only highly appreciated by his college, but acknowledged by the university. The prominent situation which his name occupies among the wranglers who graduated in the year 1783, sufficiently establishes his character as a mathematician, and his being subsequently elected a fellow of his college affords a proof of the approbation which that society entertained as well of his conduct as of his talents. In the year 1783 he was ordained deacon, by Bishop Green, in the Temple Church, London, on receiving a title for the curacy of Wintringham, in the county and diocese of Lincoln. Here in addition to his clerical duties he undertook the charge of a few pupils, and in the year 1791 published his small book of Prayers, a book which passed through sixteen large editions during the life-time of its author, and continues much in request. In the year 1794 he was presented by Lord Carrington to the small living of Humberston in Lincolnshire. Along with the curacy of Wintrington he likewise held, for some years, that of Roxby, a village in the immediate neighbourhood. These united curacies he resigned in the year 1798, on being nominated by the Rev. Dr. Coulthurst who then held the living of Halifax, to the incumbency of Trinity Church in the town, which had just been erected at the expense of the Reverend Doctor. On the decease of that gentleman, which took place in December, 1817, a memorial numerously signed by the parishioners was presented to the earl of Liverpool, then prime minister, soliciting Mr. Knight's appointment to the vacant living. Although there were instances of this mode of application for crown livings, his lordship expressed his decided disapprobation of the principle which had been acted upon, as not only tending to infringe on the patronage of the crown, but as establishing a precedent which might lead to much inconvenience. At length the high testimonials in Mr. Knight's favour, supported by the influence of the late member for Yorkshire, (William Wilberforce, Esq.) and a short correspondence with the Archbishop of York, in which his grace was pleased to speak of Mr. Knight in terms of high commendation, and fully to confirm the statements which had been made in the memorial, his lordship waved his objections to the mode of application; and on the 29th day of December, 1817, Mr. Knight received an official intimation of his appointment to the living : he died on the 7th day of January, 1827, and lies interred in the chancel.

Without entering upon the particulars which characterized the features of Mr. Knight's pastoral qualifications as a christian minister —an exemplary churchman—an able scholar—a sound divine—a kind neighbour, and a truly good and valuable member of society; the very high commendations which he received not only from his parishioners, but also from his venerable and respected diocesan, in order to obtain for him the vacant living, will fully demonstrate the deserved estimation in which he was held, not only by his parishioners, but by all who had the honor and pleasure of his acquaintance. The sermons and miscellaneous works of the deceased, arranged and revised by his son, the Rev. James Knight, A. M, perpetual curate of St. Paul's, Sheffield, have been published in two vols. 8vo, accompanied by a brief memoir of the deceased, written by his second son, the Rev. W. Knight, A. M. assistant minister of St. John's, Hull.

JOHN LAKE, D. D. was born at Halifax, in that part now dignified by the name of Russel-street; he was educated at Queen Elizabeth's free grammar school there. THORESBY says he entered St. John's College, Cambridge, before he was thirteen years of age : when there he was made prisoner, during the civil wars, with the royal party ; but escaping thence he fled to the king at Oxford, and continued four years in the royal army ; he was present at the taking of Basinghouse and Wallingford. He refused the covenant and afterwards the engagement, and entered into episcopal orders when the royal cause was at the lowest ebb. July 26, 1647, he preached his first sermon as lecturer at Halifax, but did not continue long in that employment, the town being "too deeply infected by republican and fanatical principles, to allow a place of refuge to an inflexible royalist." In 1660 he was presented to the vicarage of Leeds, but not without so much opposition by the friends of his competitor, that he found the church doors barred against him, and was compelled

T

to employ the aid of a party of soldiers to secure his induction. In 1680 he was installed archdeacon of Cleveland; in 1682 consecrated bishop of Sodor and Man; and translated in 1684 to the see of Bristol. King James ii. in 1685 nominated him to the bishopric of Chichester. Dr. Lake was one of the seven bishops, committed to the Tower for presenting a petition against one of his sovereign's papistical ordinances, and subsequently tried and acquitted, to the great joy of the people of England. On the accession of his new sovereign, William the 3rd, he refused to take the oaths of allegiance and supremacy, in the conscientious belief that it would be repugnant to the allegiance which he had sworn to his late sovereign; in consequence of this refusal he was suspended from his preferment. He did not long survive his suspension, and on his death bed dictated and subscribed a memorable declaration in support of his favourite doctrine, non-resistance and passive obedience, which he regarded as the distinguishing characteristic of the church of England. Dr. Lake died, August 30th, 1689, as he had lived, "whether mistaken or not, at least a consistent and conscientious man."

MARSH, RICHARD, D. D. was born at Finhamstead, in Hertfordshire, in 1585, and educated at Cambridge, (though some have said that he was fellow of All Souls College, Oxford.) He took the degree of D. D. at Oxford in 1636. In 1614 he was made vicar of Birstal, in the west-riding of Yorkshire: in 1625, prependary of Southwell; and in 1634, he succeeded Archbishop Bramhall in the prebend of Husthwaite, in the church of York. April 17th, 1638, he was inducted into the vicarage of Halifax, as appears by an entry written with his own hand. In 1641 the king presented him to the Archdeaconry of York, or of the west-riding of Yorkshire and in November, 1644, nominated him to the deanery, on the death of Dr. Scott, the king being then at Oxford; but the confusions of those times would not permit him to be elected, much less installed, till the Restoration, when the former of these was performed August 17th, and the other the 20th, 1660. He was also prebendary of Ripon, and as WALKER, in his *Sufferings of the Clergy*, p. 82, says, vicar of Birstal, as before.

And as the doctor had these good preferments, so he was a great and very early sufferer for his attachment to the king his patron:

for in 1642, he had his living of Halifax sequestered, for delinquency, to the use of the forces under lord Fairfax, himself narrowly escaping from the town, but taken prisoner at Blackstone-edge, and carried to Manchester, where he was confined for some time, till he made his escape from thence, and got to the king at Oxford. Thus he lost the benefit of his living for eighteen years together, and saw Halifax no more till the restoration, when he returned, Sept. 16th, 1660, and took possession of his church again. An old man, who was present, told Mr. Beckwith of York, "that the doctor went into the church with his prayer-book under his arm, and finding Eli Bentley officiating there, he turned him out of the desk, and read prayers himself." The loss which the doctor sustained at Halifax (besides other places) amounted to more than four thousand pounds. He did not live long to enjoy his deanery, for he died Oct. 13th, aged 78, and was buried the 15th, 1663, in York Minster, near the grave of Matthew Hutton, Archbishop of York, in the south aisle of the choir, and over him was an achievement with his arms, impaling Grice, of Wakefield, but that achievement is now destroyed, and there only remained, in 1766, an escutcheon hung up near his grave, with his arms, viz. gules, an horse's head couped argent. (That in Halifax church is erased.) He had resigned the vicarage of Halifax sometime before his death. He had been chaplain to king Charles I. to Archbishop Laud, and to Dr. Matthews, Archbishop of York.

The Dr. was three times married; his first wife was the daughter of Mr. Stephens, by whom he had five children; his second wife was Elizabeth, daughter of Robert Batt, of Okewell-hall, near Birstal, and fellow and vice-master of University College, Oxford, by whom one daughter, Catharine, born in trouble; for when the mother was *enceinte*, the soldiers of Cromwell coming into the house in search of Dr. Marsh, and not finding him, supposed he might be hid in bed, and therefore stabbed their swords into the bed where his wife was laid, and so frighted and wounded her, that it induced immediate parturition, but having given birth to a daughter the mother expired. The doctor fled to save himself, and a trusty maid-servant made her escape with the child in the night, with nothing but her upper garment on, carrying it in that state in the dark, for fourteen miles, to a relation of the doctor's, where it remained till the Restoration when her father was at liberty to return. This daughter, Catharine, married Mr. John Kay of Gomersal, and died at Howley-hall, about 1730, leaving a son and daughter, the latter of whom, Martha, married Dr. Robert Tomlinson, rector of Wickham and was living in 1766, being then in her 104th or 105th year. Dr. Marsh's third wife was Frances, daughter of Mr. Grice of Wakefield, She was buried in York minster, July 25, 1665.

The wives and children of delinquents being, by public ordinances allowed the fifth part of the estate and goods which had been seized upon, the following petition was sent in against Dr. Marsh, containing a set of reasons against his family receiving the said fifth part; but what was the effect of it does not appear.

"1. Dr. Marsh was long since cast out of the vicarage of Hallifax for misdemanors. 2. As wee conceive, the said Dr. Marsh was never actually sequestered, or if hee was, never yet made his composicion. 3. There was never any yett settled by authoritty in the room of the said viccor to receive the profitts, except Mr. Wayte, who was appointed viccor by the late Lord Fairfax. 4. The wholle profitts of the vicarrage doe in a manere wholy consist in Easter dewes, and comunicant two penses, which wee conceive in equitty cannot be demanded, seeing thatt Easter comunicants have soe longe seased. 5. The people in that viccarage have beene att greate charge in mayntayneing the ministers, there beeing 12 chappalreyes in the said viccarage, att which the have had for the most part preaching ministers, and very little or noe mayntayneance to most of them. 6. The said Dr. Marsh had, when hee was expelled the viccarage, severall other liveinges, as att Birstall, Yorke, Rippon, Sussex, hee was the latte Kinges chaplayen, and one of the hie comishon att Yorke, besides he hath a good estate of his owne in land, to the valeu of £30 per ann. and upwards. And whereas itt is declared, thatt this now demanded is for his childeren, being a 5ᵗ part, wee make bold humly to certiefie, thatt if itt shold bee expected, and the people forst to pay itt, the greattest part of itt must come from those thatt are in farr greater nesesitie then any of his childeren is likely yett to come too, and from those who have hazerded theire lives, and laid out their estates in the Parliment's servise, and whose suferings and loses have beene very greate.

"The peticioners unanimously, as well the inhabittants within the mother church whome the said small tithes did chiefely concerne and all the rest of the viccarage, make it theire humble request, that the said Dr. Marshe's order for his 5^t part may bee called in, and that the same, and all the rest of the said tithes or Easter oblacions may either wholy bee taken of, or otherwayes that the said tithes may bee devided amongst the several chapells and mother-church, as the was certified by the Com". for the West Rideing of the county of Yorke upon an act or order of Parliment."

It must be observed, that the estate of one John Marsh, D. D. who was said to have been late of Halifax in the county of York, was declared forfeited by treason, by an act of November 18, 1652, but this, Mr. WATSON had reason to think, was a misnomer.

MIDGLEY, SAMUEL, the real author of the history of Halifax, which goes under the name of William Bentley, was a prisoner for debt in York Castle, in 1685, where he was acquainted with Oliver Heywood. He was also three times in Halifax jayl for debt, where he wrote the above history, and where he died July 18, 1695. His poverty prevented him from printing the book which he wrote for his own support; and he not only lost the benefit of his labors in his life-time, but had another man's name put to his work when he was dead. He practised physic, and was the son of William Midgley, who was buried at Luddenden August 21, 1695, aged eighty-one.

MILNER, JOHN, B. D. was the second son of John Milner, of Skircoat. This eminent scholar was educated at the free grammar school of queen Elizabeth, there. At fourteen years of age he was sent from thence to Christ's college, Cambridge, where he took both the degrees in arts. He was elected vicar of Leeds, and inducted thereto, A. D, 1673. In 1681, he was installed prebendary of Ripon, and after an incumbency of twelve years, being dissatisfied with the oaths imposed on the accession of king William he voluntarily quitted his preferments. Continuing in communion with the church of England, he retired to St. John's college, Cambridge, where he spent the last thirteen years of his life in piety and study, beloved by the older members of the college, and reverenced for the quiet sanctity of his manners by the younger. There he died, the 16th February, 1703, aged 75. He was the author of several learned works. His character may be summed up in the following extract from a letter received by Thoresby from Dr. Gower then master of St. John's. "Great learning and piety made him really a great man; he was eminent in both, and nothing but his humility and modesty kept him from being more noted for being so. I had the happiness of much of his conversation, but still desired more. He was a blessing to the whole society by the example he gave in every good thing. He died beloved and much lamented here, and his memory is honorable and precious among us, and will long continue so."

NALSON, ROBERT, the collector of a folio manuscript, intitled, "Miscellanea sive observationes collectaniæ," and signed "Robert Nalson, 1665." This volume (which was in Mr. Watson's own collection) consists of a vast variety of subjects, chiefly transcripts, but interspersed with original papers, and others so scarce that they are nearly as valuable as if they were known originals. Wright, at page 80 of his history, says, this MS. unfortunately fell into ill hands, and had several pages, all of them relating to the gibbet executions, torn out, before the book was returned to the proper owner. Where he received that information, says Watson, I cannot tell, but it appears not from the book itself. The late Mr. Wilson, of Leeds, in his MS. account of English Historians, in two vols. folio, now at the Free Grammar School, at Leeds, says, that Mr. Nalson, left MSS, to Halifax Library, but nothing of that sort appears now, and I judge it to be a mistake. The author tells us that he received confirmation from Archbishop Freuin, in 1664, in his own chapel, at Bishopthorpe, and that he was then about thirty-nine years of age.

NETTLETON, THOMAS, son of John, born at Dewsbury, settled at Halifax, where he practised physic for several years with great success, having taken the degree of M. D. at Leyden. He and Mr. West, of Underbank, near Pennistone, in Yorkshire, were the first who instructed professor Sanderson in the principles of mathematics and the Doctor used to say, that the scholar soon became more knowing than his masters. He was author of a pamphlet, intitled "some thoughts concerning virtue and happiness, in a letter to a Clergyman." Lond. 1729, 8vo. which he afterwards much enlarged.

It was reprinted in 1736, and 1751, at London, both in 8vo., but the former of these is the more valuable, because it had the author's finishing hand. The design of this valuable work, is to shew, that happiness is the end of all our actions; how we deviate from our true happiness; and how these deviations may be prevented. He has also given us some excellent rules for the management of our several passions, and has undeniably proved, that virtue is the best and chiefest good; that it is not only the support and ornament of society, and beneficial to mankind in general, but the truest, and most substantial happiness to every particular person, as it yields the greatest pleasure, both in its immediate exercise, and in its consequences and effects: that it gives a relish to all other pleasures, and where it is wanting, there can be no true nor lasting pleasure, but all will be bitterness, horror, and remorse, without the least mixture of any thing gentle and agreeable. His other works are "Disputatio de Inflammatione;" and an account of the method of inoculating for the small pox. By a paper of Dr. Jurin's, p. 131, vol. vi. Philosophical Transactions, it appears, that Dr. Nettleton had inoculated sixty-one persons, when all others in England (as far as could be gathered) had only inoculated one hundred and twenty-one. The doctor died Jany. 9, 1742, and was buried on the 12th at Dewsbury.

The following story is told of the doctor: that being in company with several gentlemen, one of them was laying great stress on Dean Echard's account of Cromwell's selling himself to the devil before the battle of Worcester; affirming, that the bargain was intended to be for twenty-one years, but that the devil had put a trick upon Oliver, by changing the twenty-one into twelve, and then turning hastily to the doctor, asked him, "What could be the devil's motive for so doing?" The doctor without hesitation answered, "That he could not tell what was his motive, unless he was in a hurry about the Restoration."

OGDEN, SAMUEL, D. D. born in or near Manchester, July 28th, 1716, was curate of Coley, in this parish, afterwards, master of the free grammar school near Halifax, and curate of Elland. The name of Ogden was anciently Oakden, denoting a place in the township of Butterworth, near Rochdale, and their arms three slips of Oak acorned, proper, contain a proper allusion to the true orthography. He was a fellow of St. John's, in Cambridge, where he took the degree of D. D. and was made vicar of Damerham in Wiltshire. He published two sermons, preached before the university of Cambridge, in 1758, one from 1 Thess. v. 13. upon May 29, being the anniversary of the restoration or king Charles II. the other from Deut. iv. 6. on June 22, being the anniversary of the Accession of his Majesty king George II.   Both dedicated to his patron the duke of Newcastle, chancellor of the university of Cambridge.   He also published some sermons on the efficacy of prayer and intercession, printed at Cambridge.   The doctor was chosen Woodwardian professor of the university of Cambridge.   He died 22 March, 1778, and was interred in St. Sepulchre's Church, Cambridge, where a plain monument records all that will be necessary in that place. "As a preacher, (says Dr. WHITAKER,) he was an original, never yet safely imitated, and never safe to be imitated.   As a writer, he is above all praise, in short he was one of those gifted orators, who equally attract the learned and illiterate, who are heard with equal admiration and delight in the pulpit of an university, or by a congregation of peasants.   What he attempted he mastered, what he understood at all, he understood perfectly."

POWER, HENRY, M. D. practised physic in Halifax, from whence Wright, in his History, p. 171, says, he removed to New Hall, near Elland, and died there; but Wilson, in his MS. account of the English historians, already mentioned, tells us, that he removed from Halifax to Wakefield, where he died Dec. 23, 1668.   He wrote a treatise, intitled "Experimental Philosophy, in three books, containing new experiments, microscopical, mercurial, and magnetical." 4to. London, 1664.

RAMSDEN, HENRY, son of Geoffry Ramsden, of Greetland, in this parish, was admitted a commoner of Magdalen hall in Oxford, in 1610.   He took the degrees in arts, and was elected fellow of Lincoln College. in 1621, and five years afterwards, leaving that place, became a preacher in London, and was much resorted to, for his edifying and puritanical sermons.   At length, on the death of Mr. Hugh Ramsden, his elder brother, he was made vicar of

Halifax, where he continued till his death, in 1637, and was buried in the chancel of Halifax church.

The register at Halifax has this entry: "Henricus Ramsden, filius Galfridi Ramsden, de Greetland, infra vicariam de Hallifax, atq; Hugonis, nuper vicarii de Hallifax, frater natu minor, M. A. socius collegii Lincolniensis, Oxon. inductus est vicarius de Hallifax decimo calend. Septembris, anno 1629." His widow died at Elland, May 11, 1682.

ROOKEBY, WILLIAM, Dr Archbishop of Dublin, sometime vicar of Halifax, was born, as Wilson asserts in his MS. account of English historians, at Kirk Sandal in Yorkshire, though Tanner says that he was born in Halifax. He was educated, says WOOD in his *Athenæ* vol. i, p. 659, partly in an ancient hostle for the reception of Canonists in St. Aldate's parish in Oxford; he himself being afterwards doctor of the Canon law. He was made rector of Sandal and vicar of Halifax, In 1498 according to Sir James Ware, vol. i. p. 153, he was made lord chancellor of Ireland by king Henry the vii. but Wood fixes this to the year 1515, not knowing that this was his second election into that high office, which he is supposed after this to have held for life. In 1507 he was advanced to the bishopric of Meath, by Pope Julius ii. and the same year called into the privy council by King Henry the vii. And was afterwards, by the same pope, translated to the see of Dublin, Jan. 28, 1511-12, and on the 22nd of June following had restitution of the temporalties, In 1518 he convened a provincial synod, the canons of which are yet extant in the Red book of the church of Ossory. He died Nov. 29, 1521, and his body was buried (says Sir James Ware) in his own cathedral of St. Patrick's, Dublin, only his heart was conveyed into England, and deposited in the monument of his ancestors. This may be true, but it is directly contrary to the words of his will, which ordered, that he should be embowelled, and his bowels and heart buried in the church of Halifax, within the choir, and his body to be buried in the new chapel at Sandal, and thereon a tomb of stone to be made, and about the same to be written: "Ego Willielmus, Dublin. Archiepiscopus, quondam rector istius ecclesiæ, credo quod Redemptor meus vivit—Qui obiit—— cujus animæ propitietur Deus, Amen." There is no proof, it must be owned, that his body was conveyed to Sandal. That his heart and bowels were buried at Halifax seems certain, for WRIGHT, p. 43, says, they were buried in the chancel of Halifax church, and over them was laid a stone, with the figure of an heart engraved thereon; and that when the chapel, which he had ordered to be built on the north side of Halifax church, was finished, they were removed into it, with the stone which lay over them, which yet remains, though his heart and bowels may not be there, for the earth has been suffered to be opened, and once, if not oftener, the little lead box which contained them has been dug up.

The archbishop beautified and repaired the vicarage-house at Halifax.

ROOTS, HENRY, this was the person whom Mr. Tillotson (afterwards archbishop) consulted, in 1649, about taking the engagement at Clare-hall, Cambridge. He published a pamphlet, entitled " a just apology for the church of Duckenfield," 4to. This was a defence of one Eaton, who was at the head of a congregational assembly there, against the reflections of one Edwards, and is dated from Sowerby, March 2, 1646.

SAVILE, HENRY, afterwards knighted by James the First, in 1604, was one of the most profound and elegant scholars of the age in which he lived. He was born at Bradley, in this parish, Nov. 30th, 1549, and after graduating at Brazennose College, Oxford, removed on a fellowship to Merton College, in the same university. In his twenty-ninth year he made a tour on the continent, for the purpose of perfecting himself in elegant literature, and on his return was appointed tutor in Greek and mathematics to Queen Elizabeth, who held his abilities in great estimation. Seven years after, the wardenship of his college becoming vacant, he was elected to fill that situation, which he held for about six-and-thirty years, the provostship of Eton being added to it in 1596. On the accession of James to the throne of the united kingdoms, several dignified offices were offered to his acceptance by the new king, who affected to patronize all men of eminent classical attainments. The moderation of Mr. Savile was, however, as conspicuous on this occasion as his erudition; and although he accepted the order of knighthood, he steadily declined all other proposals, either of honour or emolument. In fact, the loss of an only son soon made him utterly indifferent to promotion of any kind, and from that moment he appears to have dedicated both his time and fortune solely to the advancement and encouragement of literature. In 1619 he founded two professorships in geometry and astronomy in the university of which he was a member, besides conferring several other valuable benefactions both in property and books, many of the latter forming still a part of the Bodleian library. He was the author of several learned works, of which the principal are his " Commentaries on Roman Warfare;" " Rerum Anglicarum post Bedam Scriptores," folio, to which is added a chronological account of events from Cæsar to the Conquest; " Prælectiones tredecem in Elementa Euclidis Oxoniæ habitæ;" " Oratio coram Elizabetha Regina habita;" a translation of four books of Tacitus, and that writer's life of Agricola, with a commentary, in one folio volume. He also edited Bradwardin " De Causâ Dei;" but the work by which he is principally known is his celebrated edition of the writings of St. Chrysostom, in eight folio volumes, which, including the sums paid by him for the collation of different manuscripts both in England and on the continent, was not produced at a less expense than £8000. Sir Henry Savile was the intimate friend and correspondent of J. Scaliger, Meibomius, Isaac Causabon, and most of the learned men of his day. Sir Henry is mentioned as a member of the Society of Antiquaries, in the Introduction to the Miscellaneous Tracts relating to Antiquity, published by the Society of Antiquaries of London, in 1770, p. 21. So well did he deserve the character given of him, that he was " Musarum Patronus, et Literarum Mæcenas," being an encourager of all sorts of useful learning, and universally well spoken of by all disinterested scholars. There is a painting of him in the picture gallery at Oxford. His death took place at Eton College, February 19, 1622, and his remains lie buried in the chapel belonging to that establishment. He had two brothers, JOHN SAVILE, afterwards knighted, who died in 1606, one of the barons of the exchequer, and a lawyer of considerable talent, whose reports in the courts of the exchequer and common pleas are yet referred to as books of authority: and THOMAS, of whom we record the following.

SAVILE, THOMAS, younger brother to sir John and sir Henry just mentioned, born likewise at Over Bradley, in Stainland, was admitted probationer fellow of Merton College, in 1580, and afterwards proceeding in arts, he went abroad, and travelling through various countries, improved himself in several parts of learning. After his return, he became, through the interest of his brother, one of the fellows of Eaton college, where he did credit to his brother's choice, being reckoned among the first rate scholars. He was made proctor of Oxford, April 5, 1592, and died the 12th of January following, at London; from whence his body was removed to Oxford, and interred with great solemnity in the choir of Merton College church, the following eulogium to his memory, being entered in the register of that house: "Fuit sidus lucidissimum, qui apud suos, et exteros, literarum et virtutis fama ac morum urbanitate percelebris, &c."

He wrote "Epistolæ variæ ad illustres viros." Fifteen of these were written to Camden, and are published by Dr. Thomas Smith, of Magdalen college, Oxford, in a book entitled, "V. Cl. Gulielmi Cambdeni, et illustrium Virorum ad G. Cambdenum Epistolæ, etc." London, 1691, 4to. This was the reason why Cambden, in his preliminary discourse to the Brigantes, calls this Thomas his learned friend in 1582; and it is something strange that Wood, in his *Fasti*, p. 127, should have any doubt of this being the same person, when, in his *Athenæ*, he had mentioned the above fifteen letters.

SAVILE, GEORGE, marquis of Halifax, descended of the same family as the preceding, an illustrious statesman and elegant writer, was born in 1630. On the death of Cromwell he distinguished himself by his exertions in favour of the absent king, which on the restoration of that monarch to the throne, were rewarded by a by a coronet. In 1672 he was joined in commission with the Duke of Buckingham and Lord Arlington to conduct the negociation with France for a general peace. With this view he accompanied his colleagues to Holland, but the object of their mission fatling, returned to this country, and resumed his seat at the council-board. From this situation, however, he was removed in 1675, through the influence of the Duke of York, afterwards James the Second, in consequence of his violent opposition to that Prince's measures in favour of the Roman Catholic religion. But although he appears to have been a determined enemy to that church, his loyalty to the Stuart family operated no less forcibly on him when the bill for excluding the Duke from the succession was in agitation, his strongly manifested repugnance to which measure brought him greatly into disgrace with the party with which he had hitherto acted; so much so, that they carried a vote through the Commons that a petition should be presented to the King, praying him again to dismiss the obnoxious peer from the post to which he had been but recently restored. The dissolution of the parliament, so hostile to him, soon followed, and he was raised a step higher in the peerage. In 1682 he experienced a still farther elevation, being created marquis of Halifax, keeper of the privy seal, and president of the council, which dignities he retained in the early part of the succeeding reign, till his opposition to the proposed repeal of the test acts excited the new king's displeasure, and caused his abrupt dismissal. From this moment Lord Halifax continued in opposition, till the flight of James, when he was chosen speaker of the House of Lords, in what is known as the convention parliament, and in that capacity contributed mainly to the elevation of William to the throne. His predilection for the new government, however, did not long continue: and the year following, that of the Revolution, he resigned in in disgust the privy seal, which had once more been committed to his keeping, and during the whole remainder of his life spoke and voted against the court. A mortification in the bowels carried him off in 1695. Lord Halifax was a man of great and unquestioned talents: as an orator, though powerful and convincing, his eloquence wanted that refinement which is found in his writings, his style being occasionally low, and his humour coarse. Bishop Burnet denies the then generally received opinion of his having been a freethinker, and affirms that he died a sincere Christian from conviction. He was the author of a treatise, entitled "Advice to a Daughter," as well as of a variety of political tracts, the principal of which are, "Maxims of State;" "The Character of a Trimmer:" "Character of King Charles II.;" "Anatomy of an Equivalent;" "Letter to a Dissenter," &c. Many of these were collected after his decease, and printed together in one octavo volume; an enlarged edition appeared some years after. He was succeeded in his titles and estates by his only son WILLIAM, who survived his father a little more than four years, and by whose death, without issue, the marquisate became extinct.

SAVILE, HENRY, of Shaw-hill, in Skircoat, in this parish, commonly called long Harry Savile, was of the Saviles of Bank, near Halifax, entered a student of Merton College in 1517, (his kinsman, Mr. Henry Savile, being then warden,) and was soon after made one of the portionists, commonly called postmasters. After he had taken the degree of B. A. he left Merton College, and retired to St. Alban Hall, where, in 1595, he took the degree of M. A. Being all this time under the inspection of his kinsman, he became an eminent scholar, especially in the mathematics, physic, (in which faculty he was admitted by the university to practise,) chemistry, painting, heraldry, and antiquities. Afterwards, for the completing of his knowledge, he travelled into Italy, France, and Germany, where he greatly improved himself. He wrote several things, but, I think, committed nothing to the press. He gave Camden the ancient exemplar of Asser Menevensis, which he published in 1602, and which contains the story of the discord between the new scholars which Grimbald brought with him to Oxford, at the restoration of the university by king Alfred, with the old clerks which Grimbald found there. This Henry Savile lived for some years, after his return from foreign countries, in the parish of St. Martin in the Fields, near London, and died there April 29th, 1617, aged forty nine years, and was buried in the chancel belonging to the parish church there, a monument being set over his grave on the north wall, with his bust to the middle, carved in stone, and painted, the right hand resting on a book, and the left on a death's head. The inscription worn out.

One Henry Savile, Esq. was captain of the adventure under sir Francis Drake and sir John Hawkins, against the Spaniards in the West Indies, and wrote a book called, "a libel of Spanish lies found at the sack of Cales, discoursing the fight in the West Indies between the English and the Spaniard, and of the death of sir Francis Drake; with an answer, confuting the said Spanish lies, &c." London, 1596. This was an answer to a letter wrote by the Spanish general, asserting that sir Francis Drake died of grief, because he had lost so many barks and men, and that the English fleet fled from the Spaniards in 1695. This captain Savile is supposed to have been a relation of the above.

In queen Elizabeth's time, three Henry Saviles, of Yorkshire, were matriculated as members of Merton College, Oxford, viz. one, son of Plebeian, in 1588, another, son of an Esquire, in 1593, and a third, son of an Esquire, in 1595.

TILLOTSON, JOHN, Lord Archbishop of Canterbury, was born in 1630, at Haugh End in Sowerby, in this parish, being the son of Robert Tillotson, a clothier. His father, who was a strict Calvinist, brought up his son in the same principles, and after a proper preparatory education sent him a pensioner to Clare hall, Cambridge, where he took both the degrees in arts, and was elected a fellow in 1651. Some time afterwards he became tutor and chaplain in the family of Prideaux, the attorney general to the protector, Cromwell. It is not known when he entered into orders, but his first sermon which appeared in print is dated September 1661, at which time he was still among the presbyterians. When the act of uniformity passed in the following year, he however submitted to it without hesitation, and became curate to Dr. Hacket, vicar of Cheshunt, in Hertfordshire: and was presented in 1663 to the rectory of Keddington, in the county of Suffolk, which he resigned on being chosen preacher to the society of Lincoln's inn. In 1664 he married Elizabeth, daughter to Dr. French, and niece to Oliver Cromwell, whose sister Robina was her mother. In 1666 he took the degree of D.D. and was made king's chaplain, and presented to a prebend of Canterbury. When Charles ii. in 1672 issued a declaration for liberty of conscience, for the purpose of favouring the Roman Catholics, he preached and counselled against it; but was nevertheless advanced to the deanery of Canterbury, and soon after presented to a prebend in the church of St. Paul. At the revolution, he was immediately taken into favour by king William; and in 1689 he was appointed clerk of the closet to that sovereign, and subsequently permitted to exchange the deanery of Canterbury for that of St. Paul's. On the refusal of archbishop Sancroft to take the oaths to the new government, he was appointed to exercise the archiepiscopal jurisdiction during the suspension of that prelate; and in 1691, after exhibiting the greatest reluctance, he was induced to accept the archbishopric itself.

Popery was so much the object of his dread and aversion, that in a sermon preached before the king in 1680, he was betrayed into sentiments of intolerance, which exposed him to heavy censure, implying that no man, unless divinely commissioned, and who, like the apostles, can justify that commission by miracles, is entitled to draw men away from an established religion, even although false. Several animadversions were made upon this extraordinary doctrine, which assailed the authors of the reformation itself; but the doctor made no open reply to them, although he privately acknowledged to his friends that he had hastily expressed himself in terms which could not be maintained. He warmly promoted the exclusion bill against the duke of York, and refused to sign the address of the London clergy to the king on his declaration that he would not consent to it. At the execution of lord William Russell he attended with Dr. Burnet; and though afterwards decided friends to the revolution, both these divines urged that nobleman to acknowledge the absolute unlawfulness of resistance. In the mean time, Dr. Tillotson had twice formed a scheme for the comprehension of the presbyterians within the pale of the church, both of which attempts proved abortive. He had also failed in another design for forming a new book of Homilies; and a sermon which he preached before the queen, against the absolute eternity of hell torments, still farther involved him with the advocates of rigid orthodoxy. When therefore he accepted the primacy, a large party, of course including all the nonjurors, assailed him with great animosity; and in particular he was reproached, and not unjustly, with the inconsistency of his own conduct with the doctrine he had advanced to lord William Russel. He prudently bore these attacks in silence, and even prevented some prosecutions for libel against him, directed by the crown. He was also vehemently charged with Socinianism, in answer to which he only republished four of his sermons "On the Incarnation and Divinity of our Saviour." There appears to have been no other ground for that imputation, than that he defended Christianity on rational grounds, and corresponded with such men as Limborch, Locke, and Le Clerc; to which reason Dr. Jortin adds, that he had made some concessions concerning the Socinians, which broke an ancient and fundamental rule of controversial theology, "allow not an adversary either to have common sense or common honesty." He gave the last answer to these and other strictures by doing everything he could to advance the respectability of the church, and among other things wished to correct the evils arising from non-residence. He was however counteracted in all his endeavours by the most perverse opposition, which rendered his high station a scene of much more disgust than gratification. He had indeed but little time to effect much of what he proposed, being seized with a paralytic stroke, the consequences of which carried him off after an illness of five days, on the 24th November, 1694, in his sixty-fifth year. So little had he been addicted to accumulation, that all he left his widow was the copyright of his sermons : but a pension was very properly settled on her by the crown. The temper and private character of Dr. Tillotson are entitled to great encomium ; he was open, sincere, benevolent, and forgiving ; and although in some points too compliant, and fairly liable to the charge of inconsistency, his intentions always seem to have been pure and disinterested. As a writer he is principally remembered for his sermons, which have long maintained a place among the most popular of that class of compositions in the English language. They obtained a high reputation both at home and abroad ; and though doubtless much less read than formerly, can scarcely fail of remaining a permanent part of the branch of English literature to which they belong.*

The following circumstances, in connexion with this truly great and good man, are noticed by Mr. WATSON.

It is very remarkable, that Wright, in his history of Halifax, p. 154, speaking of the dispute relating to the Archbishop's being baptized in the church, says, " I myself have twenty times looked at his name in the Register, and to the best of my remembrance, there were four others christened the same day with him, whose names were all wrote down in the same hand, and same ink, without the least interlineation." Such an information as this, one would think, might be depended upon as exact, and yet when I searched the same Register, says WATSON, I found his name to be the last of seven, who were baptized together, and entered in these words, "Bapt. Oct. 3, 1630, John Robert Tilletson, Sourb."

* Biographical dictionary.

The following original letter seems not to have been known to any of the compilers of the Archbishop's life.

"For his much respected friend, Mr. Roote, att Sorbey, are
     these.

     "SIR,   In Yorkeshire,

"To excuse the slownes and infrequency of writeing, is growne a thing soe complementall and common in the frontispeece of every letter, that I have made choice rather to put myselfe upon your candor to frame an excuse for mee, then goe about myselfe to doe it. I cannot but thankefully acknowledge my engagements to you for your kindnes showne to mee, both when I was in the country, and at other times; I shall not here let my pen run out into complementall lines, gratitude (and that as much as may bee) being all that I desire to expresse. As for our University affayres, things are as they was [so in original] before I came into the country, only wee have lesse hopes of procuring Mr. Tho. Goodwin for our master then we then had. Wee are in expectation of the visitors every day, but what will bee done at their comming wee cannot guesse. The Engagement is either comming downe hither, or (as I heare) already come, to which how soone wee shall bee called upon to subscribe, wee knowe not; as for my selfe I do not (for present) at all scruple the taking of it, yet, because I dare not confide too much to my owne judgement, or apprehension of things, and because matters of such serious consequence require no little caution and consideration, therefore I shall desire you (as soone as with convenience you can) to returne mee your opinion of it in two or three lines. Mr. Rich. Holbrooke desired me to present his respects to you and your wife, to whom alsoe I desire you to present my best respects, as alsoe to your son, Joh. Hopkinson, and his wife. Noe more, but your prayers for him who remaines.

                 Yours, whilst

                     JOH. TILLOTSON."

Clare-Hall, Dec. 6, 1649.

What sort of answer was given to the above, does not appear, but as Mr. Roote, who at that time was preacher at Sowerby Chapel, was one of the Puritans, it is probable that he would not dissuade

Mr. Tillotson from complying with the engagement here mentioned, which was an Act substituted in the room of the Oaths of Allegiance and Supremacy, and was ordered to be taken by every one who held either office or benefice, "that they would be true and faithfull to the government established, without king or house of peers."— Add to this, that Mr. Tillotson, who at that time was an undergraduate of Clare Hall, and very young, was under the care of Mr. Clarkson, a tutor there, who also was a Puritan, and attached to the government then in being. It does not appear, however, that Mr. Tillotson long adhered to the principles, (especially the religious ones,) which he may have been supposed to have received either from his father, or college tutor, for his writings breathe quite a different spirit from the stiff and rigid sentiments of those times: in particular, when Dean of Canterbury, he preached before his father at Sowerby Chapel, against the doctrine of Calvin, probably with an intent to rectify his father's notions; and one Dr. Maud, who had frequent disputes with the Archbishop's father about predestination, asking him, how he liked his son's discourse? the old man replied, in his usual way when he asserted any thing with earnestness, " I profess he has done more harm than good."

The following anecdote was told Mr. Watson by the late Rev. Mr. Tillotson, sur-master of St. Paul's School, who had it from Dr. Secker, when Bishop of Oxford :—When the famous Duke of Buckingham presented Dr. Tillotson to King Charles II. after saying, that he introduced to his Majesty the gravest Divine of the Church of England, he stepped forward, and in a lower tone said to the king, "And of so much wit, that if he chose it, he could make a better comedy than ever your majesty laughed at." But on what grounds the duke said this I cannot conceive, for the doctor has left no specimen of this kind of wit behind him. Perhaps he had an inclination to serve the doctor, and knew that this was one effectual way to recommend him to the king.

It is commonly said about Sowerby, that Robert Tillotson went to London to see his son, then dean of Canterbury, and being in the dress of a plain countryman, was insulted by one of the Dean's servants, for inquiring if John Tillotson was at home; his person, however, being described to the dean, he immediately went to the door, and in the sight of his servants fell down upon his knees to ask a blessing of the stranger.

TILSON, HENRY, D. D. bishop of Elphin, was born, it is said, in the parish of Halifax, but in what particular part is uncertain. The name has been common in several townships there, especially in Sowerby and Ovenden. He was entered a student in Baliol college, Oxford, in 1593, was made B. A. in 1596, soon after which he got a fellowship in University·College, and there took his degree of M. A. In Oct. 1615, he succeeded R. Kenion in the vicarage of Rochdale in Lancashire, where, after he had resided some years, he went chaplain to Thomas earl of Strafford, lord lieutenant of Ireland, who made him dean of Christ church in Dublin, pro vice-chancellor of the university of Dublin, and bishop of Elphin, to which he was consecrated Sept. 23, 1639 ; but this he did not long enjoy, on account of the rebellion, which soon after broke out. SIR JAMES WARE, in his *History of the Irish Bishops*, p. 635, says, that on the 16th of August, 1645, he delivered the castle of Elphin into the hands of the lord president of Connaught ; his son, Capt. Henry Tilson, who was governor of Elphin, having just before joined with Sir Charles Coot, in opposition to the king's interest. And about the same time, his library and goods were pillaged by Boetius Egan, the titular bishop of Elphin, his damages amounting to the sum of four hundred pounds. He himself fled for safety into England, and settled at Soothill-hall in the parish of Dewsbury, where some of his relations lived, and where he resided three years, intending to have returned, but never did. Having thirteen persons, however, in his family, and being stript of his income, he was obliged to have recourse to such means for subsistence, as his station in the church put in his power: for this purpose he consecrated a room in the said hall, called to this day the Bishop's parlour, where he privately ordained, and did weekly the offices of a clergyman, some of his neighbours being both hearers and benefactors to him ; till Sir W. Wentworth, of Breton, out of compassion to his distressed circumstances, employed him to preach at Comberworth, allowing him a salary to support him. Thus was this prelate obliged to stoop to become a country curate ! the following extract from the register belonging to Dewsbury church, shews when and where he was interred : " Henry, lord bishop of Elphin, buried the 2nd day of April, 1655."

WATSON, JOHN, F. S. A. was the eldest son of Legh Watson, by Esther, daughter and at last heiress of Mr. John Yates, of Swinton in Lancashire. He was born in the township of Lyme-cum-Hanley, in the parish of Prestbury in Cheshire, March 26th, 1724, (O. S.) and having been brought up at the grammar-schools of Eccles, Wigan, and Manchester, all in Lancashire, he was admitted a commoner in Brazennose College, Oxford, April 7, 1742. In Michaelmas term, 1745, he took the degree of B. A. June 27, 1746, he was elected a fellow of Brazennose College, being chosen into a Cheshire fellowship; he was ordained a deacon at Chester, by Dr. Samuel Peploe, Bishop of Chester, Dec. 21, 1746. After his year of probation was ended, he left the college, and his first employment in the church was the curacy of Runcorn, in Cheshire, from thence he removed to Ardwick, near Manchester. During his residence here, he was privately ordained a priest at Chester, by the above Dr. Peploe, May 1, 1748, and took the degree of M. A. at Oxford, in Act term, the same year. From Ardwick he removed to Halifax, where on Sept. 3, 1754, he was licensed by Dr. Hutton, on the presentation of George Legh, LL. D. Vicar of Halifax, to the perpetual curacy of Ripponden, in the parish of Halifax. Here he rebuilt the curate's house, at his own expense, laying out above four hundred pounds upon the same, which was more than a fourth part of the whole sum he there received, notwithstanding which, his successor threatened him with a prosecution in the spiritual court, if he did not allow him ten pounds for delapidations; which, for the sake of peace he complied with.

Feb. 17, 1759, he was elected a fellow of the society of antiquaries in London. August 17, 1766, he was inducted to the rectory of Meningsby in Lincolnshire, which he resigned in the year 1769, on being promoted to the valuable rectory of Stockport in Cheshire. His presentation to this, by Sir George Warren, bore date July 30, 1769, and he was inducted thereto August the 2nd following. April 11, 1770, he was appointed one of the domestic chaplains to the right hon. the earl of Dysart.

He was the author of "The history and antiquities of the parish of Halifax in Yorkshire." London : printed for T. Lowndes, in Fleet-street, 1775." In this work, p. 524-5, is a list of the several publications of his hand, amongst which is " An history of the ancient earls of Warren and Surry, proving the Warrens of Poynton, in Cheshire, to be lineally and legally descended from them." a splendidly executed work, (says Dr. Whitaker) "and forming a perfect contrast to the paper, print, and type of his history of Halifax."

WILKINSON, HENRY, was born, says Wood in his Athenæ, vol. ii. p. 112., in the vicarage of Halifax, Oct. 9, 1566; entered at Oxford in Lent term, 1581; elected probationer fellow of Merton College, by favor of his kinsman, Mr. Henry Savile, the warden, in 1586; proceeded in arts; took the degree of B. D. and in 1601 had the living of Waddesdon in Bucks. In 1643 he was elected one of the assembly of divines, and dying March 19, 1647, was buried at Waddesdon.

WILKINSON, JOHN, D. D. In BENTLEY's *history of Halifax*, p. 81, it is said, that "Doctor Wilkinson was born in Halifax parish, and brought up in Oxford, where he attained to that eminency in learning, as to become divinity professor in that university." This gentleman Mr. WATSON supposed to have been the same who is said in WOOD's *Fasti*, vol. i. p. 173., to have had the honor, when he was B. D. and fellow of Magdalen College, to be appointed tutor to Henry prince of Wales, eldest son of king James i. He was afterwards president of Magdalen Hall, and finally, president of Magdalen College, and is called by WOOD in his *Fasti*, the senior theologist of the university. It seems that the doctor fled from Oxford to the parliament, and was deprived of his presidentship.

WRIGHT, THOMAS, born at Blackburn in Lancashire, August 12, 1707, was educated in the grammar school there founded by Queen Elizabeth about 1567, took the degree of B. A. at St. John's College, Cambridge; was several years curate of Halifax, which he left in the year 1750, being then presented to the curacy of Ripponden; where he died in June 1754. He was the author of a book entitled "The Antiquities of the town of Halifax in Yorkshire, wherein is given an account of the Town, Church, and twelve chapels, the free grammar school, a list of the vicars and schoolmasters; the ancient and customary law, called Halifax Gibbet law, with the names of the persons that suffered thereby, and the times when; the public charities to church and poor; the men of learning, whether natives or inhabitants, together with the most remarkable epitaphs and inscriptions in the church and church yard. The whole faithfully collected from printed authors, rolls of courts, registers, old wills, and other authentic writings." Leeds, 1738.

It is remarkable that Mr. Wright was the immediate predecessor of Mr. Watson in the curacies both of Halifax and Ripponden, and that they both wrote a history of Halifax.

THE WOOLLEN TRADE & MANUFACTURES.

The object of the present Chapter is to present to the reader an historical account of the woollen trade and manufactures of this extensive parish, from the earliest period to which our enquiries can ascend, down to the present time.

Situated in the centre of a populous manufacturing district, in the direct line of communication between the towns of Leeds and Manchester, and the ports of Liverpool and Hull, enjoying the facility of a commercial navigation with each, and above all, possessing within herself the life and soul of manufactures, a plentiful supply of coal and water, the parish of Halifax occupies an enviable position among the manufacturing and commercial districts of the kingdom. To a right adaptation of these concurrent advantages, may be attributed her present wealth and prosperity: and in proportion as her wealth has progressed, have her manufactures improved.

Wool, the staple commodity of England, is the staple trade of the parish, and out of her large population of 109.899 souls in the year 1831, not less than 22.874 men were engaged in her manufactures, or in making manufacturing machinery. When we take this into consideration, it is impossible to calculate the advantages which are derived from this branch of trade, and the incalculable benefits which it diffuses through a large portion of the community. " Suppose, (says Mr. CHITTY) the value of English wool produced in one year to amount to three millions, the expense of working it up into various articles to be nine, its total value when manufactured will amount to twelve. Suppose the annual exportation from this country to amount to three millions, and the number of persons maintained by the manufacture, to be a million, let it be

considered that these persons expend what they earn in all the
necessaries of life, and that the procuring of such necessaries is a
source of employment and profit to the other members of the community; and then we may judge what an immense addition is made
to the national stock of industry and gain by this valuable article,
even without taking into account the sailors employed to export the
various articles into which it is wrought, and the artificers of
machines used to accelerate many parts of the manufactures."

The arts of spinning wool, and manufacturing that wool into
cloth, were doubtless introduced into England by the Romans, (in
fact they had a cloth manufactory at Winchester,) the inhabitants of
our island being only clothed in skins or leather.

In ANDERSON's *History of Commerce*, it is stated, that there was
a lawful guild fraternity of weavers in London so early as the year
1180. MADOX, in his *History of the Exchequer*, informs us that
such guild fraternities were established, not only in London but in
other places, before that period; thus—"1140, (4th Stephen,) the
weavers of Oxford pay a mark of gold for their gild. The weavers
of London for their gild, £xvi. The weavers of Lincoln two chaseurs
that they may have their rights. The fullers of Winchester £vi for
their gild."

These notices clearly indicate that fraternities of weavers were
at that time common in many parts of England; and were even then
of great antiquity. To this period may be assigned the first manufacture of broad cloths; the business of cloth making must have
been carried on to a considerable extent, when it gave rise to a fraternity of fullers. GERVASE of Canterbury, who wrote about the
year 1202, in his chronicle says, when speaking of the inhabitants
of Britain, that "the art of weaving seemed to be a peculiar gift
bestowed upon them by nature;" thus, at the period assigned to its
introduction, by modern historians; it was an art which had been
long practised; in fact, it may be safely assumed to be indigenous
of our soil.

The richness and comparative importance of the fraternity of
weavers, in the period here alluded to, may be inferred from other
circumstances mentioned in Madox of a similar import, in the years
1159, 1164, and 1189. The business of dyeing was also carried
on in these days, as a separate, honorable and profitable employment;

as appears from the following, "Anno 1201, David the dyer pays one mark, that his manor may be made a burgage."

At that early time Woad was a plant much used for dying. This plant was cultivated in Great Britain at a very early period, and more particularly so, as it came to be demanded for the Woollen manufacture; but it is a fact, that notwithstanding the extended culture, the increased demand could not be supplied, insomuch so, that it became for many years a constant article of import, as the following tables will shew;

"Anno, 1213. Sums accounted for by sundries as customs for woad imported, viz.

In Kent & Sussex (Dover excepted) £103	13	3.
Yorkshire 98	13	3.
London 17	13	4.

Other counties less: thus clearly proving that the woollen manufacture was carried on in this county and other places to a great extent.

In confirmation of the foregoing remark, is the following:

"1140. The men of Worcester pay C. shillings, that they may buy and sell dyed cloth, as they were wont to do in the time of king Henry I." This, there is every reason to believe, was British cloth, as alluded to in the ordinance of Edward the first, 1284.

"1225. The weavers of Oxford pay a cask of wine, that they may have the same privileges they enjoyed in the days of king Richard and king John."

There is another important circumstance worth noticing:

"1297. The aulnager* of cloth was displaced, and his office

---

* *Aulnager* is derived from *ulna* and *gerens*, and is the name of an officer under the King, established about the year 1350, whose business it was to measure all woollen cloths before they were brought into market, and then to fix an impression of his seal. This measure was to be the government between the buyer and seller, and to prevent all disputes about short measure. The first statute made for it is 25 Edward III. wherein it is enacted, that all cloths shall be measured by the king's aulnager; and that every buyer of cloth after the price is agreed in the halls or markets, shall have it measured by the king's aulnager, who shall put his stamp thereon, and the price of cloth shall stand for that length. And to prevent the aulnager's tumbling or defoiling them, when he measured them, he was to provide himself with a string of the length of seven yards, and the piece was to measure four times the length of that string, and he was to measure it at the creased edge. The aulnager was entitled to the following fees:—For every piece of cloth of ray, or white cloth, 28 yards and 6 quarters wide, one halfpenny, and every half piece, a farthing, to be paid by the seller. In 27 Edward III. besides the aulnage, parliament granted a subsidy, to maintain the French war, of 4d. per annum, to be collected by the aulnager; 6d. if a scarlet in grain, and 5d. if bastard or half scarlet.

given by the king to another." This (observes a learned author) indicates a very advanced state of the manufacture.

From these, and many other circumstances of the same kind that might be collected, it is evident that the woollen manufacture was carried on, as a great national object, for centuries before the days of Edward III.; at which period, it has been asserted, that it was first introduced into England.

Sir Matthew Hale enables us to account for the origin of the modern idea on this head. He remarks, "that in the time of Henry II. and Richard I. the kingdom greatly flourished in the art of manufacturing *woollen cloth*; but by the troublesome wars in the time of king John and Henry III. and also Edward I. and Edward II. this manufacture was wholly lost, and all our trade ran in wools, wool fells, and leather."

It is not reasonable to suppose that a manufacture of such indispensable utility, could be wholly lost to us. All that can be inferred from the expression, is, that it declined very much, so as in a great measure to interrupt the foreign trade in cloth, which at that time seems to have been a principal article of export from this kingdom. Edward III. restored this decayed manufacture; and hence he has come to be accounted the founder of it in England.

It was probably owing to the interruption it met with during the troublesome wars before alluded to, that the manufacture came to be so firmly established in the Netherlands, as to obtain a superiority over the woollen manufactures of Britain: and it was probably owing to this superiority that our forefathers lost the knowledge of many branches of this manufacture which it is evident they once possessed; of this kind especially may be reckoned the art of dyeing and dressing cloths, which was only revived in Britain in a very modern period.

We find the introduction of the woollen manufacture into Ireland marked under the year 1376, in Anderson's History of Commerce, but the following curious anecdote preserved by Madox shews that Irish cloth was known in England long before that period:—" In the reign of Henry III. (i. e. between 1219 and 1272,) Walter Blowburne accused Haman la Starre of a robbery, &c. whereof the said Haman had for his share two coats, viz. one of Irish cloth."

In the reign of Edward IV. Lincoln was a place noted for its fine woollen manufacture, the abbot of St. Godwins is represented by a poet of that time, as living in great pomp, his dress is thus described :—

> " His cope was all of Lycolne clothe so fine,
> With a gold button fasten'd near his chynne ;
> His autremere was edged with golden twynne."

In confirmation of this anecdote many particulars are preserved in Hackluyt's collection, that about this time a very considerable trade in cloth was carried on between Boston and Prussia, and other places of the Baltic.

A circumstance mentioned in this collection, although it may not be pertinent to my enquiry, goes far to establish the fact, that the author of the History of Commerce is wrong in some of his data : thus the discovery of the art of knitting stockings is there marked about the year 1561, when Queen Elizabeth is said to have worn the first pair of hose of this kind ; but it would seem that this art was introduced into Britain sooner than is imagined, for in the song by Sir Shybbot Gorges in the interlude of Ella, mention is thus made of it :

> " As Elynour bie the green lesselle was syttynge,
> As from the sone's heat she hurried,
> She sayde, as her whyte hands whyte hozen was knyttinge,
> What pleasure yt ys to be married."

In the year 1331 John Kemp, a master manufacturer from Flanders, received a protection to establish himself at York, with a number of dyers and fullers to carry on his trade, and in the following year several manufacturers came over from Brabant and Zealand. It is said, that the king's marriage with the daughter of the earl of Hainault enabled him to send over emissaries, without suspicion, to invite the manufacturers to this kingdom. These manufacturers were distributed over the country, at the following places :—The manufacturers of fustians (woollens) were established at Norwich, of baize at Sudbury in Suffolk, of sayes and serges at Colchester in Essex, of broad cloths in Kent, of kersies in Devonshire, of cloth in Worcestershire and Gloucestershire, of Welch friezes in Wales, of cloth at Kendal in Westmoreland, of coarse cloths, afterwards called Halifax cloths, in Yorkshire, of cloth in Hampshire, Berkshire, and Sussex, and of serges at Taunton in Devonshire.   Fresh supplies of foreigners contributed to advance the woollen trade of these districts.

The wholesome statutes that were passed in the reign of Edward III. for the regulation of trade, and the encouragement given by that monarch to this branch of it in particular, certainly entitle him to the appellation of the "Father of manufactures." The trade of the nation at this time consisted principally in the exportation of wool to Bruges and other foreign places, whence fine cloths and other products were brought back in exchange. This defect being wisely considered by King Edward III. in a parliament held at Nottingham, in the tenth year of his reign, he took the most judicious measures for improving the English manufactures; an edict was issued, inviting cloth-workers to settle in this country, for the advancement of the trade, and he granted his protection to two Brabant weavers, viz. "Willielmus de Brabant, and Hanckcinus de Brabant, textores," to settle at York, and granted them very considerable privileges. Shortly after the first emigration of the Flemings, A. D. 1335, an act was passed, prohibiting the wear of cloths made in foreign parts, and interdicting the export of English wool: this restraining act was soon repealed, but in order to support and encourage the home manufacture, a tax of 50s. per pack was imposed upon it: notwithstanding which so much continued to be exported, that the customs amounted annually to the amazing sum of two hundred and fifty thousand pounds. From this remote period the manufacture has been always regarded of the first importance, and has been the object of the especial solicitude of the legislature.

By degrees, however, the art of cloth making became more generally known and practised, and the extension of manufactures diminished the exportation of wool more effectually than could have been done by "restraining acts."

As to the precise period of the introduction of woollen manufactures into this district, we have no direct evidence; York we have shewn was one of the places assigned as the residence for the Flemish weavers. From the protection afforded them, and the encouragement given to manufactures in general, by the reigning monarch, it is evident that the trade could not be confined to the towns which were first set apart to it, but extended itself to those places where the trade had decayed, in consequence of the events I have before mentioned. That the Parish of Halifax possessed some of those peculiar advantages so favorable for manufactures is very evident: it is therefore reasonable to suppose, that it would be among the first, as the most inviting. Whether the art was brought hither from York, or some other part, is not very clear. The author of the Eboracum, says, "there is a tradition, that one of his ancestors, of the name of Drake, first brought the woollen manufactory to these parts, out of Devonshire, where it was settled by workmen brought from Flanders," but mentions no date. WRIGHT, in his History of Halifax, p. 7, affirms that the woollen trade was brought to Halifax in the time of one Mr. Waterhouse, from Ripon, for the sake of coals and water, but gives no authority for his assertion. This Mr. Waterhouse was born in 1443, and died in 1540; during which time the woollen manufactures had increased so rapidly, that the houses in Halifax were during that period, increased from 13 to 520.

On this Mr. WATSON judiciously remarks, "it is wrong to say that trade was first introduced here at that time, for by copy of court roll, dated at the court of the Prior of Lewes, held at Halifax, on the Thursday next after the feast of St. Thomas, 2 Henry V. 1414, Richard de Sunderland, and Joan his wife, surrendered into the hands of the Lord, an inclosure in Halifax, called Tenter-Croft. Also two fulling mills were erected in Rastrick, and about 17 Edward IV. 1477, Elizabeth, the widow of John Thornhill, granted a parcel of land and water in Rastrick, lying to the river Calder, called Black-greiss, to John Andrew and Nicholas Bamforth, for 30 years, on condition that they should build there two fulling mills and make a sufficient dam for the water."

From these facts I think we are justified in inferring that the trade at this early period was in a flourishing condition within this district, although the population might at that time have been too small to admit of any thing that could deserve the name of a manufactory. CAMDEN has fixed the introduction of the trade here to the end of the reign of Henry III. or beginning of Edward VI. but he depended entirely on information, and there is proof enough that his intelligence was not correct. Amongst the rest, one Richard King, who lived in this parish in the time of king Henry VIII. in a covenant of marriage, wrote himself occupier, meaning a buyer and seller of cloth. In the reign of Philip and Mary, Halifax enjoyed the peculiar protection of the legislature, it had then doubtless attained some notoriety by reason of its trade, but attempts were made by some great capitalists during this reign, to monopolize the stock of wool, and the act which was then passed exhibits the state of the parish and its trade at that time, after reciting, " that the parish of Halifax, &c. being planted in the great waste and moores, where the fertility of ground is not apt to bring forth any corne, nor good grasse, but in rare places, and by exceeding and great industry of the inhabitants; and the same inhabitants altogether doe live by cloth making; and the great part of them neither getteth corne, nor is able to keepe a horse to carry wools, nor yet to buy much wool at once, but hath ever used onely to repair to the towne of Halifax, &c. and there to buy upon the wool driver, some a stone, some two, and some three and foure, according to their ability, and to carry the same to their houses, some three, foure, five, and six miles off, upon their heads and backes and so to make and convert the same either into yarne or cloth, and to sell the same, and so to buy more wool of the wool driver, by means of which industry, the barren grounds in those parts be now much inhabited, and above five hundred households there newly increased within these forty yeares past, which now are like to be undone, and driven to beggery, by reason of the late estatute (37 Henry VIII,) that taketh away the wool driver. so that they cannot now have their wool by such small portions as they were wont to have, and that also they are not able to keepe any horses whereupon to ride, or set their wools further from them in other places, unlesse some remedy may be provided, It was enacted, that it should be lawfule to any person or persons inhabiting within the parish of Halifax, to buy any wool or wools, at such time as the clothiers may buy the same otherwise than by engrossing, and forestalling, so that the persons so buying the same, doe carry, or cause to be carried, the said wools so bought by them, to the towne of Halifax, and there to sell the same to such poore folkes of that and other parishes adjoining, as shall worke the same in cloth of yarn (to their knowledge) and not to the rich and wealthy clothier, nor to any other to sell again. Offendors against this act to forfeit double the value of the wool so sold. Justices of Peace to hear and determine the offences."

In consequence of the increase of our manufactures, the export of wool had nearly ceased before the reign of Elizabeth ; and a considerable advance appears to have taken place in the price of food, clothing and rents.

We are told by BENTLEY in his description of Halifax, that about the beginning of the last century, the lord of the manor erected a large and spacious hall, towards the upper end of the town, where the weavers and buyers of cloth met weekly, namely every Saturday morning, to transact business : the cloth sold at this hall was undrest cloth.   The lord of the manor reserved to himself a penny for every piece of cloth sold at the hall on each Saturday morning, and received weekly thirty, and sometimes forty shillings.   Great quantities of colored cloth were also sold in the butchers' shambles, before other markets began, being regularly placed on their stalls for that purpose. The market began precisely at six o'clock, between the twenty-fifth of March and the twenty-ninth of September, and at eight o'clock the rest of the year : notice whereof was given by ringing a bell, and a penalty of thirty-nine shillings and eleven pence was levied upon any one who asked the price of a piece of cloth before the bell rung.   Likewise on the Saturday market, merchants from Leeds, and other places, bought many white-dressed kerseys, to send to Hamburgh and Holland, &c.   Contracts for these were made by patterns.   Independently of the Saturday market, a considerable business was also transacted here on Tuesdays and Thursdays.

The shalloon trade was introduced here, says WATSON, about the beginning of the 17th century, and what are called figured stuffs and draw boys, about the middle of it.   Formerly much bone lace was made here, but it subsequently fell into so low a state, that few were put apprentices to the trade.   Stocking weaving or frame work knitting was first brought into Halifax in 1724, at which time a fine was paid to the corporation at Nottingham, for every apprentice.

PENNANT, in his tour to Scotland, when giving a description of Halifax, says, " the woollen manufactures flourish here greatly, such as that of the narrow cloth, bath coatings, shalloons, everlastings, a sort of coarse broad cloth, with black hair lists for Portugal, and with blue for Turkey ; sayes, of a deep blue color, for Guinea ; the last are packed in pieces of twelve yards and a half, wrapped in an oil cloth, painted with negroes and elephants, in order to cap-

tivate these poor people. Many blood red cloths are exported to
Italy, from whence they are supposed to be sent to Turkey; the blues
are sent to Norway."

For some time past the staple manufactures of the town and
neighbourhood have been shalloons, tammies, and draw boys, known
best under the title of figured lastings and amens, superfine quilled
everlastings, double russels and serges: these are all made from
combing wool. They are brought in the unfinished state to the
piece hall, where the merchants attend every Saturday to make
their purchases. Formerly the greater part of these goods were
bought by the London merchants for the supply of foreigners, but
within the present century, dye houses and other conveniences have
been erected by merchants who finish the goods upon the spot, and
are thereby able to undersell the London merchant. Of these goods
very few in proportion are sold inland; large quantities are exported
to the continent of Europe, of which those sent to Cadiz are chiefly
exported to Spanish America. Many shalloons are sent to London
for the Turkey trade.

There is, besides, a very considerable manufactory of kerseys
and half-thicks, also of bockings and baize, principally in the hands
of merchants of property in the neighbourhood of Sowerby, and
made in the valley from Sowerby-Bridge to Ripponden. The whole
of the British navy is clothed from this source. Large quantities
are exported to Holland and also to America.

But the most promising branch of manufactory is that of cloth
and coatings, which was also introduced at the latter end of the last
century by persons of enterprise, who at vast expence, erected
mills on the Calder, and other smaller streams. The success of
these factories, on their first introduction, was such as to excite
the jealousy of the Leeds merchants, who were accustomed to buy
the same articles from the lower manufacturers at their cloth hall;
and to such an extent was it carried, that in 1794 a deputation was
sent from thence to petition for an act to prevent any merchant from
becoming a manufacturer; but on consideration the absurd idea was
very properly dropt. It is evident that merchants, concentrating in
themselves the whole process of a manufactory, from the raw wool
to the finished piece, have an advantage over those who permit the
article to pass through a variety of hands, each taking a profit.

x

A custom, it is said, long prevailed in the manufacturing of broad cloth, which was that of the merchant allowing one yard in every twenty, as an indemnity for the length of the cloth being stretched beyond its length from the mill; which had the bad effect of tempting the merchant to stretch the cloth still more, in order to gain length, though the quality was injured by it. This practice threw the Yorkshire cloth into disrepute, both at home and abroad; and preference was given to the West of England fabrics, especially by the East India Company, notwithstanding the West of England cloths, which measure 48 yards in the white, do not when dyed, measure on the average so much as 45 yards. An honest and intelligent manufacturer will be able to prove "that all cloth manufactured honestly will be as long when dyed and finished, as in the white."

FULLER adverts to this practice of stretching cloth, and in his quaint way says:—"As I am glad to hear the plenty of a coarser kind of cloth is made in this county, at Halifax, Leeds, and elsewhere, whereby the meaner sort are much employed, and the middle sort inriched; so I am sorry for the generall complaints made thereof, insomuch that it is become a general by-word "to shrink as Northern cloths" (a giant to the eye, and dwarf in the use thereof) to signify such as fail their friends in deepest distress, depending on their assistance. Sad that the *sheep*, the *emblem* of innocence, should unwillingly cover so much craft under the wool thereof; and sadder that *fullers*, commended in scripture for making cloth *white*, should justly be condemned for making their own consciences *black*, by such fraudulent practices. I hope this fault, for the future, will be amended in this county and elsewhere; for sure it is, that the transporting of wool and fullers' earth (both against law) beyond the seas are not more prejudicial to our English clothing abroad, than the deceit in making cloth at home, debasing the foreign estimation of our cloth, to the invaluable damage of our nation."

About the year 1814 a considerable alteration is said to have taken place in the British wool trade: the manufacturers, finding that the foreign markets could not be supplied with cloths sufficiently fine, made from English wool, had recourse to Germany and Spain. They now use foreign wool in their broad and narrow cloths, almost to the total exclusion of the British produce; and for this, it would appear, there is an absolute necessity.

"The ancient manufacture of woollen cloth in the West Riding of the county of York, greatly increased during the war which terminated in 1815, and the advantage of machinery has combined with this circumstance, to transfer thither a great share of the West country clothing trade. In the three wapentakes of Agbrigg, Morley, and Skyrack, respectively, are found 17,000, 22,000, and 29,000 males, twenty years of age, thus employed, in all 68,000; surpassed indeed as to manufacturing population by the adjacent hundreds of Blackburn and Salford in Lancashire, where the tractable nature of cotton wool subjected it earlier to the operation of machinery. The limit of the two counties is not a very erroneous line of demarcation between the great woollen and cotton manufactories. The places most eminent in woollen fabrics and worsteds are, the parish of Halifax containing nearly 12.000 men so employed; Leeds 9.400 in the town and liberty; Bradford, 7.900; Almondbury parish, 4.500 adjacent to it; Huddersfield, worsted and silks, 3.700; Kirkburton, 2.400; Calverley, 2.100; Dewsbury parish, 1.800; Bristal, 1.700; Batley, 1.400; Kirkheaton, 1.200: and Saddleworth about 1.800; besides the same number employed in cotton factories, this being the frontier Township of the large Lancashire parish of Rochdale."*

I have purposely abstained from entering upon a statistical enquiry, as to the general state of the Wool trade and Woollen manufacture, inasmuch as it would throw little light on our local history; it may be sufficient to state, that Halifax has participated, with other districts, in the general prosperity that has attended our manufactures throughout the country, since the restrictions, connected with this particular branch of trade, have been removed.

I am indebted to Robert Baker, esq. of Leeds, superintendant of Factories, for the following interesting particulars respecting the manufactories in this parish. Mr. Baker in his communication, very properly observes, that a more detailed account of power and hands, with the number and kind of mills, would not be fair towards the manufacturers, many of whom are singular in their particular branch; however useful and important such information may be in another quarter; it would be objectionable as laying open to public view more of the private business of a man than would be either proper or

* Parliamentary Paper. 1831.

agreeable; and after all, as far as power is concerned, might be far from correct.

AN ACCOUNT, SHEWING THE NUMBER OF MILLS AND FACTORIES, IN THE PARISH OF HALIFAX, IN THE YEAR 1835; WITH THE AGGREGATE AMOUNT OF HORSE POWER EMPLOYED: ALSO SHEWING THE NUMBER OF HANDS EMPLOYED IN EACH TOWNSHIP OF THE PARISH, ITS PREVAILING MANUFACTURE, AND THE KIND OF POWER EMPLOYED.

TOWNSHIPS.	Cotton	Worsted	Woollen	Silk	Steam	Water	Aggregate Horse Power.	PERSONS EMPLOYED.							Population in 1831.
								From 9 to 12		13 to 18		Above 18		Total.	
								Male.	female	Male.	female	Male.	female		
Barkisland							155	19	8	23	32	164	144	390	2292
Elland							66	22	18	29	32	117	72	290	5500
Erringden								37	21	57	71	262	204	652	1933
North Owram } Halifax South Owram }							89	157	144	180	312	821	788	2402	31317
Heptonstall								17	4	46	64	213	250	594	4661
Hipperholme							73	56	70	69	122	261	277	855	4977
Langfield							117	64	47	83	113	341	344	992	2514
Norland							260	30	42	34	93	172	235	606	1618
Ovenden								104	100	148	203	908	739	2202	8871
Rastrick								40	45	57	54	281	135	612	3021
Rishworth								31	33	29	40	184	229	546	1536
Skircoat								49	75	59	132	268	425	1008	4060
Sowerby							122	55	31	84	57	464	204	895	6457
Soyland								99	81	165	163	918	623	2049	3589
Stansfield							164½	87	87	157	195	722	650	1898	8262
Wadsworth							118	17	26	58	80	175	204	560	5198
Warley							231½	118	145	121	207	727	508	1826	5685
								1002	977	1899	1970	6998	6081	18377	101,691

The small black line indicates, under its proper column, the prevailing manufacture of the neighbourhood, and the kind of power employed.

Of the 23 Townships comprising the Parish of Halifax, 19 may be said to be manufacturing; out of whose population, according to the census of 1831, amounting to 101,491,—18,377 are employed in the different branches of Cotton, Worsted, Woollen and Silk.

In the Parish of Halifax, there are

57 Cotton Mills employing an aggregate power of 716 horses.
35 Woollen do.   ..   ..   662 ..
45 Worsted do. ..   .. 855 ..
 4 Silk   do.   ..   ..   86 ..
 3 Mills unoccupied
 9 do. incomplete
———   ———
153   2319

From the above statement it appears that the Cotton trade is carried on here to a considerable extent; and is gradually increasing. The Silk trade, although of recent introduction, gives every promise of its becoming a very flourishing branch of manufacture in this parish; "and in reference to the manufacture of Silk, (says Mr. Baker,) it is remarkable, that Halifax from its local situation, is peculiarly adapted for the preservation of its color."

With reference to "the intellectual condition of the Factory people;" I am also indebted to Mr. Baker for the following table taken by that gentleman, which, he observes, is a fair sample of factory children generally, and an important item in any account of their moral condition.

20 mills in the Sowerby district contain 827 Males. 696 Females.

Of these are above 18 .. 464   285
        Under that age 363   411
Of these, 325 Males 400 Females read.
    ———   94 ..   37   ..   write.
    ——— 303 .. 381   ..   attend Sunday schools.
    ———   37 ..   25   ..   attend other Schools.

POPULATION.

The state of the population of this extensive parish from time to time, will be best illustrated by a simple adherence to historical facts, these will be found to be all that are necessary for every useful purpose.

As regards the town :—In the original MS. S. referred to both by WRIGHT and WATSON in their respective histories, the state of the population, at the earliest period to which our enquiries can ascend, is thus mentioned: "By this underwritten yow may gather the great encrease of howsinge and people within the towne of Halifax in not many years by paste, written by John Waterhowse, of Shipden, and some time lorde of the mannor of Halifax.

"Note, there is in Halifax this yeare 1566, of housholders that keepes fires and answers Mr. vicar in his fermours of dutyes as housholders 20 and six score and noe more (as I am crediblye enformed;) and in the time of John Waterhouse, late of Halifax, deceased, who dyed at Candlemas, 26 yeares agoe, att his deathe beinge very neare 100 yeares of age (I trow three yeares under,) and when he was but a childe there were but in Halifax in all 13 howses."

From this it would appear that there were in Halifax, about the year 1443, when Mr. Waterhouse was born, thirteen families; these in about 123 years (1566) had increased to 520. "In the year 1738 (says Mr. WRIGHT) there were above 1.100 families in the town and yet kept daily increasing ;" and in the year 1763, as will appear from the following table, they had increased to 1272 families, "and were then, says WATSON, increasing more than ever, owing to the flourishing state of their trade."

We have no evidence to shew what might be the state of the population in all the out-townships, at an early period of our history, but some inference may be drawn even as far back as the olden time when "Robert, earl of Huntingdon," ranged the forest of Sowerbyshire.

> "Nea arcir vir as him sa geud
> An pipl kauld him Robin Heud;
> Sic utlaus as he, an iz men,
> Vil Inglonde nivr si agen."

At least so says his epitaph. Tradition says, his remains lie under an ancient cross at Kirklees, where he died in 1274.

Now about this time, but unquestionably within thirteen years after, is there positive proof, that the churches of Elland and Heptonstall were both built, (a church had been erected in Halifax upwards of 130 years,) the families, therefore, in these parts of our out-townships, must have been on the increase. By an inquest taken 1284, it appears that Rastrick was then rated at 13s., and contained six freemen, the rest were "native tenantes, villaines, or bondsmen." According to another extent, there were in Fixby in the year 1314, only five houses that had fires. In the certificate of the archbishop of York and others, 2 Ed. vi. (1548) concerning chantries, &c. it is said, that "in the parrysh of Hallifaxe the nomber of houslyng people is eight thousand five hundred, and is a great wide parrysh." And during the rebellion in the north, when every protestant, who could carry arms, was zealous to shew his attachment to his religion and the queen, archbishop Gryndall says, in a letter to queen Elizabeth, that the parish of Halifax was ready to bring three or four thousand able men into the field. And it appears from CAMDEN, who was in these parts about the year 1574, and who then described the wild and mountainous districts of our parish to be "solum sterile, in quo non modo commode vivi, sed vix vivi possit;" that the number of inhabitants was then about 12.000 men.

The whole number of families in the following tables, taken from the vicar's Easter books in the year 1764, is 8244, and if we allow but five to a family, the amount will be 41.220; an amazing increase, if Camden's information was any thing near the truth.

THE NUMBER OF HOUSES AND FAMILIES IN THE PARISH OF HALIFAX,
IN THE YEARS 1763 AND 1764.

In Halifax Division, 1764.				Heptonstall Division, 1764.		
	HOUSES	EMPTY	FAMILIES		HOUSES	EMPTY	FAMILIES
Halifax......	1312	40	1272	Erringden ..	183	6	177
Hipperholme..	367	15	352	Heptonstall ..	367	15	352
Midgley	224	7	217	Langfield	139	2	137
Owram North	660	30	630	Stansfield			
—— South	466	18	448	upper third	129	3	126
Ovenden	616	19	597	Stansfield			
Shelf	186	6	180	middle third	207	4	203
Skircoat	263	12	251	Stansfield			
Sowerby	618	31	587	lower third	140	5	135
Warley......	503	16	487	Wadsworth ..	396	8	388
	5215	194	5021		1561	43	1518

In Elland Division, 1763.			
	HOUSES	EMPTY	FAMILIES
Barkisland......	267	17	250
Brighouse	77	3	74
Elland	262	23	239
Fixby.........	56	2	54
Greetland	122	6	116
Norland........	195	17	178
Old Linley......	42	2	40
Rastrick........	186	11	175
Rishworth......	131	2	129
Soyland........	264	9	255
Stainland	201	6	195
	1803	98	1705

	OCCUPATION.		
	Families chiefly employed in Agriculture.	Families chiefly employed in Trade, Manufactures, and Handicraft.	All other Families
6	10	374	
0	49	687	4
0	78	175	
3	25	33	
4	30	2125	1 1
5	64	878	
2	81	464	4
0	32	419	
2	98	199	1
3	21	198	
	60	1726	
	98	1730	
	43	746	
	71	514	
	43	191	
	24	302	
	34	702	
	107	975	
	3	589	
	25	168	
	202	1190	
	169	808	
	96	791	
	1463	15984	44

ontains 109,899 In

urers not agricultu

The following documents have been abstracted from Parliamentary papers.

COMPARATIVE ACCOUNT OF THE POPULATION OF THE PARISH OF HALIFAX, IN THE YEARS 1801, 1811, 1821, 1831; WITH THE ANNUAL VALUE OF THE REAL PROPERTY IN THE YEAR 1815.

	Annual value of the real property as assessed April, 1815.	POPULATION.			
		1801.	1811.	1821.	1831.
	£.				
Barkisland	2819	1799	2076	2224	2292
Elland with Greetland ..	7461	3385	3963	5088	5500
Erringden	2532	1313	1586	1471	1933
Fixby	1834	346	336	345	348
Halifax..............	38337	8886	9159	12628	15382
Heptonstall	4439	2983	3647	4543	4661
Hipperholme with Brighouse	7482	2879	3357	3936	4977
Langfield	2361	1170	1515	2069	2514
Midgley	2287	1209	2107	2207	2409
Norland	2883	1181	1316	1665	1618
Ovenden	7674	4513	4752	6360	8871
Owram North	9427	4887	5306	6841	10184
Owram South	8853	3148	3615	4256	5751
Rastrick	4151	2053	2442	2796	3021
Rishworth	2058	960	1211	1588	1536
Shelf	2654	1306	1553	1998	2614
Skircoat	5661	2338	2823	3323	4060
Sowerby	6763	4275	5177	6590	6457
Soyland	4757	1888	2519	3242	3589
Stainland	3155	1800	2077	2814	3037
Stansfield............	7639	4763	5447	7275	8262
Wadsworth	4425	2801	3473	4509	5198
Warley	622	3543	3958	4982	5685

TABLE OF MORTALITY, FOR THE PARISH OF HALIFAX:

DEDUCED FROM AN ACCOUNT (TAKEN FROM THE PARISH REGISTERS,) OF THE AGES OF 17,315 PERSONS (OF WHOM 8863 WERE MALES AND 8452 FEMALES,) BURIED IN THE PARISH OF HALIFAX, DURING EIGHTEEN YEARS: 1813 TO 1880.

AGE.	MALES.					FEMALES.					BOTH SEXES.				
	Living	Died	Dec. Living	Dec. Died	Each period died pr. cent	Living	Died	Dec. Living	Dec. Died	Each period died pr. cent	Living	Died	Dec. Living	Dec. Died	Each period died pr. cent
Under 5.	8863	3754	10000	4236	.42	8452	3206	10000	3793	.38	17315	6960	10000	4020	.40
5 to 9	5109	455	5764	513	.09	5246	385	6207	455	.07	10355	840	5980	485	.08
10 —14	4654	289	5251	326	.06	4861	223	5752	264	.05	9515	512	5495	296	.05
15 —19	4365	339	4925	382	.08	4638	314	5488	371	.07	9003	653	5199	377	.07
20 —29	4026	593	4543	669	.15	4324	659	5117	780	.15	8350	1252	4822	723	.15
30 —39	3433	432	3874	487	.13	3665	561	4337	664	.15	7098	993	4099	573	.14
40 —49	3001	464	3387	524	.15	3104	518	3673	613	.17	6105	982	3526	567	.16
50 —59	2537	545	2863	615	.21	2586	535	3060	633	.21	5123	1080	2959	624	.21
60 —69	1992	756	2248	853	.38	2051	757	2427	896	.37	4043	1513	2335	874	.37
70 —79	1236	812	1395	916	.66	1294	801	1531	948	.62	2530	1618	1461	931	.64
80 —89	424	395	479	446	.93	493	432	583	511	.88	917	827	530	478	.90
90 —99	29	29	33	33	1.00	61	60	72	71	.99	90	89	52	51	.98
100&upw						1	1	1	1	1.00	1	1	1	1	1.00

PARISH REGISTER BOOKS,

Earlier than the new Registers, commencing with A. D. 1813, according to 52 Geo. iii, c. 146, remain at the following churches and chapels within the parish.

SAINT ANN'S OR BRIER'S.

One book containing baptisms, A. D. 1800—1812. Entered in the registers prior to 1800. No burials or marriages.

COLEY.

Included in the registers at Halifax, prior to 1813.

CROSSTONE.

Nos. I—III. Bap. Bur. 1678—1812.

ELLAND WITH GREETLAND.

Nos. I—V. Bap. Bur. 1559, 1589, 1640, 1764. Marr. 1559, 1589, 1640, 1753; containing also the registers of Ripponden, Rastrick, Sowerby-bridge, and Norland. Nos. IV—VII. Bap. Bur. including Rastrick and Norland, 1765, 1812. Nos. VIII—XII. Marr. 1754—1812.

ERRINGDEN. SAINT JOHN'S.

No registers prior to 1821.

HALIFAX. (PARISH CHURCH.)

Nos. I—VIII. Bap. Bur. 1538—1756; Marr. 1538—1753. Nos. IX—X. Bap. Bur. 1757—1812, including the registers of all the Townships in the Parish, except Elland and Heptonstall. Nos. XI—XXIII. Marr. 1754—1812.

HEPTONSTALL.

Nos. I—IV. Bap. 1592, 1685, 1688, 1786: Bur. 1593, 1685, 1688, 1786: Marr. 1593, 1685, 1687, 1753. Nos. V. VI. Bap. Bur. 1787—1812. Nos. VIII—XII. Marr. 1754—1812.

ILLINGWORTH.

Nos. I. II. Bap. Bur. Marr. 1695—1780. No. III. Bap. Bur. 1781—1812.

LIGHTCLIFFE.

Nos. I—III. Bap. Bur. Marr. 1704—1812.

LUDDENDEN.

One register, 1653—1812. Very imperfect until 1738.

RASTRICK.

No. I. Parchment. Bap. 1719—1759. No. II. Bap. Bur. 1798—

1812. Registers partly included in Elland with Greetland.

SOWERBY.

Nos. I—VI. Bap. 1668—1812. Bur. 1643—1812.

SOWERBY-BRIDGE.

Nos. I. II. Bap. 1709—1802; Marr. 1732—1751. No. III. Bap. 1803—1812. No marriages solemnized since 1751. No burials until 1821.

THORNTON. (HALIFAX P.)

Nos. I—VI. Registers 1678, 1718, 1720, 1812.

TRINITY CHURCH, C.

Burials only, and entered in the parochial registers of Halifax.

SAINT JAMES'S CHURCH.

Baptisms and Burials, are entered in the parochial registers of Halifax.

The above is taken from a Parliamentary Paper in the year 1831 although with regard to its correctness I am rather sceptical. The parochial Registers of Halifax are, much to the credit of those in whose custody they have from time to time been placed, in an excellent state of preservation.

PAROCHIAL GOVERNMENT.

The whole Parish, in regard to its ecclesiastical purposes, being divided into three districts; viz. the Parish of Halifax; the parochial chapelry of Elland; and the parochial chapelry of Heptonstall; I shall notice them in the same order, not only because such an arrangement is more methodical than that adopted by Mr. WATSON; but also because much that relates to the township of Halifax applies to many of the other townships, and will render the work free from that verbiage which is too often connected with topographical detail.

THE PAROCHIAL DISTRICT OF HALIFAX*

Is the first or principal division of the parish, and consists of the township of Halifax, (wherein the mother church of the whole parish stands,) and nine other townships, technically called out-townships; here placed according to their estimated importance in parochial matters, viz.

SOWERBY	HIPPERHOLME-CUM-
NORTHOWRAM	BRIGHOUSE
WARLEY	MIDGLEY
OVENDEN	SKIRCOAT
SOUTHOWRAM	SHELF

* Notwithstanding I have the sanction of immemorial usage for denominating the principal division of the parish—"The Parish of Halifax;" I prefer adopting the term "Parochial district of Halifax," for my present purpose, as being more distinctive, and not liable to misconstruction.

Of these out-townships six are chapelries, viz.

SOWERBY	SOUTHOWRAM
WARLEY	HIPPERHOLME
OVENDEN	MIDGLEY

and maintain their own chapels of ease, of which there are eight, by rates unconnected with the parochial or *district* rate.

All of them are immediately dependant on the parish church, they contribute to its support and repair, and to the accustomed ordinary expenses attendant upon the performance of divine worship, in certain proportions according to the estimated importance of each township; and in legal consideration, are governed by the same principles as apply to a parish not subdivided into townships, and having one church only.   They have each pews in the North gallery of the church, appropriated to their respective inhabitants, with the name of the township to which they belong painted in the front of them: (consequently the means of attending divine service at pleasure.)

Since the year 1780, each township has received its proportion of the money given by the communicants at the church, for the use of its poor; prior to which time the wardens of Halifax distributed the whole of it to the poor of their own township.

The expences of the visitations for the Halifax wardens, and the ministers connected with the parish church, were formerly defrayed by the district; but the custom was departed from in the year 1760; and these expences are now paid by the Halifax wardens.

In regard to parochial affairs, the custom of electing churchwardens in the out-townships, Mr. WATSON states to be this:— "The vicar of the parish, as such, has a little before Easter, two names sent in from each of the seven chapels dependant on his church; and he takes which he pleases for warden, and publishes them, together with the churchwardens for Halifax, at Easter in Halifax church."   If such was once the custom, it is now not used, and each township elects its own warden; the publication of the names of the out-wardens in the church was discontinued some five or six years ago.   The custom, with regard to the election of wardens for Halifax township is clear: the vicar elects one, and the rate-payers the other, as will be seen from the following document, extracted from the parish books.

"WHEREAS great disputes and differences have already happened between the present vicar of Halifax, in the county of York, doctor of Laws, and the inhabitants of the same place for the time being, touching the right and method of nominating and chusing new churchwardens, to succeed the old ones going out from year to year. AND WHEREAS, to determine the same, many vexatious law-suits might ensue. Wherefore, to prevent the same, and that no disputes might hereafter arise between the said vicar of Halifax and the inhabitants of the said town concerning such nomination and choice as aforesaid, and that the method hereafter mentioned shall and may be a standing and constant rule of nomination and choice amongst them for the time to come: Be it known unto all men, that from this day forward public notice shall be given, by the parish clerk of Halifax aforesaid, on every Palm Sunday in the afternoon, immediately after divine service there, that a vestry meeting is thereby intended and will be had on Thursday in the afternoon then next following in every year, between the hours of four and five, for the vicar or his representative, and the inhabitants of the aforesaid town, then and there to meet and name two persons out of the whole number of the said inhabitants of the aforesaid town, who have not been in that office before, so long as a sufficient number of such persons shall remain, to serve as churchwardens for the ensuing year. And if the said vicar, or his representative, and a majority of the said inhabitants then present at such vestry, cannot agree in the choice of two : then that the said inhabitants, or such a majority as aforesaid shall be at liberty at that time, without the said vicar, to name one who shall serve for the ensuing year; and that the said vicar shall at the same time if present, if not at any other time on or before Thursday in Easter week then next following, name the other churchwarden to serve for the same year; both whose names shall immediately afterwards be returned by the old churchwardens to the parish clerk, to be published the then next Sabbath day, which said notice shall signifie who the new churchwardens are, that must succeed for the ensuing year, and by whom each of them were respectively named, in order that from thenceforth no more disputes may arise concerning the custom of the aforesaid place; but that the eighty-ninth Canon for that purpose shall be to them their guide. Witness our hands, this eighth day of September, in the year of our Lord, 1743.

GEORGE LEGH, LL.D. Vicar of Halifax.

JAS. ALDERSON,	ROBT. BUTTERFIELD,	
VAL. STEAD	JOHN CAYGILL, JUNR	Inhabitants.
JAMES WETHERHEAD	JOHN BALDWIN	
E. WINN		

It appears to have been the constant usage, whereof there is no evidence to the contrary in our parochial books (until within the last few years,) for the wardens of the out-townships to meet and consult with the churchwardens of Halifax, for the government of the parish church affairs, on the first Wednesday in every month, and on Easter Monday in every year, to pass the parish accounts and pay their respective quotas. At these meetings it was the understood practice, that the Halifax wardens could not expend above 40s. for repairs, &c. of the church, without a majority of the out-wardens agreeing thereto. The accounts were passed without calling any vestry meetings to examine the same; neither was any parish meeting called to lay a rate; but each township laid its own rate for its proportion of the money that was expended.

This mode of transacting business was not only highly irregular, and open to much abuse; but its legality was very questionable. The votes of the out-township wardens would always preponderate, and might be expected to be opposed to any disbursements however necessary, for which they did not obtain some corresponding benefit. The "expences of monthly meetings" formed a very considerable, and certainly a very objectionable, item in these accounts.

This custom prevailed until the commencement of legal parochial vestries in the year 1825. In this year the township of Northowram refused to pay its proportion of the accustomed charges; in consequence whereof they fell upon the township of Halifax to pay, and the churchwardens, finding that they had no remedy for their wrong against the township of Northowram, for the first time called a vestry meeting of the whole parishioners liable to be rated, to examine their accounts, and lay a rate for the then current year, according to an estimate laid before the meeting. A similar course was adopted in January, 1826, and this mode of calling vestry meetings has ever since been acted upon; at every such meeting each item in the accounts has been read over to the parishioners in the vestry, and at all times the parish accounts have been open for the inspection of the rate-payers; thus leaving the out-wardens without any controul over the expenditure of the church in their official capacity.

It appears from the parish vouchers that the repairs of the chancel, and other incidental expenses connected therewith, have always been charged in the churchwardens' accounts to the parish, and allowed by the vestry, until the month of June, 1832, when the usual meeting was convened for passing those accounts, and laying a new rate. In this year an item of £5, paid for some repairs in the chancel, was disallowed by the vestry, and the following resolution passed:

"Resolved. That the town and parish of Halifax will not repair the chancel, and if any churchwarden or churchwardens do at any time expend any money on the same, the parishioners will not pay it."

No specific notice appears to have been given that such a resolution would be proposed, neither is there preface or preamble to shew why or wherefore the usual practice was departed from. That the resolution is sufficiently clear and determined cannot be questioned; but its legality is very doubtful, and remains yet to be decided. When considered with the utmost candour it certainly appears to have been passed without that caution which inexperience ought to have suggested, and that regard for precedent and established custom, which even the parish ledgers would have taught its supporters it required. It is opposed to an usage long established, invariably acted upon, and of which there is no evidence to the contrary.

Each township is a distinct constabulary; the inhabitants whereof elect one constable, with the exception of Halifax which elects two. These officers are presented to the court leet of the manor to be sworn in, and are selected from among the more opulent and respectable rate-payers of the township, the office being in general performed by deputy. It is almost needless to observe that under such a system it is impossible the duties incidental to a proper discharge of the situation can be well and efficiently performed.

Y

Each township also maintains its own poor, and appoints two overseers, with the exception of Halifax, which since the year 1725 has always appointed four.

The parochial chapelries of Elland and Heptonstall are entirely independent of the mother church in all that regards what is properly called church rate; they support their respective parochial chapels without external aid, and need not now be taken into consideration.

His Majesty's Justices of the Peace for the West-Riding, who reside in the Parish, hold a petty session every Saturday at their office in the town, for the transaction of public business, and at other times when their services are required.

THE TOWNSHIP OF HALIFAX.

Having adverted to those subjects which are of a more general nature in the parochial history, it now becomes necessary to turn our attention to its topographical details. It is with diffidence I enter upon this part of my undertaking, because I feel that within the limits of a work of this description, it is impossible to do justice to an enquiry, not only in its very nature so comprehensive, and relating to a district so extensive; but presenting so many interesting objects.

As Mr. WATSON's history must form the ground-work of any attempt to elucidate this enquiry, supplying, as it does, the most interesting details of particular localities, I shall not hesitate to avail myself of his valuable assistance, particularly as in many instances the difficulty of depending on local information is so great, each informant having a different version of the same story.

The river Hebble, Halig, or Halifax brook runs through the centre of this district of the parish, in a direction from North to South, and forms the Eastern boundary of the township, dividing it from Northowram and Southowram: on the South it is bounded by Skircoat; on the West by Warley; and on the North by Ovenden. It contains 990 acres and is the smallest township in the parish, with the exception of Fixby.

The scenery, viewed from the neighbouring heights, exhibits a tract of country which perhaps more than any other in Great Britain, serves not only to shew the effect of toil and labour, but to prove as Dr. WHITAKER has well observed "how completely the wealth and industry of man can triumph over the most stubborn indispositions of nature;" instead of the place "situate at the foot of a mighty and almost inaccessible rock, all overgrown with trees and thick underwoods, intermixed with great and bulky stones standing very high above ground, in a dark and solemn grove on the bank of a small murmuring rivulet;" we are presented with the prospect of a rich and flourishing town, second only among the manufacturing towns of Yorkshire, possessing within herself every resource necessary to enable her to compete with her contemporaries, containing a population healthy, intelligent, active, industrious and inured to labour; and encircled by a country rich in every sublimity that can attest the magnificence of nature.

It appears from the MS.S. before referred to, and said to have been written by John Waterhouse, some time Lord of the manor of Halifax, that about the year 1443, "there were in Halifax in all but thirteen houses:" and that in the year 1566 there were in Halifax "of householders that kept fires, &c. 20 and six score and no more;" and we find the act of Parliament passed in the reign of Philip and Mary before mentioned, reciting that the barren grounds in these parts were much inhabited, and above five hundred householders then newly increased within these forty years past. This is all the information we have as to the state of the town, at those early periods. It may be almost superfluous to add that all traces of these thirteen houses are entirely eradicated; but nevertheless some conjecture may be formed of their probable locality. I am not expert at description, and must therefore request the indulgence of my reader if I attempt to picture in my imagination the town of Halifax as it appeared "in the time of John Waterhouse," merely to contrast it with its present appearance.

A few straggling tenements, built of wood, wattels, and thatch, near to the bank of a "crystal river," confined by no artificial barrier, and having no other limit to its overflow than what nature itself had provided, (for such was once the now polluted Hebble) stretching at irregular distances from the Bridge to the Kirkgate, and extending along the North side of the church-yard, and from thence to the lords' mill, where we may imagine the tenants "to have been well and orderly used in the grinding of their corn and grist," the principal house, called the Moote or Mulcture hall, standing on the site of the present hall, wherein dwelt the same John Waterhouse then lord of the manor or his bailiff. The vicarage house we may conceive to have been an isolated dwelling on its present site, or near it, the "road" on the south side of the church-yard between that and the vicarage then existed, and formed a continuation of the road on the West of the vicarage land down to the Kirkgate and the river; the entrance to the church being by the North porch. The present fabric was not then built, nay about this time "was the church of Halifax begun to be builded." The site now occupied by the town we may conjecture to have been mostly barren land, if at all cultivated; that on the opposite bank not having as yet been *escarted*. The tract way Wakefield doubtless existed, and a branch thereof to Shipden hall, that also belonging to the Waterhouses.*

On the introduction of the woollen trade we find the town gradually increasing in size, so that in the year 1566 there were 520 houses; of these there are still some interesting remains in good condition, and they seem in the great abundance of wood down to the reign of Henry viii. to have been constructed of oak, and generally to have consisted of three stories, the upper projecting beyond that immediately beneath, and built of strong oak framing, but destitute of all ornament, the interstices being filled up with plaster. The lower stories having undergone many alterations, it is difficult to say how they were arranged; the character of the pannelling in the wainscoat is still preserved in some parts of these houses, and here and there are to be discovered some carved foliage or other device of good workmanship.

They may now be traced at varying distances, forming something like an irregular street from the Church to the Woolshops;

---

* The name of Waterhouse is as familiar to a native of Halifax as his Parish Church. Mr. Hunter says they were a very numerous family in this Parish, so numerous as to mock the best efforts of experienced genealogists to throw them all into a strict genealogical series. The difficulty was increased, by the practice which prevailed among them, of giving the same baptismal names to children born at nearly the same period. They are descended from a Sir Gilbert Waterhouse, of Lincolnshire, who lived temp. Henry III., from whose eldest son are deduced the Waterhouses of Berkhamstead. One John Waterhouse of this branch is said by FULLER to have been a man of much fidelity and sageness ; auditor many years to Henry VIII. whom he entertained at his house. The king at his departure honored the children of this said John Waterhouse with his praise and encouragement, gave a *Benjamin's portion* of dignation to Edward, foretelling by his royal augury, "that he would be the crown of them all, and a man of great honor and wisdom, fit for the service of Princes." I much regret that my limits will not allow to trace their deduction from Gilbert, the arms are or, a pile engrailed sable, which has an allusion to the name, a house built on piles in the water. John, who is mentioned above, had two sons, Richard, of the Hollins, in Warley, and Robert, of the Moot-hall, and of Shibden Hall. The family had much to do with the affairs of the Convent and Priory of Lewes, in this Parish. The present John Waterhouse, Esq. of Well-head, is the representative at Halifax, of the male line of this once peculiarly numerous and opulent family.

(where in all probability our first artificers in wool or weavers were settled,) thence to the Old Market-place, stretching on either side into Southgate and Northgate; and proceeding onward as far as Hall End, taking that direction because the entrance from Gibbet lane was the principal highway into the town from Warley, Midgley, Wadsworth, and Heptonstall. The Gibbet then existed and was in full operation.

Many thanks are certainly due to our fellow townsman, Mr. Horner, for preserving some of these memorials of Halifax in its olden time; they are characterized by truth and well deserve a place in the library of every Halifaxonian.

Mr. WATSON says "I have a plan of the town and precincts of Halifax, which I copied from an old one drawn by the late Mr. Brearcliffe, date uncertain. The places of note marked on this plan are—the Church, Bayley hall, Moulter hall, Cross hill, Norbrigg, Stannary, and the Gibbett. No vicarage house and scarcely any houses near the church. The greater number of buildings appear to have been towards the top of the present town; but there seems not to have been a regular street in the whole place." It is very probable this plan was taken about the year 1648. (See Biography, Brearcliffe John.) It is a matter of regret that Mr. Watson did not favour us with a copy, it would have been an interesting document, and certainly a happy substitute for the ill-executed portrait of the Rev. Author.

The Rev. THOMAS WRIGHT, who published his history in the year 1738, says "so compact is now the town, and so contrived by art, that from the hill which leads to and from Wakefield it represents a cross, or rather two large beams laid cross one upon another, with the left arm rather declining; the whole consisting chiefly of four streets, (the by lanes making no alteration in the figure) in the midst whereof stands the market cross, with a large and plentiful shambles. Below the shambles, the street towards the church consists mostly of inns and woolshops. The upper part of the high street, above the shambles, is taken up with inns and shops, wherein are sold all sorts of merchandize. The left arm as you ascend from the Cross is the market for corn, salt, cheese, &c. The right arm is taken up with some shops, but most with private dwellings and houses for public entertainment.

" To the town thus described are annexed many regular and well
walled closes, variously checquered with the different beauties of
corn and grass; that from the aforesaid heights, the most curious
traveller hath not seen a more delightful landscape, if such prospects
are viewed in their proper seasons."

"In 1759, (says Mr. WATSON,) I caused a ground plan to be
taken of the town (a copy of which accompanies his work) from this
survey it appears, that from the middle of Clark-bridge, to the last
house at the bottom of King Cross-lane, measures 1156 yards:
from the beginning of Southgate, to the end of Northgate, 673
yards; from the Cross, to the last house in King Cross lane, 581
yards; from the Cross to the end of Southgate, 432 yards; from
the Cross to the end of Northgate, 205 yards; from the Cross to
the middle of Clark Bridge, 575 yards; from the Cross to the last
house on the other side of Clark Bridge, 650 yards. Mr. WATSON
also gives the names of the streets and other particular parts thereof
at that period, together with a South-east view of the town.

It then consisted of the following streets or lanes:—viz.
King-cross-lane, Hopwood-lane, Bull-green, Little-green, Bull-
close-lane, Barum top, Harrison-lane, Back-street, Lister-lane,
Cow-green, King-street, Copper-street, Swine market, Gibbet-lane,
Cabbage-lane, Pellon-lane, Loveledge-lane, Stone-trough-lane,
Snidal well-lane, Cheapside, Crown-street, Market place, North-
gate, Corn-market, Southgate, Ward's-end, Blackledge, New-road,
Woolshops, Petticoat-lane, Smithystake-lane, Jail-lane, Causey-
top, Causey, Skeldergate, Church-lane, Vicarage-lane, Well-i'th'
wall-lane, Mill-lane, Cripplegate, and Bury-lane.

WATSON mentions certain *places of note in Halifax*, as he terms
them. Amongst others,

BULL-GREEN,

"Where (he says) in former times was carried on the diversion
of Bull baiting." To say the least of it, this is very hypothetical,
it is improbable that that diversion was ever carried on here to such
an extent as to give name to the place where it was exercised: it
is much more likely to have derived its name from the place being
set apart for the sale of the animal; as was Cow-green, which he
supposes had its name from that sort of cattle being sold there,

also Swine-market, and the Corn-market, from the particular commodity there exposed to sale.

CLARKE BRIDGE.

It is probable that a bridge of some description or other has existed here from time immemorial, it may have been first built, as WATSON conjectures, by the clergy or clerks, for the convenience of passing from the church, either to their habitations, or some place set apart for religious exercises on the other side of the river. It was also the highway to Wakefield. His conjecture about the "holy well" and the "yew tree," are very problematical, the tradition "in favor of this particular spot," requires better evidence in support of it, than a modern public house sign.

CRIPPLEGATE.

It is much more probable took its name from the cripples who used to beg there, than from the cause assigned by WATSON, that it "might take its name from the lame going this way to be cured at the supposed holy place."

THE JAIL

Is appurtenant to the manor of Wakefield and kept by the lord's bailiff. The antiquity of this jail does not appear from records, but one doubtless existed in the times of the earls of Warren, not to confine debtors only, but such felons as were taken within the liberties of the forest of Hardwick, and were there triable by the custom of the said forest.

OLD MARKET-PLACE.

How long a market has been held in the town has never been ascertained, neither is there any evidence to shew that it ever had the privilege of holding one by charter. It avails but little at the present day, its prescriptive title being equally good for every useful purpose. "Here (says WATSON,) is a cross of some antiquity, though not curious; a pillory* and stocks close by it; and a little higher in the street, at what is called the Corn market-end, a square remain, in the centre of which was once fixed a May-pole.

* A Pillory seems to have been an ancient appendage to a Market, for in the 9th Edward I, we find De Furnival, (according to HUNTER,) in answer to a writ of *quo warranto*, demanding of him by what warrant he claimed to have pleas of withernam, pillory, &c. in his manor of Sheffield, replying that he made no claim to pleas of withernam; but that he had a pillory at Sheffield, and the assize of bread, because these are things always belonging to a Market.

Two centuries ago every village had a May-pole, which was in general placed in the most convenient part of the village.

> "Happy the age, and harmless were the days,
> For then true love and amity were found,
> When every village did a May-pole raise."— —1634.

Our custom "is the relic (says Mr. BOURNE) of an ancient one among the heathen, who observed the four last days of April, and the first of May in honor of the goddess Flora."

In an old calendar of the Romish church, there is the following observation on the 30th of April, "the boys go out and seek May-trees."

We read of Henry the eighth's *riding a Maying* from Greenwich to the high ground of Shooter's Hill, with Queen Katherine his wife, accompanied with many lords and ladies. Mr. BRAND also, in his *Popular Antiquities*, quotes a pamphlet entitled, *The way to things by words, and to words by things*, wherein the author tells us that "this is one of the most ancient customs, which from the remotest ages, has been by repetition from year to year, perpetuated down to our days, not being at this instant totally exploded, especially in the lower classes of life. It was considered as the boundary day, that divided the confines of winter and summer, allusively to which there was instituted a sportful war between two parties, the one in defence of the continuance of Winter, the other for bringing in the Summer. The youth were divided into troops, the one in winter livery, the other in the gay habit of spring. The mock battle was always fought booty, the Spring was sure to obtain the victory, which they celebrated by carrying triumphally green branches with May flowers, proclaiming and singing the song of joy, of which the burthen was in these, or equivalent terms,

> We have brought the summer home."

"I have more than once (adds Mr. BRAND,) been disturbed early on May morning at Newcastle, by the noise of a song, which a woman sung about the streets, who had several garlands in her hand, and which, if I mistake not, she sold to any who was superstitious enough to buy them. It is homely and low, but it must be remembered our Treatise is not "on the sublime,"

Rise up, maidens! fy for shame,
I've been four long miles from hame,
I've been gathering my Garlands gay,
Rise up, fair maids, and take in your May."

The Mayings are yet kept up by the milk maids in London, as also by the chimney sweeps, and some others of that ilk. In this part it is usual for our coachmen to decorate their persons and their horses, with flowers and ribbons, and to exhibit a superior team on the occasion. But these are nearly all the traces that now remain to perpetuate the original sport; new lights have sprung up, the innocent diversions of our forefathers are falling into disuse,

"And harmless May-poles would now be rail'd upon,
As if they were the Tow'rs of Babylon."

BATTON-ROW

Says Mr. WATSON, is the name of some ground adjoining to the church-yard, on the north side thereof. As this appellation, which is very ancient, signifies the row or street where the fair was kept, it is not unreasonable to suppose, that here was formerly a meeting every year, to celebrate the feast of the dedication of the church; for these meetings, I think, are generally looked upon as the original of fairs. And that they were anciently held in church-yards, appears from Archbishop Stafford's forbidding the holding of fairs and markets in church-yards throughout his province, in the year 1444, as they had been before 13 Edward I. by the statute of Winchester.

WARD'S END

Is a name common to many places in England, and signifies the end, or extreme part of the district, where in troublesome times, watch and ward was kept; thus if a chain of sentinels were posted round Halifax, to prevent the entrance of any but friends, one proper station would be at Ward's End.

The following survey of an house in Cheapside, Halifax, given by WATSON is too interesting to be omitted. "The date on the back part of this house is 1665; but some parts of the building seem to be much older. In a chamber window above stairs are painted on glass,—1. a dog raised on his hinder feet; 2. a cock standing on his right foot, holding in his left a pole, which he shoulders, and on which is hung an hare, about his neck is slung a bugle horn, and on his head is an high crowned hat. 3. a gentleman and lady in antique dresses, joining hands, 4, 5, and 6. fruit and birds. In the hall window, 1. A female walking. 2. a man walking; both these in antique dresses. 3. a coat of arms as supposed azure, three triple crowns, or two and one, the whole ornamented with sprigs. 4. a flower, 5. a man seated, dressing his own sore leg, having a dirk at his side, 6. a man on the sea shore flying from a mermaid in the water, who holds a glass, and seems to be tempting him to stay. 7. a cat. 8. a man armed cap-a-pie fighting with a bear, which stands erect, and he just on the point of stabbing him. 9. a wild boar. 10. a man dressed in a green doublet. 11. a man delivering to another a fish which he has just taken off the head of a barrel. 12. a bear erect, with a broad sword slung round his shoulder, and a smaller sword drawn in his right paw, a bugle horn hung round his neck. 13—17. birds. 18. the figure of a strange animal."

LOCAL ACTS OF PARLIAMENT.

Various local acts of Parliament have from time to time been passed for the benefit of the town, &c. the first of them was in the year 1762, and was entitled "an act for supplying the town with water," the object of this act was to enable certain commissioners to remove the obstructions in the watercourse issuing from a public spring called Well-head, by which the inhabitants had hitherto been supplied with water for their domestic and other uses; in consequence of these obstructions, water used to be brought into the town, from the well, in carts. The commissioners were also empowered to carry water to the town from other springs, then discovered or which might thereafter be discovered near the town, and to make reservoirs, &c. The next act was passed six years afterwards, it was an act to amend the former act and for better paving &c. the streets, and removing nuisances, &c. in the town; but both these acts have been repealed, as will be seen hereafter.

Three acts have from time to time been passed for the recovery of small debts within this and thirteen neighbouring parishes. The powers vested in the commissioners under the first acts were of a most extraordinary nature and appear to have been most shamefully abused, there are instances on record of their committing to prison within a period of eighteen months, fifty four persons for three months each, some of whose debts only amounted to 3s. 8d., and who were supported while there, out of the jailor's private purse ; and it appears from evidence adduced before a committee of the house of commons, that one person was committed for three months for a debt of one shilling and sixpence; that at one period there were fifteen persons confined in their prison, who were the parents of seventy-three children, and whose debts amounted only to £17, with many other cases of severity and oppression equally gross.

To remedy these grievances the present act was introduced in the year 1793, it repeals the former acts, and grants other powers for similar purposes. By this act certain commissioners and their successors to be elected as therein mentioned, being seised of £20 a year, real property, or £500 personally ; are appointed to hear and determine matters of debt under 40s., and to administer summary justice between the parties. There is nothing peculiar in the act to distinguish it from other local acts of a similar nature. The power of imprisonment for debts of 40s. and under is still retained, although the period of confinement is limited to forty days. On the introduction of the original bill into parliament, this clause was omitted, but it was urged by its supporters that the very spirit of the act would be left out without such a clause : it became law.

In the year 1828 the commissioners obtained leave to bring a bill into Parliament to amend the present act, and to divide the court into two separate jurisdictions; the parishes of Halifax and Huddersfield, &c. to form one division, and the parishes of Bradford, &c. to form another division, and to extend the powers of the present act. The bill did not pass into a law, but the commissioners have nevertheless divided the court into two separate jurisdictions, and have also erected an additional goal at Halifax.

The act may or may not vest in the commissioners this extraordinary power; but the same principle will equally apply to the creation of as many jurisdictions, and the erection of as many gaols as the commissioners may deem expedient : a most dangerous precedent, and the sooner the power is abrogated the better.

The number of actions entered in the Halifax and Huddersfield division of the court amounted in one year, ending February, 1831, to 10,064, the amount sued for to £9.311 0s. 11d. ; the number of actions compromised on payment of tenpence, 5664 ; the number

tried, 4400 : out of this latter number, 1837 executions were issued, viz. 427 against the goods of debtors, and 1410 against their
bodies. The executions were thus disposed of, 600 paid, 788
settled with plaintiff, 349 were imprisoned for terms not exceeding
40 days, 100 could not be levied. The costs in the majority of cases
for which executions are issued, amount to 8s. 4d. Without entering upon the question as to the expediency or policy of abolishing
imprisonment for debt in all cases, it must be confessed that some
alteration in the law by which Courts of Conscience are regulated,
is absolutely necessary ; partial in their operation, and susceptible
of being converted into instruments of oppression, their powers of
arrest and imprisonment, (if needful) ought only to be entrusted to
competent persons qualified to act in a judicial capacity. If the Court
Baron constituted as it is, be not entrusted with the exercise of that
power, it is not fitting that three commissioners should be permitted
to imprison his Majesty's subjects for debt, their only requisite
qualification for the important office of a judge being the possession
of £20 a year, or £500 personally, (putting education out of the
question,) but particularly wherein the exercise of the authority in
many cases not only requires great caution and discrimination, but
also some knowledge of the rules of law.

In consequence of the streets and footpaths in the town being
greatly obstructed by stalls and standings, several of the inhabitants
purchased the site of the present New Market-Place at considerable
expense, and erected shambles and market shops therein, and in
the year 1810 an act was passed for regulating the "NEW MARKET-
PLACE," the proprietors whereof were empowered to choose five of
their number to be trustees for managing their affairs ; and to raise
a sum not exceeding £3000 in addition to the money advanced, to
be divided into equal shares of £50 each, and applied towards paying the expences of obtaining the act, in the purchase of premises,
and in making and maintaining the Market-Place. The act prohibits
the slaughtering of cattle, &c. there, except in slaughter houses to
be set apart for the purpose ; and also the setting up of any shops
or stalls in the footpaths or high-ways. The proprietors are empowered to make such rules, regulations and bye-laws as they or
their trustees shall think fit for regulating the market, &c. provided

such rules, &c. be not repugnant to the act or to the law : the rules
are subject to appeal at the general Quarter Sessions. The proprietor's dividends are limited to £10 per cent., and there is a clause
in the act providing and enacting that when any surplus balance
shall remain after defraying all costs, &c. and the full dividend of
£10 per cent. amongst the proprietors, it shall be lawful for them
to place such surplus balance out at interest to accumulate, and
when the sum of £1500 shall be raised, to erect a Town's Hall in
some convenient situation near the New Market-Place, with suitable
offices and conveniences for the use of his Majesty's justices of the
peace for the riding, for the purpose of holding their private sessions,
and transacting their public business therein : and also if the Lords
of the Manor of Wakefield and Halifax shall think fit, for holding
the Court Leet and Court Baron therein, free from any charge by
the proprietors for the use thereof : and also for the inhabitants of
the town and parish to make use thereof, for holding any lawful
public meetings on business therein, free from any charge, on delivering to the clerk of the proprietors three days previous to such
meeting, a request in writing for the purpose, signed by ten or more
inhabitants of the town and parish who should possess or occupy
lands or tenements of the value of £20 per annum, of which number
the constable or constables of the town shall form part. The Hall is
nevertheless to be under the direction and control of the trustees, and
to be made use of by them when not wanted for the purpose aforesaid in such manner as they should appoint. Any further surplus is
to be applied in the improvement of the town, and to be suffered to
accumulate for the building of any public hospital or dispensary, or
any other purpose whatever, beneficial to the town and the inhabitants. There is a proviso in the act that no more than £1500 part
of the £3000 shall be raised until after the Town's Hall shall have
been erected. The penalties and forfeitures under the act are to be
applied one half to the informer, the other to the use of or towards
erecting a public general dispensary in the town, or such other public establishment, school, or charity, as the proprietors shall order
and direct.

In the year 1822 an act was obtained for lighting with gas the
town and township, and the neighbourhood. The subscribers were
incorporated by the name of THE HALIFAX GAS LIGHT AND COKE

Company. The joint stock of the company is not to exceed £12000, and to be divided in shares of £25 sterling each. The Gas Works are erected in Southowram, on the bank of the Hebble: there are three gasometers, capable of containing 73049 cubic feet of gas. The township is now handsomely lighted.

On the 17th June, 1823, an Act received the royal assent, "for paving, cleansing, watching, and improving the township, and for supplying the same with water:" this act repeals the two former acts. The power of carrying it into execution is invested in certain trustees to be qualified as therein mentioned, and contains several important provisions in regard to the police of the township, and the purchase of premises for widening and improving the streets, &c., My limits will not allow me to give even a summary of the act, which contains 139 sections, of too important a nature to be abbreviated, so as to answer any useful purpose. Since the passing of this act many great and useful improvements have been made in the town. Among the principal may be mentioned the widening of Bull Green; the opening of a handsome thoroughfare from Northgate to the centre of the town, called Broadstreet, and Waterhouse-street; the widening of Northgate, although this is only partially effected; the clearing away of many old houses in the vicinity of the church, and widening the streets there. The antiquated houses of the 16th century in Crown-street are not only an ornament to the place, but are interesting reminiscences of the olden time, too venerable, too intimately associated with the recollections of the old inhabitants, to be sacrificed at the modern shrine of expediency, they ought to be permitted to remain until the stern law of necessity demands their removal.—The same cannot be said of the shambles at Hall End, and the ruinous old buildings at the rear, their removal is a consummation much to be desired, and the soite they occupy would afford a most excellent situation for a handsome Exchange or other public building, not forgetting that necessary appendage,—a well regulated clock: at the rear of the building might be erected a police station and engine house, surmounted by a bell tower. These are not only conveniences in a populous commercial town, but it may be said that an absolute necessity exists for them. They should occupy a centrical situation.

Amidst the various improvements a due attention to the health of the inhabitants has not been lost sight of. The township has been well and effectually drained, and various public nuisances removed, and to these circumstances, (which it is but justice to the medical gentlemen connected with the town to say, was adopted at their recommendation,) may be attributed in a great measure, (as a means under divine providence) its preservation from that dreadful scourge which not many years ago visited the land.

The atmosphere is not so subject to those impurities arising from the smoke of steam engines which is generally the case in manufacturing towns; this may arise in a great measure from the manufactories being confined to the banks of the Hebble. A wholesome provision in the local act requires that the furnaces of all steam engines erected within the township shall consume their own smoke, although to answer any useful purpose, it should have included all steam engines within two miles of the parish church. The vicinity of the North Bridge is subject to much annoyance on this account.

The town is well supplied with water, the produce of two springs, one in the township of Ovenden, from whence it is conveyed by pipes into two reservoirs constructed for the purpose about a mile N. W. of the town, and from thence served to the inhabitants. The town possesses a better system of nightly watch and patrol than it formerly enjoyed; the present establishment is generally considered an efficient force. The system of police (so far as two honorary constables and one deputy constable to perform the duty can be called a police) is altogether ineffective, but as the subject of municipal government is under the consideration of the legislature, we may expect that something will be done to put the whole system of provincial police on a better footing.

The holding of the cattle markets on Cow Green is altogether an intolerable nuisance: if the powers of the local act are not sufficient to remove it, extended powers should be applied for: the public streets of the town should at all times be kept free and open, and not subject to those annoyances which every Saturday arise from the obstruction of the public thoroughfare: long established custom may in some degree sanction the practice, and innkeepers may be interested in the continuance of the nuisance; but it cannot be disputed that some other place should be set apart for the holding of our cattle markets. These observations will equally apply to the very dangerous and illegal practice of exercising horses in the streets at the half yearly fairs.

An annual fair is held in the town on the 24th June, being the festival of St. John the Baptist to whom the church was dedicated. In ancient times among Christians upon any extraordinary solemnity, particularly the anniversary dedication of a church, tradesmen used to bring and sell their wares, even in the church yards. I have before extracted Mr. Watson's observations on this subject, when describing "Ratton Row," p. 330.

"The custom (says Mr. BRAND in his *Antiquitates Vulgares*) our forefathers did, in all probability, borrow from their fellow heathens, whose *Paganalia* or Country Feasts were of the same stamp with that of the wake. At the conversion of the *Saxons* by *Austin* the monk, it was ordained by Pope Gregory the great, as follows :—On the day of dedication, or the birth-day of the holy martyrs whose relicks are there placed, let the people make to themselves *booths* of the boughs of trees round about those very churches which had been the temples of idols, and in a religious way to observe a feast; that beasts may no longer be slaughtered by way of sacrifice to the devil, but for their own eating and the glory of God; and that when they are full and satisfied they may return Him thanks, who is the giver of all good things." This then is the beginning of our *country wakes*. Sir H. Spelman calls them Bacchanals, because the Saxon word *Wak*, signifies drunkenness. Mr. Strutt gives a different etymology, he nevertheless deduces the origin of our fairs from these ancient wakes where great numbers attending, by degrees less devotion and reverence were observed; till at length from hawkers and pedlars coming thither to sell their petty wares, the merchants came and set up stalls and booths in the church-yards and not only those, says Spelman, who lived in the parish to which the church belonged resorted thither, but others from all the neighbouring towns and villages; and the greater the reputation of the saint, the greater were the numbers who flocked together on the occasion. KENNETT in his *Parochial Antiquities* says, that from the solemn feasting at wakes and fairs came the word *fare*, provision; good *fare*, to *fare* well.

z

The manner of holding fairs in the present day is too familiar to my readers to need any explanation here.

A fair is also held on the first Saturday in November for the sale of cattle and horses.

We now proceed to notice the places of religious worship, institutions, and public buildings within the town.

TRINITY CHURCH.

Until the year 1798, the parish church was the only place of worship belonging to the Establishment within the township. To the munificence of the late Dr. Coulthurst are we indebted for this handsome edifice: it is pleasantly and eligibly situated. The building which is altogether elegant, and the masonry excellent and elaborate, is adorned with Ionic pilasters, and has a cupola at the West end. The cemetery attached, observes Dr. Whitaker, ought to operate as an example of neatness to all the chapelries in the parish : there is considerable taste displayed in many of the tombs. It was erected under the sanction of an act of parliament passed in the year 1795; and the land purchased by Dr. C. of the trustees of Waterhouse's charities. The act empowered Dr. C. and his heirs to sell or let the pews, galleries, and a portion of not more than one fifth of the burying ground at prices to be regulated by the archbishop of York; the remaining four-fifths to be a common burying ground for the inhabitants of Skircoat and Southowram. A portion of the space within the church, with seats as the archbishop should direct, was to be provided for the poor. The act also provides an income of not less than £100 a year for the incumbent from the seats: the repairs are provided for by an assessment of the pew owners.

In the year 1810 the governors of Queen Anne's bounty granted an augmentation of £100 to meet a benefaction of £200 from Thomas Dyson, Esq. and others; and in 1816, another £100 to meet a subscription of £200; and in the year 1825 a further sum of £600 was granted by lot. Out of these augmentations a comfortable house has been erected contiguous to the church, for the residence of the incumbent. The right of presentation is vested by the act in Dr. Coulthurst and his representatives, for the term of 69 years, after which time it belongs to the vicar of the parish.

ST. JAMES'S CHURCH.

The rapid increase of the population and the great extension of the town rendered another church absolutely necessary for the accommodation of the inhabitants. Although the project was much canvassed during the incumbency of the late Rev. Samuel Knight, we are indebted to the present Rev. vicar for originating a subscription for the laudable purpose of erecting this edifice. A representation of the facts being made to His Majesty's commissioners for building, and promoting the building of additional churches, they offered to contribute a proportion of the expense, provided a sufficient sum to make up the deficiency was raised by voluntary subscription. During the life of the late Wm. Rawson, Esq. the cause of true religion never wanted a friend in the town of Halifax, his name occupied the first place in the list with a donation of £200, the good example thus set was speedily followed, and the necessary sum soon raised.

The scite being purchased, the stone was the munificent gift of Michael Stocks, Esq. the produce of his quarries at Shibden dale. The edifice is erected on raised ground in a delightful situation. It is in the pseudo-gothic style, with turrets at the West end; and was built from a design of the late John Oates, Esq. and under his superintendence. The internal arrangements consist of a spacious centre, and two side aisles; all the pews in the lower part are capable of containing five persons. There are galleries on the North and South sides and at the West end. The church will seat upwards of 1206 persons, including free seats; the cost of its erection was £4122 11s. 0d. There is a convenient cemetery attached. The whole was consecrated by the archbishop of the province in the year 1831, but not opened for public worship till January, 1832. The right of presentation is in the vicar of the parish. The Rev. John Worgan Dew was the first incumbent, whose lamented death took place Sept. 5th, 1834. The Rev. J. Gratrix, A. M. became his successor.

NORTHGATE CHAPEL.

It appears from the Rev. Oliver Heywood's diary, that the Presbyterians erected a chapel on this spot in the year 1697. The present building appears to be an enlargement of the first chapel. There are galleries on three sides, and in that at the West end there is a small organ. On the whole the interior arrangements

z 2

are strikingly neat, though the exterior presents anything but a
pleasing appearance.   It now belongs to the Unitarians.

In the cemetery attached are several tomb-stones of the early
Presbyterians, who formerly resided in this town.   Under the
East gallery is a brass plate—"To commemorate the interment in
a vault below of Ann Heywood, relict of Samuel Heywood, Esq.
attorney-at-law in Nottingham, descendant in the third degree from
Oliver Heywood, one of the founders of the Presbyterian churches
in this neighbourhood. She died Feb. 5. MDCCCXXV. Aged
LXXII.

QUAKER'S MEETING HOUSE.

The respectable society of Friends have long had a meeting
house in this town at Ward's end.   There is a burial ground attached
to the chapel.   In 1759 the number of their meeting houses exceeded
that of any other separate class of dissenters in the parish.

BAPTIST CHAPEL, PELLON-LANE.

A handsome erection has this year (1835) been built on the scite
of an old chapel there, belonging to the ana-baptists, erected in the
middle of the last century.

METHODIST CHAPEL, SOUTH-PARADE.

This chapel is the oldest place of worship in the town belonging
to the Wesleyan Methodists.   The first chapel was erected near
the present scite, in the year 1752 at a cost of £300; and the
present building finished in the year 1777. It is a spacious erection,
heavy and devoid of external ornament, but light, airy, and convenient within, and capable of containing a congregation of three
thousand persons.   A very capacious burial ground is attached to it.
Also an house for the minister.   A powerful and well-toned organ
has lately been erected.

WESLEY CHAPEL, BROAD-STREET.

This is altogether a handsome erection, and affords a perfect
contrast to the last mentioned.   The interior is well arranged, and
displays a degree of taste in the fitting up, so that on the whole,
neither the exterior nor interior appearance of the place is surpassed
by any chapels belonging to this denomination of christians in the

WESLEY CHAPEL.

Drawn by J. HORNER, Engraved by WHIMPER

SION CHAPEL.

Drawn by J. HORNER.   Engraved by WHIMPER.

HANOVER STREET CHAPEL.

Drawn by J. HORNER   Engraved by WHIMPER.

West Riding. The first stone was laid on the 3rd day of March, 1829; and the first sermon preached in it on the 6th of November following. The cost of its erection amounted to nearly £4000. An addition has lately been made of a handsome organ.

THE SQUARE CHAPEL.

This chapel belongs to the Independent Dissenters, and was founded in the year 1771, finished the following year, and first preached in May 24th, 1772. It was expressly built for the late Titus Knight the father of the late vicar. It is a lofty and spacious structure, of red brick, and presents a very handsome appearance; the interior is light, airy, and commodious, and capable of containing a very large congregation. The cost of its erection amounted to upwards of £2000. There is a cemetery attached to it.

SION CHAPEL,

Also belongs to the class of Dissenters calling themselves Independents. It was erected in the year 1819, upon the scite of an old chapel formerly used by the followers of Johanna Southcote, and other sectarians. The building is of stone, of the Doric order of architecture, and displays in its internal arrangement a degree of elegance and taste, which is generally the case in the modern chapels of this class of Dissenters. The roof is illuminated with stained glass. The cost of its erection is stated to have been upwards of £6000. There is also a spacious burial ground attached to this chapel.

SALEM CHAPEL, IN THE NORTH PARADE.

This chapel belongs to the New Connexion of Methodists, and was re-built in the year 1815, upon the scite of one erected by this denomination in 1798. It is a plain stone building, surrounded on three sides by a burial ground, on the fourth side is attached the minister's house.

HANOVER CHAPEL, KING-CROSS LANE.

This is another chapel belonging to the Methodist New Connexion. The foundation stone was laid October 1st, 1834, and is at present (August, 1835) in an unfinished state.

METHODIST CHAPEL, CARBAGE LANE.

This is a plain stone building belonging to the Primitive Methodists, or Ranters; and erected by them in the year 1822. In front there is a small burying ground.

THE NATIONAL SCHOOL,

Near to Trinity Church, is a plain brick building, erected in the year 1815, and capable of containing about four hundred scholars. The school is upheld and supported by subscription, and at present affords instruction to near two hundred scholars, who are educated in the principles of the Established Church.

LANCASTERIAN SCHOOL.

This school, for the instruction of children of all denominations, was instituted Jan. 1st, 1813. A large and commodious building was erected A. D. 1818, in Albion-street, for a school room, and it is supported by the voluntary contributions of persons of all denominations. The room is capable of containing three hundred and fifty scholars. The school has received several benefactions, and the total number of children admitted since the commencement of the institution, is 3064 boys, and 1636 girls, making a total of 4700. It is needless to observe, the Lancasterian system is adopted.

THE DISPENSARY.

This charitable institution requires no preface to shew its utility in a populous and labouring community. The inhabitants of Halifax, ever ready to attend to the call of humanity, held a meeting on the 3rd of Oct. 1807, to resolve upon a plan for the establishment of a General Dispensary, whereby the poor and industrious workman and his family should receive the aid of the physician and the surgeon, in all diseases and accidents, at their own habitations; where medicines might be regularly administered; and where, at stated hours, those who are capable of attending, might receive advice and medicine free of all expence, and with as little loss of time as possible. Its doors being always open to persons suffering from accidents, and to the sick on the recommendation of subscribers.

The building at present devoted to the purpose is a spacious well-built mansion, at Causey-head, belonging to the Governors of

Waterhouse's charities for the use of the lectures in the Parish Church. It is held now at a lease by trustees on behalf of the Dispensary, at a low rental. The charity consists of a president, two vice-presidents, a treasurer, two physicians, two surgeons, a resident apothecary, and governors. A donation of ten guineas or more constitutes a governor for life, who may have a patient continually on the books for every ten guineas contributed. An annual subscription of one guinea or more entitles the subscriber to be a governor and to have one patient continually on the books for each guinea subscribed. All ministers preaching annual sermons followed by collections, are governors, and entitled to vote on all matters relative to the institution, and also to have one patient continually on the books. The management of its affairs is entrusted to a committee of twenty-one governors chosen every year, the committee being open to the president, vice-president, treasurer, medical officers, and governors for life, who are entitled to a vote; three of them form a quorum. All ladies, as well as those governors who reside out of the district for visiting patients at their own houses, (which extends to a mile from the cross) may by letter appoint other governors to vote for them at any election by ballot; at which no person is entitled to vote who has not been a governor upwards of six months, and who has not paid his subscription on or before the day preceding the election.

It is required that every physician eligible to the Dispensary, be a medical graduate of the universities of Oxford, Cambridge, Dublin, Edinburgh, or Glasgow; and that the surgeons have obtained a diploma from some incorporated College of Surgeons. The Physicians attend at the Dispensary every Monday, Wednesday, Thursday, and Saturday; and also visit home patients at their respective places of abode, when necessary. A surgeon attends every Tuesday and Friday to examine patients labouring under surgical complaints, and also visits patients at their own houses, within the district of the Dispensary, whose cases render them unable to attend. No capital operation is to be performed without first consulting the physicians. The qualifications for the apothecary are testimonials of moral conduct and of having served a regular apprenticeship of five years to a surgeon, or surgeon apothecary: his election is made by the four medical officers; the President to collect their votes, and in case of an equality to have a casting vote. It is required that the apothecary shall reside in the house, and compound and dispense the medicines required; and devote his whole time to the duties of his office, No menial servants, nor domestic apprentices, whose masters are able to provide for them, can be admitted as proper objects of the charity.

It is obvious that in manufacturing districts the labouring poor are much exposed to accidents, and those in general of a very severe nature; arising from the complicated state of machinery; to meet cases of this description, surgical wards were opened in the Dispensary in the year 1823, and enlarged in 1827; but the number of beds at present does not exceed eight. This department, of necessity, draws largely on the funds of the institution. The numbers admitted into these wards have been very considerable.

The total number of patients admitted from the commencement of the charity till December, 1831, was 80.346. The amount of donations and collections during the same period was £4063 13 11. The annual subscriptions for the year 1834 amounted to £532 7s.

THE THEATRE.

This building has not any thing in its exterior appearance to recommend it to public notice, its frontage being occupied by the Shakspeare Tavern. It was erected about the year 1790 by voluntary subscriptions, and contains two tiers of boxes, pit and gallery. The size is sufficiently large for the town. It is open during the season under the management of Mr. Manly, whose best exertions are always put forth to cater for the amusement of his audience; but the taste for theatrical amusements does not appear to prevail here to a great extent.

THE NEW ROOMS, IN HARRISON LANE.

These rooms were erected in the year 1828, by subscription, from a design and under the superintendance of the late Mr. John Oates. The site is not only well chosen, but the building is admirably adapted to the purposes for which it was erected, and displays a degree of skill in the general arrangement of the interior. The above Vignette will better illustrate its exterior appearance than any written description.

In the centre of the ground story is an entrance hall, having on either side two spacious rooms; of those on the right side of the hall, one of them extending the whole breadth of the building, is appropriated to the use of the subscription library and has a separate entrance; the other as the temporary museum of the Literary and Philosophical Society. The rooms on the left of the hall are a handsome News room, and adjoining thereto a Billiard room, with separate entrances. There are also private apartments for the residence of the housekeeper.

From the hall are a double flight of circular stairs, lighted by a skylight of stained glass, ascending to a handsome gallery in the centre of which are folding doors opening into a suite of lofty and elegant apartments, extending the whole front length of the building, consisting of a splendid Ball room, Card room, and Supper room, forming, when united, a noble suite of Assembly rooms.

The cornices are richly and tastefully ornamented; the ceiling is arched and supported by eight fluted Corinthian pillars, so placed as to form a division of the apartments, which can be separated by invisible doors. Over the entrance is an appropriate orchestra; but on the occasion of concerts a handsome one has been built expressly for the purpose, and removeable at pleasure.

The rooms are elegantly and tastefully furnished with crimson damask curtains, sofas and ottomans, en suite; beautiful cut-glass chandeliers are suspended from the ceiling.

Adjoining the card room, and with a separate entrance from the gallery, is a Ladies' withdrawing room. There is also a dressing room for the gentlemen; a cloak and hat room; servants' waiting room, and every other requisite necessary for the convenience and accommodation of visitors.

As public rooms they have been universally admired, nor are they surpassed by any in the county, either as regards their arrange-ment, or the taste and style displayed in the fitting up. Much praise is due to the proprietors, for their spirited conduct in thus affording their fellow townsmen the opportunity of enjoying those elegant pleasures and fascinating but innocent amusements, which are the life and charm of good society.

LITERARY AND PHILOSOPHICAL SOCIETY.

The Halifax Literary and Philosophical Society was instituted in the year 1830, and is governed by certain laws and regulations settled at the first annual meeting of the society on the 7th Octo-ber, 1831. Its affairs are conducted by a president, two vice-pre-sidents, two secretaries, a treasurer, curators of the respective departments, and five members of the society, all of whom con-stituting the council, are annually elected by ballot out of the subscribing members at the annual meeting, being respectively eligible to re-election, except the vice-presidents, whose office is biennial.

General meetings of the society are held during the sessions, which extend throughout the year, with the exception of the months of July, August, and September, at stated periods, when members are elected, donations presented, communications received and read, and scientific and literary subjects discussed.

The literary character of the town may be said to have been involved in the accomplishment of so noble an undertaking as the formation of a society for the advancement of literature, science, and philosophical research; and if the encouraging and satisfactory success that attended it in its infantine state, and still attends it, be any criterion of the value the gentry of Halifax attach to the cultivation of those pursuits which ennoble the understanding and elevate the mind; the Literary and Philosophical Society, will, ere long, occupy a pre-eminent station in this country.

As the society's first annual report may be said to form the ground-work of their undertaking, I have here embodied such extracts as cannot fail to be interesting, and at the same time shew some of its principal features.

"In the society's collection in Zoology, the lover of natural history will find that facilities of a more than ordinary nature are here afforded him, of indulging and prosecuting his favorite study. The beautiful series of Foreign Birds, for the most part formed during the last few years in South America, presents numerous rare and interesting examples, and some few indeed, which there is reason to believe are, in this country, unique; whilst many individual instances occur, as perfect in their nature as those of which any other collection can boast. The Museum also contains a collection of British birds, which, though far from complete, comprises a considerable portion of the rarer species; the majority of them deriving an additional interest from their having been procured in the immediate vicinity of Halifax.

"The department of Foreign Conchology presents examples of all the Linnæan genera, in their most brilliant tints and varied forms, as well as a considerable portion of those of more modern authors; and embraces many species of unusual occurrence and beauty.

"Perhaps no district in England, hitherto explored by the naturalist, has been found more prolific in the rare and valuable productions in Entomology than that in which this institution is established, and the formation of a cabinet of British Insects which has just been effected, may be said to insure, at no distant period, a complete collection in this instructive, though minute, department of Natural History.

"In the interesting and rapidly advancing science of Geology, this immediate neighbourhood has furnished the Society with a number of specimens, consisting chiefly of Fossil plants; many, undoubtedly, of great rarity, and others, probably, unique. Some progress has thus been made towards the formation of a regular series of organic remains, from the carboniferous beds which occupy so large a portion of the parish of Halifax. It is, however, much to be regretted that these strata have not, until a very recent period, received that degree of attention from geologists, to which their importance entitled them, and the consequence is, that many of their productions remain undescribed. The establishment of this institution will, however, it is hoped, be the means of awakening a spirit of geological investigation and research, and thereby of securing not only the acquisition, but also an accurate and scientific description, of the productions of our own strata.

"Though the society's collection may be said to comprise specimens from all the Fossil-bearing strata, it is as yet deficient in examples in vertebrated animals and Mammalia."

The mineralogical department of the Museum at that time exhibited upwards of 600 specimens referable to all the four leading classes under which minerals are usually arranged—those of earthy, saline, metaliferous and inflammable substances.

"In the Cabinets set apart for the reception of coins, and other memorials and relics of former times, the antiquary will derive much gratification and instruction from a careful examination of their contents. The series of Roman and Grecian coins presents a number of interesting specimens of no ordinary beauty and value, and in the most perfect state of preservation; whilst that of the coinage of our own country comprises, with very few exceptions, examples of the currency of the English kings from the Conquest to the present period, as well as of several of the Anglo-Saxon monarchs.

"From the ruins of Athens and its vicinity, there are some beautiful illustrations of those exquisite arts which so eminently distinguished a former age; and from these it may be permitted to select, for more especial notice, the specimens of Grecian sculpture, which are not less attractive to the artist than to the antiquary.

The rude but ingenious manufactures of many uncivilized countries also ornament various parts of the museum.

In adverting to the Library, although the council could not

then continue the language of congratulation, as that important
branch of the Institution had failed to meet with its due measure of
success; they have since received from their President a well timed
and liberal donation of 50 guineas, to be applied exclusively to its
increase; together with several other donations, among which is
the munificent gift of the Public Records from His Majesty's Commissioners.   In the selection of the books, a particular reference
has been had by the Council, to the objects of the institution,
which required not a miscellaneous library for general circulation; but chiefly a collection of the most valuable standard
works on the different departments of science; and it is but justice
to the Council to state that they have appropriated the funds placed
at their disposal, with a due regard to the comparative extent, importance, and interest, of the respective subjects.   It appeared, in
the first place, desirable to obtain a suitable provision of those books
of reference, which are almost indispensable appendages to the
Museum.   Other scientific works have been, and will be, added
from time to time, possessing a more general interest.   Whether
these should be allowed to circulate beyond the bounds of the Museum is a question which will probably come under the consideration of the society.

It would be an act of injustice and ingratitude to omit particu-
larizing those of its members, to whom the society is most especially
indebted for their liberal donations,   Among these the name of the
worthy president, Christopher Rawson, Esq., occupies a prominent
place.   The acquisitions derived from this gentleman's munificence
consist of a splendid series of Roman and Grecian gold and silver
coins, medals and antiquities, various curiosities, minerals and
fossils; the value and extent of which can only be duly appreciated
by a reference to the museum: together with several expensive
and valuable books.   Nor are the interesting collections of English silver coins, and medals, the donation of Edward Nelson
Alexander, F. S. A. one of the honorary secretaries, unworthy of
especial notice.

The whole of the valuable and interesting collection of foreign
Birds, which, as a deposit, originally formed one of the bases of the
Museum, and, in fact, contributed in no small degree to its very
establishment, has been, in the most handsome manner, presented

to the society by John Smith, Esq., of Halifax; the afford an
unequivocal proof of his approbation of its proceedings, of his conviction of its permanency, and of his anxiety for its flourishing
success. To this very liberal donation, he also added the gift of
an interesting series of South American shells, which have hitherto
formed part of the contents of the Museum, and several specimens
connected with foreign natural history; merely attaching to the whole, the very proper and reasonable condition that, should so improbable an event as the dissolution of the society occur within such years, the specimens thus presented shall be restored to their former possessor.

Among the other donations which are entitled to peculiar notice, are those of Dr. Moulson, and the Rev. J. R. Walsh, who, with the view of encouraging absolute contributions to the society, and thereby augmenting its own possessions, have most kindly presented their valuable collections of Entomology; that of the former, embracing specimens, in the most perfect preservation, of Brazilian Insects; and that of the latter comprising upwards of Six Hundred British Insects, rendered particularly interesting from their being chiefly captured in our own district.

I have thus endeavoured, as briefly as possible, to set forth the advantages peculiarly enjoyed by this infant institution, and it is almost needless to add, that in proportion as those advantages are known, they cannot but be appreciated. The prosperity of this society is identified with the best interests of the Parish, and every individual who desires to promote the reputation of the one, will pride himself in the welfare of the other.

THE LITERARY AND PHILOSOPHICAL SOCIETY'S HALL.

This is a handsome classical structure, contiguous to the New Rooms. The foundation was laid on the 16th May, 1834, and the building erected from a design of Wm. Gravatt, Esq. F. R. S. Architect. On the ground floor is a good entrance hall, a spacious lecture room, and two smaller rooms, with apartments for the keeper. A circular stone stair case ascends from the hall to the museum, which exclusively occupies the first floor, and is a grand apartment well adapted for the purpose. There are only four windows on the ground floor. The roof is an entablature supported by six pilasters, in the centre is a large lanthorn sky-light to give light to the museum. The building is encircled by a handsome pallisado fence.

The day set apart for laying the foundation stone of this building was of too interesting a nature to be passed over in silence; it will long be remembered here, not only as regards the object of the undertaking, but the manner in which the ceremonial was performed. I must not omit to state that the Ladies had most kindly and considerately deputed Dr. Kenny to present to Christopher Rawson, Esq. the president of the society, a silver trowel to be used on the occasion. The day was beautifully fine; and the presence of a numerous assemblage of the fair sex (who viewed the proceedings from the adjoining rooms) gave a peculiar animation to the scene. A few short but excellent speeches having been made by some of the members of the society, and the usual muniments, and a set of coins of the present and two preceding reigns, having been deposited in a cavity of the stone, and secured by a brass plate with an appropriate inscription thereon; the worthy mason performed his interesting duty, amidst the smiles and greetings of his fair country-women, the congratulations of his friends, and the acclamations of his assembled townsmen.

The sentiment of Mr. Rawson, at the conclusion of the proceedings, is too excellent, too deeply in unison with the feelings of all who take an interest in the success of the society, to be passed over in silence, I here transcribe it, :—

"Gentlemen, the ceremony being now concluded, and the foundation laid, it remains for me to express my fervent hope, that the superstructure to be raised thereon, may to the present and succeeding generations, ever prove a scene and source of intellectual enjoyment and moral improvement: and that its walls may be ever strangers to any sentiments and opinions which do not inculcate universal philanthropy and brotherly love; sentiments and opinions, gentlemen, which, whilst they teach us to admire the wonderful works of nature, teach us at the same time, to bow with humility and reverence to that "Great First Cause," Nature's God! who made all things; who made man after His own image, and having done so, enjoined upon all mankind this sublime precept, 'love thy neighbour as thyself'; and now, in conclusion, from my heart I pray, may God bless you all."

THE MECHANICS' INSTITUTION.

The Halifax Mechanics' Institution was established in May, 1825, and owes its origin to a letter which was circulated among the principal inhabitants of the town, and signed on behalf of a small number of operatives, by one Joseph Baldwin, a respectable working mechanic,—setting forth the advantages which they expected would arise from popular institutions of this kind, when fitted up with necessary books and apparatus, and supported and countenanced by gentlemen of property and influence; expressing their desire to see an institution established in Halifax, similar in its plan and objects to those already formed in other manufacturing towns.   This appeal met with the encouragement it deserved, from a number of the more intelligent and wealthy classes of the community.   A meeting was called by public advertisement, when John Waterhouse, Esq. of Well Head, took the chair, at which a series of resolutions were agreed upon, expressive of their opinion of the beneficial results likely to arise from a society formed for the purpose of affording to the working classes the means of acquiring practical and scientific information, and their determination to encourage the desire expressed in the letter above alluded to, by co-operating with each other in forming and supporting a society which should be denominated "The Halifax Mechanics' Institution." A provisional committee was appointed to draw up rules and to obtain subscriptions, and on the 29th June, a meeting of the members and subscribers was held in the Parish church Sunday school room, when the rules for the future government of the institution were adopted and officers appointed for the ensuing year.   From this day therefore, the institution bears date, when the society consisted of seven honorary members, forty-nine members, and thirty-four subscribers.   The first annual meeting was held on the 3rd of July, 1826, and in October following a course of lectures was delivered. From this period until 1829, the subscribers to the institution gradually lessened, occasioned partly from the apathy and indifference exhibited by those for whose more especial benefit the society was formed, and partly from other causes.   In this year, however, through the active exertions of a few individuals, a deeper interest was excited, than had existed for two years previous.   In order to give a greater popularity to the institution, a few gentlemen agreed to deliver monthly, a gratuitous lecture on some important branch of science. By these means and a complete revision of the rules in the following year, the institution has become what it was originally intended to be, and instead of not having more than from twenty to thirty members on the books, as was the case in 1829, it can now boast of from 350 to 400 members.

Connected with the institution there is an evening school, three times a week; a library, consisting of upwards of 1000 volumes which is also open three times a week; and access to all lectures, apparatus, &c. &c., for the annual subscription of eight shillings.

PUBLIC LIBRARIES.

There are two public circulating subscription Libraries within the town. The principal is at the New Rooms, in Harrison Lane, and was established in the year 1769, there being at that time not more than four public libraries of this nature in the metropolis; the price of the tickets at its formation was £1. 1s. and the annual subscription 5s.: at present the value of a ticket varies from £7 7s. to £4 4s., and the annual subscription amounts to £1 5s. It is said to contain upwards of 7000 volumes, including several standard works, and many well chosen books, excluding Divinity, Law, and Physic. It is subject to a fixed code of rules, and its affairs are placed under the management of a president, vice-president, treasurer, committee, honorary secretary, and librarian, elected annually by the general body of the members. Each subscriber is at liberty to propose a work, stating its recommendations, &c., but its reception or rejection is discretionary with the committee. The library is open daily.

The other Library is in the Old Cock Yard, and was established in the year 1823, in pursuance of a resolution adopted at a meeting holden in the vestry of Sion Chapel. The price of a ticket is £1. 1s, and the annual contribution 12s.; at present the number of subscribers amounts to about 130, and there are above 1800 volumes on various subjects. Its affairs are managed by a president, vice-presidents, treasurer, committee of members, secretary, and librarian. It is opened on the afternoons of Wednesday and Saturday. By a resolution lately adopted, non-proprietors are admitted to the library for an annual subscription of 16s.

A A 2

NEWS ROOMS.

There are two public subscription News Rooms open daily in the town, one at the "Rooms" in Harrison Lane, the other in the Old Cock Yard. The former is a handsome spacious apartment appropriately furnished, and well and regularly supplied with the London and provincial daily and weekly papers. It was established in the year 1825, and is conducted on a most respectable management by a committee chosen annually from among the members. New Subscribers are admitted by ballot, seven members being required to be present at the nomination. The subscription is one guinea and a half yearly, payable in advance on the 1st of June.

The latter room is also well supplied with the London and provincial papers and is very numerously and respectably attended, it is under the management of a committee similarly chosen. New members are admitted by nomination of another member, subject however to general approval. The subscription is one guinea per annum.

THE MAGISTRATES' OFFICE.

This building, at Ward's End, is used by the Magistrates for the holding of their petty sessions and the transaction of business, until a more suitable and commodious place shall be provided under the provisions of the New Market Act. A clerk is in regular attendance and a petty sessions is holden here every Saturday, for the ordinary dispatch of business.

THE COURT OF REQUESTS.

This Court-House, in Union-street, is a building convenient for its purposes, and a considerable sum has been expended in fitting it up. The court room is well adapted for the holding of courts generally, and the transaction of judicial business. The Sheriff's Assessor, and his Deputy also hold their local courts here.

NEW MARKET PLACE.

I have before had occasion to recite the Act under which this market place was erected. It is separated from Southgate by iron pallisadoes. The West end adjoining this street is an open square, in the centre whereof stands an ornamental iron pillar, serving the useful purposes of a pump and lamp post. The market buildings are of red brick. A building extends from the centre of the

East side of the square to the bottom of the market, forming a double row of shops, and divides the market place into two compartments. The shops on both sides of the square, and on the North side of the market, together with all the shops in the centre building, are occupied as shambles. The shops on the South side have rooms above them and are occupied as dwellings. All the shops are fronted by a collonade. The Southern compartment of the market is considerably broader than the other, and in the centre thereof is a covered shed for the erection of standings, wherein are sold miscellaneous articles. In this compartment are the fish, fruit, and vegetable markets. A broad colonnade projecting from the centre building is used by the country people, for the sale of poultry, butter, eggs, &c. The vacant spaces on market days are occupied by temporary stalls. At the bottom of the market place are large and convenient slaughter houses, under proper regulations as regards their cleanliness.

THE MANUFACTURERS' HALL.

There is a boldness of conception about this building which produces an effect rather imposing than otherwise; it was erected in the year 1779. It is a large quadrangular stone structure, occupying a space of 10,000 yards, with a rustic basement story on square *cippi*, and above, two other stories fronted by two entire colonnades, within which are spacious walks leading to arched rooms, intended as repositories for the goods of the several manufactories; the number of small rooms amounting to 315. The distances of the columns is about eight feet and a half, equal to the width of the rooms, each of which has one sash window and a door to the galleries. Situated on a descent towards the East, that side is three stories high; the first story has an arcade, which is continued as far as the centre of the North and South sides: The West side consists only of two stories. The building is 110 yards in length, and 91 in breadth. The centre is occupied by a grass plot. It is proof against fire and thieves. With respect to the first adds Dr. WHITAKER, nothing about it can be consumed but the roof; and as for the latter, had the portable goods of the Foresters of Hardwic been so collected and so secured of old, the axe might have rusted and the gibbet have rotted down, in the interval between two executions.

It was erected at the expence of the merchants and manufacturers of shalloons and other woollen goods within the Parish, for the
accommodation of themselves and the merchants and buyers fre-
quenting the market of Halifax.   The hall was opened for business
on the 2nd January, 1779; and its total cost was upwards of
£12,000. Its internal management is vested in a committee of the
principal manufacturers who have an interest in the success of the
undertaking, and who have adopted a code of rules and regulations
for the observance of all who frequent it: they are posted at the
principal entrance.   Public meetings are held in the Hall, with the
permission of the proprietors, the area being admirably adapted for
the purpose.   It is also usual for the candidates for the representation of the West Riding to address their Halifax constituents in
this place.   The hustings for the election of members for the
Borough are also erected here, on the East side.

THE BATHS,

Are situated at the lower part of the town in a retired
situation, adjoining the water side.   The buildings and gardens
contain an extensive and commodious suite of cold, warm, swim-
ming, shower, and vapour baths, with appropriate dressing and
waiting rooms, and are amply supplied with fine spring water rising
near the premises. The buildings are of plain red brick, the gardens
are tastefully arranged, and a large lawn is attached for the exercise of bowls.

THE MULCTURE HALL.

This may be assigned as the oldest mansion house in the
township.   Its proper name is the Mote, or Moote Hall, and in all
probability the Lord of the Manor formerly held his court here: it
has evidently obtained its present name from the mulcture dish appertaining to the mill, being kept at the hall, for that a mill has
existed here beyond the time of legal memory there can be no doubt.
The present building is of the Elizabethan age, and has a handsome
appearance viewed from the bank above; it must have been an
enviable situation when the Hebble flowed along the valley, a
pure and uninterrupted stream.

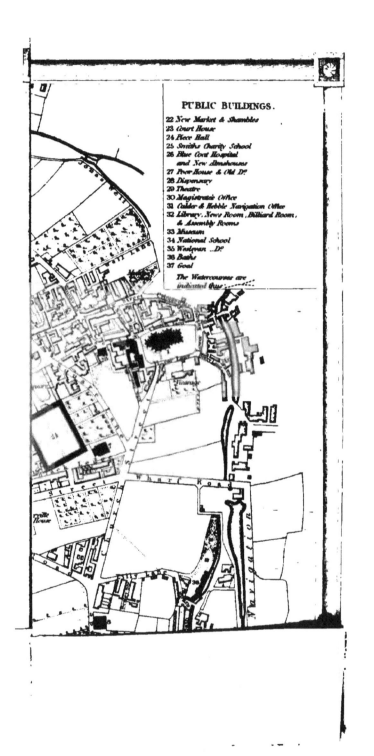

PUBLIC BUILDINGS.

22 New Market & Shambles
23 Court House
24 Piece Hall
25 Smiths Charity School
26 Blue Coat Hospital
   and New Almshouses
27 Poor House & Old D?
28 Dispensary
29 Theatre
30 Magistrates Office
31 Calder & Hebble Navigation Office
32 Library, News Room, Billiard Room,
   & Assembly Rooms
33 Museum
34 National School
35 Wesleyan ...D?
36 Baths
37 Goal

The Watercourses are
indicated thus

THE BANK.

As a private residence the Bank in George street is a handsome mansion; it was erected in the year 1766, and contains a splendid suite of apartments, ornamented with several rich and chaste devices; the back front opens into pleasure grounds tastefully arranged, and secluded from observation by a high wall. The king of Denmark, sojourned here one night on his northern tour, when in this country; hence was the name of this street, at that time called Loveledge lane, changed to the more regal appellation of George street.

The present state of Halifax certainly exhibits, in every point of view, a very different appearance from the description given of it by former historians. The immediate approaches to the Town on all sides are on the whole as good as the nature of the country will permit them to be. The North Bridge is a handsome erection; but the road-way will admit of improvement. The smoke arising from some furnaces near, and under it, is a source of much annoyance to passengers over it. The houses erected within the town during the present century are commodious, substantial, and well-built; and the masonry is of superior workmanship. The appearance of the shops is also much improved; and many of them exhibit, in a greater or less degree, a portion of metropolitan taste.

The general tendency to a dispersed population at Halifax called forth a remark from Dr. WHITAKER, who observed, that it had displayed itself in many excellent houses of stone, scattered around from the distance of two miles to a quarter of a mile from the capital, all examples of good taste and the rational application of commercial wealth. Nor has this disposition to seek for retirement in the vicinage of the town at all abated since the doctor's time; many of the principal gentry and merchants having lately erected some handsome mansions and villas in the suburbs, surrounded with luxuriant pleasure grounds and gardens.

It is much to be desired that every inducement should be held out, and every encouragement given, to this mode of investing capital; it not only concerns the comfort and respectability of the town and exhibits a substantial indication of its thriving prosperity, but is decidedly to be preferred to the rapid increase of small burgage tenements that are extending over every portion of land that can be made available for building; and compelling the inhabitants of the town to seek for air and sunshine on the moors and mountains.

In turning our attention to those parts of the Parish immediately dependant on the Parish church, it is necessary to observe, that North and South Owram, Hipperholme, and Shelf, have a character peculiar to themselves. On the North side of Ovenden brook, the whole basis of the earth becomes argillaceous, and the face of the country alters with it. The perpetual decomposition of argillaceous matter gives a rotundity and smoothness to the surface of the hills, very different from the vast projections or long and sharp ridges of quartz which characterise the vale of Calder and its dependencies. In this quarter also of the Parish there is a meanness in the appearance of the houses, produced by the same cause; as argillaceous stone rises in much thinner *laminæ*, and is far less obedient to the chisel than quartz concretions.

I shall proceed with the out-townships, according to their proximity to the capital.

THE TOWNSHIP OF NORTH OWRAM.

This township, which lies to the North-east of Halifax, is divided therefrom by the Hebble; on the West it is separated from Ovenden by a brook which falls into the Hebble at Lee Bridge. On the North it is bounded by Shelf, and on the South by South owram. Its area comprises about 3400 statute acres, in a general state of cultivation.

It is said to derive its name from having a large Bank which the Anglo-Saxons called Opep, the last syllable being derived from pam, a village; *the village on the north bank*, being situated to the North of another township called South Owram; and if the ascent from the brook by the present road and up the old Range Bank to the village of North Owram, which gives denomination to the district, was the only highway prior to the erection of the North-Bridge, we may imagine it to have been rather an arduous undertaking for our forefathers to journey from Halifax to North Owram at certain times.

The township is not mentioned in Domesday, but was originally granted by the crown to the Earl of Warren, for the history of whose title the reader is referred to the Manor of Halifax. John the 7th Earl, obtained a charter of free warren here and at Shibden from the crown, 37 Henry III. and was found to be lord thereof by Kirby's inquest, 24 Edward I. By an inquisition taken at Wakefield, 17 Edward III. it appeared, that Thomas de Totehill enfeoffed William his son, and gave him full seisin of all his lands and rents in North Owram, to hold to said William, and the heirs of his body; after whose death, Margaret, daughter and heiress of the said William, was in the wardship of Earl Warren, by reason of her minority. The manor came to the crown in the person of Edward III. in consequence of the grant from the last Earl, before referred to. By an inquisition taken at Halifax, 1577, it was found to belong

to Queen Elizabeth, as parcel of the manor of Wakefield, late
parcel of the duchy of York, and at that time annexed to the duchy
of Lancaster. By another inquisition at Pontefract, 5 and 6 Philip
and Mary, it appeared that Sir Henry Savile, knt. died seised in his
demesne as of fee of the manor. At present it is the property of
the Duke of Leeds, and parcel of his manor of Wakefield.

"The oldest mention I have seen made of this township, (says
WATSON) is in a fine, 4th of king John, between Alice, who was the
wife of Hen. de Yeland, plaint. and Robert de Sandall, Will. de
Orbur, and Roger de Thornton, who grant to Alice the third part of
the service of two oxgangs of land here."

Northowram is altogether a fine country, rich in hill and dale,
under its surface there are several large beds of coal of excellent
quality, and the collieries afford an inexhaustable supply of that
valuable mineral. It contains also some quarries of capital stone, for
building. Nor are there wanting some copious springs of good water
on the North bank, sufficient for the use of the surrounding population,—some of these springs have only latterly been brought to
light. On the whole, it is a thriving township, and ranks next to
Halifax in point of commercial importance. It participates in all
the advantages to be derived from a proximity to the town,
without being subject to its imposts, or the restrictions of its local
act. It possesses also the benefit of a most extensive traffic and
thoroughfare through its very centre to the great manufacturing
marts, and these circumstances have caused the erection of many
large and extensive manufactories in various parts, particularly on the
North bank, in the vicinity of which and Haley-hill, a considerable
population has been drawn together, and which is rapidly pro-
gressing.

This township is exclusively the seat of nonconformity within
the Parish. The first chapel was erected here by the Rev. Oliver
Heywood, in the year 1680, and with a few alterations it continues
to this day. It is a plain and humble edifice, with little to admire
as respects its outward appearance, but an interesting object so far
as it is to be regarded as a monument of the early non-conformists.
It is looked upon by the Independents with much veneration.
The Wesleyan Methodists, the New Connexion of Methodists, and
the Primitive Methodists have, severally, places of worship within

the township, and the Baptists have a small meeting house at Haley-hill. A regard for historical truth however compels me reluctantly to state, that amongst a laborious and active community of upwards of 10,000 souls, the majority engaged in manufactures, there is neither church nor chapel belonging to the establishment. This fact is of too important a nature to be looked upon with apathetic indifference, particularly in the present day.

The necessity of some ecclesiastical provision is too apparent to admit of argument, it certainly ought to be brought under the notice of the proper authorities. The wealth and respectability of the township, and the well known zeal and philanthropy of its gentry is a guarantee that if a movement was once made, the evil would soon be remedied. The central situation of Booth Town affords a most eligible and commanding scite for the erection of either church or chapel, with a convenient cemetery.

There are some places of antiquity in this township that require to be shortly noticed. The first is

BOOTH TOWN.

THORESBY, in his Topography, says, "Booth's Town, near Halifax, seems to have been so called from a sort of Tabernacles." "Whether (remarks WATSON) there was ever a fixed habitation of this sort, or the lords of the country only placed their tents on this ground whilst they took their diversion in the neighbourhood, is uncertain. It gave name, however, to a family; of whom frequent mention is made about the time of Henry VIII. It is not improbable that this village may have an high original, and have been a settlement even in the British times, for Bod, which our Saxon ancestors pronounced Borh and we Booth, in the times preceding christianity signified an habitation. A handsome, respectable old family house has long existed here.

Horley Green is remarkable for a spring I have before mentioned.

SHIBDEN HALL,

A fine old mansion, buried beneath the shades of its venerable oaks, takes its name from a rich and beautiful valley contiguous to which it is situated. The valley in all probability was so denominated from the great number of sheep depastured there. Schepe, and dene a valley, has been written various ways, Sipeden, Shepiden, Schipedene, Scheppedene, Schipden, Schepden, Shipden, and Shibden; and formerly gave name to a family, who on some account or other, changed it to Drake. WATSON gives a splendid pedigree of this family, drawn up by the author of the Eboracum, commencing with William de Schepden, of Nether Schepden, who lived temp., Edward I, as by charter dated at Schippedene in 1306, and who had John de Schipeden, alias Drake, and William. We also read that A. D. 1307, one Matthew de Schepedene, or de Halifax, was instituted into the living of Sandal Parva, on the presentation of the Prior and Convent of Lewes, in Sussex. After the Drake's, Shibden Hall became the property of the Waterhouses : the next owners were the Listers, from whom are descended its present possessors, a very respectable and ancient family, whose pedigree WATSON has also given.

HIGH SUNDERLAND

Is a very ancient farm which the Anglo-Saxons called by the name of Sunꝺep, or Sunꝺop-lonꝺ ; or it might be separated, or set apart for some particular purpose, or privilege, the knowledge of which is now lost ; for in that case they would give it this name, as being sundered or divided from the lands about it. It is called High, from its elevated situation, and is supposed to give name to a respectable and loyal family, whose descendants are still resident in the Parish.

When the present fabric at High Sunderland was erected, does not appear by any inscription upon the building ; but it is conjectured was either the work of Richard Sunderland, who married Susan Saltonstall, about 1597, or of his son Abraham, who married Elizabeth Langdale ; but more probably the latter, because we meet with the arms of Saltonstall and Langdale, impaled with those of Sunderland, in the windows. This house seems once to have been well ornamented ; there are still some statues and busts remaining, of tolerable workmanship. In a chamber window under the arms of Saltonstall, Langdale, and Thornhill, of Fixby,

> Fælix quem virtus generosa exornat avorum,
> Et qui virtute suis adjicit ipse decus.   L. S.

The initials L. S. are supposed to signify Langdale Sunderland, because in another place the arms of Saltonstall and Langdale, (as above,) are impaled with those of Sunderland. This Langdale also appears to have lived a good part of his time at Coley Hall, and to have sold the estate so late as the interregnum. Over the north door is written, *Ne subeat glis serdus*, a mistake for *surdus*; and over a door on the north side, *Ne intret amicus hirudo*. In the hall over the fire-place,

Maxima Domus utilitas, et pernicies, ignis et lingua.

Over the south door,

Hic Locus odit, amat, punit, conservat, honorat,
Nequitem, pacem, crimina, jura, probos.

Which, says Watson is also on the town-house at Delft, in Holland, and also on the town-house at Glasgow, in Scotland, with *bonos* instead of *probos*. Below the above lines, *Confide Deo. Diffide tibi.* On a pillar on the left hand of the south door, *Patria Domus.* On a pillar on the right hand of the same, *Optima Cœlum,* On the south front,

Omnipotens faxet, Stirps Sunderlandia sedes
Incolet has placide, et tueatur jura parentum,
Lite vacans, donec fluctus formica marinos
Ebibat et totum Testudo perambulet orbem !

How vain adds Mr. WATSON, are our wishes, and how uncertain the continuance of earthly things, may hence be seen, when either the writer of these, or his son, alienated this very estate, which the then owner so earnestly wished might continue in the family for ever !

Over the principal gate, *Nunquam hanc pulset portam qui violat æquum.* On the same is a cherub sounding a trumpet; and in a scroll, *Fama virtutum, Tuba perennis.* A drawing of this gateway, is to be found in Mr. Horner's views of the principal buildings in the town and parish of Halifax. Its present possessor is William Priestley, Esquire, of Lightcliffe.

SCOTE OR SCOUT HALL,

Is a square-built mansion, situated on a small eminence on the south side of the upper part of the valley of Shibden. There is no date on any part of the building, but an adjoining cottage bears date 1661, and has a dial plate inserted in it which is dated ANNO 1617.

It does not appear that this was ever the residence of any family of note, and tradition has preserved a story of the builder having been killed in hunting, while the hall was in course of erection; but of his name and family there are no traces.

The little that is related of the builder is, however, amply supported by the present appearance of the building. It is apparent that only a few of the interior apartments were fitted up contemporaneously with their erection, and of these only one retains as much of its pristine appearance as the ravages of time and the brush of the painter would allow. The pannelling on the walls, though covered with paint, are evidently of oak; and, within a projecting carved frame forming part of the decorations over the antique fire-place, there is a portrait, which tradition assigns to be that of the builder. This, to say the least, is extremely doubtful, the dress, and the trinkets displayed about his person, would better seem a hunter of an earlier date than the 17th century. In one hand there is a short hunting spear, and the other holds a hound in a leash.

That the builder was attached to the pleasures of the chase, may be inferred from the rude sculpture over the principal entrance, representing a fox pursued by dogs; and also by the fact that an adjoining building is to this day called "The dog-kennel."

Perhaps, after all, this tradition must be condemned to herd amongst the puerile stories that make the number of windows in this hall parallel the days, and its rooms equal to the number of weeks in the year.

On the top of the two fronts, East and North, there formerly was a battlement with stone globes at intervals, but this was taken down a few years since, when the hall was divided into cottages. Mr. Horner has also a faithful drawing of this building.

Adjoining the hall, and doubtless contemporaneous with it, are two sycamores, probably the largest in the parish.

This township, in opposition to North Owram, is the village on the *south* bank. It is separated from Halifax by the Hebble, and bounded on the West by Hipperholme-cum-Brighouse, and on the South by Elland. It contains an area of 2280 statute acres.

It is mentioned in Domesday book as the Terra Ilberta de Lacy, and is thus surveyed : "In Overe habuit Gamel tres carucatas terre ad geldam ubi duo caruce possunt esse. Ilbertus habet et wast. est T. R. E. val. xx solid. silva pastura tres quarentenas longitudine et trea latitudine." From this it would appear that one Gamel was lord of the territory prior to the conquest; but that at the time of William I. it belonged to Ilbert de Lacy as part of his honor of Pontefract.

"The oldest deed, (says WATSON) which I have seen relating to this subject, is in 1293, whereby Hugh de Elland, knight, gave to John de Lascye, and Margaret his wife, daughter of the said Hugh, and heirs of the said Margaret, all his land in Southowram, with his tenants, and their services, except the manor of Elland, and the service of the tenants of Eckisley and pasture in Stony-banske, for 26s. rent, and suit to mill. John Fige granted to Robert de Winhill Copeyhird, in Southowram, near Gobryllyherd on the east, and Halifax broke on the west, 1747. Another deed in 1778, describes Gobryllherd, (or Gobrylyerd) to lie on the east side of Halifax broke, between the way which leads from Halifax church towards Southowram and the way which leads from the said church towards Hipperum." These are only mentioned by Watson, as deeds of some antiquity. 24 Edward I. John de Eland was found by Kirby's inquest, to be lord of Owram. John, son of Thomas de Lacy was lord of this manor, 28 Edward III. as by deed, and in this family it continued till 16 James I. when Thomas Lacy, of Cromwelbottom, sold the full moiety or half part thereof to one Thomas Whitley. Thomas Whitley his majesty's ward, son and heir of Thomas Whitley, deceased, was lord 11 Charles I. Thomas Whitley, of Bradford, grandchild and heir of Thomas Whitley, of Cinderhills, gent. was lord of the moiety of this lordship, and let the same to farm to one Timothy Thorpe, and Mary his wife, in 1654, for ninety-nine years, at the yearly rent of £3 6s. 8d. Thomas Whitley, by will, dated Nov. 5th, 1657, gave this moiety to his son Thomas who died an infant, on which it came for want of issue of the testator, to John Thorpe and Timothy Thorpe. John survived Timothy, and left a son Timothy, grandson and heir to Mary Thorpe. Timothy died without issue. John and Timothy Thorpe, his brother, were brethren by the half-blood to Thomas Whitley, of Cinder-hills. Timothy Thorpe, of St. Dunstan's in the east, London, gent., son and heir of John Thorpe, late of Cinderhills, in Hipperholme, gent. sold to William Horton, of Barkisland, Esq. this moiety, June 27, 1711. His son, William Horton, Esq. of Coley, ordered it by will to be sold, and Robert Allenson, of Royd, in Soyland, merchant, bought it of his widow, in 1741, and sold it again to Mr. William Greame, of Heath, in Skircoat. From this family it afterwards passed by marriage to the Ingrams, and subsequently by purchase to Messrs. Holdsworth and Hall, from whom it was purchased in 1814 by Christopher Rawson, Esq. of Halifax, its present possessor.

It also appears, that Robert Lawe was joint lord of the manor of South Owram, 18 James I. with Thomas Whitley; and Toby Lawe died possessed of a moiety of this manor, as appears by his will, dated Jan. 6, 1652. Jonathan Maud, of Halifax, M. D. married Mary, the widow of Toby Lawe, and as appears by deed, dated March 25, 1654, levied a fine, "sur conusance de droit come ceo," to enable him and his heirs, in case the said Mary should die, to hold the estate left by the said Toby, by survivorship. In 1704, John Maud and Jonathan Maud, brothers, both of Halifax, sold their moiety of this lordship to William Horton, Esq. of Barkisland; who by his purchase afterwards, in 1711, became possessed of the whole. The manor of South Owram was held under the honor of Pontefract, by the hundredth part of a knight's fee.

Within and parcel of the manor of South Owram, is a reputed manor called Cromwellbottom, held of the honor of Pontefract, in free and common soccage, by fealty only, for all services; the first mention of which is 30 Edward I. when John Lacy of Cromwellbottom, and Margaret his wife, passed a fine of the manor of Cromwellbottom to the heirs of the said John; this was in consequence of the above grant of Sir Hugh de Eland. 3 Edward II. Margaret, widow of this John Lacy, covenanted with Richard de Tonge, that Thomas, her younger son, should marry Margaret, daughter of the said Richard; the mother to maintain them and their issue during life, or allow them six marks per annum out of the manor of Cromwellbottom. 27 Edward III. John, son of Thomas de Lacy, granted this manor to certain trustees, but the deed to declare the uses is probably lost. William de Mirfield also granted the same to other trustees, 41 Edward III. Oliver Wodroue quit-claimed to Richard Lacy of Cromwellbottom, his right in this manor, 4 Hen. V. John Lacy of Cromwellbottom, 14 Edward IV. enfeoffed certain trustees in this manor, with intent that it should descend to his son Thomas, on condition that he suffered his mother to enjoy her dower without molestation.

The words of the deed were these:—

"The entent of yis my present feoffement is this, that if Thomas Lacy or his heirs, or any oyther for hym or by hym, aftir the decease of me the sayd John Lacy, vexe, troble, and wolle not suffre my wyfe peasibly to occupye her dower belongyng unto her aftir my decease, or Richard Lacy or Gilbert Lacy my sons, or any oyther person or persons of or in such landes and tenementes, with yair appurt. or of any parcelle yrof, as well copyehald as freehald, gyfen by me unto yam, or any of yam, acordyng to such dedes, estates, and feoffement, and surrenders, made by me unto them, yen my sayd feoffes shal safe yam herelesse, an defende yam so vexed or trobled with the sayd manor of Cromwellebothom with yappurtenances, and if yai be not of power to defende yam, yen my sayd feoffes to make such estates and feoffments yrof over by yair discretion as shal be thoght necessarie for ye same intente; and if ye sayd Thomas or his heirs wolle suffre, performe, and fulfille myne entent afore rehersed, yen I wolle yat my sayd feoffes make such estate of ye sayd manor with yappurtenances unto ye sayd Thomas and his heirs as myne auncestres hafe hade yrin afore-tyme."

21 Edward IV. Gilbert Lacy, Esq. and Joan his wife, conveyed (inter alia) their manor of Overcrumwellbothom to Richard Symmys, vicar of Halifax, and others in trust, for what purpose uncertain. 21 Hen. VII. John Lacy was lord of this manor. 16 James I. Thomas Lacy, of Cromwellbottom, sold it to Thomas Whitley above-named, and it afterwards passed through the same hands as the first moiety of the lordship of Southowram above-mentioned, till it was purchased by the late William Greame, esq.

It remains to be enquired how Timothy Thorpe could sell a moiety of South Owram and Cromwellbottom to William Horton, in 1711, and John Maud and Jonathan Maud sell a moiety of the lordship of South Owram to the same in 1704, when it appears, from authentic evidences, that Michael Firth of Height, in Barkisland, who bought the same of John Thorpe, of Cinderhills, for £927 16s. in the reign of Charles II. sold the moiety of the manor of Cromwellbottom. and half the lordship of South Owram, to William Horton, of Barkisland, in 1685, for £941.

It does not appear that any courts were ever held for the manor of Cromwellbottom, but that the owners of lands within such manor, or reputed manor, have constantly done suit and service to the manor of Southowram; and that ways and other things within Cromwellbottom, have been presented at the court held for the manor of South Owram. There was a court baron of Jonathan Maud and William Horton, in 1686. Another of William Horton in 1689. Others of the same William, in 1691, 1705, and 1723. Another of the same William, held at Brookfoot, June 15, 1726. Another at the same place in 1728; another in 1729. There was also a court baron of Toby Lawe and Thomas Whitley, in 1633. Also, South Owram cum membris, a court baron of Jonathan Maud, M. D. and Thomas Whitley, 1657. Another of Jonathan Maud, Esq. M. D. and John Thorpe, gent. 1675; and another of the same in 1681.

This township is celebrated for its remarkably fine productive quarries of stone and slate; large quantities whereof are sent to the Metropolis where it is in great request, and also to all parts of the kingdom. Much of it is also shipped to the Continent and America. The navigation which passes through the lower part of the township affords every facility for its transmission to the out-ports. There are also several beds of good coal.

ST. ANN'S CHAPEL.

There has long been a chapel in Southowram, dedicated as above. It is also distinguished by the appellations of the Chapel in the Grove, and "the chapel in the Briers" or Breers. CAMDEN says "There is a certain chappel in the village of South Owram, belonging to this vicarage, anciently appertaining to the family of Cromblebottom of Cromblebottom and lords of the town, whereof afterwards the heirs male failing the heiress married to one of the family of Lacies, earl of Lincoln, hence was it sometimes called Lacies' chapel, as appeareth from an original deed of five hundred years old."

In the second volume of Halifax register is an extract from an inquisition, by which it was found, from a deed, bearing date the 21st of February, 21 Hen. VIII. that John Lacy, of Cromwellbottom, Esq. then living, and his neighbours, did build this chapel of St. Ann's; if so, it must have been erected before the year 1530. There is a tradition, that it is a place of great antiquity; probably therefore, the chapel might at that time have been rebuilt; but of this there is no evidence. The building is very inconveniently situated for the neighbourhood, being at a distance from the village of Southowram; but this, in all probability, was done by the owners of Cromwellbottom, who consulted in some measure their own ease and emolument.

At Howroyd is a deed by which John Lacy, of Cromwellbottom, mortgaged to Robert Lawe, of Halifax, for five marks, all that house or building commonly called the chapel, and used for a chapel in the township of Southowram, 2nd James I.

This was the grandson of John Lacy who built it, and the same who, about seven years after, sold Cromwellbottom itself, and several other estates. It seems, says WATSON, from this mortgage, "that the chapel had not been consecrated, nor have I ever seen when it was."

The present chapel was erected and consecrated in 1819: the living is valued in the parliamentary return at £123 per annum. There is a parsonage house attached. The following augmentations have been granted to this living by the governors of the bounty of Queen Anne. 1720—£200 to meet a benefaction of £200. 1756—£200 by lot, and in 1797 another £200 by lot out of the royal bounty. 1811—£1400 by lot, and in 1812 and 1823 two sums of

£200 by lot; and in 1824, a sum of £300, to meet a benefaction of £200 from the Rev. John Hope, the present respected incumbent.

The places noticed by WATSON in this township are—

ASTLEY

Corrupted from Ashdale, which was for a considerable time the property, and place of residence, of the Holdsworths, one of whom was vicar of Halifax.

BACKHALL, where lived a family of the name of Hanson.

BLAIDROYD, OR BLATHROID,

Which is at present a farm house of no great appearance: there is a tradition that certain papists, inhabitants of Halifax, not being allowed to exercise their religion in the town, or dreading a persecution if they staid longer there, retired hither, and had the present barn for their place of worship, about 1572, in the reign of Queen Elizabeth, as that date is on the building. This barn is called the New-Hall, and was larger and chambered; the places where the timber belonging to the floors was fastened being visible, and even part of the plaster in the upper rooms remaining when WATSON saw it in 1759. The windows might then be seen, and there was a fire place on the north side, which was pulled down in 1756. There was in the house, in stained glass, in a window, a sick man in bed with his arms crossed, and a man with crutches and beads, as if paying a visit to the sick man, having compassion finely expressed in his face. Near the house was a large cave or hollow, made in the side of the hill, but in Watson's time the mouth of it was choked up with a great quantity of large stones. A little distant from the house was also some ground in the delf-brow, called the Burying-place.

The name of this place seems to be derived from the Anglo-Saxon Blæð, the blade of herbs, and by synecdoche the herb itself; and royd, or land which has not been plowed; unless it may be thought to come from the British Blaidh, a wolf. It is sometimes called the Bank, and was the seat of a branch of the family of Savile, whose pedigree is referred to by Watson.

It is a very ancient situation, for Watson says, he had the copy of a deed, dated 10 Hen. IV., by which Thomas Lacy del Mere, near Castelford, grants the reversion of a messuage called Bladehous, and certain parcels of land called Bladeroides, and Bladehey, to Henry Savile, of Copley, esq.

BEACON-HILL

Is the high ground which overlooks the town of Halifax towards the East, on which there used to stand a beacon, to give notice in troublesome times of the approach of an enemy, and which could be answered by others in different parts of the country. WATSON had the copy of a deed, dated at Southowram in 1553, wherein is mentioned "le Bekyn super altitudine montis de Gletclif."

In an old parish book of accounts is the following memorandum, "That the beacon which stands in Southowram was set up att the charge of ye wapontake, for which they had £6 granted at the Sessions; but it cost near seaven pounds, and Samuel Stead took the care of getting it done, paying all ye charge of it,"

CROMWELLBOTTOM,

Signifies the foot of the crooked or winding spring. The Britons expressed the word crooked by Crwmm, and in some parts of the kingdom by Croum, Krum, and Crobm. The Saxons called it Cþumb or Cþunap. Wæl is a known Saxon word for a spring.

In a deed written in the time of Henry VIII. it is called Old Cromwellbothom. It was long the seat of the Lacy's. Mr. Watson has given an interesting pedigree of this family.

EXLEY, OR ECCLESLEY,

A district within the township of South Owram. The name of it, if Exley be the ancient way of writing it, may come from Ex, an old word for water, and ley, a pasture, because it lies upon the banks of the river Calder.

BAILEY HALL,

A corruption of Bailiff's Hall, is a respectable old mansion; and was in all probability the residence of the Lords Bailiff, who selected this spot on account of its contiguity to the river and the town of Halifax; the whole of Southowram Bank being at that time covered with wood.

TOWNSHIP OF OVENDEN.

This township lies to the North-West of Halifax, and on the West of the brook dividing it from the township of Northowram; on the West it adjoins the township of Warley, and on the North that of Thornton in the Parish of Bradford.

The name is in all probability derived from the British Avon, a brook, and the Anglo-Saxon ꝺene, a valley: this brook is called ꝼaliȝ Bpoca, or holy brook, now vulgarly distinguished by the adjective halig; it is formed by he union of the waters of Ogden and Skirden, in the district of Ogden, Oakden, or the valley of oak, from whence the stream passes through the vale of Wheatley, and forms a junction with the brook which divides Ovenden from Northowram, at Lee Bridge.

The name of Ovenden does not occur in Domesday, but Dr. WHITAKER conjectures that like Halifax it was taken out of Warley, without assigning any reason for his hypothesis. It appears to have been originally granted by the crown to the Earl of Warren. Henry III. by charter, in the 37th year of his reign, granted to John, the seventh earl, free warren in all his demesne lands (whereof Ovenden was parcel) which he then had or should acquire; from this earl it passed to the family of Thornhill, and in Kirby's inquest, 24 Edward I., John de Thornhill is returned lord of the manor. By deed s. d. Brian de Thornhill gave all his messuages, lands, &c. in Ovenden, to William de Metheley for life; and 2 Edward III. John de Metheley released the same to Brian, son of Sir John de Thornhill. From the Thornhill family it passed into that of Saville, on the marriage of Elizabeth, daughter and heiress of Simon Thornhill, with Henry Saville; in which family it still continues.

At a trial had in the Duchy Chamber, 6th Elizabeth, the crown laid claim to the wastes of Ovenden, Skircoat, Rishworth, North-land, Barsland, Wadsworth, Stansfield, and Shelf, as being within the liberties of Sowerbyshire, or in the lordship of Wakefield; and a record was produced to shew that a similar claim had been made by Henry the eighth on the townships of Ovenden, Skircoat, Rish-worth, Northland, Barsland, and Shelf, as parcel of the manor of Wakefield; and that Henry VII. died seised thereof in fee. To which Henry Saville replied that Henry VII. did not die seised thereof, and that the same were not parcel of the manor of Wake-field. The jury for the defendant: for that he proved by many court rolls and other evidences, the possession of himself and an-cestors in 1334, 1337, and 1389, as also in the reigns of Henry V. VI, VII, and VIII; and that his ancestors had, time out of mind, granted parcels of the waste lands within the said lordships and manors, receiving to them rents and services. It was there-fore decreed by the chancellor, that the said Henry Saville, his heirs and assigns, should quietly and peaceably enjoy the said townships and manors.

In the year 1814 an act of Parliament was passed, for enclosing lands in the manor of Ovenden; in consequence whereof the several commons, moors, and waste grounds called High-road well moor, Ovenden moor, Ogden moor, Skirden, Coldedge, Illingworth moor, Todmoor, Swillhill, Childwife moor, and Lee bank, with various other parcels of waste were allotted, under the award of commis-sioners, to several freeholders, and have since been enclosed: the award is deposited in Illingworth chapel.

At the time of passing this act, the area of the township was computed at 5108 statute acres, whereof the ancient enclosed lands were 3466, and the common land 1742 acres, including allotments to proprietors, occupation roads, public stone quarries, and watering places; and this agrees with the number stated in the parliamentary return of 1833. A survey of the township was made by Mr. Washington in 1825, when the area of it was found to contain 5295 statute acres, according to the admeasurement of each farm. The whole is freehold.

ILLINGWORTH.

This place gives name to the Chapelry of Ovenden: its situation is high and bleak, at the distance of two miles and an half North

West of Halifax, and on the turnpike road to Keighley. Mr. Watson's conjecture, as to the name of the place being derived from the bladness or roughness of the roads there, is extremely hypothetical.

In the village is a house, called The Cross, and distinguished by that emblem, being placed at the gable end; tradition attributes it, as an evidence of its having formerly belonged to the Knights of St. John of Jerusalem, who certainly had some possessions in these parts, and whose houses were distinguished by a cross placed in some conspicuous part, but whether this be the case in the present instance, or whether it was merely placed there for ornament, is very doubtful.

The village gave name to an old family of which there remains no pedigree, some of the descendants reside on the spot, and are in a humble situation of life; and there are some remains of the old family hall, now converted into cottages.

THE CHAPEL.

Henry Saville, lord of Ovenden, by deed dated 26 January 17, Hen. VIII. granted and confirmed to James Bawmforth, William Doughty, Wm. Illingworth, jun. John Maude, jun. Richard Best, Thomas Shaw, John Cockroft, Hy. Cockroft, John Croyser, John Greenwood, jun., Henry Illingworth, John Best, Robert Walker, jun., and Richard Deyn; one acre of land of the wastes of Ovenden as the same laid there on the east part of Chornheys, on the west part of the land of Henry Illingworth, on the north of the land of Richard Illingworth, and on the south part of the house of one John Illingworth: To hold to them, their heirs and assigns for ever, to the use of one Chapel there, in honor of the Virgin Mary built; the words are " ad usum unius Capellae ib'm in honore beata Mariae Virginis, *edifc*," not *edificand:* (the words in the grant do not warrant Mr. Watson's construction " to be built") paying yearly to the Lord one red rose.

The first edifice stood its three centuries, and in the year 1777 the present chapel was erected on the ancient scite, it is a neat plain stone structure, with a bell tower, consisting of a lobby; nave, and two side aisles, a gallery on the South side, and an organ loft at the west end, in which is a good organ; it is capable of affording further accommodation by the erection of a North gallery, and removing the pulpit to the front of the communion table.

Surrounding the Chapel is an extensive piece of ground used as a place of sepulture; this repository of the dead exhibits in its appearance a degree of cleanliness and neatness, highly creditable to those who have the care of it.

The expense of the present erection, including the stone wall round the ground, amounted to £1400.

The only vestige that remains of the old building is a fragment of broken glass in the window of the vestry.

The license to baptize and bury here was granted A. D. 1695.

The chapel is endowed with the following property:

	DW.
A Farm, called Chapel House, given by Henry Saville, 1525, containing......	5
A Farm, called Paul's Parks, given by Sir George Saville, A. D. 1561, containing, subject to a quit rent of 4 pence	15½
A Farm, called Lower Scansby, containing	43
A Farm, called Upper Scansby, containing	19
And Ainley Fields	8

Purchased by the Governors of Queen Anne's Bounty in 1731.

In 1792, the living was further augmented by lot, with £200 from the Governors.

In the year 1793, the inhabitants subscribed £200, which obtained another £200 from the Governors to meet the benefaction; with this an estate was purchased, called Reddish-house farm, containing about 33 days' work of Land, in the Township of Spotland, in Lancashire 33

In 1815, an allotment of Common near the Chapel, containing................ 6¼

Was awarded under the Enclosure Act, and in 1821, the living was further augmented by Lot with £200.

Near the chapel is a commodious building, used as a school-room, with a dwelling underneath, erected A. D. 1815. Over the door is inscribed on a stone tablet: "Erected by subscription for the purpose of educating children in the principles of the Established Church." The building is vested in trustees, and the school is in union with the national school society.

Adjoining the chapel yard is a small triangular piece of ground, called the Town's Field, but how it became the property of the public is uncertain; possession is their best and only evidence of title.

At a cottage under the wall, on the left of the stone steps leading into the chapel yard, watch and ward was kept during the rebellion of 1745; and a small detachment of soldiers were quartered at a place called Barrack castle, at present consisting of three or four cottages, on an eminence about three fields length to the right of the road leading from Illingworth to Holdsworth; from this position a communication could be kept up between Beacon-hill in South-

Ovenum and Soil hill; from whence may be seen York minster when the atmosphere is clear; and at the time of the threatened invasion from France a beacon was erected on this hill, to communicate with Almondbury bank and Otley Cheven.

HOLDESWORTH,

Is a pleasant rural village adjoining upon Illingworth, which gave name to a family of some repute. The derivation of the name is uncertain. Mr. Watson refers to a deed, s. d. whereby John, son of William de Ovenden, quit-claimed to Roger de Rastrick land in Haldewroke. (Holdeworth.) This, by the witnesses, was about 1287. 37 Hen, III. John, the seventh earl of Warren, had a charter for free warren in the township of Holdsworth; and in a survey and boundary of the copyhold land within the graveship of Hipperholme in the year 1607, it is called a township.

Holdesworth house is a fine old family mansion, long the residence of the Wadsworths: on one of the south gables is a cross similar to that before referred to. On a stone over the south porch are the initials A. B. 1633, which stand for Abraham Brigg, who sold the estate to Henry Wadsworth in 1657, Over the western gateway are ɪ W D 1680. (John and Dorothy Wadsworth.)

This estate and the two adjoining farms are, and always have been considered exempt from the custom of the soke of Ovenden.

Not far from the house, at a place called Popples, is a large commodious and handsome room, used as a national school-room, erected by the present Mrs. Wadsworth, A. D. 1816.

WHEATLEY,

Is a valley in this township lying to the North of Halifax, through which the Hebble or Halig runs. Mr. Watson says the apparent etymology of the word is the lea or meadow producing wheat; but the derivation assigned by Mr. Hunter to Wheatley in the parish of Doncaster, will equally apply to this place; namely the wet lee, when the word *wet* is pronounced according to what is the provincial enunciation of it. The lands lie low.

In a rental of the sums paid to the knights of St. John of Jerusalem, for lands, &c. within this parish is the following: Edvardus Kent, pro certis terris et ten: Whetley, infra villat. de Ovenden, 1d.

On the West side of the brook which runs through this valley,

lie Mixenden and Ovenden Wood. On Mixenden moor were discovered some remains of the British æra, which I have already adverted to; and a British road in all probability passed in this direction, as I have shown in a preceding chapter.

Within Ovenden wood are some fine springs of pure water
which are conveyed into the reservoirs that supply the town of
Halifax.

The beneficial results arising from the inclosure of the wastes,
in this township, are shewn in every point of view that presents
itself; much of the land at that time barren has not only been
considerably improved, and laid out in pasture; but exhibits in many
places a degree of cultivation which may be looked for in vain in
more favored districts. Its effect in a political point of view is more
remarkable, as will be seen by a reference to the population tables.

The turnpike road from Halifax to Keighley runs directly through
this township, and on several parts of the line there has been much
building.

Among the family mansions and modern residences within this
township, which are at present worthy of note; and of those which
are now converted into farm-houses, but still retain some distinguishing feature reminiscent of former times, are the following:—

OVENDEN HALL, a fine old mansion house, on the left of the high
road, about a mile and a quarter from Halifax, formerly the residence of the Fourness family, now belonging to Thomas Sutcliffe,
Esquire.

OVENDEN HOUSE, on the same line, a neat modern residence,
rebuilt on the scite of a former mansion, erected 1727, the property
of Mr. Bould.

PARK LODGE, a pleasant mansion, nearer Halifax, surrounded
with its pleasure grounds, the residence of Mr. Turney.

BIRK'S HALL, in the vale of Wheatley, rebuilt on the site of a
former mansion, long the residence of the Ramsbottoms, now of
Mrs. Lancashire.

JUMPLES HOUSE, now occupied as a farm-house, some time the
residence of the Ramsdens.

RYDINGS, an ancient mansion, formerly in the possession of a
family of that name, then of the Farrars, of Ewood, the last of
whom died May, 1799.

BRACKENBED, the birth place of Thomas Wilkinson, the seventh vicar of Halifax, On a stone at the end of one of the gables is I. W. 1604 : and in the old hall window are a few panes of painted glass.

FOLD, a farm-house of some antiquity, where tradition says that murder was committed prior to the building of Illingworth Chapel, while some part of the family then residing there were attending divine service on a Sunday, at Halifax church : this tradition was related to me by the late Mr. Moss, of Ovenden.

HOLDSWORTH HOUSE, the residence of Mrs. Wadsworth, I have before noticed.

SCAUSBY HOUSE, near Holdsworth, the residence of William Dean, Esq.

Of NEW HOUSE, which was formerly a large and handsome family mansion in this township, the residence of the late John Mitchell, Esq., the scite alone remains. The house was rased in the year 1808, in consequence of some family differences.

In the year 1630, Anthony Bentley, of Ovenden, gent., paid £10 composition money for not receiving the order of knighthood at the coronation of Charles I.

TOWNSHIP OF HIPPERHOLME-CUM-BRIGHOUSE.

HIPPERHOLME is so called from its elevated situation, the higher holme, in opposition to the lower and middle holme, which lie beneath it. This township is bounded on the West by North and South Owram; on the North by Shelf; on the South by Rastrick; and on the East by Hartshead-cum-Clifton. It contains 2550 statute acres, and has not been inappropriately termed the Garden of Halifax.

Hipperholme was formerly granted by the crown to the Earls Warren, and in that family it appears to have remained until the death of the 8th earl in 1347, as will be seen by a reference to the history of "The Manor." (p. 50.) being parcel thereof.

In the 22nd Henry VIII. it appears to have been in the king's hands, from the copy of a rental for this greaveship, the first article of which is, "Johannes Ryshworth de Caldeley, pro —— certis terris nuper captis de vasto domini regis juxta New Chappel." At an inquisition taken at Halifax, in the reign of queen Elizabeth, the queen was found to be possessed thereof, as parcel of the manor of Wakefield. The present duke of Leeds is its most noble possessor.

There is a court baron kept at Brighouse, by Sir George Armitage, and a court baron under Hipperholme Thorn, by the Thornhills of Fixby. A court was held under this thorn, August 22, 1688, and another, September 25, 1701; in the former of these Sir John Armitage, bart. was amerced in 2s. 6d. fine, for non-appearance; Joshua Horton, Esq. 2s. 6d. and several others 1s. each.

Hipperholme is one of the Graveships of the manor of Wakefield, within this parish. The grave is an officer or servant belonging to the lord of the manor, so called from the Anglo-Saxon Lepepe, or the German Graf. His duty is to collect the lord's rents, and his stile, in Latin deeds, is Prepositus. There are two graveships in this parish, Hipperholme and Sowerby, the former of which contains the townships and vills of Hipperholme-cum-Brighouse, Lightcliffe, and North Owram; WATSON assigns the following reasons, why the rest of this parish is exempt from the jurisdiction of graves; Halifax was, in a great measure, infranchised at different periods, but especially by the Ingrams, to whom king James I. granted the copyhold manor here. The lord of the manor has also a bailiff here who does the business of a grave. Elland, Greetland, and South Owram belong to the honor of Pontefract, and are under different regulations. The rest of the townships throughout the whole parish have been granted off by the lords of the manor of Wakefield, and do not belong to the present owner thereof; the lord's bailiff, however, at Halifax, collects yearly what are called earl Warren's rents, payable at Michaelmas, in the several townships of Fixby, North Owram, Skircoat, Midgley, Sowerby, Shelf, Hipperholme, Ovenden, and Rishworth-cum-Norland.

In a verdict of several copyholders within the graveship of Hipperholme, the jurors said, that the bailiff of the fee of Wakefield collected certain freehold rents within their graveship, called Earl's rents, which seems to point out the true original of them. In this extent is a survey of the graveship of Fekisbye and Rastricke.

"The oldest mention, adds Mr. WATSON, that I have seen made of the graveship of Hipperholm, is in the Domesday book, in 1314, the next is 21 Edw. IV. In a drawer at Howroyd, in this parish, marked No. 12, is a list of the graves for this graveship, beginning at a court held at Wakefield, 5 Oct. 21 Edw. IV. and ending at another, held 24 Hen. VII. when all the estates in the graveship having served the office in their rotation, the same Edmund Ryshworth, who had been elected 21 Edw. IV. was again chosen, that the same order might be observed as before. In the same drawer is a rental of this graveship, dated 21 Edw. IV. At the same place is also another, and more particular rental of this graveship, 22 Hen. VIII. In the above drawer is a presentment and verdict of several copyholders within this graveship, at Wakefield, Sept. 29, 1604, containing a large list of encroachments upon the waste. In the same drawer is the copy of a survey and boundary of the copyhold land within this graveship, collected by the view of the copies of every copyholder, as they presented the same to a jury sworn for enquiry on certain articles to them ministred by his majesty's commissioners, in 1607, in Coley-chapel, where the jury sat. I have the verdict of several freeholders and copyholders within this graveship, made at a great court-baron of Thomas, duke of Leedes, held at Lightcliffe, by adjournment, 24 May, 8 Ann, 1709, concerning the freehold and copyhold lands and tenements within the said graveship, which paid rents, and did service to the lord of the manor of Wakefield; when the jurors, upon enquiry into the old rentals, and evidences concerning the said graveship, did find and present, that there were twenty-seven graves within the same, and put down the names of the owners of land therein, in the order in which they ought to serve that office in their respective turns, together with their helpers. In the above drawer at Howroyd is a set of answers from several copyholders in this graveship, to a book of articles to them delivered by his majesty's commissioners, in 1617, wherein, amongst other things, they say, that they had made a particular extent, or book of survey, of the several copyhold lands within the said graveship, wherein was contained the names of every copyholder, the number of messuages, houses, cottages, oxgangs, and acres of land, as their several copies warranted the same, with most of the boundaries thereof, the particular estates or interests therein, the dates of most of their copies, and so much as contained which was oxgangland, and which was rodland, and which, and how much, was freehold land, of the late earl of Leicester's grant, with the particular tenants who then held the same."

This township is a chapelry containing two chapels, viz. Coley and Lightcliffe; they are not more than a mile distant from each other: the following may perhaps throw a little light on the reason of their proximity.

In the life of the Rev. Oliver Heywood by Mr. Slate, a paper is referred to, entitled "Particulars respecting Coley, collected by O. Heywood." The following is an extract:—

"Tradition tells us, there were two sisters, never married, that lived at Priestley Green, having large estates; who built the two chapels, Coley and Lightcliffe, a mile distant from each other, and both standing in Hipperholme township; but in what year, or by what inducements they were influenced, I cannot learn. Being built in popish times, possibly they were founded in superstition; but the work was good, and it is not our province to judge of motives at this distance."

COLEY CHAPEL.

The old chapel was built A. D. 1529, the same year with Lightcliffe, as appears from Dodsw: M. S. 117, and not 1500 as stated by Mr. Watson, neither by the joint contributions of North Owram, Shelf, and Hipperholme; if the tradition related by Mr. Heywood be correct. In the lord's rental for the graveship of Hipperholme, dated 22 Hen. VIII. (1530) it is called the new chapel.

Mr. Watson refers to a deed of feoffment, 28 Hen. VIII (1536) relating to this chapel, which he saw at Coley hall, as also to a deed declaring the uses thereof: from this deed, which is set forth in WATSON, it appears that these uses were partly superstitious. The deed alludes to Lightcliffe as a prior foundation; "and for so moch that ther is a chappel nowe newly maid within the said town of Hyperome, and that dyvers gentilmen and oders haiff gyffyn yerly rents toward the fyndyng of a Prest within the said town."

The old chapel was about twenty-eight yards long, and about thirteen and a half broad. Over the west porch was written the date when the chapel was repaired, viz. "Anno Dom. 1711." The east end was repaired the same year. On the steeple: "This end rebuilt 1711." The present fabric is a neat structure, with a cemetery attached. The incumbent is the Rev. John Watson.

The incumbency was augmented in the year 1749, by the governors of Queen Anne's bounty, with a benefaction of £200, to meet a benefaction of £200 by the Rev. Henry Whitworth: and in 1816, with £800 by lot; and again in 1817, with £600 also by lot. The present yearly revenue of the curacy is stated to be £125.

LIGHTCLIFFE CHAPEL

Is dedicated to St. Matthew. In the Harleian MS. No. 797, under the title of Lightcliffe, is this entry: "In the chapel of Lightcliffe was this inscription in red characters, 'this chapell was builded A. D. 1529.'"

In Halifax Register, at the year 1668, is the following licence to Lightcliffe chapel to baptize and bury there, from Richard Sterne, Archbishop of York. A similar licence was granted to Illingworth.

"Richardus, providentia divina Ebor. Archiep, Anglie Primas et Metropolit. dilectis nobis in Christo incolis et inhabitantibus de Hipperholme cum Brighouse, infra et juxta capellaneam de Lightcliffe, parochie de Hallifax, nostre Ebor, dioceseos, salutem in Domino sempiternam. Cum ex parte vestra nobis monstratum sit, quod incole et inhabitantes de Hipperholme cum Brighouse predicto, procul distant, scilicet per spatium quatuor aut trium milliarium ab ecclesia de Hallifax predict. ubi infantes vestri baptizari, et corpora mortuorum sepeliri olim consueverunt, et quod propter loci distantiam et viarum discrimen et proclivitatem, infantes vestri, et corpora mortuorum vestrorum, sine maximo periculo et labore convehi et asportari nequeant, et quod capella de Lightcliffe, infra parochiam de Hallifax, cum sustentatione congrua pro capellano inibi servituro fuerit, et sit induta, et quod cemeterium conveniens, cum parietibus et sepibus a prophanis inclusum, adjacens capelle predicte sumptibus propriis vestris fuerit, et sit provisum, et pro sepultura corporum mortuorum supositum: Nos igitur petitionibus vestris nobis ex parte vestra presentatis, favorabiliter inclinantes, et vos, et successores vestri, incole et inhabitantes de Hipperholme cum Brighouse predicto, infantes vestros in dicto capella de Lightcliffe predicta baptizare, et corpora mortuorum vestrorum, de tempore in tempus, in dicta capella de Lightcliffe, et cemeterio predicto. sic (ut prefertur) incluso, sepelire possitis et valeatis, absq; tamen prejudicio matricis ecclesie vestre de Hallifax, et ejusdem Vicarii (quibus omnia, et singula vadia, feoda, proficua, et emolumenta, debita consueta, et debenda, respective reservari volumus et reservamus,) licentiam et facultatem nostram concedimus et impertimur per presentes, ac vobiscum in ea parte, quantum in nobis est, dispensamus, mediante ad id decreto hoc nostro in ea parte, de et cum consensu dilecti nostri in Christo, Richardi Hooke, S.T.P. Vicarii moderni ecclesie parochialis de Hallifax, coram nobis judicialiter et personaliter adhibito interposito. In cujus rei testimonium, Sigillum nostrum Archiepiscopale presentibus apponi fecimus. Datum apud manerium nostrum, de Bishopthorpe, 8vo. die Decembris, A. D. 1680, nostreq. translationis 17º."

The present erection is a plain structure, with a bell tower, and is enclosed within a capacious cemetery.

This incumbency was augmented by the governors of Queen Anne's bounty, in the year 1749, with £200 by lot, and in the years 1758 and 1762 by two benefactions of £200 each, to meet similar benefactions by the Rev. Richard Sutcliffe, and again in 1791, with a benefaction of £200, to meet a similar one by the late Wm. Walker, Esq. The yearly value of the curacy is stated to be £140. The Rev. Robt Wilkinson, A.M. is the present incumbent.

It appears from Mr. Watson, that these Chapels have been endowed, as follows:

THE ENDOWMENT OF COLEY-CHAPEL.

"John Rysshworth, of Coley, Esq. and his son John Rysshworth of Collyn, conveyed a parcel of land in Coley, within the vill of Hipperholm, held of the capital house or hospital of St. John of Jerusalem, in England, as it lay between Edwardrode on the east, the King's common, or waste ground, on the west, Coolay Slakks on the north, and a certain inclosure called Wynters, on the south, and a yearly rent of twenty shillings, payable out of a messuage, with lands, in Shelf. At the same time also Matthew Oglethorp, of Thornton, conveyed a yearly rent of three shillings and four-pence out of all his lands and tenements in Hipperholm; Richard Rookes of Rodeshall, a yearly rent of three shillings and four-pence, out of a messuage with lands, in Shelf; Thomas Fournes, of Bothes, a yearly rent of three shillings and four-pence, out of a capital messuage, with lands, in Shelf; Richard Haldeworth, of Hipperholm, a yearly rent of three shillings and four-pence, out of his capital messuage and lands lying on the north side of Hipperholm; Henry Batte, of Haylay, a yearly rent of three shillings and four-pence out of a messuage and lands in North Owram; William Cowper, of Keighley, a yearly rent of three shillings and four-pence, out of a messuage with lands, called Deynehouse, in Shelf: John Boy, of Northowram, a yearly rent of three shillings and fourpence, out of lands and tenements in Shelf; Thomas Northend, of Hipperholm, a yearly rent of twenty-pence, out of all his free lands and tenements in Hipperholm; and William Saltonstall, of Shelf, a yearly rent of twenty-pence, out of messuages and lands in Shelf, to certain trustees named in a deed, dated the 15th of November; 21

Hen. VIII. in trust, as appears by another deed, dated the 14th of February, 21 Hen. VIII. for the use of a chapel and cemetery, to be made, founded, and built on the parcel of land above named; the aforesaid yearly rents or annuities to be received yearly at Pentecost and St. Martin in winter, by equal portions, amongst other things to the use and sustentation of Richard Northend, Capellane in the said chapel, and his successors, saying, singing, and celebrating divine offices therein for ever."

WILLIAM THORPE gave, as appears by a deed of feoffment, dated the 9th of February, 28 Hen. VIII. the yearly sum of six shillings and eightpence, payable out of his messuages, lands, tenements, &c. in the town and fields of Shelf, to be for ever bestowed at the discretion of certain feoffees therein named, to and for the amending and repairing of highways, or helping of poor maidens towards marriage, or other things necessary; and after the death of Isabel his wife, the whole rent of the above messuages, &c. to the use of a priest to sing within the township of Hipperholm, and there to pray for the soul of the said William Thorpe, and others.

ROBERT HEMINGWAY, of Overbrea, gave by will, dated March 3, 1613, forty pounds towards the maintenance of a preacher at Coley Chapel, to be bestowed at the discretion of his executors; there were also given for the same end and use, by Isabel Maud, of Halifax, widow, twenty pounds; by Agnes Royde, of North Owram, five pounds; by Matthew Whitley five pounds, by their several wills; eight pounds were likewise given to the same use, by Henry Northend and Joseph Wood; with which sums, Richard Sunderland, of Coley-hall, Esq. and seven others, as trustees, purchased of one William Kershaw, of Wike, a messuage or tenement in Wike, in the parish of Birstal, with a close of land and meadow called Mappleynne, divided into two parts, in one of which the said messuage stood; and also a house or cottage in Wike aforesaid, and also a close of land called Farhinging Royds, divided into three closes. This purchase was made with the approbation of all the inhabitants within the Chapelry of Coley, and the property was conveyed to Richard Sunderland and others, in trust that they should pay yearly the rent thereof by equal portions, at Martinmas and Pentecost, to the preaching minister at Coley aforesaid, for the time being, towards his maintenance, and in no other manner, nor to or for any other use. When only three trustees survived, they were to convey to others in three months. Mr. WATSON says, "I have seen no trust deed relating to the above, of a later date than Jan 3, 1658, which, with another made in the year 1637, were in the hands of Mr. Simpson, of Hipperholme.

RICHARD SUNDERLAND, Esq. of Coley-Hall, gave by will, A. D. 1634, thirty shillings a year, for ever, out of a tenement in Shelf, to the preaching minister of Coley chapel.

SAMUEL SUNDERLAND, Esq. by his will, as appears from Watson, gave to the successive curates of the chapel of Coley five pounds a year for ever; but Mr. THORESBY's account in his Topography of Leeds, p. 583, differs from this, for according to this author he left yearly to Coley chapel twenty shillings.

JOSHUA OATES entered into a bond of one hundred pounds, in his life time, to secure forty shillings a year to the preacher at Coley chapel for ever, out of a parcel of land in Shelf, to be paid at Martinmas and Pentecost, by equal portions.

SUSANNA DANSON was a benefactress to Coley chapel, as appears from the following inscription on a stone erected on the right hand side of the way leading from Huddersfield to Bradford, at a place called Cockhill-clough : "Mrs. Susanna Danson gave the two adjoining closes to Coley chapel for ever, and they came into possession Oct. 1730." One account says, she left fifty shillings yearly in lands within Shelf, for a sermon on Good Friday.

THE ENDOWMENT OF LIGHTCLIFFE CHAPEL.

RICHARD ROOKES, gave by indenture, dated 1 March, 20 Hen. VIII. one parcel of ground in the end of a close wherein the chapel of Lightcliffe standeth, and also 13s. 4d. a year for ever, out of the rest of the said close, towards the maintenance of a priest there. The following yearly rents were also given to the said chapel :—

	s.	d.
By John Smith, out of his chief messuage, called Royd House,	6	8
— Richard Waterhouse, out of his lands within the hamlet of Priestley	6	8
— Edmund Fairbank, out of his two messuages, and all his lands at Lidyate, in Lightcliffe,	3	4
— James Waterhouse, out of his lands and tenements in Northwood,	3	4
— John and Thomas Thorpe, out of three chief messuages, his lands, tenements, and hereditaments, in Lightcliffe	3	4
— Richard Cliffe, out of Cliff-house, and lands thereto belonging, in Lightcliffe,	3	4
— Edward Hoyle, out of Hoyle House, and all the lands, &c. thereto belonging, in Lightcliffe,	3	4

	s.	D.
By John Scolfield, out of his messuage and lands in Lightcliffe;	1	4
— Gilbert Saltonstall, out of his messuage and lands in Lightcliffe, ...	1	0
— Richard Soolsfield, out of Gibhouse, and lands thereto belonging, ...	1	0
— William Whiteley, out of his New House, and two acres of land called East field Knowle, in Lightcliffe, ...}	1	0

WILLIAM BIRKHEAD, of Brookfoot, in Southowram, gave by will, dated Dec. 29, 1638, the sum of five pounds, to Samuel Hoyle, of Hoyle House, in Lightcliffe, and Robert Hargreaves, of Hipperholme, in trust, that they should bestow the same on some parcel of land, or yearly rent of inheritance, the one half of the yearly profit should be paid yearly to the curate or preacher of God's word at Lightcliffe, and the other half to the poor people of Lightcliffe and Hipperholme, from time to time, to succeeding ages, for ever.

A considerable tract of land in this township goes by the name of Coley. It was formerly written Caldley, meaning the Ceald-ley, or cold pasture, and gave name to a family of whom Henry de Coldlay occurs in a deed dated 1313, and in several others without date.

COLEY HALL.

There is a tradition that this place was formerly a priory. The first family on record in possession of what is now called Coley Hall, was that of Rishworth. The Rishworths, of Coley, were possessed of a manor there, as appears from several deeds of different dates, one in particular of 1473, and another of 1538. WATSON says he has met with them frequently between 1371 and 1562, but never saw any pedigree of the family.

The house was lately the property, and place of residence of William Horton, Esq. of the family of Howroyd, but he and his descendants being dead, it came by inheritance to the Beaumonts, of Whitley, in Yorkshire. The present fabric is modern, and affords neither arms, inscriptions, or any thing antique.

LIGHTCLIFFE,

Takes its name from a small cliff a little to the east of it. It is a very pleasant retired village, on the road betwixt Halifax and Wakefield, near the bounds of the parish, and the residence of several opulent and respectable families.

HOILE HOUSE,

So called from standing in a hole or bottom, gave name to a family who resided here the beginning of last century, if not later.

It is said to be a very ancient situation, but there is not any thing remarkable about it at the present day.

CROW NEST.

A handsome mansion, belonging to the Walker's, surrounded with its pleasure grounds, is a delightful residence.

ROOKE'S HALL.

Here lived a considerable family of the name of Rookes, some of whom resided at Rodes-hall, in Bradford parish. Mr. WATSON has given a pedigree of the family, copied from Hopkinson. This estate called Rookes, once gave name to a family of which we meet with Richard de Rokes, in 1313, and John del Rokis in 1362. Also John Rokes, de Rokes in 1502.

WINTER EDGE,

So called, says Watson, (from whom I have taken this description) from its being situated at the edge or brink of some lands called the Winters, as by a deed dated in 1498; or from Wintep-ec3, because situated on the edge of an hill, and subject to cold winterly blasts. Under the garden-house is the following inscription :—

Garrulus insano crucietur mundus amore
Dum mea perplacide vita serena placet.

Over the door of the garden-house, "Meliora spero." Still higher over the window "Contra vim mortis, non est medicamen in hortis." In the said garden-house, in stained glass, a snake biting its tail, motto, "Sic invidia macrescit," and on the same window, a very curiously painted fly. In an out-building, called the workhouse, on stained glass, 1. A cock; 2. a rose full blown; 3. a mouse taken in an oyster: Mottos to these, 1. Loqui & tacere discas; 2. Sic virtus virescit; 3. Ob gulam captivus. In the kitchen are seven panes of glass well stained with the following subjects: 1. An Ezekiel with a book opened on an heap of sculls, in an attitude of devotion, looking up, Ezek. xxxvii. 3. 2. An old man having one hand on his breast, the other extended towards heaven, a ray of light darting on him, above his head: Si tu deseris, pereo. 3. A peacock plumed, motto, Omnia vanitas. 4. An imperfect figure of a man. 5. An angel, his right foot on a globe, his wings extended, his right hand pointing towards heaven, and in his left a laurel branch, Psalm lv. 6. 6. An old man pointing with his right hand, and in his left a staff, motto, Sicut fecit, fecere ei. 7. David crowned and dressed, looking up, weeping and praying, with hands joined, his harp with him, Psalm cxix. 136. All the above human figures are in Jewish dresses.

This Winter-Edge was held, 42 Eliz. of the crown in fee, by Samuel Saltonstall, of Huntwike, and has lately been in the possession of the Priestleys, who were originally of Priestley, adjoining to this estate.

THORESBY gives an account of one John King, of Hipperholme, who died there in January, 1675, æt. 73; he was esteemed the best archer in England, and was sent for to court in the time of Charles the 1st, "and won great wagers" during the civil wars. At Manchester he was carried on men's shoulders as the victor of the field, some of the gentry crying after him, "a King, a King," which so alarmed the republicans, they cried out "treason, treason, a plot."

BRIGHOUSE,

Is an hamlet belonging to the vill of Hipperholme, and has its name from some ancient building, or buildings, which stood near the bridge which lies over the Calder, between this hamlet and Rastrick. It gave name to a family, one of which, Roger de Brighouse, held eighteen acres of land here in 1314. They sometimes occur as witnesses to deeds at different times; in particular, Tho. Brighouse, of Brighouse, and Martin Brighouse, of Glentworth, in Lincolnshire, gent. were parties in a deed of all the freehold lands in Brighouse, 9 Eliz. There was a John Brighouse of Brighouse in 1607. John de Ealand, a younger son of Sir John de Ealand, who was slain, had the manor of Brighouse, granted him by John, the eighth earl of Warren; and 19th Edwd. III. this John regranted it to his father, Sir John, and his mother Alice, and their heirs.

"In the British Museum, (says Watson) is a MS. intituled 'Collections relating to Morley hundred, written chiefly by Mr. Jennings, No. 797,' wherein, under the article of Brighouse, it is said, that Roger Doddesworth saw at Carlinghow, a charter of the manor of Brighouse, made 19 Edwd. III. by John de Eland, knt. to John de Eland, his son, and to Alice, his wife, with a seal of the arms of Eland, being an escallop shell." In another part of the said MS. it is said that this grant was to the heirs males of their bodies, reversion to Philip de Eland, Esq. In the said MS. under the title of Hipperholm, we read, that "Robert Clarel, and William de Kenerisworth, gave to Hugh de Totehill, and Joan, his wife, the manor of Brighouses for their lives, and to John de Totehill, their younger son, after their decease, dated 1349." This seems to throw it into a different family, and yet the same MS. tells us, that 36 Edward III. "John Savile, of Eland, knt. and Isabel, his wife, (the daughter of John de Eland,) acknowledged this manor to Thomas, son of John de Eland, knt. and to the heirs of his body, remainder to the heirs of Isabel." In the same MS. mention is made of a fine, 46 Edward III. between Geoffry de Warburton, knt. and Alice, his wife, plaint. and John Savile, of Eland, knt. and Alice, his wife, deforc. of the manor of Brighouse," &c. At the inquisition at Pontefract, 5 and 6 Philip and Mary, it was found, that "Henry Savile, knt. long before his death was seized in his demesne as of fee, in this manor," amongst others: and that it was held of the manor of Wakefield in free soccage by fealty only. The Ealands of Carlinghow have held courts here. Robert Ealand held a court at Brighouse, June 28, 34 H. VIII. Marmaduke Ealand, gent. son and heir apparent of Robert Ealand, Esq. held a court at Brighouse, 9 Oct. 29 Eliz. Sir John Armitage also held a court baron there, March 5, 1661. The court leet or Sheriff's turn for the manor of Wakefield is still held here as we have seen, p. 60.

Situated on the banks of the Calder, and in the centre of the staple trade, Brighouse may be classed among the number of populous villages within this extensive parish, that have risen to opulence by reason of the woollen manufacture. The Calder and Hebble Navigation passes through it. The country around is fertile, and there are several handsome family residences delightfully situated in the vicinity.

A new church in the pseudo-gothic style has lately been erected here, on a most eligible scite: it is dedicated to St. Martin. It was built from a design of Mr. Hamerton's; the contract for its erection amounted to £8500, and it is capable of containing more than 1100 persons. The living is in the gift of the Vicar of the parish, and the Rev. Mr. Hayne is the present incumbent.

TOWNSHIP OF SHELF.

THIS Township which lies to the North East of Northowram, and adjoins the parish of Bradford, contains an area of 1350 statute acres. It is said to derive its name from its shelving situation; and about the time of Henry VIII. it was written Shelve.

Shelf seems to have been granted from the crown with the manor of Wakefield, as an appendage thereto, for by Kirkby's inquest, 24. Edw. I. earl Warren was found to be lord thereof. It is remarkable, that when the writ of Quo warranto was issued in the beginning of the reign of king Edw. I. requiring the earl to shew by what title he held several manors in this part of the country, Shelf is not mentioned; though, in the dispute in the duchy chamber at Westminster, 6 Eliz. Henry Savile, then owner of this lordship, shewed, that from an ancient roll, called Domisday-book, that the men of John Thornhill, ancestor to the said Henry, did pay for the township of Shelf of foreign service 4s. 6d. to the lord of Wakefield, which lord, as this roll was composed in 1314, is known to have been John, the last earl of Warren and Surry, who derived it from his ancestors.

The reason why Shelf was not included in the dispute between the crown and earl Warren is, that previous to this, viz. 4 Edw. II. free warren had been granted in this manor to Adam · de Swillington; which Adam, for taking part with Thomas, earl of Lancaster, against the two Spencers, was fined a thousand marks, 15 Edw. II. but that judgment being pronounced erroneous by parliament, 1 Edw. III. he came into favor, and obtained of that king a charter of free warren in all his demesne lands in this, and some other of his manors. Earl Warren had also made a grant of Shelf to another family; for amongst the escheats, 25 Edw. III. the jurors said, that it would not be for the damage of the king, if the king granted to Benedict de Normanton, that he might enfeoffe William de Mirfeild priest, of the manors of Feraley and Shelfe, held of the king *is capite*, to hold to him and heirs of the king, by the service therefore due, paying yearly to the said Benedict and heirs sixty shillings. They said also, that the said manors formerly came to the king's hands by the forfeiture of Galfrid de Feraley then adhering to the Scotch, enemies of the lord the king; and that the said Galfrid held the said manor of Shelf of John, earl Warren, as of his manor of Wakefield, by homage and fealty, which said manor of Wakefield, Edmund de Langley then held of the king's gift. These manors of Feraley and Shelf were held 50 Edw. III. by William de Mirfeild, the day he died, of the king *in capite*, by the service of one penny yearly. 16 Richard II. Roger de Swillington, son and heir of Robert de Swillington, knt. held the manor. 3 Hen. VI. John Graa, knt. and Margaret, his wife, sister and heir of John Swillington, held two parts of the manor of the king in soccage; and 6 Hen. VI. the jurors, on inquisition, said, that Joan, who was the wife of Roger Swillington, knt. held when she died, after the death of the said Roger, of the inheritance of Margaret, then wife of John Graa, knt. the third part of the manor of Shelf, the reversion thereof, after the death of the said Joan, belonging to the said Margaret, and her heirs, as to the daughter and heir of the said Roger de Swillington. After this, says WATSON, I meet with nothing relating to it, till 20 Oct. 11 Hen. VII. when Sir John Savile, knt. lord of Shelf, granted part of the waste there; as did sir Henry Savile, knt. lord of Shelf, by deed, dated 1 April, 34 Hen. VIII. At present it belongs to the Savile family.

In this township, 11 Ed. II. Henry Darcy and Hugh de Totehill had lands and tenements to the value of four pounds ten shillings, which were Geoffry de Feraley's, and which Richard Wade held for life of said Henry and Hugh. Geoffry de Shelf, residing in Shelf, gave to Robert, son of Tho. de Whitewod, one yearly rent of four shillings, and to his heirs for ever, to be perceived of one assart lying on the west part of the town of Shelf, in 1341. This the said Robert gave, in 1349, to his son Richard, and his heirs. 12 Edw. III. the king granted to Bennet de Normanton in fee, all those lands and tenements in Shelf, &c. which Will. de Midgley

late held by the service of one penny. Joan, sister of Will. Mirfield, held one messuage and sixty oxgangs of land, with a meadow
adjoining, in Shelf, of the king *in capite*, by the service of one
halfpenny for all service. No date.

Shelf-Hall is mentioned in a Deed in 1496; and a messuage
called Mounteyn, in Shelf, in another, dated in 1540; and in a
Rental of the sums paid to the Knights of St. John of Jerusalem,
in England, in 1533, is the following "Edwd. Kent supradict.
pro Shelve park, 4d."

Within this township there are several beds of good coal, from
which the manufactories in this part are principally supplied.

A new turnpike Road between Halifax and Bradford has lately
been made to pass through the township, whereby a considerable
facility has been afforded to the extension of its trade.

TOWNSHIP OF SKIRCOAT.

This Township which adjoins that of Halifax, is bounded on the South by the river Calder, by the townships of Sowerby and Warley on the West, and the river Hebble on the East. It contains an area of 1340 statute acres.

It was formerly written Schircotes, and seems, says Mr. Watson, "to have taken its name from some cots or buildings, perhaps the only one then in this division, situated near those beautiful scars or rocks which range themselves along the bank of the Calder: the habitations, as I conjecture, of swine herds, both because there were formerly plenty of oaks in the neighbourhood, and because some lands hard by, have still the name of Pighills."

It is not mentioned in Domesday Book, but was originally granted by the crown to the Earl of Warren; and it appears that John, Earl of Warren, claimed free warren here, 27 Hen. III., and that the same Earl was found to be Lord thereof by Kirby's inquest. Being part of Sowerbyshire, it was granted by Hameline, the Earl of Warren, to Jordan de Thornhill, and from that family it passed to the Savilles, on the marriage of Elizabeth, daughter and heiress of Simon Thornhill, with Henry Saville; as we have shewn under Ovenden. In the British Museum is a MS. No. 797, wherein is the following entry under Skircoat :—"43 Edw. III. Simon de Thornhill, who held of the lord in Stansfield, Skircoat, Ovenden, and Wadsworth certain tenements and lands in soocage, died, and Elizabeth, daughter and heir, of the age of two years and in the custody of Elizabeth her mother, comes and gives for relief, ten shillings."

Mr. Watson states, that there have been certain grants within this Manor, affecting the title to it, but at what time they were made does not appear. "I find, however, (says he) that John Talvas gave to Thomas, his son, the fourth part of the town of Skircoat, and the demesne lands of Copley, by deed *sans* date; and that Jordan, son of John Talvas, gave to Hugh de Copley, son of Thomas Talvas, his brother, sixteen acres of land in Skircoat wood, by deed *sans* date. In an evidence, 3 Henry VIII. express mention is made of the manor of Copley, (within this township.) The manor still continues in the possession of the noble family of Saville.

COPLEY-HALL,

Takes its name from the great copp or bank, under which it is situated; it is famous for giving name to an ancient respectable family, the first of which was Adam de Copley, slain when William the Conqueror laid siege to York, in the year 1070. Watson has given a pedigree, tracing this family of Copley, to an alliance with the Savilles, as I have shown, who it appears settled at Copley about the year 1485. A female descendant of this family intermarried with Lord Thomas Howard, brother to Henry, duke of Norfolk, who, being sent ambassador to Rome, died at sea, either on the 8th or 9th of December, 1689. They had Thomas, duke of Norfolk.

The Duke of Norfolk sold this estate to one Walker, of Huddersfield. He seems (says Watson) to have conceived a sort of prejudice against it, for having arrived at the end of Skircoat-Green, with a design to pay it a visit, and seeing that it was seated under a hill, and made but a mean appearance, he immediately turned back, and would not give himself the trouble to go to it.

KING CROSS.

On the top of a hill, something more than a mile from Halifax, in the great road from thence to Rochdale, is the remain of a stone cross of this name, which (says Watson) some of the inhabitants thereabouts think was so called, because one of the kings of England, intending to penetrate into Lancashire, was frighted with the appearance of the hills from this place, and turned back; but this traditionary, (and he might have added, absurd) story, is unsupported by any authority, and the fact seems rather to be, that it was erected by one of the name of King. So far is certain, that some time ago there was in Skircoat a considerable family of this name, who had their residence at Lower Willow Hall, beneath which is a small valley, which to this day has the name of King's Vael. In a M.S. in my

possession dated 1640, I find mention made of Samuel King, de
Willow Hall.

. But what makes this King Cross the most remarkable is, that
a little below it is an house where for some time resided the family
of Wade, of which take the following account :—CAMDEN says p.
907, "that the Wades derive their pedigree from Wada a Saxon
duke, who gave battle to king Ardulph, at Whalley, in Lancashire,
and died in 798, but of this I have seen no proof, any more than
I have that Armigel Wade, Esq. who was clerk of the council to
Hen. VIII. and Edw. VI. (as his son, Sir William, was to Queen
Elizabeth,) and one of the first discoverers of America, was, as
THORESBY, p. 155, has hinted, one of their ancestors. This
Armigel Wade died in 1568, and was buried at Hampstead, in
Middlesex, in the chancel belonging to which church, his son, Sir
William, erected a stately monument to him." In the M.S. before
referred to, I find mention made of one John Wade in Skircoat.

A church has lately been erected here by the Rev. Jonathan
Akroyd, which forms a prominent feature in the country, being
built on the brow of Skircoat moor. It has altogether an unmean-
ing appearance and is utterly devoid of architectural beauty. It
has never been consecrated, but is licenced by the Archbishop for
the celebration of divine service.

HEATH.

An account of the Free Grammar School of Queen Elizabeth
here, will be found among "the Public Charities." The School
Room which was erected in that Queen's reign still remains.

WOODHOUSE.

A very ancient situation as appears from its name. The present
building has the date 1580, erected, as supposed, by a Watmough.
It was purchased for £1800, by Simon Sterne, third son of Dr.
Richard Sterne, archbishop of York. This Simon, who was a
justice of peace, was buried at Halifax, April 17, 1703, and was
resident here, as was his son Richard, both of whom are mentioned
in a short pedigree of the family, in Thoresby, p. 215.

There is an anecdote related of Lawrence Sterne, author of
Tristram Shandy, &c.. in connection with his early life, which it is
said he passed at this place. I have given it as I find it :—"This

extraordinary character first received the rudiments of his education at Heath School, being placed there by his father previous to his going out with his regiment to the defence of Gibraltar. Sterne has recorded the following occurrence which took place while he remained at school. His master having had the ceiling of the school-room newly white washed, one unlucky day the ladder remaining there, he mounted, and wrote with a brush in large capital letters, LAU. STERNE; for which he got a sound whipping from an usher, the master however was very much hurt at this, and said before him, that never should that name be effaced, for that he was a boy of genius, and would surely come to preferment : this expression made him forget the stripes he had received."

SALTERHEBBLE,

A small hamlet within Skircoat, is not remarkable for anything worthy of notice. The Calder and Hebble Navigation, which formerly terminated here, having been continued to Halifax, what little traffic it formerly enjoyed has been removed with the company's establishment thither.

In a former part of this history I have extracted from a local newspaper, published in 1759, a short account of a wake holden in the pasture grounds of Skircoat. A fair, I am informed, is holden here to this day on the first two Sundays in May; it is called "Pickle, or Pickhill, Fair," being held, as is generally supposed, in commemoration of the cattle being taken into spring grass on the lands called Pighills, from which the fair derives its name. My informant attended this fair before the Navigation Company's warehouses were erected at Salterhebble, hundreds flocked to the place, and the scite of the warehouses was occupied by forms and other accommodations.

The situation of Skircoat is pleasant and agreeable, its proximity to Halifax renders it altogether a desirable place of residence for families of opulence engaged in mercantile and commercial pursuits.

Skircoat-moor may with propriety be termed the lungs of Halifax. Here we breathe a pure and salubrious air : here the valetudinarian may enjoy his morning's walk, and inhale the pure breezes that are wafted over its surface, uncontaminated by the smoke of steam engines : here he may take the carriage airing, or the more noble exercise of the horse, in quiet, free from interruption: here the mechanic and the artizen may enjoy those manly and athletic games and exercises which invigorate the frame and soften the toils of labour, and to which every encouragement should be given, drawing him as they certainly do from the beer-shop, and the contaminating atmosphere of the democratic club-room.

Nor is Skircoat without its attractions to the lover of nature. The scenery viewed from the high ridge on the moor is both beautiful and romantic,—the towering hills in the distance,—the Calder winding along the dale beneath, overhung in some places by deep and solemn woods, interspersed at varying distances with verdant meadows, is a delightful prospect: the mansion and the villa on the more elevated lands, environed in their park-like enclosures, add to the variety and beauty of the scene; while the thriving village of Sowerby-Bridge, immediately beneath, gives it a degree of animation—the whole constituting one perfect landscape.

TOWNSHIP OF SOWERBY.

SORBBI is mentioned in Domesday book as one of the nine bere-wics within the manor of Wakefield, in this parish. The river Calder forms its boundary on the North and East, dividing it from the townships of Midgley, and Warley : it has the Riburn on the South, and the township of Erringden on the West : and contains an area of 3670 statute acres.

"I know not" says WATSON, "how to give a better etymology of this name, than by supposing it to have meant the Seur-bye, ropb-by, (securus vicus) in modern English, the safe habitation, or settlement; for such it might well be esteemed to be, when it was defended by a fort or castle, the foundation of which may yet be seen in a field near the top of the town, adjoining to which is a piece of ground called the Hell-croft, where, no doubt, the dead were buried." In Domesday book there is no mention of the castle, but this is no proof that a castle was not there, for there are many instances of the like sort to be met with in that survey. "Its name, and that of the Hell-croft (adds Mr. WATSON) seem to prove that it was in being in the Saxon times, for that people called the grave by the name of Hell;* thus, when Jacob, Gen. xxxvii. 35. says, "I will go down into the grave unto my son, mourning;" they expressed it thus, bepenδε ιο pape το mιnum

---

* Mr. Watson ought to have proved, in support of his argument, that the word "Hell" was never used in the sense of the grave later than the Saxon times, the contrary of which however is certain. It was even doubted by THORESBY (see Duc. Leod.) whether the word Hell had any other signification in the creed—"a doubt, (says DR. WHITAKER,) which was somewhat inconsistent with the orthodoxy of his principles, and which he would not have proposed had he recollected that the burial of our Lord is mentioned in the preceding article. This interpretation, however, is countenanced by the use of the word in the old translations of the bible, so as do all they who live and confess him." So that Mr. W. need not have gone back to the Saxon version.

DD

pass to hell. Our accounts of the Anti-Normannic times are very imperfect, and therefore it cannot be expected that any thing should be said with precision about such a place as this, antecedent to that memorable æra. It is clear, however, that during the possession of the earls of Warren there was a castle here, and that the said earls frequently resorted thither for the diversions of hunting, hawking, &c. This was conveyed by John, the last earl, to king Edward II. but when the fort was suffered to decline does not appear; the most probable supposition is, that it became neglected when the lords of the manor left off to visit it. The stones which composed it have been made use of in the adjacent buildings."

Sowerby, as one of the nine berewics belonging to the manor of Wakefield, was conveyed from the crown with that manor to the earls of Warren, who made it an occasional place for their residence, on which account perhaps it was, that it was made a distinct manor or lordship of itself, and the copyholders there held, "secundum consuetudinem manerii de Sowerby;" and thus it was reputed whilst it belonged to the earls of Warren, for the last earl made a grant of it to king Edward II. in these words: "Maneria mea de Wakefeild—Sowerby—et Hallifax" (inter alia.) There are no court rolls of the manor of Sowerby in the reigns of Edw. I, II, or III, for they all perished by fire, as is said, when Pilkington, steward of that manor, had his house burned, in the reign of Hen. VI. After this event, the courts were held at Wakefield, but the style was "Cur. de Sowerby tent. apud Wakefeild;" this did not continue long, for Sowerby and Warley began to be considered as one greaveship, and parcel of the manor of Wakefield, and have continued so ever since. This township (which was entirely forest ground) was not granted to Jordan de Thornhill by earl Warren, but kept in the hands of the earls of Warren, till the last earl conveyed it to the crown.* "By an inquisition at York, 21 Edw. III, John de Warren, late earl of Surry, deceased, who held the manor of Sowerby for term of his life, remainder to the king, granted the said manor to John de Breose, for life of said earl. King Edw. III. granted said

* The fact is stated differently by Mr. WATSON, in his Memoirs of the Earls Warren and Surry. Vol. 1. p. 166, "He" (Hameline Plantagenet, the 5th Earl,) "confirmed to Jordan de Thornhill, about 1169, his inheritance in Sowerbyshire, &c. as we read in Collins' Baronetage."

manor to said John Breose and his heirs, after death of said earl.
John de Breose died seized of the premises, and said earl entered
said manor." From this it appears that the grant to Breose was
for his own life. The subsequent history of the manor of Sowerby
is the same as that of the lordship of Wakefield; the present noble
proprietor being His Grace the Duke of Leeds, for whose title
see "The Manor."

One Rustin de villa nova (Nevile) had a grant of the manor
of Sowerby for his life from Edward, Duke of York, who was
slain at Agincourt. This appears from the copy of a record dated
at Wakefield, 12 March, 9 Hen. IV. and directed to "Sir Rustin
de villa nova habenti manerium de Sowerby, ad vitam suam ex
concessione Edwardi ducis Ebor," &c. The deed is in old French,
and purporting, that the said Duke of York had granted to his
tenant Roger Banister, two parcels of pasture in Sowerbyshire,
called Mareshae and Baitings in Soyland, to hold to him and his
heirs, in base tenure, according to the custom of the manor of
Sowerby; charging the said Rustin to accept the said Roger to
make fine in the court of Sowerby, for the said parcels, and to cause
the same to be enrolled there, witnessing the grant in the said court.
This deed was dated 7th Feb. 9, Hen. IV. This record seems to
prove that a court was held at Sowerby, and yet it is added, that
by virtue of this writ, at the court of Sowerby, holden at Wakefield,
the above parcels were granted to Roger accordingly.

Mr. WATSON has some very interesting information respecting
what was once termed the forest of Sowerbyshire.

In a MS. entitled Notes and Observations, gathered from sundry
records touching the estate of the manor of Sowerby, &c. are the
following words: "It appeareth, by sundry records, that Sowerby
was a manor, forest, or free chace, severed from the manor of
Wakefield, and parcel of the possessions of the earls of Warren, and
had a castle therein, and contained many great wastes, woods,
mountains and hills, stored with wild and savage beasts, as stags,
bucks, does, wild boars, and other beasts of venerie." The reason,
in all probability, why this had the name both of forest and free
chace, was because it had beasts common to both; the hart, hind,
hare, boar and wolf, being esteemed beasts of venery; the buck,
doe, fox, marten and roe, beasts of chace. Strictly speaking, the

forest was confined to what are now called Sowerby, Erringden, and perhaps Warley; for in the reign of Edward I. John the seventh earl of Warren and Surry, (as will be seen by a reference to "the manor") was summoned to answer by what warrant he appropriated to himself, as a forest, certain divisions of the parish, not including the above townships.

There is a distinction here observed between a forest and free chace: all forest laws depended wholly on the will and pleasure of kings, and it was not fit for any subject to make such laws, and create such officers as kings did usually in their forests; and therefore where forests have devolved into the hands of subjects, as Sir Henry Spelman observes, they pass most commonly under the more humble title of chaces, though sometimes the name of forest is still retained, but without the jurisdiction. And yet, as Lord Coke has observed, if the king doth grant a forest to a subject, and also, on request made in chancery, that he and his heirs shall have justice of the forest, then the subject hath a forest in law: this seems to have been the case with regard to the forest of Sowerby. The crown, temp. Edward I. laid no claim to Sowerby, Erringden and Warley, knowing the earls of Warren had a legal right to a forest there, the same no doubt being on record; but by the earl's own confession, this power extended no farther, only that he had a right by charter to have and hunt his game in the neighbouring townships, as above related.

It appears from Kirby's Inquest in this king's reign, that the earl was possessed, (as chief lord) *inter alia*, of Fixby, Sowerby, and Warley.

In the above MS. (a copy whereof was in WATSON's possession) it is also said, that "there were proper foresters, or keepers, for the preservation of their game, and wild beasts within the manor, forest, or free chace, appointed by the lords thereof; and there are many presentments in the rolls belonging to the manor of Wakefield, for hunting, killing of deer, beating and wounding the foresters and keepers, and other misdemeanors committed against the game, and officers in that forest, in the reign of King Edward II." In another MS. (referred to by WATSON) intitled, Notes and Remembrances collected out of the manor of Wakefield touching Soyland and Warley mills, it is likewise said, that "it is manifest, by antient record, that Sowerby was a forest, or free chace, and stored with venison, and that there were foresters elected, and that the Earls Warren went often thither for pleasure in hunting, and there were many amerciaments for killing of deer." From the same MS. it also appears, that 16 Edw. I. Geppe de Dene was elected forester in Sowerbyshire, and found sureties for his fidelity, Henry Prepositus, (the Greave) of Hipperholme, W. of the same, Thomas de Shelfe, and Richard of the same. The same year divers men were taken, and imprisoned for beating and wounding Ralph, one of the foresters in Sowerbyshire, and were fined ten shillings and sixpence, and found sureties, body for body, if the said forester died before the the arrival of the Earl. Several men in Sowerbyshire were present when the above forester was wounded, but they pretended not to know who wounded him, therefore they were all attached. In the same roll two men were amerced, because they refused to be foresters in Sowerbyshire. Also Alan, son of Richard Talvas, was taken and imprisoned for taking from William del Hirst six sheaves of oats, against his will, alledging that the said William owed him the same, for preserving his corn in the night from the beasts of the woods. 35 Edw. I. Roger, vicar of Rochdale, was amerced in twenty shillings, for hunting and killing deer in Sowerbyshire, of which he paid one half, and laid in sureties for the other. 4 Edw. IV. the king granted to John Pilkington, Esquire of his body, the office of his chief forester of his chace of Sowerby. In a dispute, 6 Eliz. between the crown and Edward Savile, Esq. a deed was produced, without date, under the seal of arms of William, Earl Warren, owner of the lordship of Wakefield, whereby it appeared, that John Thornhill did grant that the said earl and his heirs for ever, should keep all his wild beasts, deer, and fowls, in the ground of the said John Thornhill, in Sowerbyshire, by the proper forester of the said earl; and the said earl, in consideration of the said liberty, did grant, by the same deed, that it should be lawful to the said John Thornhill, and his heirs, to make their whole commodity of all their lands and woods in Sowerbyshire, at their pleasure, without contradiction of the earl, or his heirs, and that the said John Thornhill and his heir should have and take yearly, within his fee in Sowerbyshire, five stags of grease, and five hinds in winter. These are sufficient proofs of a forest here : and it is worth observing, that it has sometimes been called the forest of Sowerbyshire, and sometimes the forest of Hardwic. The first, WATSON conjectures to allude to the towns within the compass of it, and the second to mean the chief place of residence within it, but of this hereafter. The liberties of the forest of Sowerbyshire, as we are told by BENTLEY, in his account of Halifax, "have their beginning on the west, from the bounds dividing the counties of Yorkshire and Lancashire; on the east, Salterhebble brook, as the same runneth from Illingworth to the river Calder; on the north it borders on the vicarage of Bradford; and on the south, on the rivers of Ryburn and Calder; and contains, within its circuit, the following towns and hamlets: Halifax, Ovenden, Illingworth, Mixenden, Bradshaw, Skircoat, Warley, Sowerby, Rishworth, Luddenden, Midgley, Eringden, Heptonstall, Rottenstall, Stansfield, Cross-stone, and Langfield;" to which WRIGHT, in his History of Halifax, p. 82, adds (very properly) Wadsworth.

That Barkisland and Norland were not within the limits of the forest is plain, from the "Domisday Booke, being an extent of the rents and services of the free men of the Soke of Wakefield, made in 1314," wherein the escape of beasts at Ryburne, into the forest, is valued at five shillings yearly; the same at Northeland, (Norland) two shillings and sixpence. Midgley also seems not to have been part of the forest, for the escape of beasts belonging to Midgley and Luddenden is valued at ten shillings yearly. The true bounds of the forest appear to have been as above described, viz. Sowerby, Erringden, and perhaps Warley. What was called Sowerbyshire was more extensive, having its denomination from the manor, and comprehended the townships and vills of Sowerby, Soyland, Erringden, Rishworth, Skircoat, Halifax, Midgley, Ovenden, Holdsworth, Stansfield, Heptonstall, Wadsworth, Routonstall, Langfield, Warley, and Saltonstall, all which were within the view or circuit of the court leet, or sheriff's turn, holden at Halifax, and the inhabitants of these towns were called men of Sowerbyshire.

"As to the name of Hardwic, (says WATSON,) I have not met with it in any ancient record, and as no place in this neighbourhood goes by that appellation now, or is known by tradition to have been called so, we must be guided by circumstances in finding it out. What then is the etymology of it? Heord-wic, or the village where herdsmen lived, differs little from it in sound, but it may be supposed that the forest would take its denomination from the most considerable place within it, and not from the huts of a few herdsmen. The most considerable place was the castle at Sowerby, where the lords of the manor had their residence when they came here to hunt, and use other diversions. But between the words Sowerby and Hardwick, there is a remarkable similarity; the former from the security which its castle gave to it, might get the name of Sureby, securus vicus; and the latter may be derived from Hart, or Hard, strong, and Wik, a village, or fort. The forest of Hardwick, therefore, is but another name for the forest of Sowerby. In this conjecture we are not a little confirmed, when it is considered that what is now called the forest of Hardwick, occurs very often in old writings, by the name of the forest of Sowerbyshire. Was this not so, there must have been two forests here adjoining to each other, and belonging to the same person, which it would be ridiculous to suppose. Besides, as above related, Earl Warren, in answer to the writ de quo warranto, in the time of king Edward II. laid no claim to a forest in the township of Halifax, and in Sowerby it was never disputed with him. When therefore it is said, that Halifax was in the forest of Hardwick, nothing more could originally be meant by it, than that Halifax was within the purlieus, or liberties of it, which it seems to have been; but the true forest of Hardwick was that of Sowerby. If any should think that the first syllable in Hardwick, or Ardwick, comes from Ard, an hill, or mountain, or from Ard, an adjective, which signified high, or lofty, the situation of the place will well agree with these opinions, and yet not overthrow the above conjecture."

Mr. Watson has certainly taken a great deal of pains to prove that Hardwick is but another name for Sowerby; now with all deference to his judgment, I would submit to the consideration of those better acquainted with the subject than myself, whether the word may not have some connection with the German Hardt-weg, or hard road in the forest.

The park of Erringden, formerly within Sowerby, I shall hereafter have occasion to notice.

The earliest account of the graveship of Sowerby, is in the

"Domisday Book" of the manor, made in 1314, from whence the following :—

"Graveship of Sowerby. Here the lord has a manor in his chase. Will. de. Townend for his lands bound to grind at the mill of Soland at the twentieth vessel, to assist in making the eldest son of the lord a knight, in marrying his eldest daughter, and shall go a hawking with the lord as often as he shall come thither, for the first day at his own charges, and if not, shall pay 1d. Several others were bound to the same service. There is in the forest an iron forge, which may continue for ever, worth 9l. 12s. yearly, viz. 4s. in each week, except fifteen days at Christmas, and fifteen days at Easter and Whitsontide. The lord may have in the forest five score cows and bulls in three vaccaries, and eight score fat beasts may be in Baytinge in Soyland, where may be agisted, besides the aforesaid beasts, an hundred great beasts between the feasts of St. Helen and St. Giles, worth yearly 40s. The pannage of the whole graveship worth yearly about 100s. The herbage in Hadreschelfe 24s. Herbage in Mankanhulls, 16s. Escape of the cattle of Midgley and Luddingden 10s. Escape at Ryburne 5s. The mill at Soland 46s. 8d. The mill of Warlulley 26s. 8d. Perquisites of court 10l. Escape of beasts out of Northland 2s. 6d. Agistments in the common pasture 36s. 8d.

"In Soland. All the rents arising from seventeen tenants here amounted to 69s. 11d. ob. These paid to the lord for foreign service 2s. Rishworth paid foreign service to the same 12d. Out of which were paid to sir John Eland for his life 2d. yearly.

"Warley. The tenants are said to hold their respective lands in this township, "per servicium de Sowerbye." In the margin is written "Skircotes & Northeland."

.At the foot of this survey was written, "The sum total of the whole extent £375 16s. 11d. ob. qa." The whole of earl Warren's rents in the north parts is also there made to amount to £668 3s. 6d. ob. qa. out of which there was paid yearly about £100 to constables, watchmen, and gate keepers at castles.

At a court held at Wakefield, Nov. 19, 1624, it was found, that there were sixty head graves within the graveship of Sowerby; of which there were forty in Sowerby, and twenty in Warley; also that every helper was to pay the head grave four pence for every penny rent, and so after that rate towards his service and charges, as had been accustomed. These graves always begin their office at Michaelmas. At the above court all the head graves, with their helpers, were formed into a list both for Sowerby, Soyland, and Warley, the sums being particularly mentioned which each were to pay, and the estate for which they were to serve. The last verdict by twelve jurymen, which Watson had heard of, summoned by the lord's steward to enquire into the rents and evidences concerning the graveship of Sowerby, was given at Sowerby-bridge, at the great court baron held there for the Duke of Leeds, May 20th, 1710.

SOWERBY CHAPEL.

Although there is no positive proof of the precise date when a chapel was first erected in Sowerby, Mr. WATSON has produced proof that there was one in existence before 35 Eliz. (Dec. 30, 1592) for one Robert Wade of Sowerby, whose will bears that date, surrendered four pounds yearly out of his lands, to feoffees in trust, that the same should be distributed to the poor of Sowerby, by the minister for the time being; and it is more than probable that it was not a new erection then, for at Whitewindows in Sowerby, is an original agreement, dated May 25th, 1622, to tax Blackwood, Sowerby, and Westfield Quarters, forty pounds each, towards enlarging, re-edifying, and beautifying the Chapel at Sowerby town. One Adam Morris is also said to have been curate there in 1572.

At the same place is another agreement, dated May 25th, 1622 between some of the chief persons in Sowerby, and one Shepherd, a carpenter, concerning the wood work in Sowerby Chapel; and there is also a third original paper there, dated Jan. 1626, wherein is recited, that the chapel of Sowerby was lately re-edified and enlarged; but situated in a mountainous country, above three miles distant from its parish-church at Halifax, by reason whereof some of the inhabitants of the same chapelry, dwelling five or six miles off (through foul and craggy ways) from the said church, were, upon occasions of christenings, weddings, and burials, put to great and extraordinary pains in travelling to and from the said church; which labor they thought might well be eased, and much expence saved; if the said chapel could be procured to be a distinct parish-church of itself, and endowed with parochial rights, viz. with all fees due for christenings, churching of women, marrying, burials, mortuaries, oblations, obventions, and such other monies and rights, as by the inhabitants of and within the said chapelry, and their predecessors, have been due and payable to the vicars of Halifax for the time being; all which divers of the said inhabitants were in great hope to obtain either in possession, by composition, or else after the death, cession, resignation, or deprivation of Robert Clay, D. D. then vicar of Halifax, if a competent sum of money could be raised for effecting thereof. Nothing however was effected till the year 1678, when another attempt was made, upon a different plan, as appears from the copy of a letter at Chaderton, written by Dr. Hooke, the then vicar, to clear himself from being a traditor of the church's rights; wherein he says, that the inhabitants of Sowerby should have liberty to bury their dead in the chapel or chapel-yard there, reserving for every burial the accustomed due of one penny to the vicar of Halifax, and to the clerk of Halifax two-pence; and also to baptise their infants, reserving to the said vicar for each infant, five pennies, and to the clerk of Halifax one penny;—that no publication of marriage be but in Halifax church, nor any marriage of any inhabitant of Sowerby but in the said church;—that the dues arising from Sowerby should be paid to the vicar quarterly; and that the churchwarden of Sowerby should attend, as formerly, the monthly meetings at Halifax, and contribute as before to all church dues. The original consent of Dr. Hooke, relating to the above, dated Oct. 8, 1678, is set forth in Watson. In consideration whereof, the people of Sowerby gave towards the purchasing of a close, annexed to the vicarage, the sum of seven pounds ten shillings, which close had been purchased of one Nicholas Elberke of Halifax, in 1688, for thirty-one pounds. It lies behind the vicarage house.

After the above consent was obtained, the archbishop granted a similar licence to Sowerby as he had done before to Lightcliffe. It is dated at Bishopthorpe, Nov. 1, 1678. See the Halifax register for that year. This grant was also registered in the archbishop's own book, and in the registry of the court at York.

June 4th, 1761, says Mr. Watson, "I had the honor to sign a certificate along with Sir George Armytage, bart. and others, that the old chapel was in bad repair, and placed in an inconvenient situation;" on which account the inhabitants obtained a Faculty from the archbishop to pull down the same, (which they did,) and in 1762 and 1763 erected the present handsome edifice, on a more commodious site than the former with a tower, "which by its elevation forms a striking object to the valley above and beneath, and by its musical bells conveys the joyful sound of the Christian Sabbath many miles around." In the interior it is one of the most elegant chapels in the North of England. The first duty done there was January 3rd, 1763. The old chapel was dedicated to St. Peter. Some remains of it are still to be seen at Field house, for which see.

In a kind of lobby at the West end is a statue of Archbishop Tillotson, erected above 40 years ago. "The situation, (says Dr. WHITAKER) is objectionable on many accounts. An archbishop should not have been placed in the lowest part of the church, or rather excluded from the church; and space might certainly have been found, if not in the centre of the apsis which encloses the communion table, yet on the North side, where a bishop always stands to perform episcopal offices. Should such a removal ever take place, the relative situation on the South side should be reserved till the chapelry of Sowerby produce another Tillotson."

ENDOWMENT OF SOWERBY CHAPEL.

It appears by an indenture at Chaderton, in Lancashire, dated March 9, 1722, that Elkana Horton, of Gray's Inn, Esq. in consideration of two hundred pounds from the governors of Queen Anne's Bounty, and one hundred pounds left by Edward Colston, of Mortlake, in Surry, Esq. sold to Nicholas Jackson, clerk, curate of Sowerby, and his successors, for ever, Lower Langley, alias Nether Langley, in Norland, containing eighteen acres, or thereabout; also a farm, called Birch Farm, in Sowerby; likewise the Lane Ends. The Bounty was obtained in 1719.

Edward Colston left a large sum for the augmentation of small livings, and his executors, at the request of the said Elkana Horton, allowed an hundred pounds to Sowerby Chapel, and Mr. Horton himself allowed another hundred pounds in the purchase. The certainty at this chapel, 3rd of Queen Anne, was seven pounds yearly, according to the return already mentioned; but in Ecton's Thesaurus, twelve pounds two shillings and eightpence.

In the year 1817, the living was further augmented by the go-vernors of the Bounty of Queen Anne, with £800 by lot. In the report of the commissioners appointed to inquire into the revenues of the church, &c. presented to Parliament by command of His Majesty, the living is valued at £199 per annum: there is a glebe-house attached. The present incumbent is the Rev. W. H. Bull. M. A.

The places within this township that have been most worthy of remark, and still retain something reminiscent of their former state, are

BALL GREEN,

Where probably was a habitation, in very early times, as Ball is a very ancient term for a place of abode. If this was the case, I conjecture that some of the foresters may have lived here.

BRECK,

So called from a break, or breach, on the side of an adjoining hill. Here some of the descendants of Archbishop Tillotson for-merly resided. At present it is the residence of the Ingrams.

BOWOOD.

The word Bau signified in ancient times, the same as Ball, but in a forest it is natural to suppose that this name has some relation to shooting.

BOWER SLACK.

In all probability an ancient settlement of some kind or other. Watson says the word will bear two interpretations, it might mean the chambered house, or a house in general, or a place of shade and retirement, being so called from the Anglo Saxon Bupe.

CALLIS.

A house which some believe to be the oldest in the vicarage, and where tradition says that Robin Hood some time resided; but no other marks of its antiquity appeared in Watson's time, than that the north part of it was studded after the manner of building in for-mer times. It might take its name from the Latin word Callis, which meant a path made by wild beasts in forests and mountains.

DEEPLEY AND DEERSTONES,

Are names which evidently took their original from the deer which inhabited this forest, and denote the places where they usu-ally frequented.

ELFABROUGH HALL,

W,ritten in deeds Elffaburghall, Elfabrough, Elphenhrough, and Ellfleteburghall, also Elfabrook, was formerly the estate of the Pilkingtons, of Bradley. It is in an orchard, and adjoins the brook from the Cragg, near Mytholmroyd bridge. It seems to have got its name in superstitious times, and to have been looked upon as an Ælpen-Bup3, or habitation of fairies, who delighted, it seems, in fountains, and streams of water, which abound at this place. Elfabright Bridge is mentioned by Harrison, the topographer. Elf is but another name for fairy, and there is a story told in this part at the present day, that a fairy house of a very beautiful construction was found near this place. It is useless wasting words in an affair of this sort, but undoubtedly the situation of the place appears to be peculiarly adapted for them, as WATSON says, if any reliance is to be placed on the tales of olden time. CHAUCER is very facetious concerning them in his Canterbury tales :

> "In the old Dayes of the King Artour,
> All was this Lond fulfilled of *Fayry*,
> The *Elf-Quene* with her jolie Company,
> Daunsed full oft in many a *grene Mede*;
> This was the old opinion, as I rede.
> I speke of many hundred yere agoe,
> But now can no man se no Elfes mo."

There is a field here which I have seen called Oldelflaburgh, and sometimes the Hall Field.

FIELD HOUSE.

The name, which is of considerable antiquity, was given by the Anglo-Saxons to a tent, and it is not improbable that something of this sort might have been fixed here by the owners of the forest, in order to command a view of the adjoining country, and to witness the diversion of hunting, hawking, &c. We find it attached to a farm-house about 200 yards from the present mansion, in the time of Charles I., with the addition of Upper or Over. At this latter place, when an old barn was removed 10 or 12 years ago, a quantity of gold coins was found, now in the possession of Robert Stansfeld, Esq. None of them are very ancient. The Jacobus' and Carolus' are most common ; these in all probability were secreted during the time of the civil wars.

Immediately contiguous to the mansion of Field-house, and partially hidden by trees, stands the Old Hall apparently built about the year 1670 or 1680. It is a regular structure, containing, like the residences of that period, a large number of small rooms, well adapted for the comforts of a numerous family, but in general the building is devoid of ornament or architectural interest. The modern mansion, built by the late George Stansfeld, Esq. in 1749, is a handsome edifice in the Grecian style, and commands an extensive view of the beautiful valley of the Riburn, and of the distant hills which separate Yorkshire and Lancashire. The arms of the family are executed in stone in relief, over what was originally the principal entrance. To the antiquarian the objects of most interest there are the remains of the old church of Sowerby, removed about the year 1760. They comprise the East window and belfry. The window consists of a gothic arch, with the usual segments forming a circle in the centre. The belfry is remarkable for the extreme beauty of its proportions and is a perfect model of architectural symmetry. One side resting on the apex of the window, the other is supported by pillars which rise out of the ground to a considerable height, and being covered with ivy, in some measure conceal the window. The effect, as seen through the large gates on approaching the house, is particularly pleasing. The belfry contains two bells, but whether or not either of them belonged to the old church is not sufficiently ascertained. Much praise is certainly due to Robert Stansfeld, Esq. the present owner of the mansion, for preserving these memorials of the old church from the hand of the spoiler.

FLONE NOOK,

From the Anglo-Saxon Fla, an arrow, pronounced in after times Flo, and in plural number Flone, where archery might have been practised in former times.

HADERSHELF OR HATHERSHELF SCOUT.

Early mention is made of this place. 10 Edward II. the earl of Warren gave to Henry de Walda a pasture in Sourby, called Hardeschelf. Hadershelf, after the conquest was so far improved that it was converted into a vaccary, where cattle were nourished and bred. These vaccaries were in length of time let forth to tenants by copy of court roll. In the year 1799 a singular discovery was made near this place. A man passing observed his

dog enter a narrow aperture, supposing him to have caught the
scent of a fox, he pursued, and found the opening gradually ex-
pand into a small cave, where he found, not a fox, but a savage,
who barred all farther approach by a pistol.   The astonished discoverer withdrew, but quickly returned with some assistants, one
of whom boldly entered, and secured the inhabitant of the cave.
The reason for his choice of this unknown retirement now appeared.
It was a repository of stolen goods ; among which were two sur-
plices taken from the parish church of Rochdale, with the scarlet
hood of a doctor in Divinity.   The plate stolen at the same time had
been previously discovered in another place.   The cave of this Cacus
was not large enough for the reception of living oxen, but it was
copiously stored with slaughtered animal food, properly cured, for
a long concealment.   The ruffian thus extracted from his lurking
place was transported for life.

<h3 style="text-align:center">HAUGH END.</h3>

It seems, by the name, as if there was an inclosure from this
place towards the town of Sowerby, and that this was the extreme
part of the bæ3.   The place will ever be regarded with veneration,
that excellent prelate, Archbishop Tillotson, having drawn his first
breath here.   WATSON has a pedigree of the family.   The present
mansion at Haugh End was erected by — Lees, Esq.

<h3 style="text-align:center">HOLLINHEY,</h3>

Where it is said a court used to be held, and the owner of it
bound to keep a white bull, a stoned horse, and a brawn.

<h3 style="text-align:center">PALLES HOUSE,</h3>

Now corrupted to Palace House, situated near the pales which
surrounded the park of Erringden.   Perhaps the Palizer's house.
It is otherwise called Motherholt.   It is on the bank of the Calder,
and overlooks the hamlet of Hebden Bridge.

<h3 style="text-align:center">POND.</h3>

A house which, report says, has belonged to the name of Stansfeld, ever since the time of the conquest.

<h3 style="text-align:center">BATTEN-ROW.</h3>

STUKELEY, in his account of Richard of Cirencester, p. 44, says,
this name is of high antiquity, and relates to panegyres, or fairs ;
and, if he is right in his conjecture, it is of high antiquity indeed,
for we cannot well suppose that any thing of that sort would be per-

mitted, after the ground was appropriated to the use of a forest.

TURVIN,

Is a valley in this township, not devoid of romantic beauty; it is so called, perhaps, from being the boundary of some kind or other, as Terfyne, and Tervyn, in the British, had this signification, as also Tarfin in the Cornish. This place is rendered remarkable from being the haunt of a most desperate gang of coiners, whom we have before noticed, and who long escaped the vigilance of government.

May 10th, 1774, the house of Commons went into a committee on the then state of the gold coin. Mr. Chamberlain,* whose evidence was corroborated by several respectable witnesses, gave the house a very entertaining account of all the persons who had been convicted of clipping, coining, filing, or otherwise diminishing the coin of the Kingdom. He was particularly severe on Yorkshire, where he said he had been down, and seen many guineas which had been reduced 5s. 3d.; some 5s. 4d.; but the general run was from 2s, 6d. to 4s. 6d. each; that almost every wool-comber in the North kept a file for the purpose; that they were at no loss to sell their filings, for there were several private mints that could coin them a guinea or half-a-guinea for a shilling. He said he had enquired into the nature of these private mints, and found they were so private that it was almost impossible for any person to find them out in their unlawful proceedings; for their houses were so situated that they could distinguish a person half a mile before he reached their house. The principal master belonging to these mints, (who was their sovereign, and, in order to give him a pre-eminence, was called king David,) had been detected and hung; but the practice still went on to a great extent. It was common, he said, in the North, to give twenty shillings for the use of twenty guineas for two hours; or they would give you two shillings for the use of two guineas for half an hour!

The coin having, since that period, been made current by weight as well by tale, the temptation to such frauds has been removed; and if they now take place, it can only be to a very inconsiderable extent.

---

* Mr. Chamberlain, solicitor to his Majesty's mint, and who prosecuted the coiners who were detected in this parish.

A small episcopal chapel was erected in this valley in the year 1815, entitled "the chapel of St. John in the Wilderness," and was consecrated by the archbishop in the year 1817; it has been endowed with the sum of £1600 by lot from the governors of Queen Anne's bounty. The living is valued at £76 per annum. The present incumbent is the Rev. Thomas Crowther.

WHITE WINDOWS.

Here is a large handsome mansion house, built by the late John Priestley, Esq. whose pedigree Mr. WATSON has given. Its present owner is George Priestley, Esq.

The township of Sowerby is divided into the three quarters of Sowerby, Westfield, and Blackwood. Sowerby, says WHITAKER, was one of the members of the first Chapelry of Luddenden, though it did not long continue to be so. It was undoubtedly the most important township within the parish, in former times, if we may judge, by the proportion it paid towards the ancient taxes and estreats. In the time of Queen Elizabeth it was rated by the justices double the amount of any of the other townships; and again for maintenance of the forces at Pontefract, during the civil wars, the proportion paid by Halifax was £6 11s., while Sowerby paid £11 5s. It also appears to have been the residence of several ancient and respectable families, the majority of them bearing arms.

A part of the principal highway which runs through this township has always been designated "Sowerby Street," and there is a tradition that it formed part of a Roman road which intersected this portion of the country. The fact not having been mentioned by WATSON, I feel some diffidence in adverting to it. I do so rather in the hope that it may incite a spirit of inquiry among my antiquarian readers, rather than from any information I am able to communicate on the subject, but I may venture to remark that such a case is not improbable, when we bear in mind that it is near upon one of the most interesting remains of a Roman station in this country, and that several coins have at various times been turned up in parts adjoining this *Street*. "Street, (says THORESBY,) is the very word that our countryman BEDE useth to signify the Roman roads."

E E

TOWNSHIP OF WARLEY.

WERLA, as it is written in Domesday Book, was another of the nine berewics belonging to Wakefield, and in all probability one of the most considerable of the nine; in fact DR. WHITAKER supposes that Skircoat and Ovenden, with Halifax, must have been taken out of it. It has sometimes been called Warlowlye or Warlully. It lies to the West of Halifax, and is divided from Midgley by the brook that empties itself into the Calder at Luddenden Foot; having the Calder on the South, and Ovenden on the North: and contains an area of 3,980 superficial statute acres.

It was originally granted by the crown to earl Warren, and in this family it remained until the re-grant by John, the eighth and last earl. It has since passed from the crown to its present noble possessor, being held under the same title as that of Halifax, &c. for which see "The Manor."

The township of Warley is altogether an interesting district. I have before had occasion to refer to some memorials of the British Era, which are to be found here, and they are well worth the inspection of the curious. Some Roman coins have also been found, and there is a remain called Camp-End, supposed to have been thrown up during the civil wars.

For parochial purposes it is divided into two districts.

Within this township is a tract of land, called

SALTONSTALL, NETHER AND OVER.

In Nether Saltonstall, twenty-four beasts might have been sustained in the winter, in the reign of Edward II.; and there were thirty acres of meadow land to mow there, for the support of the said cattle. In the summer they were removed to Baitings in Soyland. If the lord was willing to let this Nether Saltonstall to farm,

it would take yearly 43s. 8d.   In Over Saltonstall was a place for
a vaccary, and a small house in which the man who took care of it
dwelt, in the time of Edward II. also a byer or cow-house, and a
grange, or barn, to hold the hay; there were thirty acres of meadow
and pasture there, of which fifteen might be mowed, and fifteen lie
for pasture.   One bull and thirty cows, with their calves, might be
kept there, if hay was given them in the winter.   The place ought
yearly to be inclosed with a good fence, which would cost the lord
8s. and he might let the same to farm for the yearly sum of 40s.

The first grants made by copy of court-roll of Saltonstall, which
was in the latter end of the reign of Edw. II. were made upon division of the whole into six equal parts, and every part was called a
Sextondole of Saltonstall; and it appears from various accounts,
that several of the name of Saltonstall were officers of earl Warren
for Saltonstall, and to them were divers parts thereof granted.

In 1343, 17 Edward III. John de Browhirste surrendered in
court two parts of a sixth part of Saltonstall, with the reversion of
a third part of the said sixth part, which Isabel mother of said John
held as dower; the moiety of which was granted to John, son of
Thomas de Saltonstall, another moiety to Richard, son of Thomas
de Saltonstall, and William de Saltonstall, and heirs.

At Halifax, in 1376, John Cape surrendered a sixth part of Saltonstall to the use of Richard Saltonstall, and heirs.

As the last earl of Warren and Surry died June 30th, 1347, 21
Edward III. it is plain, from the first of the two instances above,
that the vaccary of Saltonstall was demised by copy before the lordship of Wakefield came to the crown.

6 Henry IV. Richard Saltonstall surrendered two sixth parts of
Saltonstall, and half a sixth part, lying between Blakebrook, Depe-
clough, the water of Luddenden, and Hoore Stones, in Sowerby,
to the use of Richard Saltonstall and heirs.   15 Edward IV. this
Richard surrendered the same to Gilbert Saltonstall, his son, which
Gilbert, 23 Hen. VII. surrendered the same to Richard Saltonstall,
his son; after the death of which Richard, son of Gilbert, Richard
Saltonstall, son and heir of the same Richard, 30 Hen. VIII. made
fine of heriot for the said lands.   This last Richard had issue Gilbert,
who died before his father, leaving a son Samuel, who, after the
death of Richard his grandfather, made fine of heriot, 40 Eliz. for

the same lands.   The pedigree of Saltonstall, is set forth in Watson under Hipperholme.

Earl Warren claimed free warren in Saltonstall, by royal charter, 37 Henry III. so that this place was, in fact, no part of the forest of Sowerby, though it lay within Warley, which appears to have been a part thereof.   This accounts for the expression above, that the place ought yearly to be enclosed with a good fence, on account, no doubt, of its being secured from the deer, and other wild beasts.

William, son of Henry de Astey, gave for ever to Ralph de Horbury, and heirs, one assart, within the bounds of Saltonstall, viz. that which Henry de Astey, his father, held, and all his right within the bounds of Saltonstall, in the name of the said assart.

Idonia, daughter of Adam, son of Philip de Shitlington, quit-claimed to said Ralph, and heirs, all her right and claim in the moiety of the town of Saltonstall, in feedings, &c. and all liberties thereto belonging.   Agnes, some time the wife of William de Astey, in her widowhood, granted to John de Horbury, and heirs, all her right and claim in six acres of land, in Saltonstall.

John de Horbury let to Richard, son of Adam de Midgley, two oxgangs of land in Saltonstall, which contain twenty six acres of land, with edifices, &c. for the term of twenty years.   This, in one of the Harleian MSS. No. 797, is said to have been done in 1278; but this in all probability was an error, as all the land, within the bounds of Saltonstall was held in demesne, till the same was granted out by copy, in the latter end of the reign of Edward II. as above-mentioned.

The name of Saltonstall, is said to be derived from Sal, or Sa, which Salmon, in his history of Hertfordshire, p. 259, says, are old words for small, or little; ꞇon, is an inclosure, and ꝼꞇal, a dwelling: as much as to say, the small habitation; agreeable to what is said above, under Over-Saltonstall, which in the original MS. is thus expressed, "Est ibidem una parva domus in qua fir-marius illius vaccarie solebat manere."   The country people pro-nounce it Satonstall.

SOWERBY-BRIDGE.

This ancient hamlet, which has now become a populous and thriving village, may be regarded as another instance of the com-mercial prosperity of these manufacturing districts.   It is seated on the banks of the Calder, within two and an half miles of Halifax, on the high road to Manchester. Possessing the advantage of a commercial navigation passing through it, connecting the Eastern and Western coasts, together with commodious and extensive wharfs for the shipment of goods; it may be said to command the traffic of the rich manufacturing vale of Sowerby. Here are also several large mills for the manufacturing of cloth, and for grinding corn, as also extensive chymical works.

A company has lately been formed for lighting the village with gas, so that a continuous lighted street may be said to connect it with the town of Halifax.

THE CHAPEL.

I have now before me a document, referred to by WATSON, connected with the first chapel built at this place. It purports to be "The feoffee copie for the ground whereon the Brigge chappell standeth, being builded in the seventeenth yeare of the reigne of king Henry the Eighth and in the yeare of our lord, 1526." It appears that there was surrendered by one John Maud and the Waterhouses of Skircote into the hands of the lord, a parcel of land containing 26 yards in length and 8 in breadth, within the township of Warley, between a fulling mill on the East and Sowerbie brigge on the West, to the use of Thomas Savile de Copley, gent. and others.

"Memorandum. That the said chappell was pulled downe and raised higher for lofting, in anno Caroli nunc anglia, &c. octavo, 1632. The charges whereof were as followeth:" the items are then set forth, the sum total amounting to £67 07s. 07d. "The townsmen of Skircoat bearing a sixth part of the charge, and the rest being equally divided between the townsmen of Norland and Warley, they having convenient seats allotted them in the said lofts, rating according to their several disbursements, "no man being mayed to give more than they pleased voluntarily to bestow; which said rooms being divided as followeth;" then follows a list of the stalls, with the names of the families among whom they were divided. I regret that my limits will not allow me to copy the list, giving as it does the names of some of the principal families who at that time lived in these parts: there are 32 stalls mentioned, 14 whereof were alletted to Warley, 13 to Norland, and 5 to Skircoate. The document concludes—

> These things of note, with other more of marke,
> Shall be recorded by your under clarke,

HEN: MAUD, 1640.

An interesting view of this old chapel has been preserved by Mr. Horner. Its situation was extremely inconvenient, and the increasing population of Sowerby-Bridge rendered further church accommodation necessary. The wealth and liberality of the principal families in the immediate vicinity did not long permit this to be a subject for complaint; a convenient scite was purchased in the centre of the village, and in the year 1819 the present handsome and commodious chapel, after the Gothic order of architecture, was erected thereon, capable of containing upwards of 1200 persons. A convenient cemetery is attached to it. The Rev. James Franks, M. A. was the first minister; on whose decease, the Rev. Thomas Rogers, the present incumbent, succeeded.

There have been some benefactions to this chapel. In a terrier belonging to Sowerby-Bridge chapel, written in 1727, are the following particulars. One chapel-house, worth one pound eight shillings per annum. One cottage-house, given to the chapel by Mr. Samuel King, eighteen shillings per annum. The queen's bounty for this chapel was obtained 18th April, 1719, to meet a benefaction of £200 by Mr. I. Taylor and others: the title-deeds belonging the bounty are dated Nov. 2, 1724. The estates bought with this money are, the Lower Brig Bottom Farm, containing nineteen days' work of land, then let for twelve pounds ten shillings a year; a farm called Earoyd, containing thirteen days' work, rent seven pounds eight shillings a year; and a farm called Gate Head, containing nine days' work, rent four pounds a year: but these rents are considerably raised since that time.

The certainty, 2nd and 3rd of Queen Anne, was six pounds a year. In the year 1775 another £200 was granted by the governors of the bounty. The present annual revenue is £166.

Among the old houses worthy of notice in this township, are

MAGSON-HOUSE,

Which probably took its name from some ancient owner of it. It has the old mark for Jesus on two parts of it, viz. IJCC.

At the North-East corner of it is an uncommon hollow in the wall, which was discovered some time ago, when a repair was made. The workmen could see that the bottom of it, which was about equal with the foundation of the house, was flagged, but did not venture down to make farther discoveries. The house stands on the side of an hill.

DEAN-HOUSE,

Where lived a family of the name of Dean; one of which, called Richard, is said to have killed, in a duel, one Brooksbank of Bank-house in Warley.

THE HOLLINS.

Is a handsome mansion, the seat of Colonel Dearden; from its elevated situation, it commands an extensive view of the surrounding country.

There are also several other handsome family residences within the township.

TOWNSHIP OF MIDGLEY.

In Domesday Book written Miclei, was another member of this parish therein described as one of the berewics of the manor of Wakefield, and was in all probability so called as being the Micel, or large ley or pasture. It lies on the west of the brook that divides it from Warley and from thence extends to another small brook that separates it from Wadsworth, having the Calder on the south, and Haworth on ·the North. It contains an area of 2110 superficial statute acres.

Midgley was also granted from the Conqueror to the earl of Warren, for we find John de Warren, earl of Surry, had free warren here by charter, 37 Hen. III. and the same earl was found to be chief lord thereof by Kirkby's inquest. 24 Edw. I. As the title of the earl of Warren will be found under " The manor" it will be unnecessary here to recapitulate it.

John Mews, alias Melsa, had free warren granted him in all his demesne lands in Midgley, 25 Edw. I. John Melsa died seized of this manor, 26 Edw. III. John de Melsa gave to John, son of Thomas de Den, of Midgley, all the land and meadow, &c. which John, the son of Thomas, held by charter in Myggeley, from Lyddingdenhead, &c. 30 Edw. III. Godfrey Mews, alias Melsa, died seised of divers lands in Midgley, which he held of Adam Everingham, of Laxton, by the eighth part of a knight's fee. After this, but whether by purchase or marriage is uncertain, it came to the family of Sotehill; for there is (says Watson) the copy of a deed from Gerard de Sotehill, dominus de Midgleye, dated at Miegleye, 3 Oct. 1392, 16 Ric. II. By an inquisition of wastes within Wakefield, 19 Edw. IV. Gerard Soothill, Esq. was found to hold the manor of Midgley, by soccage, &c. and to render by the year 2s.

Soon after this it seems to be alienated; for Gilbert Lacy, esq. and
Joan his wife, enfeoffed Richard Symmes, vicar of Halifax, and
others in this manor, by deed, dated at Southowram, 12th July,
21 Edw. IV. but for what particular purpose does not appear, excepting that it was done with intent to have it conveyed to some
one of his own family; for John Lacy of Brearley, Esq. was found
in the year 1577, by inquisition at Wakefield, to be lord of the
manor.   Soon after this it came to the Farrers, by the intermarriage
(32 Eliz.) of Henry Farrer of Ewood, with Mary, daughter of the
above John Lacy, and in this family it long continued.   The present
lady of the manor is Mrs. Campbell, formerly Miss Charlotte Wentworth, who lately intermarried with William Archibald Campbell, Esq.

The village of Luddenden partly lies within this township. The
derivation of this word appears to be somewhat doubtful. Dr.
Johnson, in his MSS. collections of Yorkshire, says—"according
to tradition it takes its name from a dane named Lordan who inhabited there, and gave it the name Lordan-den, now by corruption
Luddenden." This derivation is disputed by Mr. Watson, who
says—"it shews how inattentive the doctor was to the true grounds
of etymological learning, Lordan was not the particular name of
any dane, but a general one;" and adds, "Luddenden is derived
from the Anglo-Saxon Loð, Luð, or Lyð, which signified water;
and ðene, a valley: the last syllable appears to be redundant, unless
the stream which waters this valley was called the Loððen." But
it would seem that even Mr. Watson is not altogether right in his
conjecture, for Dr. Whitaker says—"It appears evidently to be
derived from the Saxon pluð loud, and ðene a valley, from the loud
roar of the stream which runs along it."

ST. MARY'S, LUDDENDEN.

The first licence for the celebration of masses and other divine
offices within this chapel, is to be found in the register of archbishop
Rotheram, dated A. D. 1496, in which the inhabitants of Midgley,
Sowerby and Warley are stated to have already erected at their own
expence, a chapel in the vale of Luddenden; assigning as a reason
that "frequenter cum ad suam ecclesiam parochialem de Halifax
diebus festivalibus advenerint, infra eandem ecclesiam suam parochialem, quam vis tempus fuerit pluviosum, vel aliis procellarum
turbinibus intemperatum pro multitudine populi et parochianorum

hiis diebus augmentatis intrare vix valeant." The great increase of population is here distinctly referred to. What might be the size or structure of the first chapel does not appear, but it was never consecrated nor had rights of sepulture. It appears however that archbishop Cranmer, by virtue of his legatine power, gave licence for its consecration to archbishop Lee, who died before it was performed. Yet divine service, Catholic and Protestant, continued to be performed in this chapel till the year 1624; when Archbishop Toby Mathews granted a commission to consecrate the chapel of Luddenden, to John (Bridgman,) bishop of Chester, *or* John, bishop of Sodor and Man; and *also* to Charles Greenwood, clerk, rector of Thornhill; Hugh Ramsden, B. D. rector of Methley; and Nathaniel Walsh, A. M.; accompanied by this singular clause—"quatenus dictam capellam cum caemeterio de Midgley prædicto, retroactis temporibus beate Marie virgini dedicatam ("or called by the name of,") consecretis et sanctificetis, *seu usus* vestrum consecret et sanctificet." From the first clause directed to either bishop disjunctively, with the conjunctive *necnon* applied to the priests, it was evidently intended that a bishop should be of the number. But the clause "quorum semper unus sit Episcopus" was unaccountably omitted. and the subsequent "seu unus vestrum" was understood to empower a priest alone to perform the office; and, in consequence of this understanding, the church and church-yard were actually consecrated, and the return to the mandate attested by Greenwood and Walsh alone. "Such a delegation to priests, of an office properly episcopal, is not (observes Dr. WHITAKER) to be found in the annals of the church of England." The chapel thus consecrated contained in length 28 yards, and in breadth within walls 8 yards and a foot; the circumference of the church yard, 240 yards; the breadth east and west 63 yards, and north and south 58 yards.

The chapel was invested with the same privileges as Heptonstall and Elland, and possessed the right of baptism, the nuptial benediction, and of burial.

In 1662, an arbitration was agreed upon between Halifax and the inhabitants of Midgley and Warley, because the latter refused to pay their proportion towards the repairs of the mother church, alleging that they were freed from Halifax by a grant made to St. Mary's chapel in Midgley; and it seems as if it was given against

Midgley and Warley, because it is said in an old church-book at Halifax, that "they could not make it out." After this, however, in a faculty (formerly kept in Luddenden chapel) for erecting a loft there, dated in 1703, it was called a parochial chapel.

In the year 1816 the old chapel was pulled down in consequence of its delapidated condition, and the present chapel which is a neat gothic structure was erected on its scite, and has been since consecrated. Mr. Horner has preserved a very interesting drawing of the old fabric.

ENDOWMENT OF THE CHAPEL.

RICHARD DEYNE, of Deynehouse, son and heir of John Deyne, of Myggelay, gave to John Myggelay, son of Robert Myggelay, Richard Sladen, of Myggelay, the younger, Richard Patchett of the same, William Ferroure, son and heir apparent of Henry Ferroure, Robert Shawe, son of James Shawe, and Robert Thomas, of Myggelay aforesaid, one yearly rent of thirteen shillings and four-pence, issuing out of a messuage with lands and tenements, called Herrebothlegh, in Luddyngden, within Myggelay aforesaid, to the use of John Robynson, capellane in the chapel of St. Mary of Luddyngden aforesaid, and his successors in the same chapel, for the time being, for ever, and payable at the feasts of Pentecost and St. Martin in winter, by equal portions, or within forty days after each of the said feasts, with power of distress to the above trustees, and their heirs, if the said yearly rent is unpaid for forty days after it becomes due as aforesaid.

This extract was taken, by WATSON, from the original deed, in Latin, lent by the late curate of Luddenden. It was dated at Myggelay, March 6, 17 Hen, VIII. and is in the form of a charter.

It is said that Richard Deyne left the above, because he had killed in a duel one Brooksbank, of Bankhouse, in Warley.

JOHN CROSSLEY, of Kershawhouse in Midgley, gave (as appeared from a table in Luddenden chapel) two pounds two shillings yearly, to the curate of Luddenden, for preaching a sermon every first Wednesday after the sixth day of March. One account makes this only forty shillings.

Extract from the will of JOHN MIDGLEY, of Midgley.

" I give to the curate of the chapel of Luddenden, for the time being, and his survivors, curates there, for ever, one fulling-mill or paper-mill, with one holme or croft thereto belonging, to preach a sermon yearly and every year, for ever, upon every sixteenth day of February from and after my decease; and also one loft in the said chapel which was erected therein (and is now standing) by my deceased brother William Midgley, to and for the use and benefit of the said curate for ever."

In Luddenden chapel is kept a faculty obtained by the above William Midgley, for erecting the loft here mentioned, dated in 1703.

The money arising from this benefaction, is said, in a table in Luddenden chapel, to be two pounds ten shillings yearly; but it now makes three pounds yearly, besides the loft, which raises about ten shillings more.

The following augmentations have been granted by the governors of the bounty of queen Anne to this chapel: in 1732, £200 by lot, with which, and with other contributions made in the chapelry, a farm was bought in Midgley, called Newearthhead. In the years 1772 and 1787 two further sums were obtained by lot, also £200 in the year 1810. In 1811, £300 was granted, to meet a benefaction of £200 by the chapelwardens; and in 1813 another sum of £300 was granted, to meet a benefaction by the inhabitants; and in the year 1815 a further sum of £1000 was granted by lot. The annual value of the benefice is stated to be £132 in the last parliamentary report presented by command of His majesty. The Rev. R. Jarratt, M. A. is the present incumbent.

Among the places worthy of note in this township are

BREARLEY-HALL.

The ancient seat of the Lacies, probably, says Dr. WHITAKER, a base descent from the great house of that name. The Dr. also says, the house of the Lacies stood on the scite of a farm-house at the bottom of the hill, and near the fifth milestone from Halifax, but this is not confirmed by the opinion of the neighbourhood, the old house on the top of the hill being generally denominated Brearley Hall and has always gone by that name. It was the seat of the Soothills, till it came by marriage of Isabel, daughter and heiress of Gerhard Soothill, of Brearley, esq. to Gilbert, second son of John Lacy, of Cromwellbottom, esq. in whose right he was seised of Brearley and Midgley, &c. It has sometimes been written

Brierley, which gives an easy etymology of its name. WATSON has given the pedigree of Lacy of Brearley.

EWOOD, OR EAWOOD.

Situated near the banks of the Caldar, was so named from being a woody part, as it doubtless then was, adjoining to the water, called by the Anglo-Saxons Ea. The mansion is a large substantial gentleman's house, and was long the seat of the Farrers, whose pedigree will be found set forth in WATSON. They were for some time resident here, one of the family was justice of the peace during the time of the civil wars, and there is every reason to believe that many marriages were solemnized here during the Commonwealth.

KERSHAW-HOUSE,

Is a respectable family mansion, and erected by the Midgleys of Midgley, in the year 1650; they were at one time a family of some repute here, bearing arms. A pedigree of them may be met with in THORESBY's *Topography*, p. 21.

THE PAROCHIAL

CHAPELRY OF ELLAND.

This ecclesiastical division of the parish next claims our attention. It consists of the following townships, viz.

ELLAND-CUM-GREETLAND,	BASTRICK,
BARKISLAND,	RISHWORTH,
FIXBY,	SOYLAND,
NORLAND,	STAINLAND.

I have before stated that when this division took place there is nothing to shew; but there is every reason to believe that it has existed from time immemorial. Watson says, there have been several attempts to prove Elland and Heptonstall divisions to be distinct parishes of themselves, but he has adduced no proof in support of this hypothesis; the probability is that the division was made for the convenience of the inhabitants, for it appears that even townships were divided for greater ease:—Soyland, a part of Sowerby, was allotted to Elland: and Erringden, another part, was allotted to Heptonstall.

The family at Elland having founded the chapel there for the convenience of themselves and their dependants, it is not improbable that they might have prevailed on the rectors to make the bounds of the chapelry co-extensive with those of the founders' jurisdiction; or in other words that the chaplains at Elland and Heptonstall might be allowed to baptize, marry, and bury there, the rectors paying yearly to the ministers of the chapels the sum of £4 for their maintenance, and presenting to the same as often as any vacancy happened,

I shall reserve all that further relates to ecclesiastical matters until a subsequent part of the chapter, simply remarking that in a book of accounts kept at Elland, beginning March 12th, 1561, it is said, that the order for chusing churchwardens yearly within the parish or chapelry of Elland, by the gentlemen and chief parishioners is thus. The churchwarden in Elland two years, and Greetland one. Rishworth-cum-Norland year for year. Barkisland every year. Stainland three years, and Old Linley one. Rastrick two years, and Brighouse one. Soyland three years, and Fixby one. Soyland has the presenter every year.

TOWNSHIP OF ELLAND-CUM-GREETLAND.

Elland has its name from the Anglo-Saxon Ea-land, which signifies land on the side of a river, and this is undoubtedly the correct mode of spelling it, although custom may have determined otherwise. It is thus mentioned in Domesday-book:—"In Elant habuit Gamel tres carucatas terræ et dimidium ad geldam ubi caruca potest esse. Ilbertus habet nunc, et wast. est. T. R. E. valuit xx solidos silva pastura dimidium leugæ longitudine, et quatuor quarentenæ latitudine, et quatuor acræ prati :" which is thus translated—"In Elland Gamel had three carucates of land and a half to be taxed, where there may be two ploughs. Ilbert now has it, and it is waste. Value in king Edward's time, twenty shillings. Wood pasture half a mile long and four quarentens broad, and four acres of meadow." The survey of lands belonging to this Norman, Ilbert de Lacy, occupies not less than seven pages of Domesday, and the family, afterwards earls of Lincoln, are said to have possessed 25 towns in the wapentake of Morley, of which this was one, and they held it of the king, in capite. It is within the honor of Pontefract. How the manor passed from the Lacies to the family of Elland does not appear, but that one Leisingus de Ealand had large possessions here about the time of Henry II. is certain from the fact of their holding courts for the better government of the tenants, and to prevent damage to the estate. On this account it is probable that the family became lords of the manor here. This is confirmed by the following words of an inquisition taken at Wakefield, in 1577.—

"Thomas de Thorneton quondam tenuit in Eland quintam partem unius feodi militis in qua villa clam. habere manerium cum cur. let. ratione tenuræ prædictæ." 32 Edw. I. the king granted, by charter, to Hugh de Ealand free warren in all his demesne lands in Ealand, &c. In Dodsworth's MSS. it is said Sir John Eland of Eland was a man of great account and high steward to the earl Warren, of the manor of Wakefield and other lands in the north parts. He was lord of Eland and other places.

10 Edward II. the king granted to John de Ealand a free market at his manor of Ealand. The male descendants of the Ealands having been cut off in the deadly feud that occurred about that time, (an account of which will be found hereafter,) the manor became vested in Sir John Savile on his marriage with Isabel the daughter and heiress of Ealand; for it appears in a fine levied 46 Edw. III. that John Savile, of Ealand, knt. and Isabel, his wife, were plaintiffs and John de Brumpton, parson of the church of Badsworth, deforc. of the manor of Ealand, &c. and in this family of Savile it still continues. In a MS. copy of an old survey of the knight's fees within Agbrigg and Morley, it is said, "Isabella nuper ux. Joh'is Savile Mil. ten. maner. de Elande jura hereditario, & reddit per aa. ad term. S. Martini 6s. 4d. Eadem tenet ter. & ten. nuper Tho. de Thorneton, & reddit per ann. &c. 6s. 4d."

"In the first vol. of Hopkinson's MSS. fol. 161, Edward Savile, esq. son and heir of sir Henry, knt. of the bath, is said to have held the manors of Ealand, Southowram, Greetland, and several others, of the lord Monteagle, by unknown service, 1 Eliz. And at fol. 156 of the same MS., Henry Savile, knight of the bath, is said to have held the same manors (1 Eliz.) of the queen, as of the honor of Pontefract, by military service. It seems, therefore, as if queen Elizabeth had, soon after her accession to the crown, made some kind of a grant of these manors to the family of Stanley, but I know of no such thing. Mr. Hopkinson, at p. 110, has made a mistake when he tells us, that the manor of Elland was held of the king, 20 Hen. VII. as of his manor of Wakefield, by military service."

WATSON also refers to the copy of an instrument in his possession (date omitted) wherein Robert Kaye, of Woodsome, and William Ramsden, of Langley, two justices of the peace, certify, "that whereas the kings of England had granted under the great seal, to the duke of Lancaster, that their men, tenants, servants, and all others dwelling within the liberties of the duchy of Lancaster, should be free from payment of any toll, pawnage, passage, lastage, tollage, carriage, and pickage, throughout England, the town of Elland, in the county of York, was parcel of the king's honor of Pontefract, parcel of his duchy of Lancaster, and that the inhabitants thereof ought to be free from toll accordingly.

Independently of the delightful situation of Elland, characterized by Dr. WHITAKER as the warmest and most beautiful in the Parish, the name is associated with one of those lawless outrages against the peace and order of society, which too frequently disgraced the history of our feudal times.

Situated on the southern bank of the Calder, a little beneath the union of two valleys whose sides are hung with native oak; and looking downwards a fine expanded reach of the river, the more improved husbandry around it indicates the beginning of a clearer atmosphere, and a warmer climate than those of the hills; "in fact, (says the learned Dr.) had not superstition triumphed over pleasure and convenience together, nature and common sense would have pointed it out as the proper scite for the capital of the parish."

That Elland at an early period was a place of some trade, or rather that it was the principal place of trade within this extensive parish, and maintained a rivalry with Halifax, may be inferred from the fact that it was the only town within this district that had the privilege of holding a market by charter, and that it once possessed a cloth hall. The charter was dated 10 Edw. II. when that king, at the request of John, earl of Warren, granted to John (afterward Sir John) Eland a free market on Tuesday at his manor of Eland, and two fairs there by six days, viz. one next day before the eve, on the day of the eve, and on the day of St. Peter in bonds. There is still a market-place and cross remaining, and toll is taken by the lord's steward when any thing is offered to sale in the streets; the fairs are also kept up, but no markets of any consequence have been held there for many years.

There is a tradition that the market was discontinued at the time of the plague, but after diligent enquiry I do not find that it is supported by any written authority. I think the more probable conjecture is, that as the town of Halifax not only increased in wealth and population, but became the resort of clothiers and ma-

F F

nufacturers at stated periods, who found its locality, in connection
with Leeds, Bradford, and other manufacturing places, so much
more convenient than Elland for the purposes of trade; the market
grew into disuse, its cloth hall fell into decay, the spirit of rivalry
which formerly existed between the two places ceased, and Halifax
gained that ascendancy which she continues to maintain at the
present day.

THE CHAPEL.

The parochial chapel, which is dedicated to St. Mary, is reputed
to be the oldest place of worship in the parish, with the exception
of the mother church.   None can come in competition with it except
Heptonstall, but the residence from a very early period of a great
family here, (the Ellands,) and none at Heptonstall, together with
the obscure and remote situation of the latter place, turns the scale
on the side of Elland.

In the endowment deed, however, of the vicarage of Halifax,
(see Appendix A) is recited a former confirmation by Pope Alexander
IV, of that benefice, *cum suis capellis*.   This Pope died about the year
1260, and this is the earliest evidence which appears on the subject.

The chapel has a nave, chancel, and aisle, with a tower at the
West end containing eight musical bells.   The oldest parts of the
present edifice, (notwithstanding some unskilful pretensions to an
higher antiquity,) are of much later date; "I should conjecture,"
says WHITAKER, "not earlier than the reign of Henry VII; the
columns are angular and rather slender, and the general proportions
are of that time. The fine East window which I remember much more
perfect than at present, appears to be of the same hand with that of
the Saville chapel at Thornhill.   Having been rebuilt after the first
lords, the Ellands, merged in another name, no chantry or family
burying place appears to have been retained at that time." My
limits will not allow me to particularize the armorial bearings, monuments and monumental inscriptions which are to be found within
this venerable fabric, I must content myself by simply mentioning
them. The epitaphs are entirely devoid of interest.

In the East window, are the arms of John of Gaunt, duke of Lancaster, who died in 1399, and had Elland as part of his honor of
Pontefract. The same are repeated with some difference in the supporters, crown and label. In the same window were the arms of

France and England within a garter, with Honi soit, &c. but no crown or supporters. There were also some coats of private families painted in a window in this quire, which Dr. Johnson, who surveyed the place, July 23, 1669, could not well make out, they were so defaced. Mr. WATSON has given a short account of them, and has also preserved the following inscription, taken from a window in the choir :—"Pray for the gud prosperity, mercy...... of JOHN SAVYLE, of Holly-ngezeth, Esquire, and ELIZABET his wyffe, dowzter of Robert Hopton, and all their c..lder, qwyche causyt thys wyndow to be mayde."

In a part belonging to Savile and Thornhill, a man kneeling at prayer, and in armor, his upper garment alternately white and red, behind him, in the same posture, his wife, her garment the same, only in two places thereof two bars gemells, argent ; behind her, another woman, in the same posture and dress. Under these figures in old characters :—"Orate pro prosperitate WILLIELMI THORNHILL, et ELIZABET. uxoris ejus, et JOHANNES THORNHILL, filii et heredis eorundem, et Jh̄nǣ uxoris suæ, et prosperitate NICHI.... et AGNETIS consortis suæ, filiorum et filiarum eorundem, ac omnium Benefactorum suorum." This from Dr. Johnson's MS. There were also the following inscriptions in the North quire :—"Pray for the gude prosperity, mercy, and grace of sir JOHN SAVILE, Knt. daughter and one of the heirs.... childere, and for the saul of his abovesaid wief, daughter of sir William Vernon, the which sir John causyd this window to be made the yere...." In the North window ;—"Pray ye for the souls of GEORGE SAYVELL, son of John Sayvell, Esq. and of MARGARET, his wife, daughter of Thomas Scargill, Esq. which .... caused this window to be made."

At the beginning of Elland Register (the first date of which is April 1, 1559) is this entry :—"The window over the quier or chancell dore was made in the yere of our Lord 1310, as it was written in the same window where the glass was broken, An. Dom. 1618." "This is impossible ; (says Dr. WHITAKER,) but I believe the date to have been 1510, which will agree with all the appearances of the architecture, as well as the chronology of the families who are recorded."

The chancel at Elland is called St. Mary's quire ; the North quire, St. Nicholas's quire ; and that on the South, St. John's quire.

The vicar of Halifax has from time immemorial presented to this chapel, notwithstanding attempts have been made to prove Elland a distinct parish; for which there might have been some pretence had the chapel there been erected before the mother church, which has also been contended for. There can be no doubt but that what is now called the parochial chapelry of Elland, was looked upon as part of the parish of Halifax, before any place of religious worship was erected at Elland, otherwise it had been a parish of itself to all intents and purposes, and totally unconnected with Halifax.

The minister receives a yearly stipend of four pounds from the vicar of Halifax, which has been paid from time immemorial; and which, at the time it was originally given, was a sufficient maintenance for a clergyman in that station. Heptonstall receives the same pension.

The chapelry supports its own chapel, and is entirely independant of the mother church in all that relates to the church-rate: it possesses the rights of baptism, marriage, and sepulture. The incumbent also appropriates the surplice fees to his own use, not of right but of indulgence, which was originally granted A. D. 1663, as appears from the register. A similar indulgence was granted to Heptonstall. These two chapelries also contended for the mortuaries within their respective divisions, but the right to these was clearly with the vicar prior to their extinguishment.

This chapel was in 1736 returned by the governors of Queen Anne's bounty, to have had, 3rd of Anne, a clear yearly value of £26 10s. In the year 1724, the governors granted a bounty of £200, to meet a benefaction of £200 by Mr. Lancaster and others, with which sum a farm was subsequently purchased by the then curate, called Blean Farm, in the parish of Askarth, near Askrig, containing about thirty days work of land, with liberty of thirteen cattle gates in four different pastures, and a common right for an hundred sheep. In the year 1824 the governors granted a further augmentation of £400 by lot. WATSON mentions two sums of 20s. each payable yearly to the curates of Elland; one sum payable out of Marshall hall, the other out of a close in Stainland. The yearly revenue of the curacy, as stated in the report before alluded to, is £147, there is also a glebe house attached. The Rev. C. Atkinson is the present Incumbent.

There was formerly a Chantry at Elland, which by inquisition taken at Pontefract, 19 Richard II. appears to have been founded for one chaplain, presentable by sir John Savill, knt. and Isabel his wife, and their heirs, within fifteen days from the time of any vacation, for the said chaplain to celebrate therein, at the altar of St. John Baptist, for the good estate of John duke of Acquitain and Lancaster, of John Sayvill, knt. and Isabel his wife, and the children of the said John and Isabel, and for the souls of the said duke, and said John and Isabel, and the souls of their children after death; and for the souls of Henry late earl of Lancaster, John Sayvill, and Margery his wife, parents of said John Sayvill, knt. also of Thomas de Eland, and Joan his wife, parents of the said Isabel, of John Rylay, Thomas Cross, Chaplain, and Richard Schepard, of Eland, and the friends and benefactors of said John Sayvill, knt. and Isabel, and for the souls of all the faithful deceased.

The deed by which the above was founded, may be seen in Mr. Watson's history, its length precludes its insertion here: it was confirmed by archbishop Scroope.

In the certificate of the archbishop of York and others concerning chantries, &c. 2 Edw. VI. this chantry is thus described;—
"The Chuntrie in the Chapell of Heland, in the Poch of Hallifaxe. John Sysson, incumbent of the foundacon of John Savyle, Knt. to the entent to pray for the sowle of the Founder, and all Xpen sowles, and to do dyvyne service in the said chapell, and to mynystre Sacrements in the same, havynge thereunto belonginge 1800 people.

"The same is in the Poch abovesaid, distunte from the Poch Church two myles. The necitie is to have divyne service and sacrements and sacrementalls done and mynystred ther. Ther is no land alienate or sold aithence the 4th day of Februarye, Anno R. R. Hen. 8vi. 28o.

"Goods, ornaments and plate perteynynge to the same, as apperyth by the inventorye, viz. Goodes valued at 13s. 8d. Plate at 52s. First, the Mancon-house of the said Incumbent, rented at 2s. 6d. and one annuall rente, goynge furth of the lands of Sir Henrie Savell, Knt. lienge in Wyke, of 106s. 8d. Sum of the said Chuntrie 109s. 2d. wherof payable to the King's Maᵗⁱᵉ. for the tenths 10s. 11d. And so remanyth £4 18s. 3d." In the list of pensions and annuities paid in 1553, to incumbents of chantries, published in WILLIS's *History of Abbies*, vol. ii. p. 291, the pension to John Scisson, at Elland, is only called £5; but, from other authorities, I judge this to be a mistake.

From what has been said it is evident, that Elland chapel was not erected purely as a chantry chapel, since it was more than a century after its being first built that we hear of a chantry priest there. The argument, therefore, made use of to exclude the vicar of Halifax from presenting to this chapel, because it has been a chantry chapel, and privately endowed, is ill founded, both because it was set up merely as a chapel of ease to Halifax; and supposing it had been otherwise, yet we find, that the priory of Lewis first granted it to the vicar of Halifax, and afterwards the king himself did the same, when, after the dissolution, he was impowered by statute to present to this living.

There was a light kept up here in former times, as I find by deed, but when founded does not appear. The original deed was at Okes, in Rishworth, importing that Walter de Frith granted to John his son a moyety of his land in Arnaldelyes, and a moyety of the land which he bought of Tho. de Thornton, lying within Boynley (Bottomley) and Barkeslond, and a moyety of the land which he bought of Hugh, son of Julian, and others, paying yearly to Hugh de Eland a farthing and half farthing (quadrant et dim. quadrant.) to Thos. Thornton two pence of silver and one halfpenny, to John de Barkislond one arrow feathered with a goose feather; and also paying yearly to the said Walter three-pence and one halfpenny of silver at Martinmass, and after the death of the said Walter the same to go to the light of the Blessed Virgin Mary of the church of Eland, (debent reverti ad Lumen beate Marie Virginis ecclesie de Eland.) There is no date to this deed, but amongst the witnesses are Hugh de Eland, Hen. de Risseworth, and Tho. de Coppeley, all whom were contemporary about the year 1287.

The testamentary burials at Elland, it appears from Torr's MS. are of an earlier date than at Halifax; the first is A. D. 1399, John Sayvill, of Eland, Chevalier.

ELLAND HALL,

Is within the township, but on the North side of the Calder; in many maps it is put down on the South side of that river through mistake. It was, for several generations, the seat of the ancient and honorable family of the Elands; who, there is every reason to believe, lived here in great splendor until the deadly feud hereinafter mentioned, when it became vested by marriage in the Savile family. A barn belonging to the house was pulled down in Mr. Watson's time, supposed to have been a chapel from the form of the window. In one of the lodging-rooms several scripture sentences had been written on the pannels of the wainscot, but were then almost defaced. Some very ancient furniture remained in the house, which is now inhabited by tenants; in particular, there were two massy bedsteads with a great deal of carved and inlaid work about them, on one of which was the date 1566. The building was of timber, as was the custom some hundred years ago, and between two of the walls was a vacancy of a considerable size, and perhaps deeper than the foundation of the edifice, which no doubt had its use in troublesome times. "It is not likely (says Dr. Whitaker) that the Savilles ever wholly deserted Elland hall, on account of the large estates in the neighbourhood. It had, like every other mansion of the same rank in ancient times, a park; and a very few aged oaks may perhaps have been contemporary with the Ellands, and with the deadly affray by which the name became extinct."

The best account, says Watson, I can give of this once famous family is this :—"Leisingus de Eland, as by deed sans date, and who gave name to Lasing-croft in Yorkshire, married, and had Henry de Eland, who married the daughter and coheir of Whitworth of Whitworth. By her he had sir Hugh de Eland, as by deed sans date. He married and had sir John de Eland, who was living 30 Hen. III. and also 3 Edw. I. for in this latter year a riot was presented at Brighouse Turne, upon John Eland and John Quermby, about a distress which Eland had taken from Quermby, for aid to make his son a knight, for lands in Stainland. This sir John married, and had sir Hugh de Eland, who married Joan, daughter and coheir of sir Richard Tankersley, knt. This sir Hugh is said to have died 3 Edw. II. He was witness to a deed of John earl Warren, dated at Koningsburgh, 5 Oct. 1 Edw. II. 1307, wherein the earl confirmed to the free burgesses of Wakefield and their heirs, their privileges, viz. to each a toft of an acre in free burgage, for six-pence rent per ann. with liberty of free trade in all his lands in

Yorkshire, and wood to burn; for which charter they gave to earl Hamelin, his countess, and son, seven pounds; and amongst the witnesses was Hugh de Elond, the grandfather of this sir Hugh. Besides this confirmation, the said earl John, by the deed above-named, granted to the said burgesses to be toll free in all his lands for all wares and merchandize of their own manufacture, and that they should not be obliged to answer at any court but his, called Burman-court, in Wakefield, unless for trespasses against himself; and that whatsoever goods should be bought of any burgess for him or his use, at certain rates, should be paid for within forty days, and pawnage for every hog 2d. and pig 1d. and to have commonage for all cattle but goats, in all woods, moors, &c. except New and Old Park, and the great meadow, (only not in fawning time,) and that they might inclose and hedge their corn ground, and fright away his deer from thence without horn. Sir Hugh had by Joan his wife, 1. sir Thomas de Eland. 2. Richard, 3. Margaret, and 4. Wymark. Of these, Margaret married to her first husband, John Lacy, to whom, and to his heirs by the said Margaret, her father gave, by deed in 1293, all his land in South Owram, and all his tenants there and their services, except his manor of Eland, and the service of his tenants in Eckisley, and the pasture in the Stony-bancke, for a rent of 26s. yearly, and suit to his mill. They had issue. The said Margaret married, to her second husband, William the constable of Nottingham castle, when earl Mortimer was there taken prisoner. In a book, intitled "The Cronicles of Englonde, with the fruyte of tymes, imprynted at London by Wynkyn de Worde, in 1528," folio 114 and 115, is an account how this William de Eland betrayed earl Mortimer: an extract will be found in Watson, p. 167.

The existence of the other daughter is proved from a deed in the chartulary of Whalley Abbey, folio 234, wherein Robert de Mitton grants to Gilbert de Notton, for his homage and service, and 20s. of silver, two bovats of land in Wordelword, and two bovats in Heleye, which Hugh de Elond, father of Richard de Elond, gave with Wymark his daughter, in free marriage to Jordan de Mitton, grandfather to the said Robert, paying yearly 4s. of silver at the feast of St. Oswald, of which 2s. was to be yearly paid at Martin-mas to Hugh de Elond. From hence also it appears that Richard de Eland, by the manner of his being mentioned here, was the eldest son of sir Hugh, but dying perhaps in his minority without issue in the life time of his father, the said sir Hugh was succeeded in title and estate by his son, sir Thomas de Eland, who married and had sir John de Eland, knight of the shire for Yorkshire, with sir William Grammary, 14 Edw. III.; and sheriff of Yorkshire, 15 Edw. III. in which year it is said, that he marched privately in the night, at the head of a body of his tenants, and put to death three neighboring gentlemen in their own houses, an account of which will be given below. This sir John married three wives, 1. Alice, daughter of sir Robert Lathom. 2ndly. Ann, daughter of . . . . . . Rygate, s. p. 3dly. Olive. . . . . . By Alice, his first wife, he had 1. Sir John de Eland, who had a son, name unknown, and Isabel. 2. Thomas de Eland, esq. 3. Henry. 4. Margery. 5. Isabel. and 6. Dionysia. In the account of the feodary of the honour of Pomfret, of the lands and tenements in Eland in the hands of the lord, by the minority of the heir of Thomas de Eland, is 61. 18s. 2d. for the term of Whitsuntide, 1350. After the death of sir John de Eland, and his son and heir, sir John Savile, of Tankersley, purchased in 1350 the wardship of Isabel Eland, daughter of the said sir John, from the lord of the honour of Pontefract, for £200. See Comput. seneschall. honoris de Pomfrete, p. 17. After this purchase he married her, and in her right became possessed of the estates belonging to that family.

There are two narratives of the hereditary feud, before alluded to, one in prose and the other in verse. Both have been printed, and no less distinguished antiquaries than WATSON our own historian, BEAUMONT of Whitley, and DR. WHITAKER, have written commentaries upon it. WRIGHT would not print it in his history of Halifax, because he disbelieved it, stating as his reason that the whole seemed to have been done in defiance of law; but we are informed that this mode of executing private revenge was not infrequent among the Norman barons and their descendants. In BRADY's *History of the reign of king Stephen*, p. 281, it is there said—" if any earl or great man found himself aggrieved by another, they frequently got together all their men-at-arms or knights that held of them, their other tenants and poor dependants, and as much assistance from their friends and confederates as they could, and

burnt one another's castles and houses, &c." and an instance of it
is mentioned in the history of "the Manor," (p. 53) where the king
interfered : and it will be shewn in the sequel that this very feud,
as it is called, arose out of a quarrel between the earl of Lancaster
and the earl of Warren, regarding Alice de Laci, the heiress of
Pontefract.

The following metrical record of the event was transcribed by
Mr. Hopkinson about the year 1650, and has nothing but internal
evidence to support the truth of the story which it relates.

HISTORY OF SIR JOHN ELAND, OF ELAND, AND HIS ANTAGONISTS.

1 NO worldly wight can here attain   always to have their will;
But now in grief, sometimes in pain,   their course they must fulfil

2 For when men live in worldly wealth,   full few can have that grace,
Long in the same to keep themselves,   contented with their place.

3 The Squire must needs become a Knight,   the Knight a Lord would be,
Thus shall you see no worldly wight,   content with his degree.

4 For pride it is that pricks the heart,   and moves men to mischief,
All kind of pity set apart,   withouten grudge or grief.

5 Where pride doth reign within the heart,   and wickedness in will,
The fear of God quite set apart,   their fruits must needs be ill

6 Some cannot suffer for to see,   and know their neighbours thrive,
Like to themselves in good degree,   but rather seek their lives.

7 And some must be possess'd alone,   and such would have no peer,
Like to themselves they would have none   dwell nigh them any where.

8 With such like faults was foul infect,   one sir John Eland, knight;
His doings make it much suspect   therein he took delight.

9 Some time there dwelt at Crossland hall,   a kind and courteous knight,
It was well known that he withal   sir Robert Beaumont hight.

10 At Eland sir John Eland dwelt   within the manor hall,
The town his own, the parish held   most part upon him all.

11 The market-town was Eland then,   the patent hath been seen,
Under king Edward's seal certain,   the first Edward I ween.

12 But now I blush to sing for dread,   knowing mine own country
So basely stor'd with Cain his seed   there springing plenteously.

13 Alack, such store of witty men   as now are in these days,
Were both unborn, and gotten then,   to stay such wicked ways.

14 Some say that Eland sheriff was   by Beaumont disobey'd,
Which might him make for that trespass   with him the worse appaid.

15 He rais'd the country round about,   his friends, and tenants all,
And for this purpose picked out   stout, sturdy men and tall.

16 To Quarmby hall they came by night,   and there the lord they slew,
At that time Hugh of Quarmby hight,   before the country knew.

17 To Lockwood then the self same night,   they came and there they slew
Lockwood of Lockwood, that wiley wight,   that stirr'd the strife anew.

18 When they had slain thus suddenly   sir Robert Beaumont's aid,
To Crossland they came craftily,   of nought they were afraid.

19 The hall was water'd well about,   no wight might enter in;
Till that the bridge was well laid out,   they durst not venture in.

20 Before the house they could invade,   in ambush they did lodge;
And watch'd a wench with wiley trade,   till she let down the bridge.

21 A siege they set, assault they made   heinously to the hall;
The knight's chamber they did invade,   and took the knight withal.

22 And this is for most certainty   that slain before he was,
    He fought against them manfully,   unarmed as he was.

23 His servants rose, and still withstood, and struck with might and main;
    In his defence they shed their blood,   but all this was in vain.

24 The lady cry'd, and shriek'd withal,   when as from her they led
    Her dearest knight into the hall,   and there cut off his head.

25 But all in vain, the more pity,   for pity had no place,
    But craft, mischief, and cruelty,   these men did most embrace.

26 They had a guide that guided them,   which in their hearts did dwell,
    The which to this that moved them,   the very Devil in Hell.

27 See here in what uncertainty   this wretched world is led;
    At night in his prosperity,   at morning slain, and dead.

28 I wis a woful house there was,   the lord lay slain, and dead,
    Their foes then eat before their face   their meat, ale, wine, and bread.

29 Two boys sir Robert Beaumont had   there left alive unslain;
    Sir John of Eland he them bade   to eat with him certain.

30 The one did eat with him truly,   the younger it was, I think;
    Adam, the elder, sturdily,   would neither eat nor drink.

31 See how this boy, said Eland, see   his father's death can take;
    If any be, it will be he,   that will revengement make.

32 But if that he wax wild anon,   I shall him soon foresee;
    And cut them off by one and one,   as time shall then serve me.

33 *The first Fray here now have you heard,* *the second doth ensue ;*
    And how much mischief afterward   *upon these murders grew.*

34 *And how the mischief he contriv'd*   *his wicked heart within,*
    Light on himself shall be describ'd,   *mark now—for I begin.*

35 The same morning two messengers   were sent to Lancashire,
    To Mr. Towneley and Brereton,   their helps for to require.

36 Unto the mount beneath Marsden,   now were they come with speed,
    But hearing that their friend was slain, they turn'd again indeed.

37 When Eland with his wilful ire   thus Beaumont's blood had shed,
    Into the coasts of Lancashire,   the lady Beaumont fled.

38 With her she took her children all,   at Brereton to remain;
    Some time also at *Townley* hall   they sojourned certain.

39 *Brereton* and *Townley*, friends they were to her, and of her blood;
    And presently it did appear   they sought to do her good.

40 They kept the boys till they increas'd in person and in age,
    Their father's death to have redrest   still kindled their courage.

41 Lacy and Lockwood were with them   brought up at Brereton green,
    And Quarmby, kinsman unto them,   at home durst not be seen.

42 The feats of fence they practiced,   to weild their weapons well,
    Till fifteen years were finished,   and then it so befel.

43 Lockwood, the eldest of them all,   said, Friends, I think it good,
    We went into our country all,   to venge our father's blood.

44 If Eland have this for well done,   he will slay mo indeed,
    Best were it then we slew him soon,   and cut off Cain his seed.

45 I saw my father Lockwood slain,   and Quarmby in the night,
    And last of all they slew certain   sir Robert Beaumont, knight.

46 O Lord, this was a cruel deed !   who could their hands refrain;
    For to pluck out such wicked weed,   tho' it were to their pain !

47 To this the rest then all agreed.   devising day by day,
    Of this their purpose how to speed,   what was the readiest way.

48 Two men that time from Quarmby came,   Dawson and Haigh, indeed,
    Who then consulted of the same   of this how to proceed.

49 These countrymen, of course only,   said Eland kept alway
    The Turn at Brighouse certainly   and you shall know the day.

50 *To Cromwelbottom* you must come,   in the wood there to wait;
    So you may have them all and some,   and take them in a strait.

51 The day was set, the *Turn* was kept   at Brighouse by sir John;
    Full little wist he was beset,   then at his coming home.

52 Dawson and Haigh had play'd their parts, and brought from Brereton green,
Young gentlemen with hardy hearts, as well were known and seen.
53 Adam of Beaumont there was laid, and Lacy with him also,
And Lockwood, who was nought afraid to fight against his foe.
54 In Cromwelbottom woods they lay a number with them mo,
Armed they were in good array, a spy they had also.
55 To spy the time when Eland came, from Brighouse turn that day,
Who play'd his part, and shew'd the same to them there as they lay.
56 Beneath Brookfoot a hill there is to Brighouse in the way, .
Forth came they to the top of this, there prying for their prey.
57 From the lane end then Eland came, and spied these gentlemen,
Sore wonder'd he, who they could be, and val'd his bonnet then.
58 Thy court'sy 'vails thee not, sir knight, thou slew my father dear,
Some time sir Robert Beaumont, hight, and slain thou shalt be here.
59 Said Adam Beaumont, with the rest thou hast our fathers slain,
Whose deaths we mind shall be redrest of thee, and thine certain.
60 To strike at him still did they strive, but Eland still withstood,
With might and main, to save his life, but still they shed his blood.
61 They cut him from his company, belike at the Lane end;
And there they slew him certainly, and thus he made his end.
62 Mark here the end of cruelty, such fine hath falshood lo!
Such end forsooth himself had he, as he brought others to.
63 But Beaumont yet was much to blame, tho' here he play'd the man,
The part he play'd not in the same of a right christian.
64 A pure conscience could never find an heart to do this deed,
Tho' he this day should be assign'd his own heart's blood to bleed.
65 But kind, in these young gentlemen, crept where it could not go,
And in such sort enforced them their fathers bane to slo.
66 *The second Fray now here you have,* *the third now shall you hear;*
Of your kindness no more I crave, *but only to give ear.*
67 When sir John Eland thus was slain indeed the story tells,
Both Beaumont and his fellows then fled into Furness fells.
68 O cruel Mars, why wert thou nought contented yet with this;
To shed more blood, but still thou sought, for such thy nature is.
69 Their young conscience corrupt by thee, indeed could never stay,
Till into extreme misery they ran the readiest way.
70 For Cain his seed on every side, with wicked hearts disgrac'd;
Which to shew mercy hath denied, must needs be now displac'd.
71 In Furness fells long time they were boasting of their misdeed,
In more mischief contriving there, how yet they might proceed.
72 They had their spies in this country nigh Eland, who then dwell'd,
Where sir John Eland liv'd truly, and there his household held.
73 Mo gentlemen then were not there, in Eland parish dwell'd,
Save Savile half part of the year his house at Rnahworth held.
74 He kept himself from such debate removing thence withal.
Twice in the year by Savile gate unto the Bothom hall.
75 Adam of Beaumont then truly, Lacy and Lockwood eke,
And Quarmby came to their country, their purpose for to seek.
76 To Cromwelbottom wood* they came, there kept them secretly,
By fond deceit there did they frame, their crafty cruelty.
77 This is the end in sooth to say, . on Palm Sun. e'en at night,
To Eland miln they took their way about the mirke midnight.
78 Into the milne house there they brake, and kept them secretly,
By subtilty thus did they seek, the young knight for to slay.
79 The morning came, the miller sent his wife for corn in haste,
These gentlemen in hands her hent, and bound her hard and fast.
80 The miller sware she should repent she tarried there so long,
A good cudgel in hand he hent to chastise her with wrong.

* Some read "hall".

81 With haste into the miln came he and meant with her to strive,
But they bound him immediately, and laid him by his wife.

82 The young knight dreamt the self-same night with foes he were bested,
That fiercely fettled them to fight against him in his bed.

83 He told his lady soon of this, but as a thing most vain;
She weigh'd it light, and said, I wis we must to church certain,

84 And serve God there this present day, the knight then made him bown,
And by the miln-house lay the way that leadeth to the town.

85 The drought had made the water small, the stakes appeared dry;
The knight, his wife, and servants all, came down the dam thereby.

86 When Adam Beaumont this beheld, forth of the miln came he,
His bow in hand with him he held, and shot at him sharply.

87 He hit the knight on the breast plate, wherest the shot did glide;
William of Lockwood, wroth thereat, said, Cousin, you shoot wide.

88 Himself did shoot, and hit the knight, who nought was hurt with this,
Whereat the knight had great delight, and said to them, I wis,

89 If that my father had been clad with such armour certain,
Your wicked hands escap'd he had, and had not so been slain.

90 O Eland town, alack, said he, if thou but knew of this,
These foes of mine full fast would flee, and of their purpose miss.

91 By stealth to work needs must they go, for it had been too much,
The town knowing, the lord to slo for them, and twenty such.

92 William of Lockwood was adread the town should rise indeed;
He shot the knight quite thro' the head, and slew him then with speed.

93 His son and heir was wounded there, but yet not dead at all;
Into the house convey'd he were, and died in Eland-hall.

94 A full sister forsooth had he, an half brother also;
The full sister his heir must be, the half brother not so.

95 The full sister his heir she was and Savile wed the same;
Thus lord of Eland Savile was, and since in Savile name.

96 Lo here the end of all mischief, from Eland, Eland's name
Dispatch'd it was, to their great grief, well worthy of the same.

97 What time these men such frays did frame, deeds have I read, and heard
That Eland came to Savile's name in Edward's days the Third.

98 But as for Beaumont, and the rest, they were undone utterly;
Thus simple virtue is the best and chief felicity.

99 By Whittle-lane end they took their flight, and to the old Earth-yate;
Then took the wood, as well they might, and spy'd a privy gate.

100 Themselves conveying craftily, to Anneley-wood that way,
The town of Eland manfully pursued them that day.

101 The lord's servants throughout the town, had cry'd with might and main,
Up, gentle yeomen, make you bown, this day your lord is slain.

102 Whittle, and Smith, and Rimmington, Bury with many mo:
As brimme as boars they made them bown, their lord's enemies to slo.

103 And, to be short, the people rose throughout the town about;
Then fiercely following on their foes, with hue and cry, and shout.

104 All sorts of men shew'd their good wills, some bows and shafts did bear;
Some brought forth clubs, and rusty bills, that saw no sun that year.

105 To church now as the parish came, they join'd them with the town,
Like hardy men to stand all sam, to fight now were they bown.

106 Beaumont and Quarmby saw all this, and Lockwood where they stood;
They fettled them to fence, I wis, and shot as they were wood.

107 Till all their shafts were gone and spent, of force then must they flee;
They had dispatch'd all their intent, and lost no victory.

108 The hardiest man of them that was, was Quarmby, this is true;
For he would never turn his face, till Eland men him slew.

109 Lockwood, he bare him on his back, and hid him in Anely wood;
To whom his purse he did betake, of gold and silver good.

110 Here take you this to you, said he, and to my cousins here;
And in your mirth, remember me, when you do make good cheer.

111 If that my foes should this possess, it were a grief to me;
 My friends welfare is my riches, and chief felicity.
112 Give place with speed, and fare you well, Christ shield you from mischief;
 If that it otherwise befal, it would be my great grief.
113 Their foes so fiercely follow'd on, it was no biding there:
 Lockwood, with speed, he went anon, to his friends where they were.
114 With haste then towards Huddersfield, they held their ready way;
 Adam of Beaumont the way he held, to Crosaland hall that day.
115 When Eland men returned home through Aneley wood that day;
 There found they Quarmby laid alone, scarce dead, as some men say.
116 And then they slew him out of hand, dispatch'd him of his pain;
 The late death of their lord Eland inforced them certain.
117 Learn, Savile, here, I you beseech, that in prosperity
 You be not proud, but mild and meek, and dwell in charity;
118 For by such means your elders came, to knightly dignity;
 Where Eland then forsook the same, and came to misery.
119 Mark here the breach of charity, how wretchedly it ends;
 Mark here how much felicity, on charity depends.
120 A speech it is to ev'ry wight, please God who may or can;
 It wins always with great delight, the heart of ev'ry man.
121 Where charity withdraws the heart, from sorrow and sighs deep:
 Right heavy makes it many a heart, and many an eye to weep.
122 You gentlemen, love one another, love well the yeomanry;
 Count ev'ry Christian man his brother, and dwell in charity.
123 Then shall it come to pass truly, that all men you shall love;
 And after death then shall you be in heav'n, with God above.
124 To whom always, of ev'ry wight, throughout all years and days;
 In heav'n and earth, both day and night, be honor, laud, and praise.

The late Mr. Beaumont supposed the whole to be a fiction, because at the very period of the tragedy the different parties appear to have been at peace, so far as it may be inferred from their attesting each other's charters. But this argument is not conclusive, there was an interval of fifteen years, in which though the flame was not extinct, it was smothered under embers, so that decent appearances were kept up between the survivors of the families. "In my opinion (says WHITAKER) the poem authenticates itself. Let the reader turn to DODSW. MS., and at that part of the pedigree which refers to this period he will find, what Mr. Watson never observed, that though the estate passed by marriage of a sister of the last Elland to the Savilles, there was a brother Henry. This is not accounted for: but the poem informs us that this Henry was a brother of the half blood, and therefore, the immediate ancestor having died intestate, could not inherit. This could not be invented." Then again, the story is so circumstantial, the places, dates, &c. so specific and so consistent, that he could not conceive it a fable.

Yet the present poem, wherever the writer procured his materials is later by little less than two centuries than the events which it

records. Tradition could never have carried down so many probable and consistent facts from the reign of Edwd. III to that of Hen.
III. and not have failed to gather in its course much of the wonderful and fabulous. The ballad is certainly precisely in the style of
Sternhold and Hopkins, and can claim no affinity with Chaucer.

There is mention made in Dods. MSS. that the event which gave
rise to this tragedy was a fray between the retainers of Earl Warren
and Thomas Earl of Lancaster on the account of Alice de Lacy,
daughter of the Earl of Lincoln, and wife of Thomas Earl of Lancaster, Grandson to Henry III. The Earl was beheaded 1332.
She died A. D. 1348. This nearly fixes the date of the transaction.
"Sir John Eland of Eland was a man of great account, and high
steward to the earl Warren, of the manor of Wakefield, and other
lands in the north parts. He was lord of Eland, Tankersley, Ful-
bridge, Hinchfield, and Ratchdale: and being sheriff of Yorkshire, he
slew Robert Beaumont in his own house at Crossland Hall, 24 Edw.
III, and was himself slain by sir Robert Beaumont's sons, as he
came from keeping the sheriff's turn at his own manor of Brighouse,
and not long after the said Beaumont slew the said sir John Eland's
son and heir as he came over Elland mill dam, on Palm Sunday
morning, there being at that time no bridge there. This appeareth
by evidence and pedigrees in the keeping of John Armytage, of
Kirklees, Esquire, *and they have a play and song thereof in the country still.* The quarrel was about the earl of Lancaster, and the earl
Warren, that took away the said earl of Lancaster's wife, there
being a man slain of the said earl Warren's party, in a hurley-bur-
ley betwixt the said lords for that matter. Eland came to search
for the murderer, in the said Beaumont's house, who belonged to
the said earl of Lancaster, and slew him there."

Mr. WATSON has made some judicious observations on this poem
which I cannot omit, inasmuch as he seems to have bestowed more
than ordinary attention on the subject, although it appears that the
MSS. of Dods. before referred to escaped his attention, he says,
"The origin of this bloody quarrel is not very clear; our poet, at
verse 14, gives us one cause of it, but he speaks very doubtfully
about it. I have read in other MSS. that one Exley had killed the
brother's son of sir John Eland, and that sir Robert Beaumont
screened him from the resentment of sir John, also that the affair

was, in some measure, made up, sir John Eland having accepted
of a compensation in lieu of justice being done upon the murderer,
but that he afterwards violated the agreement in the manner above
related.   It seems not unlikely that some fresh provocation was
given, from what is said in verse 17, Lockwood of Lockwood being
there charged with something of this sort, when he is called "a
wiley wight," and said to have "stirred the strife anew."   He
appears, indeed, to have been a person of a bad character, for in
the court rolls at Wakefield, 35 Edw. I. John de Lockwood was
presented, and afterwards found guilty, of having forcibly ejected
one Matthew de Linthwaite from his free tenement, and when the
earl's grave and bailiff came to take possession thereof, he made an
attempt, with others unknown, to have slain them, so that they
barely escaped with their lives.   I have one MS. which says, that
Exley above named was a relation of sir Robert Beaumont's, and
that he happened to kill a sister's (not brother's) son of sir John
Eland's, for which Exley gave to the Elands a piece of land for satisfaction; yet notwithstanding sir John sought to slay him, and
he fled thereupon to sir Robert Beaumont for protection; on which
sir John got together a considerable number of armed men, and in
one night, in the month of May, put to death the said sir Robert,
and two old gentlemen, his near relations, sir Hugh de Quarmby
and old Lockwood.   This is so far confirmed, that in Mr. Hopkinson's MS. collections at North Bierley, in Yorkshire, it is said,
"that with sir Robert Beaumont were slain his brother Wilham,
and———Exley, who had killed the brother's son of sir John
Eland."

"The description given at verse 19, of Crossland hall is true, the
remains of a wet ditch surrounding it are visible to this day; but
neither Quarmby nor Lockwood houses had the same advantage.
It is said in Hopkinson's MSS. above quoted, "that when sir John
Eland gave bread to Adam Beaumont he threw it at him with dis-
dain; on which sir John said, He would weed out the offspring of
his blood, as they weed out the weed from corn;" but this threat-
ning was so far from being verified, that sir John's male issue were
entirely cut off, whilst that of Beaumont continued.   It seems that
William de Beaumont, of Whitley, in the parish of Kirkheaton,
married, and had sir Robert Beaumont, knt. who, about 20 Edw.

II. married Grace, daughter and heiress of sir Edward Crossland, of Crossland, knt. by whom Adam above mentioned, Thomas, and John, according to a MS. pedigree in my possession; though, at verse 29, only two boys are mentioned, but the third might be too young to be noticed, or possibly at that time not born. Adam and Thomas both died without issue; John married Alice, daughter of John Soothill, esq; by whom Richard, from whom descended a race, who lived in splendor to the reign of king Charles I. If any stress may be laid on particular words in a poem of this sort, where we have one word for rhyme, and another for reason, there is proof, in the 38th verse, that sir Robert Beaumont might have a third son : for after shewing that lady Beaumont fled into Lancashire, it follows, "With her she took her children all, at Brearton to remain." At verse 42, the writer tells us, that these young gentlemen were brought up at Brereton green "till fifteen years were finished," soon after which they contrived to kill sir John Eland, as it is said, 21 Edw. III. or 1347; if therefore sir Robert Beaumont was married 20 Edw. II, or 1326, (as in the pedigree of that family is asserted,) his son Adam would be, at the death of sir John, about twenty years of age, and consequently about five years old at the decease of his father, a circumstance which accounts for the different behaviour of the two boys described at verse 30, in a very satisfactory manner; but at the same time invalidates the reason contained in verse 14, for sir John Eland was not sheriff of Yorkshire till 15 Edw. III. or 1341, and indeed that reason seems on all accounts inadmissible.

"The Lacy mentioned in verse 53, was no doubt of the Lacys of Cromwelbottom, the head of which family had just before married the aunt of sir John Eland, it is not therefore likely that it was he, unless we read in verse 76, as in some copies, "Cromwelbottom hall," instead of "wood," for then it will seem to follow that he was involved in the scheme, and permitted the conspirators to meet privately at his house, to consider of a plan for their operations; but as he was a neighbour and relation, and is not represented as having received any injury from sir John, it is hard to say why he was concerned. It is remarkable, that he is only named when the ambush was laid for sir John on his return from Brighouse, and when they came back from Furness Fells to their own country, but is not said to have borne any part in the transaction at Eland mill; perhaps he had either repented of what he had done, or thought it sufficient to assist in taking off the actual murderer of Beaumont, and the rest, without punishing the sin of the father on the second and third generation.

"Verse 93 cannot well be explained, for no authority which I have seen shews the name of sir John's son and heir; the half brother there mentioned was a son of sir John's lady, who was daughter of Gilbert Umfravile, and widow of Robert Coniers, of Sockborn, in the county of Durham.

"In verse 98, the lord's servants are represented as calling on the yeomanry throughout the town to arm to revenge their master's death; but in Hopkinson's MSS. it is said, that the town and neighbourhood were raised by sound of horn, and ringing the bells backward.*

"After Quarmby was wounded, he is said in Hopkinson's MSS. to have been hid in an ivy tree in Aneley wood, with an intent to have been saved, but was discovered by the Eland men on their return from pursuing, and killed.

"At the end of the printed account of these remarkable transactions, is "A relation of the lives and deaths of Wilkin (or William) Lockwood, and Adam Beaumont, esqrs. and what adventures happened to them after the battle with the Eland men, in Anely wood as the same is recorded in a very ancient manuscript," but evidently written in the same style as the former. The substance of that story is this; that Lockwood after his escape from the pursuit of the Elanders, retired to a solitary place called Camel-hall, near Cawthorn, (now pronounced Cannon-hall,) where he commenced an amour with a young woman of loose principles, whose father rented Camel-hall, and they had frequent meetings in a large hollow oak in Emley park, but were discovered by the keeper, who soon made the neighborhood acquainted with what he had seen; on which Lockwood thought fit to retire to Ferry-bridge, where he remained for some time in security, and might have continued to have done so, if his passion for his mistress had not put him upon paying her a visit, and venturing for that purpose into the common road towards the place of her habitation, he casually met with two young gentle-

* Although these statements differ, there is no inconsistency.

women of his kindred, as they were travelling from Lepton to Whitley, who informed him that diligent search was made after him by the sheriff and his men, and several others, and therefore advised him to go directly to Crossland-hall, to Adam Beaumont, where he might live safely, and hunt with him and other gentlemen both the red and fallow deer, at Hanley and Holm-forth, but by no means to go any more to this woman, for she would certainly betray him. To this he so far agreed, that he promised to be at Adam Beaumont's before he eat or drank, but he no sooner had parted with them than he posted speedily through the woods to Camel-hall, thus hasting to his own ruin, (which during his absence his enemies had contrived); for Bosville, who at that time was under-sheriff, and owner of Camel-hall, had, a little before Lockwood's arrival, been with his tenant, to contrive how he might take him prisoner at his next coming, threatening him, that if he would not discover him, he would not only take the farm from him, but do him farther mischief; whereas, if he gave information of him, he should continue to be tenant there, and have other considerable favors done him. Influenced by these motives, the tenant, on Lockwood's arrival, gave notice thereof to Bosville, who presently assembling a great company of men, beset the house, and in the king's name commanded Lockwood to surrender, who replied, that 'he scorned to do it so long as he had life and strength to defend himself,' and making a stout resistance, they threatened to burn the house over his head; disregardless however of that, he continued to defend himself with his bow, and so successfully annoyed his assailants that they began to despair of taking him, and as the writer thinks, would have withdrawn their men, if his Dalilah had not, under the color of a feigned embrace, got the opportunity of cutting his bow-string in sunder with a knife which she had concealed in her hand; notwithstanding which he found means to protect himself, till by fair promises he was prevailed upon to surrender himself; but no sooner did the ungenerous conquerors get him in their power, than they first bound him and then cruelly put him to death, to the utter extirpation of the ancient family of Lockwood of Lockwood.

"The other champion, Adam Beaumont, as we are told in the poem, retired after the engagement at Elland, to his paternal seat

e g 2

at Crossland-hall. Here for some time he lived in security, diverting himself with hunting and other exercises, not doubting but the storm had been blown over; but hearing of the death of Lockwood, he began to fear for his own safety, and the more so as he had not a friend left to apply to for council and assistance, for his cousin Lacy had retired into the north country, and many unexpected enemies appeared against him, as precepts were sent from London to the sheriff to arrest him; he therefore took the resolution to leave the country, and having landed safe in France, by some means or other he got into the service of the knights of Rhodes, to fight, with no mean command, in defence of the Christian faith, in the kingdom of Hungary, against a numerous army of the Turks; in which adventure he gave signal proofs of his great strength and courage. And to so high a degree of fame and dignity did he arrive, that some have even asserted that the name of Beaumont is to be found registered amongst the knights of Rhodes. However that is, this (says the same writer) is undoubtedly true, that out of Hungary he wrote a private letter of the great successes and honors which he had obtained in that country, all of it written, and subscribed with his own hand, directed to Jenkyn Dixson, dwelling at the Hole-house, within the parish of Almondbury, in the county of York; and not many years after, his friends received a true and full narrative of his life and death, namely, that his residence was sometimes at Rhodes amongst the knights there, and sometimes in Hungary, where, in one of the engagements against the Turks, he honorably ended his life."

Attached to Elland Hall although in the township of Southowram is a Park, called Elland Park, of which says WATSON the first mention is in a deed without date, of Hugh de Ealand, wherein this park is excepted. By an inquisition at Pontefract 5 and 6 of Philip and Mary, it was found that Henry Saville, sen. deceased, gave the custody of his park of Ealand to Thomas Saville, of Exley, afterwards of Welburne. It was in all probability dispailed when the family left this neighbourhood, but it at present retains the name of Elland park.

Among other houses worthy of note in this township, are

ANELEY HOUSE.

Once the residence of Edward Saville, fourth son of Nicholas

Saville of New Hall. This place in ancient deeds is written Alnald-ley, Awnley, and Avenley.

BURTON, in his *Monasticon Eboracence*, p. 138, says, "That Abulay-grange, in the chapelry of Eland, in Halifax parish, belong-ed to the abbey of Fountains; and that on July 12, 1478, 18 Ed-ward IV. Thomas de Swinton, the abbot thereof, granted it to John Nesfield, prior of Nostel, for life." "This Abulay (says WATSON) I take to be what is now called Aneley, contracted from Avenley: and in the Ledger book of Fountains, under the title of Yeland, it was said, 'that by an indenture, 14 Edward IV. the grange of Ain-ley, in the chapelry of Eland, was divided equally between John Savile, of Hullenedge, esq. and William, son of Robert Wilkinson, by sir John Savile, knt. and Thomas Savile, esq. his son.' It is men-tioned again by BURTON, p. 152, under the name of Awndelay." The abbey of Fountains appear to have had other possessions in this township and chapelry, for the particulars whereof I must refer the reader to WATSON, p. 319.

HULLENEDGE,

Perhaps from Hollin-edge, was formerly the seat of a branch of the Saviles, the first of whom was Thomas Savile of Hullenedge, second son of Henry Savile, of Copley. It gave name to a family, of whom Hugh de Hollingegge occurs in a deed dated in 1316.

NEW HALL was also the seat of a branch of the Saviles of Hul-lenedge.

Independently of the endowment of the parochial chapel before referred to, the following devises to the incumbent there have from time to time been made; they were omitted in the account of public Charities because they concerned, only, the minister of the chapel.

ROBERT INMAN, of Elland, by will dated April 12th, 1638, gave and devised to his brother, George Ramsden, of Greetland, and Jo-seph Ramsden, of the same, his nephew, their heirs and assigns, one annuity or yearly rent of twenty shillings, to be issuing out of two messuages or tenements, called the Lee, with the appurtenan-ces, in Old Linley, within the township of Stainland, in the county of York, payable yearly on the feasts of Pentecost and St. Martin the bishop in winter, by equal portions. In trust and confidence, that the said George Ramsden and Joseph Ramsden and their heirs should dispose of the same yearly rent of twenty shillings, and all the profits thereof, from time to time, to and for the use and better maintenance of a preacher, who should preach the word of God at the parochial chapel of Elland aforesaid, from time to time, to succeeding ages for ever. A clause was added empowering a distress to be made in case of non-payment.

HENRY WILSON, of Elland, by his will dated June 28th, 1652, gave, devised and bequeathed unto Gilbert Savile, of Greetland, gent. and others, and to their heirs for ever, five closes of new land in the Broad Carr, as also one house or cottage, with the appurtenances in Elland, and one backside thereunto belonging; and also one ruinated house, or house-stead thereunto adjoining, with the appurtenances, in Elland, between the smithy then in the tenure of John Gillot, and the house then in the tenures of Jonas Clay and Brian Rawnsley; and also all his parts and purports of the said smithy, and the two houses then in the tenures aforesaid; and also one whole chamber then in the tenure of Sarah Hinchliffe, or her assigns, and one whole shop, with the appurtenances, in Elland, then in the tenure of John Hanson or his assigns, unto the said Gilbert Savile and others, at the rent of one red rose, in the time of roses, should it be asked; upon trust, that they should first pay out of the same all such rents as were accustomed to be paid by the testator, and the profits of the said premises his will and mind was should be used and employed by and for the benefit of the stipendiary preacher at the parochial chapel of Elland, the said preacher having the consent of the trustees or any three of them. The testator also gave to the said trustees fifty pounds, towards building a house near the cross in Elland, to be paid when the foundation of the house should be laid, which house his will and mind was should be used and employed by his trustees for the use of the preacher aforesaid. It was Henry Wilson's will that during the time there was not a preacher as the trustees should approve of, that the profits should be disposed of to such a minister as they should think fit, the said minister officiating and doing service for the same in the parochial chapel of Elland aforesaid.

Jeremy Bently, one of the trustees, took upon him the care of building the house, and laid out, besides the fifty pounds left by the will, forty-five pounds of his own money, for which he had a quit rent of three pounds per annum out of the house and land left by Henry Wilson, granted him by the rest of the trustees, till he should be satisfied some other way.

PROTESTANT DISSENTERS.

Joseph Brooksbank, of Hackney, in the county of Middlesex, Esq. by indenture, dated June 5th, 1756, conveyed to the Rev. Joseph Brooksbank and others, a messuage or tenement, and cottage, called Cinder hills, in South Owram, and also eight closes of land to the same belonging, known by the names of the Upper Ing, the Lower Ing, the Long field, two Coal pit brows, the Little Steass Mires, the Sough Mires, and the Small Long close, in trust that they, and the survivors and survivor of them, should yearly out of the rents and profits of the said messuage, cottage and lands, (after the necessary charges of repairing and supporting the same, and of the execution of the trusts thereby created) in the first place, pay, or cause to be paid, by two equal half-yearly payments, the clear yearly sum of ten pounds, without deduction, to the minister for the time being, of the congregation of protestant dissenters meeting or assembling for the worship of God, in the meeting-house made use of for that purpose at Elland, so long as there should be such a minister, and the exercise of divine worship by protestants dissenting from the church of England should be permitted therein by the laws of this realm, and no longer. And on this further trust that the said trustees, for the time being, should yearly out of the said rents expend the sum of forty shillings, in the purchase of such books of piety and devotion as they should think fit, to be by them given and distributed amongst the forty poor children taught at the free school in Elland, which was formerly founded and endowed by Joseph Brooksbank, deceased, grandfather of the above named Joseph Brooksbank, owner of Cinder-hills aforesaid. And upon trust to pay the remainder of the said clear rents and profits of the said premises yearly unto the Schoolmaster, for the time being, of the said school, as an addition to his allowance, or salary, for teaching and instructing the said children in manner directed by the said Joseph Brooksbank, founder of the said school, and to and for no other use whatsoever.

When the trustees were by death, reduced to two, or under, the survivor or survivors were to convey to as many as were necessary to make the number seven. There is a proviso in the deed, that the premises should revert to the right heirs of Brooksbank, in the event of divine worship by protestant dissenters not being permitted in the chapel.

GREETLAND.

This Township adjoins Elland on the West, and is an independent township, presenting its own constable, choosing its own chapel warden and overseer, although it seems at the present day to be considered as an hamlet within the vill of Elland. It appears from time immemorial to have been held under the same lords as Elland, of the honor of Pontefract.

The modern pronunciation of the name is Greetland, but it has often been written Gretland; and may have had its name either as being the great land, or from the number of stones in it, which, in the Islandic language, were called Grioot, or Griot, or from the Saxon Gryt, or Greot, sand or gravel.

The only places of note in this township are Clayhouse and Crawstone.

CLAYHOUSE,

Which from its appellation, seems not to have had a very noble origin. It gave name to a family of repute, now extinct, who are parties to deeds, &c. between the years 1313, and 1687; they had the title of gentlemen, and bore arms; and one of the family, Robert Clay, D. D. was vicar of Halifax. The estate at Clayhouse belongs to the trustees of Wheelwright's Charity, and is now occupied by the Dysons, a very respectable family, who have long resided there.

CRAWSTONE,

Where lived some time ago, an ancient and apparently wealthy family, of the name of Ramsden, bearing arms.

The township of Elland-cum-Greetland is not a party to the Vicar Act, nor has it since availed itself of the privilege of becoming a party thereto within the time therein limited. The Vicar is possessed in right of his vicarage to a piece of land, called the Vicar's park, situate on Greetland moor, containing 75 acres.

TOWNSHIP OF BARKISLAND.

THIS township, which lies to the West of Stainland, is bounded on the North by Norland, and the West by the Ryburn, and contains an area of 2420 statute acres. It is sometimes called Barsland; and has its name (says WATSON) from the Anglo-Saxon Biɲce or Beoɲce a birch tree, and lonð, a territory or district ; in the same manner as some have derived the word Barkshire. The c was anciently pronounced like k. In confirmation of this etymology, some part of the township has at this day the name of Birch or Birk-closes, and there is an ancient situation therein, called Barkesay, or Barsey, (meaning the inclosure where the birch trees grew.) After all, if Barsland is really the original name of this district, it may be derived from the Anglo-Saxon Bæɲs, a wolf, and lonð, (ut supra :) as much as to say, the country remarkable for wolves ; in this case, the place in this township called the Wolf-fold, must be looked upon as having actual reference to this animal, and not as a druidical remain, as already described.

It is worth remarking, that several townships in this neighbourhood, which lie contiguous to each other, are called by the name of some land or other ; as Elland, Greetland, Barkisland, Norland, Soyland, Stainland, an instance very rarely met with.

Barkisland is not mentioned in Domesday Book by name. The oldest deed, (says WATSON) in my possession relating to it, is an agreement in 1288, between Thomas de Thorneton and Henry de Risheworthe, whereby the former conveyed to the latter the fourth part of all the vill of Barkisland, if he did not repay to the said Henry, in six years, three marks and forty pence, which he had borrowed of him ; this clearly indicates that the land was not then in a very improved state. In a few years after, it appears this Henry was possessed of

a still greater part of the township, for Hugh, son of John de Ba-
land, by deed dated at Elland, A. D. 1306, quit claimed to Thomas
de Langfeld, and Ellen his wife, Jordan de Insula, and Isabel his
wife, John de Sayvill, and Margery his wife, his claim in the yearly
payment of ten marks for the moiety of the vill of Barkisland, which
Henry de Rishworth, father of the said Ellen, Isabel, and Margery
was bound to pay him.   This is the commencement of the Savile's
title to the manor, who by this match, became possessed of part,
and subsequently lords of the whole.   Between the 3rd and 6th of
Edward II. William de Langfeld, and Agnes his wife, levied a fine
of a third part of the manors of Rishworth, Barkisland, Bothomley,
and Scamonden : if he die without heir, remainder to the right
heirs of the said William, with remainder over to Gilbert de la Legh,
and his heirs.   This shews what manors Henry de Rishworth
died possessed of, and that they were equally divided among his
three daughters, who were his coheiresses.   19 Edward IV. by an
inquisition of wastes in Wakefield it appeared, that Thomas Saville, knt. held divers lands and tenements in Stainland, Berkaland,
and Northland, by soccage, paying yearly thirteen shillings and
four pence.   This was doubtless paid to the lord of the manor of
Wakefield, for in a deed without date, to which the above Thomas
de Thorneton was witness, Thomas de Gledhill, and Adam, son of
Roger de Barkislande, grant to Richard, son of William de Barkislande, for his homage and service, &c. three parts of an assart
called Huieterode, in Barkislande, and give a general warranty,
" salvo tamen servicio domini comitis Warreni."   In a deed 7 Henry VII. sir John Sayvile, knt. is called Dominus de Barsland, and
grants part of his waste there, reserving an annual rent to himself
and heirs, also suit to his court at Barsland, and mill in Northland,
to hold of the capital lords of the fee by the accustomed services ;
here he seems to hold the whole manor, under the lord of Wakefield.   By an inquisition taken at Pontefract, 5 and 6 Philip and
Mary, the jurors found that Henry Savile, knt. before his death,
was seized (inter alia) in fee tail of the manor of Barkaland, held of
the manor of Wakefield, in free soccage by fealty, and thirteen
shillings and four-pence for this and others.   Also at a trial in the
duchy chamber, 6 Elizabeth, it appeared that the crown laid claim
as will be seen under Ovenden, to the manors and wastes, inter alia,

of Ovenden, Rishworth, Norland, Barsland; but the decree was in favor of Henry Savile.

It appears, from fines levied in the 8th and 9th of Elizabeth, that this manor was to remain to the heirs male of the body of Thomas Savile, of Lupset, deceased, for want of issue male in the line of Savile of Thornhill, which failed in the person of Edward Savile, the sixth lineal descendant from Henry Savile, which Henry married Elizabeth, daughter and heiress of Simon Thornhill, of Thornhill, whereby the manor passed from the name of Thornhill to that of Savile. 16 Eliz. an estate in Barkisland was said, in an inquisition *post mortem*, to have been held of the heir of Henry Savile, knt. "ut de manerio suo de Barkisland;" this must have been Edward, son of the said sir Henry. 19 Eliz. George, earl of Shrewsbury, joined with the said Edward Savile, and Henry Savile, in conveyances within this manor. The trust reposed in this noble family arose from sir George Savile, knt. and bart. son of Henry Savile, of Lupset, esq. above named, marrying Mary, daughter of the said George Talbot, earl of Shrewsbury. 33 Eliz. an estate was conveyed within this manor, and another 41 Eliz. by Gilbert, earl of Shrewsbury, Edward Savile, esq. lord of the manor of Barkislande, son and heir of Henry Savile, knt. deceased, and George Savile, knt. son and heir of Henry Savile, late of Lupset, esq. deceased. In 1605, 3 James, George Savile, knt. the elder, is in a deed called lord of the manor of Barkisland; this was a direct ancestor of sir George Savile, of Rufford, bart. to whom the manor passed. The present claimant is the Right Honorable the Earl of Scarborough.

I have shewn that this manor was formerly divided between Thomas de Langfeld, Jordan de Insula, and John de Sayvile, who married the three daughters coheiresses of Henry de Rishworth, to whom the lordship of Barkisland belonged. Sir John Savile, who married the daughter and heiress of sir John Ealand, is said to have bought the family of Insula's share, but the other third part passed from the Langfelds to the Hamertons by marriage, and in that family it continued till sir Stephen Hamerton was attainted, and it came to the crown in the reign of Henry VIII. This, in some measure appears from an inquisition taken at Ilkley, 14th April, 6 Henry VIII. after the death of John Hamerton, esq. when it was found that the said John died seised in his demense as of fee of the third part of the manor of Barkisland, and that Stephen Hamerton, esq, aged twenty-one years, was son and heir; but how the Saviles became possessed of this third part is not shewn.

Within the township are some interesting Druidical remains, before referred to.

On the 24th May, 1814, an act received the royal assent for inclosing lands in the manor of Barkisland, the Hon. and Rev. Jno. Lumley Saville being the then Lord; the following are the names of the commons, moors, and wastes enclosed, they may prove interesting to the topographer,—Wisket hill, Gillipole hill, Coney garth hill, Hill house hill, Barkisland cross, Height common, Ringstone edge, Birch green, Hiley hill, Flocktons, Cliff hill, Horse pasture, Whole stones, Withen's pike, Law and Bog holes, containing altogether about 1000 statute acres.

RIPPONDEN,

Formerly written Ribournden, is the name of a village in this township, lying on the great road over Blackstone-edge, between Rochdale and Halifax, in a beautiful valley, which, having the peculiar features of the neighbourhood, rich meadows, hanging oak woods and quick changes of landscape, finely contrasted by the barren and purple hills beyond, is the most pleasing among the dependencies of the Calder.

From whence it has its name is not easy to determine. Rhe or Rey signify a river, and Rhy is the British for a ford; Boupne is a brook, and bene a valley. Rhi also, in the ancient language of this country, denoted a king, as if the valley through which the river Rybourn directs its course, was, on some account or other, a royal vale. That this was ever distinguished by the residence of a crowned head, (says WATSON) I have no authority to say, but I have seen the name, in a very ancient evidence, written Riburghe or the King's borough. Possibly some king, in the Saxon times, might encamp here, as there is a large hill hanging over this village, called to this day by the name of the Konygarth, or King's mountain.

THE CHAPEL,

Which is dedicated to St. Bartholomew, cannot fail to attract the attention of the passing traveller: viewed from the high road it has truly an "interesting appearance." It is of the Tuscan order of architecture, and the chapel yard is surrounded with one of the finest yew hedges in the country, cut in the form of Saxon arches. Within the yard are several tomb-stones cut with considerable taste and neatness by the celebrated John Collier, who, under the fictitious name of Tim Bobbin, was the author of the well-known work, "The Lancashire dialect."

There is no account in what year the chapel was first founded, but MR. WATSON has produced the following licence from the register of archbishop Nevil at York ;—"Georgius, etc. dilectis in Xpo filiis incolis et inhabitantibus villarum de Sowland, Risheworth, Bothomley, et Barsland, de parochia de Halifax, nostre Dioceseos, salutem, gratiam, benedictionem. Ut in Capella situata in Riburneden, de parochia de Halifax predicta, missas et alia divina officia, voce submissa, per quoscunq. Capellanos idoneos in vestra aut alicujus vestrum et aliorum quorumcunq. ibidem advenientium presentia licite valeatis facere celebrari, duntamen locus ad hoc decens fuerit et honestus, ac Ecclesie parochiali de Halifax predicte, et Capelle de Elande, ejusdem parochie, in decimis, oblationibus, et aliis obventionibus et emolumentis, debitis, et consuetis, prejudicium nullum inde generetur, si aliud canonicum non obsistat, licentiam tam vobis audiend. quam Capellanis hujusmodi quibuscunq. divina ut prefertur celebrand. concedimus specialem per presentes quousq. duxerimus revocandam duraturam. Dat. nostro sub Sigillo, in Castro nostro de Cawode, 8vo. die mensis Jan^{ii}. An. Dom. 1465."

"This" observes DR. WHITAKER, "is so clear and definite that I can only suppose the witness to the following deposition, which is extracted from DODS. MSS. v. 58. to have labored under a defect of memory when it was taken."

"Primo die Jul. 1580. Edwd. Firth, late of Tootill, born at Ryponden, of the age of 93 years, saith that he hath seen Sowerby Church and Rybonden Chapel to build, and that there was a pair of Butts in the Plaine where Rybonden Chapel standeth, and that it was about 88 years since Ripponden Chapel was first builded, and that he has seen the chapel 3 times enlarged since the first erection which was about the 12 Hen. VII." The witness seems to have been mistaken. To contradict this account the reader will observe the word "situata" in the licence, which implies the chapel to have been already built.

It was rebuilt in 1610, and soon after the rebuilding of it, an

old man then living in Barkisland, whose name was John Waterhouse, being childless, and bearing a charitable mind, (as said in a
paper at Howroyd) gave the sum of ten pounds to be bestowed in
erecting and setting up a chamber in the lower end of the said
chapel, which was accordingly performed, and used for that purpose
for several years.

The second chapel extended itself from the old Bridge-end, along
by the present chapel-yard wall towards the South-East, and the
rivulet called the Cob-clough ran under it, and this was so much
damaged by the inundation in May, 1722,* that it was the cause of
the chapel being demolished.

The archbishop's licence for rebuilding Ripponden chapel was
dated April 6, 1729. The sum got by brief was £541 0s. 4d.
besides the subscriptions of the neighbouring gentlemen. There
was collected by brief on the erection of the edifice, £83 6s. The
chapel and cemetery were consecrated, Septr. 9th, 1737, by Dr.
Martin Benson, bishop of Gloucester, when a sum was collected,
to be laid out in the purchase of a piece of plate for the use of the
chapel.

The tower contains four fine-toned bells which bear the following inscriptions;—on the first bell, "The gift of Elkanah Hoyle,
gent. A. R. 1715." On the second, "Venite, exultemus Domino,
1708." On the third, "Gloria Pax Hominibus, 1708." On the
fourth, "O may their souls in heaven dwell, who made the least a
tenor bell. 1701."

There are no burials allowed within this chapel.

Attached to the incumbency is a minister's manse, built on land
surrendered by one Thomas Priestley, 35 Eliz. to the use of the
preacher or minister of Ripponden chapel for the time being, or such
as should celebrate divine worship therein: a yearly rent of 6s. 8d.
is payable thereout. The curates of Ripponden have generally,
since that time, lived in the above house; but, "in the year 1754,
(says MR. WATSON) when I took possession of this curacy, the
building was so ruinous and inconvenient, that it was found necessary to rebuild it, which I did at my own expence, to the amount

---

* May 18th. In this flood not only the chapel of Ripponden was destroyed, but all
the mills upon the brook; twelve persons, eight in one family, were drowned, and several
corpses washed out of their graves. See John Collier's story of the Lady of the Booth.

of more than £400, the inhabitants not giving the least assistance."

THE ENDOWMENT.

It appears from the report of the Commissioners before referred to, that a yearly rent of £24 is paid to the minister of this chapel, arising from land purchased with money, the gift of Thomas Gledhill, in commemoration whereof the said minister, or ministers, should preach one sermon yearly, upon the first day of May, if it be not of the Lord's day, and if so, then in the week following, at the minister's choice of the day."

ELIZABETH HORTON, of Barkisland, by will dated July 13, 1670, gave and devised to the minister of the gospel of Ripponden chapel, five pounds per annum for ever, he preaching a sermon there on every Good Friday yearly for ever, to be paid forth of the rents, issues, and profits of a messuage and lands called Pearce-hey, in Barkisland aforesaid, provided such minister for the time being be an orthodox person, and such as the owner of Barkisland-hall for time being for ever should approve of, and in case of non-approbation, and so long as such dislike should continue, then the said sum to be distributed to the poor people of Barkisland aforesaid."

THOMAS HORTON, Esq. who died about 1698, left by deed one half-part of a farm or tenement called the Hill-top, near Steel-lane in Barkisland, to the minister of Ripponden chapel, who, in consideration thereof, was to preach yearly for ever a sermon upon St. Thomas's day. This account is taken from the copy of an old terrier without date, in the register book belonging to Ripponden chapel. The whole is regularly fulfilled; and the rent paid yearly to the minister of Ripponden is four pounds five shillings.

A quit-rent of £1 10s, is payable "unto the curate of Ripponden for the time being, on every twenty-fourth day of June, for ever, to preach a sermon in Ripponden chapel, on every the said twenty-fourth day of June for ever." It was purchased under the will of William Horton, of Howroyd, Esq. dated 8th Oct. 1713."

THOMAS HOLROIDE, of Halifax, by codicil to his will, dated March 8, 1729-30, gave a rent-charge of five pounds per annum out of his two farms in Bottomley in the township of Barsland, to the curate of the chapel of Ripponden, for the time being, for ever, for reading the prayers according to the liturgy of the church of England, every Wednesday and Friday, in the morning, throughout the year. These farms are called by the name of Wormald.

It appears from the copy of an old terrier without date, in the register-book of the chapel that Richard Firth, of Ripponden, gave (but whether by deed or will is uncertain) two messuages or cottages at Ripponden, for which the minister of the chapel there was to preach five sermons upon the first Wednesday in the several months of April, May, June, July, and August, in the said chapel at Ripponden successively and annually for ever.

ELKANA HOYLE, of Soyland, by will dated March 28, 1718, gave and devised unto the curate of Ripponden for the time being, for ever, one annuity or yearly sum of three pounds, to be for ever issuing, going forth, and payable out of his messuage, hereditaments, and premises, with appurtenances, at or near Lighthazels, called Lower Hoyle Heads, to be yearly paid to such curate as aforesaid for ever, on Ascension-day; provided such curate preach a sermon on that day in Ripponden chapel aforesaid, and provided such curate be a sound orthodox preacher and divine according to the usages of the present church of England as by law established, and should have had university education, and have come to be curate there with the consent and good liking of the owners of Upper Swift Place. "The money" says WATSON, "has generally, if not always, been paid to the curate of Ripponden, except from the year 1755 to 1761 inclusive, when it was given to the poor; the Rev. Geat's principles not corresponding with those of the owner of Upper Swift place." It is but justice to MR. WATSON to say that the soundness of his orthodoxy was never called in question.

The chapel received an augmentation from the governors of queen Anne's bounty in the year 1724, to meet a benefaction of £200 from Mrs. Mary Horton and others. By Indenture dated the 22nd day of September, 1730, between Nathan Fielden, of the first part, the governors of the bounty of queen Anne, Mary Horton, of Howroyd, widow, Charles Radcliffe, Elkana Hoyle, and Samuel Hill of the second part; and William Sunderland, clerk, curate of Ripponden, of the third part; in consideration of £400 the said Nathan Fielden sold, for the use of the curates of Ripponden, Blackshaw-clough, and the customary or copyhold messuage or tenement called Crosswells, both in Soyland; also the houses and little croft, which he had at Ripponden. A memorial of this deed was registered at

Wakefield, October 16, 1730, in Lib. 200, p. 126, and No. 173.

The clear yearly value of this chapel, as stated by the governors of Queen Anne's bounty, in their parliamentary return, (1736) pursuant to an order of the house of Lords, was twenty-two pounds, thirteen shillings, and fourpence. It is not stated in the last return. The present respected incumbent of Ripponden chapel is the Rev. Frederic Custance.

The places worthy of notice in this township are

BARKESBY, OR BARSEY,

Just mentioned. The family which it gave name to, had considerable possessions, and may have been the first improvers of the land in this part. Some of their names appear during a great part of the fourteenth century. At Oaks, in Rishworth is a deed, wherein John son of Alan de Barkesay, grants to John, son of Richard de Barkesay, certain lands lying near the brook called Blakeborne, within the divisions of Stainland, Barkesland, and Greteland. Dated at Barkesay, in 1326. At the same place is a deed of release, which for its conciseness, (says WATSON,) is worth preserving. "Sciant presentes & futuri, quod ego Matild. de Hues, dedi, concessi, relaxavi, & omnino de me & heredibus meis quietum clamavi, Johanni filio Roberti de Clay, & heredibus suis, vel suis assignatis, totam terram quam emi de Ada patre meo in Barkesay, pro quadam summa pecuniæ mihi propriis manibus data. In cujus rei testimonium sigillum meum apposui. Hiis testibus Ric. de Schaye, Tho. Cler. Rog. del Haye, Joh'e de Ponte, & aliis."

A John de Barksey entered into possession of Clogh-houses in Barkisland, (which John de Clay had held,) at the court of the prior of the hospital of St. John of Jerusalem, in England, held at Batley, 41 Edw. III, 1367.

BARKISLAND HALL,

Takes its name from a small village wherein it is situated, lying in one of the roads between Ripponden and Huddersfield. This village arose on account of the most considerable person in the district making his habitation here, and probably building a few houses in the vicinity for his dependants. At Howroyd is a beautiful pedigree on vellum of this family, &c. entitled "The pedigree of John Gledhill, of Barkisland, collected out of antient deeds and evidences, finished, perased, and confirmed by William Seager, knt. alias

H H

Garter, principal king of arms, in 1632." From the Gledhills the estate passed by marriage, in 1636, to William Horton, esq. who became, in right of Elizabeth his wife, (a Gledhill) possessed of it. There is an interesting pedigree of the ancient family of Horton in WATSON, p. 151.

The hall was probably built about the year 1640, by John Gledhill, who married Sarah, daughter of William Horton, for he lived there in the reign of king Charles I. and in the window of the hall part are the painted figures of a man and two children : under the first, ætat. 36, 1641 ; under one of the children, ætat. 4, 1641 ; under the other, ætat. 2½, 1641. Over the back door is cut in stone, "Nunc mea, mox hujus, sed postea nescio cujus;" which may be seen in CAMDEN's Remains, p. 125, edit. 1636. If this was put there by the above John Gledhill, the observation was soon remarkably verified, when the estate passed into the name of Horton, and after a very short possession to that of Bold, in which family it still remains.

BOTTOMLEY, OR BOTHOMLEY,

A large district of land in the township of Barkisland, so called from the Anglo-Saxon Botm, an hollow place, and Leaȝ, a field or pasture; a definition which agrees with the situation of it. This place gave name to a family, who lived here from the year 1326 to 1593, and how much longer is uncertain.

BOWERS,

Called so either from the Anglo-Saxon Bupe, a chamber, because the house here might be chambered over, contrary to the ancient custom of this county, or it may mean an house in general, or a place of shade and retirement, for that word has all these significations.

FIRTH-HOUSE,

Anciently written Frit, or Frith-house, signifies, in all probability, the house in the wood. A place a little above is still called Woodhead.

HEIGHT,

Probably takes its name from its situation, standing high on the side of a steep hill. Dr. JOHNSON, in his MSS. collections for an history of Yorkshire, says, this is a place of great antiquity.

HOWROYDE,

Written also in deeds Holerode, Hooleroid, Holeroyde, Howleroid, Holroide, and Howroyde, has its name from the Anglo-Saxon Hou, an hill, and Rois, which word, when applied to land, signified such as was barren and uncultivated, and which, on that account, paid only about two-pence an acre, and was freed from the service of grave, and other taxes.

The present house, (with the exception of some additions) was built in 1642, by the purchaser of it, William Horton, who married Elizabeth, daughter of Thomas Gledhill, of Barkisland, and who, besides the arms of Horton and Gledhill, put in the hall window, in stained glass, the following devices. The mottos attached to these devices may be found in WATSON: there is not any thing to recommend them to the reader's notice.

A female figure, called Auditus, (or Hearing,) playing and singing to a guitar.

Visus, (or Sight,) at her toilet.

Odoratus, (Smelling,) with flowers before her on a table.

Tactus, (Touch,) having just cut her finger.

Gustus, (Taste,) a female figure smoking and drinking.

To make the above emblems the stronger, near to Hearing is a buck and hare, alluding to the music in hunting ; near to Seeing, a king's fisher, which is a quick-sighted bird ; near to Smelling, a parrot, holding fruit to its beak ; near to Feeling, a greyhound, with an hare lying at its feet ; and near to Tasting, a wolf devouring a lamb.

The mansion is surrounded by an extensive park, and is at present the seat of a younger branch of the Horton family ; having been occupied by the late Colonel Horton, a most active and intelligent magistrate of the West Riding, and colonel of the Halifax Volunteers. Its present occupier is William Horton, Esq. Mr. Horner has an excellent drawing of Howroyde in his series of views in and about Halifax.

PARROCK-NOOK,

A small house, mentioned here to ascertain the etymology of it, as it occurs in other parts of the parish, Peappoc signified, in the Saxon, a small park, but none of the places in this neighbourhood, called by this name, have their derivation from thence. THORESBY, in his *Topography*, p. 89, seems to think that a place near Leeds, called Parrack, had its name from the lord, or his

H H 2

bailiff and tenants meeting there at certain seasons to hold a Paroc, a kind of court, not much unlike the forest Swain-mote, where an account was taken of the pannage for the year past. WATSON says "I am rather of opinion, that as we meet with such names as Parrock-nook and Parrock-foot, and fields are called by the name of Parrock, where no building has ever been, we should rather derive it from the above Peappoc or Peappuc, and understand it in the sense either of a wood or inclosure."

PIKE-LOW,

Is an hill, where formerly a beacon was fixed. Of these, this neighbourhood once contained a considerable number, as appears by the *rudera* where they stood, and the names by which the places are still distinguished, such as Pike-low, Pike-end, Beacon-hill, &c.

TOWNSHIP OF FIXBY.

IT adjoins Elland on the East, and contains 890 statute acres, being the smallest township in the Parish.

It seems to be the better opinion that "Feslei," described in Domesday Book is the present town of Fixby, although WATSON says the name does not occur there, and that it must be surveyed as part of Elland, or some other neighbouring district, having got the name of a township since that event, as seems to be the case of several others in the vicarage or parish of Halifax.

Mr. WATSON'S conjecture as to the derivation of the word is certainly ingenious, that it takes its name from some considerable person who had his residence here, for Fek-his-bye is the same as Fek-his-habitation. The word *bye* was used both by the Saxons and Danes to denote a dwelling, nor is it more clear who were the immediate possessors of this place before the conquest. Nor are there wanting instances in confirmation of this opinion. All the nine berewicks within the manor of Wakefield belonged to king Edward, prior to the conquest, and "Feslei" in all probability was granted by the crown to the earls of Warren and Surry, as by Kirkby's Inquest, temp. Edward I. earl Warren was returned by the Sheriff of Yorkshire, lord of Fekisbye. In a tax recorded in Kirkby's book it is called villa de Fekisbye, and even at that time it seems to have been little improved, for the whole sum received from it was but five shillings, which (Skircoat excepted) was less than was received from any township or vill in the whole parish.

In the survey taken in 1314, before referred to, it appears that the lord received here yearly 18s. 4d. besides other advantages : at that time there were only five houses in which fires were kept, in a mediety of the said vill, part of the lands being held by those who resided out of the vill.

It is remarkable that in this survey eight bovates of land are said to make two carucates, whereas they have generally been supposed to make but one; either therefore this was the custom at this particular time, or place, or a mistake is made in two ancient manuscripts from whence this account is taken.

It has been said, by WATSON, that the chief habitation in the township gave name to a family which had a good estate here, till William de Toothill married the daughter and heiress of Thomas Fixby, of Fixby. How considerable this family was does not appear; WATSON tells us he has not met with any pedigree, coat of arms, nor title of knight belonging to them. But he had copies of many deeds wherein the name occurs, between the years 1255, and 1312, as also deeds without date; but in the extent of all the lands within the soke of Wakefield, already said to have been made in 1314, there is no mention of the family at all.

It appears that one Sampson de Wriglesford was lord of at least a part of the town of Fekisby for he granted certain acres of the woods there. Walter de Wriglesford granted a carucate, or plow land, in Fekisby, which he had of the grant of John Wriglesford, to one Michael Brertwisell, in the time of Henry III. or before, and Henry son of Henry de Fekisby, granted to the said Michael all his lands in Fekisby, and the marriage of the heir. It continued in the name of Wriglesford for a long time, till the above Michael Brertwisell married Maud, sister of John de Wriglesford, who procured the above grant of all the Wriglesford's lands in Fekisby, as well in demesne as in service, with homages, wards, &c. It afterwards came to William de Bellomonte (Beaumont) in whose family it continued till William Beaumont, knt. granted to Thomas de Totehill, and William his son, the moiety of the town of Fekisby, with wards, marriages, &c. From the family of Totehill it came to that of Thornhill, by the marriage of Richard de Thornhill with Margaret daughter and heiress of William de Totehill. This moiety of the town is called in some old deeds, South-Fekisby. By an inquisition taken at Wakefield, August 1577, it was found that Brian Thornhill held in Fekisby certain lands of the queen, as of her demesne of Wakefield; and it appeared by roll of court, 14 Edward III. that they were held by military service, viz. the tenth part of a knight's fee. The jury also certified, that the said Brian Thornhill claimed to have a manor in this town. The said Brian was also found to be lord of the manor of Fixby, by an inquisition taken at Halifax in

the reign of queen Elizabeth. The present lord of the manor is
Thomas Thornhill, Esq. THORESBY has given a splendid pedigree
of this family from the conquest; it is set forth by WATSON, and
cannot fail of being interesting to the genealogist.

The following will also prove interesting to the topographer;
some of the names, but particularly the termination of many of them
are of such frequent occurrence in the parish, that I have given Mr.
WATSON's derivations without alteration.

Bradewallsike. The termination Sike signifies, according to
common usage in this country, a small rill of water, from the Anglo-saxon ƀich; Brade is broad, and wall is either from walle, which
formerly denoted a well of water, or was written for vall which
meant a ditch.

Brenehill. The place where wood used to be burnt into charcoal
Ƀpenniaᵹ in the anglo-saxon meant burning. It is a wood to this day.

Bromecroft, 35 Edward III, the herb Broom grew plentifully
here; but by croft we are not to understand a small inclosure only,
but a farm in general, for three acres were conveyed here, and there
might be much more.

Brocholes. From Ƀroc, a badger, and Ƀolh, which signifies a cave,
den, or hollow in the earth, where wild beasts secrete themselves.

Buttgreen. The place where probably the bowmen of this neighbourhood used to exercise themselves by shooting at a mark, which
was fixed on artificial banks of earth, called to this day Butts, particularly in Lancashire, where the custom in WATSON's time was in
some measure kept up for the sake of diversion, and the common
distances were four, eight, twelve, and sixteen roods, eight yards
to the rood.

Crossgate. This might be taken to mean a place where two
ways intersected each other, but for this expression in the deed,—
"ter. que iacet apud crucem," there was therefore, according to the
superstition of those times, a cross fixed here by the way side, as
there were also several others in different parts of this parish.

Felinge. Fell, in the Saxon, as Camden has observed in his *Remains*, page 117, signified a craggy, barren or stony place. Fœlsted
in Dutch means the same thing, and Fels, in German is a rock.
Inge is a Danish word for a meadow, and is sometimes used for low
ground, or a common.

Fordell. The farther dole, or division of land, perhaps in the public field, from the Anglo-saxon *bælan,* to divide, or distribute. Unless it comes from the British Dol, a low fertile piece of ground, either meadow or pasture. The Vandals said Dol for a valley, and Dall is the same in Teutonic.

Gillerode. Camden in his *Remains,* p. 117, says Gill is a small water. Rode, or Royde, has already been explained under How-royde, in Barkisland.

Lydate. This occurs several times in the parish, and other parts of the kingdom, and has had various significations affixed to it. ꝉlıꝺ-ᵹeaꞇ, in Saxon, is a false gate, a postern, a back door, and Luꝺ-ᵹæꞇ is the same. Verstigan derives it from the Saxon, Lᴇᴏꝺ-ᵹaꞇᴇ, quasi porta populi, in which sense it seems to have been a gate on or near a public road, or else the road itself. "But the most probable interpretation, I think, is from Laꝺe, or Loꝺ, both which used to signify a watercourse, and there happens to be this at all the places of this name which I have seen ; Ludgate, in London, not excepted, for after all, it seems to be so called from the water which emptied itself into Fleet-ditch, at a small distance from it." In this sense it answers very well to the Porta Fluentana at Rome.

Netherton Pighells. The first of these words signifies either the nearer inclosure, village, farm, or dwelling-house. The Saxon Ton or Tun, is a common termination in many parts of England, for as Verstigan, p. 295 has observed, " In ford, in ham, in ley, and tun, the most of English surnames run." The same author has likewise told us, that our ancestors cast up for safety a ditch, and made a strong hedge about their houses, and the buildings so environed about with tunes (or hedges) got by a metaphor, the name of tunes annexed to them. The custom of surrounding houses with fences or guards, seems to be alluded to in our English translation of the book of Job, i. 10. where it is said, "hast thou not made an hedge about him. and about his house, and about all that he hath on every side ?" The difference between Ham and Tun seems to have been this, that the former was the mansion house of the lord such as the romans called Villa Urbana, and the latter the Rustica Villa, let out to tenants or farmers. Pighills does sometimes denote a small parcel of land enclosed, called also a Pingle, and perhaps may be the same as in Lancashire is denominated a Pingot. It is frequently pronounced Pickle. An hog-stye is also to this day, in some parts of Yorkshire, called a Pig-hull, from the Saxon helan, or the Icelandic hil, both which signify to cover. It is therefore probable that some large herd of swine were fed here, and that a convenient building called a Pig-hull, was erected to receive them at proper times; which gave name to the place after this was destroyed. The name Highill is of frequent occurrence in the Parish.

Old Rode. So called, either as it was the Old Royde land, or because some ancient way led through it; probably the latter, as the Roman military way passed through this township, and I know not any such distinction as that of Old royd land and New royd land.

Ryding. A place cleared of wood; as we to this day say, to rid a piece of ground; either from the Islandic, rid, to pluck up, or the Saxon apeban, which signified the same. In the same sense, likewise do the Danes use the word Redde, and the Dutch, Redden. The German Ried also is locus è sylva excisus.

Staniforlang. The Stony furlong. This measure, still used in several parts of England, was sometimes computed at forty poles, which made the eighth part of a mile, yet at other times it was used for a quantity of ground of more or fewer acres.

Thwerlands. The word Thwer may anciently have been used for three, as Thwertwick for third night; so that these lands might belong to three different persons, or be divided into so many different parts. It is very rarely met with.

Tofts. A toft meant formerly either a dwelling-house, or the place where such house had stood. The owner of such house was called a Toftman, and he who had neither house nor land, was said to have, Ne toft, ne croft. Tofts also signified groves of trees, now called tufts, answering to the French Touffe du bois.

Wytehalge. Thoresby, in his Topography, page 90, says that white rents were such as were paid in silver, and black mail such as were paid in cattle, or provisions. This Halge or Haghe, was a piece of ground, the rent of which was paid in money. The distinction of Whiteley and Blackley, so common in this Parish, tend to verify the above observation.

There is a park in this township, the seat of the Thornhills; which has been of long standing.

TOWNSHIP OF NORLAND.

THIS township adjoins Greetland on the West, and contains an area of 1140 statute acres. It is sometimes called Northland, from a great part of the township facing the North, and not from its lying to the North of any considerable place. It was granted from the crown to the earls of Warren, whose title may be seen under the manor; for John earl of Warren and Surrey claimed free warren in Northland by charter, dated June 27, 37 Hen. III. And in the pleas of the crown, 21 Edw. I. the jurors presented, that John earl of Warren and Surry appropriated to himself the free chace in Northouram, Fikisby, Northland, Rishworth, &c. and it was not known by what warrant. Sir John de Ealand, in the reign of Edw. III. held of the lord certain lands and rents, and Stainland, Barkisland, Norland, and Rishworth, by the service of thirteen shillings by the year. After the death of sir John, his lands came to a daughter, married to John Savile, esq. shortly after knighted. In the year 1543, Aug. 9, 35 Hen. VIII. sir Henry Savile, "dominus de Northlande," grants a part of the waste or common there. 6 Eliz. the crown laid claim to the manor, (as may be seen under Ovenden,) but the jury found for the Saviles. 1568, 4 Aug. 10 Eliz., Edward Savile, esq. son and heir of Sir Henry deceased, Richard Gascoigne, of Sotehill, esq. and dame Elizabeth, late wife of the said Henry, and then wife of the said Richard, granted part of the wastes or commons of Northland and Barkisland, reserving suit to the courts of Northland and Barkisland, &c. Fines 8 and 9 Eliz. between Edward Savile, esq. &c. comp. and Henry Savile, esq. and others, deforc. of the manors of Elland, Stainland, Greetland, Barkisland, Rishworth, Norland, (inter alia,) the right of Edward Savile, from whom, it passed into the line of sir George Savile, of Rufford. The present noble owner is the Honourable the

Earl of Scarborough. Mr. WATSON tells us " that no gentleman's family settled in this township." There is mention of a mill here, temp. Henry VII.

Within the township is

SOWERBY CROFT.

Which has been remarked on account of its name, and the singularity of its being called Sowerby-Croft, when it lies so far from Sowerby, and within the township of Norland; and perhaps it can no otherwise be accounted for, than by considering that both Sowerby and Norland were the estate of the earls of Warren, and that as they frequently came to Sowerby for their diversion, it was necessary for them to have a farm (which at that time of the day was called a croft,) for the purpose of raising hay, corn, &c. and this piece of ground might be deemed to be the most proper in that neighbourhood, either on account of its soil, or its being out of the forest; and in that case, as the profits of it were constantly taken to Sowerby, it would get the name of Sowerby Farm or Sowerby Croft.

TOWNSHIP OF RASTRICK.

This township lies to the South of Elland, in the fertile vale of Calder, by which river it is separated from Brighouse, and contains an area of 1290 statute acres.

The supposed etymology of the name will be found in the Saxon Æra, (p. 43,) some remains of the work of that people having existed here in WATSON's time, although now destroyed. Here also lived a considerable family, who took their name from the vill, and whose pedigree WATSON has set forth at length, taking it from a MS. at Fixby, another in his own possession, and a third mentioned in Wright's History, p. 135, intitled, "Observationes quædam collectæ tam ex antiquis chartis, & rotulis curiarum, & aliis scriptis, & genealogiis, quam de progenia & familia in Rastricke, olim vocata Rastricke, ac modo Hanson," together with a grant of arms to the Hanson's of Rastrick, and a certificate to one Elias Rastricke of his having visited Jerusalem.

Rastrick was likewise granted from the crown to the earls of Warren, as shewn under the manor. John earl of Warren and Surrey claimed free warren here by charter, 37 Hen. III. and I presume it came by means of a grant from the last earl, at his death, to king Edward III. and long remained in the crown as chief lords; for in a deed, 3 James, 1605, it is called, " parcell of his highnes mannor or lordshippe of Wakefeilde, and parcell of the annexed possessions of his majesties duchie of Lancaster." The present lord of the manor is Thomas Thornhill, of Fixby, esq.; it is not improbable, that the Toothills, of Toothill, had some grant thereof; for the Thornhills, of Fixby, obtained a great part of their possessions here by the marriage of Richard Thornhill, with Margaret, daughter and heiress of William Toothill, of Toothill, by Sibil, daughter and heiress of Thomas de Fixby. Within Rastrick is the reputed manor of Toothill, which William de Rylay had of the gift and feoffment of Henry de la Welda, and conveyed in trust to Richard de Northland the chaplain, and John, son of Eve, by the name of " manerinm de Tothill, in villa de Rastrike," dated at Toothill, on Wednesday, next after the feast of the Annunciation of the virgin Mary, 5 Edw. III.

It is evident, from various deeds, that Henry de la Weld, jun. was possessed of the manor of Totehill; that he enfeoffed William de Rylay with the same; and that the said William gave it to Richard de Northland, and John, son of Eve, who also conveyed it in trust to Henry de Savile and others. About thirty years after this, it was the property of Toothill, of Toothill, from which family it passed by marriage to that of Thornhill, and became in the same manner the property of John Leventhorpe, of Leventhorpe, whose wife, with the consent of her husband, caused it to be reconveyed to her brother William Thornhill, whose posterity have enjoyed it ever since. Mr WATSON has inserted the following deed to shew the nature of feoffments in trust in these early times; with all deference to this gentleman's opinion, it is not a feoffment, but it appears to be a certificate by the priest that a feoffment had been made. " Forasmuche as it is meritory and needful to every xp̃tian man of every doubtful matter to bere record and wittnes of the truthe, that whereas John Leventhorpp was possessid and seisid of a mannor callid Totehill, with all their appurt: within the towneshippe of Rastrike, as in the right of Katerin his wieff, of the which mannor with all their appurt: beforesaid, by thassent and consent of Katerin, the wieff of the sayd John, mad a feoffment and graunt unto William Leventhorpp, son of the said John and Katerin, with other, under the forme and condicion that followes; that is for to say, that the sayd William, with other feoffers, shold make a lawefull estate of the sayd mannor, with all their appurt: to William Thornhill, brothta to the said Katerin, and to the heirs of his body laghfully begotten, and that the children of the said John and Katerin to the said William Thornhill, and his heirs, might more worhsippfullye be receyvid and welcomid, I, sir Thomas Strenger, pariah preiste of Eland, recordeth, that the said Katerin disclosid hir will unto me att Schingildhall, that this said feoffment was made to the use and profitte of William Thornhill, brother to the sayd Katerin, in the form beforesaid: of the which will beforsaid

to repeat and beare record, the sayd Katerin gav me the sayd Thomas Strenger, fifteen pence. Sealled in the presents of John
Gleidhill, of Eland, and Alice his wieff, and many others." In
consequence of this William Leventhorp, Esq, son of John Leventhorp, and Katharine his wife, of the vill of Sabrigeford, in Hertfordshire, with the consent of Katharine his mother, quit claimed
to William Thornhill, Esq. late of Fixby, and his lawful heirs, this
manor of Toothill, and for want of such remainder, to the heirs of
the said Katharine. Dated 12th November, 7 Hen. VI.

This manor also belongs to the Thornhills, of Fixby.

The oldest mention of the township of Rastrick, in any dated
instrument, is in the tax of the wapontake of Agbrig and Morley,
in 1284, recorded in Kirkby's book, where it is called a vill, and rated at 13s.

In an extent of the rent and service of the freemen of the soke
of Wakefield, made in 1314, the lord received of William, the son
of Annabil, 5s. 3d. of William, son of Walter, 1d. ob. and of Alexander de Rastrick, 2d. of John del Okes, for one tenement and one
bovate of land, 4d. of Alexander del Okes for one tenement of eight
acres, 1d. and of Richard, son of Maud, for five acres, 2s. ob. These
were all the freemen at this time in Rastrick; the rest were, according
to this roll, nativi tenentes, villains, or bondmen, some perhaps by
birth, such as were at the arbitrary pleasure of the lord, both in
their persons, children, and goods; others so by contract, holding
their lands, and tenements, by doing certain stated servile offices,
such as plowing the lord's land, mowing his grass, and reaping his
corn. But the general badges of slavery in the graveship of Fixby
and Rastrick, were, that all the nativi tenentes, of what condition
soever, were tied to the repair of Wakefield mill-dam, and paid
marchetum, which is a word of various significations; but here implying maiden-rents, or a certain sum of money paid by the tenant
to the lord for liberty to marry a daughter.

THE CHAPEL.

There is certain evidence that a chapel existed at Rastrick so
early as the year 1411. Dr. WHITAKER says "there is, or was, the
base of a Saxon cross, with scrolls and other ornaments resembling
that of Hartshead, on the south side of this chapel, from which I
am led to conclude that there was an ancient unrecorded place of

worship here prior to the foundation of the parish of Halifax, and dependant during an unknown period, upon the parish of Dewsbury."

WATSON refers to an old MS. relating to this chapel, it is to the following effect :—

"M^{dum.} that in the thirtye neyne yeare of Queene Elizabeth a Parlyamente was begon at Westminster the 24 of October, A°. Domⁱ. 1597, and divers statuts there enacted and agreid upon, amongeste which was a godlye statute made, intituled, An Acte to reforme deceits and breaches of truste, touching lands gyven to charitable uses, &c. by virtue of which Acte a Commission was awarded for the of hir Maties. heighe Cowrte of Chauncerye to the righte reverend father the lord archbishoppe of Yorke, and divers other noblemen and gentilmen in Yorckeshier, to enquiere of the breaches aforsaid, &c.

"By vertue of whiche Comission, Sir John Savile, of Bradley, Knt. one of the Barons of Thescheques, Sir John Savile, of Holoye, Knt. John Favor, Doctor of Lawe, Vicar of Halifax, Roberte Kaye, and Will. Ramesden, Esquier, two Justices of Peace, &c. sate in Eland, and inpanelled a Jurye, to enquire of the breaches aforsaid, which Jurye amongeste other things presented as followeth.

"Item, we presente, that in the towne of Rastricke there is one awneyente chappell, buyldid as is thoughte above two hundreth yeares since by the inhabitants of Rastricke, whiche was dedicated to St. Mathewe, and wherein devine service hath bane used within the memorye of man, whiche is converted to a lathe, or banne, to the great hurte of the inhabitants there, and late solde unto Roberte Ramesden, late of Rastricke, by Will. Tusser, Cleroke of the Duchye, under color of a comission made unto hym, in the two and twentye yeare of his Heighnes reigne, for sale of some improvements. Theye do not knowe of anye lands or ten^{ts} gyven to the maintenance of the service ther, save one chappel-yeard, and one howse-steede, now in ruyne, wherein somtyme (as reporte is) dwellyd a Hermit, who was a principal founder of that Chappell. But the inhabitants be desyerous, in regard theye be two miles from the Churche, that it be to them agayne restored, and theye meane, by a voluntarye stipend, to mainteyne divine service there againe, as was in former tymes used.

"This presentement was, amongest other things, returned by force of the said comission unto the heighe Courte of Chauncerye.

"M^dum. that it was the good .... of the said Mr. Baron Savile, upon suite to hym made by yong Mr. Thornehill and John Hanson, upon the laste days of Julye, A° 43 Elis. to call before hym Henrye Ramesden, sonn and haire of the said Roberte, being his coosen, sheweing unto hym that nether his late father nor he had anye right in that Chappell, (but as other inhabitants bade,) nor Mr. Tusser had anye right to grannte it, being a Chappell of such antiquitye as it was; and he orderyd, by assent of the said Mr. Thornehill, John Hanson, and Henrye Ramesden, that the inhabitants of Rastricke shold peye unto hym forty shillings, in regard his father had disbursed som charge to Mr. Tusser, and that he shold surrender his right in the Chappell, and a parcell of land lickrind for a garth to it, to the use of the inhabitants of the towne. This order was made in wrytinge, and thereunto the said Baron sett his hand, and the said Henrye Ramesden also. The moneye was paid unto Henrye, and he surrendrid accordinglye, as appeareth by the order and by the cowrtinge of this surrender."

Then follows an account of the charges of repairing this chapel; under which it appears that a common day wo'k was made by most of the inhabitants of Rastrick, March 28, 1602, when the old wall about the garth was pulled down, and a new one begun. In April following Rastrick chapel was fesoyd to be walled to the square, after the rate of 3s. 4d. a roode, to be begun the day after Palm Sunday, and to be finished before the 20th day of August. August 2nd, another common day work was made, and one end of the chapel pulled down, and enlarged in length six yards, the breadth being the same as the old chapel. It then proceeds thus:—

"M^dum, that the olde Chappell in Rasiricke was buyldid of two heights, to witt, the Chappell of one rate, and the Queere of another. The breadthe of the olde Chappell was the same the nowe is; yt conteynid in lenthe .... yeards, and in height two yeards and a half besyde the Queere. The Queere of the olde Chappell before it was pulled downe, conteynid in lenght fower yeards and a foote, and in height to the square two yeards and half a foote.

"Theer was placed in this Chappell the image of owre Ladye, graven in wood, the image of St. Mathewe, unto whome it was dedicated, and the image of one other Sancte. And theer stood in the street, nye to the Chappell-doore, one Cross of stone, very fine-lys graven with fretted worck." This ancient cross yet remains, in the chapel yard, though with the top broken off.

Then follow more accounts, amongst which are these remarks: "the 17th daye of Auguste, 1602, the resydue of the Chappell was pulled downe, and the old Queer. John Thornhill, yonger, and John Hanson, fescid the Queere to wall at 8s. 4d. a roode, and they bare the charge of a great stone windowe. Henrye Ramesden made another windowe, and walled about the same."

Whole charges of the Chappell to the square 48s. 4d. Of the gavell end, above the sqhare, 4s. 6d. Walling the Queere (besides the two windows) 23s. 4d. For stones getting and labourers wages 5s. 6d. Total £4 1s. 8d. The roof cost in workmanship 30s. Sufficient timber was given to the old to make it with. The 14th day of November, 1602, the chapel was fescid to theake for 20s. Some slate was given. The whole charge of this was 35s. 11d. Charge of plastering at 1½d. a yard, 39s. 4d. The seating of the chapel, besides timber, (which was mostly given) cost £3 13s. 4d. Amongst the rest a good ash tree was at that time forced down the river by a flood, froa Copley hall to Rastrick, which Mr. William Savile, the owner of Copley, thought fit to give towards seating the chapel. Paving is the chapel cost 9s. 10d. For pulpit making 5s. 4d. viz. 2s. 8d. for workmanship, and the same for diet; the wood was given. Glass for windows 14s. 10d. A bell was borrowed of Mr. Will. Ramsden for a time.

"M^dum, that Gilberte Tomson, of Mirfeilde, aged threscore and .... yeeres, who had servid as a Clercke in .... for manye yeares, was toleratid by Mr. Doctor Faver, vicar of Halifax, to reed devine service theere, durante bene placito of hym and the inhabitants, and he did the first service 1°. Jan. A°. 1603.

"M^dum, that the stales were twentye besyd the Queere, and the tax of the townshippe 13s. 4d. being twentye tymes 8d. And the wear thus intendid:

"Mr. Thornehill, for all his landes in Rastricke, 3s. 4d. being one fourth part of the towne, fyve stales.—Henrye Ramesden and his tenants, 20d. two stales and an half; and in the like proportion for all the rest.

"M^dum, that theere was ordinarye service so distincklye done and redd, and psalmes so well tuned and songe in that Chappell, that pleasyd Mr. Doctor Favor (to encorage the people in welduinge) to preache there in May, 1606, and Mr. More, parson of Giseleye, and divers other, had preached theer before. Note, that before his com'ynge the great windowe next the pulpitt, which was the Queere windowe in the olde Chappelle, beeing of wodd, was taken downe, and a newe windowe of stone theere made and glassed at the charges of Johann, the wieff of John Hanson; that window cost 30s. besyde the carryage from Greetland.

"M^dum, that theere was suche resorte of people to this Chappell, that the twenty seates made wold not place them, and the inhabitants thought good to stale the nether end of the Chappell. John Hanson bore the charges of an outshott on the north side of the Queere."

In Feb. 1606, Mr. Ramsden calling for his bell which he had lent, the inhabitants bought a new one, which cost £3 13s. and with the whole expence attending it £4 12s. The above is the only account that can be given of the antiquity of this chapel; except that in two deeds, dated in 1411, there is mention of the Chapel-yard and the Chapel-croft.

The present chapel was erected about 40 years since. It is a handsome stone edifice, with a bell tower attached, and is surrounded by a cemetery.

THE ENDOWMENT.

From a recital in a deed, dated 11th June, 1605, it appears that ten acres of the waste and commons of the manor of Rastrick were granted by the steward of the manor of Wakefield, to be inclosed and improved, for the maintenance of some honest person to say divine service in the chapel, paying yearly four-pence to the grave of Rastrick.

The chapel has received the following augmentations from the governors of queen Anne's bounty: before the year 1720 the returned certainty was five pounds per annum; in 1720, £200 was granted to meet a benefaction of £200 from sir George Armytage, bart. and John Bedford, esq.; in 1760, three sums of £200 each to meet three benefactions of the like sums from George Braithwaite and George Thornhill, esqrs., and Dr. Strafford's executor; and in 1822 a further sum of £200 was granted by lot. The present annual value of the incumbency, as stated in the last Report presented to

Parliament, is £135. There is also a glebe-house attached. The present incumbent is the Rev. Thomas Burton, M. A.

Amongst the ancient estates in this township are the following:

ACRE,

A piece of ground lying near Linlands, by the side of the river Calder, conveyed by Isabel Scot, of Rastrick, in her widowhood, and Ellen and Alice, daughters of the said Isabel, in their pure virginity, by deed without date, to John de Totehill, to hold freely and hereditarily, paying yearly three half-pennies for all services and demands. They also conveyed to him, by another deed, half an acre in the same place; from whence it is plain, that the above name did not here signify a fixed quantity of land, but an open piece of ground, from the Saxon Aceþe, a field, or as the Germans say, Acker, by which they mean any sort of arable land, and call the tiller of it Ackermann, agreeable to the Anglo-Saxon Aceþ-mon. It is supposed that in early times an acre did not necessarily signify any determined quantity of land, and when, by degrees, it was brought to do this, the measure still varied, till it was fixed by the statute called the Ordinance for measuring of land, passed in the reign of king Edward I.

BLACKGREENS

Is a parcel of land and water before-mentioned, lying to the river Calder, where two fulling mills were erected, 17 Edw. IV.

BENERODE,

Called otherwise Boneroyd, says WATSON, because perhaps it was a boon bestowed by the lord on some favourite tenant, or follower; bene, amongst the Anglo-Saxons, and bone in the old English, signifying a petition or boon; but if it is a little corrupted from Binn-royd, it will signify the place which afforded shelter, or security to cattle. Rode, or royd, is said to be uncultivated land, which in respect of its original barrenness paid but two-pence per acre, and was freed from the grave's service, and other impositions; all which may be true, but still we want its etymon. It is one of the many words which the Saxon Vocabularies, not having met with in any Saxon MSS. have honestly omitted.

BOTHEROYD.

Gave name to a family, who, as we are told by Dr. Johnson in his MS. Collections, had a privilege belonging to their lands, that they might hawk and hunt between Worset Pole, four miles above Rastrick westward, and to Spend Bridge, four miles from Rastrick eastward; which privilege was bought by one Mr. Law.

LINLANDS.

Here, on the bank of the river Calder, was the seat of the Rastricks, of Rastrick, the most distinguished family which is known to have resided in this township. The place is at present corruptly called Lilands. It might have its name from the Ling, or Heath, which originally grew here, but it seems more probable that it was so called from Llynn, which in the ancient British (as Lin does in the Cornish and Armoric languages) signifies a lake or pond of water, and such an one there once was here, for in a copy of a deed without date, Isabel, widow of John Scot, and Ellen and Alice her daughters, granted to John de Toythill, four acres of land in Linlands, abutting on the south on the *magnum puteum*, and on the water of Calder.

NEWLAND

Is mentioned by the name of an assart, 34 Edw. III. It was so called, because from being a wood it was newly made arable; for in old deeds where the word terra occurs, it means, says COKE, arable ground only, being so called, a terendo, quia vomere teritur. Hence appears the reason of the distinction we so often meet with in deeds, between the words terra, pratum, and pastura.

TOOTHILL,

Is a remarkable round-copped hill, which attracts the eyes of every one travelling between Wakefield and Elland. It is a natural mount, though the top of it looks as if it was artificial. It has a good command of the country, and had its name, very probably, from the neighbourhood being called together, on public occasions, from the top of it, by the sound of an horn. Tuyte, or Tote, in the Belgic language, signifies an horn; and tuyten or toten (in English, to tote or toot) to blow with an horn, as to toot means, in the Swedish, inflare cornu. As it lies at a moderate distance above Castle-hill, at Rastrick, and was a much more elevated situation, it might serve to collect the inhabitants together, or give them notice to secure themselves in the fort, on any sudden alarm. Or if it answered no military purpose, it might be done as a signal to those who were to attend the Lord when he came there for the diversion of hunting, &c. In the forest of Sowerby, is a piece of high ground called also Toothill, which it is also said was made use of for this latter purpose ; and there are many such like situations in other forests which have the same name of Toothill, particularly one in the forest of Macclesfield, in Cheshire, near Lime-hall, which was the residence of the Lords of that part of the forest.

Near this hill (in Rastrick) lived the family before-mentioned who took the surname of Toothill.

WOODHOUSE,

A very ancient mansion which long since gave name to a family of some account, as already mentioned. It has its name from the materials of which it is built to distinguish it from such as were made of stone, a custom seldom used until after the Norman Era.

TOWNSHIP OF RISHWORTH,

Or RUSHWORTH, so called from the number of rushes therein, adjoins the township of Barkisland on the back, and contains an area of 6,190 statute acres. The name is not modern, as appears from the Saxon orthography, and pronunciation of Rish for Rush.

John, earl of Warren and Surry, claimed free warren here by charter, 37 Henry III. in the dispute 9 Edwd. I. and pleaded, that he had this amongst others of ancient tenure, so that it seems to have been granted from the crown with the manor of Wakefield. Earl Warren was found to be lord thereof by Kirkby's inquest, 24 Edw. I. It is very probable that the family of Rishworth acquired a manor here, for in the fines from the 3rd to the 6th of Edward II. it appears that William de Langfield, and Agnes his wife, were parties concerning the third part of the manors of Rishworth, Barkisland, Bothomley, and Scamonden, which claim came from the family of Rishworth, as stated under Barkisland. Another third part went with a coheiress of Henry de Rishworth to Jordan de Insula, and sir John Eland is said to have bought his part. By the copy of a deed, dated at Elande in 1326, John de Eland, knt. grants to John, son of Robert de Claye, and the heirs of his body lawfully begotten, the sixteenth part of all the waste of Risseworthe. This came to sir John Savile, when he married the heiress of Eland; but another third part had come to John Savile, father of this sir John, on account of his marrying Margaret, daughter, and one of the three co-heiresses of the above Henry de Rishworth. A fine was levied 13 Edw. II. between John de Savile, and Margaret, his wife, concerning twenty-seven shillings, to be paid from lands in Barkisland, Bothomley, Northland, and the third part of the manor of Rishworth, which Alicia the wife of Henry de Rishworth, held for life. Another third part of this manor went to Thomas de Langfeld, who married another of the daughters, and from that family, by marriage, to the Hamertons, as also stated under Barkisland. It then became the property of sir George Savile, of Rufford: and subsequently of the Right Honorable the Earl of Scarborough.

RISHWORTH HALL.

A small building is all that remains to remind the topographer that Rishworth Hall formerly existed. Here lived a family of that name, of which there is no pedigree; from them it passed to the Saviles. In that unfortunate feud between sir John Eland and most of the neighbouring gentry, already mentioned, the owner of Rishworth Hall, John Savile, very prudently kept himself clear of the quarrel, residing one half of the year at Rishworth Hall, and removing thence, by Savile-gate, to Bothom Hall in the parish of Huddersfield. This Savile-gate, or road, was first made and used by John Savile, (who married Margaret, daughter and co-heiress of Henry de Rishworth,) after he came to spend part of his time at Rishworth Hall. His way from Bothom Hall to this place was by Outlane, where begins the Dane's road, and which stretching over the township of Stainland, enters that of Barkisland, crossing the brook near the bridge: in this township, at no great distance from the remain called Meg-dike, Savile-gate branches out from the Dane's road, and points directly upon Rishworth Hall, going by Rishworth Mill. This road seems to have been made new only from the place where it left that attributed to the Danes, and appeared in MR. WATSON's time, to have been only laid out for travelling on horseback. A good part of the ground it went over is now inclosed.

The following observations of Mr. WATSON are certainly deserving of attention and consideration, because they seem to be the result of much practical experience, although I fear the correctness of some of his conclusions, may be called in question,

"*Stable.* On Booth-moor, in this township, is a piece of ground inclosed within trenches, the side of which, to the south-west, is about sixty yards long, that to the south-east, an hundred and three yards; the side opposite to the first of these about fifty yards, and that opposite to the second also about an hundred and three yards; there is a round piece of raised ground near one of the angles, and there is something like a passage through the whole. This I conjecture was made, in former times for the use of cattle, and the name of it seems to confirm this opinion. There are several of these remains in different parts of the country, which have been taken for military stations by antiquaries, particularly one on Wike-moor mentioned in HEARNE's edition of *Leland's Itinerary*, Oxford, 1744, vol. i. page 146. This seems originally to have been of an oblong form, but part of it is destroyed by some inclosures. Its smaller diameter was about seventy-seven yards; of its larger there only remain at present about forty-eight yards. The ditch has been about eight yards wide, but could never be intended for defence, for there is not any water in the neighbourhood to fill it with, and the whole lies upon a flat common, without any sort of rising ground in any of the approaches to it, which yet has generally been thought necessary in the choice of situations to make places of defence.

"But what gives us the clearest idea of this subject, is a couple of remains, at a very small distance from each other, on Crossland moor in the parish of Huddersfield; one of these is seventy-seven yards by sixty-four; but the greatest part of it, when I saw it in 1759, was inclosed with a wall, and intended to be plowed up. The other is ninety-eight yards by eighty-seven. The vallum of this last was six yards and about one foot wide. The smaller has the appearance of a quadrangle, the larger was rounded off a little at the corners. In the larger of them was found, when it was plowed up, three ancient mill-stones, each a foot in diameter, and eleven hollow places, two or three yards long a-piece, and three quarters deep or thereabouts. Now these, one would think, if any thing of this sort could put in its claim for a military station, might be looked upon in that light; and yet most assuredly they never were intended for any such purpose. Their name shews their use; the country people call them the Stot-folds, without knowing the meaning of the expression, which proves them to be of some antiquity. Our Saxon ancestors, it is well known, were fond of horses, and took great pains in the breeding of them, both for war and private purposes; they had numbers of them taken care of together, and made proper inclosures for that purpose, with suitable conveniences therein, both for the cattle, and those who attended them; these inclosures they called Ꞩꞇoꝺ-ꝼolꝺꞃ, the very name of the places in question. For proof of this see Monasticon, vol. i. p. 260. These on Crossland-moor were so considerable that the people who were to make some stay here, found it necessary to have mill-stones with them to grind their corn ; and no doubt but the hollows above mentioned, were where their huts were placed.   To me it seems likely that these works belonged to the garrison at Castle hill, near Almondbury, from which they were not very far distant, and the roads through each of them pointed that way.   If this be so, it affords a presumptive argument that Castle-hill was, what I have attempted to prove it in the first volume of the Archæologia, p. 221, a Saxon station."

It appears from the Couchir book of Fountains Abbey, fol. 207, that Thomas, son of William de Horbury, gave to Ivo Talvas and his heirs, all his land in Wulfrunwall, (now called Wormald,) without retention, with all commodities thereto belonging, in the town of Rishworth ; and from fol. 111, that Ivo Talvas, of Fekisby, gave to John the Clerk, his son, the said land : both without date.

An account of the excellent charitable foundation, called Rishworth School, will be found among the "Public Charities."

There are some very interesting druidical remains in this township.

TOWNSHIP OF SOYLAND.

This township which lies to the South of Sowerby, and to which it is said formerly to have belonged, is sometimes written South-land, and by contraction Soland, because a considerable part of it inclines to the South. It contains an area of 4960 statute acres.

In lord Kirkby's book (1284) it was taxed in Sowerby as an hamlet belonging to that vill; but it is an independant manor: for in the dispute between the crown and earl Warren, temp, Edw. 1. the earl pleaded that he and his ancestors had used free warren in Soyland, but named not Sowerby. By other accounts also he claimed free warren in Soyland, by charter 37 Hen. III. which never was claimed for Sowerby: the reason of which might be, because Sowerby was an ancient forest, and therefore the crown knew they had no right to it; but Soyland being divided from this by a small rivulet, and considered in some respects as a territory of itself, they might think there was some chance of its not being included in the earl's title to the forest. The services which the tenants in Soyland were bound to render to the lord are stated under Sowerby.

The following places are worth mentioning :—

BAITINGS,

Has for a long time past been a public-house, a welcome place where the weary traveller might rest, and refresh himself after the great fatigue of crossing Blackstone-edge, in his road from Lancashire to Yorkshire, before the roads over this craggy mountain were improved to that degree of perfection in which they are now to be seen. As the house has so long been put to this use, both by bipeds and quadrupeds, the name would appear to have been derived from thence, was there not the strongest reason to suppose that the place was so called before it was ever applied to the purpose of an inn; in short, that it had its denomination from the land, and not from housing here; for whatever may be the meaning of the first syllable, the latter comes, undoubtedly, from the Saxon Inʒe, called yet, in many parts of the North of England, Ing, and in the plural number Ings, which signify meadows or pastures. This was a summer vaccary, or feeding for cattle, and held, on that account, as domain land by the earls of Warren, under this title, "Tenementa que sunt in manibus Domini in Dominico." This vaccary was so considerable, that in 1314, in the book called Domisday, or an extent of the rents and services of the free men of the soke of Wake-field, it was returned that there might be in Baytinge twenty-eight fat beasts, and besides them ten fat beasts might be agisted (or pastured) there, between the feasts of St. Helen and St. Giles, which was yearly worth forty shillings; another account says, it was worth yearly twenty-six shillings and eight pence. This, with other vaccaries in the forest, was afterwards granted, or let out by copy of court roll, not by any certain number of acres, but by the name of such a vaccary, lying within such and such boundaries. The following is a grant of this vaccary; at a court held at Wake-field, 12th of March, 9th Henry IV. (translated from the French.)

"Edward, duke of York, earl of Cambridge, Rutland, and of Cork, and lord of Tindall, to our trusty and well-beloved Lord Rustin, of Nevill, greeting. Know you that we have granted to our tenant, Roger Banister, two parcels of pasture, lying out of our park of Erringden, in Sowerbyshire, lying towards the south, called Mareshae, and the Baitings: To have and to hold to the said Roger, his heirs and assigns, in base tenure, according to the custom of our said manor of Sowerby, yielding yearly to us and our heirs twenty-six shillings and eight-pence, at terms usual. We charging you that you accept the said Roger to make fine in our court of Sowerby for the said parcels. To have and to hold, to him and to his heirs, in form as is said, and that you cause the same to be en-rolled there, witnessing our grant in the said court, In witness whereof we have hereunto put our seal, dated the seventh day of February, in the ninth year of the reign of our Sovereign Lord, king Henry the Fourth after the conquest." The said Roger gave to the lord, for fine for entry, five shillings, which he paid in court.

At the Turn at Halifax, Oct. 12, 14 Hen. IV. a grant was made of two messuages, called Baitings, and also one old pasture, called Baitings, as this lay within the following bounds. Beginning at Baytingclough, and from that place as far as to Shokeforthebroke, and so as far as to Lyttil Manneshede, and from that place lineally across the way at Mireshaclough, and from thence as far as Blakestonedge, even where the water falls and parts, and so on the south side of a certain way called the Causaye, as far as to Shokeforthebroke aforesaid. And the present owner of Baitings claims so much to this day.

In one of the fields belonging to this estate, was formerly the foundations of a building which goes by the name of the chapel. In the time of Hen. VIII. the estate belonged to one Richard Gledhill, and in the reign of king James I. to the Priestleys, of White-Windows. 1 William & Mary, Mrs. Everild Thornhill was admitted to the premises in fee, on the surrender of Henry Priestley, subject to a proviso of redemption. 1693, William Horton, gent. was admitted in fee to the same, on the surrender of the said Mrs. Thornhill, and Martha Priestley, widow. June 1st, 1711, Thomas Priestley, son and heir of the said Henry Priestley, deceased, released his equity in the said premises to the said William Horton, in fee, from which family it came by devise to Musgrave Brisco, Esq. the present owner,

FORGE-HOUSE.

Which probably is the same mentioned in the survey of the manor of Sowerby in the year 1314.

LADYWELL.

A house so called, near which is a remarkable fine spring which in former time seems to have been appropriated to superstitious uses, and to have been dedicated to the Virgin Mary, honored at that time with the title of our Lady; if indeed the country in this part was not the property of some religious house, for a considerable part of it went by the name of Lady-land, as appears from the following entry in a MS, in the Harleian Collection, No. 797.—"Turn at Brighouse, 1st Feb. 44 Edwd. III, John, son of Thomas Culpan, died seized of six oxgangs of land in Soland, which lies in Ladyland, which are held by eighteen-pence rent, and suit of court of Wakefield, from three weeks to three weeks." It belonged formerly to the name of Whiteley.

LIGHTHAZLES.

A house which gives name to a large district around it. On one of the gable ends, says WATSON, "is what I take to be intended for the name of Jesus, which I have observed on several old houses in Halifax parish, and might in that credulous age, be made use of to drive away evil spirits." This place might take its name from Lyre a few, and hæfl, an hazle, as being a place where a small wood of hazles grew.

ROYD.

A house surrounded with good land, though doubtless it took its name from its having been terra debilis & inculta.

SWIFT-PLACE.

Once the property of a family of the name of Swift, one of whom erected a cross above the house by the road side, still called Swift-cross.

TOWNSHIP OF STAINLAND.

THIS township lies to the West of Elland, and contains an area of 1730 statute acres. The name is in all probability derived from the nature of the land here, a corruption of Stony-land; although in point of fertility it is not inferior to the neighbouring townships.

Within this township is an ancient cross, of which the following sketch is here inserted, the remarks will be found in a subsequent page.

At the court at Wakefield, 6 Edw. III. Roger, son and heir of Thomas de Thornton, who held the fourth part of the town of Stainland by the service of ten shillings, did his homage. 7 Rich.

II. Hugh Annesley, and Joan, his wife, gave to Brian Stapleton, knt. (inter alia) the manors of Linley, Stainland, &c. which some time were William de Quermby's, late husband of said Joan, for term of her life, rendering to said Hugh and Joan, and to the assigns of said Joan, for her life, seventeen pounds fifteen shillings.

John de Heton claimed the custom of the body and lands of Joan, daughter of William de Quermby, alleging that the said William held of him in Quermby certain lands and tenements, and the moiety of the town of Stainland by homage, fealty, escuage, and service of four-pence by the year, or of one pair of gilt spurs. They made an agreement at Pontefract, Sept. 5, 10 Ric. II.

In the decree 6 Elizabeth before referred to, Edward Savile, his heirs and assigns, were allowed peaceably to enjoy the manor of Stainland, though it does not appear from the proceedings, that any other person had laid claim to it. In 1577, by an inquisition taken at Wakefield, it was found that this manor was held of the queen, as of her lordship of Wakefield, but by what service the jury were ignorant; it appears by records, that it was by foreign service. By another inquisition taken at Halifax, in some part of the reign of queen Elizabeth, the heirs of Sir Henry Savile, knt. and lady Elizabeth, his wife, were found to hold this manor, (inter alia) being deemed to be within the lordship or dominion of Wakefield, but not parcel thereof, neither parcel of the duchy, by reason of annexing the same lordship to the duchy, as was supposed. Stainland and Barkisland were found, by an inquisition at Pontefract, 5th and 6th Phil. and Mary, to be held of the manor of Wakefield, in free soccage by fealty and thirteen shillings and four-pence yearly; and that Henry Savile, knt. before his death was seized in fee tail of this manor of Stainland amongst others; how it descended afterwards may be seen under Barkisland, which descended with it. It belongs at present to the same noble owner.

There are two Charities connected with Stainland, which are omitted in the Commissioners' Report. I have here stated them in the words of my informant. JAMES GLEDHILL, late of Holy-well-green, (who died July 27th, 1792,) bequeathed £100, the interest arising therefrom to be disposed of annually in the following manner —40s. to the minister of Stainland for preaching a sermon on good-Friday; the remainder to be laid out in linen cloth and given to the poor of Stainland.

MRS. PRESTON left £2 16s. 8d. annually to the poor of Stainland, called *Lady-Dole*, vested in the earl of Mexborough.

BRADLEY-HALL.

The present owner of which is Savile, earl of Mexborough; was doubtless in days gone by, a noble residence, well befitting that illustrious house. The chapel here, says Dr. Johnson, was pulled down at the time of the civil wars, but the hall was burnt down in 1629. There is a tradition in the neighbourhood about this fire, and it is likewise said, that it caused the family to remove to Methley. The bells are also said to have been removed to Methley church, near which this branch of the Savile family have a seat. Only a small part of the hall now remains, but the ground about it shews, by its inequality, that it has been more extensive. Over the gate are the figures 1577, and the letters I. S. John Savile. On the kitchen wall is 1598. In Watson's time, the chapel which had been re-edified, served the the tenant for a barn; a few large stones in an adjoining fence are supposed to have belonged one entrance to the church.

LINLEY,

Is a division within the township of Stainland. It was called Old Linley, to distinguish it from another Linley, in the neighbouring parish of Huddersfield, which goes by the name of New Linley: in a deed dated in 1326, is this expression, "in campo de Stayneland, & in divisis de Lyndeleye;" and in another, 23 Eliz. it is called Old Linley, alias Over Linley.

By indentures of fine, in 1309, Thomas, son of Richard de Wakefield, granted to William, son of Adam del Lee, an annual rent of 5s. 11d. of silver, with homages, wards, reliefs, escheats, &c. to be taken from certain of his tenants therein mentioned, within the vill of Linnley; which seems to imply the right of manor in the granter. And in a deed, sans date, John le Harpur de Wakefield, and Eleanor his wife, (of the same family, no doubt,) grant to Thomas de Touthill an annual rent of 8s. which he had recovered, 14 Edw. II. (1230) from William, son of Adam del Lee, in Hold Linley, with wards, reliefs, and escheats, "simûl cum dominio de Hold Linley & vasto, sicut Ric. clericus de Wakefield quondam·tenuit." By another date, sans date, the said John grants to the said Thomas, 5s. 11d. to be received from all his tenants in Hold Linley, with wards, &c. " et dominio de Hold Linly, sicut

Rise de Wakefeld quond. tenuit." By another deed he grants to him "moram turbarum et boscum de Old Linley." From the Toot-hills the manor of Old Linley descended to the Thornhills, on ac-count of Richard de Thornhill marrying Margaret, daughter and heiress of William de Toothill, in the reign of Edw. III. and accor-dingly, by an inquisition taken at the court at Wakefield. 4 Hen. IV. (1402) Margaret, late wife of Richard Thornhill, held, at the time of her decease, (inter alia) " Linley cum mora turbaria & bosco de Old Linley, cum wardis, &c."

In the 47 Geo. III, an act was passed for enclosing lands in this township. The lands enclosed under the authority of this act, comprised two several open fields or mesne inclosures, called the Upper Town Field and the Lower Town Field, and divers open commons, moors, and waste grounds, called Old Linley edge, Lind-ley moor, Lee hill, Jaggar Green, Dean and Gosforth Clough, and other parcels of waste ground containing in the whole 200 statute acres or thereabouts. Thomas Thornhill, esq. is the present lord of the manor.

ST. HELEN'S.

WATSON informs us, that here was once a Popish chapel, and tradition says that it was also used by the Protestants in the reign of queen Elizabeth. It was dedicated to St. Helen, whose name a remarkably fine well, just by the remains of the chapel, retains to this day. The chapel has been converted into a cottage, and it can only just be seen that it once was a place of greater account. In one of the walls of the house they shew you a large stone, which is called the Cross, and which is sometimes visited by strangers, who at the same time enquire for the well; and, adds WATSON, "from the behaviour of some of them, the inhabitants concluded they were Papists, whose zeal brought them thither, to behold this once famous place, of which their forefathers were despoiled."

STAINLAND CHAPEL.

In the year 1755 a chapel was erected in this township " for the convenience of those who lay at so great a distance from any church, chapel, or other place of public devotion." It is vested in nine trus-tees upon trust to be " appropriated to and made use of as a chapel of ease for the lawful assembly and meeting of the inhabitants of the said township of Stainland, and of the vills and hamlets contiguous thereto, and of all and every other person and persons who should be desirous and willing to make use of and frequent the same, for the celebration of divine worship therein, after the manner of the true protestants of the church of England, and who should be subject to the rites, ceremonies, payments, customs, and services as in the said church is used and practised."

There is a cemetary attached. The trustees from time to time to be appointed are to be "true protestants, according to the church of England as now by law established."

STAINLAND CROSS,

On the road side, and within half a mile of St. Helen's, stands this interesting structure, which appears to have escaped the notice of either WRIGHT or WATSON.

It represents a saltier or St. Andrew's cross, carved on a block of stone; the block is scooped out in the form of a cup, but the cover that was formerly attached to it has been removed. The shaft is circular and plain, without any of that rich, uncouth sculpture, or scroll ornament, which antiquarians generally attribute to Saxon or Danish structures. Its height from the base to the top of the column is about ten feet, the shaft does not exceed five feet.

Neither tradition nor history have preserved the date or purpose of its erection, and the oldest inhabitant only knows that his paternal sire spoke of it as a very old affair. Since therefore we are left in the dark on the subject, we may indulge in a harmless antiquarian speculation; in the hope that it may induce a more extended enquiry among those who are qualified to form an opinion on its merits.

It will be observed that one of the peculiar features of this structure is its simplicity, and although that very circumstance may be adduced as an argument in favor of its antiquity, the fact that the shaft has none of that interlaced and curious tracery work before referred to, is against the probability of a Saxon origin.

Old HEARNE, the antiquary, tells us that "among us in Britain crosses became most frequent, when, after William the conqueror's time, great crusades were made into the Holy Land. Then crossings or creasings were used on all occasions. 'Twas not looked upon as enough to have the figure of the cross both on and in churches, chapels, and oratories, but it was put also in church yards, and in every house, nay many towns and villages were built in shape of it, and it was very common to fix it in the very streets and highways."

Crosses were not uncommon in the parish. Watson mentions one in Fixby which he seemed to think was placed by the wayside, "according to the superstition of the times;" also "the cross of Mankynholes," this was in existence prior to the Reformation, and the presumption is that all of them were, for it was the custom of the Romish church to erect crosses in public situations, to remind the traveller of his religious duties; so far Mr. Watson's conjecture may be correct, but it is open to doubt whether if this cross had been used as a symbol of faith, it would have escaped the mistaken zeal of the Reformists; or the fanatical fury of the Puritans, when they attacked Bradley-hall, had there been a tradition that it was originally placed for a superstitious use.

It is not improbable that it was placed there to mark the boundary of some land. Crosses were made use of in former times for this purpose, particularly where lands belonged to monasteries or religious houses, and it is certain that the knights of St. John of Jerusalem had lands in this part of the country, as also the nuns of Kirklees. There is a statute in existence to prevent the removal of these species of land-marks. Other descriptions of crosses called memorial crosses are to be found in many parts of the country, but being in general erected to perpetuate a particular event, tradition has preserved the history of their erection.

HOLY WELL.

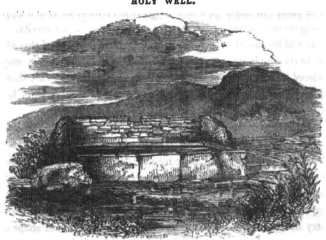

This well gives name to Helliwell (or Holy-Well) green.   It is sometimes called St. Helen's well from its supposed connection with St. Helen's chapel.   There is no evidence to shew when it was first formed, nor is there any thing peculiar in its construction that it should excite the attention of the passing traveller.   That "it is no new conceit, but a real piece of antiquity" the following, from Watson, will satisfy the most incredulous.

"I have the copy of a deed without date, but which, by the witnesses, must have been executed between the years 1279 and 1324, wherein William de Osesete grants an assart in Linley to Henry *de Sacro Fonte de Staynland*."   Its original use must be matter of conjecture, although there can be little doubt it was honored in the dark ages of Popery with the peculiar designation of Holy. The custom of giving names to wells is of great antiquity and prevailed in the days of the patriarchs, see Gen. 21—31.   "It was a custom if any well had an awful situation, and was seated in a lonely, melancholy vale; if its water was clear and limpid, and beautifully margined with the tender grass, or if it was looked upon as having a medicinal quantity, to dedicate it to some saint."

Hence is it that at this day we have St. John's well, St. Mary's well, St. Peter's well, &c. &c.   The superstitious practice of paying adoration to wells and fountains was forbidden in the early ages, and there was a canon made in the reign of king Edgar to that effect. The custom of affixing ladles of iron, &c., by a chain to wells is also of great antiquity, and still retained in many parts of the North.

THE PAROCHIAL

CHAPELRY OF HEPTONSTALL.

THIS third and last ecclesiastical division of the Parish consists of the following townships, viz.

HEPTONSTALL,	STANSFIELD,
ERRINGDEN,	WADSWORTH.
LANGFIELD,	

The chapelry which possesses the same parochial rights as Elland, is subject to similar impositions, and under the same ecclesiastical jurisdiction. The vicar of the parish has the right of presentation, and pays the incumbent an ancient yearly stipend of £4. Attached to the parochial chapel is a chapel of ease at Crosstone, within Stansfield; and another has recently been erected within the same township, under the sanction of the Commissioners for building and promoting the building of additional churches.

The chapelry comprises a larger district of country than either Halifax or Elland, and over which nature has indeed been lavish of her gifts. "Were it in the power of taste (says DR. WHITAKER,) for one moment, to separate the inelegance which ever accompanies manufactures, from natural scenery, it would be impossible to traverse this portion of the vale of Calder, without pleasure. There are, in particular, two scenes, one West of Hebden-bridge and the other of Todmorden, which, in countries free from such associations, would be compared to very fine Highland glens; the latter in particular strikingly resembles the pass of Killikranky."

TOWNSHIP OF HEPTONSTALL.

The township is bounded on the North and East by the Hepton, on the South by the Calder, and partly on the West by a brook which separates it from Stansfield, and comprises an area of 5320 statute acres.

As to the etymology of the name WATSON says it is a little uncertain, it may come from the anglo-saxon Ƀeap, an heap of any thing, and tun, an habitation or settlement, the word "stall" having been since added. Be that as it may, Hep, in Saxon, is high, and Heptonstall the high place; unless we are to understand by it the place on the Hepton, for in a charter S. D. referring to an ancient dispute between the prior of Lewes, as rector impropriate of Halifax, and sir John de Thornhill, as mesne lord, mention is made of "Joh. prior de Lewes, & Dñ's Joh de Thornhill, super stagnum de Heptonstall super aquam quæ vocatur Hepton (not Hebden*) quæ currit inter Heptonstall et Wadsworth." The date does not appear, but a deed is referred to dated 1313, 9 Edward II, whereby sir John granted to the prior and convent of Lewes, in Sussex, and their successors licence to attach their mill dam of Heptonstall on his soil in Wadsworth, over the water called Hebden, where it should please the said prior and his successors.

Mr. Watson appears to have fallen into an error respecting Heptonstall, when he says it is thus mentioned in Domesday book. "In Heptone duo fratres habuerunt tres carucatas terre ad geldam, et tres caruce possunt ibi esse. Ilbertus habet, et Gamel de eo, sed wast est. T. R. E. valuit xx solidos, silva pastura 1 leuga et dimidium longitudine, et leuga latitudine." This is not the Heptone described in Domesday, says DR. WHITAKER, "but another place in Agbrigg wapontake;" therefore Mr. Watson's hypothesis must fall to the ground. It is not improbable that it was granted from the crown to earl Warren, for in Kirkby's inquest, 24 Edw. I. earl Warren was found to be the lord of the manor of Heptonstall; and in a MS. in the British Museum, No. 797 of the Harleian MSS. being collections relating to Morley hundred, chiefly written by Mr. Jennings, it appears that John Warren, earl of Surry, claimed free warren in Heptonstall, by charter, 37 Henry III. By an inquisition taken at Pontefract, 25 August, 5 and 6 Philip and Mary, it was found that sir Henry Saville, knight, died seized in fee tail of the manor of Heptonstall, and from him it passed by

* DR. Whitaker thinks the latter the true orthography.

degrees to sir George Saville, of Rufford, deceased. 5 Charles, 1629, a court was held at Heptonstall, by Charles Greenwood, clerk, rector of Thornhill, lord of the manor of Heptonstall. The present possessor of the manor is The Right Honorable the Earl of Scarborough.

The village, from which the township takes its name, is situated on a bleak and barren hill, frequently rendered inaccessible by the inclemency of the weather, the only safe approach being the new road branching from the Todmorden and Halifax Turnpike Road, the old highway over the Hepton is steep and dangerous. It is difficult to conceive how a large and populous village should have arisen on a site so cold, barren, and difficult of access. "The place is the very counterpart of Haworth." But it is not without its redeeming qualities, the scenery viewed from the various points of this elevated station is indeed grand, romantic, beautiful and picturesque; and the ascent by the new road commands a most pleasing view of the rich vale of Calder. Tradition tells us that a battle was formerly fought here between the Cavaliers and Roundheads, and that a great part of the town was burnt. To its honor be it recorded that it it formed a garrison for the king. The appearance of the town indicates that it has seen better days, and trade was once so good here that it maintained some kind of a market. WATSON refers to a deed, 2 Charles I. wherein it is recited, that John Sunderland, late of the Hossalde in Ayringden, purchased of sir Arthur Ingram, of London, knight, William Ingram, doctor of laws, and Richard Golthorpe, of London, gent. all that house and building commonly called Heptonstall Cloth-hall, in Heptonstall aforesaid, by indenture dated Nov. 10, 9th James I. As the prescriptive market at Halifax came into repute this might decline, and there is the greater reason for this presumption, as the reign of queen Elizabeth is the very time when trade began more particularly to flourish at Halifax. This the owners above named being sensible of, in the succeeding reign of James I. and there being no probability of the hall being ever used for the like purpose again, rather than suffer it to sink down into unprofitable ruins, they conveyed it as above.

THE CHAPEL.

This chapel was originally dedicated to St. Thomas à Becket, and DR. WHITAKER says, "though there is no certain evidence of it, it was probably erected not long after his murder." (Dec. 30, 1172.) A well in the neighbourhood is called Becket (for Becket) well, and seems to have been dedicated to the saint of the place. WRIGHT says, this chapel was built about the year 1840 : but WATSON thinks it to be coeval with Elland, and to have been erected before the year 1260, for the reason already mentioned. It may not be amiss to take notice here, that Joseph Wilkinson, vicar of Halifax, in the chancery-suit about Heptonstall, swore, that he had heard, and believed it to be true, that the family of Saviles did formerly build and endow the chantry chapels of Heptonstall and Elland, and did build and repair part of the parish church of Halifax ; and that there was some agreement between the inhabitants of Elland and Heptonstall chapelries, and the rest of the inhabitants of Halifax parish, and the Saviles, that the said inhabitants should repair their several chapels, and that the other inhabitants in the parish of Halifax, who were nearer to the parish church, should repair the same at their own charge. This may or may not be true, but it is improbable that the Saviles built Elland chapel, for it was erected long before the Saviles had any estate there ; and the same is also true of Heptonstall. Another assertion, made use of in the same dispute by the vicar of Halifax, was equally false, that Heptonstall was originally a chantry chapel, but afterwards became parochial ; for there is reason to believe, that it had parochial rights before a chantry was ever founded in it.

Of the original fabric there are no remains, the whole having been rebuilt about the end of Henry VII's reign (1500.) It is a singular edifice, and very judiciously, though awkwardly constructed, low and on a broad base to resist the outrageous tempests which oft assail it. The tower if left to itself is strong enough to defy the fury of the elements for many centuries : the masonry is excellent. The chapel itself has four aisles, of which two, with a row of angular columns running up the middle, occupy the ordinary place of the middle aisle ; on the outside of these are two others, low and sloping to the eaves. The date of the present erection, which from its extent implies that the chapelry attached to it was then become very populous, may I think be ascertained from some fragments of painted glass, yet preserved in the East window, with the date MDVIII. Every thing about the architecture agrees with this.

In one of the aisles is an ancient grave-stone, the inscription round which is worn out, but a Calvary cross is still visible thereon. On one of the windows are the arms of Stansfield, of Stansfield; date in old numerals, 1508. Also sufficient remains to shew, that the twelve apostles have been painted there, and with each of them, in antique character, the part of the creed inscribed to him. On a pillar towards the North is the ancient mark for Jesus.

There was once an organ here, as appears from the following entry in the register book: "Mem. The 21 day of April, Ano Dom!. 1572, in the parish church of Heptonstall there were laid up in the coffer, with the register book, 120 organ pipes; and 16 great pipes, 5 wood pipes, and 15 lead pipes, were laid up with Richard Bentley, in Heptonstall, for the use of the parish, in the presence of, &c." WATSON says "the chapel of Heptonstall was made uniform in 1634, and every man's particular form or seat appropriated to him," but I have a grant in my possession, dated 33 Elizabeth, (1596) of "one half of a short form and stall, as the same was then builded, standing on the South side of the church, betwixt the stalls or forms of, &c." which goes far to prove that an appropriation of seats took place before the time specified by Watson.

There is inserted in archbishop Scott's register at York, fo. 29, a licence granted by the ordinary, in 1482, for the celebration of masses and other divine offices, without the chapel of Heptonstall, till it should be restored, having been polluted by the effusion of blood. The chapel was restored on the 10th of January following, by a commission for that purpose. The following is a copy of the original:—"Will. Poteman, etc. Reverendo in Xpo Patri et Domino, Domino Willielmo, Dei gracia Dromoren. Episcopo, dicti Reverendi Patris Saffraganeo, salutem in omnium Salvatore. Quia, ut accepimus, Capella de Heptonstall, Parochie de Hallyfax, Ebor, Dioces. cum cimiterio ejusdem, nuper fuerunt et sunt violenta sanguinis consueta, vestre Paternitati Reverende tenore presentium concedimus facultatem, et plenam in Domino potestatem. Dat. Ebor. effusione notorie polluta, ad reconcilandam igitur dictam Capellam, cum cimiterio ejusdem, ut prefertur, violenta sanguinis effusione polluta, ceteraq; omnia et singula facienda, exercenda et expedienda, que in hujusmodi solempnitate necessaria fuerint et fieri decimo die mensis Januarii, Anno Dom. millesimo quatercentissimo octogesimo secundo." From the same Register, fol. 30.

DR. WHITAKER has indulged in some very severe remarks on the usage to which he alleges the chapel and its cemetery was formerly subject. A vulgar notion exists among some of the inhabitants, that the belfry or steeple of this chapel belongs to the churchwardens for the time being as of right. I should not have adverted to the fact, had not that supposed right been attempted to be exercised on a recent political occasion, when the keys were obtained from the incumbent and possession of them held against his express remonstrance; the bells not being permitted to be used for ecclesiastical purposes. It is needless to add there is no foundation for such an extravagant and absurd notion, but the ignorance of its partizans.

The chantries which were founded in this chapel were these, as inserted in the archbishop's certificate mentioned under Elland:—1. A chantry there (no founder's name mentioned) worth yearly five pounds. 2. The service of our lady there, worth four pounds yearly. From this there is a variation in WILLIS's *History of Abbies*, v. ii, p. 292; for under the title of Heptonstall is this: "Virgin Mary's chantry. To Richard Michell, incumbent, £8 12s." But there is an old MS, wherein the sums to both agree with the archbishop's certificate, as does STEVEN's *Supplement to the Monasticon*, vol. i. p. 68. In a list of the tithes paid in the vicarage of Halifax, in the reign of Hen. VIII. is the following entry: "For the lands in Stansfeld belonging to the Chauntry of the blessed Virgin Mary in the church of Heptonstall, 12d."

The old chapel-yard is filled up, but a considerable addition was made some years back, The present cemetery is large and commodious, and surrounded by a wall and iron fence.

Of the Testamentary burials at Heptonstall, the oldest appears to be "Robert Shagh, buried in the church-yard of the chapel of St. Thomas the Martyr, of Heptonstall, 1467, 7 Edw. IV." This from a MS in the British Museum, Harleian Collection, No, 797; and from hence may be seen, among numberless other instances which might be produced, what little distinction was formerly made in this parish, between the words church and chapel.

THE ENDOWMENT.

The chapel has from time to time been endowed with the following property and gifts.

By the will of Richard Naylor of Erringden, dated May, 1609, an annuity of thirty-two shillings and six-pence, charged upon three closes of land, meadow and pasture, called the Gould pit, the Great hey, and the South end of the Crag in Mixenden in Ovenden, containing about seven acres, for and towards the keeping and maintaining a preacher at Heptonstall for the time, so as he be a master of Arts, to be paid at the feast of St. John the Baptist, for all the year.

JOHN GREENWOOD, of Learings, in Heptonstall, by will, dated Feb. 10, 1687, gave to the owner or inheritor of Learings, in Heptonstall, and to the churchwardens and overseers of the same for the time being, and to their heirs and successors for ever, one annuity of forty shillings a year, issuing out of a messuage and tenement, with appurtenances, in Stansfield, commonly called Dovescout, in trust to pay the one moiety or half part thereof unto Daniel Town, curate at Heptonstall, for preaching every year a sermon upon the first Wednesday in June yearly, at Heptonstall, during his natural life, if he be able in body, and can be admitted; and after his decease, to the curate of Heptonstall for the time being, he performing as aforesaid for ever.

JOHN GREENWOOD, of Hippings in Stansfield, by will dated 13 Decr. 1705, willed that he who should be lawfully admitted as parson or minister of Heptonstall, to officiate there, should preach a sermon upon the first Wednesday in August yearly for ever, in lieu of which sermon, and his yearly wages for Hippingsland, he gave him and his successors twenty shillings yearly, for ever.

THOMAS SUNDERLAND, of Hathershelf in Sowerby, by will dated Nov. 13, 1721, gave and devised one annuity or yearly rent of twenty shillings, payable out of a messuage and lands thereunto belonging, called New house, in Turvin, yearly to such orthodox curate or parson of Heptonstall church or chapel, in this county, for the time being, as should be conformable to the present Established church of England, both in doctrine and discipline, and should on the second Wednesday in the month of March, for ever, preach one commemoration sermon, for, or on account of, the testator's only child, Thomas Sunderland, who died in that month.

The chapel has received the following augmentations from the governors of the bounty of queen Anne; in 1747, £200 by lot, in consequence of which, a purchase was made of a messuage and lands thereto belonging, called West croft head, in the parish of

Bradford, chapelry of Haworth, and township of Oxnop, yielding the clear yearly rent of £8. 10s. In 1736, its clear yearly value was returned to have been ten guineas, 3rd queen Anne. In 1780 another £200 by lot, in 1809, £200 to meet a benefaction of £200 from Mr. Marshall's trustees. In 1810 two sums of £200 each to meet two benefactions of £200 each, one from the Hon. and Rev. J. Lumley Saville and others, the other from H. Cockroft, Esq. and others, In 1810, £600 by lot. In 1824, £200 by lot. And in 1825 £200 to meet a benefaction of £200 from the Rev. Joseph Charnock, the present incumbent. According to the last Report of the Commissioners for enquiring into the revenues of the church, the income is stated to be £120 per annum.

About half a mile beyond the town is a straggling hamlet called Heptonstall Slack, where it is said there are the remains of some earth-works, but of what nature I have not been able to ascertain. There is also a place called The Lea, (or meadow) below the town, so called from its situation on the bank of the Hepton: the scenery in this part of the country is peculiarly fine and romantic.

TOWNSHIP OF ERRINGDEN.

This township comprises a very mountainous country, bounded by the Calder on the North, partly by a brook and partly by the township of Sowerby on the East, and by Langfield on the West; and contains an area of 2,980 statute acres.

The etymology of the name is uncertain. In the time of Edw. III. it appears to have been written Heyrikdene, as also in letters patent 11th of the same king; this possibly may be corrupted from Here-wic-dene, Anglo-Saxon words, the first of which signifies a company of armed men, the second a fortress, and the last a valley; if so, says WATSON, "it takes its name from an adjoining valley, where formerly was a castle, already described in the Saxon Era; or the army, which came to attack this fort, might encamp on this ground, which is the more probable, as there are yet the remains of a redoubt at some distance from the Castle-hill, thrown up to defend the passage of the river Calder from an attack on the Erringden side of the water. But if Heyrikdene be thought a greater corruption of the true name than Erringden, as it is now generally written, it might be the Earing-dene, from the Anglo-Saxon Epian to plow, to till or eare." I have letters patent of queen Elizabeth, wherein it is spelt Aeringdene alias Earingdene. And this name it might acquire when it was enclosed as a park, as being expressive of the chief purpose for which it was enclosed; for the country, to a considerable extent, being a forest, and stored with beasts of various kinds, for the purpose of hunting, there could not be much corn grown where these had liberty.

In Erringden was formerly a park appurtenant to the forest of Sowerbyshire, the oldest express mention of which (says WATSON) is in a deed between William de Langfeld, and John de Metheleye,

9 Edward III. wherein the former grants to the latter, "omnes terras et tenementa q: habuit ex dono Dom. Johannis comitis Warren. in le Withens, Tornelymosse et Mankanholes in Sourbischire extra parcum de Heyrikdene." Of this deed there was an ancient attested copy at the late Mr. Cockcroft's, of Mayroid. At what time this park was first inclosed does not appear, but in all probability it must have taken place before the erecting of Heptonstall chapel, (which was prior to the year 1260,) because it was allotted thereto at the division of the parish, which could not have been, had it not been inclosed. Probably it was not very long after the date of the forest: and the ground of which this forest consisted, is said, by the late Mr. Robert Nalson, of Halifax, at fol. 128 of his MS. entitled, *Miscellanea, sive observationes collectanea*, to have been granted by king Henry I. to earl Warren, in 1116. The park was dispailed about the 27 Henry VI. as appears from certain letters patent of that monarch, as follows :—"Richard, duke of York, earl of March and of Ulnstre, lord of Wiggemore and of Clare, to all those that these letters shall see or hear, greeting. Forasmuch as for certain reasonable causes moving us thereunto, and also for to eschewe the debate and controversy, which of long time hath continued amongst our officers and tenants of our lordship of Sowerby, unto the great hurt of us, and them also, because of our game within our park of Ayringden, to the reformation of which, and also to improve our said park, and the herbage of the same from henceforth, to our most profit and avail; We therefore trusting in the truth, wisdom, and diligence of our right trusty and well-beloved sir John Seville, knt. our steward in Yorkshire, Thomas Willughby, our auditor in England, and John Vincent, our receiver in the said shire, have ordained and committed them, and given them full power and authority, by these our letters, for to divide our said park in divers parts or in parcels, and let it to ferme to good and sufficient men for term of life, or for term of years, or otherwise, after the custom of the manor, as their discretions shall think to our most avail, destroying our game there, so that we bear hereafter no more charge thereof, holding firm and stable whatsoever our commissioners shall do in our name in the matter abovesaid. In witness whereof we have set our seal to these our letters. Given at our castle of Fodringham, the seventeenth (one copy says sixteenth) day of

March, in the twenty-seventh year of the reign of our sovereign lord Henry Sixth," &c.

In consequence of the above, we find by the court rolls, that Thomas Stansfeld came to the court and took of the lord a fourth part of the said park, as it lay between Birnedakirygate (Burnt-acreesgate) and Beamonde-cloughe; to hold to him, his heirs and assigns for ever, by service, according to the custom of the manor, paying yearly to the lord six pounds sterling at Michaelmas; and for a fine at entrance, eight pounds six shillings and eight-pence. Also Thomas Southcliffe took another fourth part of the said park, as it lay between Beamonde-cloughe and Hawks-clough. Rent and fine as above. Also the said Thomas Southcliffe took a part of the said park lying between Hoohoile and Brodehedeclough, to the three stones on Eringden moor, which is called Mandike, where the division of the park ends. Yearly rent three pounds eight shillings. Fine four pounds ten shillings. Also Richard Fourness took another parcel called Sexokekerres, lying between Hawkesclough and Hoohoile, to the aforesaid stones in Mandike. Rent two pounds ten shillings. Fine three pounds. Also Ralph Estwodd took another parcel lying between Brodehedeclough and the white stone in the Cragg, and to the aforesaid stones in Mandike; and another small parcel near Simmewifeclough. Rent one pound seven shillings. Fine one pound eighteen shillings and fourpence. Also John Ryleye took another parcel lying between the white stone in the Cragg, and another stone beyond Gunerwalle-nase, (now called Nase-end.) Rent one pound seven shillings. Fine one pound eighteen shillings and four-pence. Also Robert Akeroyd took another parcel lying between Le Great Oller and Hawks-cloughe. Fine one pound ten shillings; no rent mentioned. Also John Sunderland took another parcel, lying between the said stone beyond Gunerwalle-nase and Lez Withennes, and so to Bannesterdike. Rent two pounds ten shillings. Fine four pounds six shillings and eight-pence. And it was agreed, that the said tenants, their heirs, and assigns, should pay at the death of a chief tenant, or an alienation, after the rate of twenty shillings for the fourth part of the said park; and should yearly chuse one of the tenants amongst themselves to be the lord's greave to collect the above rent of twenty-four pounds. And the said tenants were not to do suit at the lord's mill, unless he built a new mill on the river Calder, or the water of Ayringden. And they gave the lord for fine at entrance fifty marks.

This Richard, duke of York, was soon after slain at the battle of Wakefield, in 1460, and the above copyholders became tenants to the crown in the person of his son, King Edward the Fourth, who by patent, 9 Edw. IV. part 1. m. 4. (one account says, 4 Edw. IV.) granted to John Pilkington, an esquire of his body, the office of chief forester, or master of his chase of Sowerby, and keeper of his park of Erringden, for term of life. It is very likely that the place was a sinecure after the accession of Edward IV. the park being dispailed, or at least all the game destroyed, and even the forest itself so neglected, as such, that Watson says he cannot even meet with the name of forester after the death of this John. The Pilkingtons seem to have been highly in favor with the lords of this forest and park, for Robert Pilkington had a considerable post under the above-named duke of York, in the reign of Henry VI. as will appear from the following dispute which happened in his time, and which tending very much to shew the forest customs, is here translated from the barbarous Latin of the times :—"Be it known in the court of Sowerby, held there the third day of May, in the twenty-first year of the reign of king Henry VI. after the conquest of England. A controversy having arisen between Robert Pilkington, steward and governor of Sowerbyshire, of the one part, and the tenants of Sowerby and Warley, of the other part. The said steward alleging, that the lord shall take his profit of the common, without the agreement of the tenants, in what manner he shall think fit, and make fine for his own uses, as he himself shall please to fix the same ; the tenants answer, and say, that it is not so by their custom, which they will prove by law, for they say their custom is, that no man shall inclose any parcel of the waste without the view of twelve men sworn in the court, and without proclamation being there thrice made, when the people are assembled, to see whether it be for the hurt of the tenants, or not. And if it shall be found by those twelve men, or by the tenants, that it is for their harm, it shall not be inclosed. And if any tenant shall trespass in the demesne lands, he shall be presented by the foresters, and four sworn tenants, who he is, and what trespass he hath committed, and the steward shall fine him according to the fact.

And that custom was in the days of our ancestors, in the reign of king Edward III. The said steward taking this declaration of the tenants into consideration, agreed, that a writing indented should be made between him and them, and two or four tenants should go to the lord, and shew him the writing, and solicit for their customs, and what good writings he should know to come from his lord, he should confirm, and they would take him for their good master," The answer to which was in English thus :—" Be it known by this writing, that we, Richard Langley, duke of York, Edward, son and heir of the said duke, and earl of Marshe, with our full and noble council of our family, greeting. We command our well-beloved servant, Robert Pilkington, steward and governor of Sowerbyshire. Whereas our tenants have given us a bill indented between you and them, to have their commons and customs, as their ancestors had in the reign of king Edward III. by our full, and noble council, we grant to them according to that writing, and their desires, as the custom of right requires, viz. when any tenant, or tenants, doth or do desire any parcel of our commons, in our court, that there be sworn twelve tenants, and proclamation be there thrice made, where a multitude of the people are assembled, whether it be for the hurt of the tenants, or not, and if it be found for the hurt it shall not be received in the said court; and if there be any dispute there, concerning any common or custom between tenant and tenant, or between vill and vill, they shall abide tryal by twelve men in the said court where the dispute was received, as was customary in former times. And if any shall make fine in our courts within our lordships, for any waste, twelve men not first sworn on the occasion, nor proclamation made in such form as is aforesaid, that then those tenants to whom it is hurtful, and other tenants with them, shall go to the inclosure, and make it common again, not inclosed, nor at any time after to be inclosed. Their fines for entrance shall be made agreeable to their customs. And if any officer, or greave, or bailiff, or suitor to the court, who sit in the said court, do disagree with any tenant there present, they shall rise to allege their matters at the bar, and put them to the judgment of twelve men. So that all matters which are in variance in our lordships, which belong to our courts, shall be determined by twelve men as before recited. Furthermore we desire and admonish you to fulfil that writing, as you would have our good lordships, and remain in your office, so that our tenants do not come again to us for these matters."

, The park of Erringden was granted from king Edward VI. to sir William Willoughby, knt. lord Willoughby, and sir Thomas Hennage, knt. by letters patent under the great seal of England, dated at Burnedisley, August 17, in the second year of his reign, These sold it afterwards, by deeds dated 10th and 12th of November. 2 Edward VI, to Richard Whalley, Esq; of Welbeck, in the county of Nottingham. WATSON says, April 6th, 2 Eliz. a royal licence was given to this Richard Whalley, to alienate seven messuages, and certain lands here, to Edward Stansfield, of Ayringden, clothier in which licence, as also in the deed of conveyance, it is called Aryngden parke, in parochia de Heptonstall, and said to be held of the queen in capite. But he does not find when it passed from the name of Whalley. It is not improbable that this Richard Whalley alienated portions of it to divers persons. I have in my possession a similar royal grant and licence to that mentioned by WATSON, dated 28 Eliz., from the queen to Richard Whalley, armiger, and Anne, to alienate three messuages, &c. in Aerynden, alias Earynden, Parke, holden of the queen in capite, to Richard Thomas, senr. Richard Thomas, junr. and Edward Thomas ; and also another deed prior to the enfranchisement deed of the 4th James I. set forth in WATSON. This deed is important on account of its recitals. It is dated 1st James I., Nov. 6th, 1603, and is a deed under the hands and seals of George Halstead, John Sunderland, William Sutcliffe, of Ayringden, Richard Naylor, of Wadsworth, and Edward Radcliffe, of Sowerby ; reciting that the late queen of famous memory, Elizabeth, late dread sovereigne, had by her highness letters patent, bearing date at Westminster, the 6th day of February, in the foure and fourtieth yeare of her late highness reigne, gyven, granted and confirmed unto the said George Halstead, John Sunderland, William Sutcliff, beinge tenants of Ayringden their heirs and assigns, all that the park of Ayrenden, late Earingden in the county of Yorke, with all the rights, members, and appurts, being by a particular thereof of the yearly value of £24, by yeare, sometyme parcel of the lands and possessions of the duchy of York and then or late parcel of the lordship of Wakefield, in the said county of York, beinge and all and singular the messuage, milnes, houses, edifices, barns, stables, dovehouses, orchards, gardens, lands, tenements, meadows, feedings, pastures, hereditaments whatsoever, to the said parke of Ayrenden in the said county of York appertaining or belonging, reputed, taken or known to be part, parcel or member thereof, as further by the said letters patent may appear, which said letters patent were so accepted of for the avoidinge of suite, trouble, question, ambiguity and controversy that was like to have grown by reason of a supposed imperfection or concealment in a former grant thereof, by the late king Edward the sixth, unto sir Thomas Heneage, sir William Willoughby, knight, lord Willoughby, bearing date at Burndisley the seaventh day of August in the second yeare of his reign. The deed declares the uses of a fine previously levied concerning the three messuages, &c.

4 James I. the said George Halstead, John Sunderland, William Sutcliffe, and one Henry Naylor, clothiers, obtained an enfranchisement deed from that king, which recites, that in consideration of the sum of threescore and twelve pounds, twenty-four pounds of which were paid for the grant of Erringden park, and forty-eight pounds for a release and discharge of the service and tenure mentioned, and reserved in certain letters patent of king Edward VI. bearing date the 17th day of August, in the second year of his reign; as also in other letters patent bearing date the 6th day of February, 44 Eliz. the said king did grant to the said George Halstead, &c. all the park of Erringden, of the yearly rent or value of twenty-four pounds, some time parcel of the lands and possessions of the duchy of York, and then or late belonging to the lordship or manor of Wakefield, and late annexed to the duchy of Lancaster, with all messuages, milnes, houses, edifices, buildings, barns, stables, dovehouses, orchards, gardens, lands, tenements, meadows, feedings, pastures, and hereditaments whatsoever; And also commons, demesne lands, wastes, heaths, moors, marshes, woods, underwoods, commodities, waters, fishings, fish-ponds, suits, soccages, mulctures, free warrens, mines, quarries of stone, rents, reversions, and services, rents charge, rents soke, and rents and services as well of free as customary tenants, works of tenants, free farms, annuities, knights fees, wards, marriages, escheats, relieves, heriots, fines, amerciaments, courts leets, view of frank pledge, perquisitions, and profits of courts and leets, and all things

to the court leet and view of frank pledge belonging, waifs, estrayes, bondmen and bondwomen, villains with their posterities, estovers, and commons of estovers, fairs, markets, tolls, tributes, customs, rights, jurisdictions, franchises, privileges, profits, commodities, advantages, emoluments, and hereditaments whatsoever. And the said George Halstead, &c. their heirs and assigns, for ever might by this grant have, hold, and keep within the premises, and any parcel thereof, all such courts leets, view of frank pledge, law days, assize, and assizes of bread, wine, and ale, waives, estraies, and of all the goods and chattels of felons and fugitives, and all manner of deodands, knights fees, wards, marriages, relieves, escheats, heriots, free warrens, liberties, parks, and all other rights, &c. in as ample manner and form, as any duke of York, or any other possessing the said park, ever had, held, or kept. To hold to the said George Halstead, &c. their heirs and assigns for ever, of the said king, his heirs, and successors, as of the manor or lordship of Wakefield, in the county of York, parcel of the duchy of Lancaster, in free and common soccage, by fealty only, and not in capite, nor by knights service, for all rents, services, and demands whatsoever, "This (says Mr. WATSON) was only a trust deed in Halstead, Sunderland, Sutcliffe, and Naylor, for they afterwards conveyed back what had been made over to them by different owners. In consequence however of the above enfranchisement deed, the landholders in Erringden acknowledge no lord of the manor, nor pay suit or service to any court."

I have another deed dated 16th April, 1607, James I. which, seems to confirm this statement of Watson's; it purports to be made between the said Halstead, Sunderland, Sutcliffe, and Naylor of the one part, and Richard Thomas of the other part, and recites the enfranchisement deed from the king, and that Halstead, Sunderland, and Naylor, as well for themselves as for the rest of the inhabitants of Earingden, and at the charge of all the said inhabitants, obtained from His Majesty, under the great seal, &c. all that the parke of Earingden, &c. as before set forth; this deed declares that so much of the said land, &c. as was, at the time of making the grant, reputed to belong to said Halstead, &c. should continue to them, and as to the residue thereof, to the uses of Richard Thomas and of others, the freeholders, tenants, and inhabitants of Aerynden, alias Earynden Parke.

The present state of this once famous park is, that it constitutes the township of Erringden, and has no waste ground in it, but is all enclosed, though not improved. It lies entirely in the township of Sowerby, and for a considerable way there is but a small slip of land between this and the bounds of Sowerby township, which, in that part, are formed by the river Calder. The reason of this is, because the limits of Erringden are where the pales stood; and the rest must belong to Sowerby, out of which the park was originally taken. Tradition says, that the park held a great many sheep, as well as deer.

The following places in this township are worthy of note:—

GUNERWALLNASE

Which has the modern name of Nase-end. Here is a flat piece of ground, whereon, tradition says, a tower once stood, and the situation seems favorable enough for an erection of this sort, for it commands a great part of the country.

THE LODGE.

Here doubtless lived some of the keepers, as tradition informs us they did likewise at Bell-house, within this park. This Lodge, which is near Height, in Erringden, is said to be the oldest house in the township, which confirms the above opinion.

OLD CHAMBER.

The habitation, as I take it, of Pilkington, Seneschal, and rector of Sowerbyshire, whose house was burned in the reign of Hen. VI. It is certain that he lived in Erringden, and at this place more likely than any other, because of its being a chambered house, which, as THORESBY, in his *Ducatus*, Appendix, p. 606, has justly observed, "was a rare matter of old amongst the sylvicolæ in the forest of Hardwick," where the chaumer mon signified an inhabiter of the chambered house, the very place we are describing. In the neighboring forest of Rossendale is a house called Chamber, from the convenient situation of which it is probable that the chaumer-mon was here, as in the above instances, the keeper of the forest.

THE MANSION-HOUSE

In this township, is a respectable old fabric, at Hoo-hoile, it has been long in the possession of the present family of Sutcliffes; who have considerable possessions in this part, we find them taking part of the park at the time it was dispailed.

TOWNSHIP OF LANGFIELD.

THIS township which adjoins Erringden on the East, the parish of Rochdale, in Lancashire, on the West, and the Calder on the North, contains an area of 2620 statute acres.

It is mentioned in Domesday book as one of the nine berewicks belonging to the manor of Wakefield, by the name of Langsfelt, (otherwise Langfield.) From the crown it passed to the earls of Warren, and they justified their right to the exercise of free warren here in a writ of quo warranto by charter 37 Henry III.

3 Edward I, Tho. de Langfeld held in capite of earl Warren, in the town of Mancanholes, thirteen oxgangs of land, paying yearly 3s. 4d. 9 Edward III. Will. de Langfeld conveyed to John de Metheleye and Henry de Langfeld, all his lands which he had of the gift of John earl Warren in le Withens, Tornelymosse and Mankanholes in Sourbeschire, without the park of Heyrikdene, viz. between Mankanhole-edge on the one side and Southstrindsbrae on the other, and in 11 Edward III, the king confirmed this grant to them in fee for the yearly rent of 26s. 8d. In this confirmation they are called waste lands.

From the Langfeld's it passed to sir Richard Hamerton, of Hamerton, knt. who married the heiress of Langfeld about the time of Edward III. Sir Richard had Sir Stephen, who had John, who had Sir Stephen : the estate of this Sir Stephen Hamerton, of Hamerton, knt., (he being attainted of high treason in the reign of Henry VIII, and executed at Tyburn,) came into the hands of the crown. HOLINSHEAD in his *Chronicle*, p. 1569, says, "about the latter end of this 28th year, the lord Darcy, Aske, sir Robert Conestable, sir John Bulmer, and his wife, sir Tho. Percye, brother to the earl of Northumberlande, sir Stephen Hamilton, (it should be Hamerton,) Nicholas Tempest, Esq. William Lomley, son to the lord Lomley,

began eftsoons to conspire, although every of them before had received their pardons ; and now were they all taken, and brought to
the tower of London as prisoners." Sir Stephen, therefore, had
been in Aske's first rising, called the Pilgrimage of Grace, and had
been pardoned with the other ringleaders of that conspiracy. After
the attainder of Sir Stephen, the manor of Langfield never returned
to the Hamertons.

By an inquisition, taken in the year 1577, it appears to have been
in the hands of the Queen, per attincturam Step. Hamerton, mill. How
it became vested in the Savilles, whose property it now is, is not
shewn : the present lord is the Right Honorable the Earl of Scarborough.

MANCANHOLES,

Within this township, has its name as " I conjecture, (says WATSON)
from the British Mawn, a turf, or peat, being probably the place
from whence the ancient British inhabitants of this neighbourhood
fetched their fuel." After the Conquest it was so far improved, that
it was converted, along with Cromptonstall, Fernside, Oversalton-
stall, Nethersaltonstall, Hadershelf, and Baitings, all in Sowerbyshire, into a vaccary, where cattle were nourished and bred, as appears by surveys taken in the time of the earls of Warren, and by
the accounts of the officers of the said earls ; which likewise shew
that they were held in demesne. These officers were called In-
stauratories, and gave the yearly accounts of the revenues of their
cattle, as the graves gave of their rents at every audit, to the earl's
other officers. These vaccaries were, in length of time, let forth
to tenants by copy of court roll. The herbage of Mancanholes, in
1314, was valued at 16s. per annum. WATSON had the copy of a
deed in 1519, wherein the " cross of Mankynholes" is mentioned.

On the highest point of this township called Stoodley Pike, has
been erected a lofty column, in honor of the Duke of Wellington,
which forms a conspicuous object from the valley beneath, and many
miles round. From its summit there is a most extensive prospect.

TOWNSHIP OF STANSFIELD.

This township extends six miles along the banks of the Calder, that river partly dividing it from Lancashire, on the East it is separated from Heptonstall by a brook which empties itself into the Calder at Mytholm. It contains an area of 5920 statute acres; the name characterizes the place (Stoney-field,) and it possesses many fine druidical remains, an account of which will be found in the chapter devoted to the "British Æra."

Stansfield is also mentioned in Domesday book, as one of the nine berewics belonging to Wakefield, by the name of Stansfelt, and therefore was conveyed along with that manor. It was in the hands of earl Warren at the time of Kirkby's inquest. Hameline Plantagenet, earl of Warren and Surry, granted by deed under seal, without date, his inheritance in Sowerbyshire, of which Stansfeld was a part, to Jordan, son of Askolf de Thornhill, and in that family it continued till it was transferred to that of Savile, on account of the marriage of Henry Savile with Elizabeth, daughter and heiress of Simon Thornhill, of Thornhill. The present lord of the manor is the right Hon. the earl of Scarborough, who succeeded to the late earl. This manor in some ancient evidences is called Stansfeld cum Blackshawe et Rowtonstall; and that the last of these was a reputed manor is plain, because earl Warren claimed free warren there by charter 37 Henry III. And in the fines 8 and 9 Elizabeth the manor of Rowtonstall, amongst others, is said to be the right of Edward Savile. The manors of Stansfeld and Wadsworth are said, in an Inquisition taken at Pontefract, 5 and 6 Phil. and Mary, to be held of the lordship of Wakefield, by the rent of two shillings yearly, and to be worth beyond reprises thirty pounds.

An act for enclosing lands within the township received the royal assent on the 25th day of May, 1815. The lands enclosed comprise divers commons, moors, and waste grounds called the Stumps or Chisley stones, Keelham height, Bride stones, Hawk-stones, Mount hill, Red mines, Salt pie, Red mine clough, Field head moor, Brown hill, Pole hill, Clunter, and Cowside, containing together 1000 acres.

STANSFIELD-HALL.

Or more properly speaking, Stansfeld-hall, is situated in a very beautiful part of the vale of Todmorden. A part of the old house still exists, and there are some remains of the arms over the mantle piece in the hall, in plaister work, irregularly placed along with those of Lascels, a cross flory; from which last circumstance it is probable that it was built by Thomas Stansfeld who married Barbara the daughter of John Lascels.

A family of considerable repute lived here, who took their name from their situation. The original of them was one Wyons Marions, lord of Stansfield, who probably came from Normandy with William the Conqueror, and in all likelihood a follower of earl Warren, on whom this lordship was bestowed.

It appears from certain writings in the possession of the Sutcliffe family, the present owner of it, that in 1675 one John Pilling sold Stansfield Hall, with its appurtenances, to Joshua Horton, Esq. of Sowerby, and that the widow Pilling released her right of dower in the said hall to Dr. Thomas Horton, in 1693. This Pilling is supposed to have bought of Stansfeld, and Sutcliffe, of Horton.

John, son of Essolf, gave to Roger son of Warin, and to Amabella his daughter, five oxgangs of land in Stansfeld, with the mill in the same town, with what was fixed to the mill, which, with the appurtenances, amounted to seven oxgangs of land, to be held in free marriage, with wastes, woods, and paying fifteen shillings yearly.

John de Thornhill held forty oxgangs of land in Stansfeld and Wadsworth, paying ten shillings yearly, 3 Edw. I.

CROSTONE CHAPEL.

WRIGHT, p. 74. says he cannot tell whether this is as old as Sowerby chapel or not; however, it is certain that there was a chapel here in 1616. There is a tradition of the neighbourhood, that it was built by a Stansfeld, of Stansfield-hall; if so, it must have been in being before the year 1526, for at that time James Stansfeld, of Stansfeld, (the last of that name who resided here,) removed to Hartshead. Others say, that on account of the great distance from the mother church, the inhabitants of Stansfield and Langfield obtained leave to build this chapel, and that, in order to raise a provision for a curate there, they did, at the founding and consecrating of it, endow it with a yearly salary of twenty pounds, which salary, in a pamphlet published at London, by Archdeacon Hayter, in 1741, being an account of a dispute with the body of Quakers concerning their payment of tithes, church rates, &c. is said to have been paid in 1572, as appeared by a chapel rental of that date. It is however most probable, as Dr. Whitaker says, that the first chapel was erected about the time of Henry VIII. and so denominated from a much more ancient cross of which the base and socket now remains near the place.

The late structure was perhaps of the time of James I. and was remarkable for nothing but the peculiarity of cross arches springing from the ground which supported the wood work instead of principals. In consequence of the late fabric being very much out of repair and further accommodation required, a subscription was lately raised and a representation made to the commissioners for building and promoting the building of churches, who granted a sum of money to meet the subscription.   A new chapel has since been erected which was consecrated by the archbishop of the province in September, 1835.

Nov. 1st, 1678, a licence was obtained from the Archbishop of York to the inhabitants of Stansfield and Langfield, for the allowance of baptisms and burials at Crostone, similar to the licence given under Lightcliffe.

In the Register at Heptonstall is an injunction, dated June 28, 1682, from the Archbishop of York, to the curate and chapel-wardens of the chapel of Crostone, reciting, that information had been given, that under colour of the above licence, the curate of Crostone had presumed to join persons together in holy matrimony in the said chapel, and that several persons dying in the said chapelry, had been carried to an adjacent church or chapel, called Todmorden, in Lancashire, and there interred, without a certificate from the curate of Heptonstall, or his being any way acquainted therewith ; and that the inhabitants of the said chapelry of Crostone had refused to pay the parish clerk his usual fee for such burials at Crostone and Todmorden as aforesaid; and that the said curate or chapel-wardens of Crostone had neglected to return the names of such persons so married, baptized, and buried, to the curate or clerk of Heptonstall, by reason whereof the said curate and clerk were likely to be defrauded of their ancient and accustomed dues; and commanding them to redress those grievances for the future.

As to the Endowment of the chapel, it appears there is 10s. paid annually to the incumbent for preaching a sermon yearly in the said chapel, on Whit-sunday, from a farm in Harley-wood, in Stansfield, called the Jumps.

The inhabitants of Stansfield and Langfield, as it is said, did at the first building of the chapel, charge their estates therein with the annual payment of twenty pounds to the curate, which, as appears from an old chapel rental, was paid in 1572, and is continued to this day. The living has been augmented by the governors of the bounty of queen Anne with the following sums; in the year 1810, £200 by lot; 1813, £1400 by lot; 1816, two sums of £300 each to meet two benefactions of £200 each from the inhabitants; 1820, £800 by lot; and 1824, a sum of £300 to meet a benefaction of £200 from the Rev. J. Fennell, the present incumbent. The value of the living, as stated in the Report of the Commissioners presented to Parliament in June, 1835, by command of His Majesty, is £130 per annum.

MYTHOLM.

A small hamlet in this township, embedded in the mountain scenery of the vale of Todmorden. The want of an ecclesiastical place of worship in this vale had long been felt, and the inconvenient access to the parochial chapel of Heptonstall, as also to Crostone in inclement weather was a matter of complaint. A new chapel, in the pseudo gothic style, from a design of the late Mr. John Oates, has within the last year, (1835,) been erected on a most eligible spot of ground at Mytholm adjoining the brook there, and at the foot of a high ridge of hills that overlook the valley. The scite was handsomely presented by the Rev. James Armytage Rhodes (at the back of whose mansion it is situate;) as also the stone from the neighbouring quarry: the funds were provided by the commissioners for building churches.

There is a dissenting chapel in this township at Eastwood, which has been in existence upwards of a century, and is endowed with some property, but to what extent I am not aware. It arises from the Will of MARY HUTTON, of Pudsey, dated July 26th, 1720, who gave and devised to Robert Milnes, of Wakefield, and others, (7 trustees,) their heirs and assigns, all her tenements at Horton, Bowling, or either of them, upon trust that her said trustees should after her decease, receive the rents, &c. deducting thereout the money disbursed in the reparation or improvement of the premises, and yearly pay over the clear remainder of such rents and profits to such protestant dissenting ministers of the presbyterian or congregational persuasion, who should be respectively the settled preachers at the respective chapels then used, and duly recorded at the general or quarter sessions, as places of religious worship, (then follows the names, &c. of seven chapels, amongst which is Eastwood Chapel in the township of Stansfield,) and their respective successors, who should reside within the parish in which the chapel wherein he officiates is situate, for the benefit, better maintenance, and support of such preachers, to be equally divided amongst them. There is a proviso, that in case the said seven chapels, or any of them should cease to be made use of as places of religious worship by protestant dissenters from the church of England, having such preachers as aforesaid, by the space of four years, either through the restraint and prohibition of the civil government, or otherwise, that then, from and immediately after such discontinuance of religious worship there, her said trustees, their heirs and assigns, should convey over the premises to the use of such preachers, in manner therein mentioned.

On the decease of four trustees, the survivors are, within three calendar months to choose four honest able persons, protestant dissenters from the church of England, as by law established, and so on from time to time.

TOWNSHIP OF WADSWORTH.

THIS township, which is separated on the North by a watercourse from the township of Oxenhope in the parish of Bradford, and is bounded on the South by the river Calder, is the largest in the Parish, occupying no less than 10.080 statute acres, though its population is by no means proportionate.

The name, says WATSON, "I take to mean Woodsworth, on account of the woods which once abounded here, though the present appearance of the country does not much justify this etymology:" but with all deference to that gentleman, I think it may be derived from the Saxon patronymic Wada, and is probably the name of some person who established here his *worth*, or residence. We learn from CAMDEN that there was a Saxon duke, named Wada, who gave battle to king Ardulph, at Whalley in Lancashire, and died in 798.

Wadsworth is mentioned also in Domesday-book as one of the nine berewics belonging to the lordship of Wakefield, by the name of Wadesuurde. Earl Warren was allowed free warren in this township, by charter, 37 Hen. III. And it was also one of the towns which Hamelin earl Warren granted in Sowerbyshire to Jordan de Thornhill, about 1169. Simon de Thornhill had lands here; and Richard de Thornhill gave to Adam de Redicar, estovers in the wood of Wadsworth, date uncertain. John de Thornhill held, 3 Edw. I. forty oxgangs of land in Stansfeld and Wadsworth, paying yearly ten shillings. 30 Hen. III. a fine was passed between John, son of William de Whitley, plaintiff, and Ivo de Methley, defendant, of twelve oxgangs of land, in Thornhill, Ovenden, and Wadsworth. In a survey of the honor of Pickering, in 1577, it appeared, that 43 Edw. III. Simon de Thornhill, who held of the lord in Stansfeld, Skircoat, Ovenden, and Wadsworth, certain lands, &c.

in socoage, died, and Elizabeth, his daughter and heir, of the age of two years, and in the custody of Elizabeth, her mother, came and gave for relief ten shillings. Sir Brian de Thornhill, parson of the church of Bedall, enfeoffed John de Methley, and Cecily his wife, of nine acres of the waste of Wadsworth, and other tenements, which Beatrice, who was the wife of sir John de Thornhill, held in name of dower, 2 Edw. III. 46 Edw. III. John Snithall, chaplain, gave to John de Wodhead, of Clifton, forty-five shillings rent, and the fourth part of a mill, which said John had of the gift of William de Normanton, and Isabel his wife, by fine thereof levied in the King's court in Wadsworth, Ovenden and Illingworth, in Sowerby-shire, to hold to the said John, to the full age of Thomas, son and heir of Adam de Metheley, of Thornhill. Otto de Rivill gave to Richard de Stansfeld, for his homage and service, one oxgang of land in Wadsworth, which Richard Talvas some time held, lying in the field of Waddesworth, and in Crimlishworth. Jordan le Vavasor, and Katharine his wife, were summoned to answer to the king, by what warrant they claimed to have free warren in all their demain lands in Wadsworth, and they came not, therefore it was commanded to the sheriff to distrain them by all their lands, &c.

18 Hen. VI. Thomas Sayvyll, of Thornyll, esq. and Margaret, his wife, granted to Richard de Waddesworth the elder, and heirs, certain lands in Waddesworth, and liberty when, and as often as they pleased, to hunt, hawk, fish, and fowl, within the vill and dominion, (dominium,) of Waddesworth, as freely as if he the lord was there in person, with liberty, if the lord inclosed any of the waste, or common pasture, for said Richard, and heirs, to inclose likewise "quantum sibi acciderit secundum liberum redditum suum," and to be free from suit of mill, to hold in feodo militari.

From the Pipe Rolls it appears, that John de Nevill had lands in Waddeswort and Stanesfield, which he held of the king, as of his manor of Wakefield.

Abraham Sunderland, of High Sunderland, sold to Richard Waddesworthe, of Waddesworthe, a farm in Waddesworthe, called Sn'aboyth, 24 Eliz. the sum of £40 to be paid the last day of June, 1586, in the south part of Halifax church, upon the tomb-stone in Dr. Haldesworth's work there, betwene ten of the clock afore noone, and foure of the clock at after noon of the same day. How this, and other manors within Sowerbyshire, granted by earl Warren, passed from the family of Thornhill to that of Savile, where it now remains, (the present possessor being The Earl of Scarborough,) we have shewn under Barkisland.

Within this township is a district called Crimsworth, formerly Crimlishworth, Crimsonden, or Crimsworthden, I have had occasion to mention it in the chapter on the British Era. Whether Mr. WATSON's hypothesis, that the place is so called from Cromlech, be correct or not, I must leave others to determine. This is in all probability the place (Crumbestonestun) which has been supposed by the translator of Domesday to be Crosstone. Dr. WHITAKER is mistaken in stating it to be within Heptonstall.

HEBDEN-BRIDGE,

Formerly a hamlet in the valley between Halifax and Todmorden, on the bank of the Calder and Hepton. It has now become a populous manufacturing village. The Rochdale canal, which passes through it, enables it to carry on a considerable trade with the manufacturing towns of Lancashire.

MAYROID,

Belonging to the family of Cockcroft. The following will shew that the family was of some account two centuries ago. "1630, Henry Cockcrofte, of Mayroides, in the county of Yorke, gent. paid the somme of fifteene pounds. And it is discharge of a composicon by him made with myselfe and others, his Ma^{ts.} Comissioners for compounding the fynes and forfetures for not attending and receaveing the order of Knighthood at his Ma^{ts.} Corenacon, according to the lawe in that case provided."

The name was originally Cowcrofte, and is so written in a general livery, under value granted to the heirs of William Cowcrofte, dated 26 Elizabeth. The original at Mayroid.

OLD TOWN.

A remain of a place once more considerable. At present it consists of a very few houses. As it lies just opposite to Heptonstall, it is possible that it may have got the name of Old Town, to shew that it was an older settlement than that. SALMON, in his *Antiquities of Surrey*, has remarked, p. 46, that the curiosity of the Saxons was not strong enough to preserve any particulars. They called Roman settlements by the name of Old Town, "but whether that was the case here, (says WATSON,) I have not an opportunity to examine, only if I recollect right, there is a place near it called Green gate, and another which goes by the name of the Tower, which I deliver as an hint to such lovers of antiquity as have leisure and inclination to correct and enlarge these my imperfect remarks."

It is not improbable that Old Town was formerly a settlement of this description. I have before ventured on a conjecture, (see p. 39) (see p. 39) "that the broken causeway over the wild moors of Heptonstall, pointing towards Ilkley" passed in the direction of Old Town; and to the remarks then made I beg to refer my reader, because I there brought forward evidence of the existence of generations, who some "two thousand years ago" peopled our wild solitudes and moorlands. My conviction remains the same, that the enquiry is well worth the attention of those who have a taste, a spirit, a feeling, and an interest, in the antiquities of their native parish. Although the very word "antiquities" has a dry and musty look, it cannot but afford gratification to traverse a land covered with the memorials of the past, and anxiously to enquire what kind of beings they were that have left behind them such palpable proof of their existence and power as is to be found in this extensive parish. "Far from me, and from my friends, (exclaims DR. JOHNSON,) be such frigid philosophy as may conduct us indifferent and unmoved over any ground which has been dignified by wisdom, bravery, or virtue. That man is little to be envied whose patriotism would not gain force upon the plain of Marathon, or whose piety would not grow warmer among the ruins of Iona."

BOROUGH of HALIFAX.

Halifax — Printed & Published by Hartley & Walker.

THE BOROUGH OF HALIFAX.

" HALIFAX.—From the point on the North of the Town, at which the respective boundaries of the several townships of Halifax, North Owram, and Ovenden meet, westward
along the boundary of the township of Halifax, to the point at which the same meets the
road leading from a house called Shay to Bank Top; thence along the said Road from
Shay to Bank Top to the point at which the same meets the road leading from South
Owram to North Owram; thence along the said road from South Owram to North Owram
to God Lane Bridge; thence in a straight line to the South Eastern corner of New Town,
on the Bradford road; thence in a straight line to the point first described."

Boundary Act. 2nd Will. IV. c. 46:

THE important changes that have from time to time taken place
in our social institutions, whether arising from a love of novelty, or
considered as the revolutions of human society, having in general
been designated as the commencement of a new Era, might have
justified the adoption of a different title from that which distinguishes
this chapter, and permitted me to say something on that never-fail-
ing topic :—"PARLIAMENTARY REFORM;" but feeling that it is a
subject for political speculation rather within the province of the
general, than the local historian, I have spared my reader the pain of
forcing upon his exhausted attention for "a thousandth time," an argument, either on the policy of the measure, or the merits of the
enactment considered as one of modern legislative wisdom; because
these are questions on which not only the ablest statesmen, and the
profoundest lawyers differ; but upon which public opinion itself
is also much divided.

Viewed in the light of an important constitutional measure framed
for the avowed purpose of conferring upon the people one of the
most invaluable privileges which they can possess, it was not to be
expected that it should come from the birth perfect in all its parts;
the work of any present legislature is at the best but a provision of
political expediency, which presuming speculators will often ques-

M M

a resolution unanimously passed to form a permanent association, denominated "*The Halifax Constitutional Election Committee*;" the avowed object of which should be (and that only) "not only at that eventful period, but from time to time thereafter, to promote the return of one representative of the borough in Parliament, who was firmly and unalterably attached to the sacred and solemn compact entered into between the king and the people, at the glorious revolution." Such was the spirit which animated the Tories, and such appeared to be a most unexceptionable plan for promoting the prosperity and comfort of the borough; preserving its peace and harmony, and allaying the bitterness of party feeling.

It is certainly to be regretted that this conciliatory spirit was not responded to by the Whigs; too transported to share with others the political boon that had been granted to all, they maintained their original purpose, determined to make the new constituency subservient to their views. It is true they had a right to adopt that course which best subserved their interests, the question of policy resolved itself into one of expediency; they rejected the aid of the Radicals, although there was only a difference of shade in their political systems; in fact, they knew their strength and trusted in their majority.

The Radicals resolved to give their support to a candidate whose political principles were in accordance with those of the Union.

The first candidate in the field was MICHAEL STOCKS, ESQ., a native of the parish. He had resided within it all his life, and was possessed of considerable landed property : having formerly been an active magistrate for the district, his personal influence was extensive, and he might be said to have an intimate acquaintance with the borough and its interests. This gentleman made a bold and explicit declaration of his political principles. They were decidedly liberal; but he was friendly to an ecclesiastical establishment supported by the state.

The Tories felt the necessity of selecting at this important crisis, as their representative, a gentleman of sound constitutional principles, who was not only identified in some degree with the interests of the borough, but whose family, respectability, and station fully entitled him to look forward to such an honorable distinction.* In compliance with the resolution of the Constitutional Election Committee, a deputation waited upon George Horton, Esq. of Howroyde, with a request that he would allow himself to be put in nomination; a disinclination, however, on the part of this gentleman, to undertake so arduous and important a trust, would not allow him to accede to the wishes of the requisionists. Similar applications were subsequently made to John Waterhouse, Esq. and Christopher Rawson, Esq. successively, to allow themselves to be put in nomination : but both these gentlemen (the former most positively) declined the proffered honor. The brilliant parliamentary career of Lord Wharncliffe, particularly during the period he had represented the county of York in the Lower House, his intimate acquaintance with her commerce, and the deep interest he had at all times taken in her staple trade and manufactures; his enlightened views and patriotic spirit, but above all, his firm attachment to the civil and ecclesiastical institutions of the land, induced the Tories to turn their attention to a scion of his Lordship's house. The Hon. JAMES STUART WORTLEY, his Lordship's third son, had been educated to the bar and had given early promise that he had profited by the excellent example of his noble parent. A requisition, numerously and very respectably signed was accordingly presented to him, he consented to be put in nomination, and at the same time made a frank and open avowal of his political sentiments, declaratory of his unalterable attachment to the British Constitution in church and state ; and his appreciation of the manifold blessings we enjoy under it.

The Whigs had resolved to return two members who were decidedly friendly to the Reform Act, and who supported the measures of that administration of which Earl Grey was then Premier. The Hon. Mr. WENTWORTH, the eldest son of Viscount Milton, and grandson of the venerable Earl Fitzwilliam, was fixed upon. The name was an assurance that Whig principles would ever find a

* It may be proper to state, that the Tories, in anticipation of the borough being authorised to return two members, had first turned their attention to the Hon. William Seabright Lascelles, third son of the Earl of Harewood, who had consented to stand for the honor of representing it in Parliament; and a requisition to that gentleman was very generally signed: but in consequence of an illiberal observation made in a debate in the House of Lords by Lord Brougham, on the occasion of the removal of a Magistrate of the West Riding, connected with the Borough, from the Commission of the Peace, Mr. Lascelles, through the medium of a friend, begged that the requisition to him might not be presented.

steady supporter in this gentleman, although as yet he had not appeared in public life. It was objected by some that he had not attained his majority, but this objection merged in the honor of the connection and a requisition was accordingly presented by a deputation appointed for the purpose.

The other gentleman selected by the Whigs was CHARLES WOOD. Esq. of Hickleton hall, Doncaster, the member for Grimsby & Wareham, eldest son of Sir Francis Lindley Wood, Bart, of Barnsley, in the county of York, son-in-law of the Premier, (Earl Grey,) and one of the joint secretaries to the treasury. This gentleman's principles, connection, and office were a sufficient guarantee that the interests of the Whigs would not be compromised in his hands, and he consented to be put in nomination. The selection of these gentlemen did honor to the judgment of the Whigs, and would have reflected credit on older constituencies than the Borough of Halifax. But Mr. Wentworth declined to become a candidate for the suffrage of the electors, and it became necessary to supply his place.

It was said that the principles of Mr. Stocks did not exactly suit the more aristocratic portion of the Whigs, but I am not prepared to say wherein they did not harmonize. RAWDON BRIGGS, JUNR. Esq, an eminent Banker in the town, had promised his strenuous support to Mr. Wood, and had avowed himself a reformer. This gentleman was solicited to become a candidate in the place of Mr. Wentworth. Mr. Briggs had neither mixed himself much in public life nor at any time taken a very active part in politics; but he was well acquainted with the local interests of the place, its trade and commerce; was possessed of considerable wealth; and above all, an high and unimpeachable character. He had every reason to look forward to the support of his fellow-townsmen, for setting aside political differences, in private life he was respected by all parties. Mr. Briggs stated his willingness to be put in nomination in conjunction with Mr. Wood, but having pledged himself to support the return of that gentleman he begged to be explicitly understood that by so doing he did not prejudice Mr. Wood's eventual success.

The Revising Barristers held their court at the Magistrates' Office, in the month of October, 1832, and the first Register of Voters for the new borough, shewed a constituency of 536 electors, (of these 5 are named twice.)   The King, by his Royal Proclamation, dated the 3rd December, 1832, having dissolved the old Parliament, the new precept directed to John Drumelzier Tweedy, Esq., the returning officer for the borough, shortly after arrived in Halifax. This gentleman lost no time in issuing the formal notices, and making the necessary preparations.   The time and place appointed for proceeding with the election, was Tuesday, the 11th December, in the manufacturer's piece-hall; and the two following days for taking the poll; for this purpose the borough was divided into two districts, and two polling places provided, one at a house in Cow Green; and the other at the Magistrates' office, Ward's End.

The nomination day, at length arrived, and the arrangements that had been made by the returning officer were highly judicious.   Few towns possess so eligible a convenience for holding popular assemblies, (particularly of this description) as the town of Halifax. Commodious hustings were erected on the east or lower side of the Manufacturers Hall, and to these hustings and the adjoining galleries, many were admitted by tickets.   The area of the hall began to be filled at an early hour, and about eleven o'clock the respective candidates, attended by music and banners, entered the hall.   The returning officer occupied the centre of the hustings; Messrs. Wood and Briggs, and their supporters the right; Michael Stocks, Esq., and his supporters the extreme right; and the Hon. Jas. Stuart Wortley and his supporters the left.   The orange party with their colours, took their station on the right of the area, and the blues who on this occasion did not exhibit any colours, on the left.

Notwithstanding the state of the weather was rather unpropitious, and a cold December morning ill calculated to draw together a large outdoor assemblage, the Manufacturers' Hall, exhibited a truly animating and interesting appearance, rendered doubly so by being graced with the presence of many ladies, who occupied the rear of the hustings.

Mr. Tweedy opened the business by commanding silence, while the Precept was read.   The usual oath was then administered to him, and the act against bribery and corruption read.   After a few preliminary observations from the returning officer, Mr. Copperthwaite, a surgeon, proposed Mr. Stocks as a fit and proper person to represent the borough in Parliament, Mr. George Haigh, of the Mount, seconded the proposition.   G. B. Browne, Esq., of Myrtle Grove, proposed Charles Wood, Esq., and Mr. Samuel Hodgson, an eminent woolstapler in the town, seconded the nomination.   Christopher Rawson, Esq., proposed, and John Waterhouse, Esq., seconded the nomination of the Hon. James Stuart Wortley; Mr. Jonathan Akroyd, an extensive manufacturer, proposed Mr. Briggs, and Mr. Binns, of Norland, seconded the motion.   The respective candidates addressed the electors in the order of nomination, in speeches explanatory of their political principles, each receiving a share of applause and disapprobation; Mr. Wortley, as might be expected, his full share of the latter.   The returning officer having called for the usual show of hands, declared the same in favour of Mr. Stocks and Mr. Briggs.   The result was received with shouts by the Radicals. Messrs. Wood and Wortley forthwith demanded a poll, which being granted, was appointed to commence on the following morning, and the meeting was adjourned, each party returning to their respective committee rooms.

At nine o'clock on Wednesday morning the poll was opened at both booths, and the polling continued leisurely during the day. The next morning it was renewed at eight, and in the course of the afternoon the friends of Mr. Wortley finding there was no chance of continuing it open with any prospect of that gentleman's ultimate success declined to bring up more voters; the contest then lay between the three other candidates, and was carried on until the final close at four o'clock with considerable vigour, when there appeared for Rawdon Briggs, Jun. Esq. 242, Charles Wood, Esq. 235, Michael Stocks, Esq. 186, and the Hon. J. S. Wortley, 174.

Friday the 14th having been appointed by the Returning Officer for announcing the result, the respective candidates (with the exception of Mr. Wortley) and their supporters appeared on the hustings.   The usual formalities were gone through, the numbers as before stated, officially announced, and Messrs. Briggs and Wood declared duly elected burgesses for the borough.   The friends of the successful candidates having provided for the occasion a triumphal car richly caparisoned with orange ribbon, &c. and drawn by six horses, the new members were chaired through the town, preceded by music, banners, flags, &c. and everywhere greeted with the usual demonstrations of approbation; in the evening they sat down with their supporters to a sumptuous entertainment, the Tories having very prudently adopted that excellent old English custom on the first day. The analysis of the poll may be stated thus :—

No. of Voters.	No. of Votes.	Description of Votes.	Votes for Briggs.	Votes for Wood.	Votes for Stocks.	Votes for Wortley.
149	149	Plumpers	4	6	59	80
343	688	Splits	238	229	127	94
492	837		242	235	186	174

The following is an extract from the return furnished by the Returning Officer to the House of Commons, of the expenses incurred in this election.

	£.	s.	d.
Sum paid by each Candidate for the expenses incurred by the Returning Officer	26	5	0
Total amount paid..	106	0	0
Particulars of the expenses incurred by the Returning Officer :— Carpenters and Masons' expenses for the Hustings and Polling places, and use of Piece-Hall	38	17	6
Deputies, Polling Clerks and attendants at the hustings and Polling places..	34	14	0
Poll Books, and Printing, &c.	19	12	3
Refreshments, by order, for Deputies, &c.	8	11	5
Sundries	0	13	6
Reserved for small bills not come in; if the whole be not wanted, to be returned proportionally to each candidate	2	11	4
	£106	0	0

Halifax, 26th February, 1833.   J. D. TWEEDY.

Thus terminated the first election of members to the Reformed Parliament, for the borough of Halifax; and each party looked forward for the enjoyment of those incalculable blessings they were led to expect would be derived from the possession of this (if properly exercised) invaluable privilege, this Reform in the Constitution : how far these anticipations have been realised, it is not my province to enquire.

The register of persons qualified to vote within the borough, from the 1st November, 1833, to the 1st November, 1834, contained 630 names. That between the 1st November, 1834, and November, 1835, 648 names, thus shewing a gradual increase in the constituency.

Scarcely however had the general registration for the last year been completed, when the King dismissed the Reform Administration from his majesty's councils. This circumstance rendered a speedy dissolution of Parliament extremely probable ; and a spirit of activity began to manifest itself throughout the country, in anticipation of another general election.

The note of preparation was sounded in Halifax. Mr. Wood in compliance with the wishes of his friends, solicited a renewal of the trust with which he was then honored; and The Honorable J. S. Wortley again responded to the call of a requisition most numerously and respectably signed. Mr. Briggs had determined to retire from public life, in consequence of the precarious state of his father's health, and who did not long survive.

In taking a short review of Mr. Briggs's parliamentary career, it does not appear that he joined in any of the debates; but he was nevertheless a constant attendant in his place, and an active member on the various committees it was his duty to attend; at all times ready of access to his constituents and ever attentive to their requests: while he avowed himself a Reformer, (and his votes on the leading public questions of the time sufficiently testify the liberality of his principles) he was by no means a blind supporter of the administration; to be brief, in the discharge of his senatorial duties he ever proved himself, what cannot be said of all in the first reformed parliament,—a consistent and independent member.

The Radicals had determined to profit by this opportunity and to supply the vacancy with a candidate of their own choosing. EDWARD PROTHEROE, JUN, ESQ. who had formerly sat in Parliament for Evesham and Bristol, was honored with their approval.

Three candidates were now in the field, representing the three great political parties in the state; and the approaching dissolution was looked forward to by all with an intensity of interest never equalled in this place on any previous occasion. The contest to be decided was in truth a "contest of principles." The excitement that prevailed throughout the country at the late election had in some degree subsided, and the reflecting spirit of the people was returning to its natural state.

Whether the Whigs and Radicals were distrustful of their strength as separate parties is not for me to determine; certain it is they coalesced; but whether at a sacrifice of principle on the part of each to secure the ultimate success of both, is a political secret within the breasts of those who were parties to that coalition.

Although the adoption of this course did not fail to excite the indignation of the Tories, who saw in it an attempt to grasp the representation of the borough regardless of consequences, it appeared to give an additional impetus to their exertions, and they had within a few days a list of upwards of 200 electors who pledged themselves to plump for Mr. Wortley at the ensuing election.

On Monday, the 29th December, 1834, the proclamation for dissolving the first reformed Parliament was issued, and on the Thursday following the Writ for Halifax was received by George Stansfeld, Esq. the Returning Officer, (who had been appointed in the room of Mr. Tweedy, deceased.)   The following Monday was fixed for the day of nomination, and the two next days for taking the poll. Two Polling Places, one at the Magistrate's Office, and the other at Cow Green were appointed, and the Borough divided as on the former occasion.

The activity of all parties was unprecedented, as the time approached. The Tories had to fight single handed against a most powerful coalition.   On the day of nomination the friends of each candidate assembled at their respective committee rooms at an early hour, and at ten o'clock preceded by their music and banners, moved towards the Manufacturer's Hall.   Hustings were erected on the East side of the Hall as on the previous occasion : the Returning Officer occupied the centre; Mr. Wortley and his supporters the left; and Messrs. Wood and Protheroe and their supporters the right; several ladies occupied the rear of the hustings, and it must be conceded that celestial blue appeared the favorite color with the fair sex.   The blue colours were planted on the left of the area fronting the hustings, and the orange on the right, each occupying a part of the front centre; at the rear was posted a party of non-electors, with a large yellow banner, on which were inscribed divers sentences, fully demonstrating that they were by no means impartial spectators. There were not less than six thousand persons in the Hall at this time.

The preliminary proceedings having been gone through, George Buxton Browne, Esq. proposed Charles Wood, Esq., and Mr. D. Ramsden, a corn dealer, seconded the nomination. Mr. Nicholson, a printer, proposed Edward Protheroe, Jun. Esq. which was seconded by Wm. Briggs, Esq. the banker ; and C. Rawson, Esq. again proposed the Hon. Jas. Stuart Wortley, and the nomination was again seconded by J. Waterhouse, Esq. as at the first election.

The respective candidates having addressed the electors, the Returning Officer called for the usual shew of hands, which was declared in favor of Messrs. Wood and Protheroe. Mr. Wortley forthwith demanded a Poll. The parties having retired from the Hall the remainder of the day was occupied by the respective candidates

and their committees in making active preparations, while the state
of party feeling shewed itself in the town, by those manifestations
which usually characterize a contested election.

On Tuesday morning, the polling commenced at 9 A. M. and
closed at 4 P. M.: when the numbers stood thus—Wood, 295;
Protheroe, 273; Wortley, 259. Each candidate then addressed
the electors from their respective committee rooms. Disheartening
as these numbers might appear to the Tories, they were not cast
down; experience seemed to have taught them that the time occupied by a public dinner, as on the former occasion, after the first
days' poll, might be much more profitably employed, they continued
at their posts until the morning dawned: the other party was
equally on the alert; and intense interest prevailed as to the ultimate
result. Wednesday arrived, and the contest was renewed at 8
o'clock with redoubled vigour. Mr. Wood was considered secure,
and the struggle between Mr. Wortley and Mr. Protheroe was desperate as it was glorious. Messengers were dispatched from the
polling places to the head quarters of their committees, with an
account of every vote, as the contest drew to a close. The fickle
goddess at length smiled on the Tories, and at 4 o'clock presented
them with a majority of one. At the close of the poll the numbers
stood thus, Wood 336, Wortley 308, Protheroe 307.

On Thursday morning, the returning officer appeared on the
hustings, accompanied by Mr. Wood and Mr. Wortley, and their
respective supporters. The area of the hall was closely filled. The
seals of the poll books having been opened, Mr. Stansfeld in the
presence of the candidates, numbered the amount of voters, each
party being satisfied of the correctness of the calculation; during
the time occupied in these proceedings, four protests were handed
in by the Radicals against the decision of Mr. Stansfeld, in the case
of four votes. The returning officer then announced the gross poll
to be as before stated, and accordingly declared Charles Wood,
Esq., and the Hon. James Stuart Wortley, to be duly elected, and
executed the usual indentures of return. No sooner had this been
completed than the chairman of Mr. Protheroe's Committee pro-
tested against Mr. Wortley's return, and stated that the affair would
come before the House of Commons. The new members then came
forward, and respectively returned thanks; the chairman of Mr.

Protheroe's committee performing the duty for that gentleman.

The following is a correct analysis of the votes :—

No. of Voters.	No. of Votes	Description of Voters	Votes for Wood.	Votes for Wortley.	Votes for Protheroe.
251	251	Plumpers	5	223	13
75	150	Split Votes	56	75	19
274	550	Coalition Splits	275		275
601	951		336	308	307

and happy should I have been to have added, thus passed over and terminated, one of the severest struggles that ever distinguished an election contest ; but while I lament that it is my duty not only to record one of the most lawless and unjustifiable attacks on the property of Mr. Wortley's supporters by the sovereignty of the people, that ever disgraced such a contest ; it is also my duty to state that ulterior proceedings were adopted by the friends of the defeated candidate, ill calculated to allay the bitterness of party feeling, and give the passions that calm repose which it is so desirable to enjoy after a period of strong excitement.

The partizans of each candidate, or rather of Messrs. Wood and Protheroe, and Mr. Wortley, had paraded the town during the election in separate divisions, accompanied by music and flags, as is usual on such occasions ; and it was not to be expected, considering the strong excitement that prevailed, as the contest drew to a close, that these parties should meet from time to time without coming into personal collision. I do not state this with a view to extenuate either party, where either party might have been to blame, but to shew that however each might have fared in a trial of strength, it did not appear on a subsequent investigation of facts before a jury, that any provocation was given to justify the outrageous breach of the peace that disgraced alike the town, and the cause the rioters espoused.

From the noon of Wednesday until six in the evening, the town was at the mercy of a mob of not less than 500 ruffians, armed with various weapons and missiles, who made a general attack upon the dwellings of those who had rendered themselves obnoxious to the popular cause.

I shall shortly trace the mob in their lawless career, although I am unable to particularize the various acts of mischief that they committed ; among other places that were attacked, and windows broken, may be numbered the following—The Blucher public house, where a blue flag was hauled down and the staff converted into blud-geons; the White Horse, Southgate; the Shakespeare Tavern; the White Swan Inn; the Talbot, (in which every window was broken;) Mr. Lister's, the auctioneer; the Vicarage, where much damage was done; the Three Pigeons; Mr. Staveley's, Beanfield, windows broken and other damage done; C. Rawson's, Esq. Hope-house, windows &c. broken; Mr. J. Rawson's, the Shay, windows, furniture, &c. broken; Mr. J. Holdsworth's, Shaw-hill, windows broken, house rifled. Hence they directed their course to Mr. J. E. Norris's, Saville-hall, where the dining and drawing rooms were both broken into and rifled, and the furniture, books, &c., scattered over the lawn and garden: some valuable paintings were also destroyed, and silver-plate stolen: for the latter no compensation could be recovered from the wapontake. The mob then proceeded to the Bee-Hive, in King Cross-Lane, where they broke the windows; hence, through the town, to Mr. Atkinson's spirit-shop, North Bridge, where they also broke the windows.

During part of the time the mob were employed in their work of mischief, it appeared from evidence subsequently adduced before a jury, that they were accompanied by music.

The following short abstract of the judicial proceedings that fol-lowed, will shew the nature of the damage done. On Monday, February 10, a special session was held in the magistrates' office for the purpose of deciding upon the claims for compensation for damage done under thirty pounds. The following is a list of the claimants who had given the usual notices, and whose claims were considered by the magistrates assembled:—Joseph Bottomley, Sun Inn, £30; John Holdesworth, Pigeons, £30; Mr. John Lister, sur-geon, £26 15s. 6d.; Messrs. F. H. and W. Nicholson, drapers, £17 17s.; Thomas Atkinson, spirit merchant, £17 0s. 8d.; Wm. Akroyd, King of Prussia, £15; James Balmforth, Britannia, £12; John Helliwell, beer-seller, £12; Mr. John Staveley, merchant, £11 5s. 11d.; Thomas Mann, White Hart, £8 9s. 6d.; Joseph Bairstow, Union Cross, £7; Jas. Brier, White Horse, £6 9s. 10d.; John Smithson, King's Head, £6. 3s.; Mrs. Mary Bairstow, Shak-speare, £5 11s.; Benjamin Wood, druggist, £3; William Firth, Black Bull, £3; making a sum of £241 12s. 5d.

The usual notices were proved to have been given; and it was stated that the claim of C. Rawson, Esq., would be taken to the assizes, the damage having been ascertained to amount to seventy-six pounds. All these claims were allowed with some trifling deductions.

On Tuesday the 10th March, a court was held at York-castle, before William Gray, junr. Esq. under sheriff, for the assessment of damages suffered by other parties, owing to the riots. The following cases were disposed of :—

	Sum Assessed.
Norris, gent. *v.* The inhabitants of Agbrigg & Morley..	£799
Holdsworth, *v.* the same	£230
Staveley and others, *v.* the same	£240
Musgrave, *v.* the same	£ 80
Sugden, *v.* the same	£ 90
Metcalfe, *v.* the same	£133

On the 31st March, another court was holden, when the remainder were disposed of :—

	Sum Assessed.		
	£.	s.	D.
Rawson,C.Esq. *v.* the inhabitants of Agbrigg&Morley	73	9	11
Rawson, J. *v.* the same	250	0	0
Carr, *v.* the same	124	12	7
Sutcliffe, *v.* the same	45	0	0

From the foregoing facts, it would appear that the ruling passion of the mob was an insatiable love of mischief; and it cannot be disputed, from the evidence produced on these enquiries, that had any thing like an efficient and organised police force, been directed to act with vigor and effect at the first breaking out of the disturbance, the mob might have been effectually dispersed; but unfortunately encouraged by non-resistance, they increased in strength until the constabulary force of the town, (which was never brought to bear upon them until the mischief was done,) was of little or no avail. The magistrates at one o'clock had dispatched a messenger to the commanding-officer at Leeds, for a party of the king's troops, requiring their immediate assistance, and a troop of lancers arrived at seven o'clock, from Dewsbury. The mob however had by this time considerably dispersed, and the presence of the military for a few days, effectually restored tranquility.

I have stated that ulterior proceedings were adopted by the supporters of Mr. Protheroe to unseat Mr. Wortley. On the 19th February the new parliament assembled, and on the 9th of March following a petition was presented to the house of Commons against the hon. gentleman's return. On the following night a petition was also presented against the return of Mr. Wood, and both these petitions were referred to a committee, to be ballotted for on the 12th May. Both parties were once more actively engaged in preparing for a species of warfare which is perhaps more calculated than any other to perpetuate party strife. Whether the petitioners against Mr. Wortley's return found that they could not invalidate that return, or whether they thought the better part of valour was discretion, I am not prepared to say; but on the 25th of April they gave formal notice to the friends of that gentleman, that they intended to abandon their petition: and on the following day a similar notice was given to the friends of Mr. Wood.

The excitement caused by the election was also productive of legal proceedings that had much better have been buried in oblivion. An action was brought by G. B. Browne, Esq., against the proprietors of the Halifax Guardian newspaper, to recover damages for an alleged libel, which appeared in that paper, in the shape of certain letters explanatory of the plaintiff's conduct when soliciting an elector, of the name of Waddington, for his vote on behalf of Mr. Protheroe. This action was followed up by another, brought by Waddington against Mr. Browne and another, for an assault arising out of the same transaction. Both cases were tried at the York Spring assizes before Mr. Baron Parke, and a special jury; when a verdict for the defendants was found in the first case; and a verdict by consent for the plaintiff, in the second case.

In the month of April a change in His Majesty's councils led to a rumour, that Mr. C. Wood was about to take office under the new administration, of which the Viscount Melbourne was premier. A requisition to Christopher Rawson, Esq. was prepared unknown to that gentleman, and numerously signed, calling upon him to supply any vacancy that might arise in the representation of the borough, should Mr. Wood's acceptance of office compel him to vacate his seat. To this requisition Mr. Rawson required a short time for consideration and ultimately returned an answer stating his

readiness to comply with the wishes of the requisitionists should
the contemplated event take place.   This however did not happen.
I must not omit to mention that the friends of Mr. Wood expressed
their fixed determination to defend any attempt that might be made
to contest the Hon. member's seat in the event of its being vacated.

The Revising Barristers held their annual court in the borough
on the 20th October, 1835.   At the preceding courts there had
been little to occupy their attention beyond formal business; but
on this occasion their proceedings were viewed with more than ordinary interest.   The decisions of various Election Committees of the
House of Commons on cases arising under the Reform act, rendered it
necessary that a more than ordinary attention should be paid to a correct revision of the overseer's lists, inasmuch as the insertion of a
voter's name in the register was in these tribunals considered *primâ
facie* evidence of a legal right to the elective franchise.

The result of the late election was important to both parties,
for it proved beyond a doubt that a re-action had taken place since
the first election, in favor of the Tories. The scales at this time were
nearly balanced.   The overseer's lists presented a considerable increase in the number of claimants, many of whom it was notorious
had no *bonâ fide* qualification.   Not less than 260 notices of objection were given by the Tories, and 130 by their opponents : of these
some were paired off previous to the sitting of the court.   On the
morning of the 20th the court met at the Magistrates' Office, and
thence by adjournment at the Talbot Inn, where three separate
courts were formed for the dispatch of business, each objection
being generally separately argued.   The result of the decisions
reduced the list to 757 voters; thus shewing an increase of 109
above the constituency of the preceding year.

During the last session, an act was passed, to limit the time
of taking the Poll in Boroughs; henceforth the polling shall commence at eight o'Clock a. m. of the day next following the day fixed
for the election; and continue such one day only, and no poll shall
be kept open later than four o'clock p. m. not more than three hundred voters shall be allowed to poll in each booth, nor more than one
hundred in one booth, if required by any candidate, or the proposer
or seconder of any candidate.

N N

APPENDIX.

A

See page 82.

THE deed of endowment of the vicarage of Halifax is in Latin: the following is a translation:—

To all the sons of the Holy Mother Church to whom this writing shall come, Gilbert the venerable vicar of father William, by the grace of God, Archbishop of York, and primate of England, wish health in Christ Jesus. By how much more carefully the enemy of the human race goes about seeking whom he may devour, and contriving for the supply of his unsatiable lust, so much more studiously and watchfully ought we to resist his wicked efforts, with all our power, lest the deceitful craftiness of the betrayer should draw the sheep into sudden destruction. Hence it comes to pass that on account of the great produce and revenue of the Mother Church of Halifax, (which Church together with its chapels and dependencies, has been for a long time in the patronage of foreigners, who were more eager for the milk and wool, than for the salvation of souls, and have shamefully neglected its spiritual concerns:) frequently the *Court Clergy* * and sometimes foreigners, unacquainted with the English language, have wrested the said church by violent threats, by oppression, and by the powerful entreaties of princes, from the hands of the prior and convent of Lewis, its rightful patrons, and when admitted to the same, have miserably disregarded their pastoral office. Wherefore the Reverend Father, our lord Archbishop, observing and regretting this miserable negligence, and much grieved on account of so many persons destitute of the consolations of a pastor, has often and deeply meditated how he might administer permanent relief to this disease. He perceived these—That if a perpetual vicar should be appointed, who might continually reside there and have portions assigned him from the revenue of the said church, sufficient for the maintenance of hospitality, and for the other burthens incumbent on so rich a benefice and if the remainder of the profits of the living should go to the patrons for their use; by such arrangement, both the advantage of souls would be consulted, and also the said religious would exceedingly rejoice at the happy increase of their means of hospitality. Often the said Archbishop, when about to set off to the Council of Lyons, enjoined us to cause the forementioned things to be executed especially since William de Chameur, the then rector of that church, had been just appointed to the bishopric of Lofon. We therefore with great care estimated the just profits of the said church, and we have ordained and appointed, that a perpetual vicar should be established in the above mentioned parish, who together with his successors, shall receive certain portions of the revenue, amounting to 50 marks a year, according to the accustomed and common taxation; and that the remainder shall go to the patrons for their perpetual use. Moreover at the decease of any vicar, the aforesaid prior and convent, shall present according to the Canons, fit persons to the Archbishop and his successors. Besides what has been already mentioned, we here enumerate some other things which shall be granted to the vicar for ever, viz.—

(* Clerici curiales,) qu. practising lawyers in holy orders.

That he shall have a piece of ground extending in length from the road, along the river side, towards the east as far as another road towards the west, and in breadth from the road along side of the church yard, to the land of Richard de Gunar, towards the south; on this piece of ground, a vicarage house shall be built, in which the vicar for the time being shall reside. Also that if any dispute shall arise concerning the said land or any part of it, the expenses shall be paid by the patrons, so that the vicar for the time being may not be deprived of any part of the said land: also the vicar for the time being shall receive all offerings and profits arising from alterage, except the tenth of wool and of lambs and of kids, every thing else relating to alterage we decree shall fall to the use of the vicar absolutely. But the vicar shall at his own expence, provide for the service of the mother church and its chapels; the repair of the Chancel, the Procurations and Synodals, and all the ordinary burthens, and the whole remainder, viz. all the profits proceeding from the above church, shall, as aforesaid, go for the use of the patrons, saving always the rights of the church of York, and the dignity of the Archbishop for the time being.

Since a dispute has arisen between the vicar and convent of Lewes, on the one hand, and Ingolard Turbard, vicar of the church of Halifax, on the other, concerning the tithes of Mills and of calves and mortuaries, in vivis animalibus, in respect of which the prior and convent assert that they have been enormously injured by the order formerly made at the taxation of the vicarage. We therefore for the sake of peace and concord, by the consent of Julian de Landona and Richard de Meltona, the Procurators of the prior and convent appointed for this purpose, and of the aforesaid vicar summoned before us, do appoint and ordain that the same vicar and his successors, shall for ever be bound to receive in full the aforesaid tenths of Mills and calves, and mortuaries, but the vicar himself and his successors shall for ever be bound to pay to the prior and his successors, and the convent or their attorney, or agent, four pounds and thirteen shillings every year, at two periods of the year, viz: one half at the feast of St. Oswald, and another half at Easter, &c. &c.

See page 82.

With respect to the changing the church of Halifax from a rectory to a vicarage, the following Bull of Pope Alexander is inserted in the register of archbishop Corbrigge, fol. 9.

" Alexander Episcopus, Servus Servorum Dei, dilectis filiis Priori et Conventui Lewicensibus, Cluniacensis Ordinis, Cicestriencis Dioceseos, Salutem et Apostolicam Benedictionem. Cum Ecclesia vestra hospitalitate habeatur conspicua, et in ea specialiter vigeat observantia regularis, dignum arbitramur et decens, ut ipsam donis extollamus specialium gratiarum; hinc est, quod nos vestris supplicationibus inclinati, presentium vobis tenore concedimus, ut cedente aut decedente Willielmo, Rectore Ecclesie de Halifax, Ebor. Dyoces. in qua jus optinetis, ut asseritis, patronatus, Ecclesiam ipsam, cum pertinentiis suis, in usus vestros perpetuo retinere, ac ipsius corporalem possessionem, per vos, vel per alium, seu alios, ordinarii, vel cujuscunq. irrequisito consensu, ingredi libere valeatis; Vicario ipsius Ecclesie pro sustentatione sua, et ejusdem Ecclesie oneribus supportandis, congrua portione de ipsius proventibus reservata. Non obstante, si felicis recordationis J. Papa, predecessor noster, vel nos mandavimus, sub quacunq. forma verborum alicui de beneficio, aut beneficiis, ad vestram collationem seu presentationem spectantibus provideri, quibus quoad assecutionem aliorum beneficiorum pro tempore vacantium, nolumus aucthoritate presentium prejudicium generari. Nos e'm' (perhaps etiam, or etenim) decernimus irritum et inane, si quod contra hujus concessionis nostre tenorem a quocunq. contigerit attemptari. Nulli ergo omnino homini liceat hanc paginam nostre concessionis infringere, vel ei ausu temerario contraire. Si quis hoc attemptare presumpserit, indignationem omnipotentis Dei et Beatorum Petri et Pauli Apostolorum ejus se noverit incursurum. Dat. Viterbii, ... Idus Augusti, Pontificatus nostri anno tertio."

The following also (entered in the same register-book) was sent to the Abbot of St. Alban's, empowering him to give possession of the church of Halifax to the prior and convent of Lewis.

"Alexander Episcopus, Servus Servorum Dei, dilecto filio Abbati Sancti Albani, Ordinis Sancti Benedicti, Lincolniensis Diocoseos, Salutem et Apostolicam Benedictionem. Cum Ecclesia Lewicensis, Cluniacensis Ordinis, Cicestriensis Dyoceseos, hospital. habeat conspic. et in ea special. vigeat observantia regularis, dignum arbitramur et decens ut ipsam donis extollamus donis speci alium gratiarum; hinc est quod nos dilectorum filiorum Prioris et Conventus ipsius Ecclesie supplicationibus inclinati eis per nostras literas duximus concedendum, ut cedente aut decedente Willielmo, Rectore Ecclesie de Halifax, Ebor. Dioc. in qua iidem Prior et Conventus jus optinent, sicut asserunt, Ecclesiam ipsam cum pert. suis in usus suos perpetuo retinere, ac ipsius corporalem possessionem per se vel per alium, seu alios, Ordinarii cujuscunq. alterius irrequisito consensu ingredi libere valeant, Vicario ipsius Ecclesie pro sustentatione sua, et ejusdem Ecclesie oneribus supportandis, congrua portione de ipsius proventibus reservata. Non obstante, si felicis recordationis J. Papa, predecessor noster, vel nos mandavimus, sub quacunq. forma verborum alicui de Beneficio, aut Beneficiis, ad ipsorum collationem seu presentationem spectantibus provideri, quibus quoad assecutionem aliorum beneficiorum pro tempore vacantium, nolumus aucthoritate literarum nostrarum prejudicium generari. Nos etiam decernimus irritum et inane si quod contra hujus concessionis nostre tenorem a quocunq. contigerit attemptari. Quocirca discretioni tue per Apostolica scripta mandamus, quatenus cedente aut decedente Rectore predicto, eosdem Priorem et Conventum, vel Procuratorem suum, eorum nomine in corporalem possessionem ipsius Ecclesie ac pert. ejusdem, per te vel per alium inducas et defendas inductos, amoto ab ea quolibet illicito detentore, contradictores per censuram ecclesiasticam apostolice propo'ita compescendo; non obstante si aliquibus personis communiter vel divisim a sede apostolica sit indultum, quod interdici, suspendi, vel excommunicari non possint per literas dicte sedis, nisi in eis de indulto hujus et toto tenore ipsius plena et expressa mentio habeatur, et qualibet alia indulgentia generali vel speciali per quam effectus presentium impediri valeat. vel differri, et de qua vel cujus toto tenore facienda esset in presentibus mentio specialis. Dat. Viterbii, ... Idus Augusti, Pontificatus nostri anno tertio."

See page 85.

A TERRIER of all the glebe lands, hereditary endowments, &c. belonging to the vicarage of Halifax in the county and diocese of York, exhibited at the primary visitation of the Most Reverend Edward, lord archbishop of York, holden at Wakefield on the 23rd day of June, A. D. 1809.

Halifax is a vicarage endowed. The king is patron.

Imprimis, The vicarage house is of stone, inhabited by the vicar. Then follows an internal description of the vicarage house.

Item, belonging to the vicarage on the south side, adjoining to the vicarage house, is one field and a small pleasure ground. One paddock to the West. One croft to the east. These fields contain about two acres. The track on the other side of the hedge belongs to the said field.

Item, a field called Hawkin Royd now divided into two portions by upright flag stones. This field is in the township of Southowram; to the south abuts on Halifax old bank, to the north and east on land belonging to the heirs of the late Robert Parker, esq., to the west on the brook which separates the township of Halifax and Southowram. This field contains about five acres and a half.

Item, in the town of Halifax in Southgate, a field called the vicarage field, or Shackfield, or Blackledge. This field, by authority of an act of Parliament passed in the year of our lord 1781, has been leased out by the present vicar upon building leases for the term of 99 years to twelve separate tenants, each of whom pays a certain annual rent to the vicar for the time being. These leases by the aforesaid act are renewable at the pleasure of the vicar. Then follows an accurate abstract of such leases.

N. B. The land tax of the vicarage house and the above property has been redeemed.

Item, an allotment of land called the vicar's park, consisting of seventy-five acres upon Greetland moor. This allotment is described.

Item, an allotment of land called the Vicar's Penand, and consisting of seven acres upon Old Linley moor. The allotment is then described.

The allotments were so made to the vicar in lieu of all vicarial and small tithes whatsoever within Elland-cum-Greetland or within Old Linley.

THE ANCIENT ENDOWMENT of the vicarage of Halifax, as entered in the church register, consists of the Easter dues, mortuaries, tithes of corn mills and all small tithes save those of wool and lamb, and of all surplice dues throughout the parish and vicarage. The surplice fees from the parochial chapels of Elland and Heptonstall have been gratuitously uncalled for by the present vicar and his two immediate predecessors, though due. (Vide said register.)

N. B. The tithe of Halifax corn mills is a load of malt yearly at Christmas, and all the corn the vicar uses in his own house, ground toll free.

The vicar of Halifax receives also a portion of the surplice fees from the church of the Holy Trinity, which portion the late archbishop of York ascertained under the authority of the act of parliament for building the said Trinity church.

Then follows an account of two annuities of forty shillings, one of which was sold in 1799 and the money appropriated as therein mentioned: the other which was given for eighty years is now extinct.

In Halifax church are a crimson velvet cushion, and hangings for the pulpit and reading desk, nine bells in good order, a good clock and chimes, two large flagons, one large salver, two large plates, four less, and cups, all silver, weighing about three hundred and thirty ounces.

There is also a small cup in the vicarage house with this inscription—" the legacy of Mr. Nathaniel Waterhouse to the vicar."

There are not any lands or money in stock for the repair of the church.

The following townships are and have been from time immemorial charged with the repairs of Halifax church and the church yard fence, viz. Halifax, Sowerby, North Owram, Ovenden, Warley, South Owram, Hipperholme, Skircoat, Shelf, Midgley; and their respective proportions are entered in a book of accounts for the said church. These said townships have lately levelled and repaired the church-yard of Halifax; Mr. Wm. Lawrence and Mr. Saml. Hodgson were then churchwardens. For a further account of this proceeding see the board put up at the West end of the church near to the font.

The vicar for the time being always appoints the clerk, sexton, grave-digger, and verger. Their wages are paid by custom.

D

AN ACCOUNT

SHEWING THE NUMBER OF CHURCHES AND CHAPELS BELONGING TO VARIOUS DENOMINATIONS, WITHIN THE PARISH OF HALIFAX, IN THE YEAR 1836.

Those Churches and Chapels marked thus * were in existence in 1756.

PAROCHIAL DISTRICT OF HALIFAX.

TOWNSHIP OF HALIFAX.

Churches or Chapels.	Where Situate.	Denomination.
*The Parish Church,	St. John's,	The Parish Church.
Trinity Church	Harrison Lane,	Ecclesiastical.
St. James's Church,	North Parade,	Ditto.
Square Chapel,	Church Lane,	Independent Dissenters.
Sion Chapel,	Wade Street,	Ditto Ditto.
*Chapel,	Northgate,	Unitarian.
*Chapel,	South Parade,	Wesleyan Methodist.
Wesley Chapel,	Broad Street.	Ditto Ditto.
Chapel,	Pellon Lane,	Baptist

Churches or Chapels.	Where situate.	Denominations.
Salem Chapel,	North Parade,	Methodist New Connexion
Hanover-Street Chapel,	King Cross Lane,	Ditto Ditto.
Ebenezer Chapel,	Cabbage Lane,	Primitive Methodist.
*Chapel,	Ward's End,	Society of Friends.

TOWNSHIP OF NORTHOWRAM.

*Chapel,	Northowram,	Independent Dissenters.
Chapel,	Northowram,	Methodist New Connexion
Chapel,	Haley Hill,	General Baptist.
Chapel,	Blackmires,	Wesleyan Methodist.
Chapel,	Ambler Thorn,	Methodist New Connexion
Chapel,	Round Hill,	Primitive Methodist.

TOWNSHIP OF SOUTHOWRAM.

*St. Anne's Church,	Southowram	Ecclesiastical.
Chapel,	Ditto.	Wesleyan Methodist.
Chapel,	Southowram Bank,	Primitive Methodist.

TOWNSHIP OF OVENDEN.

*St. Mary's Church,	Illingworth,	Ecclesiastical.
Chapel,	Ovenden,	Wesleyan Methodist.
Chapel,	Illingworth Moor,	Ditto.
Mount Tabor Chapel,	Mount Tabor,	Ditto.
Chapel,	Mixenden,	Independent Dissenters.
Mount Zion Chapel,	Upper Brockholes,	Methodist New Connexion
Chapel,	Bradshaw Lane,	Methodist New Connexion

TOWNSHIP OF HIPPERHOLME-CUM-BRIGHOUSE.

*Church,	Coley,	Ecclesiastical.
*St. Matthew's Church,	Lightcliffe,	Ditto.
St. Martins' Church,	Brighouse,	Ditto.
Chapel,	Ditto,	Wesleyan Methodist.
Chapel,	Ditto,	Society of Friends.
Chapel,	Ditto,	Methodist New Connexion
Chapel,	Bramley Lane,	Independent Dissenters.
Chapel,	Near Lightcliffe,	Wesleyan Methodist.

TOWNSHIP OF SHELF.

Chapel,	Shelf,	Independent Dissenters.

TOWNSHIP OF SKIRCOAT.

Christ Church,	Skircoat Moor,	Licensed by the Archbishop
Chapel,	Bolton Brow,	Wesleyan Methodist.
Chapel,	Salterhebble,	Ditto.
Chapel,	King Cross,	Methodist New Connexion

TOWNSHIP OF SOWERBY.

*St. Peter's Church,	Sowerby Town,	Ecclesiastical.
St. John's Church,	Wilderness,	Ditto.
Chapel,	Sowerby,	Wesleyan Methodist.
Chapel,	near Mytholmroyd Bridge,	Ditto.
Chapel,	Sowerby,	Independent Dissenters.
Chapel,	Boulderclough,	Methodist New Connexion
Chapel,	Steep Lane, near Sowerby,	Baptist.

TOWNSHIP OF MIDGLEY.

*St. Mary's Church,	Luddenden,	Ecclesiastical.
Chapel,	Luddenden Dean,	Wesleyan Methodist.
Booth Chapel,	near Luddenden,	Independent Dissenters.
Chapel,	Midgley,	Methodist New Connexion

Churches or Chapels.	Where situate.	Denominations.

TOWNSHIP OF WARLEY.

*Church,	Sowerby Bridge,	Ecclesiastical.
Chapel,	Warley,	Johnsonians.
Chapel,	Warley Town,	Independent Dissenters.
Chapel,	near Luddenden Foot,	Wesleyan Methodist.
Chapel,	Luddenden,	Ditto.

PAROCHIAL CHAPELRY OF ELLAND.

TOWNSHIP OF ELLAND-CUM-GREETLAND.

*St. Mary's Church,	Elland,	Ecclesiastical.
Chapel,	New Street, Elland,	Seceding Methodists.
Chapel,	New Road, do.	Independent Dissenters.
Chapel,	Dog Lane, do.	Wesleyan Methodist.
Chapel,	Townfield Lane, do.	Methodist New Connexion
Chapel,	Blackley, in Elland,	Baptist.
Chapel,	Elland,	Unitarian.
*Chapel,	Greetland,	Wesleyan Methodist.

TOWNSHIP OF BARKISLAND.

*St. Bartholomew's Church,	Ripponden,	Ecclesiastical.
Chapel,	Do.	Society of Friends.

TOWNSHIP OF NORLAND.

Chapel,	Mount Pleasant,	Wesleyan Methodist.

TOWNSHIP OF RASTRICK.

*St. Matthew's Church,	Rastrick,	Ecclesiastical.
Building used as a Chapel,	Bridge End,	Independent Dissenters.

TOWNSHIP OF RISHWORTH.

Chapel,	Ripponden Bank,	Wesleyan Methodist.
Chapel,	Parrock Nook,	Independent Dissenters.
Chapel,	Rishworth,	Baptist.

TOWNSHIP OF STAINLAND.

*Chapel,	Stainland,	True Protestants of the Church of England.
Providence Chapel,	Stainland,	Independent Dissenters.
Bethel Chapel,	Outlane, Stainland,	Primitive Methodist.

TOWNSHIP OF SOYLAND.

Chapel,	Mill Bank,	Wesleyan Methodist.
Chapel,	Soyland Town,	Methodist New Connexion
Chapel,	Stones, Soyland,	Independent Dissenters.

PAROCHIAL CHAPELRY OF HEPTONSTALL.

TOWNSHIP OF HEPTONSTALL.

*St. Thomas's Church,	Heptonstall,	Ecclesiastical.
Chapel,	Do.	Wesleyan Methodist.
Chapel,	Heptonstall Slack,	General Baptist.
Chapel,	Hebden Bridge,	Baptist.
Chapel,	Hebden Bridge Lanes,	Wesleyan Methodist.

Churches or Chapels.	Where situate.	Denomination.
	TOWNSHIP OF ERRINGDEN.	
Chapel,	Cragg,	Wesleyan Methodist.
	TOWNSHIP OF LANGFIELD.	
Chapel,	York Street, Todmorden,	Wesleyan Methodist.
Chapel,	Mankinholes,	Ditto.
	TOWNSHIP OF STANSFIELD.	
*Church,	Cross Stone,	Ecclesiastical.
St. James's Church,	Mytholm,	Ditto.
*Chapel,	Eastwood,	Presbyterian or Congregational persuasion.
Chapel,	Blackshaw Head,	Wesleyan Methodist.
Chapel,	Gronny Stones, near Shaw	Baptist.
Chapel,	Millwood,	Baptist.
Chapel,	Line Holme,	General Baptist.
Chapel,	Blind Lane,	
	TOWNSHIP OF WADSWORTH.	
Chapel,	Longfield or Blackhill,	Wesleyan Methodist.
*Chapel,	Wainsgate,	Baptist.
Chapel,	Birchcliffe,	General Baptist.

ERRATA.

Since writing my observations on the Roman Æra, I have been supplied by the kindness of a friend with some information, respecting the Bath referred to in page 38. Among the buildings to which WATSON's attention was directed, there appears to have been the remain of a Roman bath, with a vapour room or sudatorium. This room, according to the report of some workmen who destroyed it, was four yards long and about two yards and a half broad. The floor is said to have been between three and four yards below the present surface of the ground; and the pavement was nearly a yard in thickness, composed of lime and bricks, brayed together exceedingly hard. In one corner of this room was a drain about five inches square, into which as much water was conveyed as would have turned an overfall mill, yet no vent could be discovered, nor did it raise a large spring about twenty yards below, and about four yards lower than the foundation of the building.

The remains of the bath were discovered about twelve years ago, by a person who was getting stone for the repair of the neighbouring fences. The property upon which the bath was found, belonged to the late B. Allen, Esq., of Huddersfield, who had it taken up at a considerable expense, and placed in the grounds adjoining his mansion, where it now stands, under an arch composed of stones, tiles, &c., found at Cambodunum, over which ivy has grown, giving to the whole a venerable appearance.

INDEX.

Lightning Source UK Ltd.
Milton Keynes UK
UKOW07f1854110316

270061UK00011B/175/P